Beginning PHP, Apache, MySQL® Web Development

Beginning PHP, Apache, MySQL® Web Development

Michael Glass
Yann Le Scouarnec
Elizabeth Naramore
Gary Mailer
Jeremy Stolz
Jason Gerner

Wiley Publishing, Inc.

Beginning PHP, Apache, MySQL® Web Development

Published by
Wiley Publishing, Inc.
10475 Crosspoint Boulevard
Indianapolis, IN 46256
www.wiley.com

Copyright © 2004 by Michael Glass, Yann Le Scouarnec, Elizabeth Naramore, Gary Mailer, Jeremy Stolz, and Jason Gerner

Published by Wiley Publishing, Inc., Indianapolis, Indiana

Published simultaneously in Canada

Library of Congress Control Number: 2004101426

ISBN: 0-7645-5744-0

Manufactured in the United States of America

10 9 8 7 6 5 4 3 2 1

1MA/SV/QS/QU/IN

For general information on our other products and services or to obtain technical support, please contact our Customer Care Department within the U.S. at (800) 762-2974, outside the U.S. at (317) 572-3993 or fax (317) 572-4002.

Wiley also publishes its books in a variety of electronic formats. Some content that appears in print may not be available in electronic books.

About the Authors

Michael "BuzzLY" Glass

Michael Glass has been a gladiator in the software/Web site development arena for more than eight years. He has more than ten years of commercial programming experience with a wide variety of technologies, including PHP, Java, Lotus Domino, and Vignette StoryServer. He divides his time between computer programming, playing pool in the APA, and running his Web site at www.ultimatespin.com. You can usually find him slinking around on the PHPBuilder.com forums, where he is a moderator with the nickname BuzzLY.

Thanks, Staci, for putting up with long and late hours at the computer. Elizabeth and Jason, it wouldn't have been the same project without you two. And thanks to my code testers at www.ultimatespin.com: Spidon, Kaine, Garmy, Spidermanalf, Ping, Webhead, and FancyDan. You guys rock!

To Donna and Gerry, who have influenced my life more than they can ever know, and who taught me the importance of finishing what you've started.

Yann "Bunkermaster" Le Scouarnec

Yann is the senior developer for Jolt Online Gaming, a British gaming company. He is a moderator at PHPBuilder.com and a developer of open source PHP software for the gaming community. He has also worked for major software corporations as a software quality expert.

I thank all the innocent bystanders who got pushed around because of this project: Debra and Nancy, who were patient enough not to have homicidal thoughts; and my wife and kids, who barely saw me for six months.

Elizabeth Naramore

Elizabeth has been programming with computers since a very young age, and, yes, she remembers when software was packaged on cassette tapes. Graduating from Miami University at age 20 with a degree in Organizational Behavior, she found a world of opportunity awaiting her—in corporate marketing. Her first love was always computers, however, and she found herself sucked back to the programming world in 1997 through Web site design and development (once a computer geek, always a computer geek). While she plans to return to Miami to get her Masters in Computer Science, she currently stays busy running several Web sites. Her main focus is in e-commerce and running www.giftsforengineers.com.

Elizabeth has spent the past six years developing Web sites and coordinating all phases of Web site publication and production. She is currently a moderator at PHPBuilder.com, an online help center for PHP. Her other interests include poetry, arts and crafts, camping, and juggling the many demands of career, family, and the "other duties as assigned" that come along in life. She lives in Cincinnati, Ohio, with her husband, beautiful daughter, and a new baby on the way.

Gary "trooper" Mailer

After graduation from university in 1998, Gary worked in a major software house in central London as a quality assurance engineer, and also as the departmental Web developer (using ASP). This gave him a taste of Web development. After a few years, he made the jump into full-time Web development and has not looked back since.

Gary has worked in a few different sectors, including communications (Siemens) and hotels (Hilton), as well as in "traditional" development houses.

He is currently a freelance developer for a European communications company. Gary has been and continues to be an active member of and contributor to the PHPBuilder.com site.

Jeremy "stolzboy" Stolz

Jeremy is a Web developer at Cloverfish Inc. (`www.cloverfish.net`), a Web development company in Fargo, North Dakota. Jeremy is primarily a PHP/MySQL developer, but he has also worked with many other languages. When not working, he frequents the Internet and tries to keep up his programming skills. He is a contributor to and moderator at PHPBuilder.com. He also frequents many other computer-related Web sites to keep his skills sharp and up to date.

Thanks to my employer and colleagues for giving me the time and space to participate in this project. Also, thanks to Debra Williams Cauley at Wiley for getting me involved in this project for Wrox.

I dedicate this book to my wife and family for helping me get through the long hours of preparation and writing.

Jason "goldbug" Gerner

Jason currently spends his days working as a Web developer in Cincinnati and burns free time complaining about lack of support for Web standards and abusing XML. He can often be found lurking in the PHPBuilder.com discussion forums, waiting to chime in with nagging comments about CSS or code efficiency.

Credits

Acquisitions Editor
Debra Williams Cauley

Development Editor
Nancy Stevenson

Production Editor
Eric Newman

Technical Editor
Jason Gerner

Copy Editor
Nancy Rapoport

Editorial Manager
Mary Beth Wakefield

Vice President & Executive Group Publisher
Richard Swadley

Vice President and Executive Publisher
Robert Ipsen

Vice President and Publisher
Joseph B. Wikert

Executive Editorial Director
Mary Bednarek

Project Coordinator
Kristie Rees

Graphics and Production Specialists
Sean Decker
Carrie Foster
Joyce Haughey
Jennifer Heleine
Kristin McMullan

Quality Control Technicians
Andy Hollandbeck
Susan Moritz
Carl William Pierce
Brian Walls

Proofreading and Indexing
TECHBOOKS Production Services

Contents

Contents

Part II: Movie Review Web Site

Contents

Chapter 7: Validating User Input   191

Chapter 8: Handling and Avoiding Errors   215

Part III: Comic Book Fan Site

Chapter 9: Building Databases   237

Contents

Contents

Contents

Contents

Contents

Introduction

Welcome to *Beginning PHP, Apache, MySQL® Web Development*, your guide to developing dynamic Web sites using these popular open source solutions. Consider us your tour guide as we travel through the various adventures that await you. Okay, so perhaps it won't be that glamorous or exciting, but we do promise an enjoyable learning experience.

The main purpose of this book is to provide you with a taste of what can be done with Web development using these three modules together. While we've given you only the tip of the iceberg, it will be enough to get you started and to get those creative juices flowing when designing and developing your own site. Each of these modules is complex in and of itself, and this book merely covers the basics of all three. This book is not meant to be an in-depth and comprehensive resource but rather an introduction.

Who's This Book For?

We assume that anyone reading this book has some experience with Web site development concepts and a basic working knowledge of HTML. Knowledge of other programming languages besides PHP is not a prerequisite for this book, but certainly any programming experience you have will help you understand and apply the concepts.

This book is geared toward the "newbie" to these three areas, and we've brought many of the concepts and code snippets to the most basic level. As your experience and comfort level grow with your knowledge and practical applications, you will find more complex and perhaps more efficient ways of doing things. When that happens, you will know that you have come over to the dark side and joined us as PHP, Apache, and MySQL enthusiasts.

What's Covered in the Book

A variety of topics are covered in this book:

- ❑ Installation and configuration of PHP, Apache, and MySQL
- ❑ Basic introduction to each module and how the modules interact with one another
- ❑ Gathering input from and interacting with your Web site visitors
- ❑ Handling and avoiding errors and general troubleshooting tips
- ❑ User registration and logins
- ❑ E-mailing and setting up e-mail lists using the three modules
- ❑ Content management systems
- ❑ Adding e-commerce to a Web site
- ❑ Incorporating a discussion forum into your site
- ❑ Using activity logs and error logs to enhance your Web site
- ❑ Locating a third-party Web host
- ❑ Finding the text editor that's right for you
- ❑ Using PEAR to enhance your Web site

As you read through the chapters and learn about these topics, you will be creating two complete Web sites. The first is a movie review Web site that displays information about films and their respective reviews. This project will cover the basics, such as writing PHP code, creating a MySQL database, filling it with data, and showing it to your visitors based on what they want to see.

The second project is a comic book fan Web site, which acts as a resource for any comic book fan. This site will be developed in the latter part of the book and will incorporate some of the more complex topics. You will create a truly interactive Web site, where your visitors can interact with you and with other members of the site.

We take you step by step through the development of each of these sites, and you will continually build upon them as new concepts are introduced. Note, however, that each of the chapters is a stand-alone chapter, so that if you are not particularly interested in reading a specific one, you won't be left in the dust.

If you thought the days of the "pop" quiz were over, you might want to think again. We have provided handy-dandy exercises at the end of some of the chapters to test your knowledge of the chapter topics and to challenge you to think one step further. Don't worry, however, as we've provided the answers in Appendix A.

Other general references are provided for your reading pleasure in additional appendixes. These are not intended to be comprehensive resources, but they are great for referencing the general topics covered in the meat of the chapters.

As any programmer knows, software is constantly being improved and debugged, and while we used the latest and greatest versions of our modules at the time of publishing, chances are those versions won't be around for long. It is important for you to visit the source Web sites for PHP, Apache, and MySQL (URLs provided frequently for you throughout this book) to get the most updated versions and recent release notes. When developing Web sites using applications, we recommend that you always use the most recent stable release. Using software versions that have not been fully tested can be dangerous to your application and leave bugs in your code. The same is true for the new learner—you should be learning on a stable release of the application, not on a beta version.

The most recent stable versions that were in effect at the time of this book's writing were:

- ❑ **PHP:** Version 4.3.3 (PHP5 is still in beta at this writing, although we do address it and its current implications)
- ❑ **Apache:** Version 2.0.47
- ❑ **MySQL:** Version 4.0.15a

Future editions of this book will address changes and improvements in these programs as they become available.

What You Need to Use This Book

This book is designed to be multiplatform and covers topics and issues for both Windows- and Linux-based systems. We have provided you with instructions for downloading and installing all three components onto your machine. Each is an open source program, so you can download and use them free of charge.

The only other external piece of software needed is a text editor. If you're not sure what that is or what you should be using, don't worry—we cover that topic, too.

Source Code

We have provided the two applications and accompanying code that are discussed in the text. The complete source code from the book is available for download from www.wrox.com. As PHP5 is in beta production at the time this book was written, we will update the code and applications on the companion Web site with any pertinent changes that come as a result of the stable release of PHP5. We encourage you to visit the companion site periodically to view these updates. Although all the code you need is listed in the book, we suggest you download a copy of the code to save yourself a lot of typing.

Conventions

Throughout the book, we have used certain typographic conventions to get our points across. While you don't need a secret decoder ring to get the gist of what we mean, knowing *how* we say what we're saying will certainly help.

> Boxes like this one hold important, not-to-be-forgotten, mission-critical information that is directly relevant to the surrounding text.

Filenames, field names, and commands or functions are shown in monospaced type—for example, "Open the `create.php` file and . . ."

We present code in two ways:

```
//This is an example of code that is being seen for the first time
```

```
//This is an example of code that you have already seen, but is being referenced
later
```

```
//or code that we're quoting from another source, such as from a configuration file
```

Changes to an existing program created earlier in a chapter will be shown in bold:

```
//This is old code here.
//This is the line we want you to add.
```

You will be prompted to get your fingers typing and your brain working in our "Try It Out" sections, which entice you to actually apply the concepts we're covering and get a firsthand glimpse into coding. We then follow up with a "How It Works" section to explain what you just accomplished.

Customer Support

We offer source code for download, errata, and technical support from the Wrox Web site at www.wrox .com. In addition, you can join mailing lists for author and peer discussion at http://p2p.wrox.com (see the last section in this introduction for more info on the P2P site).

Source Code and Updates

As you work through the examples in this book, you may choose either to type all the code manually or to use the source code files that accompany the book. All of the source code used in this book is available for download at www.wrox.com. Once at the site, simply locate the book's title (either through the Search utility or by using one of the title lists) and double-click the Download Code link on the book's detail page and you can obtain all the source code for the book.

Errata

We have made every effort to ensure that there are no errors in the text or in the code. However, we are human, so occasionally something will come up that none of us caught prior to publication.

To find the errata page for this book, go to www.wrox.com and locate the title using the Search utility or one of the title lists. Then, on the book details page, click the Book Errata link. On this page you will be able to view all errata that have been submitted for this book and posted by Wrox editors. You can also click the Submit Errata link on this page to notify us of any errors that you might have found.

While we're on the subject of submitting errata, we want to hear about any error you find in this book. Simply e-mail the information to techsupwrox@wrox.com. We'll check the information and, if appropriate, post a message to the book's errata page and fix the problem in subsequent editions of the book.

If you do e-mail us, your e-mail should include the following things:

❑ In the Subject field, include the book's title, the last six digits of the ISBN (557440 for this book), and the number of the page upon which the error occurs.

❑ In the body of the message, tell us your name, contact information, and the problem.

We won't send you junk mail, we promise. We need these details to help you as quickly as possible.

> Note that the Wrox support process can offer support only for issues that are directly pertinent to the content of our published title. Support for questions that fall outside of the scope of normal book support is provided by the community lists of our http://p2p.wrox.com forums.

p2p.wrox.com

For author and peer discussion, join the P2P mailing lists at wrox.com. Our unique system provides programmer-to-programmer contact on mailing lists, forums, and newsgroups, all in addition to our one-to-one e-mail support system discussed in the previous section. Wrox authors and editors and other industry experts are present on our mailing lists.

At http://p2p.wrox.com you will find a number of different lists that will help you, not only while you read this book but also as you develop your own applications. To subscribe to a mailing list, follow these steps:

1. Go to http://p2p.wrox.com and choose the appropriate category from the left menu bar.
2. Click the link for the mailing list you want to join.
3. Follow the instructions to subscribe and fill in your e-mail address and password.
4. Reply to the confirmation e-mail that you receive.
5. Use the subscription manager to join more lists and set your e-mail preferences.

Part I: Getting Started

Chapter 1: Introduction and Installation Configuration

Introduction and Installation Configuration

You've spent your hard-earned money and purchased this book, so you undoubtedly know the enormous benefits of using PHP, Apache, and MySQL together to create your Web site. But in the event that this book was placed on your desk one Monday morning with a sticky note that read, "Learn this!" in this chapter we look at the basics of PHP, MySQL, and Apache to show you what makes the "AMP" combination so popular. We also walk you through the procedure for installing all three components of the AMP module and advise you on how to best configure the software to meet your specific needs.

Installation Configuration

You can choose to install one, two, or all three components of the AMP package based on your specific needs. For example, if you are responsible for providing a company-wide intranet and/or hosting your own Web site, you should probably install all three. If your site is hosted by a third-party Web hosting company, however, you do not necessarily need to install all three components (or, for that matter, any).

Installing the three components, even if you don't have to, enables you to develop and test your site in the comfort of your own workspace without having to upload to the file server just to test at every little step. If you do a lot of off-line testing, however, we highly recommend that you still perform a complete test once your site is live and running, as your settings may differ from those on your Web-hosting company's server. Even a small difference can cause you big headaches.

Over the course of this book, you will develop two complete Web sites:

❑ **Movie Review Web site.** Developing this site introduces you to writing a PHP program, making your pages look professional, working with variables and includes, and integrating PHP with MySQL to make your site truly dynamic as pages are created "on the fly" for your Web-site visitor. You will also get experience in error handling and data validation while working on this site.

❏ **Comic Book Fan Web site.** The creation of this Web site takes you through the steps of building databases from scratch, sending out e-mails using PHP, authenticating users, managing content through CMS, creating a mailing list, setting up an e-commerce section, and developing and customizing a discussion forum.

Finally, this chapter covers how to learn about your visitors through the use of log files and how to troubleshoot common mistakes or problems. The appendixes in this book provide you with the necessary reference materials you'll need to assist you in your Web site development journey, and offer tools to make you more efficient.

Because PHP5 is in beta release only at the time of this writing, we will touch on how your code may be affected by upgrading, but we will not discuss PHP5 in depth.

After reading this book, you will be able to create a well-designed, dynamic Web site by utilizing tools available for free. Although this book is not intended to be a detailed analysis of Apache, PHP, and MySQL, it points you in the right direction to explore further issues you may wish to delve into.

Brief Intro to PHP, Apache, MySQL, and Open Source

Let's take a moment to explore the history of each of these three components and how they work together to help you create a professional, dynamic Web site.

What Is Open Source?

PHP, Apache, and MySQL are all part of the *open source* group of software programs. The open source movement is basically a collaboration of some of the finest minds in computer programming. By allowing the open exchange of information, programmers from all over the world contribute to make a truly powerful and efficient piece of software available to everyone. Through the contributions of many people to the publicly available source code, bugs get fixed, improvements are made, and a "good" software program becomes a "great" one over time.

A Brief History of Open Source Initiatives

The term "open source" was coined in 1998 after Netscape decided to publish the source code for its popular Navigator browser. This announcement prompted a small group of software developers who had been longtime supporters of the soon-to-be open source ideology to formally develop the Open Source Initiatives (OSI) and the Open Source Definition.

Although the OSI ideology was initially promoted in the hacker community, upon Netscape's release of Navigator's source code, programmers from all walks of life began to offer suggestions and fixes to improve the browser's performance. The OSI mission was off and running, as the mainstream computing world began to embrace the idea.

Linux became the first operating system to be called open source (although BSD was a close runner-up, distributed from Berkeley in 1989), and many programs followed soon thereafter. Large software corporations, such as Corel, began to offer versions of their programs that worked on Linux machines.

Although there are now numerous classifications of OSI open source licenses, any software that bears the OSI Certification seal can be considered open source because it has passed the Open Source Definition list. These programs are available from a multitude of Web sites; the most popular is www.sourceforge.net, which houses more than 66,000 open source projects.

Why Open Source Rocks

Open source programs are very cool because:

- ❑ **They are free.** The greatest thing about open source software is that it is free and available to the general public. Software developers and programmers volunteer their time to improve existing software and create new programs. Open source software cannot, by definition, require any sort of licensing or sales fees.

- ❑ **They are cross-platform and "technology-neutral."** By requiring open source software to be non–platform specific, the open source community has ensured that the programs are usable by virtually everyone. According to the Open Source Definition provided by the Open Source Initiative at http://opensource.org/docs/definition.php, open source programs must not be dependent on any "individual technology or style of interface" and must be "technology-neutral." As long as the software can run on more than one operating system, then it meets the criteria.

- ❑ **They must not restrict other software.** This basically means that if an open source program is distributed along with other programs, those other programs may be open source or commercial in nature. This gives software developers maximum control and flexibility.

- ❑ **They embrace diversity.** Diversity of minds and cultures simply produces a better result. For this reason, open source programs cannot, by definition, discriminate against any person or group of persons, nor against any "field of endeavor." (For example, a program designed for use in the medical profession cannot be limited to that field if someone in another field wants to take the program and modify it to fit his or her needs.)

For a complete list of the criteria a piece of software must meet before it can be considered "open source," or for more information about the OSI or the open source community, visit the OSI Web site at www.opensource.org.

How the Pieces of the AMP Module Work Together

Now that we have covered some of the history of open source, it's important to understand the role each of these programs (Apache, MySQL, and PHP) plays in creating your Web site.

Imagine that your dynamic Web site is a fancy restaurant. Diners come to your place, and each one wants something different and specific. They don't worry so much about how the food is prepared, as long as it looks and tastes delicious. Unlike a buffet-type spread, where everything is laid out and your patrons simply choose from what's available (the analogy being a more static, informational Web site with little interaction and input from your visitors), a nice restaurant encourages patron/waiter interaction and complete customization for any specific dietary needs (a dynamic Web site where the visitor can choose what he or she wants to see).

In this scenario, we can attribute the three components of the AMP module as follows:

❑ **Apache:** This is your highly trained master of culinary arts, the chef. Whatever people ask for, she prepares it without complaint. She is quick, flexible, and able to prepare a multitude of different types of foods. Apache acts in much the same way as your HTTP server, parsing files and passing on the results.

❑ **PHP:** This is the waiter. He gets requests from the patron and carries them back to the kitchen with specific instructions about how the meal should be prepared.

❑ **MySQL:** This is your stockroom of ingredients (or in this case, information).

When a patron (or Web site visitor) comes to your restaurant, he or she sits down and orders a meal with specific requirements, such as a steak, well done. The waiter (PHP) takes those specific requirements back to the kitchen and passes them off to the chef (Apache). The chef then goes to the stockroom (MySQL) to retrieve the ingredients (or data) to prepare the meal and presents the final dish to the patron, exactly the way he or she ordered the meal.

Apache

Apache acts as your Web server. Its main job is to parse any file requested by a browser and display the correct results according to the code within that file. Apache is quite powerful and can accomplish virtually any task that you, as a Webmaster, require.

The version of Apache covered in this book is the most recent and stable at the time of this writing: version 2.0.47. The features and server capabilities available in this version include the following:

❑ Password-protected pages for a multitude of users

❑ Customized error pages

❑ Display of code in numerous levels of HTML, and the capability to determine at what level the browser can accept the content

❑ Usage and error logs in multiple and customizable formats

❑ Virtual hosting for different IP addresses mapped to the same server

❑ DirectoryIndex directives to multiple files

❑ URL aliasing or rewriting with no fixed limit

According to the Netcraft Web site (www.netcraft.com), at the time of this writing Apache is running over 27 million Internet servers, more than Microsoft, Sun ONE, and Zeus combined. Its flexibility, power, and, of course, price make it a popular choice. It can be used to host a Web site to the general public, or a company-wide intranet, or for simply testing your pages before they are uploaded to a secure server on another machine. Later in this chapter, we discuss how to configure your Apache setup to accommodate all of these options.

PHP

PHP is a server-side scripting language that allows your Web site to be truly dynamic. PHP stands for *PHP: Hypertext Preprocessor* (and, yes, we're aware PHP is a "recursive acronym"—probably meant to confuse the masses). Its flexibility and relatively small learning curve (especially for programmers who have a background in C, Java, or Perl) make it one of the most popular scripting languages around. PHP's popularity continues to increase as businesses and individuals everywhere embrace it as an alternative to Microsoft's ASP language and realize that PHP's benefits most certainly outweigh the costs (three cheers for open source!). According to Zend Technologies, Ltd., the central source of PHP improvements and designers of the Zend Engine, which supports PHP applications, PHP code can now be found in approximately 9 million Web sites.

The version of PHP referenced in this book is the most recent stable release at the time of publication: version 4.3.3. Although we discuss several of the most common uses and functions of PHP, you can find a complete list of PHP functions in Appendix B of this book. As you continue to program in PHP and your comfort level increases (or the demands of your boss grow), we encourage you to expand your use of built-in PHP functions to take advantage of its tremendous power. You can download the PHP software from PHP's Web site at www.php.net.

MySQL

Another open source favorite, MySQL is the database construct that enables PHP and Apache to work together to access and display data in a readable format to a browser. It is a Structured Query Language server designed for heavy loads and processing of complex queries. As a relational database system, MySQL allows many different tables to be joined together for maximum efficiency and speed.

This book references version 4.0.15a, the most stable release of MySQL at the time of publication. While a complete list of features can be found at the MySQL Web site (www.mysql.com), some of the more popular features of this program are as follows:

- Multiple CPUs usable through kernel threads.
- Multi-platform operation.
- Numerous column types cover virtually every type of data.
- Group functions for mathematical calculations and sorting.
- Commands that allow information about the databases to be easily and succinctly shown to the administrator.
- Function names that do not affect table or column names.
- A password and user verification system for added security.
- Up to 32 indexes per table permitted; this feature has been successfully implemented at levels of 60,000 tables and 5,000,000,000 rows.
- International error reporting usable in many different countries.

MySQL is the perfect choice for providing data via the Internet because of its ability to handle heavy loads and its advanced security measures.

For more information on how MySQL was developed, or other specific information not covered in this book, visit the resource Web site at www.mysql.com.

PHP5: The Future of PHP

At the time of this writing, PHP5, the newest version of PHP, is in the beta-testing phase. While we can't speculate on which changes, if any, will be made to the final release, we would be negligent if we did not prepare you for some changes that will most likely be in store for those who choose to upgrade. Knowledge of these changes is especially important for those of you who have your Web sites hosted by a third-party hosting company; if that company decides to upgrade, you will be along for the ride. Like it or not, their decisions ultimately affect how you code your programs.

Throughout this book, we draw attention to concepts or syntax that will change in PHP5. This information is for your benefit only and does not affect the PHP version most commonly used today, the one discussed in this book.

A Brief Overview of PHP5

With the development of PHP5, Zend brings some new methodologies to the PHP table. The biggest change to note is the switch in focus from procedural programming to OOP (object oriented programming). While procedural programming has served PHP well thus far, large and complex programs are much better served with OOP. Currently, PHP4 passes variables by value instead of reference. PHP5 changes all that. The new PHP5 provides for improved error handling and integration of objects from external sources, such as Java.

How Changing to PHP5 Affects This Book

PHP5 will change the way you do some things, and although it's still in beta testing at the time of this writing, we have tried to isolate specific code and circumstances that are most likely to need alteration if and when you upgrade to PHP5. In each chapter that covers a topic that may be affected should the upgrade take place, we will bring this information to your attention.

Installation Configuration of Apache

For the purposes of working through this book, we assume that you have installed Apache on your computer. If you haven't done so but would like to, you can find detailed installation instructions in Appendix I.

Before you begin configuring and customizing your installation, take a minute to make sure you have installed everything correctly.

You can access the Apache executable file in three ways:

❑ Open Windows Explorer and go to the directory where you have installed Apache, the default being c:\program files\Apache Group\Apache2\; click `Apache.exe` to start your Apache HTTP server.

❑ At the DOS prompt, change directories to the location where the Apache file has been loaded, and type **apache**. This starts the server.

❑ During installation, the default option is to add Apache to your Start menu, so unless you disabled this, you can locate the Apache HTTP Server listing directly from your Start button. This gives you shortcuts to starting the server and to testing and configuring features, as well.

To test installation of your Apache server, open your Web browser and type the following:

```
http://localhost/
```

If your installation was successful, you will see an Apache "success" page in your browser. If not, check your error log by opening the `error.txt` file, which you can find in c:\program files\ApacheGroup\Apache2\logs\. This gives you an indication of where your installation went wrong.

If you had installation problems, note that you might experience problems if Apache is trying to share port 80 with another Web server or application, such as a firewall.

Customizing Your Installation

Now that you know that everything works okay, you can adjust the configuration file to better suit your needs. The main configuration file you use to make changes is `httpd.conf`; this is found in the c:\program files\Apache group\Apache2\conf directory by default or wherever you have installed Apache. This file can be opened with any common text editor, such as Notepad.

Adding PHP to the Equation

In order for Apache to recognize a PHP file as one that needs to be parsed with the PHP engine, you need to add the following two lines to your `httpd.conf` file:

```
AddType application/x-httpd-php .php3 .php
AddType application/x-httpd-php-source .phps
```

While you can add these lines anywhere in the program, we recommend that you scroll down through the program to find the correct "AddType application" section to avoid human error.

Now add the PHP module into your `httpd.conf` program so that Apache can properly parse PHP.

In your program, add the following line:

```
LoadModule php4_module c:/php/sapi/php4apache2.dll
```

Make sure your path matches the location of this file.

Document Root

By default, the directory under which Apache looks for files is c:\program files\ApacheGroup\Apache2\htdocs\. You can change this to whatever is applicable for your directory structure, but for the purposes of this discussion, let's create a directory named c:\program files\Apache Group\Apache2\test\ where you can put files to test them.

In order to point Apache to the new directory, you must change the document root in your httpd.conf file by following these steps:

1. Locate the section of the file that resembles this text:

    ```
    #
    # DocumentRoot: The directory out of which you will serve your
    # documents. By default, all requests are taken from this directory, but
    # symbolic links and aliases may be used to point to other locations.
    #
    DocumentRoot "C:/Program Files/Apache Group/Apache2/htdocs"
    ```

2. Change the last line of this section to:

    ```
    DocumentRoot "C:/Program Files/Apache Group/Apache2/test"
    ```

    Notice that this uses forward slashes instead of backslashes.

3. Locate the section of the file that resembles this text:

    ```
    #
    # Note that from this point forward you must specifically allow
    # particular features to be enabled - so if something's not working as
    # you might expect, make sure that you have specifically enabled it
    # below.
    #

    #
    # This should be changed to whatever you set DocumentRoot to.
    #
    <Directory "C:/Program Files/Apache Group/Apache2/htdocs">
    ```

4. Change the last line of this section to:

    ```
    <Directory "C:/Program Files/Apache Group/Apache2/test">
    ```

5. Save your file and restart Apache so it can recognize the changes you made to the config file.

Now create a small "test" program to make sure Apache can find your directory.

Open Notepad and type the following:

```
<HTML>
<HEAD>
<TITLE>Apache testing</TITLE>
</HEAD>
<BODY>
```

```
If this works, we did it!
</BODY>
</HTML>
```

Save this as `index.html` in the "test" directory you created. Now open your browser, and type **http://localhost**. You should see the screen shown in Figure 1-1.

Figure 1-1

Installation Configuration of PHP

Once PHP has been installed on your computer, you can customize it to fit your needs. Although some of the configuration settings deal with how the information is shown through the browser, a great many of the settings relate to how the server handles errors and how those errors are displayed to you and your users. You will also be able to have some control over how PHP interacts with MySQL.

Testing Your Installation

To ensure that both PHP and Apache have been installed together, write another test program. Open Notepad and type the following program:

```
<HTML>
<HEAD>
<TITLE>PHP Testing</TITLE>
</HEAD>
<BODY>
<?php
echo "If this works, we <i>really</i> did it!";
?>
</BODY>
</HTML>
```

Save this file as `phptest.php`. Open your browser and type **http://localhost/phptest.php** and you should see the screen shown in Figure 1-2.

Figure 1-2

Customizing Your Installation

The configuration file that holds the key to how PHP runs on your computer is named php.ini; it can be found in the root directory where you extracted your installation files. For the purposes of our discussion, we assume that you extracted the files to c:\ and then renamed the installation directory to c:\php\.

The php.ini file includes a brief explanation of each of the configuration settings, which are beyond the scope of this discussion. However, you are encouraged to read through the entire introduction of the php.ini file before you begin making changes. In the table that follows, we touch on some of the more commonly changed settings.

Setting	What It Does
short_open_tag	Allows short tags to be parsed (<? and ?> as opposed to <?php and ?>)
asp_tags	Allows ASP-style tags to be parsed (<% and %>)
precision	Determines the number of digits to be displayed in floating point numbers. Default is 12, and this should suffice for most applications.
output_buffering	Allows header lines to be sent after HTML has already been sent to the server. The default is "Off," and most third-party hosts maintain this default. It is not advisable to change this setting, especially if you depend on a third-party host.
max_execution_time	Sets the limit for how long a script can take to run. Expressed in seconds.
max_input_time	Sets the limit for how long a script can take to parse the data. Expressed in seconds.
memory_limit	Sets the limit for how much memory a script can use to run. Expressed in MB.
error_reporting	There are many levels you can use to set what errors will be shown to you, but for the purposes of our book, we assume that error_reporting is set to E_ALL. When set to E_ALL, all errors and warnings are shown.
display_errors	Determines whether or not errors will be printed. Let's leave this feature on while you develop your site and you learn PHP, but once the site is ready to go live, we recommend that this setting be switched to "off" for security purposes.
log_errors	Allows errors to be written into a log file for future reference. We recommend that you switch this setting to "on."
error_log	Points to the name of your PHP error log file.

Table continued on following page

Setting	What It Does
variables_order	Determines the order in which variables are registered. The default is EGPCS, which translates into Environment, GET, POST, COOKIE, and Built-in variables. We recommend that you leave this as the default setting until you are more familiar with PHP and the way variables work. In addition, your third-party host will most likely keep the default setting. This setting applies to all variables on all PHP pages, which we discuss in greater detail in Chapter 2.
register_globals	Determines whether variables sent through forms are available globally. This was a recent change from "on" to "off" as the default, and we recommend you leave this set to "off." You can read more about register_globals in Chapter 2.
file_uploads	Enables Web site visitors to upload files to your server.
upload_max_filesize	Sets the limit for how large a file that is uploaded may be.
mysql.allow_persistent	Determines whether or not a persistent connection can be established with the MySQL server.
mysql.max_persistent	Sets the limit of how many persistent connections are allowed. For no limit, set this to -1.
mysql.max_links	Sets the limit of how many total links are allowed (persistent and non-persistent together). For no limit, set this to -1.
session.save_path	Determines where session information will be stored on your computer. You must specify a valid path, such as c:\php\sess\tmp or c:\tmp if you are using Windows. You must also create this directory beforehand, as PHP will not set this up for you.

There are numerous other varables in your file that can be altered; we encourage you to work with the defaults until you feel more comfortable with PHP and your Web site setup. Changing these defaults can raise functionality, security, and performance issues, adversely affecting your site.

Installation Configuration of MySQL

MySQL needs TCP/IP protocols to run properly, regardless of the Windows environment. You must install this before you can continue if it is not already on your computer. (Most computers have this set up already by default.)

Testing Your Installation

As before, it's a good idea to test your installation. You can do this from a DOS prompt so that you can view any error messages your MySQL server encounters.

Follow these steps to test your installation:

1.   For Windows 95/98/Me, at the DOS prompt, change directories until you are in the MySQL server main directory (the default is c:\mysql\bin\). Then type:

```
c:\mysql\bin>mysqld
```

2.   For Windows 2000/XP/NT, at the DOS prompt, change directories until you are in the MySQL server main directory and type:

```
C:\>C:\mysql\bin\mysqld —install
```

You should see a screen that looks similar to the one shown in Figure 1-3.

Figure 1-3

3.   To start the MySQL server, type the following:

```
c:\>NET START MySQL
```

Your screen will look like the one shown in Figure 1-4.

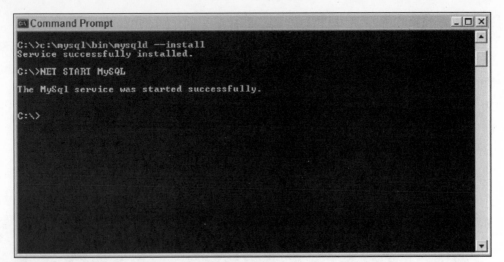

Figure 1-4

4. To stop the server from running, type the following:

```
c:\>NET STOP MySQL
```

5. Let's test to make sure your MySQL server is running. While there are many possible commands to test the server, to keep things simple, let's use the following:

```
C:\>c:\mysql\bin\mysql test
```

Your screen should look something like the one shown in Figure 1-5.

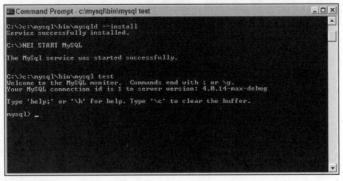

Figure 1-5

6. To return to the DOS prompt, enter the following:

```
mysql>exit
```

or

```
mysql>quit
```

7.   To shut down the MySQL service, type:

```
C:\>c:\mysql\bin\mysqladmin -u root shutdown
```

It's time to configure your system to improve security, set up some user permissions, and alter your settings according to your preferences.

Configuring Your Installation

Before you configure any of your settings, start the MySQL service again.

1.   Enter the following:

```
c:\>c:\mysql\bin\mysql mysql
```

And now your screen should look like Figure 1-6.

Figure 1-6

2.   By default, MySQL on Windows sets up all users with all privileges. In order to change this, enter the following:

```
mysql> DELETE FROM user WHERE Host='localhost' AND User='';
```

You will get a response from MySQL that states:

```
Query OK, 1 row affected (0.46 sec)
```

The time it takes to process the query may differ based on the speed of your computer, but the important thing here is that you get the "OK" from the MySQL gods.

3.   Then get out of MySQL again and reset the users by entering the following:

```
mysql> quit
c:\>c:\mysql\bin\mysqladmin reload
c:\>c:\mysql\bin\mysqladmin -u root password choose_a_password
```

4.   Insert whatever password you would like for your root access; in our example, we chose mysql-pass, as shown in Figure 1-7.

Figure 1-7

5. To reconnect to the server, try your new password:

```
C:\>c:\mysql\bin\mysql -h localhost -u root -p
```

You will be prompted for your password; in this case, we entered "mysqlpass," but you should enter whatever you chose for your root password; you should then see the prompt shown in Figure 1-8.

Figure 1-8

The my.cnf File

The my.cnf file, which can be opened with any text editor, such as Notepad, is the main file that MySQL uses to read configuration options you have set up in your installation. You may alter this file at any time to tweak your configuration down the road.

By default, the installation of MySQL provides us with four sample my.cnf configuration files to use as examples: my-small.cnf, my-medium.cnf, my-large.cnf, and my-huge.cnf. If you used the default directory during installation, these were all saved under the c:\mysql\ directory.

The difference in these files is presumably the amount of space you have on your computer dedicated to processing query requests and so on. For the purposes of the Web sites used in this book, the my-medium.cnf file will suffice, so save it to your root c:\ directory so it can be accessed by the MySQL server. Be sure to rename this file my.cnf so the server can find it.

Your my.cnf file looks like this:

```
# Example mysql config file.
# Copy this file to c:\my.cnf to set global options
#
# One can use all long options that the program supports.
# Run the program with -help to get a list of available options

# This will be passed to all mysql clients
[client]
#password=my_password
port=3306
#socket=MySQL

# Here is entries for some specific programs
# The following values assume you have at least 32M ram
# The MySQL server
[mysqld]
port=3306
#socket=MySQL
skip-locking
set-variable      = key_buffer=16M
set-variable      = max_allowed_packet=1M
set-variable      = table_cache=64
set-variable      = sort_buffer=512K
set-variable      = net_buffer_length=8K
set-variable      = myisam_sort_buffer_size=8M
server-id         = 1

# Uncomment the following if you want to log updates
#log-bin

# Uncomment the following rows if you move the MySQL
      distribution to another
# location
#basedir = d:/mysql/
#datadir = d:/mysql/data/


# Uncomment the following if you are NOT using BDB tables
#skip-bdb

# Uncomment the following if you are using BDB tables
#set-variable      = bdb_cache_size=4M
#set-variable      = bdb_max_lock=10000

# Uncomment the following if you are using Innobase tables
#innodb_data_file_path = ibdata1:400M
#innodb_data_home_dir = c:\ibdata
#innodb_log_group_home_dir = c:\iblogs
#innodb_log_arch_dir = c:\iblogs
#set-variable = innodb_mirrored_log_groups=1
#set-variable = innodb_log_files_in_group=3
#set-variable = innodb_log_file_size=5M
```

```
#set-variable = innodb_log_buffer_size=8M
#innodb_flush_log_at_trx_commit=1
#innodb_log_archive=0
#set-variable = innodb_buffer_pool_size=16M
#set-variable = innodb_additional_mem_pool_size=2M
#set-variable = innodb_file_io_threads=4
#set-variable = innodb_lock_wait_timeout=50

[mysqldump]
quick
set-variable       = max_allowed_packet=16M

[mysql]
no-auto-rehash
# Remove the next comment character if you are not familiar with SQL
#safe-updates

[isamchk]
set-variable       = key_buffer=20M
set-variable       = sort_buffer=20M
set-variable       = read_buffer=2M
set-variable       = write_buffer=2M

[myisamchk]
set-variable       = key_buffer=20M
set-variable       = sort_buffer=20M
set-variable       = read_buffer=2M
set-variable       = write_buffer=2M

[mysqlhotcopy]
interactive-timeout
```

While you can find a complete reference of configuration at the source (www.mysql.com), the options a beginner will be most concerned with follow. To set any of these options, simply type the appropriate line directly in your my.cnf file under the appropriate section.

First, let's discuss the local-infile option, which can be found in the my.cnf file as follows:

```
[mysqld]

local-infile     =1
```

This allows you to load large amounts of data from a tab-delimited file or .csv file directly into your MySQL database. While this option can be very helpful if you are running your own Web site, or if you are the only one accessing the MySQL configurations, many third-party hosts have this set to 0 to block their MySQL hosts from accessing this command, primarily for security reasons. If you are contemplating having your Web site hosted by a third party and you will need this feature, you may want to verify that they have this setting enabled to save yourself some major headaches later on, such as having to manually input large amounts of data a bit at a time, or having to write a subroutine that inputs the data for you. If you haven't yet chosen your third-party host, this will be an important selling point.

Second, let's discuss altering the `log-bin` configuration option that can be found in the following section of the `my.cnf` file:

```
# Uncomment the following if you want to log updates
#log-bin
```

This is very important if you care at all about monitoring which updates are made to your MySQL tables (and you should). This logs all activity to the tables, and this topic is covered in greater detail in Chapter 16. We recommend that you uncomment the `log-bin` line to at least make the data available. Whether or not you do anything with it is another story.

Setting Up Users and Privileges

Hackers (or the malicious breed known as "crackers") can be quite crafty in the ways in which they break into your system, especially if you are directly connected to the Internet. MySQL allows you to pick and choose what user is allowed to perform what function based on the "privileges" that you establish. All user privilege information is stored in a database called mysql, which is located, by default, in your c:\mysql\data directory.

If you're the only one accessing the MySQL database, you may not have to worry about adding users. However, what if you have, say, an Aunt Edna who is going to help you out by inputting some back-logged information? You want her to be able to go into the tables and look at things, and even insert some information. But you probably don't want her to be able to delete your entire database. By restricting her privileges as a user, you help to protect your data.

Try It Out   Setting Up Privileges

In order to set up the initial privileges parameters, you need to make sure you're logged on as "root." Then you're going to GRANT Aunt Edna some privileges as a new user, so type the following:

```
mysql> GRANT SELECT,INSERT,UPDATE
    -> ON *.*
    -> TO edna@localhost
    -> IDENTIFIED BY 'ednapass';
```

How It Works

You have now established that "edna" is a valid user who will be allowed access to your MySQL system, provided two things:

❑ She attempts her connection from the "localhost" host—not a different connection from somewhere else.

❑ She supplies the correct password: "ednapass".

Your Aunt Edna will now be allowed to select information from the database, insert new information in the database, and update old information in the database. By giving her access to all the tables in the database (via the use of ON *.*), we have allowed her to modify any table in existence.

As you become more familiar with working with tables and MySQL commands, modifying privileges or user information will become easier for you, as the information is all stored in a table (just like everything else in MySQL).

A complete list of privileges that you can grant is available at the MySQL Web site, www.mysql.com.

Where to Go for Help and Other Valuable Resources

While we've certainly tried to make this as easy as possible for you, there are so many different variables in computers and their setups that it is virtually impossible to cover every possible situation. Anyone who works with computers on a regular basis is surely aware that, while in theory everything seems relatively simple, things don't always go as planned (or as we think they should). To your advantage, there are several avenues for help should you find yourself in a difficult situation.

Help within the Programs

Before getting online and searching for help, you may try looking for answers to your problems within the programs themselves.

In Apache, the manual was installed with the standard installation and can be accessed in c:\program files\apache group\apache2\manual. A check of your error log will be most helpful as well.

In MySQL, you can enter this realm by typing the following at your DOS prompt:

```
c:\>c:\mysql\bin\mysql —help
```

This provides a multitude of commands that will help you find what you need, or at the very least, provide a valuable "cheat sheet" for administering your MySQL server. In addition, this will allow you to see the current settings for your server at a glance so you can potentially troubleshoot any problem spots.

Source Web Sites

You undoubtedly know where to find these by now, but just in case, the Web sites associated with each of our three components have incredibly detailed information to help you work out any issues, or report any bugs you may find in the programs:

- ❑ For Apache questions and information: www.apache.org
- ❑ For PHP questions and information: www.php.net
- ❑ For MySQL questions and information: www.mysql.com

AMP Installers

Now that we've taken your entire Saturday afternoon to install and configure each of these components, we can tell you about some third-party software programs that will complete the installation for you. You can find an extended list of these types of installers at www.hotscripts.com.

Foxserv

This is an Apache/MySQL/PHP installer that can be found at www.foxserv.net. It is offered as an open source program and is free to the general public. Foxserv allows you to customize your configuration files during installation and also allows for PEAR modules to be downloaded. (You can read more about the use of PEAR in Appendix H.) This installer is compatible with both Windows and Linux systems.

PHPTriad

This is another open source installer that is available at no charge. It is available for download at http://sourceforge.net/projects/phptriad/ but is currently applicable to Windows systems only. Along with Apache, PHP, and MySQL, the package includes Perl and phpMyAdmin (another powerful database administration system we discuss in Chapter 3).

NuSphere Technology Platform

The creators of the popular PHP editing program PHPEd have also developed an AMP installer, which they provide as a free download on their Web site at www.nusphere.com. This installer covers Apache, MySQL, PHP, and PERL, and offers downloads for both Windows and Linux systems.

Summary

By now, you should be well versed in AMP and open source. You know that the abbreviation AMP refers to Apache, MySQL, and PHP, all of which work together to help you develop dynamic Web sites.

So now you've installed, configured, and tested the installation for Apache, MySQL, and PHP and should be ready to start making some Web sites!

Part II: Movie Review Web Site

2

Creating PHP Pages

In this chapter, we discuss the basics of PHP and start you on your way to creating your first complete Web site, one featuring movie reviews. After you complete your Web site, your visitors will be able to locate information about a particular movie, and you will be able to program in PHP.

In this chapter, we cover the following basic PHP commands and structures:

- ❑   Using echo to display text
- ❑   Formatting text with both HTML and PHP
- ❑   Constants and variables
- ❑   Using a URL to pass variable values
- ❑   Sessions and cookies
- ❑   HTML forms
- ❑   if/else statements
- ❑   Includes
- ❑   Functions
- ❑   Arrays and foreach
- ❑   while and do/while

By the end of this chapter, if you actually try all the "Try It Out" exercises, you will be able to create a simple login form, give your users an option to either see a review of your favorite movie or see a list of your top favorite movies, and offer them a numbered list of your movies based on how many they decide they want to see. You can even alphabetize the list for them, if so desired.

Overview of PHP Structure and Syntax

PHP programs are written using a text editor, such as Notepad or WordPad, just like HTML pages. However, PHP pages, for the most part, end in a *.php* extension. This extension signifies to the server that it needs to parse the PHP code before sending the resulting HTML code to the viewer's Web browser.

In a five-star restaurant, patrons see just a plate full of beautiful food served up just for them. They don't see where the food comes from, nor how it was prepared. In a similar fashion, PHP fits right into your HTML code and is invisible to the people visiting your site.

How PHP Fits with HTML

We assume that you know some HTML before you embark on your PHP/Apache/MySQL journey, and you've undoubtedly seen how JavaScript code and other languages can be interspersed within the HTML code in an HTML page. What makes PHP so different is that it not only allows HTML pages to be zcreated on the fly; it is invisible to your Web site visitors. The only thing they see when they view the source of your code is the resulting HTML output. This gives you more security for your PHP code and more flexibility in writing it.

HTML can also be written inside the PHP section of your page; this allows you to format text while keeping blocks of code together. This will also help you write organized, efficient code, and the browser (and, more important, the viewer) won't know the difference.

PHP can also be written as a standalone program, with no HTML at all. This is helpful for storing your connection variables, redirecting your visitors to another page of your site, or performing other functions that we discuss in this book.

The Rules of PHP Syntax

One of the benefits of using PHP is that it is relatively simple and straightforward. As with any computer language, there is usually more than one way to perform the same function. Once you feel comfortable writing some PHP programs, you can research shortcuts to make yourself and your code more efficient. For the sake of simplicity, we cover only the most common uses, rules, and functions of PHP.

You should always keep in mind these two basic rules of PHP:

❑   PHP is denoted in the page with opening and closing tags as follows:

```
<?php
?>
```

❑   PHP lines end with a semicolon, generally speaking:

```
<?php
// First line of code goes here;
// Second line of code goes here;
// Third line of code goes here;
?>
```

Comments can be added into your program as we just did through double slashes (//) for one-liners or /* and */ for opening and closing comment tags that may extend over several lines of code. Indents don't matter, and, generally speaking, neither do line returns. This gives you freedom as a programmer, but a little freedom can be a dangerous thing, as we discuss in the next section.

And there you have it! Now you're an expert. Okay—there might be a few more things you need to learn, but this gets you started.

The Importance of Coding Practices

Before we jump in, it is important to realize how the structure of your code can affect your program. As far as the Web server parsing the PHP code, the structure of your code really doesn't matter. To the server, your code will show up as one continuous line regardless of tabs, indents, and line returns. But to the human eye, how well your code is organized can really make a difference.

Take a look at the following examples:

```php
<?php
if ($_POST["fname"] == "Joe") {
  echo "<p>Hi $_POST['fname']</p>";
}
else {
  echo "<h2>Your name's not Joe, so you can't enter the Web site.</h2>"
}

//check to make sure the first name is equal to Joe before granting access
     if ($_POST["fname"] == "Joe")
          {
          echo "<p>";
          echo "Hi ";
          echo $_POST['fname'];
          echo "</p>";
          }
     else
          {
          echo "<h2>";
          echo "Your name's not Joe, so you can't enter the Web site!";
          echo "</h2>";
          }
?>
```

You can see that although it involves more typing, it will be much easier to spot any missing syntax or a specific portion of the code for troubleshooting purposes.

What Makes a Great Program?

Truly professional code follows three general guidelines:

❑ **Consistency:** Blocks of well-written code always look the same and have the same indents and ways of coding, such as syntax shortcuts that use bracket placement and formatting styles consistently throughout the program. The great thing about PHP is that it really doesn't care about tabs or indents, so you are free to create a style all your own, one that works best for you.

In addition, while there may be more than one syntax for accomplishing the same goal, good coders will be consistent throughout their code with whichever method they choose. For example, as far as PHP is concerned, the following two snippets of code mean the same thing:

```
<?php
// php code goes here;
?>

<?
// php code goes here;
?>
```

You should simply pick one and stick with it throughout your program.

❏ **Frequent comments:** The more you use comments throughout your code, the better off you will be. While it's not so important in smaller, simpler programs, when your programs become more and more complex, it will be hard for you to remember what you did, where you did it, and why you did it the way you did.

❏ **The use of line numbers:** Some text editors insert line numbers for you, but others do not. We discuss text editors later in this chapter, but you should know that it is important to denote line numbers somehow in your code, if they are not provided for you, because PHP lets you know when your program generates errors, and it notifies you of the line number in which the error occurs. If you have to count the lines manually every time you encounter an error, you can imagine how time consuming and inefficient your debugging will be.

Why Should You Care About What Your Code Looks Like?

It's important to follow good coding practices for three reasons:

❏ **For efficiency:** The easier your code is to read and follow, the easier it will be to keep track of where you are with your code, and the quicker it will be to pick up where you left off after a break.

❏ **For debugging:** Knowing where your problem lies is a major debugging tool. If you have used comments, you can easily follow your own logic, and if you have line numbers and consistent formatting, you can easily scan your document to pinpoint a trouble area.

❏ **For future expansions and modifications:** Utilizing comments in your code is especially important for future changes, as not all of us can remember the logic behind code that was written years or even just months ago. Also, if you are working on code that involves a team, if everyone is utilizing the same coding styles, it will be much easier to make changes or additions to someone else's work down the road.

Okay, enough preaching about good code—let's get to it.

Creating Your First Program

You can't get much simpler than this first program, but try it out to get a feel for what the results look like. The PHP function echo, seen in the material that follows, is one of the most commonly used PHP functions and one that, undoubtedly, you will become intimate with. It is used to send text (or variable values or a variety of other things) to the browser.

Using echo

Try using echo to see what results you achieve:

1. Enter the following program in your favorite text editor (Notepad, WordPad, or whatever), and save it as firstprog.php.

Make sure you save it in a "plain text" format to avoid parsing problems, and double-check to ensure that the file is not saved as firstprog.php.txt by default.

```
<HTML>
<HEAD>
<TITLE>My First PHP Program</TITLE>
</HEAD>
<BODY>
<?php
echo "I'm a lumberjack.";
?>
</BODY>
</HTML>
```

2. Open this program using your browser.

Your resulting screen should look like the one in Figure 2-1.

Figure 2-1

Now view the source of the HTML code so you can see what happened with the PHP portions of the code. As you can see, the PHP portion of the code has vanished, leaving only the resulting HTML code.

Now add the line noted in bold text so you can get a better feel for how your PHP code will be parsed.

```
<HTML>
<HEAD>
<TITLE>My First PHP Program</TITLE>
</HEAD>
<BODY>
<?php
echo "I'm a lumberjack.";
echo "And I'm okay.";
?>
</BODY>
</HTML>
```

Save the revised file and open it in your browser. As you can see, the line runs together without a line break, even though you had your PHP code on two different lines.

How It Works

When a browser calls a PHP program, it first searches through the entire code line by line to locate all PHP sections (those encased in the appropriate tags) and it then processes them one at a time. To the server, all PHP code is treated as one line, which is why your two lines of code were shown as one continuous line on the screen. After the PHP code has been parsed accordingly, the server goes back and gobbles up the remaining HTML and spits it out to the browser, PHP sections included.

While the .php extension commands the server to check for and parse any PHP code contained in the program, if you are running your own Web site or if you have access to your own httpd.conf *file, you can change what file extensions are able to parse PHP code. For example, if you have an existing Web site and you simply want to add a small PHP section to your HTML page, you can revise the following line in your* httpd.conf *file to include .html or .htm files on your server so that they are considered to be PHP files:*

```
AddType application/x-httpd-php .php3 .php .html .htm
AddType application/x-httpd-php-source .phps
```

This can also cause a heavy load on your server, so we recommend that you create your site in such a way that only .php files are parsed.

Using HTML to Spice Up Your Pages

From the previous example, you can see that it is wise to use HTML to make your pages look more professional and less utilitarian. HTML can be inserted within your PHP block of code using the echo function. Anything you can code in HTML, from frames, to tables, to font characteristics, can be inserted within a PHP section of code.

Integrating HTML with PHP

You will be better able to see how easily we can use HTML in the PHP program with the following practical example.

Using PHP within HTML

Let's modify the following lines to the current program, as shown in bold:

```
<HTML>
<HEAD>
<TITLE>My First PHP Program</TITLE>
</HEAD>
<BODY>
<?php
echo "<h1>I'm a lumberjack.</h1>";
echo "<h2>And I'm okay.</font>";
?>
</BODY>
</HTML>
```

Your screen now looks something like the one in Figure 2-2.

Figure 2-2

You can see that by inserting some HTML code within the PHP section of the program, you accomplish two things:

❑ You can improve the look of your site.

❑ You can keep PHP lines of code together without having to jump back and forth between HTML and PHP.

If you view the source of your HTML code you will see the HTML code you inserted using the `echo` function displayed just as you intended.

Considerations with HTML Inside PHP

Let's discuss some pitfalls commonly seen with the practice of inserting HTML inside PHP.

❑ **You'll have to check for double quotes.** As you may have noted when you worked through the previous example, using the `echo` function involves the use of double quotation marks. Because HTML also uses double quotes, you can do one of two things to avoid problems:

   ❑ Use single quotes inside your HTML.

   ❑ Escape your HTML double quotes with a backslash, as in the following:

```
echo "<font size=\"2\">";
```

This is especially useful if you want to display double quotes in your text, such as:

```
echo "He was about 6'5\" tall.";
```

❑ **Remember that you still have to follow PHP rules, even though you're coding in HTML.** Sometimes when you begin to code in HTML within your PHP section, you can temporarily forget that you need to follow PHP guidelines and end your sentences with a semicolon, as well as closing all quotes at the end of your `echo` statements.

❑ **Don't try to cram too much HTML into your PHP sections.** If you find yourself in the middle of a PHP portion of your program, and your HTML is becoming increasingly complex or lengthy, consider ending the PHP section and coding strictly in HTML. Consider the following examples:

```
<?php
    echo "<table width='100%' border='2' bgcolor='#FFFFFF'>";
    echo "<tr>";
    echo "<td width='50%'>";
    echo "<font face='Verdana, Arial' size='2'>";
    echo "First Name:";
    echo "</font></td">;
    echo "<td width='50%'>";
    echo "<font face='Verdana, Arial' size='2'>";
    echo $_POST["fname"]
    echo "</font></td>";
    echo "</tr>";
```

```
            echo "</table>";


    ?>
    <table width="100%" border="2" bgcolor="#FFFFFF">;
         <tr>
              <td width="50%">
              <font face="Verdana, Arial" size="2">
              First Name:
              </font>
              </td>

              <td width="50%">
              <font face="Verdana, Arial" size="2">
              <?php
                   echo $_POST["fname"];
              ?>
              </font>
              </td>
         </tr>
    </table>
```

Although we have not yet discussed variables, you can see in the first example that the only thing PHP was really needed for was to give us the value held in the variable fname and display it on the screen. The rest of the related code was in HTML. In this type of instance, you're better off just staying in HTML and pulling out the PHP line when you need it, instead of coding the HTML inside the PHP. While it really doesn't matter to the server, it makes for easier formatting, easier debugging, and less typing (which is always a good thing!). In essence, it is up to you to balance your HTML with PHP and discover what works best for your coding style.

Using Constants and Variables to Spice Up Your Pages

We've covered the basics of using the echo function to display text the way you want it. Really, this works no differently from coding an HTML page. However, utilizing constants and variables allows you to take advantage of the power of PHP.

Overview of Constants

A constant is a placeholder for a value that you reference within your code. Constants are typically named with capital letters (so you can easily find them within your code), and the values are usually formally defined before using them. Constant names must begin with a letter or underscore and cannot begin with a number. Names are also case-sensitive.

The values assigned to constants are defined with the PHP function define(). Once they've been defined, they can't be changed or undefined.

Try It Out   Using Constants

Let's see how you can use constants in your program.

1.   Open your text editor and type the following program:

```
<HTML>
<HEAD>
<TITLE>My Movie Site</TITLE>
</HEAD>
<BODY>
<?php
    define ("FAVMOVIE", "The Life of Brian");
    echo "My favorite movie is ";
    echo FAVMOVIE;
?>
</BODY>
</HTML>
```

2.   Save this file as `moviesite.php` and open it in your browser. You should see the text shown in Figure 2-3.

Figure 2-3

How It Works

By defining the constant known as FAVMOVIE, you have set the value as "The Life of Brian," which can be recalled and displayed later on. While this constant can't be changed or reset throughout your program, it is available for use by any part of your program.

Overview of Variables

Unlike constants, variables are obviously meant to be variable—they are meant to change or be changed at some point in your program. Variables also do not need to be defined or declared and can simply be assigned when needed.

Variables are denoted with a dollar sign ($) and are not case-sensitive as are constants. The first letter of the variable name must be an underscore or letter and cannot be a number.

In PHP4, by default, variables are not passed by reference unless you preface them with an ampersand to force use of that practice. In PHP5, all variables will be passed by reference with no additional syntax required. This significantly increases the speed and power of your PHP programs.

Try It Out **Using Variables**

Let's use variables in the program.

1. Open your text editor and make the following changes to your moviesite.php file (noted in bold text):

```
    <HTML>
<HEAD>
<TITLE>My Movie Site</TITLE>
</HEAD>
<BODY>
<?php
    define ("FAVMOVIE", "The Life of Brian");
    echo "My favorite movie is ";
    echo FAVMOVIE;
    echo "<br>";
    $movierate=5;
    echo "My movie rating for this movie is: ";
    echo $movierate;
?>
</BODY>
</HTML>
```

2. Save the changes and access the file in your browser. Your screen should now look like the one in Figure 2-4.

Figure 2-4

How It Works

The value "5" is assigned to the variable `movierate`, and it is assigned as an integer value instead of a string. The following line of code would cause the value of "5" to be seen as a string:

```
$movierate="5";
```

By keeping this as an integer, you can then perform mathematical calculations on this number later on (such as giving the viewer the average movie rate), as in this example:

```
<?php
    $bobsmovierate=5;
    $joesmovierate=7;
    $grahamsmovierate=2;
    $zabbysmovierate=1;
    $avgmovierate=(($bobsmovierate+$joesmovierate+$grahamsmovierate
        +$zabbysmovierate)/4);
    echo "The average movie rating for this movie is: ";
    echo $avgmovierate;
?>
```

PHP also has numerous built-in mathematical functions such as:

- **rand([min],[max]):** Generates a random integer.

- **ceil(number):** Rounds a decimal up to the next highest integer.

- **floor(number):** Rounds a decimal down to the next lowest integer.

- **number_format(number [,dec places] [,dec point] [,thousands]):** Formats the number based on the chosen number of decimal places, and uses the designated decimal point and thousands separator, if applicable.

- **max(argument1, argument2, ...):** Returns the maximum value of the supplied arguments.

- **min(*argument1, argument2, . . .*):** Returns the minimum value of the supplied arguments.

For a complete listing of PHP's mathematical functions, please refer to Appendix C.

Passing Variables Between Pages

We've talked about how to use variables in code, but wouldn't it be great if you could move the variable value from page to page? There are basically three ways to accomplish this task, and the method you choose is based on the situation and what best fits your needs at the time.

A Word About register_globals

Before we begin discussing the three methods of parsing variables between pages, it is important understand a little concept we call `register_globals`. This is a configuration setting in your php.ini file that, when turned off, prevents the variable value from being falsely inserted by an outside source (because PHP doesn't require variable initialization). While previous versions of PHP set the default setting in `php.ini` to "on," ever since version 4.2 the default has been switched to "off." This was the cause of many a programmer's sleepless night, as you must refer to your variables differently if `register_globals` is turned off, or else find all your variables' values coming up empty.

While many third-party Web hosts have turned on `register_globals`, for security reasons not everyone does; thus the decision was made to make the assumption that `register_globals` is off for the purposes of our tutorial. Coding with the assumption that `register_globals` has been turned off is the safest way to code because your program will work regardless of the server's setting.

Instead of calling variable values by the standard $varname syntax, when `register_globals` is "off" and you need to pass variables across pages, in the receiving page only you need to refer to them in a different way. You will see this in action in the next "Try It Out" section, but the various ways to refer to variables depend on how they are being sent.

Syntax	When to Use It
`$_GET['varname']`	When the method of passing the variable is the `"GET"` method in HTML forms
`$_POST['varname']`	When the method of passing the variable is the `"POST"` method in HTML forms

Table continued on following page

Syntax	When to Use It
$_SESSION['varname']	When the variable has been assigned the value from a particular session
$_COOKIE['varname']	When the variable has been assigned a value from a cookie
$_REQUEST['varname']	When it doesn't matter ($_REQUEST includes variables passed from any of the above methods)
$_SERVER['varname']	When the variable has been assigned a value from the server
$_FILES['varname']	When the variable has been assigned a value from a file upload
$_ENV['varname']	When the variable has been assigned a value from the operating environment

If you do not retrieve the variables using this syntax, the variable value will appear to be empty in your program and can cause you much grief in debugging!

Passing Variables Through a URL

The first method of passing variables between pages is through the page's URL. You've undoubtedly seen URLs such as this:

```
http://www.mydomain.com/news/articles/showart.php?id=12345
```

This is an example of passing variable values through the URL. In the preceding example, we are requesting that the article with the ID number of "12345" be chosen for the showart.php program. The text after the URL is called the *query string*.

You can also combine variables in a URL by using an ampersand (&), as in this example:

```
http://www.mydomain.com/news/articles/showart.php?id=12345&lang=en
```

This asks to retrieve the file with an ID of "12345" and the language presumably equal to "en," for English.

There are a few disadvantages to passing variables through a URL:

- ❏ Everyone can see the values of the variables, so passing sensitive information isn't really very secure using this method.

- ❏ The user can change the variable value in the URL, leaving your site potentially open to showing something you'd rather not show.

- ❏ A user might also pull up inaccurate or old information using a saved URL with older variables embedded in it.

Using URL Variables

Let's modify your program to show the URL variables in action.

1.   Modify your `moviesite.php` file as follows (changes are in bold text):

```
<HTML>
<HEAD>

<TITLE>My Movie Site - <?php echo $favmovie ?></TITLE>
</HEAD>
<BODY>
<?php
     //delete this line: define ("FAVMOVIE", "The Life of Brian");
     echo "My favorite movie is ";
     echo $favmovie;
     echo "<br>";
     $movierate=5;
     echo "My movie rating for this movie is: ";
     echo $movierate;
?>
</BODY>
</HTML>
```

2.   Save your `moviesite.php` file and start a new document in your text editor.

3.   Type the following code:

```
<HTML>
<HEAD>
<TITLE>Find my Favorite Movie!</TITLE>
</HEAD>
<BODY>
<?php
     echo "<a href='http://localhost/moviesite.php?favmovie=Stripes'>";
     echo "Click here to see information about my favorite movie!";
     echo "</a>";
?>
</BODY>
</HTML>
```

4.   Save this file as `movie1.php` and open it in your browser. Your screen should look like the one in Figure 2-5.

5.   Now click the link and see what you get (see Figure 2-6).

Figure 2-5

You see the value for $favmovie as "Stripes" in the URL, as shown in Figure 2-6, but notice there is nothing shown for the value in the body of your page, nor in the title as it's supposed to be.

What went wrong? You guessed correctly if you said "register_globals"! This is a prime example of how not retrieving the variables in the correct way can leave your pages not working and you perplexed. Let's modify the moviesite.php file to fix the mistake.

1. Edit the following lines in your program (as shown in bold text):

```
<HTML>
<HEAD>
<TITLE>My Movie Site - <?php echo $_REQUEST['favmovie'] ?></TITLE>
</HEAD>
<BODY>
```

```php
<?php
    echo "My favorite movie is ";
    echo $_REQUEST['favmovie'];
    echo "<br>";
    $movierate=5;
    echo "My movie rating for this movie is: ";
    echo $movierate;

?>
</BODY>
</HTML>
```

2. Now save your file and reopen `movie1.php`. The link should now work fine, and your screen should look like the one in Figure 2-7.

Figure 2-6

Figure 2-7

How It Works

A few notes about your program we should point out:

- ❑ As you can see from the "Title" section of your program, PHP code can be inserted in a straight line in the midst of your HTML code. This is helpful when you just need to insert one tidbit of information grabbed from PHP.

- ❑ Also from that same line, you can insert PHP information anywhere in your HTML program, including the title.

- ❑ You saw firsthand the effects of not taking into account register_globals when accessing a variable from another page, but did you notice that when we referred to $movierate, we did not have to include the register_globals syntax? This is because we kept the variable's value within our page and did not get the information from another page or source.

- ❑ We chose $_REQUEST for our variable syntax because it really didn't matter to us in our example where the value for $favmovie came from. We were not trying to validate anything or prevent an unauthorized user from entering this page of the site: We simply wanted to pass the value across.

Special Characters in URLs

Passing variables through a URL poses an interesting problem if there are spaces, ampersands, or other special characters in the value of your variable. Luckily, there are substitutes for special characters that maintain the integrity of the variables' values. There is a special function to use when passing these values through a URL called `urlencode()`. If you wanted to change your favorite movie from "Stripes" to "Life of Brian," you would use `urlencode()` to encode the value and insert the proper HTML special characters.

To try this out, perform these steps:

1. Add the following line in your `movie1.php` file:

```
$myfavmovie=urlencode("Life of Brian");
```

2. Change this line:

```
echo "<a href='http://localhost/moviesite.php?favmovie=$myfavmovie'>";
```

3. Save the file and open it again in your browser. Clicking the link now displays the page shown in Figure 2-8.

Figure 2-8

Passing Through Sessions

As mentioned before, passing a value through a URL is fine if the information is not of a particularly sensitive nature or if it is relatively static and there is no danger of a user pulling up old information from a previously saved page. If you are transmitting information such as usernames or passwords, however, or personal information such as addresses and phone numbers, there are better methods for passing the information while keeping it private.

What Is a Session?

A *session* is basically a temporary set of variables that exists only until the browser has shut down (unless you set this up differently in your php.ini file, which is another story altogether). Examples of session information include a session ID, and whether or not an authorized person has "logged in" to the site. This information is stored temporarily for your PHP programs to refer back to whenever needed.

Every session is assigned a unique session ID, which keeps all the current information together. Your session ID can either be passed through the URL or through the use of cookies. Although for security reasons, it is preferable to pass the session ID through a cookie so that it is hidden from the human eye, if cookies are not enabled, the backup method is through the URL.

This setting is determined in your `php.ini` file. If you would like to force the user to pass variables through cookies (instead of allowing a backup plan), you would set the following line in your file:

```
session.use_only_cookies = 1
```

To begin a session, use the function `session_start()`. Because we have `register_globals` set to "off," you should not use the `session_register()` function you may have seen in other PHP scripts. Make sure before using sessions that your php.ini file has been modified to show a valid path in the `session.save_path` variable, as described in Chapter 1.

First, you need to decide what information will be stored in your session. Anything that has been stored in a database can be retrieved and stored temporarily along with your session information. Usually, it is information such as username and login information, but it can also be preferences that have been set at some point by the user. An SID (session ID) will also be stored in the session array of variables.

Try It Out   Passing the Visitor's Username

Let's say you want to pass your visitor's username and whether or not he or she has authentically logged into the site between the first page and the second page. Because we won't discuss the use of forms until later in this chapter, we'll fake it for now.

Follow these steps:

1. Change your `movie1.php` file to include the following lines (shown in bold).

```
<?php
session_start();
$_SESSION['username']="Joe12345";
$_SESSION['authuser']=1;
```

```
?>
<HTML>
<HEAD>
<TITLE>Find my Favorite Movie!</TITLE>
</HEAD>
<BODY>
<?php
    $myfavmovie=urlencode("Life of Brian");
    echo "<a href='http://localhost/moviesite.php?favmovie=$myfavmovie'>";
    echo "Click here to see information about my favorite movie!";
    echo "</a>";
?>
</BODY>
</HTML>
```

2. Now save your `movie1.php` file.

3. Open `moviesite.php` to make the following changes (shown in bold text).

```
<?php
session_start();
//check to see if user has logged in with a valid password
    if ($_SESSION['authuser']!=1) {
    echo "Sorry, but you don't have permission to view this page, you loser!";
    exit();
    }
?>
<HTML>
<HEAD>
<TITLE>My Movie Site - <?php echo $_REQUEST['favmovie'] ?></TITLE>
</HEAD>
<BODY>

<?php
    echo "Welcome to our site, ";
    echo $_SESSION['username'];
    echo "! <br>";
    echo "My favorite movie is ";
    echo $_REQUEST['favmovie'];
    echo "<br>";
    $movierate=5;
    echo "My movie rating for this movie is: ";
    echo $movierate;

?>
</BODY>
</HTML>
```

4. Click the link in `movie1.php`, and you should see the text for `moviesite.php` shown in Figure 2-9.

Figure 2-9

How It Works

There are a few important things to point out about this procedure:

❑ All the session information is at the top of the page, before any HTML code. *This is very important!* If there is even a leading space before the PHP code at the top of the page, you will get this error:

Warning: session_start(): Cannot send session cache limiter - headers already sent
(output started at c:\program files\Apache Group\Apache2\test\moviesite.php:1) in
c:\program files\Apache Group\Apache2\test\moviesite.php on line **2**

There are some other situations that will give you the "headers already sent" error, which we discuss in Chapter 17.

❑ Refer to the session variables using the register_globals syntax, $_SESSION['varname']; if you don't, the variables will contain empty values.

❑ You must use the function session_start() at the beginning of every page that references the session variables.

❑ We used an if statement, which we delve into later in this chapter. It's a good idea to take a quick glance at this syntax, just to familiarize yourself with it.

What Is a Cookie?

Cookies are tiny bits of information stored on your Web site visitor's computer. There appears to be some sort of paranoia about using cookies; thus, many people choose to disable this feature in their Web browsers. While cookies can, in theory, be intercepted to gain information such as a person's IP address and operating system, cookies are primarily used for storing information only. There are also a few ad campaigns that have developed technology to utilize cookies to track your browsing habits, and many people see this as an invasion of privacy. Also, because cookies are stored in a commonly named directory, anyone with access to someone else's computer (either via a hack or physical location) can potentially open cookie files and glean information about the owner. Because of these possibilities it's not a good idea to store any potentially private information on a computer.

> *For more information on cookies and the potential security risks (however minute), you are encouraged to visit the W3 Security FAQ Web site at* www.w3.org/Security/faq/wwwsf2.html.

All that being said, because your visitors may either have cookies turned off or may physically delete cookies from their computers, relying on cookie information from a Web development standpoint probably isn't the brightest idea.

So why do developers use cookies, anyway? The advantage to storing information in a cookie versus a session is longevity. Sessions alone can't store information for more than the length of time the browser window is open. Like the elusive and mean-spirited video game that loses all high scores once it's unplugged, once a browser closes, all session information is lost. Cookies, on the other hand, can live on a person's computer until the developer has decided it's been long enough and they automatically "die." It is because of this longevity that cookies are fabulous for storing information such as a visitor's username or language preferences. These are the pieces of information that users won't have to retype every time they visit your site, but if for some reason someone did get wind of the information, it wouldn't be the end of the world.

We mentioned earlier that sessions alone can't store information for very long. However, we can alter this limitation if we use sessions in conjunction with cookies. If your sessions are passing variables using cookies, you *can* set the life of these cookies to longer than the life of the browser using the session.cookie_lifetime configuration in your php.ini file. Keep in mind, however, that not only will the session information be stored on the person's computer; the session ID will be stored, and that can cause you problems later on.

To set a cookie, you use the appropriately named setcookie() function. When setting a cookie, you can determine that the following information be set along with it:

- ❏ Cookie name (this is mandatory).
- ❏ Value of the cookie (such as the person's username).
- ❏ Time in seconds when the cookie will expire. (Based on a UNIX timestamp, but you can set it using the following syntax: time()+60*60*24*365 keeps the cookie alive for a year. This is optional, but if it is not set, the cookie will expire when browser is closed.)
- ❏ Path (the directory where the cookie will be saved—default is usually sufficient; this is optional).
- ❏ Domain (domains that may access this cookie—this is optional).
- ❏ Whether a cookie must have a secure connection to be set (defaults to 0; to enable this feature set this to 1).

You make each of these settings as follows:

```
setcookie('cookiename', 'value', 'expiration time', 'path', 'domain',

    'secure connection');
```

As you know by now, those values will be referenced in the script as $_COOKIE['cookiename'].

Try It Out   Setting a Cookie

Let's have the Web site set a cookie on Joe's machine so that he (theoretically) doesn't have to type his username (Joe12345) every time he comes back to visit. To do this, follow these steps:

1.   Modify your movie1.php file as shown:

```php
<?php
setcookie('username', 'Joe', time()+60);
session_start();
//delete this line: $_SESSION['username']="Joe12345";
$_SESSION['authuser']=1;
?>
<HTML>
<HEAD>
<TITLE>Find my Favorite Movie!</TITLE>
</HEAD>
<BODY>
<?php
    $myfavmovie=urlencode("Life of Brian");
    echo "<a href='http://localhost/moviesite.php?favmovie=$myfavmovie'>";
    echo "Click here to see information about my favorite movie!";
    echo "</a>";
?>
</BODY>
</HTML>
```

2.   Save the file.

3.   Make the following changes to your moviesite.php file:

```php
<?php
session_start();
//check to see if user has logged in with a valid password
    if ($_SESSION['authuser']!=1) {
    echo "Sorry, but you don't have permission to view this
        page, you loser!";
    exit();
    }
?>
<HTML>
<HEAD>
<TITLE>My Movie Site - <?php echo $_REQUEST['favmovie'] ?></TITLE>
</HEAD>
<BODY>
```

```
<?php
    echo "Welcome to our site, ";
    echo $_COOKIE['username'];
    echo "! <br>";
    echo "My favorite movie is ";
    echo $_REQUEST['favmovie'];
    echo "<br>";
    $movierate=5;
    echo "My movie rating for this movie is: ";
    echo $movierate;

?>
</BODY>
</HTML>
```

4. Save the file.

5. Open a new browser window (in case we have any session information from the previous example lingering about) and open the `movie1.php` file. Your screen should look like the one in Figure 2-10.

Figure 2-10

How It Works

When using cookies, remember the following:

❑ Like sessions, cookies must be placed at the very tip-top of the page, before your first <HTML> line. Otherwise, you get the ol' "headers already sent" error.

❑ If you didn't notice, we changed the username from Joe12345 when we were using sessions, to Joe when we were using cookies. This was to double-check that the information was coming from the cookie and not the session.

❑ We set the expire time for the cookie to 60 seconds so we could play with and test our cookies without having to wait around for them to kick off. For a normal application storing usernames, it would be logical to set this higher.

❑ Unlike sessions, cookie information can't be accessed in the current page where the cookies have been set. You have to move on to the next page for the cookie to be set and accessible to your program.

Passing Through Forms

Up until now, we've passed information among pages successfully, but we've been the ones to supply all the information, not the visitor. While it would be a great world if we really knew that much about our Web site visitors, it might get a little labor-intensive on our part. What do you say we let them supply us with information for a change?

If you've never filled out a form online, then you have probably been living in a cave somewhere with no Internet access. Forms are the great Venus Fly Traps just lying in wait to gobble up useful information from Web site visitors. Forms allow your Web site to be truly interactive; they take data from the user and send it off somewhere where it gets massaged, manipulated, perhaps stored, and then some result is sent back to the user. While we discuss forms in greater detail in Chapter 5, we will briefly touch on them here so you get a basic understanding of how they work.

Fast Primer on Forms

In case you are a bit rusty on the syntax of forms, or if you just need a quick reference, here is a quick, down-and-dirty discussion of forms.

Forms are coded in HTML and stay in HTML.

A form is made up of four parts:

❑ **Opening tag line, indicated by <FORM> tag.** This tag line must include an *action* and a *method*. An action gives the form a URL or path to another program that will take the data included in the form and carry it from there. A method (GET or POST) tells the form how the data is to be carried. (POST is, generally speaking, the preferred method because it's more secure.)

❑ **Content of the form, including input fields.** Input fields are the areas where the user types in the information (or selects it in the case of a checkbox or radio button). An input field must include a *type* and a *name*, and can include other parameters, such as maxlength.

The type of input field can be one of many different selections, the most common being:

- **Text.** Used for collecting from 2 characters up to 2,000 characters. The parameter used to limit the number of accepted characters for a particular input field is `maxlength`. For large input fields (such as comments) the input field text area is recommended over text.

- **Checkbox.** Used to allow users to make a selection from a list of choices; also permits users to make more than one choice. Individual choices must be indicated with a value parameter.

- **Radio.** Also known as radio buttons. Used for allowing users to choose from a list, but they permit only one choice. Individual choices must be indicated with a `value` parameter.

- **Options.** Also known as drop-down boxes. Used for allowing users to choose from a list, Individual choices must be indicated with a `value` parameter.

- **Password.** Hides what the user is typing behind asterisks, but does not compromise the value of the variable.

The name of the input field will be known as your variable name in your PHP program. In order to avoid issues with PHP parsing, you should name your input fields according to the PHP variable naming guidelines covered earlier in this chapter.

- **Action button(s) or images typically submit/clear or user-defined button, technically considered input types as well.** These are indicated with the input types `submit`, `reset`, and `image` for user-created buttons.

- **Closing tag line, indicated with </FORM> tag.**

Got it?

Try It Out   Using Forms to Get Information

Because our program is slowly increasing in size, for this section switch to a text editor that will add line numbers to your document. If you are using a text editor that inserts these line numbers already, you do not need to worry about adding these in. Otherwise, you may want to add periodic line numbers as comments to help you keep track. Besides adding line numbers to our program, you are also going to insert comments to help you keep track of what is going on.

Now let's look at how to use forms to get information from visitors:

1. Open your `movie1.php` file and make the following changes:

```
<?php
//delete this line: setcookie('username', 'Joe', time()+60);
session_start();
$_SESSION['username']=$_POST['user'];
$_SESSION['userpass']=$_POST['pass'];
```

```php
$_SESSION['authuser']=0;

//Check username and password information

    if (($_SESSION['username']== 'Joe') AND
        ($_SESSION['userpass']== '12345'))
    {
    $_SESSION['authuser']=1;
    }
    else
    {
    echo "Sorry, but you don't have permission to view this
        page, you loser!";
    exit();
    }
?>
<HTML>
<HEAD>
<TITLE>Find my Favorite Movie!</TITLE>
</HEAD>
<BODY>
<?php

$myfavmovie=urlencode("Life of Brian");
    echo "<a href='http://localhost/moviesite.php?favmovie=$myfavmovie'>";
    echo "Click here to see information about my favorite movie!";
    echo "</a>";
?>
</BODY>
</HTML>
```

2. Now make these changes to your `moviesite.php` file.

```php
<?php
session_start();
//check to see if user has logged in with a valid password
    if ($_SESSION['authuser']!=1) {
    echo "Sorry, but you don't have permission to view this
        page, you loser!";
    exit();
    }
?>
<HTML>
<HEAD>
<TITLE>My Movie Site - <?php echo $_REQUEST['favmovie'] ?></TITLE>
</HEAD>
<BODY>
<?php
    echo "Welcome to our site, ";
    //delete this line: echo $_COOKIE['username'];
```

```
        echo $_SESSION['username'];
        echo "! <br>";
        echo "My favorite movie is ";
        echo $_REQUEST['favmovie'];
        echo "<br>";
        $movierate=5;
        echo "My movie rating for this movie is: ";
        echo $movierate;

    ?>
    </BODY>
    </HTML>
```

3. Start a new file:

```
    <?php
    session_unset();

    ?>
    <html>
    <head>
    <title>Please Log In</title>
    </head>

    <body>
    <form method="post" action="http://localhost/movie1.php">
      <p>Enter your username:
        <input type="text" name="user">
      </p>
      <p>Enter your password:
        <input type="password" name="pass">
      </p>
      <p>
        <input type="submit" name="Submit" value="Submit">
      </p>
    </form>
    </body>
    </html>
```

4. Save this file as `login.php`.

5. Load this file into your browser and login with the username of Joe12345 and the password 12345.

Let's see what happens; if the authorization script works, the screen you should see looks like the one shown in Figure 2-11.

Now try logging in with the correct Username=Joe/Password=12345 combination. Your `movie1.php` site should load as it did before, and the link should take you to the `moviesite.php` page.

Figure 2-11

How It Works

In `login.php`, we first release any variables from sessions that may be lingering around with the command `session_unset()`. Then we ask for two variables from the user: username and password (variable names `user` and `pass`, respectively). These are submitted to `movie1.php` (the "action" in the form) via the `POST` method (the "method" in the form). This is why we have to refer to them using the `$_POST` syntax beginning of `movie1.php`.

Our file `movie1.php` actually accomplishes several things. It:

❑   Starts the session and, by default, registers the variables. Values are set based on the information sent from the form in `login.php`.

❑   Checks to see if the username and password are acceptable. In real life we would match this information to a database for authentication and verification.

❑   Sets the `authuser` to 1 if the acceptable username/password combination has been supplied, which grants the user permission to then proceed to other pages in the site, such as `moviesite.php`.

❑   If the username/password combination is not acceptable, a tactful error message is displayed to the user.

As the information is passed on to `moviesite.php` as before, the only thing `moviesite.php` has to check for is that the user is authorized through the `authuser` variable.

Using if/else Arguments

You've just seen how `if/else` arguments can be used to set variables and display messages; you will find this an invaluable tool for doing many other things. Like a big floppy-eared, slobbery hound dog, `if` and `if/else` statements can be a programmer's best friend.

Using if Statements

Unlike with some other programming languages, in PHP, the `if` statement can be used alone. The syntax is as follows:

```
if (condition1 operator condition2) action to be taken if true;
```

As in this example:

```
if ($stockmarket >= 10000) echo "Hooray! Time to Party!";
```

If you are creating more than a simple statement that will easily fit on one line, you must use brackets ({}) to enclose your "action to be taken if true" section:

```
if ($stockmarket >= 10000) {
    echo "Hooray! Time to Party!";
    $mood = "happy";
    $retirement = "potentially obtainable";
    }
```

Operators

The operators used to compare the two conditions are similar to those you're likely to be familiar with. A list of these operators follows. Please note that these are only for use within the `if` statement itself and are not to be used when assigning values to variables.

Operator	Appropriate Syntax
equal to	==
not equal to	!= or <>
greater than	>
less than	<
greater than or equal to	>=
less than or equal to	<=
equal to, and data types match	===

Special Syntax Considerations

You should pay special attention to the use of semicolons in `if` statements. Please note semicolons are needed in individual lines within the `if` statement, but not at the end of the `if` statement itself. Also, please take special note of the use of the double equals sign when comparing condition1 and condition2. This takes some getting used to for the newbie and can slip you up if you're not careful.

The way you indent your lines does not matter to PHP, but it matters to the human eye, so if possible, try to keep your indents consistent and easy to read.

Try It Out   Using if

Let's start off by trying a brief program to illustrate `if` by itself.

1. Open your text editor and type the following program:

```
<html>
<head>
<title>How many days in this month?</title>
</head>
<body>
<?php
$month=date("n");
if ($month==1) echo "31";
if ($month==2) echo "28 (unless it's a leap year)";
if ($month==3) echo "31";
if ($month==4) echo "30";
if ($month==5) echo "31";
if ($month==6) echo "30";
if ($month==7) echo "31";
if ($month==8) echo "31";
if ($month==9) echo "30";
if ($month==10) echo "31";
if ($month==11) echo "30";
if ($month==12) echo "31";
?>
</body>
</html>
```

2. Save this as `date.php` and open it in your browser.

The result should display the number of days in the current month.

How It Works

We get the value for variable `$month` by tapping in to one of PHP's numerous built-in date functions; `date("n")` returns a value equal to the numerical equivalent of the month as set in your server, such as 1 for January, 2 for February, and so on. (We talk more about `date()` in Appendix C.)

Then we test the `if` statements on each potential value for `$month` until we get the right answer. If the first `if` statement is false, the program immediately goes to the next line and executes it. When it gets to the right month, it carries out the rest of the statement in the line, and then goes to the next line and executes it as well. It does not stop once it comes across a true statement, but continues on as if nothing happened.

Using if and else Together

Using if by itself is fine and dandy in some cases, but there are other times when the if/else combination is more appropriate. For example, suppose you want to show a certain message on your site, but have a holiday message you'd like shown for the month of December? Or suppose that on your movie review site you want to show an abbreviated version of a movie review for those who haven't yet seen the movie? It's these "either/or" cases where you need to whip out the all-powerful if/else combination.

Try It Out   ### Using if and else

Let's keep with the date theme to let the user know whether or not the current year is a leap year.

Follow these steps to accomplish this:

1.   Open your text editor and enter the following code:

```
<html>
<head>
<title>Is it a leap year?</title>
</head><body>
<?php
$leapyear=date("L");
if ($leapyear==1) echo "Hooray! It's a leap year!";
else echo "Aww, sorry, mate. No leap year this year.";
?>
</body>
</html>
```

2.   Save this file as leapyear.php and open it in your browser.

You should now see a statement based on whether or not the current year is a leap year.

How It Works

When the program evaluates the if statement, if it is false, it jumps down to the next line of code as in the previous example. When the program reads the else part of that statement, it executes it and moves down to the next line. This part is basically the same as when if is used alone. However, when the if statement is true, the rest of the line is executed and the program jumps down to the next line. Upon seeing the else statement, it skips over that and continues on with the program.

If you were to take out the word else and leave the rest of the statement, the "Aww, sorry, mate" message would appear every time, which is something we don't want to happen.

Using Includes for Efficient Code

Are you getting sick of typing the same things over and over again? The makers of PHP have blessed us frustrated developers with a little time-saving device called "includes" that save you from reentering frequently used text over and over.

Includes are PHP files tucked into other PHP files. Imagine that you wanted to type the same message on every page of your site. Perhaps it is your company's name and address, or maybe today's date. If you are coding each page of your site from scratch, this is not very efficient for a couple of reasons:

❑ You are typing the same information over and over again, which is never good.

❑ In the case of an update or a change, you have to make the change in every single page of your site. Again, this is redundant and time consuming, and it elevates the potential for human error.

A solution to this problem is to use an include. Includes can use any extension, but are sometimes referenced as .inc files. If you are adding potentially sensitive information, for example server variables such as passwords, then it is advisable to save these in .php files so they are never accessible to anyone because the information is parsed before it is sent to the browser. An "include" is included in another file while it is being parsed, and then the final output is sent to the browser. You can add an include in any other file, and it doesn't have to be inserted all the time.

Try It Out   Adding a Welcome Message

Let's say we want every page in the movie review site to show a welcome message and perhaps today's date. We want to create a file that includes this information, so follow these steps:

1. Open your text editor and type the following:

```
<div align="center"><FONT SIZE="4">Welcome to my movie review site!</font>
<br>
<?php
echo "Today is ";
echo date("F d");
echo ", ";
echo date("Y");
?>
</div>
```

2. Save this file as header.php.

3. To include this file in the three existent movie Web site files, add the following line in the beginning of the <body> section of the HTML to login.php, movie1.php, and moviesite.php:

```
<?php include "header.php" ?>
```

4. Save your files.

Let's look at the files again. If you open login.php, you should see the screen shown in Figure 2-12.

You will see the same two lines on every page where you have included the header.php file.

Figure 2-12

How It Works

When PHP comes across an include line in a script, it stops working on the current program and immediately shoots on over to whatever file it's told to include. The server parses that second file and carries the results back to the original file, where the parsing continues from where it left off.

Suppose we decided we didn't really want the date to be shown with the trailing zeroes. Luckily, PHP has a solution for that when formatting the date function. Make the following change to your `header.php` file and see what happens:

```
<div align="center"><FONT SIZE="4">Welcome to my movie review site!</font>
<br>
<?php
```

```
echo "Today is ";
echo date("F j");
echo ", ";
echo date("Y");
?>
</div>
```

Your problem is fixed, and it's fixed in all the pages in your site, in one fell swoop.

Using Functions for Efficient Code

As with includes, using functions makes your code (and your typing) more efficient and easier to debug.

Functions are blocks of code that can be called from anywhere in your program. They enable you to execute lines of code without having to retype them every time you want to use them. Functions can help set or update variables, and can be nested. You can also set a function to execute only if a certain criterion has been fulfilled.

Functions are mini-programs within themselves. They don't know about any other variables around them unless you let the other variables outside the function in through a door called "global." We use the `global $varname` command to make an outside variable's value accessible to the function. This does *not* apply to any variables passed with any variables that are global by default, such as `$_POST`, `$_GET`, and so on.

Your function can be located anywhere within your program and can be called from anywhere within your program (this is a change from PHP3). Therefore, you can list all your commonly used functions at the top of your program, and they can all be kept together for easier debugging. Better yet, you can put all your functions in a file and *include* them in your programs. Now we're rolling!

> *PHP provides you with a comprehensive set of built-in functions (which can be found in Appendix C), but sometimes you need to create your own customized functions.*

Try It Out   **Working with Functions**

Let's see functions in action by following these steps:

1.   Open your `movie1.php` page and modify it as shown in bold text:

```
<TITLE>Find my Favorite Movie!</TITLE>
</HEAD>
<BODY>
<?php include "header.php"; ?>
<?php
    $myfavmovie=urlencode("Life of Brian");
    echo "<a href='http://localhost/moviesite.php?favmovie=$myfavmovie'>";
    echo "Click here to see information about my favorite movie!";
    echo "</a>";
    echo "<br>";
    echo "<a href='http://localhost/moviesite.php?movienum=5'>";
    echo "Click here to see my top 5 movies.";
```

```
        echo "</a>";
        echo "<br>";
        echo "<a href='http://localhost/moviesite.php?movienum=10'>";
        echo "Click here to see my top 10 movies.";
        echo "</a>";
    ?>
    </BODY>
    </HTML>
```

2. Now modify `moviesite.php` as shown:

```php
<?php
session_start();
//check to see if user has logged in with a valid password
    if ($_SESSION['authuser']!=1) {
    echo "Sorry, but you don't have permission to view this
            page, you loser!";
    exit();
    }
?>
<HTML>
<HEAD>
<TITLE>My Movie Site - <?php echo $_REQUEST['favmovie'] ?></TITLE>
</HEAD>
<BODY>
<?php include "header.php"; ?>
<?php
function listmovies_1()
{
    echo "1. Life of Brian<br>";
    echo "2. Stripes<br>";
    echo "3. Office Space<br>";
    echo "4. The Holy Grail<br>";
    echo "5. Matrix<br>";
}

function listmovies_2()
{
    echo "6. Terminator 2<br>";
    echo "7. Star Wars<br>";
    echo "8. Close Encounters of the Third Kind<br>";
    echo "9. Sixteen Candles<br>";
    echo "10. Caddyshack<br>";
}

if (ISSET($_REQUEST['favmovie'])) {
    echo "Welcome to our site, ";
    echo $_SESSION['username'];
    echo "! <br>";
    echo "My favorite movie is ";
    echo $_REQUEST['favmovie'];
    echo "<br>";
    $movierate=5;
    echo "My movie rating for this movie is: ";
    echo $movierate;
```

```
}
else {
    echo "My top ";
    echo $_REQUEST['movienum'];
    echo " movies are:";
    echo "<br>";

    listmovies_1();
    If ($_REQUEST['movienum'] == 10) listmovies_2();
}
?>
</BODY>
</HTML>
```

3. Now you must go through the `login.php` file before you can see your changes. Log in as Joe and use the password 12345. Your `movie1.php` page should look like the one in Figure 2-13.

4. Click the "5 Movies" link. Your screen should look like Figure 2-14.

5. Go back and click the "Top 10" link; your screen will look like the one in Figure 2-15.

Figure 2-13

Figure 2-14

How It Works

This has been a rudimentary look at how to use functions, but you can see how they work. The moviel.php page gave users the option of looking at five or ten of our favorite movies. Whichever link they choose sets the value for $movienum.

In addition, moviesite.php accomplishes several other tasks:

❑   It sets up the functions listmovies_1() and listmovies_2(), which prints a portion of the total top 10 list.

❑   We also added this line:

```
if (isset($_REQUEST['favmovie'])) {
```

The isset function checks to see if a variable has been set yet (this doesn't check the value, just whether or not it has been used). We didn't want to show users the information about our favorite movie if they didn't click on the link to see it, so we if/else'd it right outta there. If the variable favmovie has not yet been sent, the program jumps on down to the else portion.

❑ The program performs another if statement to check the value of movienum to run the correct corresponding functions.

❑ It also references the movienum variable for the title of our list, so the program displays the correct number of movies in the list.

As you get more advanced in your PHP programming skills, you might store a list of all your favorite movies in a database and reference them that way, changing your listmovies() function to list only one movie at a time and running the function movienum a number of times. You could also give your users the option of choosing how many movies they want displayed, perhaps through a drop-down box or radio buttons. That would be your new movienum variable.

Figure 2-15

A Word About Arrays

We've talked about variables and how they are used, but what if we had more than one value assigned to that variable? That, my friends, is a good old-fashioned array. Arrays are nothing more than lists of bits of information mapped with keys and stored under one variable name. For example, you can store a person's name and address or a list of states in one variable.

Array Syntax

Let's store a person's name and age under one variable name. We can do this as follows:

```php
<?php
$name = array("firstname"=>"Albert", "lastname"=>"Einstein", "age"="124");

echo $name["firstname"];

?>
```

This gives you an output of "Albert" and all the values are still stored in the variable name name. You can also see how we keep track of the information inside the variable with the use of keys such as "firstname" and "lastname."

You can also set an array value in the following way:

```php
<?php
$name["firstname"] = "Albert";
$name["lastname"] = "Einstein";
$name["age"] = 124;
?>
```

This is the equivalent of the preceding example.

If you wanted to simply store a list and not worry about the particular order, or what each value should be mapped to (such as a list of states or flavors of shaved ice), you don't need to explicitly name the keys and PHP will assign invisible internal keys for processing. This would be set up as follows:

```php
<?php
$flavor[] = "blue raspberry";
$flavor[] = "root beer";
$flavor[] = "pineapple";
?>
```

Sorting Arrays

PHP gives us many easy ways to sort array values. We've listed some of the more common array-sorting functions in the table that follows, although a more extensive list can be found in Appendix C.

Function	Description
arsort(array)	Sorts the array in descending value and maintains the key/value relationship
asort(array)	Sorts the array in ascending value and maintains the key/value relationship
rsort(array)	Sorts the array in descending value
sort(array)	Sorts the array in ascending value

Try It Out   **Sorting Arrays**

Before we go further, let's do a quick test on sorting arrays so you can see how the array acts when it is sorted. Type the following program in your text editor and call it sorting.php.

```php
<?php
$flavor[] = "blue raspberry";
$flavor[] = "root beer";
$flavor[] = "pineapple";

sort($flavor);
print_r($flavor);
?>
```

How It Works

Notice anything weird in the preceding code? Yes, we've introduced a new function: print_r. This simply prints out information about a variable so that people can read it. It is frequently used to check array values, specifically. So the output would look like that in Figure 2-16.

You can see that the sort() function has done what it's supposed to and sorted the values in ascending alphabetical order. You can also see the invisible keys that have been assigned to each value (and reassigned in this case).

foreach Constructs

There exists a foreach command that will apply a set of statements for each value in an array. What an appropriate name, eh? It works only on arrays, however, and will give you a big old error if you try to use it with another type of variable.

Your syntax for the foreach command looks like this:

```php
<?php
$flavor[] = "blue raspberry";
$flavor[] = "root beer";
$flavor[] = "pineapple";
echo "My favorite flavors are:<br>";
foreach ($flavor, as $currentvalue) {
     //these lines will execute as long as there is a value in $flavor
     echo $currentvalue "<br>\n";
}
?>
```

74

Figure 2-16

This produces a list of each of the flavors in whatever order they appear in your array.

Try It Out   Adding Arrays

Let's see what happens when we add arrays to the `moviesite.php` file. Let's also sort them and use the `foreach` construct. Changes are in bold:

```php
<?php
session_start();
//check to see if user has logged in with a valid password
    if ($_SESSION['authuser']!=1) {
    echo "Sorry, but you don't have permission to view this
        page, you loser!";
    exit();
    }
?>
<HTML>
<HEAD>
<TITLE>My Movie Site - <?php echo $_REQUEST['favmovie'] ?></TITLE>
</HEAD>
```

```
<BODY>
<?php include "header.php"; ?>
<?php
$favmovies = array("Life of Brian","Stripes","Office Space","The Holy Grail",
 "Matrix", "Terminator 2", "Star Wars", "Close Encounters of the Third Kind",
 "Sixteen Candles", "Caddyshack");

//delete these lines:
function listmovies_1()
{
     echo "1. Life of Brian<br>";
     echo "2. Stripes<br>";
     echo "3. Office Space<br>";
     echo "4. The Holy Grail<br>";
     echo "5. Matrix<br>";
}

function listmovies_2()
{
     echo "6. Terminator 2<br>";
     echo "7. Star Wars<br>";
     echo "8. Close Encounters of the Third Kind<br>";
     echo "9. Sixteen Candles<br>";
     echo "10. Caddyshack<br>";
}
//end of deleted lines


if (ISSET($_REQUEST['favmovie'])) {
     echo "Welcome to our site, ";
     echo $_SESSION['username'];
     echo "! <br>";
     echo "My favorite movie is ";
     echo $_REQUEST['favmovie'];
     echo "<br>";
     $movierate=5;
     echo "My movie rating for this movie is: ";
     echo $movierate;
}
else {
     echo "My top 10 movies are:<br>";

     if (ISSET($_REQUEST['sorted'])) {
     sort($favmovies);
     }

     //delete these lines
     echo $_REQUEST['movienum'];
     echo " movies are:";
     echo "<br>";

     listmovies_1();
     If ($_REQUEST['movienum'] == 10) listmovies_2();
```

```
        //end of deleted lines

        foreach ($favmovies as $currentvalue) {
            echo $currentvalue;
            echo "<br>\n";
        }
    }
    ?>
    </BODY>
    </HTML>
```

And let's change movie1.php as shown here:

```
<?php
session_start();
$_SESSION['username']=$_POST['user'];
$_SESSION['userpass']=$_POST['pass'];
$_SESSION['authuser']=0;

//Check username and password information

    if (($_SESSION['username']== 'Joe') AND
        ($_SESSION['userpass']== '12345'))
    {
    $_SESSION['authuser']=1;
    }
    else
    {
    echo "Sorry, but you don't have permission to view this page, you
        loser!";
    exit();
    }
?>
<HTML>
<HEAD>
<TITLE>Find my Favorite Movie!</TITLE>
</HEAD>
<BODY>
<?php include "header.php" ?>
<?php

$myfavmovie=urlencode("Life of Brian");
    echo "<a href='http://localhost/moviesite.php?favmovie=$myfavmovie'>";
    echo "Click here to see information about my favorite movie!";
    echo "</a>";
    echo "<br>";
    //delete these lines
    echo "<a href='http://localhost/moviesite.php?movienum=5'>";
    echo "Click here to see my top 5 movies.";
    echo "</a>";
    echo "<br>";
    //end of deleted lines
```

```
              echo "<a href='http://localhost/moviesite.php'>";
              echo "Click here to see my top 10 movies.";
              echo "</a>";
              echo "<br>";

              echo "<a href='http://localhost/moviesite.php?sorted=true'>";
              echo "Click here to see my top 10 movies, sorted alphabetically.";
              echo "</a>";

      ?>
      </BODY>
      </HTML>
```

Now let's log in with the `login.php` file (logging in as Joe, with password 12345), and when we get the choice, let's click both links that list the top 10 movies.

How It Works

Your screens should look like Figures 2-17 and 2-18.

Figure 2-17

Figure 2-18

We first put the movie list in one variable, `$favmovies`, with the array function. Then we were able to list them individually using the `foreach` construct in `moviesite.php`. We also added a link that would allow users to show the list sorted alphabetically, by adding a variable named `$_REQUEST[sorted]`. When this variable was set to "true," the `sort()` function would execute, and we passed that "true" variable through the URL in the link.

You may have noticed a shortcoming in the program . . . okay, you may have noticed many shortcomings, but one in particular stands out. We can no longer control how many movies are shown in our list. We are stuck with showing the total number of movies in our array. There's a way to fix that, which we talk about next.

While You're Here . . .

If you've had any background in programming, you've undoubtedly had *some* experience with a `while` or `do/while` function. Just in case you've never heard of this (and maybe been living on Mars or something), let's give a brief synopsis of this concept. A `while` command simply tells the server to execute a command or block of commands repeatedly, as long as the given condition equals "true."

while checks for the condition at the beginning of the block of code, but do/while checks for the condition at the end of the block, guaranteeing that the block executes at least once.

The following is an example of the while and do/while commands:

```
$num = 1;
while ($num <= 5) {
      echo $num;
      echo "<br>";
      $num = $num + 1;
}

$num = 1;
do {
      echo $num;
      echo "<br>";
      $num = $num + 1
} while ($num <= 5);
```

Both of the preceding snippets of code print the numbers 1 through 5, each on a separate line.

Try It Out — Using the while Function

Let's allow users to tell us how many movies they want to see, and let's number the list as we did before, using the while function.

Make the following changes to your movie1.php program:

```
<?php
session_start();
$_SESSION['username']=$_POST['user'];
$_SESSION['userpass']=$_POST['pass'];
$_SESSION['authuser']=0;

//Check username and password information

      if (($_SESSION['username']== 'Joe') AND
          ($_SESSION['userpass']== '12345'))
      {
      $_SESSION['authuser']=1;
      }
      else
      {
      echo "Sorry, but you don't have permission to view this
            page, you loser!";
      exit();
      }
?>
<HTML>
<HEAD>
<TITLE>Find my Favorite Movie!</TITLE>
</HEAD>
<BODY>
```

```php
<?php include "header.php" ?>
<?php

$myfavmovie=urlencode("Life of Brian");
echo "<a href='http://localhost/moviesite.php?favmovie=$myfavmovie'>";
echo "Click here to see information about my favorite movie!";
echo "</a>";
echo "<br>";

        //delete these lines
        echo "<a href='http://localhost/moviesite.php'>";
        echo "Click here to see my top 10 movies.";
        echo "</a>";
        echo "<br>";
        echo "<a href='http://localhost/moviesite.php?sorted=true'>";
        echo "Click here to see my top 10 movies, sorted alphabetically.";
        echo "</a>";
        //end of deleted lines

        echo "Or choose how many movies you would like to see:";
        echo "</a>";
        echo "<br>";
?>
<form method="post" action="http://localhost/moviesite.php">
  <p>Enter number of movies (up to 10):
    <input type="text" name="num">
    <br>
    Check here if you want the list sorted alphabetically:
    <input type="checkbox" name="sorted">
  </p>
  <input type="submit" name="Submit" value="Submit">
</form>
</BODY>
</HTML>
```

And make the following changes to `moviesite.php`:

```php
<?php
session_start();
//check to see if user has logged in with a valid password
    if ($_SESSION['authuser']!=1) {
    echo "Sorry, but you don't have permission to view this
          page, you loser!";
    exit();
    }
?>
<HTML>
<HEAD>
<TITLE>My Movie Site - <?php echo $_REQUEST['favmovie'] ?></TITLE>
</HEAD>
<BODY>
<?php include "header.php"; ?>
<?php
$favmovies = array("Life of Brian","Stripes","Office Space","The Holy Grail",
```

```
      "Matrix", "Terminator 2", "Star Wars", "Close Encounters of the Third Kind",
      "Sixteen Candles", "Caddyshack");

  if (ISSET($_REQUEST['favmovie'])) {
        echo "Welcome to our site, ";
        echo $_SESSION['username'];
        echo "! <br>";
        echo "My favorite movie is ";
        echo $_REQUEST['favmovie'];
        echo "<br>";
        $movierate=5;
        echo "My movie rating for this movie is: ";
        echo $movierate;
  }
  else {
        echo "My top ". $_POST["num"]. " movies are:<br>";

        if (ISSET($_REQUEST['sorted'])) {
        sort($favmovies);
        }

        //list the movies
        $numlist = 1;
        while ($numlist <= $_POST["num"]) {
              echo $numlist;
              echo ". ";
              echo pos($favmovies);
              next($favmovies);
              echo "<br>\n";
              $numlist = $numlist + 1;
              }

        //delete these lines
              foreach ($favmovies as $currentvalue) {
              echo $currentvalue;
              echo "<br>\n";
        }
        //end of deleted lines
  }
  ?>
  </BODY>
  </HTML>
```

Now let's play around with our new `movie1.php` and `moviesite.php` files.

How It Works

Your code should show a list of the top movies based on how many you as the user chose to see and whether or not you wanted them listed alphabetically.

You'll notice several things in our code:

❑ We added a little trick to our normal echo statement: the use of periods to amend the statement as such:

```
echo "My top ". $_POST["num"]. " movies are:<br>";
```

This way we can slip in and out of quotes virtually undetected.

❑ We set $numlist to 1, and this will keep track of what number we're on.

❑ We are using the variable $_POST["num"] to place a limit on the number of movies to be listed; this is the number the user input from the form in movie1.php.

❑ The function pos($favmovies) is also a new one for you. This function returns the current value where the array "pointer" is (starts at the beginning). We echo'd this function because we wanted to see the current value.

❑ The function next($favmovies) is another new array function that moves the array pointer to the next value in line. This gets us ready for the next iteration of while statements.

Now see, that wasn't so hard, was it? We're really cooking now!

Alternate Syntax for PHP

As a programmer, it's always great when you can find a quicker and easier way to make something happen. We have included some useful shortcuts or alternate syntax for tasks you are already familiar with.

Alternates to the <?php and ?> php Tags

You can denote PHP code in your HTML documents in other ways:

❑ **<? and ?>.** This must be turned on in your php.ini file with the short open tags configuration.

❑ **<% and %>.** This must be turned on in your php.ini file with the ASP tags configuration.

❑ **<script language="PHP"> and </script>.** These are available without changing your php.ini file.

Alternates to the echo Command

You already got a taste of print_r(), but you can also use the print() command to display text or variable values in your page. The difference between echo() and print() is that when using print(), a value of 1 or 0 will also be returned upon the success or failure of the print command. In other words, you would be able to tell if something didn't print using the print() command, whereas echo() just does what it's told without letting you know whether or not it worked properly. For all other intents and purposes, the two are equal.

Alternates to Logical Operators

You may remember that and and or are obvious logical operators we use when comparing two values, but there are other ways to express these operators:

❑ && can be used in place of and, the only difference being the order in which the operator is evaluated during a mathematical function.

❑ || can be used in place of or, the only difference being the order in which the operator is evaluated during a mathematical function.

Alternates to Double Quotes: Using heredoc

Besides using double quotes to block off a value, you can also use the heredoc syntax:

```
$value = <<<ABC
This is the text that will be included in the value variable.
ABC;
```

This is especially helpful if you have double quotes and single quotes within a block of text, such as:

```
$value = <<<ABC
Last time I checked, I was 6'-5" tall.
ABC;
```

This keeps us from having to escape those characters out, and keeps things much simpler. Your "ABC" syntax can consist of any characters.

Alternates to Incrementing Values

You can have variable values incremented automatically in two different ways:

```
$value = $value+1
```

or

```
$value++
```

These are equivalent and both add 1 to the current value of $value.

Summary

Although we've covered many different topics in this chapter, our goal was to give you enough ammunition to get started on your own Web site. Our hope is that you are beginning to realize the power of PHP and how easy it is to jump in and get started. As we talk about database connectivity in Chapter 3, you will start to see how PHP can work with a database to give you a very impressive site.

PHP is straightforward, powerful, and flexible. There are numerous built-in functions that can save you hours of work (date() for example, which takes one line to show the current date). You can find a complete list of PHP functions in Appendix B; browse that list to find bits and pieces you can use in your own site development.

Exercises

To build your skills even further, here is an exercise you can use to test yourself. The answers are provided in Appendix A, but keep in mind that there is always more than one way to accomplish a given task, so if you choose to do things a different way, and the results display the way you want, more power to you.

Try modifying your PHP files in the following ways:

1. Go back to your date.php file and instead of displaying only the number of days in the current month, add a few lines that say:

The month is _____.

There are ____ days in this month.

There are _____ months left in the current year.

2. On your movie Web site, write a file that displays the following line at the bottom center of every page of your site, with a link to your e-mail address. Set your font size to 1.

This site developed by: <u>ENTER YOUR NAME HERE</u>.

3. Write a program that displays a different message based on the time of day. For example, if it is in the morning, have the site display "Good Morning!"

4. Write a program that formats a block of text (to be input by the user) based on preferences chosen by the user. Give your user options for color of text, font choice, and size. Display the output on a new page.

5. In the program you created in Step 4, allow your users the option of saving the information for the next time they visit, and if they choose "yes," save the information in a cookie.

6. Using functions, write a program that keeps track of how many times a visitor has loaded the page.

Using PHP with MySQL

So now that you've done some really cool stuff with PHP in Chapter 2, such as using includes and functions, it's time to make your site truly "dynamic" and show users some real data. You may or may not have had experience with databases, so we'll take a look at what MySQL is and how PHP can tap into the data. We will also show you what a MySQL database looks like in terms of the different tables and fields, and give you some quickie shortcuts to make your life much easier (you can thank us later for those).

By the end of this chapter, you will be able to:

- ❑ Understand a MySQL database
- ❑ View data contained in the MySQL database
- ❑ Connect to the database from your Web site
- ❑ Pull specific information out of the database, right from your Web site
- ❑ Use third-party software to easily manage tables
- ❑ Use the source Web site to troubleshoot problems you may encounter

Although some of this information is expanded upon in later chapters, this chapter lays the groundwork for more complex issues.

Overview of MySQL Structure and Syntax

MySQL is a relational database system, which basically means that it can store bits of information in separate areas and link those areas together. You can store virtually anything in a database. Information such as the contents of an address book, product catalog, or even a wish list of things you want for your birthday can be stored in your database.

In the sites you create as you work through this book, you are storing information pertinent to a movie review site (such as movie titles and years of release) and comic book fan information (such as a list of authentic users/comic book fans and their passwords).

MySQL commands can be issued through the command prompt, as you did in Chapter 1 when you were installing it and granting permissions to users, or through PHP. We primarily use PHP to issue commands in this book and will discuss more about this shortly.

MySQL Structure

Because MySQL is a relational database management system, it allows you to separate information into tables or "areas of pertinent information." In nonrelational database systems, all the information is stored in one big area, which makes it much more difficult and cumbersome to sort and extract only the data you want. In MySQL, each table consists of separate *fields,* which represent each bit of information. For example, one field could contain a customer's first name, and another field could contain his last name. Fields can hold different types of data, such as text, numbers, dates, and so on.

You create database tables based on what type of information you want to store in them. The separate "areas" or *tables* of MySQL are then linked together with some common denominator, where the values of the common field are the same.

For an example of this structure, imagine a table that includes a customer's name, address, and ID number, and another table that includes the customer's ID number and past orders he has placed. The common field is the customer's ID number, and the information stored in the two separate tables would be linked together via fields where this number is equal. This enables you to see all the information related to this customer at one time.

Let's take a look at the ways in which you can tailor database tables to fit your needs.

Field Types

When you create a table initially, you need to tell MySQL server what types of information will be stored in each field. The different types of fields and some examples are listed in the table that follows.

MySQL Field Type	Description	Example
char(length)	Any character can be in this field, but the field will have a fixed length.	Customer's State field always has two characters.
varchar(length)	Any character can be in this field, and the data can vary in length from 1 to 255 characters. Maximum length of field is denoted in parentheses.	Customer's Address field will has letters and numbers and varies in length.
int(length)	Numeric field that stores integers that can range from -2147483648 to +2147483647, but can be limited with the length parameter. The length parameter limits the number of characters that can be shown, not the value. Mathematical functions can be performed on data in this field.	Quantity of a product on hand.

MySQL Field Type	Description	Example
int(length) unsigned	Numeric field that stores positive integers (and zero) up to 4294967295. The length parameter limits the number of characters that can be displayed. Mathematical functions can be performed on data in this field.	Customer ID (if entirely numerical).
text	Any character can be in this field, and the maximum size of the data is 65536 characters.	Comments field that allows longer text to be stored, without limiting field to 255 characters.
decimal(length,dec)	Numeric field that can store decimals. The length parameter limits the number of characters that will be displayed, and the dec parameter limits the number of decimal places that can be stored. For example, a price field that would store prices up to 999.99 would be defined as decimal(6,2).	Prices.
enum("option1", "option2", . . .)	Allows only certain values to be stored in this field, such as "true" and "false," or a list of states. 65535 different options are allowed.	Gender field for your users will have a value of either "male" or "female."
date	Stores a date as yyyy-mm-dd.	Date of order, birthday, date joined as a registered user.
time	Stores time as hh:mm:ss.	Time a news article was added to the Web site.
datetime	Multipurpose field that stores date and time as yyyy-mm-dd hh:mm:ss.	Last date and time a user visited your Web page.

While the preceding field types should suffice for most needs, we've listed some perhaps less-often-used types in the table that follows.

MySQL Field Type	Description
tinyint(length)	Numeric field that stores integers from -128 to 127. (Adding the unsigned parameter allows storage of 0 to 255.)
smallint(length)	Numeric field that stores integers from -32768 to 32767. (Adding the unsigned parameter allows storage of 0 to 65535.)
mediumint(length)	Numeric field that stores integers from -8388608 to 8388607. (Adding the unsigned parameter allows storage of 0 to 16777215.)

Table continued on following page

MySQL Field Type	Description
bigint(length)	Numeric field that stores integers from -9223372036854775808 to 9223372036854775807. (Adding the unsigned parameter allows storage of 0 to 18446744073709551615.)
tinytext	Allows storage of up to 255 characters.
mediumtext	Allows storage of up to 1677215 characters.
longtext	Allows storage of up to 4294967295 characters.
blob	Equal to a text field, except it is case-sensitive when sorting and comparing. Stores up to 65535 characters.
tinyblob	Equal to the tinytext field, except it is case-sensitive when sorting and comparing.
mediumblob	Equal to the mediumtext field except it is case-sensitive when sorting and comparing.
longblob	Equal to the longtext field except it is case-sensitive when sorting and comparing.
year(length)	Stores a year in four-character format (by default). It is possible to specify a two-year format by signifying that with the length parameter.

Believe it or not, there are even more data types supported by MySQL; a comprehensive list of them can be found in Appendix D.

Checklist for Choosing the Right Field Type

Although you won't actually be creating a database from scratch just yet, it's important to understand how to figure out what field type will best serve your needs. We've put together a list of questions about fields that you can ask yourself before your database tables have been created. As you answer each of these questions, keep in mind the potential values that could exist for the particular field you're setting up.

Will the field contain letters and numbers both?

❑ Yes (look at char, varchar, text, tinytext, mediumtext, longtext, blob, tinyblob, mediumblob, longblob).

  ❑ How many characters will need to be stored? Will it vary from entry to entry?

  ❑ **Less than 255 characters, fixed length:** Use char.

  ❑ **1–255 characters, variable length:** Use varchar if you want to delete any trailing spaces, or if you want to set a default value. Use tinytext if you don't care about trailing spaces or a default value or if your text does not need to be case-sensitive. Use tinyblob if you don't care about trailing spaces or a default value, but your text does need to be case-sensitive.

  ❑ **256–65536 characters:** Use text if your text does not need to be case-sensitive in searches, sorts, or comparisons, use blob if your text is case-sensitive.

❑ **65537–1677215 characters:** Use `mediumtext` if your text does not need to be case-sensitive, use `mediumblob` if your text is case-sensitive.

❑ **1677216–4294967295 characters:** Use `longtext` if your text does not need to be case-sensitive, use `longblob` if your text is case-sensitive.

❑ Yes. It may contain letters or numbers, but it must be one of a finite number of values. Use enu.

❑ No. It will consist of dates and/or times.

Use `timestamp` if you need to store the time and date the information was entered or updated. Any other, date only: use `date`. If you need to store date and time both, use `datetime`. If you need only the year, use `year`.

❑ No. It will consist only of numbers, and mathematical functions will be performed on this field.

❑ Integers from -127 to 127, use `tinyint`.

❑ Integers from -32768 to 32767, use `smallint`.

❑ Integers from -8388608 to 8388607, use `mediumint`.

❑ Integers from -2147483648 to 2147483647, use `int`.

❑ Integers from -9223372036854775808 to 9223372036854775807, use `bigint`.

❑ Integers from 0 to 255, use `tinyint` unsigned.

❑ Integers from 0 to 65535, use `smallint` unsigned.

❑ Integers from 0 to 16777215, use `mediumint` unsigned.

❑ Integers from 0 to 4294967295, use `int` unsigned.

❑ Integers from 0 to 18446744073709551615, use `bigint` unsigned.

❑ Decimals with fixed decimal places, use `dec`.

❑ No. It will consist of only numbers, but mathematical functions will not be performed on this field. Use the preceding guidelines for text/number mix in the field.

If your field requirements do not fall into any of the previous categories, check Appendix D for a complete list of all available field types. If you are still unsure about what type of field you need, you can also check the documentation at the MySQL source Web site, www.mysql.com.

null/not null

Your MySQL server also wants to know whether or not the field can be empty. You do this with the `null` or `not null` option. `null` tells MySQL that it is okay if nothing is stored in the field, and `not null` tells MySQL to require something, *anything*, to be stored there. If a field has been defined as `not null` and nothing is entered by the user, an error pops up.

Don't forget that a number zero is different from a `null` entry.

Indexes

MySQL uses indexes to expedite the process of searching for a particular row of information. Here's how indexes work: Imagine you have a room full of stacks and stacks of receipts from everything you have ever bought in your life. Then you find you have to return some zippered parachute pants you bought in 1984, but unfortunately you need the receipt. So you start sifting through the massive stacks of papers. Lo and behold, five days later you find the receipt in the last pile in the room. After cursing to yourself that perhaps you should get a little more organized, you realize you could at least group them by year of purchase. And then you start getting *really* organized and group them further into categories, such as apparel, 8-track tapes, and so on. So the next time you need to return something you purchased many years ago, you can at least jump to the correct pile and even know what category to look in. Makes sense, right?

Now imagine that your data is stored willy-nilly in your table so that every time you wanted to search for something, it would start at the first record and make its way down through all the rows until it found what it was looking for. What if you had 10,000 rows and the one you happened to be looking for was at the very end? Pull up your chair and take your shoes off, because it could be a while.

By using an internal filing system, MySQL can jump to the approximate location of your data much more quickly. It does this through the use of indexes, also known as *keys*. In our preceding "receipt" example, you decided to group your receipts by year, so if your receipts were stored in a database, an index entry would be "year." You also decided to further group your receipts, so another index would be "category."

MySQL requires at least one index on every table, so that it has *something* to go by. Normally, you would use a *primary key*, or unique identifier that helps keep the data separate. This field must be "not null" and "unique"; an example would be a customer ID number to keep your customers separate. (You could easily have two "John Smiths," so you need a way to tell the difference.) In your "receipts" table example, you would create a primary key and assign each receipt its own identifying number so you can tell each receipt apart.

MySQL also provides a feature that allows a value in a field to be automatically incremented by one. This `auto_increment` parameter is useful for making sure your primary key is being populated with unique numbers.

Unique

We all like to think we're unique, but when this parameter is turned on, MySQL makes sure that absolutely no duplicates exist for a particular field. Typically, this is used for only the primary key in your table, but it can be used with any field.

For example, what if you ran a contest in which only the first person from every state who visited would be allowed to join your Web site? You could use the `unique` parameter; then anyone who tries to insert data into your database from a state where someone has already filled the slot will get an error message.

Auto Increment

Say you have a field that you want to automatically increase by one whenever a new record is added. This can be a quite useful function when assigning ID numbers. You don't have to worry about what the last ID number was; the field automatically keeps track for you.

You can designate a field to be auto incremented by simply adding this command when setting up your table. You can also determine what the first number in the count will be, if you don't want it to be 1. You will see this in action later in the chapter.

Other Parameters

There are other specifications you can make when creating your database, but these are for more advanced MySQL users. For a complete list of these parameters, we encourage you to visit the source: www.mysql.com.

Types of MySQL Tables

Now that you understand some of the general features of tables, you should know that there are different types of tables. There are five main types of tables in the current version of MySQL:

- ❏ MyISAM
- ❏ ISAM
- ❏ HEAP
- ❏ InnoDB
- ❏ BDB

A brief summary of each of these types follows, but if you would like to find out more about them, we encourage you to visit the source at www.mysql.com.

MyISAM

This is the default table and will usually be sufficient for the average user's needs. It supports all the field types, parameters, and functions we've talked about.

ISAM

This is basically the same as the MyISAM table, except that it can't handle data larger than 4GB and the data is stored in a machine-specific format; this means it isn't portable across operating systems. The maximum key length is 256, which means that blob and text fields can't be indexed.

There are other differences that you can read about at the mysql.com Web site.

This table type will no longer be available in PHP5.

HEAP

These are mostly used for temporary tables because of their incredible speed, but they don't support a lot of the common features of the MyISAM table, such as auto_increment and blob/text columns. This type should be used in unique circumstances only. You might use it, for example, if you were working with user logs and you wanted to store the information in a temporary table to massage the data, but you didn't necessarily need to keep the data long-term.

InnoDB

This type, along with the BDB type, is considered to be "transaction safe," which means that you can recover data from crashes. It is meant for extremely large and frequently accessed applications. It features a "row-locking" mechanism to prevent users from attempting to change or add the same row to the table. According to the source Web site, one instance of this type of table has been shown to support 800 inserts and updates per second—not too shabby! You can also read more about this type at its own Web site: www.innodb.com.

BDB

BDB, or BerkeleyDB, is the other type of table that is "transaction safe." It is actually its own entity that works closely with the MySQL server and can be downloaded from www.sleepycat.com. Like InnoDB tables, it is meant to support very large applications with literally thousands of users attempting to insert and update the same data at the same time. There is a complete reference manual available at its source Web site, which we invite you to read.

MySQL Syntax and Commands

Although it is quite possible to access MySQL directly through a shell command prompt, for the purposes of this book, we are going to access it through PHP. Regardless of the mode by which the MySQL server gets its information and requests, the syntax is basically the same.

Typically, you keep the MySQL commands in all caps, although this is not necessary. The purpose of this is to help keep the MySQL syntax separate from the variables and table or database names.

Common commands we will be using in this book include:

- ❑ **CREATE:** Creates (duh) new databases and tables
- ❑ **ALTER:** Modifies existing tables
- ❑ **SELECT:** Chooses the data you want
- ❑ **DELETE:** Erases the data from your table
- ❑ **DESCRIBE:** Lets you know the structure and specifics of the table
- ❑ **INSERT INTO tablename VALUES:** Puts values into the table
- ❑ **UPDATE:** Lets you modify data already in a table
- ❑ **DROP:** Deletes an entire table or database

How PHP Fits with MySQL

You can use MySQL commands within PHP code almost as seamlessly as you do with HTML. There are numerous PHP functions that work specifically with MySQL to make your life easier, a comprehensive list of which can be found in Appendix C.

Some of the more commonly used functions are:

- ❑ **mysql_connect ("hostname", "user", "pass"):** Connects to the MySQL server.
- ❑ **mysql_select_db("database name"):** Equivalent to the MySQL command USE; makes the selected database the active one.

❑ **mysql_query("query"):** Used to send any type of MySQL command to the server.

❑ **mysql_fetch_rows("results variable from query"):** Used to return a row of the entire results of a database query.

❑ **mysql_fetch_array("results variable from query"):** Used to return several rows of the entire results of a database query.

❑ **mysql_error():** Shows the error message that has been returned directly from the MySQL server.

You will most likely become very familiar with these commands, and many more!

You can also send any MySQL command to the server through PHP and the `mysql_query` command, as in the preceding example. You do this by sending the straight text through PHP either through a variable or through the `mysql_query` command directly, like this:

```
$query = "SELECT * from TABLE";
$results = mysql_query($query);
```

or

```
$results = mysql_query("SELECT * from TABLE");
```

The results of your query are then put into a temporary array known as `$results`, which you'll learn more about later.

Connecting to the MySQL Server

Before you can do anything with MySQL, you must first connect to the MySQL server using your specific connection variables. Connection variables consist of the following parameters, which you must know before you can connect successfully:

❑ **Host name.** In our case, it's the local host because we've installed everything locally. You will need to change this to whatever host is acting as your MySQL server.

❑ **User name.** We've used just the root user for simplicity's sake, but you may have another user name that you'll need to insert to access your specific server.

❑ **User name's password.** Again, we've used the password that we set up in Chapter 1, but you need to use your own password.

We issue this connection command with the PHP function called `mysql_connect`. As with all of our PHP/MySQL statements, you can either put the information into variables, or leave them as text in your MySQL query.

Both of the following snippets have the same effect; first:

```
$host = "localhost";
$user = "root";
$pass = "mysqlpass";
$connect = mysql_connect($host, $user, $pass);
```

then:

```
$connect = mysql_connect("localhost", "root", "mysqlpass");
```

For the most part, your specific needs and the way you are designing your table dictate what piece of code you use. Most people use the first method, for security's sake, and they may even put those variables in a different file and include them wherever they need to, to make a connection to the database.

So now that we've hooked you up with the server, whaddya say we actually do something with a database?

Looking at a Ready-Made Database

Let's create the database that you will be using for your movie site. It consists of three tables:

❑   `movie` table, which stores the names of the movies and information about them

❑   `movietype` table, which stores the different categories of movies

❑   `people` table, which stores the names of the actors and directors in the movies

Try It Out   Creating a Database

Perform the following steps to create the database and tables:

1.   Open your browser and type the following code. This creates our database and the tables you need to hold the data.

```
<?php
//connect to MySQL; note we've used our own parameters- you should use
//your own for hostname, user, and password
$connect = mysql_connect("localhost", "root", "mysqlpass") or
    die ("Hey loser, check your server connection.");

//create the main database
mysql_create_db("wiley")
    or die(mysql_error());

//make sure our recently created database is the active one
mysql_select_db ("wiley");

//create "movie" table
$movie = "CREATE TABLE movie (
  movie_id int(11) NOT NULL auto_increment,
  movie_name varchar(255) NOT NULL,
  movie_type tinyint(2) NOT NULL default 0,
  movie_year int(4) NOT NULL default 0,
  movie_leadactor int(11) NOT NULL default 0,
  movie_director int(11) NOT NULL default 0,
  PRIMARY KEY  (movie_id),
  KEY movie_type (movie_type,movie_year)
```

```
) TYPE=MyISAM AUTO_INCREMENT=4 ";

$results = mysql_query($movie)
    or die (mysql_error());

//create "movietype" table
$movietype = "CREATE TABLE movietype (
  movietype_id int(11) NOT NULL auto_increment,
  movietype_label varchar(100) NOT NULL,
  PRIMARY KEY  (movietype_id)
) TYPE=MyISAM AUTO_INCREMENT=9" ;

$results = mysql_query($movietype)
    or die(mysql_error());

//create "people" table
$people = "CREATE TABLE people (
  people_id int(11) NOT NULL auto_increment,
  people_fullname varchar(255) NOT NULL,
  people_isactor tinyint(1) NOT NULL default 0,
  people_isdirector tinyint(1) NOT NULL default 0,
  PRIMARY KEY  (people_id)
) TYPE=MyISAM AUTO_INCREMENT=7";

$results = mysql_query($people)
    or die(mysql_error());

echo "Movie Database successfully created!";

?>
```

2. Save this file as createmovie.php.

3. Fill the database with this file, which you should save as moviedata.php:

```
<?php
//connect to MySQL
$connect = mysql_connect("localhost", "root", "mysqlpass") or
    die ("Hey loser, check your server connection.");

//make sure we're using the right database
mysql_select_db ("wiley");

//insert data into "movie" table
$insert="INSERT INTO movie (movie_id, movie_name, movie_type, movie_year,
    movie_leadactor, movie_director)
      VALUES (1, 'Bruce Almighty', 5, 2003, 1, 2),
      (2, 'Office Space', 5, 1999, 5, 6),
      (3, 'Grand Canyon', 2, 1991, 4, 3)";
$results = mysql_query($insert)
    or die(mysql_error());

//insert data into "movietype" table
$type="INSERT INTO movietype (movietype_id, movietype_label)
      VALUES (1,'Sci Fi'),
```

```
              (2, 'Drama'),
              (3, 'Adventure'),
              (4, 'War'),
              (5, 'Comedy'),
              (6, 'Horror'),
              (7, 'Action'),
              (8, 'Kids')" ;
$results=mysql_query($type)
      or die(mysql_error());

//insert data into "people" table
$people="INSERT INTO people
          (people_id, people_fullname, people_isactor, people_isdirector)
      VALUES (1, 'Jim Carrey', 1, 0),
      (2, 'Tom Shadyac', 0, 1),
      (3, 'Lawrence Kasdan', 0, 1),
      (4, 'Kevin Kline', 1, 0),
      (5, 'Ron Livingston', 1, 0),
      (6, 'Mike Judge', 0, 1)";
$results=mysql_query($people)
      or die(mysql_error());

echo "Data inserted successfully!";
?>
```

4. First, run `createmovie.php` from your browser; then run `moviedata.php`.

How It Works

We hope you didn't have too many errors when running the previous files and you saw the two "success" statements. Although we tried to insert useful comments throughout the code, let's dissect this thing one step at a time.

First, we connected to the MySQL server so that we could begin sending MySQL commands and working with the database and tables. We also wanted to be told if there was an error, and we wanted our program to immediately stop running. We did this in the first few lines of code:

```
<?php
//connect to MySQL; note we've used our own parameters- you should use
//your own for hostname, user, and password
$connect = mysql_connect("localhost", "root", "mysqlpass") or
      die ("Hey loser, check your server connection.");
```

Then we actually created the database itself, and if for some reason the database could not be created, we told the server to stop running and show us what the problem was:

```
//create the main database
mysql_create_db("wiley")
      or die(mysql_error());
```

We also made sure to select our database so the server would know which database we would be working with next:

```
//make sure our recently created database is the active one
mysql_select_db ("wiley");
```

Then we began making our individual tables, starting with the movie table. We defined the individual field names and set up their parameters. We also set the database type and started the table auto incrementing of the `movie_id` at 4 (because we will be entering records 1–3 with the `moviedata.php` file). We discuss much more about this feature later on in this chapter, but this gives you a glimpse of things to come:

```
//create "movie" table
$movie = "CREATE TABLE movie (
  movie_id int(11) NOT NULL auto_increment,
  movie_name varchar(255) NOT NULL,
  movie_type tinyint(2) NOT NULL default 0,
  movie_year int(4) NOT NULL default 0,
  movie_leadactor int(11) NOT NULL default 0,
  movie_director int(11) NOT NULL default 0,
  PRIMARY KEY (movie_id),
  KEY movie_type (movie_type,movie_year)
) TYPE=MyISAM AUTO_INCREMENT=4 ";
```

Once we had our MySQL statement ready to go, we just had to send it to the server with the `mysql_query` command. Again, we told the server to stop executing the program and let us know what the error was, if there was one:

```
$results = mysql_query($movie)
    or die (mysql_error());
```

We also created a movie type and people tables in much the same way:

```
//create "movietype" table
$movietype = "CREATE TABLE movietype (
  movietype_id int(11) NOT NULL auto_increment,
  movietype_label varchar(100) NOT NULL,
  PRIMARY KEY (movietype_id)
) TYPE=MyISAM AUTO_INCREMENT=9" ;

$results = mysql_query($movietype)
    or die(mysql_error());

//create "people" table
$people = "CREATE TABLE people (
  people_id int(11) NOT NULL auto_increment,
  people_fullname varchar(255) NOT NULL,
  people_isactor tinyint(1) NOT NULL default 0,
  people_isdirector tinyint(1) NOT NULL default 0,
  PRIMARY KEY (people_id)
) TYPE=MyISAM AUTO_INCREMENT=7";

$results = mysql_query($people)
    or die(mysql_error());
```

We assume that everything was successful if our program runs all the way to the end, so we echoed ourselves a success statement, just so we know:

```
echo "Movie Database successfully created!";

?>
```

With our `moviedata.php` file, we populated the tables with information. As always, we have to connect to the MySQL server and select the database. (Hint: Wouldn't this be great as an *included file*?!)

```
<?php
//connect to MySQL
$connect = mysql_connect("localhost", "root", "mysqlpass") or
    die ("Hey loser, check your server connection.");

//make sure we're using the right database
mysql_select_db ("wiley");
```

Then we began by inserting data into the movie table. We first listed the columns we would be accessing. We then listed the values for each record, as follows:

```
//insert data into "movie" table
$insert="INSERT INTO movie (movie_id, movie_name, movie_type, movie_year,
    movie_leadactor, movie_director)
      VALUES (1, 'Bruce Almighty', 5, 2003, 1, 2),
      (2, 'Office Space', 5, 1999, 5, 6),
      (3, 'Grand Canyon', 2, 1991, 4, 3)";
$results = mysql_query($insert)
      or die(mysql_error());
```

We did the same with the other tables, movie type, and people.

```
//insert data into "movietype" table
$type="INSERT INTO movietype (movietype_id, movietype_label)
        VALUES (1,'Sci Fi'),
      (2, 'Drama'),
      (3, 'Adventure'),
      (4, 'War'),
      (5, 'Comedy'),
      (6, 'Horror'),
      (7, 'Action'),
      (8, 'Kids')" ;
$results=mysql_query($type)
      or die(mysql_error());

//insert data into "people" table
$people="INSERT INTO people
        (people_id, people_fullname, people_isactor, people_isdirector)
      VALUES (1, 'Jim Carrey', 1, 0),
      (2, 'Tom Shadyac', 0, 1),
      (3, 'Lawrence Kasdan', 0, 1),
      (4, 'Kevin Kline', 1, 0),
      (5, 'Ron Livingston', 1, 0),
```

```
      (6, 'Mike Judge', 0, 1)";
$results=mysql_query($people)
    or die(mysql_error());
```

Then, because we instructed our program to die if there is any error, we echoed a success statement to ourselves to let us know that the entire program executed and we received no errors:

```
echo "Data inserted successfully!";
?>
```

Querying the Database

Once you have some data in the database, you may want to actually retrieve it once in a while. You use the SELECT statement to choose data that fits your criteria.

Typical syntax for this command is as follows:

```
SELECT [fieldnames]
    AS [alias]
    FROM [tablename]
    WHERE [criteria]
    ORDER BY [fieldname to sort on] [DESC]
    LIMIT [offset, maxrows]
```

You can set numerous other parameters, but these are the most commonly used:

❑ **SELECT [fieldnames]:** First decide what specific fieldnames you want to retrieve; if you want to see them all, you simply insert *.

❑ **AS:** You use the alias to group two or more fieldnames together so that you can reference them later as one giant variable. An example would be:

```
SELECT first_name, last_name AS full_name. . . ORDER BY full_name . . .
```

You cannot use the AS parameter with the WHERE parameter, as this is a limitation of MySQL. When the WHERE clause is executed, the column value may not be known.

❑ **FROM:** This is pretty self-explanatory: You just need to name the table or tables you are pulling the data from.

❑ **WHERE:** List your criteria for filtering out the data.

❑ **ORDER BY:** Use this parameter if you want the data sorted on a particular field; if you want the results returned in descending order, add DESC.

❑ **LIMIT:** This enables you to limit the number of results returned and offset the first record returned to whatever number you choose. An example would be:

```
LIMIT 9, 10
```

This would show records 10–19. This is a useful feature for showing only a certain number of records on a page, and then allowing the user to click a "next page" link to see more.

For a complete reference, you are advised to—yet again—visit the source at www.mysql.com.

WHERE, oh WHERE

The beast clause called WHERE deserves its own little section because it's really the meat of the query. (No offense to the other guys, but they are pretty much "no brainers.") WHERE is like a cool big brother that can really do some interesting stuff:

❑   **Comparison operators** are the heart of the WHERE clause, and they include the following:

❑   =, <, >, <=, >=, !=

❑   **LIKE and %:** Oh how we like LIKE. LIKE lets you compare a piece of text or number and gives you the % as a wildcard.

Example:

```
SELECT * FROM products WHERE description LIKE "%shirt%"
```

This gives you any records that have the word or text pattern of "shirt" in the description. Fabulous. (Like, totally.)

❑   **Logical operators** are also accepted in the WHERE clause:

```
SELECT * FROM products WHERE description LIKE "%shirt%" AND price < 25
```

This gives you all the products that have the word or text pattern of "shirt" in the description and that have a price of less than $25.

Now that you have the SELECT query down to a science, let's look at this baby in action, shall we?

Try It Out   **Using the SELECT Query**

Open your text editor and save this file as select.php:

```php
<?php
//connect to MySQL
$connect = mysql_connect("localhost", "root", "mysqlpass") or
     die ("Hey loser, check your server connection.");

//make sure we're using the right database
mysql_select_db ("wiley");

$query="SELECT movie_name, movie_type
     FROM movie
     WHERE movie_year>1990
     ORDER BY movie_type";
$results=mysql_query($query)
```

```
        or die(mysql_error());

while ($rows=mysql_fetch_array($results)) {
     extract($rows);
     echo $movie_name;
     echo " - ";
     echo $movie_type;
     echo "<br>";
}

?>
```

How It Works

You should see the screen shown in Figure 3-1 after running `select.php`.

Figure 3-1

First, as always, we had to connect to the MySQL server and the specific database. Next we plan out our query and assign it to the $query variable.

We wanted to choose only the fieldnames `movie_name` and `movie_type` because we decided we didn't care about seeing the rest of the information contained in the table at this time. If we wanted to retrieve everything, we simply would have written:

```
SELECT * FROM ...
```

but instead we wrote:

```
$query="SELECT movie_name, movie_type
```

Next, we told the server from what table we want to retrieve the information.

```
    FROM movie
```

Then we gave it the conditions of our query. In this case, we wanted to see only movies made since 1990, so we wrote:

```
    WHERE movie_year>1990
```

And we asked the server to sort the results by movie type and ended our query and the PHP line:

```
    ORDER BY movie_type";
```

Pretty easy, eh? Let's try using the `foreach` function instead of the `while` function and see how it works.

Working with PHP and Arrays of Data: foreach

We touched upon arrays in the previous chapter, but there is a handy-dandy PHP function we didn't discuss. It's the `foreach` function, and it is quite helpful when working with arrays of data from the database.

The `foreach` function is similar to the `while` function if you're using `while` to scroll down through a list of results from your query. Its purpose is to apply a block of commands to every row in your results set. It is used in this way:

```
foreach ($row as $value) {
    echo $value;
    echo "<br>";
}
```

The preceding code would take all the variables in the `$row` array and list each value with a line break in between them. You can see this in action in Chapters 4 and 5 and get a better idea of how it can be used.

Try It Out   Using foreach

In your `select.php` file, make the following changes (shown in bold).

```
<?php
//connect to MySQL
$connect = mysql_connect("localhost", "root", "mysqlpass") or
```

```
            die ("Hey loser, check your server connection.");

    //make sure we're using the right database
    mysql_select_db ("wiley");

    $query="SELECT movie_name, movie_type
        FROM movie
        WHERE movie_year>1990
        ORDER BY movie_type";
    $results=mysql_query($query)
        or die(mysql_error());

    while ($rows=mysql_fetch_assoc($results)) {
        foreach($rows as $val1) {
        echo $val1;
        echo " ";
        }
    echo "<br>";
    }
    ?>
```

You should see the same results as before, except that there is now no dash between the elements. Pretty sneaky, huh? Because using `mysql_fetch_array` actually returns two sets of arrays (one with associative indices, one with number indices), you see duplicate values if you use this function without clarifying. You can therefore either use `mysql_fetch_array(MYSQL_ASSOC)` or `mysql_fetch_assoc` to perform the same thing and return only one array at a time. We still need to use the `while` function to proceed through the selected rows one at a time, but you can see that using `foreach` applies the same sets of commands to each value in the array regardless of their contents.

Sometimes you will need to have more control over a specific value, and can't apply the same formatting rules to each value in the array, but the `foreach` function can also come in handy when using formatting functions such as creating tables. Let's create another version of the `select.php` program that illustrates this.

Open your text editor and save the following as `select2.php`:

```
    <?php
    //connect to MySQL
    $connect = mysql_connect("localhost", "root", "mysqlpass") or
        die ("Hey loser, check your server connection.");

    //make sure we're using the right database
    mysql_select_db ("wiley");

    $query="SELECT *
        FROM movie
        WHERE movie_year>1990
        ORDER BY movie_type";
    $results=mysql_query($query)
        or die(mysql_error());
    echo "<table border='1'>\n";
    while ($rows=mysql_fetch_assoc($results)) {
```

```
echo "<tr>\n";
     foreach($rows as $value) {
     echo "<td>\n";
     echo $value;
     echo "</td>\n";
     }
echo "</tr><br>\n";
}
echo "</table>\n";
?>
```

You can see that this would easily show a long string of array variables with a few lines of code, whereas if we had to echo out each separate variable with the accompanying HTML code, this script would be quite lengthy.

A Tale of Two Tables

The preceding code is all nice and neat and pretty, but it doesn't do you a whole lot of good if you don't have a secret decoder ring to tell you what those cryptic "movie type" numbers correspond to in plain English. That information is all stored in a separate table, the `movietype` table. So how do we get this information?

There are two ways to get information from more than one table:

❑ Reference the individual tables in your query

❑ Join the individual tables in your query

Let's try out these methods and then talk about each of them in more detail.

Try It Out   Referencing Individual Tables

You can distinguish between two tables in your database by referencing them in the SELECT statement as follows:

```
$query = "SELECT table1.field1, table2.field2
          FROM table1, table2
          WHERE table1.field1 = table2.field3
```

Change your `select2.php` program as shown here in bold:

```
<?php
//connect to MySQL
$connect = mysql_connect("localhost", "root", "mysqlpass") or
     die ("Hey loser, check your server connection.");

//make sure we're using the right database
mysql_select_db ("wiley");

$query="SELECT movie.movie_name, movietype.movietype_label
    FROM movie, movietype
```

```
        WHERE movie.movie_type = movietype.movietype_id
            AND movie.movie_year>1990
        ORDER BY movie_type";
$results=mysql_query($query)
        or die(mysql_error());
echo "<table border='1'>\n";
while ($rows=mysql_fetch_assoc($results)) {
echo "<tr>\n";
        foreach($rows as $value) {
        echo "<td>\n";
        echo $value;
        echo "</td>\n";
        }
echo "</tr><br>\n";
}
echo "</table>\n";
?>
```

How It Works

You should now see a table with the movie names and actual words for the type of movie instead of our cryptic code. The common fields were linked in the WHERE portion of the statement. ID numbers from the two different tables (fieldname movie_type in the movie table and fieldname movietype_id in the movietype table) represented the same thing, so that's where we linked them together.

Try It Out   Joining Two Tables

In life as in code, regardless of the circumstances under which two things join together, it is rarely a simple thing, and more often than not, it comes with conditions and consequences.

In the world of MySQL, joins are also complex things that we discuss in greater detail later; meanwhile, we walk you through a very simple and commonly used join so you can get a taste of what joining is all about.

Make the following changes to select2.php, as shown in bold:

```
<?php
//connect to MySQL
$connect = mysql_connect("localhost", "root", "mysqlpass") or
        die ("Hey loser, check your server connection.");

//make sure we're using the right database
mysql_select_db ("wiley");

$query="SELECT movie_name, movietype_label
    FROM movie
    LEFT JOIN movietype
    ON movie_type = movietype_id
    WHERE movie.movie_year>1990
    ORDER BY movie_type";
$results=mysql_query($query)
        or die(mysql_error());
```

```
echo "<table border='1'>\n";
while ($rows=mysql_fetch_assoc($results)) {
echo "<tr>\n";
        foreach($rows as $value) {
        echo "<td>\n";
        echo $value;
        echo "</td>\n";
        }
echo "</tr><br>\n";
}
echo "</table>\n";
?>
```

How It Works

You should see the same result as in the previous example. As you can see, we simply listed all the fields we wanted to see, regardless of the table they were in. (MySQL will find them as long as the tablename is referenced there somewhere.) We did this in the first line of the SELECT statement:

```
SELECT movie_name, movietype_label
```

Then we told MySQL what tables we wanted to access and what type of join should be used to bring them together in these statements:

```
        FROM movie
    LEFT JOIN movietype
```

We used the most common LEFT join statement in this case. Although there are other things that go along with this, the LEFT join in layman's terms simply means that the second table (movietype in our example) is dependent on the first table (movie). We are getting the main information from movie, and "looking up" a bit of information from movietype.

We then told the server which field to use to join them together in this line:

```
ON movie_type = movietype_id
```

Again, we don't need to clarify which table is being used, but if you have overlapping fieldnames across tables, you can add this if you like, to avoid confusion.

We kept our condition about only showing the movies that were made after 1990, and sorted them by numerical movie type with these lines:

```
WHERE movie.movie_year>1990
ORDER BY movie_type";
```

And the rest of the code is the same. See, joining wasn't that bad, was it?

Helpful Tips and Suggestions

Now and then, we all get into a little trouble. Instead of sitting in the corner and sucking your thumb, or banging your fist against your keyboard (as seen in the infamous "bad day" mpeg floating around the Internet), relax! We are here to help.

Documentation

The guys over there at MySQL have provided wonderfully thorough documentation covering more than you ever wanted to know about its capabilities, quirks, and plans for the future. We have stated this time and time again, but the source Web site really can provide you with the most up-to-date and accurate information.

You can search the documentation, or even add your own comments if you've discovered something especially helpful that might help out other folks just like you. Because this is all open source, you really do get a community feeling when you read through the documentation.

Once again, the manual can be found at www.mysql.com.

Using PHPMyAdmin

Okay, now that we've given you the task of learning MySQL and PHP on your own from scratch, we're going to let you in on a dirty little secret: It's called PHPMyAdmin and it will probably be your new best friend.

PHPMyAdmin is another wonderful open source project that enables you to access your MySQL databases through a GUI. It's easy to set up and manage, and it makes administering your databases, tables, and data a breeze. It does have some limitations, but for the most part, it will make you a lot more efficient.

With this software, you can easily:

- ❑ Drop and create databases
- ❑ Create, edit, and delete tables
- ❑ Create, edit, and delete fields
- ❑ Enter any MySQL statements
- ❑ View and print table structure
- ❑ Generate PHP code
- ❑ View data in table format

You can download the software by visiting the source Web site at www.phpmyadmin.net. This software works whether your MySQL server is on your local machine, or if it is hosted by a third party.

Summary

We've covered some pretty fundamental programming concepts here and delve more into those in future chapters. But for now you should have a pretty good handle on the basics, anyway.

You should have a good understanding of databases and tables and how to insert and retrieve information stored within those tables. You should also have a good understanding of how MySQL works with PHP to make dynamic pages in your Web site. In the next few chapters, we build on this knowledge to create more complex applications.

Exercises

We have started you on the MySQL/PHP journey, and in the next few chapters we take you places you've never dreamed of. To fine-tune your skills, here are a few exercises to really make sure you know your stuff.

1. Create a PHP program that prints the lead actor and director for each movie in the database.

2. Pick only comedies from the movie table, and show the movie name and year it was produced. Sort the list alphabetically.

3. Show each movie in the database on its own page, and give the user links in a "page 1, page 2 . . . " type navigation system.

4

Using Tables to Display Data

So now that you can successfully marry PHP and MySQL to produce dynamic pages, what happens when you have rows and rows of data that you need to display? You need to have some mechanism for your viewers to easily read the data, and it needs to be in a nice, neat, organized fashion. The easiest way to do this is to use tables.

In this chapter, we cover the following:

❑ Creating a table to hold the data from the database

❑ Creating column headings automatically

❑ Populating the table with the results of a basic MySQL query

❑ Populating the table with the results of more complex MySQL queries

❑ Making the output user-friendly

Creating a Table

Before you can list your data, you need to set up the structure, column headings, and format of your table.

Try It Out Defining the Table Headings

Let's define the table headings for our table.

1. Open your favorite text/HTML editor and enter the following code.

```php
<?php
    $movie=<<<EOD
    <h2><center>Movie Review Database</center></h2>
    <table  width='70%' border='1' cellpadding='2'
      cellspacing='2' align='center'>
        <tr>
<th>Movie Title</th>
```

```
                    <th>Year of Release</th>
                    <th>Movie Director</th>
                    <th>Movie Lead Actor</th>
                    <th>Movie Type</th>
            </tr>
        </table>
EOD;

        echo $movie;
    ?>
```

2. Save this file as `table1.php` and upload it to your Web server.

3. Load your favorite browser and view the page that you have just uploaded.

   Your table should look like the one shown in Figure 4-1.

Figure 4-1

How It works

All the code between `<<<EOD` and `EOD;` is held in the variable `$table`, so instead of printing each element of the HTML table, we are adding that element to the variable `$table`. Incidentally, we have left the border on just to show ourselves that it is actually working.

Then we simply echo the contents of `$table`. And finally, we close the PHP script using the `?>` tag.

By using these two tags, we can use raw HTML code (that is, HTML code that does not need any modification at all).

As you may recall from Chapter 2 in the discussion regarding using `heredoc`, we can change the text "EOD" to whatever we'd like, but the beginning and ending tags must match. For example, this will work fine:

```
$table =<<<HAHAHA
        code here
HAHAHA;
```

but this:

```
$table =<<<HAHAHA
        code here
BOOHOO;
```

will not work. You will receive an error such as the one shown in Figure 4-2.

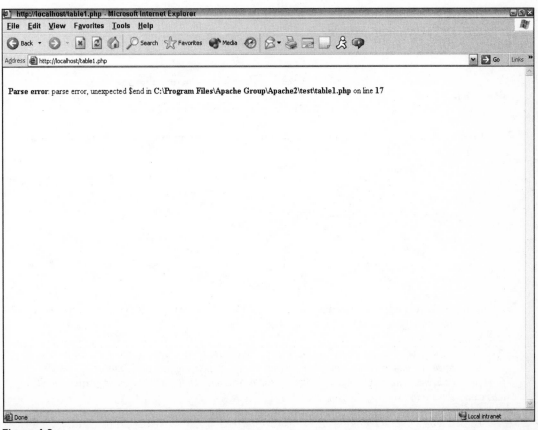

Figure 4-2

Note that there must be *no* spaces after the =<<<EOD and the EOD; tags. In addition, there can be no leading space, indents, or any other characters on the closing tag line (semicolons are permissible). If there is even one space, you'll receive an error. (You can potentially spend *hours* trying to fix an error as a result of having a single space after these tags!) Always remember to delete all spaces after these tags.

Now that you can create a table, let's fill it with some data from your movie review database. After all, that's what you're here for!

Populating the Table

Looking at our empty skeleton of a table gives us the blueprint for how our data will be laid out once it is retrieved from the database.

Try It Out   **Filling the Table with Data**

As this is quite a large piece of code, we'll explain what's going on as we go through it. All changes are in bold. A few things are taken out from the original script (we'll soon see who has been paying attention).

1. Open the file `table1.php`, and with your favorite text/HTML editor make the following changes to the existing code. We use the databases created in Chapter 3 for the purposes of the example here.

   Remember to replace `servername`, `username`, `userpassword`, and `databasename` with your own values.

```php
<?php
    $link = mysql_connect("servername","username","userpassword") or
die(mysql_error());
    mysql_select_db("wiley") or die (mysql_error());
```

2. Start by making a connection to the database. (You have remembered to change the settings to reflect your own, haven't you? Good.)

```php
$query = "SELECT
                movie_name,
                movie_director,
                movie_leadactor
        FROM
                movie";

$result = mysql_query($query,$link) or die(mysql_error());
$num_movies = mysql_num_rows($result);
```

3. Run a SQL query against the database and get the results. And while you are at it, count how many records were returned from the query.

   As we discuss in Chapter 3, we've put the SQL words in capital letters. This is good practice, as it allows you to easily identify what words are field names and which ones are SQL keywords. It is also good practice to make your SQL query as easy to read as possible. That is why we have written the SQL query over several lines.

```
$movie_header =<<<EOD
<h2><center>Movie Review Database</center></h2>
<table  width='70%' border='1' cellpadding='2' cellspacing='2' align='center'>
    <tr>
        <th align='left'>Movie Title</th>
        <th align='left'>Movie Director</th>
        <th align='left'>Movie Lead Actor</th>
    </tr>
EOD;
```

4.   Then enter the block of code that was originally there (minus the echo statement).

Pay attention to the fact that it's called $movie_header, *not* $movie (as it was in the first example).

```
while($row = mysql_fetch_array($result))
{
    $movie_name = $row['movie_name'];
    $movie_director = $row['movie_director'];
    $movie_leadactor = $row['movie_leadactor'];

    $movie_details .=<<<EOD
<tr>
        <td>$movie_name</td>
        <td>$movie_director</td>
        <td>$movie_leadactor</td>
    </tr>
EOD;
    }

$movie_details .=<<<EOD
<tr>
        <td> </td>
</tr>
<tr>
        <td>Total :$num_movies Movies</td>
</tr>
EOD;
```

How It Works

The preceding code does quite a lot of work for us, so let's look at it in more detail.

As you know, the while { } statement loops through the records that have been returned. For each record, it executes the block of code that is between the brackets. Don't worry; PHP is smart enough to know how many records there are and what record number is currently on in this case. There is no danger of having the wrong values assigned to the wrong record.

The first line within the while loop (after the {) tells the script to pull out the value of the field movie_name in the current record and put it into a variable called $movie_name. The next four lines do the same thing (well, almost the same—they simply assign different field values to differently named variables).

Then you come across the familiar tag that you saw at the beginning of this chapter. It's not quite the same as the one before because this one has `.=<<<EOD` instead of just `=<<<EOD`. So instead of just having one record's values, `$movie_details` contains all of the record values that have been returned. Then at the end we have included the total number of movies in our database.

> *By adding a period (.) in front of `=<<<EOD`, you are adding the current value to the existing values. If you forget to add the period (.) then all you will get is the last record's values. That's because in PHP `$var = "1"` means "make $var become equal to the value of 1."*

In the preceding example, notice that we've assigned the name of the movie to the variable `$movie_name` and then used `$movie_name` instead of doing the following.

```
while($row = mysql_fetch_row($result))
{
    $movie_details .=<<<EOD
    <tr>
        <td>$row['movie_name']</td>
    </tr>
EOD;
}
```

The preceding snippet does exactly the same thing, but it would then limit you if you wanted to do any formatting on the variable's values (you'll see what we mean a bit later on).

Try It Out   Putting it All Together

The data has now been retrieved, but we need to send it all to the browser so it will display in the table.

1. We assign the `$movie_footer` variable by entering the following:

```
$movie_footer ="</table>";

$movie =<<<MOVIE
                $movie_header
                $movie_details
                $movie_footer
MOVIE;

    print "There are $num_movies movies in our database";
    print $movie;
?>
```

2. Save this file as `table2.php` and upload it to your Web server.

3. Load that page into your Web browser.

You should see something similar to the screen shown in Figure 4-3.

Figure 4-3

Try It Out   **Improving Our Table**

The table may look pretty, but as in Chapter 3, it doesn't do us much good if we don't have our secret decoder ring to decipher what actors and directors were associated with our movies. You need to link your tables to pull this information.

1.   Modify your `table2.php` file as shown in bold text:

```php
<?php
$link = mysql_connect("localhost","root","mysqlpass") or die(mysql_error());
    mysql_select_db("wiley") or die (mysql_error());

$query = "SELECT
      movie_name,
    movie_director,
    movie_leadactor
    FROM
```

```
movie";

     $result = mysql_query($query,$link) or die(mysql_error());
$num_movies = mysql_num_rows($result);


$movie_header=<<<EOD
     <h2><center>Movie Review Database</center></h2>
     <table  width='70%' border='1' cellpadding='2'
      cellspacing='2' align='center'>
          <tr>
               <th>Movie Title</th>
               <th>Movie Director</th>
               <th>Movie Lead Actor</th>
          </tr>

EOD;

function get_director() {
     global $movie_director;
     global $director;

     $query_d = "SELECT people_fullname
          FROM people
          WHERE people_id='$movie_director' ";
     $results_d = mysql_query($query_d) or die(mysql_error());
     $row_d = mysql_fetch_array($results_d);
     extract ($row_d);
     $director = $people_fullname;
}

function get_leadactor() {
     global $movie_leadactor;
     global $leadactor;

     $query_a = "SELECT people_fullname
          FROM people
          WHERE people_id='$movie_leadactor'";
     $results_a = mysql_query($query_a) or die(mysql_error());
     $row_a = mysql_fetch_array($results_a);
     extract ($row_a);
     $leadactor = $people_fullname;
}

while($row = mysql_fetch_array($result))
{
     $movie_name = $row['movie_name'];
     $movie_director = $row['movie_director'];
```

```
        $movie_leadactor = $row['movie_leadactor'];

        //get director's name from people table
        get_director($movie_director);

        //get lead actor's name from people table
        get_leadactor($movie_leadactor);

        $movie_details .=<<<EOD
        <tr>
            <td>$movie_name</td>
            <td>$director</td>
            <td>$leadactor</td>
        </tr>
EOD;
    }


$movie_details .=<<<EOD
<tr>
    <td>Total :$num_movies Movies</td>
</tr>
EOD;

$movie_footer ="</table>";

$movie =<<<MOVIE
            $movie_header
            $movie_details
            $movie_footer
MOVIE;

    print "There are $num_movies movies in our database";
    print $movie;
?>
```

2. Save your file and reload it in your browser. Your screen should now look like that in Figure 4-4.

How It Works

With the functions `get_director` and `get_leadactor` added, the script requests that specific information be requested from the server for each separate row in the table. This enables you to pull the information you want without muddling up your original query. You also cleaned up the formatting for the last two rows with the change in code near the end of the script.

Congratulations! You have successfully developed a powerful script that will query a database and put its contents into an HTML table. Give yourself a pat on the back. But like all good explorers, onward we must go.

Figure 4-4

Who's the Master?

Now let's build on the good work that you've done so far and add more information and functionality to your table.

Adding Links to the Table

The steps in this section will enable you to load extra information depending on the movie that you click. This requires you to do the following:

1. Open `table2.php` in your favorite text/HTML editor and add the lines of code that appear in bold.

   We haven't displayed the whole page of code, as we're sure you know it by heart already.

```
$query = "SELECT
    movie_id,
    movie_name,
    movie_director,
    movie_leadactor
    FROM
```

```
        movie";

        $result = mysql_query($query,$link) or die(mysql_error());
        $num_movies = mysql_num_rows($result);

    while($row = mysql_fetch_array($result))
    {
        $movie_id = $row['movie_id'];
        $movie_name = $row['movie_name'];
        $movie_director = $row['movie_director'];
        $movie_leadactor = $row['movie_leadactor'];

        //get director's name from people table
        get_director($movie_director);

        //get lead actor's name from people table
        get_leadactor($movie_leadactor);

        $movie_details .=<<<EOD
        <tr>
            <td><a href='movie_details.php?movie_id=$movie_id'title=
    'Find out more about $movie_name'>$movie_name</td>
            <td>$director</td>
            <td>$leadactor</td>
        </tr>
EOD;
    }
```

2. Save the file as table3.php, upload the file to your Web server, and open the page with your browser.

Your screen should look like that in Figure 4-5.

How It Works

You should notice a change between Figure 4-4 (table2.php) and Figure 4-5 (table3.php). You now have links to more detailed information about each movie for your visitor to click.

The first change made in the previous section altered the MySQL query to include the $movie_id field.

Then we added the new field to the results set returned from the query. (Otherwise, we'd just be selecting a field and not actually doing anything with it, and what's the point of that?)

The final change created the HTML code that produces a hyperlink on the movie name. We've also added a nice little touch with the inclusion of "tooltips" for each of the movies in the list. Unfortunately, some Web browsers don't support this (apologies to those of you who have such browsers).

So now that the changes have been made, what does it actually do?

Place your mouse over some hyperlinks, and if you view your status bar, you'll see that each link is unique and is created dynamically.

This page is known as the "master page," and the page that we are going to link to is known as the "child page."

Good, eh? No more having to type lots of different hyperlinks (what a bore that used to be).

Figure 4-5

Adding Data to the Table

Before you can go any further, you need to add some data to your existing database that you can use for your movie details. If you recall from Chapter 3, for each movie, you currently have the movie name, director, lead actor, type, and year of release. Let's also add the running time, how much the movie made, and how much it cost to produce. For all you sticklers out there, a word of warning: the dollar amounts we are using are *for instructional purposes only*. In fact, we have no idea how much money these movies actually made, nor how much they cost to produce. Work with us on this one, okay?

1.   Open your text editor and type the following code:

```php
<?php
$link = mysql_connect("localhost","root","mysqlpass") or die(mysql_error());
    mysql_select_db("wiley") or die (mysql_error());

//alter "movie" table to include running time/cost/takings fields
$add = "ALTER TABLE movie ADD COLUMN (
    movie_running_time int NULL,
     movie_cost int NULL,
```

```
        movie_takings int NULL)";
$results = mysql_query($add)
    or die(mysql_error());


//insert new data into "movie" table for each movie
$update="UPDATE movie SET
    movie_running_time=102,
    movie_cost=10,
    movie_takings=15
  WHERE movie_id = 1";
$results = mysql_query($update)
    or die(mysql_error());

$update="UPDATE movie SET
    movie_running_time=90,
    movie_cost=3,
    movie_takings=90
  WHERE movie_id = 2";
$results = mysql_query($update)
    or die(mysql_error());

$update="UPDATE movie SET
    movie_running_time=134,
    movie_cost=15,
    movie_takings=10
  WHERE movie_id = 3";
$results = mysql_query($update)
    or die(mysql_error());

?>
```

2. Open this file in your browser. Don't worry—you will see a blank screen, but your table has been altered and the information has been entered automatically.

How It Works

First, the script used the ALTER TABLE command to add the appropriate fields into the existing movie table, and then it used the UPDATE command to insert the new data into those fields. If you aren't familiar with these commands, you might try rereading Chapter 3.

Try It Out   **Calculating Movie Takings**

Now that you have the data in place, you need to create a new page that you'll use to display the extra movie information (movie_details.php).

1. Open your text editor and type the following program:

```
<?php
$link = mysql_connect("localhost","root","mysqlpass")
 or die(mysql_error());
    mysql_select_db("wiley") or die (mysql_error());

/* Function to calculate if a movie made a profit,
loss or broke even */
```

```
function calculate_differences($takings,$cost)
{
    $difference = $takings - $cost;

    if($difference <0)
    {
        $difference = substr($difference,1);
        $font_color ='red';
        $profit_or_loss = "$".$difference."m";
    }elseif($difference >0){
        $font_color ='green';
        $profit_or_loss = "$".$difference."m";
    }else{
        $font_color ='blue';
        $profit_or_loss = "Broke even";
    }
    return "<font color='$font_color'>".$profit_or_loss."</font>";
}
?>
```

This function will make life easier for you. This will become clearer as we proceed through the rest of this example.

2. Save this file as `movie_details.php`.

How It Works

The line that contains the code `substr` is placed before the `$profit_or_loss` line because a loss will return a negative number, and no one actually says, "The movie made a loss of minus 10 million dollars." Instead we say, "The movie lost 10 million dollars." However, what happens when the movie takings are the same as the movie production costs? That's where the last "else" comes into play. We've covered all eventualities.

The important thing to remember is that in PHP you can very easily create new variables by performing actions on existing ones. Just because you don't hold the information in the database doesn't mean you can't create it.

Try It Out   Displaying the New Information

Now you are going to alter the original master table to include the new data, and this will serve as your new "child" table.

1. Add the following code to `movie_details.php`:

```
/* Function to get the director's name from the people table */
function get_director() {
    global $movie_director;
    global $director;

    $query_d = "SELECT people_fullname
        FROM people
        WHERE people_id='$movie_director' ";
    $results_d = mysql_query($query_d) or die(mysql_error());
    $row_d = mysql_fetch_array($results_d);
    extract ($row_d);
```

```
        $director = $people_fullname;
}


/* Function to get the lead actor's name from the people table */
function get_leadactor() {
    global $movie_leadactor;
    global $leadactor;

    $query_a = "SELECT people_fullname
        FROM people
        WHERE people_id='$movie_leadactor'";
    $results_a = mysql_query($query_a) or die(mysql_error());
    $row_a = mysql_fetch_array($results_a);
    extract ($row_a);
    $leadactor = $people_fullname;
}

$query = "SELECT
                *
        FROM
                movie
        WHERE
                movie_id ='".$_GET['movie_id']."'";

$result = mysql_query($query,$link) or die(mysql_error());

$movie_table_headings=<<<EOD
    <tr>
        <th>Movie Title</th>
        <th>Year of Release</th>
        <th>Movie Director</th>
        <th>Movie Lead Actor</th>
        <th>Movie Running Time</th>
        <th>Movie Health</th>
    </tr>
EOD;


while($row = mysql_fetch_array($result))
{
    $movie_name = $row['movie_name'];
    $movie_director = $row['movie_director'];
    $movie_leadactor = $row['movie_leadactor'];
    $movie_year = $row['movie_year'];
    $movie_running_time = $row['movie_running_time']." mins";
    $movie_takings = $row['movie_takings'];
    $movie_cost = $row['movie_cost'];

    //get director's name from people table
    get_director($movie_director);

    //get lead actor's name from people table
    get_leadactor($movie_leadactor);

}
```

How It Works

Because we've already written the functions to get the director's and lead actor's names, we "borrowed" this from the `table2.php` file. Then we've changed the query to return everything in each record, as opposed to only a few fields. It does mean that we are returning one field that we are not actually using. The query now contains a WHERE clause. This determines which record we are going to retrieve the data from.

Take a look at the WHERE clause (it's not as daunting as it first seems).

We have used `$_GET['movie_id']` in the WHERE clause. This is the ID of the movie that was passed from the hyperlink in `table3.php`.

We've also created the variable `$movie_table_headings` to contain the headings for the fields that we'll be using.

The rest of the code is very similar to the code in `table3.php`. We've added four extra fields to the `while` control loop.

Didn't we say previously that returning fields that you don't need is not good practice? Yes, we did. However, in this case we are returning only one more field than we need, as opposed to returning many redundant fields. So are we going against our own advice? Well, to be 100 percent truthful, yes. However, as we are using the vast majority of fields in each record, PHP will not suffer from this tradeoff and it is worth it. You would *not* want to do this when, for example, you want the values of (say) 5 fields and the record structure contains 50 fields. If you did this in that instance, PHP would be "wasting" resources to return the other 45 fields.

Try It Out   Displaying Movie Details

So now that you've arranged to return information from records, what next? Now you put this extra information to work.

1. Add the following lines of code to `movie_details.php`.

```
$movie_health =
    calculate_differences($movie_takings,$movie_cost);
$page_start =<<<EOD
<HTML>
    <head>
        <title>Details and Reviews for: $movie_name</title>
    </head>
    <body>
EOD;
$movie_details =<<<EOD
<table width='70%' border='0' cellspacing='2' cellpadding='2' align='center'>
    <tr>
        <th colspan='6'><u><h2>$movie_name: Details</h2></u></th>
    </tr>
        $movie_table_headings
    <tr>
        <td width='33%' align='center'>$movie_name</td>
        <td align='center'>$movie_year</td>
        <td align='center'>$director</td>
        <td align='center'>$leadactor</td>
```

```
            <td align='center'>$movie_running_time</td>
            <td align='center'>$movie_health</td>
        </tr>
</table>
<br />
<br />
EOD;
$page_end =<<<EOD
    </body>
</HTML>
EOD;
$detailed_movie_info =<<<EOD
    $page_start
    $movie_details
    $page_end
EOD;

echo $detailed_movie_info;
mysql_close();
```

2. Save the file as movie_details.php, upload the file to your Web server, and browse to table3.php.

3. Click a movie name and you should see a page similar to Figure 4-6.

Bruce Almighty: Details

Movie Title	Year of Release	Movie Director	Movie Lead Actor	Movie Running Time	Movie Health
Bruce Almighty	2003	Tom Shadyac	Jim Carrey	102 mins	$5m

Figure 4-6

How It Works

Remember the function we created at the top? When we add the line in Step 1 of the previous "Try It Out" section, we call the function and ask it to execute. Whatever value is returned from the `calculate_difference` function will be placed in the variable `$movie_health` (after all, if a movie is healthy then it has made a profit). Passing the `$movie_takings` and the `$movie_costs` to the function will produce the correct result.

When we define the `$page_start` variable, we start sorting out the actual page structure. By adding the variable `$movie_name`, we can get it displayed in the browser's title bar. You can see now how handy the `=<<<EOD` syntax is becoming.

Next, we define the `$movie_details` variable. This should be fairly self-explanatory. Remember the `$movie_table_headings` variable we created previously? All we've done is slot it into place within the `$movie_details` variable and, hey presto, it appears.

Finally, we define the `$page_end` variable and bring it all together in the closing lines.

Phew! That was a lot of code there! Now is a good time to take a break and reward yourself (mine's coffee with milk and two sugars, thanks).

A Lasting Relationship

What if you wanted to find all the reviews for a particular movie? As it stands, you'd need to create a new SQL query in the `movies_details.php` page and execute it when the page loads, which would make a total of two SQL queries in one page. It would work, but it would not be very efficient. (We're all efficient coders, aren't we?) This also results in unnecessary code.

It's time for us to answer the question, what's a relationship?

A *relationship* is a way of joining tables so that you can access the data in all those tables.

The benefit of MySQL is that it is a relational database and, as such, supports the creation of relationships between tables. When used correctly (this can take a bit of time to get your head around) relationships can be very, very powerful and can be used to retrieve data from many, many tables in one SQL query.

The best way to demonstrate this is to build upon what we have done so far, so let's do it.

Try It Out   Creating and Filling a Movie Review Table

Before you can access movie reviews in your movie review table, you need to create the table and then fill it with data.

1. Open your text editor and type the following code:

```php
<?php
//connect to MySQL
$connect = mysql_connect("localhost", "root", "mysqlpass") or
    die ("Hey loser, check your server connection.");
mysql_select_db ("wiley");
```

```
//create "reviews" table
$reviews = "CREATE TABLE reviews (
  review_movie_id int(11) NOT NULL,
  review_date date NOT NULL,
  review_name varchar(255) NOT NULL,
  review_reviewer_name varchar(255) NOT NULL,
  review_comment varchar(255) NOT NULL,
  review_rating int(11) NOT NULL default 0,
  KEY  (review_movie_id),
  ) TYPE=MyISAM";

$results = mysql_query($reviews)
    or die (mysql_error());

//populate the "reviews" table
$insert = "INSERT INTO reviews
    (review_movie_id, review_date, review_name,
        review_reviewer_name, review_comment, review_rating)
    VALUES
    ('1', '2003-08-02', 'This movie rocks!',
        'John Doe','I thought this was a great movie even though
        my girlfriend made me see it against my will.' ,'4'),
    ('1','2003-08-01','An okay movie',
    'Billy Bob','This was an okay movie. I liked Eraserhead better.','2'),
    ('1','2003-08-10','Woo hoo!',
    'Peppermint Patty','Wish I\'d have seen it sooner!','5'),
    ('2','2003-08-01','My favorite movie',
    'Marvin Marian','I didn\'t wear my flair to the movie but I loved
    it anyway.','5'),
    ('3','2003-08-01','An awesome time',
    'George B.','I liked this movie, even though I thought it was
     an informational video from our travel agent.','3')";

$insert_results = mysql_query($insert)
    or die(mysql_error());

?>
```

2. Save this file as `createreviews.php`, upload it to your server, and open it in your browser. Your reviews table has now been created and filled!

How It Works

By now you should be familiar with creating tables using MySQL and PHP, and this should be pretty self-explanatory. If you're having trouble, you might try going back to Chapter 3.

Try It Out   **Querying for the Reviews**

In this example, you're going to link two tables (movies and reviews) to show the reviews for a particular movie. This requires a lot of changes to the `movie_details.php` page, so you'd best make a copy of the file (can't ever be too careful). Then follow these steps:

1. Open `movie_details.php` in your favorite text/HTML editor.

2. Make the following changes to the code (changes are in bold):

```
$movie_query = "SELECT
                    *
            FROM
                    movie
            WHERE
                    movie_id ='".$_GET['movie_id']."'

$movie_result = mysql_query($movie_query,$link) or die(mysql_error());
```

And later in the code, change the following:

```
while($row = mysql_fetch_array($movie_result))
{
    $movie_name = $row['movie_name'];
    $movie_director = $row['movie_director'];
```

3. Add the following lines:

```
$review_query = "SELECT
                    *
            FROM
                    reviews
            WHERE
                    review_movie_id ='".$_GET['movie_id']."'
            ORDER BY
                    review_date DESC";

$review_result = mysql_query($review_query,$link) or die(mysql_error());
```

How It Works

We've changed the name of $query to $movie_query, and also changed $result to $movie_result. This was done to ensure that we do not confuse ourselves when accessing the relevant results set returned from a SQL query. There is also an "order by" clause, which ensures that the most recent reviews are at the top of the page.

A fundamental mistake that a lot of beginners make is to simply use the same variable names when creating SQL queries (for example, $sql = "SELECT ..."). Let's assume that we simply copied and pasted, and then modified the movie query and movie result when it was called query. We'd have two SQL queries called query and two results sets called $result. When the first result ran it would produce the expected results, as would the second one. However, if we ever wanted to refer to the results set that was returned from the first SQL, we'd have a big problem.

Why? The first results set would have been overwritten by the results of the second SQL query. For this reason, always ensure that you use different names for additional SQL queries and results sets returned from the query.

Try It Out   **Displaying the Reviews**

The next chunk of code is the function that allows you to display a cool little graphic for the rating that each film received from the reviewer.

1. Enter this code:

```
function generate_ratings($review_rating)
{
    for($i=0;$i<$review_rating;$i++)
    {
        $movie_rating .= "<img src='thumbsup.gif'> ";
    }
    return $movie_rating;
}
```

2. Now add the code in the following lines immediately below the $movie_table_headings variable.

```
$review_table_headings=<<<EOD
    <tr>
        <th>Date of Review</th>
        <th>Review Title</th>
        <th>Reviewer Name</th>
        <th>Movie Review Comments</th>
        <th>Rating</th>
    </tr>
EOD;
```

3. You need to add the next few lines to the page following the review table headings:

```
while($review_row = mysql_fetch_array($review_result))
{
    $review_flag =1;
    $review_title[] = $review_row['review_name'];
    $reviewer_name[] = ucwords($review_row['review_reviewer_name']);
    $review[] = $review_row['review_comment'];
    $review_date[] = $review_row['review_date'];
    $review_rating[] = generate_ratings($review_row['review_rating']);}
```

4. Next, you need to add the following lines to the page:

```
$i=0;
while($i<sizeof($review))
{
    $review_details .=<<<EOD
    <tr>
        <td width='15%' valign='top' align='center'>$review_date[$i]</td>
        <td width='15%' valign='top'>$review_title[$i]</td>
        <td width='10%' valign='top'>$reviewer_name[$i]</td>
        <td width='50%' valign='top'>$review[$i]</td>
        <td width='10%' valign='top'align='center'>$review_rating[$i]</td>
    </tr>
EOD;
    $i++;
}
```

5. Make the changes (in bold) as shown here. Go slowly, and ensure that you make all the changes correctly.

```
      <td>$movie_health</td>
</tr>
</table>
<br />
<br />
EOD;

if($review_flag)
{
    $movie_details .=<<<EOD
        <table width='95%' border='0' cellspacing='2'
          cellpadding='20' align='center'>
        $review_table_headings
        $review_details
    </table>
EOD;
}
```

6. Save the file as `movie_details.php` (overwriting the existing one—we hope you have made a backup copy as suggested).

7. Upload to your Web server and load `table3.php`.

8. Click a movie and you'll see something similar to Figure 4-7.

Figure 4-7

How It Works

The `generate_ratings` function is fairly straightforward. You send it the value that is in the ratings field for a movie and it creates a "rating" image for that movie and returns it. Notice that we are using `.=` (which is similar to `.=<<<`). This ensures that movies with a rating of more than 1 will get additional images added to the single rating image

The `$review_table_headings` variable contains the table headings for the reviews that we have just pulled out via the previous SQL query. This uses exactly the same concept as the movie table headings in the previous example. So now we have all the review table headings in a nice, neat variable.

While the script is collecting rows of reviews, if there are any reviews for the movie, you set a flag indicating this using the `$review_flag` variable. The code creates arrays to hold the values that will be returned. Why are we putting them into arrays and not just ordinary variables? This allows the variables to hold data for more than one review for the movie. After all, we expect that there'll be many, many reviews for each film. If you didn't create the review variables as arrays, then you'd return only the last review for the movie. In the previous discussion, we looked at why we preferred to put the field values into a variable rather than echo out the field values. Take a look at the line `reviewer_name`. You'll notice that we have placed the line `$review_row['review_name']` inside the PHP function `ucwords`. This allows us to automatically perform the `ucwords` function (which capitalizes the first letter of each word) on the value returned from that field.

The code then loops through the array and assigns values to each of the fields that we are going to display to the user for the review. We use the PHP `sizeof` function to calculate how many records have been returned.

Finally, we've broken the `$movie_details` variable up into several smaller chunks and added them through the use of `.=<<<`. Just as we have done before, we used an already-defined variable (in this case, `$review_table_headings` and `$review_details`) and just slotted it into the correct place. If the review flag has been set, then we'll see the items that make up the reviews (review table headings and the reviews).

We've made quite a few changes in this section. But as you can see, the changes have been well worth it. Now you know how to use MySQL to create relationships between tables. We successfully retrieved all the reviews from the review table depending on the `movie_id` variable. We also looked at using the `$_GET` superglobal variable to pass values from one page to another.

Summary

We've shown you how to work with HTML tables to display your data, how to pull data from more than one database table and have it displayed seamlessly with data from another table, and how to create dynamic pages that display detailed information about the rows in your database. You should also be able to include those nifty little images to graphically display data to your Web site visitors.

What more could you possibly need to know about PHP and MySQL? Plenty!

Form Elements: Letting the User Work with Data

An interactive Web site requires user input, which is generally gathered through forms. As in the paper-based world, the user fills in a form and submits its content for processing. In the Web-application instance, the processing is performed by a PHP script, not a sentient being. Hence, the script requires coded intelligence.

When you fill in a paper form, you generally use a means to deliver its content (for example, the postal service) to a known address (such as a mail order bookstore). The same logic applies to online forms. An HTML form is sent to a specific location and processed.

In HTML, the form element is rather simple; it states where and how it will send the contents of the elements it contains once submitted. At this point, PHP comes into play. Your PHP script receives the data from the form and uses it to perform an action, such as updating the contents of a database, sending an e-mail, testing data format, and so on.

PHP uses a set of simple yet powerful expressions that, once combined, provide you with the means to do virtually anything you want.

In this chapter, you begin to build a simple application that allows you to add, edit, or delete members of a data set (in this instance, movies, actors, and directors). This chapter welcomes you into a world of PHP/MySQL interaction by covering:

- ❑ Creating forms using buttons, text boxes, and other form elements
- ❑ Creating PHP scripts to process HTML forms
- ❑ Mastering $_POST and $_GET to retrieve data
- ❑ Passing hidden information to the form processing script via hidden form controls and a URL query string

Your First Form

As a wise man once said, every journey starts with a single step. To start this particular journey, we will focus on a very simple form. It will include only a text field and a submit button in a table layout. The processing script will display only the value entered in the text field.

Try It Out   **Say My Name**

In this exercise, you are going to get PHP to respond to a name entered in a form. This is a simple variation of the typical "hello world," allowing you to take your first step into interactivity.

1. Create a text file named `form1.html` and open it in your favorite text editor.

2. Enter the following code:

```html
<html>
<head>
   <TITLE>Say My Name</TITLE>
</head>
<body>
<form action="formprocess1.php" method="post">
   <table border=0 cellspacing=1 cellpadding=3 bgcolor="#353535" align="center">
      <tr>
         <td bgcolor="#ffffff" width="50%">
            Name
         </td>
         <td bgcolor="#ffffff" width="50%">
            <INPUT type="TEXT" name="Name"><br />
         </td>
      </tr>
      <tr>
         <td bgcolor="#ffffff" colspan=2 align="center">
            <INPUT type="SUBMIT" name="SUBMIT" value="Submit">
         </td>
      </tr>
   </table>
</form>
</body>
</html>
```

3. Create another empty file named `formprocess1.php` and enter the following code:

```php
<html>
<head>
   <title>Say My Name</title>
</head>
<body>
<?php
   echo "Hello ".$_POST['Name'];
?>
   <PRE>
```

```
      DEBUG :
<?php
    print_r($_POST);
?>
    </PRE>
</body>
</html>
```

4. Upload the files to your Apache work directory.

5. Type **test** in the name text box (as shown in Figure 5-1) and click the Submit button.

You can see two distinct parts on the resulting page: the "Hello Test" portion and the DEBUG *part shown in Figure 5-2.*

You just coded your first form processing script.

Figure 5-1

```
Hello Test

DEBUG :
Array
(
    [Name] => Test
    [SUBMIT] => Submit
)
```

Figure 5-2

How It Works

As with any recipe, it's a good idea to start working on forms by understanding the ingredients. To familiarize yourself with forms, you'll need some background information about HTML form elements and a few new PHP functions.

Let's start with the HTML form.

HTML references can be found at the World Wide Web Consortium Web site at www.w3.org/MarkUp.

FORM Element

First, we'll introduce the first HTML element you'll need: FORM. It delimits the form area in the page and holds the fields you want your Web site users to fill in.

```
<FORM action="formprocess1.php" method="post">
<!-form controls here->
</FORM>
```

Notice that the FORM element has an ending tag and two attributes.

The first attribute (action) is the recipient page address (the form processing script).

The second attribute (method) is the way in which you will send the data to the recipient. There are two separate ways of sending a form to its processing script: the POST and the GET methods.

The POST method (see Figure 5-3) takes the data from the form fields and sends it through an HTTP header. In this case, the data cannot be seen in the URL.

```
foo.php
    <form action="bar.php" method="POST">
    <input type="text" name="movie_name">
    </form>


                  http://localhost/bar.php


bar.php
    The movie is called <?=$_POST["movie_name"]?>.
```

Figure 5-3

The GET method gets the data from the form fields, encodes it, and adds it to the destination URL, as shown here:

```
http://localhost/formprocess1.php?field1=valuea&field2=value%20b
```

As you can see, the field names and their values are easy to read inside the script URL.

INPUT Element

The second new HTML element included here is INPUT. This is the basis of most forms and can be used in many different ways to gather many different types of information.

In this case, we use two different types of INPUT: the text and submit types.

Here's the INPUT TEXT type:

```
<INPUT type="TEXT" name="Name">
```

The INPUT text type is a standard, single-line text box. As with all form controls, it needs a name so that the processing script can access its content using the following syntax:

```php
<?php
    echo $_POST['Name']; // will display the value typed in
?>
```

And here's the INPUT submit type:

```
<INPUT type="SUBMIT" name="SUBMIT" value="Submit">
```

As its name cleverly hints, the submit element displays a button that, when pressed, submits the form. The button text is set through the value attribute. As mentioned for the text INPUT, this form control needs a name for a processing reference.

Processing the Form

In this little script, you may have noticed a few new functions and syntaxes, and you are probably curious about them.

The first form processing script is an interactive variation of the famous "hello world," but in this case it displays "hello" and the name you type in the text box.

To make this happen, you need to print the value of the text field you filled in on the form. You know the echo command, so let's move on to the other piece, $_POST['Name'].

The $_POST global array contains all form data submitted with the POST method. The array index of the field is its name. See the next item for hints on checking the content of your $_POST array using the print_r() function.

```php
<?php
    echo "Hello ".$_POST['Name'];
?>
```

In this example, $_POST['name'] displays what you entered in the "Name" box.

```
Hello test
```

(A debugging tip: Dump the global arrays.)

You might wonder what print_r($_POST) does. It simply dumps the whole contents of the super global $_POST array to the output. This is a great way to debug your forms, as you will see.

The $_POST array, as with all arrays, has case-sensitive indexes. Use this tip to check for case and display the state of your objects when building a script.

Your formprocess1.php script outputs something similar to the following:

```
Hello test
DEBUG :
Array
(
```

```
    [Name] => test
    [SUBMIT] => Submit
)
```

When receiving the submitted form, PHP sets the POST array with the data that the form sends. As with any array, you can directly access any of the indexes by name. In this instance, you can clearly see that the Name index contains the value test. This trick works for all forms, even the most complicated ones.

Let's move on to see how you can use more HTML elements during form input to interact with the user.

Driving the User Input

The form in this example allows you to lead the user to choose values from a set of values you provide. Defining a value set is done through the use of specific HTML elements, such as list boxes, radio buttons, and checkboxes.

Two kinds of predefined user input are in HTML forms. The first kind allows you to choose one item from the available options; the second allows the user to choose multiple items. Drop-down list boxes and radio buttons allow for one selection only. Checkboxes and multiline list boxes provide for multiple choices.

Try It Out   **Limiting the input choice**

Let's start with the simple type of input. Follow these steps to create a single selection list:

1. Create a text file named form2.html and open it in your favorite text editor.

2. Enter the following code:

```html
<html>
<head>
    <TITLE>Greetings Earthling</TITLE>
</head>
<body>
<form action="formprocess2.php" method="post">
    <table border=0 cellspacing=1 cellpadding=3 bgcolor="#353535"
    align="center">
        <tr>
            <td bgcolor="#ffffff" width="50%">
                Name
            </td>
            <td bgcolor="#ffffff" width="50%">
                <INPUT type="TEXT" name="Name">
            </td>
        </tr>
        <tr>
            <td bgcolor="#ffffff">
                Greetings
            </td>
            <td bgcolor="#ffffff">
                <SELECT name="Greeting">
```

```
                        <option value="Hello">Hello</option>
                        <option value="Hola">Hola</option>
                        <option value="Bonjour">Bonjour</option>
                    </SELECT>
                </td>
            </tr>
            <tr>
                <td bgcolor="#ffffff" width="50%">
                    Display Debug info
                </td>
                <td bgcolor="#ffffff" width="50%">
                    <INPUT type="checkbox" name="Debug" CHECKED>
                </td>
            </tr>
            <tr>
                <td bgcolor="#ffffff" colspan=2 align="center">
                    <INPUT type="SUBMIT" name="SUBMIT" value="Submit">
                </td>
            </tr>
        </table>
    </form>
    </body>
    </html>
```

3. Create another empty file named `formprocess2.php` and enter the following code:

```
<html>
<head>
    <TITLE>Greetings Earthling</TITLE>
</head>
<body>
<?php
    if ($_POST['Debug'] == "on"){
?>
<PRE>
<?php
        print_r($_POST);
?>
</PRE>
<?php
    }
?>

<p align="center"><?php echo $_POST['Greeting']?> <?php echo $_POST['Name']?></p>
</body>
</html>
```

4. Save `formprocess2.php` and upload it to your work folder.

5. Call the page from your browser.

    As you can see from the resulting page displayed in Figure 5-4, the form got a bit more complicated.

Figure 5-4

6.   Enter your name and click the Submit button.

The display page that appears, shown in Figure 5-5, is rather simple; it holds only debug information and a greeting.

How It Works

As you see, this code uses logic similar to that in `formprocess1.php`. Two fields have been added (a drop-down list box and a checkbox).

`formprocess2.php` does the same thing as `formprocess1.php` but with an added twist. It displays the debugging information only if the Debug checkbox is selected and greets you using any of the drop-down list choices in the subsections that follow.

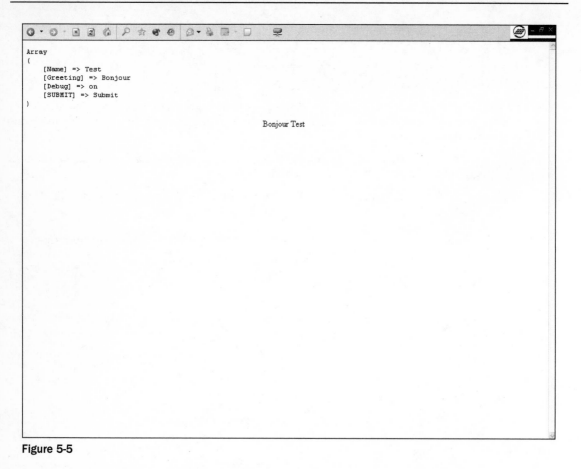

Figure 5-5

INPUT Checkbox Type

The checkbox can represent only two possibilities: When checked, it passes the value `on` to the `$_POST` array, but otherwise it just doesn't send anything. This is a great way to represent Boolean typed data.

```
*    SELECT element
<SELECT name="Greeting">
   <option value="Hello">Hello</option>
   <option value="Hola">Hola</option>
   <option value="Bonjour">Bonjour</option>
</SELECT>
```

The SELECT element (also known as list) allows you to display a fixed list of choices from which the user has to choose an element. The item selected won't be sent as displayed but will be sent as its value. In this example, the value and its display are identical, but in a database-driven system you would probably see record IDs as the values and their text label as list choices. A good example is a product number and its name.

When using lists, be sure to set the value part of the OPTION items. If these are not set, the list looks all the same but is totally useless because all choices will send the same null value.

One Form, Multiple Processing

Forms always react in a predefined way based on how you code your processing script to handle the data that the user sends to the system. A single form can have more than one defined action by using different submit buttons.

| Try It Out | Radio Button, Multi-Line List Boxes |

In the following example, you create a form that prepares a search and creates a movie/actor/director interface.

1. Create a text file named `form3.php` and open it in your text editor. Then type the following code:

```html
<html>
<head>
   <TITLE>Add/Search Entry</TITLE>
</head>
<body>
<form action="formprocess3.php" method="post">
   <table border=0 cellspacing=1 cellpadding=3 bgcolor="#353535" align="center">
      <tr>
         <td bgcolor="#ffffff" width="50%">
            Name
         </td>
         <td bgcolor="#ffffff" width="50%">
            <INPUT type="TEXT" name="Name">
         </td>
      </tr>
      <tr>
         <td bgcolor="#ffffff">
            What you are looking for
         </td>
         <td bgcolor="#ffffff">
            <SELECT name="MovieType">
               <option value="" SELECTED>Select a movie type...</option>
               <option value="Action">Action</option>
               <option value="Drama">Drama</option>
               <option value="Comedy">Comedy</option>
               <option value="Sci-Fi">Sci-Fi</option>
               <option value="War">War</option>
               <option value="Other">Other...</option>
            </SELECT>
         </td>
      </tr>
      <tr>
         <td bgcolor="#ffffff">
            Add what?
         </td>
```

```
            <td bgcolor="#ffffff">
                <INPUT type="radio" name="type" value="Movie" CHECKED>
                Movie<BR>
                <INPUT type="radio" name="type" value="Actor">
                Actor<BR>
                <INPUT type="radio" name="type" value="Director">
                Director<BR>
            </td>
        </tr>
        <tr>
            <td bgcolor="#ffffff" width="50%">
                Display Debug info
            </td>
            <td bgcolor="#ffffff" width="50%">
                <INPUT type="checkbox" name="Debug" CHECKED>
            </td>
        </tr>
        <tr>
            <td bgcolor="#ffffff" colspan=2 align="center">
                <INPUT type="SUBMIT" name="Submit" value="Search">
                <INPUT type="SUBMIT" name="Submit" value="Add">
            </td>
        </tr>
    </table>
</form>
</body>
</html>
```

2. Create another file named `formprocess3.php` and edit it to add the following code:

```php
<?php
    if ( $_POST['type'] == "Movie" && $_POST['MovieType'] == ""){
        header("Location:form3.php");
    }
    $title = $_POST['Submit']." ".$_POST['type']." : ".$_POST['Name'];
?>
<html>
<head>
    <TITLE><?php echo $title?></TITLE>
</head>
<body>
<?php
    if ($_POST['Debug'] == "on"){
?>
<PRE>
<?php
        print_r($_POST);
?>
</PRE>
<?php
    }
    $name = $_POST['Name'];
    $name[0] = strtoupper( $name[0]);
```

```
    if ($_POST['type'] == "Movie"){
        $foo = $_POST['MovieType'] ." ". $_POST['type'];
    } else {
        $foo = $_POST['type'];
    }
?>

<p align="center">
    You are <?php echo $_POST['Submit']?>ing
    <?php echo $_POST['Submit'] == "Search" ? "for " : "";?>
    a <?php echo $foo ?>
    named "<?php echo $name?>"
</p>
</body>
</html>
```

3. Start your browser and open `http://localhost/myform3.php`.

The form shown in Figure 5-6 appears. Notice that the form has two submit buttons. One is labeled Search, the other Add.

Figure 5-6

4. Type **Kevin Kline** in the Name field.

5. Leave `Movie Type` as is; then move on to the `Item Type` field, in which you'll select Actor.

6. Clear the Display Debug Dump checkbox if you like; then click the Search button.

The results appear, as shown in Figure 5-7.

```
Array
(
    [Name] => Kevin Kline
    [MovieType] =>
    [type] => Actor
    [Debug] => on
    [Submit] => Search
)

            You are Searching for a Actor named "Kevin Kline"
```

Figure 5-7

Now play around a bit with the form. Look at the output and how it changes when you modify the data.

How It Works

You just coded a simple form with two possible actions. Depending on the button you click and the data you choose to enter, this code outputs different information.

What's new in the form page itself? A group of radio buttons and a new submit button have been added. Let's have a closer look at these.

Radio INPUT Element

The radio button is a very simple element. By default, if no radio button is specified as CHECKED, no default choice is made. Always remember that choosing the default value is a very important part of building a form. Users often leave defaults in forms. (It is a form of laziness, so to speak.)

```
<INPUT type="radio" name="type" value="Movie" CHECKED>
Movie<BR>
<INPUT type="radio" name="type" value="Actor">
Actor<BR>
<INPUT type="radio" name="type" value="Director">
Director<BR>
```

For multiple radio buttons to be linked together to form a group and be processed as a single form element, they need to share the same name and different values (quite obviously). In the preceding code, the name is always type. This tells the browser that selecting one of the radio buttons clears the others.

Multiple Submit Buttons

As with radio buttons, submit buttons share the same name with a different value. Clicking one of these buttons simply submits the form.

```
<INPUT type="SUBMIT" name="Submit" value="Search">
<INPUT type="SUBMIT" name="Submit" value="Add">
```

As you can see in the DEBUG block, the submit button sends its own information to the script. You can access the submit button value through the $_POST['Submit'] array.

Basic Input Testing

What about the processing script? What's new in there?

The following code checks that the item type is Movie, and, if it is, it checks that the user has selected a valid movie type from the list. If he or she has not, he or she is redirected to the form page.

The test is a simple if with an and operator. (In simple Monopoly parlance, if the item type is movie and the movie type is not specified, you go back to square one and you do not collect $2,000.)

```
if ( $_POST['type'] == "Movie" && $_POST['MovieType'] == "" ){
   header("Location:form3.php");
}
...
```

The header function allows you to send a raw HTTP header. It is useful for handling security problems and access restrictions. In this instance it redirects the user to the specified page.

A very common error with beginning PHP users is that they fail to understand a very simple fact: Once sent, the headers cannot be sent again. This means that any echo, any space, any tabulation left before the call to the header function will trigger a warning in the script execution. Here are a few typical errors:

```
<?php
header("Location:form3.php");
?>
```

This code will fail. The empty line starting the script will send the headers with a carriage return and a line feed (depending on the operating system).

```
<?php
echo "foobar";
header("Location:form3.php");
?>
```

This code will fail. The echo function will send the headers with the text "foobar".

Dynamic Page Title

This code is rather simple to understand: You don't start outputting as soon as you start executing the PHP script. What often happens is that at the start of the scripts there will be a check for intrusion and context verification. In this instance, you dynamically set the page title using the action type and item type you will use to handle the page.

```
...
    $title = $_POST['Submit']." ".$_POST['type']." : ".$_POST['Name'];
?>
<html>
<head>
    <TITLE><?php echo $title?></TITLE>
...
```

Manipulating a String as an Array to Change the Case of the First Character

Single string characters can be accessed through a very simple syntax that is similar to array index access. Specify the index of the character you want to access and voilà! To change the case of a character or an entire string, use the strtoupper() function:

```
...
$name = $_POST['Name'];
$name[0] = strtoupper( $name[0]);
...
```

We could have used the ucfirst() function (which essentially does what the code explained previously did), but a bit of creativity can't hurt.

Ternary Operator

This line holds a ternary comparison operation. Ternary operators are not PHP-specific; many other languages, such as C, use them.

```
...
<?php echo $_POST['Submit'] == "Search" ? "for " : "";?>
...
```

These work in a very simple way and can be compared to an if-else structure:

```
[expression]?[execute if TRUE]: [execute if FALSE];
```

The ternary operator is a known maintainability hazard. Using this operator will make your code less readable and will probably cause errors during maintenance stages.

Using Them All

Now that you know most of the form elements, let's create a skeleton for the application. The system will add new items or search for existing ones. As we have no database interfacing so far, this form will just display the information typed in.

Try It Out   **Hidden and password input**

   1.   Create a file named form4.php and open it in your text editor.

   2.   Enter the following code:

```php
<?php
// Debug info Display
function debugDisplay(){
?>
<PRE>
$_POST
<?php
   print_r($_POST);
?>
$_GET
<?php
   print_r($_GET);
?>
</PRE>
<?php
}

// Switch on search/add wizard step
switch( $_GET['step']){
// #################
//  Search/Add form
// #################
   case "1":
      $type = explode(":",$_POST['type']);
      if ($_POST['Submit']=="Add"){
         require($_POST['Submit'].$type[0].'.php');
      } else {
         if ( $_POST['type'] == "Movie:Movie" &&
```

```php
                    $_POST['MovieType'] == ""){
                header("Location:form4.php");
            }
?>
<h1>Search Results</h1>
<p>You are looking for a "<?php echo $type[1]?>" named "<?php echo
$_POST['Name']?>"</p>
<?php
        }
        if ($_POST['Debug'] == "on"){
            debugDisplay();
        }
        break;
// ################
//  Add Summary
// ################
    case "2":
        $type = explode(":",$_POST['type']);
?>
<h1>New <?php echo $type[1]?> : <?php echo $_POST['Name']?></h1>
<?php
        switch( $type[0] ){
            case "Movie":
?>
<p>Released in <?php echo $_POST['MovieYear']?></p>
<p><?php echo nl2br(stripslashes($_POST['Desc']))?></p>
<?php
                break;
            default:
?>
<h2>Quick Bio</h2>
<p><?php echo nl2br(stripslashes($_POST['Bio']))?></p>
<?php
                break;
        }
        break;
// ##############
//  Starting form
// ##############
    default:
        require('startform.php');
        break;
}
?>
```

3. Create a new file called `startform.php`, and enter the following code:

```html
<html>
<head>
    <TITLE>Multipurpose Form</TITLE>
</head>
<body>
<FORM action="form4.php?step=1" method="post">
```

```
    <table border=0 width="750" cellspacing=1 cellpadding=3 bgcolor="#353535"
align="center">
    <tr>
        <td bgcolor="#ffffff" width="30%">
            Name
        </td>
        <td bgcolor="#ffffff" width="70%">
            <INPUT type="TEXT" name="Name">
        </td>
    </tr>
    <tr>
        <td bgcolor="#ffffff">
            Item Type
        </td>
        <td bgcolor="#ffffff">
            <INPUT type="radio" name="type" value="Movie:Movie" CHECKED>
            Movie<BR>
            <INPUT type="radio" name="type" value="Person:Actor">
            Actor<BR>
            <INPUT type="radio" name="type" value="Person:Director">
            Director<BR>
        </td>
    </tr>
    <tr>
        <td bgcolor="#ffffff">
            Movie type (if applicable)
        </td>
        <td bgcolor="#ffffff">
            <SELECT name="MovieType">
                <option value="" SELECTED>Movie type...</option>
                <option value="Action">Action</option>
                <option value="Drama">Drama</option>
                <option value="Comedy">Comedy</option>
                <option value="Sci-Fi">Sci-Fi</option>
                <option value="War">War</option>
                <option value="Other">Other...</option>
            </SELECT>
        </td>
    </tr>
    <tr>
        <td bgcolor="#ffffff" width="50%">
            Display Debug Dump
        </td>
        <td bgcolor="#ffffff" width="50%">
            <INPUT type="checkbox" name="Debug" CHECKED>
        </td>
    </tr>
    <tr>
        <td bgcolor="#ffffff" colspan=2 align="center">
            <INPUT type="SUBMIT" name="Submit" value="Search">
            <INPUT type="SUBMIT" name="Submit" value="Add">
        </td>
    </tr>
</table>
```

```
</FORM>
</body>
</html>
```

4.   Create another new, empty file named `AddMovie.php`, in which you will add this code:

```php
<?php
   if ( $_POST['type'] == "Movie:Movie" &&
        $_POST['MovieType'] == ""){
      header("Location:form4.php");
   }
   $title = $_POST['Submit']." ".$_POST['type']." : ".$_POST['Name'];
   $name = $_POST['Name'];
   $name[0] = strtoupper( $name[0]);
?>
<html>
<head>
   <TITLE><?php echo $title?></TITLE>
</head>
<body>
<FORM action="form4.php?step=2" method="post">
   <input type="hidden" name="type" value="<?php echo $type[1]?>">
   <input type="hidden" name="action" value="<?php echo $_POST['Submit']?>">
   <table border=0 width="750" cellspacing=1 cellpadding=3 bgcolor="#353535"
align="center">
      <tr>
         <td bgcolor="#ffffff" width="30%">
            Movie Name
         </td>
         <td bgcolor="#ffffff" width="70%">
            <?php echo $name?>
            <input type="hidden" name="Name" value="<?php echo $name?>">
         </td>
      </tr>
      <tr>
         <td bgcolor="#ffffff">
            Movie Type
         </td>
         <td bgcolor="#ffffff">
            <?php echo $_POST['MovieType']?><br />
            <input type="hidden" name="type" value="Movie: <?php echo
$_POST['MovieType']?>">
         </td>
      </tr>
      <tr>
         <td bgcolor="#ffffff">
            Movie Year
         </td>
         <td bgcolor="#ffffff">
            <SELECT name="MovieYear">
               <option value="" SELECTED>Select a year...</option>
<?php
for ($year=date("Y"); $year >= 1970 ;$year-){
?>
```

```
                    <option value="<?php echo $year?>"><?php echo $year?></option>
<?php
}
?>
            </SELECT>
        </td>
    </tr>
    <tr>
        <td bgcolor="#ffffff">
            Movie Description
        </td>
        <td bgcolor="#ffffff">
            <textarea name="Desc" rows="5" cols="60"></textarea>
        </td>
    </tr>
    <tr>
        <td bgcolor="#ffffff" colspan=2 align="center">
            <INPUT type="SUBMIT" name="SUBMIT" value="Add">
        </td>
    </tr>
    </table>
</FORM>
</body>
</html>
```

5.   Create a file named `AddPerson.php` and enter the following code:

```
<?php
    $title = $_POST['Submit']." ".$_POST['type']." : ".$_POST['Name'];
    $name = $_POST['Name'];
    $name[0] = strtoupper( $name[0]);
?>
<html>
<head>
    <TITLE><?php echo $title?></TITLE>
</head>
<body>
<FORM action="form4.php?step=2" method="post">
    <input type="hidden" name="type" value="Person: <?php echo $type[1]?>">
    <input type="hidden" name="action" value="<?php echo $_POST['Submit']?>">
    <table border=0 width="750" cellspacing=1 cellpadding=3 bgcolor="#353535"
align="center">
    <tr>
        <td bgcolor="#ffffff" width="30%">
            <?php echo $type[1]?> Name
        </td>
        <td bgcolor="#ffffff" width="70%">
            <?php echo $name?>
            <input type="hidden" name="Name" value="<?php echo $name?>">
        </td>
    </tr>
    <tr>
        <td bgcolor="#ffffff">
        Quick Bio
```

```
            </td>
            <td bgcolor="#ffffff">
               <textarea name="Bio" rows="5" cols="60"></textarea>
            </td>
         </tr>
         <tr>
            <td bgcolor="#ffffff" colspan=2 align="center">
               <INPUT type="SUBMIT" name="SUBMIT" value="Add">
            </td>
         </tr>
      </table>
   </FORM>
   </body>
   </html>
```

6. Upload the files to your Apache server and launch a browser, entering the address `http://localhost/chapter5/form4.php` (adapt this URL to your setup).

A new form, shown in Figure 5-8, pops up, asking for more details.

Name	Grand Canyon
Item Type	⦿ Movie ○ Actor ○ Director
Movie type (if applicable)	Drama ▾
Display Debug Dump	☑
	Search Add

Figure 5-8

7. Enter the name of the movie you want to add: "Grand Canyon."

8. Select a date for the year the movie was made (1998, if memory serves).

9. Select Drama in the Movie type list

10. Click the Add button; this takes you to the add form shown in Figure 5-9.

Figure 5-9

11. Type a quick movie description, making sure you enter multiple lines, and press the Enter key between them.

12. Click the Add button and see how the information is displayed (see Figure 5-10).

New Drama : Grand Canyon

Released in 1998

Grand canyon, a master piece.
Two thumbs up.

Figure 5-10

How It Works

This script is designed around a simple idea: one skeleton script and multiple flesh-and-muscle scripts doing the job under one URL with query strings.

This raises a question, however: Why use one skeleton script and multiple flesh-and-muscle scripts? One word: maintainability. One of the things most beginners never think about when they start a new language is maintainability. It is a very common error that most people regret.

Let's say that you have a site you made in the month after reading this book and you made a darn good job of it for a first site. Six months later you've learned a lot and want to improve this site.

At this very moment, the full force of chaos theory hits you square in the face: You can't read your code anymore. How unfortunate. Our goal now is to help you to separate things out in such a way that, when you come back to your code in six months, you won't have to start from scratch (which, trust me, happens to most of us).

So, let's get back to work. How does this thing work, anyway? We discuss the elements you must decipher in the sections that follow.

The Skeleton Script

The skeleton here is the `form4.php` script. It all revolves around a use of the switch case structure. It starts with a function definition for the debug display (which now holds the display of the $_GET super global array).

The trick resides in the fact that the forms will use the POST methods and thus transmit their information through the $_POST array; the actual page content switching will be made through query strings passed through the $_GET array.

Each step in the building of the data is guided by the $_GET['step'] index value. It holds the information passed on by the ?step=1 part of the URL.

Each value of the step has a specific script attached to it.

Default Response

What happens when you call the page the first time and the step URL parameter is not set? Logically enough, it evaluates the switch condition and finds that it doesn't match any of the specified cases, so it executes the default behavior:

```
switch( $_GET['step']){
...
   default:
       require('startform.php');
       break;
}
```

The `require()` function gets the content of the file that is specified and includes it in the script at interpretation time. The `require()` function differs from the `include()` in that it triggers a fatal error instead of a warning if the file is not found. In this instance, not having the form script would slightly reduce our script's functionality, so we want to know if it doesn't find the file.

Adding Items

When adding a person or a movie, you need two different forms (at least if you consider that you store the same data in the database for the actors and directors). So you need a second branching (the first branching being the step switch) to determine which form will be displayed.

Now we hit a part of the script in which there is a little trick. The list item value is used to store two values instead of one. The trick is to use a separator, and then to explode the value into an array and access the piece you need (the `explode()` function takes each bit of text delimited by the separator and inserts it as new array elements). Let's take a closer look.

In this case we have three types of items (Actors, Directors, and Movies), each of which requires a form to create. But we have decided that, so far, an Actor and a Director form hold the same information. So we don't need two different forms, just one. You handle this by adding a tree structure level above the item level, Person or Movie. Under Person you include the Actor and Director level. The whole point is to be able to use the new hierarchy level name to name the file so that the including is automatic and you can add new levels later without too much effort.

In startform.php we have:

```
<INPUT type="radio" name="type" value="Person:Actor">
Actor<BR>
```

You can clearly see that the value part of the type element is composed of two different values, separated by a semicolon.

In form4.php you have:

```
...
$type = explode(":",$_POST['type']);
if ($_POST['Submit']=="Add"){
    require($_POST['Submit'].$type[0].'.php');
}
...
```

In this script, you retrieve the type element value using the $_POST['type'] array index and then use the explode() function on its content. The explode() function is fairly easy to use; it just needs a string that specifies the delimiter and a string that holds the text to be exploded.

For example, we have "Person:Actor" as the value to explode and a colon (:) as the delimiter. The resulting $type variable will be an array holding the pieces of the string cut at each instance of the semicolon. If you represent it in the print_r format, you have:

```
Array
(
    [0] => Person
    [1] => Actor
)
```

The goal of having simple file names inclusion is achieved. We have two Add scripts, and one name: AddPerson.php and AddMovie.php.

```
require($_POST['Submit'].$type[0].'.php');
```

This line recomposes our filenames automatically.

Summary

You've learned a lot of about forms in this chapter. Forms are composed of fields. Each field type has a specific purpose and allows a certain data type to be entered. Text fields can be used to enter text or numeric data. Lists can be used to enter any type of data and have a limited set of possible values. Lists are a good way to drive user input when multiple choices are available.

Forms are processed by the PHP script using the super global array $_GET and $_POST, which is a sub-array of $_QUERY. Each super global array has its use, as you saw, and contributes to making your script access the form data.

Always remember to keep your forms simple. Some studies have shown that a form with more than 15 items is often too complex for many users to use. (Readability and layout are the keys to having a usable system.)

Letting the User Edit the Database

Retrieving data from a database is all well and good when you've fed the database some data. Most databases don't generate their own contents (well, none do), and only a few get fed data by other systems (integrated systems and so on). So we have to feed our system with data that comes from PHP.

Our database of choice (out of many available) is MySQL, as you have probably figured out. (It's in the title of the book, right?)

All database interaction is based on SQL (you will one day encounter XML and other sources, but let's not go there now). You know the basic SQL syntax to get data from a table; now let's look at the other side of the equation.

Most people use SQL to insert data that PHP modifies or generates. We will try a slightly different approach and let SQL do its thing.

This chapter covers database editing, including:

- ❑ Adding entries, which is quite simple, but you will find that adding entries in a relational database is yet another exercise
- ❑ Deleting entries without corrupting the database structure and referential integrity
- ❑ Modifying entries to replace some existing fields with new content in an existing record

Preparing the Battlefield

This may sound a bit Vulcan, but if you want to manage a database, the first logical thing to do is to create one. To save time, let's use an existing database to avoid any problems in the coming exercises. Create a new empty database in phpMyAdmin named chapter6. In the new-born database, execute the chapter6.mysql script, which holds the database definition and its start data.

Then you're ready to go.

Try It Out   Setting Up the Environment

First, you need a start page. Follow these steps to create one:

1.   Create a new directory called chap6 under your htdocs (or create an alias, if you wish).

2.   Create an index.php script and enter the following code:

```php
<?php
   $link = mysql_connect("localhost", "root", "")
      or die("Could not connect: " . mysql_error());
   mysql_select_db('chapter6', $link) or die ( mysql_error());
?>
<html>
<head>
   <TITLE>Movie database</TITLE>
</head>
<body>
   <table border=0 width="600" cellspacing=1 cellpadding=3 bgcolor="#353535"
align="center">
         <td bgcolor="#ffffff" colspan=2 align="center">
            Movies <a href="movie.php?action=add&id=">[ADD]</a>
         </td>
<?php
   $moviesql = "SELECT
                  *
               FROM
                  `movie`
               ";
   $result = mysql_query($moviesql)
      or die("Invalid query: " . mysql_error());
   while( $row = mysql_fetch_array($result, MYSQL_ASSOC) ){
?>
      <tr>
         <td bgcolor="#ffffff" width="50%">
            <?php echo $row['movie_name']?>
         </td>
         <td bgcolor="#ffffff" width="50%" align="right">
            <a href="movie.php?action=edit&id=<?php echo
$row['movie_id']?>">[EDIT]</a>
            <a href="delete.php?type=movie&id=<?php echo
$row['movie_id']?>">[DELETE]</a>
         </td>
      </tr>
<?php
```

```
        }
?>
            <td bgcolor="#ffffff" colspan=2 align="center">
                People <a href="people.php?action=add&id=">[ADD]</a>
            </td>
<?php
    $moviesql = "SELECT
                    *
                FROM
                    `people`
                ";
    $result = mysql_query($moviesql)
        or die("Invalid query: " . mysql_error());
    while( $row = mysql_fetch_array($result, MYSQL_ASSOC) ){
?>
        <tr>
            <td bgcolor="#ffffff" width="50%">
                <?php echo $row['people_fullname']?>
            </td>
            <td bgcolor="#ffffff" width="50%" align="right">
                <a href="people.php?action=edit&id=<?php echo
$row['people_id']?>">[EDIT]</a>
                <a href="delete.php?type=people&id=<?php echo
$row['people_id']?>">[DELETE]</a>
            </td>
        </tr>
<?php
    }
?>
    </table>
</body>
</html>
```

3. Now open your browser and go to http://localhost/chapter6/index.php as shown in Figure 6-1.

Remember that all links are broken, so do not worry; that's perfectly normal because we haven't yet created the pages.

How It Works

You must always have a central administration interface that allows you to perform actions on the data and easily see the content. This script is the admin interface. It shows you everything and allows you to manage everything in sight.

What does it do and how does it do what it does? As in Chapter 4, where we connected to the database and displayed its contents, we will do the same thing here. The table holds the name of each known movie and person, and generates EDIT and DELETE links.

Figure 6-1

Inserting a Simple Record from phpMyAdmin

Note that in the following scripts, we will follow a simple rule concerning SQL: Always try the query in MySQL before trying to insert it in your code. The simple reason is that you are probably better off debugging one language at a time.

Try It Out   Inserting Simple Data

Now follow these steps to insert some data:

1. Open your database in phpMyAdmin and enter the following SQL code (yes, there is an error) as in Figure 6-2.

```
INSERT INTO
    `movie`
( `movie_name` , `movie_type` , `movie_year` )
    VALUES
( 'Bruce Almighty','1','2003' )
```

Figure 6-2

2. The following message appears (see Figure 6-3 for details):

```
You have an error in your SQL syntax.  Check the manual that corresponds to your
MySQL server version for the right syntax to use near ''2003 )' at line 5
```

3. Fix the error as this suggests (quite simple to do with the line number reference) and run.

   phpMyAdmin then displays the executed SQL and takes you back to the table content display as shown in Figure 6-4.

Before doing any SQL query in PHP, you should always test your SQL statement in phpMyAdmin. It will enable you to debug the SQL before inserting it in your code and prevent debugging in two different languages at the same time.

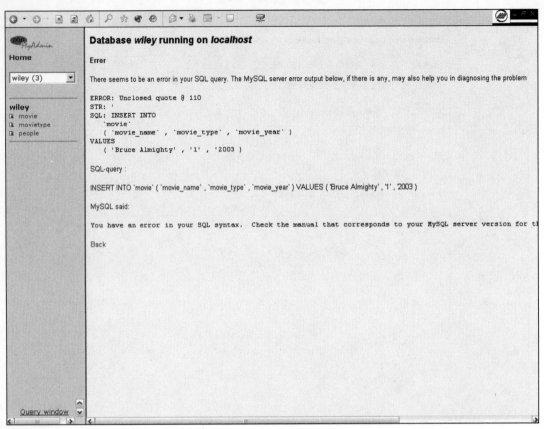

Figure 6-3

How It Works

When inserting a record in a table, you don't need to insert the id if you set the primary key field to auto increment. The engine will gladly handle that for you. This enables you to be sure you don't have duplicate keys in the table.

To get the just-inserted record auto increment id, just use the PHP `mysql_insert_id()` function right after the `mysql_query()` function call. This function returns the primary key field when inserting a new record.

The `mysql_insert_id` *function syntax can be found on the PHP site at* www.php.net/ `mysql_insert_id`.

Because we have created the SQL query on more than one line, we can use the line number returned in the following error message.

```
You have an error in your SQL syntax.  Check the manual that corresponds to your
MySQL server version for the right syntax to use near ''2003 )' at line 5
```

Figure 6-4

This line corresponds to the value part of our SQL statement, as shown here:

```
( 'Bruce Almighty','1','2003 )
```

If our SQL query had been on one line, we'd have had only a useless "error in line 1" message. Here you can see that on the guilty line we forgot to close a quote in the movie_year value.

Now you can see that we omitted the `movie.``movie_id` field. We did this on purpose (yes, we did). Not specifying the primary key value forces the MySQL engine to automatically determine the auto increment value. Thanks to this trick, we don't need to know what the next key will be.

Inserting a Record in a Relational Database

Databases often hold more than just one table. All those tables can be totally independent but that would be like using your car to store some things in the trunk but never to drive you around.

In old systems in which relational databases didn't exist, every row held all the information. Imagine your system running with only one table holding all the information. Your movie table would store all the data about the actors and the directors and the movie types. Let's say that one day you were to decide that a movie category should change from action to adventure (things change). You would then have to go through all records to change the movie type label.

In modern RDBMS (relational database management systems), this is not the case anymore; you will create a `movietype` table storing a reference of all movie types possible, and you will link movies to the relevant movie type.

To link those tables, you will use a primary key/foreign key team. The primary key of the `movietype` table is a numeric identification of each type of movie. For example, in our database the id 1 references comedy. The foreign key is the reference in the movie table to the `movietype` primary key.

In the following exercise, you use PHP and SQL to insert a movie in your database. This movie is of a known movie type from the `movie type` reference table.

Try It Out   Inserting a Movie with Known Movie Type and People

This time, let's do something a bit more complicated. You need to be able to add a movie to the system while specifying an existing movie type and existing actor and director.

1.   Create a new empty file named `movie.php` and enter the following code:

```php
<?php
$link = mysql_connect("localhost", "root", "")
    or die("Could not connect: " . mysql_error());
mysql_select_db('chapter6', $link) or die ( mysql_error());
$peoplesql = "SELECT
            *
        FROM
            `people`
        ";
$result = mysql_query($peoplesql)
    or die("Invalid query: " . mysql_error());
while( $row = mysql_fetch_array( $result , MYSQL_ASSOC )){
    $people[ $row['people_id'] ] = $row['people_fullname'];
}
?>
<html>
<head>
    <TITLE>Add movie</TITLE>
</head>
<body>
<FORM action="commit.php?action=add&type=movie" method="post">
    <table border=0 width="750" cellspacing=1 cellpadding=3 bgcolor="#353535"
align="center">
        <tr>
            <td bgcolor="#ffffff" width="30%">
                Movie Name
            </td>
            <td bgcolor="#ffffff" width="70%">
                <input type="text" name="movie_name">
            </td>
        </tr>
        <tr>
            <td bgcolor="#ffffff">
```

```
                    Movie Type
          </td>
          <td bgcolor="#ffffff">
          <SELECT id="game" name="movie_type" style="width:150px">
<?php
          $sql = "SELECT
                    `movietype_id`,
                    `movietype_label`
                FROM
                    `movietype`
                ORDER BY
                    `movietype_label`
                ";
          $result = mysql_query($sql)
              or die("<font color=\"#FF0000\">Query Error</FONT>".mysql_error());
          while ( $row = mysql_fetch_array($result) ){
              echo '<OPTION
value="'.$row['movietype_id'].'">'.$row['movietype_label'].'</OPTION>'."\r\n";
          }
?>
          </SELECT>

          </td>
        </tr>
        <tr>
          <td bgcolor="#ffffff">
            Movie Year
          </td>
          <td bgcolor="#ffffff">
            <SELECT name="movie_year">
              <option value="" SELECTED>Select a year...</option>
<?php
for ($year=date("Y"); $year >= 1970 ;$year--){
?>
              <option value="<?php echo $year?>"><?php echo $year?></option>
<?php
}
?>
            </SELECT>
          </td>
        </tr>
        <tr>
          <td bgcolor="#ffffff">
            Lead Actor
          </td>
          <td bgcolor="#ffffff">
            <SELECT name="movie_leadactor">
              <option value="" SELECTED>Select an actor...</option>
<?php
foreach( $people as $people_id => $people_fullname ){
?>
              <option value="<?php echo $people_id?>" ><?php echo
$people_fullname?></option>
<?php
}
?>
```

```
            </SELECT>
          </td>
      </tr>
      <tr>
          <td bgcolor="#ffffff">
              Director
          </td>
          <td bgcolor="#ffffff">
              <SELECT name="movie_director">
                  <option value="" SELECTED>Select a director...</option>
<?php
foreach( $people as $people_id => $people_fullname ){
?>
                  <option value="<?php echo $people_id?>" ><?php echo
$people_fullname?></option>
<?php
}
?>
              </SELECT>
          </td>
      </tr>
      <tr>
          <td bgcolor="#ffffff" colspan=2 align="center">
              <INPUT type="SUBMIT" name="SUBMIT" value="Add">
          </td>
      </tr>
    </table>
</FORM>
</body>
</html>
```

2. Save your file and upload it to a new chapter6 directory on your server.

3. Create a new empty file named commit.php and enter the following code:

```php
<?php
// COMMIT ADD
    $link = mysql_connect("localhost", "root", "")
        or die("Could not connect: " . mysql_error());
    mysql_select_db('chapter6', $link) or die ( mysql_error());
    switch( $_GET['action'] ){
        case "add":
            switch( $_GET['type'] ){
                case "movie":
                    $sql = "INSERT INTO
                            `movie`
                            ( `movie_name` ,
                            `movie_year` ,
                            `movie_type` ,
                            `movie_leadactor` ,
                            `movie_director` )
                        VALUES
                            ( '".$_POST['movie_name']."' ,
                            '".$_POST['movie_year']."' ,
                            '".$_POST['movie_type']."' ,
                            '".$_POST['movie_leadactor']."' ,
                            '".$_POST['movie_director']."' )
```

```
                     ";
            break;
        }
        break;
    }
    if ( isset( $sql ) && !empty( $sql )){
        echo "<!-".$sql."->";
        $result = mysql_query( $sql )
            or die("Invalid query: " . mysql_error());
?>
        <p align="center" style="color:#FF0000">
            Done. <a href="index.php">Index</a>
        </p>
<?php
    }
?>
```

4. Save your file and upload it to a new chapter6 directory on your server.

5. Open your browser on the index.php page and click ADD next to the `movie` table header.

6. Add a movie named "Test" with random type, actor, and director in the form shown in Figures 6-5 and 6-6.

Figure 6-5

Figure 6-6

7. Click the "add" button and you will see the confirmation message as in Figure 6-7.

How It Works

Inserting data is always easier when you have an actual method to insert (remember these wise words). We generally use HTML forms.

HTML forms allow us to drive the way the user enters the data. Once submitted, the form sends the server information that PHP can use to generate and run the SQL INSERT statement.

As you see in the movie insertion form in movie.php, we have four combo boxes and a text field. The text field content is left to your discretion, but the combos are quite directive. Let's review the content of the combos generated from the database contents.

Figure 6-7

First, let's concentrate on the people combos. Each combo lists all persons present in a `people` table.

```php
<?php
    $link = mysql_connect("localhost", "root", "")
        or die("Could not connect: " . mysql_error());
    mysql_select_db('chapter6', $link) or die ( mysql_error());
    $peoplesql = "SELECT
            *
            FROM
                `people`
            ";
    $result = mysql_query($peoplesql)
        or die("Invalid query: " . mysql_error());
    while( $row = mysql_fetch_array( $result , MYSQL_ASSOC )){
        $people[ $row['people_id'] ] = $row['people_fullname'];
    }
?>
```

At the beginning of the form script, we query the `people` table and put its content in an array. The data regarding people known to the system is stored in the `people` table.

To generate the list of people, we simply query the database, retrieve all the known people in the system, and display the names in the combo and reference their primary key as the item value. Each known person will have an item in the combo box:

```
<SELECT name="movie_director">
    <option value="" SELECTED>Select a director...</option>
<?php
foreach( $people as $people_id => $people_fullname ){
?>
    <option value="<?php echo $people_id?>" ><?php echo $people_fullname?></option>
<?php
}
?>
</SELECT>
```

Here we've used the `foreach` syntax to walk the array to generate all the options.

Now we'll generate the movie type combo box. This is a more conventional use of SQL to generate contents. We'll reuse this code soon to create a generic form to edit and add, so you need to understand the details of how this works.

```
        <SELECT id="game" name="movie_type" style="width:150px">
<?php
        $sql = "SELECT
                `movietype_id`,
                `movietype_label`
            FROM
                `movietype`
            ORDER BY
                `movietype_label`
            ";
        $result = mysql_query($sql)
            or die("<font color=\"#FF0000\">Query Error</FONT>".mysql_error());
        while ( $row = mysql_fetch_array( $result , MYSQL_ASSOC ) ){
            echo '<OPTION
value="'.$row['movietype_id'].'">'.$row['movietype_label'].'</OPTION>'."\r\n";
        }
?>
        </SELECT>
```

This code generates the options in combo box by querying the `movietype` table to extract all available movie types. Each option will have the movie type id as a value and the movie type itself as a label.

Now that our form is ready, we need to have a script that uses this data to create records. As you can see, the `switch case` on `$_GET['action']` is totally useless for now. In the next exercises, we add a lot of code to the `movie.php` script so we can use it to edit the movies.

Deleting a Record

Deleting records is easy (a bit too easy at times—you will know what I mean soon). As we said before, always be sure to test your queries on a test database. Deleting records in a test database never threatens your system, and testing your query helps you find any SQL error before deleting all the records in your production database because you forgot a little thing such as a WHERE clause. MySQL deletes everything that matches the SQL statement. If you omit a WHERE clause in your query, all the records will match the SQL statement and thus will be deleted.

Deleting always means losing data. To delete a record you need to point the record to the database engine through a set of conditions in a WHERE statement. Once this statement is executed, there is no turning back. The record(s) will be deleted without hope of return; that's why we advise caution when using the DELETE statement.

Try It Out   Deleting a Single Record

Before asking PHP to delete anything, you will try deleting a record from phpMyAdmin to familiarize yourself with the DELETE statement. Follow this step to delete a record:

❑   Open phpMyAdmin and enter the following code:

```
DELETE FROM
    `movie`
WHERE
    `movie_id` = '12'
LIMIT 1
```

phpMyAdmin returns a nice message saying you deleted a record from the `movie` table.

How It Works

The DELETE SQL statement is very simple to use. As you see, we used the LIMIT 1 statement to limit the deletion to only one record (just in case).

Cascade Delete

As you know, a database often holds related records in different tables. Deleting some records without consideration of relations introduces you to chaos and heavy database manual tweaking. MySQL unfortunately doesn't manage relations for you, and thus will not automatically preserve referential integrity.

To avoid that problem, we use a more elaborate form of the DELETE statement, the *Cascade Delete,* as discussed in the following section.

Try It Out   Cascade Delete

Now that you know how to use DELETE, you will add it to your system to delete a known person from the system. As you store references to known people in the `movie` table, you will need to update the `movie` table content so you don't reference deleted people. (The update-specific exercises come next in this chapter.)

Follow these steps to implement the Cascade Delete:

1. Create a new text file named `delete.php` and enter the following code:

```php
<?php
    $link = mysql_connect("localhost", "root", "")
        or die("Could not connect: " . mysql_error());
    mysql_select_db('chapter6', $link) or die ( mysql_error());
// DELETE SCRIPT
    if ( !isset( $_GET['do'] ) || $_GET['do'] != 1 ){
?>
        <p align="center" style="color:#FF0000">
            Are you sure you want to delete this <?php echo $_GET['type']?>?<br/>
            <a href="<?php echo $_SERVER['REQUEST_URI']?>&do=1">yes</a> or <a
href="index.php">Index</a>
        </p>
<?php
    } else {
        if ( $_GET['type'] == "people" ){
            // delete references to people from the movie table
            // delete reference to lead actor
            $actor = "UPDATE
                        `movie`
                    SET
                        `movie_leadactor` = '0'
                    WHERE
                        `movie_leadactor` = '".$_GET['id']."'
                    ";
            $result = mysql_query( $actor )
                or die("Invalid query: " . mysql_error());
            // delete reference to director
            $director = "UPDATE
                        `movie`
                    SET
                        `movie_director` = '0'
                    WHERE
                        `movie_director` = '".$_GET['id']."'
                    ";
            $result = mysql_query( $director )
                or die("Invalid query: " . mysql_error());
        }
        // generate SQL
        $sql = "DELETE FROM
                    `".$_GET['type']."`
                WHERE
                    `".$_GET['type']."_id` = '".$_GET['id']."'
                LIMIT 1";
        // echo SQL for debug purpose
        echo "<!--".$sql."-->";
        $result = mysql_query( $sql )
            or die("Invalid query: " . mysql_error());
?>
        <p align="center" style="color:#FF0000">
```

```
        Your <?php echo $_GET['type']?> has been deleted. <a
href="index.php">Index</a>
        </p>
<?php
    }
?>
```

2. Save delete.php and upload it to your chap6 directory.

3. Open index.php in your browser. You will see the [DELETE] links next to each movie or person as in Figure 6-8.

	Movies [ADD]	
Bruce Almighty		[EDIT] [DELETE]
Office Space		[EDIT] [DELETE]
Grand Canyon		[EDIT] [DELETE]
Test		[EDIT] [DELETE]
	People [ADD]	
Jim Carrey		[EDIT] [DELETE]
Tom Shadyac		[EDIT] [DELETE]
Lawrence Kasdan		[EDIT] [DELETE]
Kevin Kline		[EDIT] [DELETE]
Ron Livingston		[EDIT] [DELETE]
Mike Judge		[EDIT] [DELETE]

Figure 6-8

4. Try deleting the test movie you added in the previous exercise by clicking the DELETE link next to the "Test" movie name. You will be asked for confirmation as in Figure 6-9.

5. Click the "yes" link to confirm the deletion and wait for the confirmation message as in Figure 6-10.

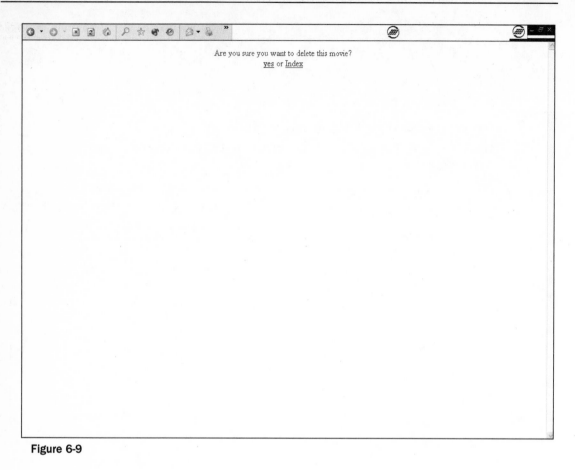

Figure 6-9

How It Works

Here we are, planning the annihilation of an innocent set of data. Putting any moral issues aside, let's see how this script works.

First, you need to understand that in a relational database you cannot delete records and just forget about them. Deleting has to be considered carefully. For example, if you delete a person from the `people` table, this prevents you from finding a potential reference to that person in the `movie` table. If you delete Jim Carrey from the `people` table, who will "Bruce Almighty's" lead actor be? If you don't do anything, Jim Carrey's id will remain in the record and you will have a corrupted database. You don't want that, do you? (The answer is no.)

The solution to this problem is to make sure that you always have the round peg (the round peg being a foreign key) in the round hole (the round hole being a record). In the code that follows, we update the `movie` table with a 0 value (the default value telling the script we have not set the people part) before deleting the `people` record. This also allows us to check the behavior of the UPDATE SQL statement. (Isn't life great?)

Your movie has been deleted. Index

Figure 6-10

```php
// delete reference to lead actor
$actor = "UPDATE
        `movie`
    SET
        `movie_leadactor` = '0'
    WHERE
        `movie_leadactor` = '".$_GET['id']."'
    ";
$result = mysql_query( $actor )
    or die("Invalid query: " . mysql_error());
// delete reference to director
$director = "UPDATE
        `movie`
    SET
        `movie_director` = '0'
    WHERE
        `movie_director` = '".$_GET['id']."'
    ";
$result = mysql_query( $director )
    or die("Invalid query: " . mysql_error());
```

In the preceding code, we set any field in the `movie` table that might hold a reference to our unfortunate, soon-to-be-deleted person. The UPDATE statement works in a very simple way. It sets the fields specified to the new value specified in all records, meeting the requirements of the WHERE statement.

You might wonder what would happen if someone were to forget the WHERE part. Well, curiosity is a fine quality: This would update all records in the table, which is probably not something you want to do in real life.

Once our tidying up is done, we do the deleting:

```
// generate SQL
$sql = "DELETE FROM
        `".$_GET['type']."`
    WHERE
        `".$_GET['type']."_id` = '".$_GET['id']."'
    LIMIT 1";
// echo SQL for debug purpose
echo "<!--".$sql."-->";
$result = mysql_query( $sql )
    or die("Invalid query: " . mysql_error());
```

This DELETE query is a bit dynamic, but it's fairly understandable. We don't want to code a SQL statement for each type. (Well, we did for the movies update, but it doesn't count, does it?) So we use the information passed through the URL to generate our SQL statement. The table and primary key field are generated dynamically from the item type to delete.

Editing Data in a Record

Having data in the database is all well and good, but data has a mind of its own and tends to want to be updated. To update data, we need to identify the data to update and present the system user with a nice interface to do so. Using the same interface as was used to create the data is often a good practice.

Try It Out   **Editing a Movie**

In this exercise, you create a script that enables you to edit a movie. You will build on the existing movie.php script you created earlier.

1. Open movie.php in your favorite text editor and enter this code:

```
<?php
    $link = mysql_connect("localhost", "root", "")
        or die("Could not connect: " . mysql_error());
    mysql_select_db('chapter6', $link) or die ( mysql_error());
    $peoplesql = "SELECT
            *
        FROM
            `people`
        ";
    $result = mysql_query($peoplesql)
        or die("Invalid query: " . mysql_error());
    while( $row = mysql_fetch_array( $result , MYSQL_ASSOC )){
```

```php
            $people[ $row['people_id'] ] = $row['people_fullname'];
        }

    switch( $_GET['action'] ){
        case "edit":
            $moviesql = "SELECT
                            *
                        FROM
                            `movie`
                        WHERE
                            `movie`.`movie_id` = '".$_GET['id']."'
                        ";
            $result = mysql_query($moviesql)
                or die("Invalid query: " . mysql_error());
            $row = mysql_fetch_array( $result , MYSQL_ASSOC );
            $movie_name = $row[ 'movie_name' ];
            $movie_type = $row[ 'movie_type' ];
            $movie_year = $row[ 'movie_year' ];
            $movie_leadactor = $row[ 'movie_leadactor' ];
            $movie_director = $row[ 'movie_director' ];
            break;
        default:
            $movie_name = "";
            $movie_type = "";
            $movie_year = "";
            $movie_leadactor = "";
            $movie_director = "";
            break;
    }
?>
<html>
<head>
    <TITLE><?php echo $_GET['action']?> movie</TITLE>
</head>
<body>
<FORM action="commit.php?action=<?php echo $_GET['action']?>&type=movie&id=<?php
echo $_GET['id']?>" method="post">
    <table border=0 width="750" cellspacing=1 cellpadding=3 bgcolor="#353535"
align="center">
        <tr>
            <td bgcolor="#ffffff" width="30%">
                Movie Name
            </td>
            <td bgcolor="#ffffff" width="70%">
                <input type="text" name="movie_name" value="<?php echo $movie_name?>">
            </td>
        </tr>
        <tr>
            <td bgcolor="#ffffff">
                Movie Type
            </td>
            <td bgcolor="#ffffff">
            <SELECT id="game" name="movie_type" style="width:150px">
<?php
```

```
        $sql = "SELECT
                `movietype_id`,
                `movietype_label`
            FROM
                `movietype`
            ORDER BY
                `movietype_label`
            ";
        $result = mysql_query($sql)
            or die("<font color=\"#FF0000\">Query Error</FONT>".mysql_error());
        while ( $row = mysql_fetch_array($result) ){
            if ( $row['movietype_id'] == $movie_type){
                $selected = " SELECTED";
            } else {
                $selected = "";
            }
            echo '<OPTION
value="'.$row['movietype_id'].'"'.$selected.'>'.$row['movietype_label'].'</OPTION>'
."\r\n";
        }
?>

        </SELECT>

        </td>
    </tr>
    <tr>
        <td bgcolor="#ffffff">
            Movie Year
        </td>
        <td bgcolor="#ffffff">
            <SELECT name="movie_year">
                <option value="" SELECTED>Select a year...</option>
<?php
for ($year=date("Y"); $year >= 1970 ;$year--){
            if ( $year == $movie_year){
                $selected = " SELECTED";
            } else {
                $selected = "";
            }
?>
            <option value="<?php echo $year?>"<?php echo $selected?>><?php echo
$year?></option>
<?
}
?>
            </SELECT>
        </td>
    </tr>
    <tr>
        <td bgcolor="#ffffff">
            Lead Actor
        </td>
```

```
                <td bgcolor="#ffffff">
                    <SELECT name="movie_leadactor">
                        <option value="" SELECTED>Select an actor...</option>
<?php
foreach( $people as $people_id => $people_fullname ){
            if ( $people_id == $movie_leadactor){
                $selected = " SELECTED";
            } else {
                $selected = "";
            }
?>
                    <option value="<?php echo $people_id?>"<?php echo $selected?>><?php
echo $people_fullname?></option>
<?php
}
?>
                    </SELECT>
            </td>
        </tr>
        <tr>
            <td bgcolor="#ffffff">
                Director
            </td>
            <td bgcolor="#ffffff">
                <SELECT name="movie_director">
                    <option value="" SELECTED>Select a director...</option>
<?php
foreach( $people as $people_id => $people_fullname ){
            if ( $people_id == $movie_director){
                $selected = " SELECTED";
            } else {
                $selected = "";
            }
?>
                    <option value="<?php echo $people_id?>"<?php echo $selected?>><?php
echo $people_fullname?></option>
<?php
}
?>
                    </SELECT>
            </td>
        </tr>
        <tr>
            <td bgcolor="#ffffff" colspan=2 align="center">
                <INPUT type="SUBMIT" name="SUBMIT" value="<?php echo
$_GET['action']?>">
            </td>
        </tr>
    </table>
</FORM>
</body>
</html>
```

2. Open the `commit.php` script and edit its content to match this new code:

```php
<?php
// COMMIT ADD AND EDITS
    $link = mysql_connect("localhost", "root", "")
        or die("Could not connect: " . mysql_error());
    mysql_select_db('chapter6', $link) or die ( mysql_error());
    switch( $_GET['action'] ){
        case "edit":
            switch( $_GET['type'] ){
                case "movie":
                    $sql = "UPDATE
                                `movie`
                            SET
                                `movie_name` = '".$_POST['movie_name']."',
                                `movie_year` = '".$_POST['movie_year']."',
                                `movie_type` = '".$_POST['movie_type']."',
                                `movie_leadactor` = '".$_POST['movie_leadactor']."',
                                `movie_director` = '".$_POST['movie_director']."'
                            WHERE
                                `movie_id` = '".$_GET['id']."'
                            ";
                    break;
            }
            break;
        case "add":
            switch( $_GET['type'] ){
                case "movie":
                    $sql = "INSERT INTO
                                `movie`
                                ( `movie_name` , `movie_year` , `movie_type` ,
`movie_leadactor` , `movie_director` )
                            VALUES
                                ( '".$_POST['movie_name']."' , '".$_POST['movie_year']."' ,
'".$_POST['movie_type']."' , '".$_POST['movie_leadactor']."' ,
'".$_POST['movie_director']."' )
                            ";
                    break;
            }
            break;
    }
    if ( isset( $sql ) && !empty( $sql )){
        echo "<!--".$sql."-->";
        $result = mysql_query( $sql )
            or die("Invalid query: " . mysql_error());
?>
        <p align="center" style="color:#FF0000">
            Done. <a href="index.php">Index</a>
        </p>
<?php
    }
?>
```

3. Now open your browser and go to `http://localhost/chapter6/index.php` as shown in Figure 6-11.

Movies [ADD]		
Bruce Almighty		[EDIT] [DELETE]
Office Space		[EDIT] [DELETE]
Grand Canyon		[EDIT] [DELETE]
People [ADD]		
Jim Carrey		[EDIT] [DELETE]
Tom Shadyac		[EDIT] [DELETE]
Lawrence Kasdan		[EDIT] [DELETE]
Kevin Kline		[EDIT] [DELETE]
Ron Livingston		[EDIT] [DELETE]
Mike Judge		[EDIT] [DELETE]

Figure 6-11

4. Try clicking the EDIT link next to the "Bruce Almighty" movie, change a few boxes and the movie name, and press the "edit" button in the form shown in Figure 6-12.

5. Edit the "Bruce Almighty" entry again with the procedure in Step 4, and fix it so it's back to its own old self.

Now the EDIT links for movies will actually do something!

You see that the script loads the stored values and allows you to edit the data easily. Play around a bit, and get a feel for the way it all works.

Movie Name	Bruce Almighty
Movie Type	Sci-Fi
Movie Year	2003
Lead Actor	Jim Carrey
Director	Tom Shadyac
	edit

Figure 6-12

How It Works

The `commit.php` code is very much the same as what you saw already, but there is an interesting twist in `movie.php`. Let's look at it in some detail.

First, look at the switch at the start of the script. We defined a switch on a query string parameter named `action`. If the action is `edit`, we query the database for a record corresponding to the id specified in the id query string parameter and set some variables. These variables are set to void if `action` is not `edit`.

```
switch( $_GET['action'] ){
    case "edit":
        $moviesql = "SELECT
                *
            FROM
                `movie`
            WHERE
                `movie`.`movie_id` = '".$_GET['id']."'
        ";
    $result = mysql_query($moviesql)
        or die("Invalid query: " . mysql_error());
    $row = mysql_fetch_array( $result , MYSQL_ASSOC );
```

```
                    $movie_name = $row[ 'movie_name' ];
                    $movie_type = $row[ 'movie_type' ];
                    $movie_year = $row[ 'movie_year' ];
                    $movie_leadactor = $row[ 'movie_leadactor' ];
                    $movie_director = $row[ 'movie_director' ];
                    break;
                default:
                    $movie_name = "";
                    $movie_type = "";
                    $movie_year = "";
                    $movie_leadactor = "";
                    $movie_director = "";
                    break;
            }
    ?>
```

The variables set in the preceding code are used to set the default value of the form fields. Each field has a known value if you are editing a record and has a void value if you are creating a record.

```
<tr>
    <td bgcolor="#ffffff" width="30%">
        Movie Name
    </td>
    <td bgcolor="#ffffff" width="70%">
        <input type="text" name="movie_name" value="<?=$movie_name?>">
    </td>
</tr>
```

In this example, the movie_name field takes the $movie_name variable content as a default value. This allows us to reload the form with data from the record to edit it.

Editing a text field is pretty straightforward. Editing a value in a list is another story. You can't just display the list and hope the user will reset the value to the original when he or she edits the record. You need to reload the whole list and make the previously set value as a default in the list so the user can just forget about it if he or she doesn't want to edit it.

How do you do this? The script holds the solution:

```
<tr>
    <td bgcolor="#ffffff">
        Movie Type
    </td>
    <td bgcolor="#ffffff">
        <SELECT id="game" name="movie_type" style="width:150px">
<?php
$sql = "SELECT
            `movietype_id`,
            `movietype_label`
        FROM
            `movietype`
        ORDER BY
            `movietype_label`
        ";
$result = mysql_query($sql)
```

```
  or die("<font color=\"#FF0000\">Query Error</FONT>".mysql_error());
while ( $row = mysql_fetch_array($result) ){
   if ( $row['movietype_id'] == $movie_type){
      $selected = " SELECTED";
   } else {
      $selected = "";
   }
   echo '<OPTION
value="'.$row['movietype_id'].'"'.$selected.'>'.$row['movietype_label'].'</OPTION>'
."\r\n";
}
?>
      </SELECT>
   </td>
</tr>
```

We load the list as we would have done if adding a record, but we compare the current value to the default value. If they are identical, add a simple SELECTED flag to the option value. This sets the default list value to the current value in the table.

```
if ( $row['movietype_id'] == $movie_type){
   $selected = " SELECTED";
} else {
   $selected = "";
}
```

What Next?

The next thing you might do is to create the edit/delete code for the `people` table. This code is available in Chapter 17, "Troubleshooting."

Summary

As you've learned in this chapter, there are three basic actions in modifying the content of a database:

- ❑ Insert
- ❑ Delete
- ❑ Update

These actions are performed by the database itself through SQL queries PHP executes on MySQL. Read up on the SQL statements used in this chapter to get a good feel for how far they can take you and at what level you feel confident using these commands.

Often, using MySQL revolves around the same few PHP functions. The SQL executed through those commands on the database changes the way the system reacts. Don't hesitate to learn more about SQL to enhance your PHP systems.

And finally, always remember that testing your query alone in phpMyAdmin saves you a lot of time debugging it when working in a PHP script.

Validating User Input

Accepting user inputs means being prepared to react to human error and human habit. The fact is that users acquire habits pretty fast. If a person uses an application often enough, the brain starts creating automation for well-known application paths. As the system evolves, user habits will have a bearing on the changes you make. Try switching two fields on a form and see what happens in any widely used system. Users will just go insane until their brains reinitiate the automated path. This problem also exists in new systems because of the users' habits regarding certain commonly used data formats (dates, for example). If you use a format that is not familiar to your users, you will confuse them and force them to change their usual habits to match your new format. It's vital to consider user input when creating a system.

In this chapter, we cover user input validation, including:

- ❑ Validating simple string values
- ❑ Validating integer values
- ❑ Validating formatted text input

Users Are Users Are Users . . .

Let's consider an example here: You work in a bank. You are developing a new system to allow the employees to manage a customer account updating process on the company intranet. You use your well-known MM-DD-YYYY format for the date. It all works quite well when testing, but when put in production, your users say it doesn't work. Why? Because all your company systems use the ISO 8601 YYYY-MM-DD date format (a standard used in many systems because the date can be sorted alphabetically). Your users are confused between the two different formats and input wrong information in the system. If you fail to implement the correct input validation methods, you can end up with a corrupted database or trigger errors in your application.

You can avoid this by using well-known formats and validating the user input. When you expect an integer value, for example, you can check that it is an integer before you try to use it. Simple enough rule.

What Now?

To really understand the role of user input and validation, you need to see it in action. So, first we need to add a few fields to our beloved movie database. The modifications are all in the `movie` table.

The movie application provides us with a lot of opportunities to check for user input. We will need to add a few features to the application, however, to provide more case studies. It will also help you to review what you learned in the previous chapters.

Add a movie_release field INT(11) with default value 0 after the existing movie_year field, as shown in Figure 7-1. This allows you to store a timestamp for the movie release date. Then add a field named movie_rating at the end of the table type TINYINT(2). That information holds the movie rating we gave the movie when viewing it (see Figure 7-2). This rating goes from 0 to 10.

Figure 7-1

Figure 7-2

Forgot Something?

Sometimes, when a user enters data in a form, he or she forgets to fill in a field. When this happens, the system has to react so that the insertion of the invalid or incomplete data will not corrupt the database. In some cases, these errors are made on purpose. In fact, these attempts to find cracks in the walls around your system are quite frequent. You need to design your system so it can react to such errors or malicious attempts to corrupt the database.

Try It Out   Setting Up the Environment

Start by making sure your users enter a movie name when creating a new movie entry.

1.   Open the `movie.php` script and modify it as follows (modifications are shown in bold):

```
<?
$link = mysql_connect("localhost", "root", "")
    or die("Could not connect: " . mysql_error());
mysql_select_db('wiley', $link) or die ( mysql_error());
```

```php
    $peoplesql = "SELECT
                *
            FROM
                `people`
            ";
    $result = mysql_query($peoplesql)
        or die("Invalid query: " . mysql_error());
    while( $row = mysql_fetch_array( $result , MYSQL_ASSOC )){
        $people[ $row['people_id'] ] = $row['people_fullname'];
    }

    switch( $_GET['action'] ){
        case "edit":
        $moviesql = "SELECT
                *
            FROM
                `movie`
            WHERE
                `movie`.`movie_id` = '".$_GET['id']."'
            ";
        $result = mysql_query($moviesql)
            or die("Invalid query: " . mysql_error());
        $row = mysql_fetch_array( $result , MYSQL_ASSOC );
        $movie_name = $row[ 'movie_name' ];
        $movie_type = $row[ 'movie_type' ];
        $movie_year = $row[ 'movie_year' ];
        $movie_leadactor = $row[ 'movie_leadactor' ];
        $movie_director = $row[ 'movie_director' ];
        break;
        default:
            $movie_name = "";
            $movie_type = "";
            $movie_year = "";
            $movie_leadactor = "";
            $movie_director = "";
            break;
    }
?>
<html>
<head>
    <TITLE><?php echo $_GET['action']?> movie</TITLE>
</head>
<body>
<FORM action="commit.php?action=<?php echo $_GET['action']?>&type=movie&id=<?php
echo $_GET['id']?>" method="post">
<?php
if ( !empty($_GET['error']) ){
    echo "<div align=\"center\" style=\"color:#FFFFFF;background-color:#ff0000;font-
weight:bold\">".nl2br(urldecode( $_GET['error']))."</div><br />";
}
?>
    <table border=0 width="750" cellspacing=1 cellpadding=3 bgcolor="#353535"
align="center">
        <tr>
```

```
            <td bgcolor="#ffffff" width="30%">
                Movie Name
            </td>
            <td bgcolor="#ffffff" width="70%">
                <input type="text" name="movie_name" value="<?php echo $movie_name?>">
            </td>
        </tr>
        <tr>
            <td bgcolor="#ffffff">
                Movie Type
            </td>
            <td bgcolor="#ffffff">
            <SELECT id="game" name="movie_type" style="width:150px">
                <option value="" SELECTED>Select a type...</option>
<?php
        $sql = "SELECT
                `movietype_id`,
                `movietype_label`
            FROM
                `movietype`
            ORDER BY
                `movietype_label`
            ";
        $result = mysql_query($sql)
            or die("<font color=\"#FF0000\">Query Error</FONT>".mysql_error());
        while ( $row = mysql_fetch_array($result) ){
            if ( $row['movietype_id'] == $movie_type){
                $selected = " SELECTED";
            } else {
                $selected = "";
            }
            echo '<OPTION
value="'.$row['movietype_id'].'"'.$selected.'>'.$row['movietype_label'].'</OPTION>'
."\r\n";
        }
?>
            </SELECT>

            </td>
        </tr>
        <tr>
            <td bgcolor="#ffffff">
                Movie Year
            </td>
            <td bgcolor="#ffffff">
                <SELECT name="movie_year">
                    <option value="" SELECTED>Select a year...</option>
<?php
for ($year=date("Y"); $year >= 1970 ;$year--){
            if ( $year == $movie_year){
                $selected = " SELECTED";
            } else {
                $selected = "";
            }
```

```
?>
                <option value="<?=$year?>"<?=$selected?>><?=$year?></option>
<?php
}
?>
            </SELECT>
        </td>
    </tr>
    <tr>
        <td bgcolor="#ffffff">
            Lead Actor
        </td>
        <td bgcolor="#ffffff">
            <SELECT name="movie_leadactor">
                <option value="" SELECTED>Select an actor...</option>
<?php
foreach( $people as $people_id => $people_fullname ){
    if ( $people_id == $movie_leadactor){
        $selected = " SELECTED";
    } else {
        $selected = "";
    }
?>
                <option value="<?php echo $people_id?>"<?php echo $selected?>><?php
echo $people_fullname?></option>
<?php
}
?>
            </SELECT>
        </td>
    </tr>
    <tr>
        <td bgcolor="#ffffff">
            Director
        </td>
        <td bgcolor="#ffffff">
            <SELECT name="movie_director">
                <option value="" SELECTED>Select a director...</option>
<?php
foreach( $people as $people_id => $people_fullname ){
    if ( $people_id == $movie_director){
        $selected = " SELECTED";
    } else {
        $selected = "";
    }
?>
                <option value="<?php echo $people_id?>"<?php echo $selected?>><?php
echo $people_fullname?></option>
<?php
}
?>
            </SELECT>
        </td>
    </tr>
```

```
            <tr>
                <td bgcolor="#ffffff" colspan=2 align="center">
                    <INPUT type="SUBMIT" name="SUBMIT" value="<?=$_GET['action']?>">
                </td>
            </tr>
        </table>
    </FORM>
    </body>
    </html>
```

2. Save the file as `movie.php` and upload the new code to your work directory.

3. Open the `commit.php` script and modify it as follows (modifications are shown in bold):

```
<?php
// COMMIT ADD AND EDITS
    $error = '';
    $link = mysql_connect("localhost", "root", "")
        or die("Could not connect: " . mysql_error());
    mysql_select_db('wiley', $link) or die ( mysql_error());
    switch( $_GET['action'] ){
        case "edit":
            switch( $_GET['type'] ){
                case "people":
                    $sql = "UPDATE
                            `people`
                        SET
                            `people_fullname` = '".$_POST['people_fullname']."'
                        WHERE
                            `people_id` = '".$_GET['id']."'
                        ";
                break;
                case "movie":
                    $movie_name = trim($row[ 'movie_name' ]);
                    if( empty($movie_name)){
                        $error .= "Please+enter+a+movie+name%21%0D%0A";
                    }
                    if (empty($_POST['movie_type'])){
                        $error .= "Please+select+a+movie+type%21%0D%0A";
                    }
                    if (empty($_POST['movie_year'])){
                        $error .= "Please+select+a+movie+year%21%0D%0A";
                    }
                    if ( empty($error) ){
                        $sql = "UPDATE
                                `movie`
                            SET
                                `movie_name` = '".$_POST['movie_name']."',
                                `movie_year` = '".$_POST['movie_year']."',
                                `movie_type` = '".$_POST['movie_type']."',
                                `movie_leadactor` = '".$_POST['movie_leadactor']."',
                                `movie_director` = '".$_POST['movie_director']."'
                            WHERE
                                `movie_id` = '".$_GET['id']."'
                            ";
```

```php
                        } else {
                            header(
"location:movie.php?action=edit&error=".$error."&id=".$_GET['id'] );
                        }
                        break;
                }
                break;
        case "add":
            switch( $_GET['type'] ){
                case "people":
                    $sql = "INSERT INTO
                                `people`
                                ( `people_fullname` )
                            VALUES
                                ( '".$_POST['people_fullname']."' )
                            ";
                    break;
                case "movie":
                    $movie_name = trim($row[ 'movie_name' ]);
                    if( empty($movie_name)){
                        $error .= "Please+enter+a+movie+name%21%0D%0A";
                    }
                    if (empty($_POST['movie_type'])){
                        $error .= "Please+select+a+movie+type%21%0D%0A";
                    }
                    if (empty($_POST['movie_year'])){
                    $error .= "Please+select+a+movie+year%21%0D%0A";
                    }
                    if ( empty($error) ){
                        $sql = "INSERT INTO
                                    `movie`
                                    ( `movie_name` ,
                                    `movie_year` ,
                                    `movie_type` ,
                                    `movie_leadactor` ,
                                    `movie_director` )
                                VALUES
                                    ( '".$_POST['movie_name']."' ,
                                    '".$_POST['movie_year']."' ,
                                    '".$_POST['movie_type']."' ,
                                    '".$_POST['movie_leadactor']."' ,
                                    '".$_POST['movie_director']."' )
                                ";
                    } else {
                        header( "location:movie.php?action=add&error=".$error );
                    }
                    break;

            }
            break;
    }
    if ( isset( $sql ) && !empty( $sql )){
        echo "<!-".$sql."->";
        $result = mysql_query( $sql )
```

```
              or die("Invalid query: " . mysql_error());
    ?>
          <p align="center" style="color:#FF0000">
          Done. <a href="index.php">Index</a>
          </p>
    <?php
       }
    ?>
```

4. Save the file as `commit.php` and upload it to your server.

5. Now open your browser and go to `http://localhost/chapter7/index.php` (adapt this URL to fit your setup) and try adding a movie with no name, as shown in Figure 7-3.

Movie Name	
Movie Type	Action
Movie Year	2001
Lead Actor	Jim Carrey
Director	Ron Livingston
Movie release date (dd-mm-yyyy)	29-10-2003
Movie rating (0 to 10)	9
	add

Figure 7-3

6. Now try to enter a new movie without setting the year and the movie type (see Figure 7-4).

7. Edit a movie from the index and try deleting the name and submitting the form (see Figure 7-5).

8. Notice the error message stating the mistake made in filling in the form (Figure 7-6).

Figure 7-4

How It Works

When the form passes information to the commit script, the data has to be verified. In this case, we use a simple verification method: The `empty()` function returns `true` if the string is empty and `false` if not. To ensure that the user did not submit the form with a simple space in the movie name field, we `trim()` the field's content to eliminate any space leading or trailing the string. (Some people like to trigger errors in Web sites by entering erroneous input; let's not make their job easy.)

At the same time, if an error is detected, we add a message to the `$error` variable that collects all the error messages. The error messages are URL encoded before being added to the code. (See `urlencode` and `urldecode` functions in the manual; for more information, check the PHP Web site at www.php.net/url.)

```
if( empty($movie_name)){
    $error .= "Please+enter+a+movie+name%21%0D%0A";
}
```

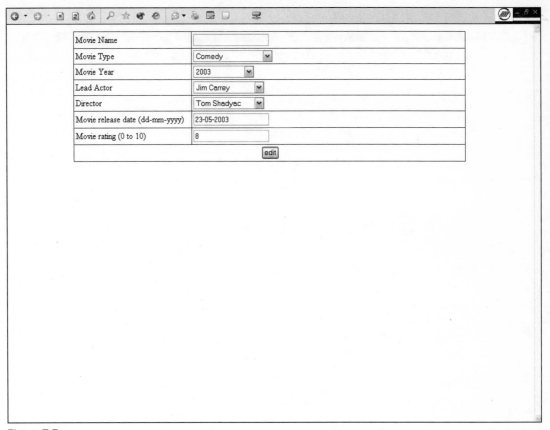

Figure 7-5

Once we are sure that an error has occurred, we redirect the user to the form with an error message stating the problem. The error message is URL encoded to ensure that it will be passed to the movie.php script without being corrupted.

```
if ( empty($error) ){
} else {
    header( "location:movie.php?action=add&error=".$error );
}
```

Once redirected to the form, the system needs to display the decoded error message.

```
<?
if ( !empty($_GET['error']) ){
    echo "<div align=\"center\" style=\"color:#FFFFFF;background-color:#ff0000;font-
weight:bold\">".nl2br(urldecode( $_GET['error']))."</div><br />";
}
?>
```

Figure 7-6

This causes a rather colorful message that your user will not miss to be displayed by the browser.

The update itself is performed at the end of the code, along with all the controls and debug messages we need.

```php
if ( isset( $sql ) && !empty( $sql )){
    echo "<!--".$sql."-->";
    $result = mysql_query( $sql )
        or die("Invalid query: " . mysql_error());
?>
    <p align="center" style="color:#FF0000">
        Done. <a href="index.php">Index</a>
    </p>
<?php
}
```

If the $sql variable is not previously set (which could happen if the page is called out of context), the code will not try to execute and will do nothing. (Note that it would be a good exercise for you to code a response to this occurrence, such as a message or a logging of the error in the database.)

Checking for Format Errors

Checking for errors in dates or other formatted data is a requirement in most systems because users can't always be guided in their input. You should always check for what is entered if you require a specific format or set of values.

At this point, we need the feared and powerful regular expressions. The regular expressions allow us to define a pattern and check to see if it can be applied to our data. It's very useful to check for dates, social security numbers, and any data that has to respect a predefined set of format requirements. (It helps to be sure to always indicate the format in the source field.)

Try It Out   **Checking Dates and Numbers**

First, you need to modify the database and a few pages slightly:

1. Open the well-known `movie.php` and modify it as follows (modifications are shown in bold):

```php
<?php
    $link = mysql_connect("localhost", "root", "")
        or die("Could not connect: " . mysql_error());
    mysql_select_db('wiley2', $link) or die ( mysql_error());
    $peoplesql = "SELECT
                *
            FROM
                `people`
            ";
    $result = mysql_query($peoplesql)
        or die("Invalid query: " . mysql_error());
    while( $row = mysql_fetch_array( $result , MYSQL_ASSOC )){
        $people[ $row['people_id'] ] = $row['people_fullname'];
    }
    switch( $_GET['action'] ){
        case "edit":
         $moviesql = "SELECT
                    *
                FROM
                    `movie`
                WHERE
                    `movie`.`movie_id` = '".$_GET['id']."'
                ";
        $result = mysql_query($moviesql)
            or die("Invalid query: " . mysql_error());
        $row = mysql_fetch_array( $result , MYSQL_ASSOC );
        $movie_name = $row[ 'movie_name' ];
        $movie_type = $row[ 'movie_type' ];
        $movie_year = $row[ 'movie_year' ];
        $movie_release = $row[ 'movie_release' ];
        $movie_leadactor = $row[ 'movie_leadactor' ];
        $movie_director = $row[ 'movie_director' ];
        $movie_rating = $row[ 'movie_rating' ];
        break;
        default:
            $movie_name = "";
```

```php
                $movie_type = "";
                $movie_year = "";
                $movie_release = time();
                $movie_leadactor = "";
                $movie_director = "";
                $movie_rating = "5";
                break;
        }
?>
<html>
<head>
    <TITLE><?php echo $_GET['action']?> movie</TITLE>
</head>
<body>
<FORM action="commit.php?action=<?php echo $_GET['action']?>&type=movie&id=<?php
echo $_GET['id']?>" method="post">
<?php
if ( !empty($_GET['error']) ){
    echo "<div align=\"center\" style=\"color:#FFFFFF;background-color:#ff0000;font-
weight:bold\">".nl2br(urldecode( $_GET['error']))."</div><br />";
}
?>
    <table border=0 width="750" cellspacing=1 cellpadding=3 bgcolor="#353535"
align="center">
        <tr>
            <td bgcolor="#ffffff" width="30%">
                Movie Name
            </td>
            <td bgcolor="#ffffff" width="70%">
                <input type="text" name="movie_name" value="<?php echo $movie_name?>">
            </td>
        </tr>
        <tr>
            <td bgcolor="#ffffff">
                Movie Type
            </td>
            <td bgcolor="#ffffff">
            <SELECT id="game" name="movie_type" style="width:150px">
                <option value="" SELECTED>Select a type...</option>
<?php
        $sql = "SELECT
                    `movietype_id`,
                    `movietype_label`
                FROM
                    `movietype`
                ORDER BY
                    `movietype_label`
                ";
        $result = mysql_query($sql)
            or die("<font color=\"#FF0000\">Query Error</FONT>".mysql_error());
        while ( $row = mysql_fetch_array($result) ){
            if ( $row['movietype_id'] == $movie_type){
                $selected = " SELECTED";
            } else {
```

```
            $selected = "";
        }
        echo '<OPTION
value="'.$row['movietype_id'].'"'.$selected.'>'.$row['movietype_label'].'</OPTION>'
."\r\n";
    }
?>
        </SELECT>

        </td>
    </tr>
    <tr>
        <td bgcolor="#ffffff">
            Movie Year
        </td>
        <td bgcolor="#ffffff">
            <SELECT name="movie_year">
                <option value="" SELECTED>Select a year...</option>
<?php
for ($year=date("Y"); $year >= 1970 ;$year-){
        if ( $year == $movie_year){
            $selected = " SELECTED";
        } else {
            $selected = "";
        }
?>
                <option value="<?php echo $year?>"<?php echo $selected?>><?php echo
$year?></option>
<?php
}
?>
            </SELECT>
        </td>
    </tr>
    <tr>
        <td bgcolor="#ffffff">
            Lead Actor
        </td>
        <td bgcolor="#ffffff">
            <SELECT name="movie_leadactor">
                <option value="" SELECTED>Select an actor...</option>
<?php
foreach( $people as $people_id => $people_fullname ){
        if ( $people_id == $movie_leadactor){
            $selected = " SELECTED";
        } else {
            $selected = "";
        }
?>
                <option value="<?php echo $people_id?>"<?php echo $selected?>><?php
echo $people_fullname?></option>
<?php
}
?>
```

205

```
                        </SELECT>
                    </td>
                </tr>
                <tr>
                    <td bgcolor="#ffffff">
                        Director
                    </td>
                    <td bgcolor="#ffffff">
                        <SELECT name="movie_director">
                            <option value="" SELECTED>Select a director...</option>
<?php
foreach( $people as $people_id => $people_fullname ){
            if ( $people_id == $movie_director){
                $selected = " SELECTED";
            } else {
                $selected = "";
            }
?>
                            <option value="<?php echo $people_id?>"<?php echo $selected?>><?php
echo $people_fullname?></option>
<?php
}
?>
                        </SELECT>
                    </td>
                </tr>
                <tr>
                    <td bgcolor="#ffffff" width="30%">
                        Movie release date (dd-mm-yyyy)
                    </td>
                    <td bgcolor="#ffffff" width="70%">
                        <input type="text" name="movie_release" value="<?=date( "d-m-Y" ,
$movie_release )?>">
                    </td>
                </tr>
                <tr>
                    <td bgcolor="#ffffff" width="30%">
                        Movie rating (0 to 10)
                    </td>
                    <td bgcolor="#ffffff" width="70%">
                        <input type="text" name="movie_rating" value="<?=$movie_rating?>">
                    </td>
                </tr>
                <tr>
                    <td bgcolor="#ffffff" colspan=2 align="center">
                        <INPUT type="SUBMIT" name="SUBMIT" value="<?=$_GET['action']?>">
                    </td>
                </tr>
            </table>
        </FORM>
    </body>
</html>
```

2. Now open `commit.php` and modify it as follows (modifications are shown in bold):

```php
<?php
// COMMIT ADD AND EDITS
   $error = '';
   $link = mysql_connect("localhost", "root", "")
      or die("Could not connect: " . mysql_error());
   mysql_select_db('wiley2', $link) or die ( mysql_error());
   switch( $_GET['action'] ){
      case "edit":
         switch( $_GET['type'] ){
            case "people":
               $sql = "UPDATE
                     `people`
                   SET
                     `people_fullname` = '".$_POST['people_fullname']."'
                   WHERE
                     `people_id` = '".$_GET['id']."'
                   ";
            break;
            case "movie":
               $movie_rating = trim($_POST['movie_rating']);
               if ( !is_numeric ( $movie_rating )){
                 $error .= "Please+enter+a+numeric+rating+%21%0D%0A";
               } else {
                 if ( $movie_rating < 0 || $movie_rating > 10 ){
                    $error .= "Please+enter+a+rating+between+0+and+10%21%0D%0A";
                 }
               }
               if ( !ereg ("([0-9]{2})-([0-9]{2})-([0-9]{4})",
$_POST['movie_release'] , $reldatepart) ){
                    $error .= "Please+enter+a+date+with+the+dd-mm-
yyyy+format%21%0D%0A";
               } else {
                    $movie_release = @mktime ( 0, 0, 0, $reldatepart['2'],
$reldatepart['1'], $reldatepart['3']);
                    if ( $movie_release == '-1' ){
                       $error .= "Please+enter+a+real+date+with+the+dd-mm-
yyyy+format%21%0D%0A";
                    }
               }
               $movie_name = trim($_POST[ 'movie_name' ]);
               if( empty($movie_name)){
                  $error .= "Please+enter+a+movie+name%21%0D%0A";
               }
               if (empty($_POST['movie_type'])){
                  $error .= "Please+select+a+movie+type%21%0D%0A";
               }
               if (empty($_POST['movie_year'])){
                  $error .= "Please+select+a+movie+year%21%0D%0A";
               }
               if ( empty($error) ){
                  $sql = "UPDATE
                        `movie`
```

```
                        SET
                            `movie_name` = '".$_POST['movie_name']."',
                            `movie_year` = '".$_POST['movie_year']."',
                            `movie_release` = '$movie_release',
                            `movie_type` = '".$_POST['movie_type']."',
                            `movie_leadactor` = '".$_POST['movie_leadactor']."',
                            `movie_director` = '".$_POST['movie_director']."',
                            `movie_rating` = '$movie_rating'
                        WHERE
                            `movie_id` = '".$_GET['id']."'
                        ";
                } else {
                    header(
"location:movie.php?action=edit&error=".$error."&id=".$_GET['id'] );
                }
                break;
        }
        break;
    case "add":
        switch( $_GET['type'] ){
            case "people":
                $sql = "INSERT INTO
                        `people`
                        ( `people_fullname` )
                    VALUES
                        ( '".$_POST['people_fullname']."' )
                    ";
                break;
            case "movie":
                $movie_rating = trim($_POST['movie_rating']);
                if ( !is_numeric ( $movie_rating )){
                    $error .= "Please+enter+a+numeric+rating+%21%0D%0A";
                } else {
                    if ( $movie_rating < 0 || $movie_rating > 10 ){
                        $error .= "Please+enter+a+rating+between+0+and+10%21%0D%0A";
                    }
                }
                $movie_release = trim($_POST['movie_release']);
                if ( !ereg ("([0-9]{2})-([0-9]{2})-([0-9]{4})", $movie_release ,
$reldatepart) || empty( $movie_release )){
                    $error .= "Please+enter+a+date+with+the+dd-mm-
yyyy+format%21%0D%0A";
                } else {
                    $movie_release = @mktime ( 0, 0, 0, $reldatepart['2'],
$reldatepart['1'], $reldatepart['3']);
                    if ( $movie_release == '-1' ){
                        $error .= "Please+enter+a+real+date+with+the+dd-mm-
yyyy+format%21%0D%0A";
                    }
                }
                $movie_name = trim($row[ 'movie_name' ]);
                if( empty($movie_name)){
                    $error .= "Please+enter+a+movie+name%21%0D%0A";
                }
```

```
                        if (empty($_POST['movie_type'])){
                            $error .= "Please+select+a+movie+type%21%0D%0A";
                        }
                        if (empty($_POST['movie_year'])){
                            $error .= "Please+select+a+movie+year%21%0D%0A";
                        }
                        if ( empty($error) ){
                            $sql = "INSERT INTO
                                    `movie`
                                    ( `movie_name` ,
                                      `movie_year` ,
                                      `movie_release` ,
                                      `movie_type` ,
                                      `movie_leadactor` ,
                                      `movie_director` ,
                                      `movie_rating`)
                                VALUES
                                    ( '".$_POST['movie_name']."' ,
                                      '".$_POST['movie_year']."' ,
                                      '$movie_release'
                                      '".$_POST['movie_type']."' ,
                                      '".$_POST['movie_leadactor']."' ,
                                      '".$_POST['movie_director']."',
                                      '$movie_rating' )
                                ";
                        } else {
                            header( "location:movie.php?action=add&error=".$error );
                        }
                            break;

                    }
                break;
            }
    if ( isset( $sql ) && !empty( $sql )){
        echo "<!-".$sql."->";
        $result = mysql_query( $sql )
            or die("Invalid query: " . mysql_error());
?>
        <p align="center" style="color:#FF0000">
            Done. <a href="index.php">Index</a>
        </p>
<?php
    }
?>
```

3. Now save the files, upload them, and open your browser to the site index.

4. Click any movie and try entering **2003-10-10** in the release date field. You will be brought back to the form with a nice, yet very explicit, message telling you what format to respect, as shown in Figure 7-7.

5. Try entering alphanumeric values in the rating field, as in Figure 7-8 (which could easily have been a drop-down but is a text field for the purpose of the exercise).

Figure 7-7

If the entered value is not in the 0 to 10 range, it will be refused. (Note that the decimals are not managed in this code and will be lost.)

How It Works

This requires some explaining. First, let's look into the type validating functions.

In the `commit.php` code, we use the `is_numeric()` function. This function returns a Boolean TRUE if the value is indeed numeric and FALSE if not. There are more of these validating functions available, including:

❑ **is_string,** which checks to see if the value is of the string format

❑ **is_bool,** which checks for Boolean type (TRUE, FALSE, 0 or 1)

❑ **is_array,** which tells you if the variable holds an array

❑ **is_object,** which determines if the variable stores an object (remember this one when you try object oriented coding using PHP; it is very useful)

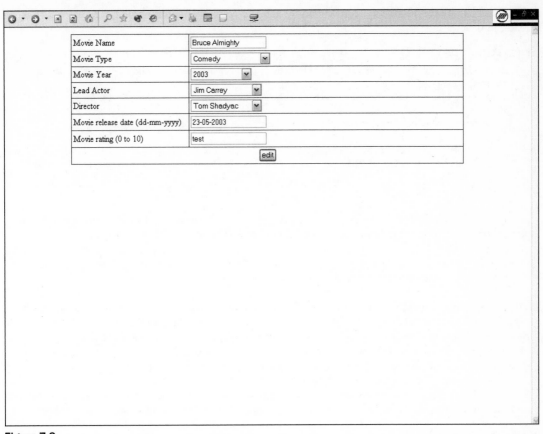

Figure 7-8

These functions are all documented in the PHP manual at www.php.net/variables.

In this instance, the use of is_numeric allows us to make sure our user has entered a numeric value (remember that we are expecting a numeric value between 0 and 10).

```
$movie_rating = trim($_POST['movie_rating']);
if ( !is_numeric ( $movie_rating )){
    $error .= "Please+enter+a+numeric+rating+%21%0D%0A";
} else {
    if ( $movie_rating < 0 || $movie_rating > 10 ){
        $error .= "Please+enter+a+rating+between+0+and+10%21%0D%0A";
    }
}
```

The code first cleans up the value of leading and trailing spaces (always try to be prepared for typos and mishaps) and then tests to see if the value is numeric. If it's not, the error message queue is fed; if it is, we test the value to see if it is between 0 and 10. If the value is not between 0 and 10, we add an error message to the error message queue.

The date validation is almost as simple to understand, if you know about regular expressions. Here's a closer look at it:

```
$movie_release = trim($_POST['movie_release']);
if ( !ereg ("([0-9]{2})-([0-9]{2})-([0-9]{4})", $movie_release , $reldatepart) ||
empty( $movie_release )){
    $error .= "Please+enter+a+date+with+the+dd-mm-yyyy+format%21%0D%0A";
} else {
    $movie_release = @mktime ( 0, 0, 0, $reldatepart['2'], $reldatepart['1'],
$reldatepart['3']);
    if ( $movie_release == '-1' ){
        $error .= "Please+enter+a+real+date+with+the+dd-mm-yyyy+format%21%0D%0A";
    }
}
```

As you saw in this chapter's first exercise, we use the `trim()` function to clear all leading and trailing spaces in the received string to make sure our user entered something other than just a space.

> *The string manipulation functions are found at the PHP Web site at* `www.php.net/strings`. *You can find* `trim` *and some other very useful functions there.*

The next statement contains two conditions. The first condition tests for a regular expression match. The regular expression is `"([0-9]{2})-([0-9]{2})-([0-9]{4})"`. What does this do? `[0-9]{2}` specifies that we want to check for numbers between 0 and 9 with two occurrences. For example `02` will match but not `2`. The same logic applies to the `[0-9]{4}` statement: The only difference is that we are expecting four digits in our number. These four digits are the year part of the date.

So, in English, it means: I want my string to start with a number with two digits, followed by a hyphen (-), and then another group of two digits, and then a hyphen (-), and finish with a four-digit number.

```
if ( !ereg ("([0-9]{2})-([0-9]{2})-([0-9]{4})", $movie_release , $reldatepart) ||
empty( $movie_release )){...
}
```

Now, this is not exactly what our regular expression says. It says that if it matches our condition, we will split it in three different chunks, each chunk delimited with the parentheses.

This cutting is performed by the `ereg()` function. If the `$movie_release` string matches the pattern, `ereg` will cut the string into parts and then store each part as an element of the `$reldatepart` array in our example.

> *Be sure to read the PHP manual about regular expressions at* `www.php.net/regex` *and consult a few tutorials to understand the real power of using regular expressions. (A good starting tutorial can be found at* `www.phpbuilder.com/columns/dario19990616.php3`.)

If our date were 02-03-2003, the array would be as follows:

```
Array
(
    [0] => 02-03-2003
    [1] => 02
```

```
    [2] => 03
    [3] => 2003
)
```

As you can see here, the first index holds the whole string, and each chunk holds a cut-off part of the string, delimited by the parentheses.

Now that we have our date in an understandable format, we can change it into a timestamp using the `mktime()` function, which allows you to create a timestamp from chunks of dates. It is also a very useful function to manipulate dates.

```
$movie_release = mktime ( 0, 0, 0, $reldatepart['2'], $reldatepart['1'],
$reldatepart['3']);
```

This code stores a timestamp from the day, month, and year information fed to the system in the `$movie_release` variable. The format is `int mktime` (`int hour`, `int minute`, `int second`, `int month`, `int day`, `int year`). The returned value is the number of seconds between January 1, 1970, and the specified date.

> See documentation at www.php.net/mktime for additional information regarding optional parameters such as daylight saving flag.

If `mktime` fails to create a timestamp from the date you passed to it, it will return -1. This happens when the input is invalid, although it matches the regular expression (for example 99-99-9999 will pass the regular expression test, but is obviously not a valid date). To be sure that the date is indeed a date, we will test for the return value from `mktime` and respond accordingly.

```
if ( $movie_release == '-1' ){
    $error .= "Please+enter+a+real+date+with+the+dd-mm-yyyy+format%21%0D%0A";
}
```

In this case, a false date entry triggers an error message asking for a valid date.

Here's an alternate technique: The same timestamp generation could have been performed using SQL. Many things that PHP does on the string manipulation side can be done straight from SQL, as shown here:

```
if ( !ereg ("([0-9]{2})-([0-9]{2})-([0-9]{4})", $movie_release , $reldatepart) ||
empty( $movie_release )){...
}
$reldate = $reldatepart['3']."-".$reldatepart['2']."-".$reldatepart['1']."
00:00:00";
$sql = "INSERT INTO
        `movie`
            (`movie_release`)
    VALUES
        (UNIX_TIMESTAMP('$reldate'))
    ";
```

In this code, the SQL does the timestamp generation. The `UNIX_TIMESTAMP()` SQL function expects a YYYY-MM-DD HH:MM:SS (2003-12-05 02:05:00) format and creates a timestamp from it. In the code, we force the creation of the timestamp at 00:00 on the date of the movie release. You can save yourself some lengthy coding by using SQL features wherever possible.

> *See documentation on MySQL* date *and* time *functions at* www.mysql.com/doc/en/ Date_and_time_functions.html.

Summary

Validating user data is all about being prepared for the worst. Users make mistakes—that's the nature of users. Most errors are unintentional. Some errors are made intentionally to deny the service. It happens every day. The developer has to help the system deal with user input errors.

Regular expressions help you meet many user input validation challenges. Learning how to use them is often the key to success in an interactive system.

Handling and Avoiding Errors

You will probably be spending a fair amount of time contemplating errors in your code, as do most Web developers when they start programming. No matter how good you are, how good your code, how long you have been coding, or how hard you try, you will encounter times when you have errors in your code.

It is of the utmost importance that you know how to handle your errors and debug your own code. Being able to efficiently and properly debug your code is an invaluable time-saver; and in Web development, $time == $money!

Luckily, PHP comes with a full-featured API (Applications Programming Interface) that provides you with many ways to trap and resolve those unwanted errors. PHP also allows you to use the API to capture the errors and create your own custom error functions or pages. These features are useful when debugging your code and when notifying your Webmaster about errors that seem to be happening to your applications as users are running them. Not only can you use PHP code to trap errors and customize them; you can use the Apache Web Server to help do this.

How the Apache Web Server Deals with Errors

Apache has a directive, the ErrorDocument, that you can configure in the `httpd.conf` file to create custom error pages with PHP so visitors to your site don't see the old boring server-created error pages. There are limitless possibilities when creating these custom messages. As with the PHP error-catching pages, you can have the ErrorDocument call PHP pages to do whatever you would like them to do—from simply displaying a friendly error message to the user to e-mailing a system administrator to notify him or her of the failure.

Now, unlike PHP error pages, the Apache ErrorDocument pages are used more for instances of missing pages (that is, a "Page Not Found" error or Forbidden access error pages and other requests of that sort). So, if someone visits your site, and he or she runs into the "Page Not Found" error page, the script will e-mail the administrator and he or she can in turn check to see if this was a valid request and there is something wrong with the page or server, or if someone was just looking for pages or trying to sniff around where they weren't supposed to be.

Apache's ErrorDocument Directive

Error handling is an invaluable resource and a "must have" for Web developers to keep their sites up and running with the fewest end-user problems or complaints. If you rely on people contacting you to tell you about errors on your site, you will never get any decent input. Allowing the server to do this for you will greatly increase your success at running a smooth server. We will first look at Apache's ErrorDocument method of error handling.

Try It Out   Using Apache's ErrorDocument Method

First of all, you need to make some changes to the `httpd.conf` file to allow you to create a custom error page. Apache is usually set up by default to go to its own internal error pages, but you don't want that. You want Apache to go to your custom error page, no matter what error has occurred.

To do this, you change the default settings to your own specific settings by following these steps:

1. Open up your `httpd.conf` file, and you will find some lines around line 750 or so that look like this:

```
# Customizable error responses come in three flavors:
# 1) plain text 2) local redirects 3) external redirects
#
# Some examples:
#ErrorDocument 500 "The server made a boo boo."
#ErrorDocument 404 /missing.html
#ErrorDocument 404 "/cgi-bin/missing_handler.pl"
#ErrorDocument 402 http://www.example.com/subscription_info.html
```

2. Change that information to the following:

```
# Customizable error responses come in three flavors:
# 1) plain text 2) local redirects 3) external redirects
#
# Some examples:
ErrorDocument 400 /error.php?400
ErrorDocument 401 /error.php?401
ErrorDocument 403 /error.php?403
ErrorDocument 404 /error.php?404
ErrorDocument 500 /error.php?500
```

There are many ErrorDocument codes, but we will focus on the error messages you see typically in everyday Web browsing. The following is a list of all server codes and what they stand for, including the five we will be addressing in these examples.

- **Successful Client Requests:**
  - **200:** OK
  - **202:** Accepted
  - **203:** Non-Authorative Information
  - **204:** No Content
  - **205:** Reset Content
  - **206:** Partial Content
- **Client Request Redirected:**
  - **300:** Multiple Choices
  - **301:** Moved Permanently
  - **302:** Moved Temporarily
  - **304:** Not Modified
  - **305:** Use Proxy
- **Client Request Errors:**
  - **400:** Bad Request
  - **401:** Authorization Required
  - **402:** Payment Required
  - **403:** Forbidden
  - **404:** Not Found
  - **405:** Method Not Allowed
  - **406:** Not Acceptable
  - **407:** Proxy Authentication Required
  - **408:** Request Timed Out
  - **409:** Conflicting Request
  - **410:** Gone
  - **411:** Content Length Required
  - **412:** Precondition Failed
  - **413:** Request Entity Too Long
  - **414:** Request URI Too Long
  - **415:** Unsupported Media Type

- ❑ **Server Errors**:

    - ❑ **500:** Internal Server Error

    - ❑ **501:** Not Implemented

    - ❑ **502:** Bad Gateway

    - ❑ **503:** Service Unavailable

    - ❑ **504:** Gateway Timeout

    - ❑ **505:** HTTP Version Not Supported

Although we are showing you just a few of these, you can catch others as well by simply adding another ErrorDocument to the `httpd.conf` *file. For example, say you want to implement the 501 error code, you would simply add* **ErrorDocument 501 /error.php?501** *to your code and add the error handling in the* `error.php` *page, which you'll see shortly.*

Now we will look at a simple way to show the user error messages, and then get into some more complex ways to notify the Webmaster of errors occurring on the Web site by using the `mail()` command that you learned previously.

To show the user error messages, follow these steps:

1. Open your text editor and save a page called `error.php`.

2. Enter the following code:

```php
<?php
$error_no = $_SERVER['QUERY_STRING'];

switch ($error_no)
{
    case 400:
        $error_output = "<h1>&quot;Bad Request&quot; Error Page - (Error Code
            400)</h1>";
        $error_output .= "The browser has made a Bad Request<br>";
        $error_output .= "<a href=\"mailto:sysadmin@localhost.com\">Contact</a>
            the system administrator";
        $error_output .= " if you feel this to be in error";
    break;
    case 401:
        $error_output = "<h1>&quot;Authorization Required&quot; Error Page -
(Error Code
            401)</h1>";
        $error_output .= "You have supplied the wrong information to access a
            secure area<br>";
        $error_output .= "<a href=\"mailto:sysadmin@localhost.com\">Contact</a>
            the system administrator";
        $error_output .= " if you feel this to be in error";
    break;
    case 403:
        $error_output = "<h1>&quot;Forbidden Access&quot; Error Page - (Error Code
```

```
                        403)</h1>";
            $error_output .= "You are denied access to this area<br>";
            $error_output .= "<a href=\"mailto:sysadmin@localhost.com\">Contact</a>
                    the system administrator";
            $error_output .= " if you feel this to be in error";
        break;
        case 404:
            $error_output = "<h1>&quot;Page Not Found&quot; Error Page - (Error Code
                    404)</h1>";
            $error_output .= "The page you are looking for cannot be found<br>";
            $error_output .= "<a href=\"mailto:sysadmin@localhost.com\">Contact</a>
                    the system administrator";
            $error_output .= " if you feel this to be in error";
        break;
        case 500:
            $error_output = "<h1>&quot;Internal Server Error&quot; Error Page -
(Error Code
                    500)</h1>";
            $error_output .= "The server has encountered an internal error<br>";
            $error_output .= "<a href=\"mailto:sysadmin@localhost.com\">Contact</a>
                    the system administrator";
            $error_output .= " if you feel this to be in error";
        break;
        default:
            $error_output = "<h1>Error Page</h1>";
            $error_output .= "This is the custom error Page<br>";
            $error_output .= "You should be <a href=\"index.php\">here</a>";
    }
    ?>
    <html>
    <head>
        <title>Beginning PHP, Apache, MySQL Web Development</title>
    </head>
    <body>
    <?php
    echo $error_output;
    ?>
    </body>
    </html>
```

How It Works

Now, to test one of these, simply open your browser and type **http://localhost/asdf/qwerty/page.html**, or any other page you know for certain doesn't reside on your server, into the address bar. You should see the "Page Not Found" message on the screen similar to the message shown in Figure 8-1.

Another way to test or simulate the error messages so that you can ensure you coded the page correctly is to supply the page with the query string information via the browser. For example, if you want to simulate an "Internal Server Error" error message, type **http://localhost/error.php?500** into your address bar. The page will use the query string information and run the code just as if there was an Internal Server Error on one of your pages. The result will look pretty similar to the previous example, but will contain a different message. The "Internal Server Error" page will look like the one shown in Figure 8-2, displaying the "Internal Server Error" message on the screen.

Apache's ErrorDocument: Advanced Custom Error Page

Up until this point, we've been showing the user a custom error message only. You can do countless other things, such as e-mailing the administrator or Webmaster of the site so he or she can look into the issue further should there be a problem with certain pages. This is a great way for you to keep track of your pages without having to check up on the server periodically. More than likely, if you haven't received any error e-mails, there haven't been problems with your server.

Now we generate an automatic e-mail that tells the administrator what time the error occurred, on what day, what the error was, what page generated the error, and what error message was displayed to the user who navigated to the page. We will be adding this functionality to the same error.php file, so if you wish to keep them separate, name the original page error_old.php or whatever you prefer.

Figure 8-1

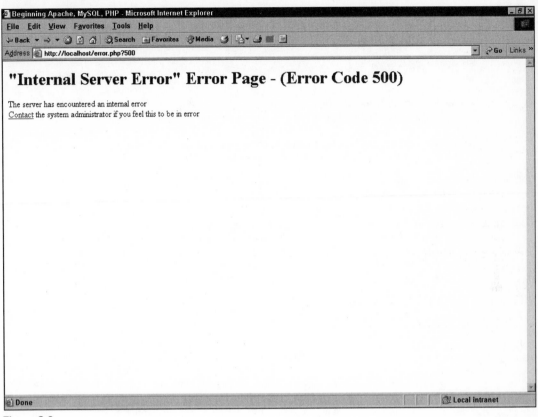

Figure 8-2

The full code will look like this:

```
<?
function e-mail_admin($error_no, $error_output, $full_date, $full_time,
$request_page)
{
     $to = "Administrator <admin@yourdomain.com>";

     $subject = "Apache Error Generation";

     $body = "<html>";
     $body .= "<head>";
     $body .= "<title></title>";
     $body .= "</head>";
     $body .= "<body>";
     $body .= "Error occurred on <b>" . $full_date . "</b> at <b>" . $full_time .
"</b><br>";
```

```
        $body .= "Error received was a <b>" . $error_no . "</b> error.<br>";
        $body .= "The page that generated the error was: <b>" . $request_page .
    "</b><br>";
        $body .= "The generated error message was:" . $error_output;
        $body .= "</body>";
        $body .= "</html>";

        $headers = "MIME-Version: 1.0\r\n";
        $headers .= "Content-type: text/html; charset=iso-8859-1\r\n";

        $headers .= "From: Apache Error <host@yourdomain.com>\r\n";
        $headers .= "Cc: webmaster@yourdomain.com\r\n";

        mail($to, $subject, $body, $headers);
}

$date = getdate();
$full_date = $date['weekday'] . ", " . $date['month'] . " " . $date['mday'] . ", "
    . $date['year'];
$full_time = $date['hours'] . ":" . $date['minutes'] . ":" . $date['seconds'] . ":"
    . $date['year'];

$error_no = $_SERVER['QUERY_STRING'];
$request_page = $_SERVER['REQUEST_URI'];

switch ($error_no)
{
    case 400:
        $error_output = "<h1>\"Bad Request\" Error Page - (Error Code
    400)</h1>";
        $error_output .= "The browser has made a Bad Request<br>";
        $error_output .= "<a href=\"mailto:sysadmin@localhost.com\">Contact</a>
            the system administrator";
        $error_output .= " if you feel this to be in error";

        e-mail_admin($error_no, $error_output, $full_date, $full_time,
    $request_page);
    break;
    case 401:
        $error_output = "<h1>\"Authorization Required\" Error Page - (Error
    Code 401)</h1>";
        $error_output .= "You have supplied the wrong information to access a
    secure area<br>";
        $error_output .= "<a href=\"mailto:sysadmin@localhost.com\">Contact</a>
    the system administrator";
        $error_output .= " if you feel this to be in error";

        e-mail_admin($error_no, $error_output, $full_date, $full_time,
    $request_page);
    break;
    case 403:
        $error_output = "<h1>\"Forbidden Access\" Error Page - (Error Code
    403)</h1>";
        $error_output .= "You are denied access to this area<br>";
```

```
            $error_output .= "<a href=\"mailto:sysadmin@localhost.com\">Contact</a>
the system administrator";
            $error_output .= " if you feel this to be in error";

            e-mail_admin($error_no, $error_output, $full_date, $full_time,
$request_page);
        break;
        case 404:
            $error_output = "<h1>\"Page Not Found\" Error Page - (Error Code
404)</h1>";
            $error_output .= "The page you are looking for cannot be found<br>";
            $error_output .= "<a href=\"mailto:sysadmin@localhost.com\">Contact</a>
the system administrator";
            $error_output .= " if you feel this to be in error";

            e-mail_admin($error_no, $error_output, $full_date, $full_time,
$request_page);
        break;
        case 500:
            $error_output = "<h1>\"Internal Server Error\" Error Page - (Error Code
500)</h1>";
            $error_output .= "The server has encountered an internal error<br>";
            $error_output .= "<a href=\"mailto:sysadmin@localhost.com\">Contact</a>
the system administrator";
            $error_output .= " if you feel this to be in error";

            e-mail_admin($error_no, $error_output, $full_date, $full_time,
$request_page);
        break;
        default:
            $error_output = "<h1>Error Page</h1>";
            $error_output .= "This is the custom error Page<br>";
            $error_output .= "You should be <a href=\"index.php\">here</a>";
}
?>
<html>
<head>
    <title>Beginning PHP, Apache, MySQL Web Development</title>
</head>
<body>
<?
echo $error_output;
?>
</body>
</html>
```

Now we will explain what we just did. The output that you see in the browser will be the same as you saw before, but behind the scenes, we used the mail() function to send an e-mail to the administrator. We also used some other PHP functions, such as getdate(), to note the time and day the error occurred. We threw in some function practice for you to get the hang of sending variables as parameters to and from functions. Now the administrator or Webmaster will be getting an HTML-formatted e-mail concerning the error message that the user received when he or she happened to go to that page.

That's it: You just used Apache's ErrorDocument Directive to help you maintain your server.

Error Handling and Creating Error Handling Pages with PHP

Now let's look at how you can troubleshoot your PHP scripts using simple logical steps. First, however, you need to understand what PHP does when it encounters an error and what it does with certain errors.

When a PHP script gets executed and encounters an error, it displays a message in the browser showing you what the error was. Depending on what type of error occurred, the script may no longer finish executing. You are likely to run into these sorts of errors when writing your own scripts. Don't feel ashamed if you receive errors; everybody makes errors when writing code, no matter what the level of expertise. Even though it is normal to receive errors during the development of your script, you don't want errors (which are normally complicated to understand for the lay person) to be popping up to end users when your site has gone live. For this reason, it's important to know how to catch those unwanted errors and generate more user-friendly errors that let the user know that there will be a solution forthcoming.

Error Types in PHP

There are 11 types of errors in PHP listed in the following table, along with the Report All Errors option. Each of these can be called by either an integer value or a named constant.

Error	Integer Value	NAMED CONSTANT
E_ERROR	1	Fatal runtime error
E_WARNING	2	Non-fatal runtime error
E_PARSE	4	Compile-time parse error
E_NOTICE	8	Non-fatal runtime notice
E_CORE_ERROR	16	Fatal errors occurring at startup
E_CORE_WARNINGS	32	Non-fatal runtime error caused by initial startup
E_COMPILE_WARNING	128	Non-fatal compile-time error
E_USER_ERROR	256	User-generated error by PHP function `trigger_error()`
E_USER_WARNING	512	User-generated warning by PHP function `trigger_error()`
E_USER_NOTICE	1024	User-generated notice by PHP function `trigger_error()`
E_ALL	2047	All errors and warnings reported

Typically, you don't have to worry about all of the error types; your main concern is with runtime errors such as notices, warnings, and errors, along with the user-generated equivalents. Your error-handling code helps resolve these cryptic errors to offer helpful, user-friendly messages.

There are three main types of errors that we will discuss in full here:

❑ **Fatal errors:** Fatal run-time errors. These indicate errors that the program can't recover from. Script execution is halted.

❑ **Warnings:** Runtime warnings (non-fatal errors). Script execution is not halted.

❑ **Notices:** Runtime notices. These indicate that the script has encountered something that could indicate an error, but could also happen in the normal course of running the script.

Generating PHP Errors

Now let's generate some errors so that you can check out what you need to do to resolve them. Consider this code snippet, for example:

```php
<?php
//set string with "Wrox" spelled wrong
$string_variable = "Worx books are great!";

//try to use str_replace to replace Worx with Wrox
//this will generate an E_WARNING
//because of wrong parameter count
str_replace("Worx", "Wrox");
?>
```

Now if you run this snippet, you should see the following error:

Warning: Wrong parameter count for str_replace() in
c:\FoxServ\www\errorhandling\error1.php on line 8

Because this is a nonfatal error that does not halt script execution, you can still run code after the point where the error occurred. If you change the snippet to this:

```php
<?php
//set string with "Wrox" spelled wrong
$string_variable = "Worx books are great!";

//try to use str_replace to replace Worx with Wrox
//this will generate an E_WARNING
//because of wrong parameter count
str_replace("Worx", "Wrox");

//this is a non-fatal error, so the original
//variable should still show up after the warning
echo $string_variable;
?>
```

it will produce the following output:

Warning: Wrong parameter count for str_replace() in
c:\FoxServ\www\errorhandling\error1.php on line 8
Worx books are great!

Next, we throw out a fatal error to show you how it produces different results when the error occurs. Let's create a fatal error by using the following code:

```php
<?php
//beginning of page
echo "Beginning";

//we are going to make a call to
//a function that doesn't exist
//this will generate an E_ERROR
//and will halt script execution
//after the call of the function
fatalerror();

//end of page
echo "End";
//won't be output due to the fatal error
?>
```

This produces the following output:

```
Beginning
Fatal error: Call to undefined function: fatalerror() in
c:\FoxServ\www\errorhandling\error2.php on line 10.
```

Notice that Beginning was output because it was before the function call, but End was not because the fatal error halted the script execution. You can suppress the fatal error calls by putting an ampersand in front of the function call, like so: @fatalerror(). This suppresses the error, but the script still halts its execution.

> Note that as of PHP 4 the default error reporting does not show E_NOTICE errors. However, you may want to show them during development. Enabling E_NOTICE errors for debugging can warn you about possible bugs and/or bad programming practices. For example, you might use something such as $row[variable], but actually it is better to write this as $row['variable'] because PHP will try and treat "variable" as a constant. If, however, it isn't a constant, PHP assumes it to be a string for the array.

If you don't know what your error reporting level is set at, you can simply run the error_reporting() function without any arguments, like this:

```php
<?php
echo error_reporting();
?>
```

By default, all error handling is handled by PHP's built-in error handler, which tells you the error and displays the message associated with that error. The message displays the error type, the error message, the filename, and the line number where the error occurred.

You may have noticed an error similar to this one in a previous code snippet:

```
Warning: Wrong parameter count for str_replace() in
c:\FoxServ\www\errorhandling\error1.php on line 8
```

Usually, letting PHP generate its own errors is fine, but with complicated applications, you may want to catch the errors so you can do whatever you want to do with the error, such as notifying an administrator so he or she can look into the problem further. We will now create a custom error handler to catch the errors and display a more friendly error message.

We will be expanding on the code snippet we created for this example:

```php
<?php
//create your error handler function
function handler($error_type, $error_message, $error_file, $error_line)
{
        echo "<h1>Page Error</h1>";
        echo "Errors have occurred while executing this page. Contact the ";
        echo "<a href=\"mailto:admin@yourdomain.com\">administrator</a> to report
              errors<br><br>";
        echo "<b>Information Generated</b><br><br>";
        echo "<b>Error Type:</b> $error_type<br>";
        echo "<b>Error Message:</b> $error_message<br>";
        echo "<b>Error Filename:</b> $error_file<br>";
        echo "<b>Error Line:</b> $error_line";
}

//set the error handler to be used
set_error_handler("handler");

//set string with "Wrox" spelled wrong
$string_variable = "Worx books are great!";

//try to use str_replace to replace Worx with Wrox
//this will generate an E_WARNING
//because of wrong parameter count
str_replace("Worx", "Wrox");
?>
```

Now the output should look similar to that in Figure 8-3.

Because your error handler is user-defined, you can catch the errors, and you can re-create the error messages based on the error type. Let's create a snippet for this sort of error handler:

```php
<?php
//create your error handler function
function handler($error_type, $error_message, $error_file, $error_line)
{
        switch($error_type)
        {
                //fatal error
                case E_ERROR:
                        echo "<h1>Fatal Error</h1>";
                        die("A fatal error has occured at line $error_line of file
                            $error_file.<br>
                        Error message created was &quot;$error_message&quot;");
                        break;
                //warnings
                case E_WARNING:
                        echo "<h1>Warning</h1>";
```

```
                echo "A warning has occured at line $error_line of file
                        $error_file.<br>";
                echo " Error message created was &quot;$error_message&quot;";
            //notices
            case E_NOTICE:
                //don't show notice errors
                break;
        }
    }

    //set the error handler to be used
    set_error_handler("handler");

    //set string with "Wrox" spelled wrong
    $string_variable = "Worx books are great!";

    //try to use str_replace to replace Worx with Wrox
    //this will generate an E_WARNING
    //because of wrong parameter count
    str_replace("Worx", "Wrox");
    ?>
```

Figure 8-3

The previous code snippet we created produced a fatal error, which is why the E_ERROR case was called in the switch statement. This sort of handler is nice to use to trap any sort of error and perform different actions based on the error. The output should look similar to Figure 8-4.

Figure 8-4

Even though you can trap the errors and display whatever you want to display, you may not want the user to see the error message we have created previously. You can create an error message that simply says there was an error on the page. Then you can apologize for the inconvenience and allow the user to go to another page. Finally, you can write the error message to a log file, write it to a database, or send it to the Webmaster or administrator via e-mail so that person can further review the error.

We personally prefer the e-mail method because it requires that the person be notified of the problem right away, and it doesn't require him or her to check the database or log files periodically. The only problem with this method is if there are a lot of requests to the page where the error is occurring; in that case the admin will be bombarded with e-mails.

For this last exercise, let's set up your full-featured error handler to do just what you want it to. You can then include this page in all your pages so you can trap all the errors without using PHP's built-in handler.

Follow these steps:

1. Create the code as follows:

```php
<?php
//create your error handler function
function handler($error_type, $error_message, $error_file, $error_line)
{
    global $_SERVER['HTTP_HOST'], $_SERVER['HTTP_USER_AGENT'],
$_SERVER['REMOTE_ADDR'], $_SERVER['REQUEST_URI'];

    switch($error_type)
    {
        //fatal error
        case E_ERROR:
            $to = "Administrator <admin@yourdomain.com>";

            $subject = "Custom Error Handling";

            $body = "<html>";
            $body .= "<head>";
            $body .= "<title></title>";
            $body .= "</head>";
            $body .= "<body>";
            $body .= "<h1>Fatal Error</h1>";
            $body .= "Error received was a <b>" . $error_type . "</b>
error.<br>";
            $body .= "The page that generated the error was: <b>" . $error_file
. "</b>";
            $body .= " and was generated on line: <b>" . $error_line .
"</b><br>";
            $body .= "The generated error message was:" . $error_message;
            $body .= "</body>";
            $body .= "</html>";

            $headers = "MIME-Version: 1.0\r\n";
            $headers .= "Content-type: text/html; charset=iso-8859-1\r\n";

            $headers .= "From: Apache Error <host@yourdomain.com>\r\n";
            $headers .= "Cc: webmaster@yourdomain.com\r\n";

            mail($to, $subject, $message, $headers);
            die(); //kill the script
            break;
        //warnings
        case E_WARNING:

            $to = "Administrator <admin@yourdomain.com>";

            $subject = "Custom Error Handling";

            $body = "<html>";
            $body .= "<head>";
            $body .= "<title></title>";
```

```
                    $body .= "</head>";
                    $body .= "<body>";
                    $body .= "<h1>Warning</h1>";
                    $body .= "Error received was a <b>" . $error_type . "</b>
                            error.<br>";
                    $body .= "The page that generated the error was: <b>" .
                            $error_file . "</b>";
                    $body .= " and was generated on line: <b>" . $error_line .
                            "</b><br>";
                    $body .= "The generated error message was:" . $error_message;
                    $body .= "</body>";
                    $body .= "</html>";

                    $headers = "MIME-Version: 1.0\r\n";
                    $headers .= "Content-type: text/html; charset=iso-8859-1\r\n";

                    $headers .= "From: Apache Error <host@yourdomain.com>\r\n";
                    $headers .= "Cc: webmaster@yourdomain.com\r\n";

                    mail($to, $subject, $message, $headers);
                    break;
                    //script will continue

            //notices
            case E_NOTICE:
                    //don't show notice errors
                    break;
        }
    }
    /*
    set error handling to 0
    we will handle all error reporting
    only notifying admin on warnings and fatal errors
    don't bother with notices as they are trivial errors
    really only meant for debugging
    */
    error_reporting(0);

    //set the error handler to be used
    set_error_handler("handler");

    /*
    Create the rest of your page here.
    We will not be displaying any errors
    We will be e-mailing the admin an error message
    Keep in mind that fatal errors will still halt the
    execution, but they will still notify the admin
    */
    ?>
```

Once you run this page and you receive an error, the script e-mails the admin with the error and some useful information about the user who visited the page that generated the error.

Other Methods of Error Handling

You've just seen some of what you can do with custom error messages, but there are other ways to deal with errors.

Not Meeting Conditions

Error trapping cannot catch all problems in your code. It will catch only problems related to PHP itself. Any problems you are having with conditions in your code will not be caught by simple error trapping. This will have to be manually done by using several different methods of troubleshooting in your code.

For example, let's say you are submitting a form and you are wondering why the condition isn't true when you are checking for submission. Let's say you have an input such as this:

```
<input type="submit" name="submit" value="Submit">
```

You are checking to see whether the submit button has been pressed to then see whether or not you should process the form information. You are probably doing a check similar to this:

```
if($_POST['submit'] == "submit")
{
//form has been submitted
}
else
{
//form has not been submitted
}
```

Now, see if you can figure out what is wrong with the code causing you not to get the if statement. Here's a hint: The value of the submit button is "Submit", not "submit". To troubleshoot to see if your condition is working or not, you can simply put a line in your if statement such as this:

```
echo "In the if statement";
```

Should you get into the if statement, the echo'd line is output to the browser. If you don't change the lowercase "submit" to an uppercase "Submit," you don't see that echo in the browser, so you can then further investigate why you aren't getting into the if statement. Let's hope that you realize the error and change the case and test it again, and voilà, the line has been echoed.

You will find that you need to do this to establish where in your code actions are happening. Not only do you want to do this with if statements, but you will probably be using it to test for loops, while loops, foreach loops, do while loops, and many others at other times when you are running conditions, or are expecting results and you can't figure out why something isn't working.

When Variables Aren't Being Output

Another common problem is when variables aren't being output. Most of the time, the variables are just fine, but the programmer can't figure out why they aren't being output. Again, the conditions aren't being met, and if a condition isn't met and the expected variables are in the condition, they obviously aren't going to be output. Many programmers run into this problem and have a hard time figuring it out. They tend to lay blame on the variables before checking to see whether or not their conditions have been met.

There are also times when the variables are the reason for the condition not being met, as shown in the previous paragraph. The programmer uses the wrong value to check the `if` statement and the condition fails. The best thing for a programmer to do in this situation is to troubleshoot. Throw an `echo` here and an `echo` there to see where your problems are. Don't give up at the first sign of defeat: You should exhaust all of your own programming resources before you go looking for help elsewhere.

Parse Errors

A parse error is another main error type. Parse errors occur when you forget a semicolon, when curly braces are mismatched, when square brackets aren't used properly, and so on. These parse errors usually don't have to do with a condition statement; they are mainly syntax errors that will cause the script to halt execution. Parse errors are worse than fatal errors because they won't even let the script run at all; they merely give you the error information.

Summary

You have read through a lot of useful information in this chapter. Learning from your own mistakes and errors will help you to be quicker at noticing small, trivial mistakes that are causing problems in your code. I believe the single best action a programmer can learn is how to troubleshoot. Once you have that figured out, nothing can hold you back from creating seamless applications that will impress you and your clients.

Exercises

Here are three short snippets of code to sift through. You should spot the errors and figure out how to fix them. The answers are provided in Appendix A. Once you are finished, based on what you have learned, create a little error-catching script to catch the errors.

1.

```
<?
$query = "select * from table_name where name = '" . $_POST['name'] . "';"
$result = mysql_query($result) or die(mysql_error());
?>
```

2.

```
<?
if ($_POST['first_name'] = "Jethro")
{
echo "Your name is " . $_POST['first_name'];
}
?>
```

3.

```
<?
$full_name = $_POST['mrmiss'] ". " $_POST['first_name'] " " $_POST['last_name'];
?>
```

Part III: Comic Book Fan Site

Building Databases

In previous chapters, you created a very nice movie review Web site, but now the hand-holding is over, my friend. It's time for us to push you out of the nest. In this chapter, you will have the opportunity to create your own databases, and your own Web site.

We show you how to put together a comic book appreciation Web site, but you can certainly take the concepts we teach you and branch off to create that online auction or antique car site you have always dreamed about. We think the comic book appreciation Web site is cooler, but *whatever*. You do your thing.

In this chapter, we are going to cover the basics of creating your own database. Topics we discuss include:

- ❏ Planning the design of your database
- ❏ Database normalization
- ❏ Creating your database
- ❏ Creating and modifying tables in your database
- ❏ Building Web pages to access your data with PHP

Getting Started

You have a great idea for a site, right? Excellent. Open up your PHP editor and start coding! Believe it or not, many people approach the creation of a Web site in just this way. You may be tempted to yourself. It is not impossible to create a good site in this manner, but you are seriously handicapping your chances for greatness. Before you begin, you need a plan.

We're not going to tell you how to plan out an entire Web site, complete with charts and maps and business models. That's not what this book is all about. We are going to assume that you or somebody in your company has already done that by reading other great books on business models, attending seminars, reading great articles on the Web, and perhaps even hiring a business consultant who will help you with everything but building the site (because that's what we're going to teach you how to do).

So you have a great idea for a Web site *and* a plan. What do you suppose is the first step in creating a successful Web application using PHP, Apache, and MySQL? We'll give you a clue: Look at the title of this chapter.

We need to build the database this site will be based on. Don't worry—one of the great things about relational database design is that you don't have to create *every* table your site will use. You can start with a few, and build on it. As long as you follow the basic principles of good database design, your database should be quite scalable (that is, expandable to any size).

Nam et Ipsa Scientia Potestas Est!

That is, *knowledge is power*. Very profound words, coming from a man who wore a big, ruffled collar. Francis Bacon coined the phrase 400 years ago, and it still holds true today.

Of course, information is the foundation of knowledge. Knowledge consists of having information available to you and knowing what to do with it. Data is the building blocks—the facts and figures—that we piece together to create useful sets of information.

We must be sure to store this data in an easily accessible place and in a way that allows us to relate that data to any other data fairly easily. We also want to be able to modify or remove each piece of data quickly and efficiently, without disturbing other data. With proper database design, all of this is possible.

Sound like a daunting task? Don't worry. You see, we know a secret that has been kept hidden like the magician's code: *Efficient database design is easy.* No, really, we promise! You see, most of us computer geeks like to seem invaluable and very intelligent, and it sounds quite impressive to most interviewers to see on a resume "Designed a comprehensive Web site utilizing an RDBMS backend." When you are done with this chapter, you will be able to put that on your resume as well!

What Is a Relational Database?

Let's first cover a few basics of database design. The relational database is a concept first conceived by E. F. Codd of IBM, in 1970. It is a collection of data organized in tables that can be used to create, retrieve, delete, and update that data in many different ways. This can be done without having to reorganize the tables themselves, especially if the data is organized efficiently.

Take a look at the first table that follows. You can see that we have a very simple collection of data consisting of superheroes' aliases and real names, and their superhero ID. Nothing too amazing, of course, but notice how we relate it to the league table that follows it. Each superhero user has a League_ID that corresponds to an ID in the league table. Through this link, or *relationship*, you can see that Average Man is a member of the Dynamic Dudes League because the ID in the league table matches his League_ID in the superhero table.

ID	League_ID	Alias	Real Name
1	2	Average Man	Bill Smith
2	2	The Flea	Tom Jacobs
3	1	Albino Dude	George White
4	3	Amazing Woman	Mary Jones

ID	League
1	Extraordinary People
2	Dynamic Dudes
3	Stupendous Seven
4	Justice Network

At first glance, it may seem silly to create a table with one data column and an ID. Why not just put the league name in the superhero table? Imagine that you had a database of 10,000 superheroes, and 250 of them were in the Dynamic Dudes league. Now imagine that the Superhero Consortium decided to do a reorganization and "Dynamic Dudes" was changed to the "Incredible Team." If the league name were in the superhero table, you would have to edit 250 records to change the value. With the leagues in a separate, *related* table, you have to change the name in only one place.

That is the key to a relational database. And speaking of keys . . .

Keys

A key is a column that identifies a row of data. In the superhero table, the first column is a key called "ID," as it is in the league table. In both cases, because they are unique, and in the table of the data they represent, they are called *primary keys*.

Most of the time, the primary key is a single column, but it is not uncommon to use more than one column to make up a primary key. The important distinction is that for each row, the primary key must be unique. Because of that characteristic, we can use the key to identify a specific row of data.

The primary key must contain the following characteristics:

❑ They cannot be empty (null).

❑ They will never change in value. Therefore, a primary key cannot contain information that might change, such as part of a last name (for example, smith807).

❑ They must be unique. In other words, no two rows can contain the same primary key.

239

The `League_ID` column in the superhero table is also a key. It matches the primary key of the league table, but it is in a different, or *foreign*, table. For this reason, it is called a foreign key. Although not a requirement, many programmers will give the foreign key a name that identifies what table it refers to ("League"), and some identifier that marks it as a key ("_ID"). This, along with the fact that keys are usually numeric, makes it fairly clear which column is the foreign key, if one exists in the table at all.

> *Keys do not have to be purely numeric. Other common values used as primary keys include Social Security numbers (which contain dashes), e-mail addresses, and ZIP Codes. Any value is valid as a primary key as long as it is guaranteed to be unique for each individual record in the table, and will not change over time.*

Keys can enable your tables to be recursive. You might, for example, have a `sidekick_ID` column in the superhero table that we could link to the `ID` column in the same table. Sidekicks are heroes, too, you know . . .

Relationships

In order to be related, the two tables need a column they can use to tie them together. The superhero and league tables are related to each other by the `League_ID` column in the superhero table, and the ID field in the league table. There is no explicit link created in the database; rather, you create the relationship by linking them with a SQL statement:

```
SELECT * FROM superhero s, league l WHERE s.League_ID = l.ID
```

In plain English, this statement tells the MySQL server to "select all records from the superhero table (call it 's') and the league table (call it 'l'), and link the two tables by the superhero `League_ID` column and the league `ID` column."

There are three types of relationships: one-to-one (1:1), one-to-many (1:M), and many-to-many (M:N). Our previous example is a one-to-many relationship. To figure out what type of relationship the tables have, ask yourself how many superheroes you can have in a league. The answer is more than one, or "many." How many leagues can a superhero belong to? The answer is "one." That is a one-to-many relationship. (Of course, in some universes, a superhero might belong to more than one league. But for our example, our superheroes exhibit league loyalty.)

One-to-many is the most common database relationship. Such 1:1 relationships don't happen often, and a many-to-many relationship is actually two one-to-many relationships joined together with a linking table. We explore that further later in the chapter.

> *Although they are more rare, here's an example of a one-to-one (1:1) relationship just so you know. Say you have a link between a company and its main office address. Only one company can have that exact address. In many applications, however, the main office address is included in the company table, so no relationship is needed. That's one of the great things about relational database design. If it works for your needs, then there is no "wrong" way to do it.*

Referential Integrity

The concept of referential integrity may be a little lofty for a beginner book like this, but we think it is important to touch on this briefly. If your application has referential integrity, then when a record in a table refers to a record in another table (as the previous example did), the latter table will contain the corresponding record. If the record is missing, you have lost referential integrity.

In many cases, this is not disastrous. You might have an article written by an author whose name no longer exists in the author table. You still want to keep the article, so losing the referential integrity between authors and articles is okay. However, if you have an order in your database that can't be related to a customer because the customer was deleted, then you might be hard pressed to figure out where to send the product, and who to charge for it!

There are ways to enforce referential integrity in a MySQL database. However, these concepts and procedures are beyond the scope of this book. If you are interested in obtaining more information about referential integrity and foreign keys, visit www.mysql.com/doc/en/InnoDB_foreign_key_constraints.html.

Normalization

"Database normalization" is one of those big fancy terms that database administrators like to throw around, along with "Boyce-Codd Normal Form," "trivial functional dependency," and "Heisenberg compensator." They aren't really important terms to know to be able to design a good database, but we'll touch on normalization here.

For our purposes, we will simply define normalization as the process of modifying your database table structure so that dependencies make sense, and there is no redundant data. In a moment, we are going to go through this process. The best way to learn is to do!

Designing Your Database

It's time to design your application. This will be a relatively simple application, but it will help you learn important concepts such as normalization and expose you to various SQL commands.

Typically, this is where we would take you through a "Try It Out" section and tell you How It Works. When first designing a database, however, you do not need your computer. All you need is a pad of paper and a pencil. So, go get a pad of paper and a pencil. We'll wait.

Let's draw some tables.

The application you are going to design is a comic book character database. You will store a little bit of information about various characters, such as their alter ego's alias, their real names, the powers they possess, and the location of their lair. (Yes, that's right. I said "lair.")

Creating the First Table

Before we open MySQL and start mucking around with tables, we need to figure out how we are going to store all of the data. For simplicity, let's create one big table with all of the relevant data. You can draw it out on your piece of paper, or if you just can't stay away from your computer, use your favorite spreadsheet program. Copy the information you see in the table that follows.

name	real name	power 1	power 2	power 3	lair address	city	st	zip
Clean Freak	John Smith	Strength	X-ray vision	Flight	123 Poplar Avenue	Townsburg	OH	45293
Soap Stud	Efram Jones	Speed			123 Poplar Avenue	Townsburg	OH	45293
The Dustmite	Dustin Huff	Strength	Dirtiness	Laser vision	452 Elm Street #3D	Burgtown	OH	45201

We'll call that table "zero," because we're not even at the first step yet, and that data is just *ugly* (from a relational database standpoint).

The first thing you should notice is that there are multiple power columns. What would you do if you had to add a character with more than three powers? You would have to create a new column, and that's not good. Instead, let's combine all the powers into one column, and then separate each power into its own separate row. The other columns are duplicated in these additional rows (so, Clean Freak would have three rows instead of one, each row including a different power in the power column, but the name, address, and so on would remain identical among the three listings). This concept is called *atomicity*. Each value (cell) is *atomic*, or has only one item of data.

Let's also create a unique primary key for each character. Yes, you could use the character's name, but remember that a primary key should never be something that could change, and it must be unique. To handle this requirement we'll create an ID column.

Because in this pass we have multiple rows with the same character and the multiple rows are a result of the existence of multiple powers, we'll combine the ID column with the power column to create the primary key. When more than one column makes up the primary key, it is called a *composite primary key*. We'll mark the primary key columns with an asterisk (*) to highlight them for you.

Your table should look like the one that follows. We'll call this table "one" because it's our first pass at normalizing. (Yes, you are in the middle of a normalization process. We told you it wasn't difficult.)

id*	name	real name	power*	lair address	city	st	zip
1	Clean Freak	John Smith	Strength	123 Poplar Avenue	Townsburg	OH	45293
1	Clean Freak	John Smith	X-ray vision	123 Poplar Avenue	Townsburg	OH	45293
1	Clean Freak	John Smith	Flight	123 Poplar Avenue	Townsburg	OH	45293
2	Soap Stud	Efram Jones	Speed	123 Poplar Avenue	Townsburg	OH	45293

id*	name	real name	power*	lair address	city	st	zip
3	The Dustmite	Dustin Hare	Strength	452 Elm Street #3D	Burgtown	OH	45201
3	The Dustmite	Dustin Hare	Dirtiness	452 Elm Street #3D	Burgtown	OH	45201
3	The Dustmite	Dustin Hare	Laser vision	452 Elm Street #3D	Burgtown	OH	45201

Looking better, but there is still repeated data in there. In fact, the power column is what is causing the duplicate data. Let's separate out the power column and use a foreign key to relate it to the original table. We will also further normalize the power table so that we get rid of duplicate data. This is pass number "two." See the three tables that follow.

id*	name	real name	lair address	city	st	zip
1	Clean Freak	John Smith	123 Poplar Avenue	Townsburg	OH	45293
2	Soap Stud	Efram Jones	123 Poplar Avenue	Townsburg	OH	45293
3	The Dustmite	Dustin Hare	452 Elm Street #3D	Burgtown	OH	45201

id*	power
1	Strength
2	X-ray vision
3	Flight
4	Speed
5	Dirtiness
6	Laser vision

char_id*	power_id*
1	1
1	2
1	3
2	4
3	1
3	5
3	6

As you can see, we have much less repeated data than we did before. The powers have been separated out, and a link table has been created to link each power to each appropriate character.

It may seem a bit nitpicky, but you still have some duplicate data that you can take care of in the character table. It is quite possible for more than one character to be in the same lair, as is the case with Clean Freak and Soap Stud. Let's create a lair table, and link it to the character table with keys. Let's also add a new column to the character table for alignment. See the two tables that follow.

id*	lair_id	name	real name	align
1	1	Clean Freak	John Smith	Good
2	1	Soap Stud	Efram Jones	Good
3	2	The Dustmite	Dustin Hare	Evil

id*	lair address	city	st	zip
1	123 Poplar Avenue	Townsburg	OH	45293
2	452 Elm Street #3D	Burgtown	OH	45201

We waited to add the alignment column to illustrate a point. If you are in the middle of the normalization process, and discover that there is some other data you need to add, it isn't difficult to do so. You could even add a completely new table if you needed to. That is the great thing about relational database design.

The City and State fields are not only duplicates, but they are redundant data with the ZIP Code (which is in itself a representation of the City/State). City and State are also not directly related to the lairs (because other lairs could exist in the same city). For these reasons, we will put City and State in a separate table. Because the ZIP Code is numeric, and a direct representation of City/State, we will make the Zip column a primary key. This is pass "three," shown in the three tables that follow.

id*	lair_id	name	real name	align
1	1	Clean Freak	John Smith	Good
2	1	Soap Stud	Efram Jones	Good
3	2	The Dustmite	Dustin Hare	Evil

id*	zip_id	lair address
1	45293	123 Poplar Avenue
2	45201	452 Elm Street #3D

id*	city	st
45293	Townsburg	OH
45201	Burgtown	OH

You may have noticed that we have created a many-to-many (M:N) relationship between the characters and their powers (a character can have multiple powers, and many characters may have the same power). There are two tables with primary keys, and a linking table between them has two foreign keys, one for each of the tables. The combination of the foreign keys is a primary key for the char_power table. This enables the M:N relationship.

Just for fun, let's add a small table that links the superheroes to villains, and vice versa. This is another M:N relationship because any superhero can have multiple villain enemies, and any villain can have multiple superhero enemies. Of course, we have the character table as one of the "many" sides of the equation—can you figure out what table we will use for the other "many" side? If you said the character table, you are correct! This is just like the character-power relationship, but this time we reference the table to itself via a good_bad linking table. The goodguy_id and badguy_id columns *each* link to the id column in the character table. Each column in the good_bad table is a foreign key, and both columns make up a composite primary key.

goodguy_id*	badguy_id*
1	3
2	3

And just like that, you have created your database design. Congratulations! You now have a "map" that will help you create your database tables on the server. Not only that, but you just normalized your database design as well by modifying your database table structure so that dependencies make sense, and there is no redundant data. In fact, you have actually gone through the proper normalization steps of First, Second, and Third Normal Form.

What's So Normal About These Forms?

Remember we told you that we were calling the first table "zero"? That's called Zero Form. It is basically the raw data, and is usually a very flat structure, with lots of repeated data. You see data like this sometimes when a small company keeps records of its customers in a spreadsheet.

The first pass through the table, which we called pass "one," was the first step of normalization, called "First Normal Form," or 1NF. This step requires that you eliminate all repeating data in columns (which we did with the power column), create separate rows for each group of related data, and identify each record with a primary key. Our first step satisfies the requirements of 1NF.

You can see where we're going with this, can't you? The Second Normal Form (2NF) requirements state that you must place subsets of data in multiple rows in separate tables. We did that by separating the power data into its own table. Second Normal Form also requires that we create a relationship with the original table by creating a foreign key. We did that in pass "two," when we satisfied the requirements for 2NF.

On our third pass, we removed all the columns not directly related to the primary key (City and State), and used the ZIP Code as the foreign key to the new city_state table. Third Normal Form (3NF) is then satisfied. Congratulations! You normalized a database just like the pros do.

There are further requirements for database normalization, but Third Normal Form is generally accepted as being good enough for most business applications. The next step is Boyce-Codd Normal Form, followed by Fourth Normal Form and Fifth Normal Form. In our case, the other Forms don't apply—the database is as normalized as it needs to get. All tables are easily modifiable and updateable, without affecting data in the other tables.

We know there are some database gurus out there who would tell you that in order to completely satisfy the Forms of normalization, that the align column should be put into its own table and linked with a foreign key. While that may be true in the strictest sense of the rules, we usually think of normalization as a guideline. In this case, we have only two values, good and evil. Those values will never change, and they will be the only values available to the user. Because of this, we can actually create a column with the ENUM datatype. Because the values good and evil will be hardcoded into the table definition, and we don't ever see a need to change the values in the future, there is no problem with keeping those values in the char_main *table.*

Standardization

When you are designing a new application, it is a very good idea to come up with standards, or design rules, that you adhere to in all cases. These can be extensive, such as the standards published by the W3C for HTML, XML, and other languages. They can be very short, but very strict, such as the list of ten standards brought down from a mountain by an old bearded man. For now we'll just standardize our table structure. For this application, we came up with the following table standards:

❑   **Table names:** Table names should be descriptive, but relatively short. Table names will be in lowercase. They should describe what main function they serve, and what application they belong to. All six of our tables should start with "char_" to show that they belong to the character application.

❑   **Column names:** Table columns are similar to table names. All column names will be in lowercase. They will be kept short, but multiple words (such as lair and address) will be separated by an underscore "_" (lair_addr).

❑   **Primary keys:** Single primary keys will always be called "id". Except in special cases, primary keys will be an integer datatype that is automatically incremented. If they consist of a single column, they will always be the first column of the table.

❑   **Foreign keys:** Foreign keys will end with "_id". They will start with the table descriptor. For example, in the char_lair table, the foreign key for the char_zipcode table will be called zip_id.

Finalizing the Database Design

One other thing we like to do during the database design process is put the datatypes into the empty cells of each table. We can print these tables and easily refer to them when we are writing the SQL code. You may want to do this yourself (or just use the tables provided).

If you don't understand datatypes, you can learn about them in Chapter 3, and we discuss datatypes in more detail a little later in this chapter as well. For now, just understand that datatypes are the type of data stored in each table column, such as INT (integer), VARCHAR (variable-length character string), or ENUM (enumerated list). When appropriate, they are followed by the length in parentheses; for example, varchar(100) is a character column that can contain up to 100 characters.

If you have been working in a spreadsheet, simply erase all of the actual data in those tables. If you used a pad and pencil, just follow along. Reduce the tables to two rows, one with column names, the other row blank. If you want, you can make a copy before erasing the data.

In keeping with the previously listed table standards, we arrive at the following tables. Yours should look very similar.

id*	lair_id	name	real_name	align
int(11)	int(11)	varchar(40)	varchar(80)	enum('good','evil')

id*	power
int(11)	varchar(40)

char_id*	power_id*
int(11)	int(11)

id*	zip_id	lair_addr
int(11)	varchar(10)	varchar(40)

id*	city	state
varchar(10)	varchar(40)	char(2)

good_id*	bad_id*
int(11)	int(11)

We think it is about time we actually created these tables on the server. Ready? Not so fast: We have to create the database first.

Creating a Database in MySQL

There are a number of ways to create a database. All require the execution of a SQL statement in one way or another, so let's look at that first:

```
CREATE DATABASE yourdatabase;
```

What, were you expecting something more complicated? Well, an optional parameter is missing: IF NOT EXISTS. We're pretty sure you know whether or not it exists, but if it makes you feel better, you can certainly add that:

```
CREATE DATABASE IF NOT EXISTS yourdatabase;
```

That's all there is to it. Think of the database as an empty shell. There is nothing special about it, really. The interesting stuff comes later, when you create the tables and manipulate the data.

That said, we still have to figure out how we are going to execute that SQL statement. Here are a few suggestions:

❑   From the MySQL command prompt. Do it this way only if you have access to the server on which MySQL is installed. If you are running your own server, or you have telnet access to the server, this may be an option for you.

❑   If you are being hosted by an ISP, you may need to request that the ISP create a database for you. For example, on one author's site the ISP has CPanel installed, and he simply clicks the module called MySQL Databases. From the next page, he simply types in the database he wants to create and clicks a button, and it's created for him.

     ISPs will usually give you this option because you have a limit in your contract on how many databases you are allowed to create. On one of our sites, for example, the limit is ten databases.

❑   If you have PHPMyAdmin installed (either on your own server or through your ISP), you can then run the SQL command from there. PHPMyAdmin is a valuable tool, and we recommend you use it if that is an option for you. It allows you to see your table structures and even browse data. It is a dangerous tool, however, because you can easily drop tables or entire databases with the click of a button, so use it carefully.

❑   Another option is to run your SQL statement from a PHP file. Most likely, if you are hosted by an ISP, they won't allow the creation of databases in this manner. However, almost any other SQL statement will work using this method. This is the way we will be running SQL commands through the rest of this chapter.

Once you have determined how you are going to run that SQL command, go ahead and do it. Make sure you substitute your own database name for yourdatabase. Because we are going to develop a comic book appreciation Web site, you could call it comic_book_app:

```
CREATE DATABASE IF NOT EXISTS comic_book_app;
```

Now that we have a design mapped out and a database created in MySQL, it is time to create some tables.

Try It Out   Create the Table

First, we're going to create the file that will hold the hostname, username, password, and database values.

1. Open your favorite text editor, and enter the following code (making sure you use the proper values for your server):

```php
<?php

define('SQL_HOST','yourhost');
define('SQL_USER','joeuser');
define('SQL_PASS','yourpass');
define('SQL_DB','yourdatabase');

?>
```

2. Save the file as config.php.

This file will be included on each subsequent PHP file that needs to access the database.

3. Type the following code in your favorite PHP editor, and save it as make_table.php:

```php
<?php
require('config.php');

$conn = mysql_connect(SQL_HOST, SQL_USER, SQL_PASS)
 or die('Could not connect to MySQL database. ' . mysql_error());

mysql_select_db(SQL_DB,$conn);

$sql1 =
 "CREATE TABLE IF NOT EXISTS char_main (
  id int(11) NOT NULL auto_increment,
  alias varchar(40) NOT NULL default '',
  real_name varchar(80) NOT NULL default '',
  lair_id int(11) NOT NULL default 0,
  align enum('good','evil') NOT NULL default 'good',
  PRIMARY KEY (id)
 )";

$sql2 =
 "CREATE TABLE IF NOT EXISTS char_power (
  id int(11) NOT NULL auto_increment,
  power varchar(40) NOT NULL default '',
  PRIMARY KEY (id)
 )";

$sql3 =
 "CREATE TABLE IF NOT EXISTS char_power_link (
  char_id int(11) NOT NULL default 0,
  power_id int(11) NOT NULL default 0,
  PRIMARY KEY (char_id, power_id)
 )";

$sql4 =
 "CREATE TABLE IF NOT EXISTS char_lair (
  id int(11) NOT NULL auto_increment,
```

```
  zip_id varchar(10) NOT NULL default '00000',
  lair_addr varchar(40) NOT NULL default '',
  PRIMARY KEY (id)
 )";

$sql5 =
 "CREATE TABLE IF NOT EXISTS char_zipcode (
  id varchar(10) NOT NULL default '',
  city varchar(40) NOT NULL default '',
  state char(2) NOT NULL default '',
  PRIMARY KEY (id)
 )";

$sql6 =
 "CREATE TABLE IF NOT EXISTS char_good_bad_link (
  good_id int(11) NOT NULL default 0,
  bad_id int(11) NOT NULL default 0,
  PRIMARY KEY (good_id,bad_id)
 )";

mysql_query($sql1) or die(mysql_error());
mysql_query($sql2) or die(mysql_error());
mysql_query($sql3) or die(mysql_error());
mysql_query($sql4) or die(mysql_error());
mysql_query($sql5) or die(mysql_error());
mysql_query($sql6) or die(mysql_error());
echo "Done.";
?>
```

4. Run this file by loading it in your browser.

Assuming all goes well, you should see the message "Done" in your browser. The database now should contain all six tables.

How It Works

Every PHP script that needs to access your database on the MySQL server will include `config.php`.

These constants will be used in your scripts to gain access to your database. By putting them here, in one file, you can change the values any time you move servers, change the name of the database, or change your username/password. Any time you have information or code that will be used in more than one PHP script, you should include it in a separate file. That way, you'll need to make your changes in only one location.

```
define('SQL_HOST','yourhost');
define('SQL_USER','joeuser');
define('SQL_PASS','yourpass');
define('SQL_DB','yourdatabase');
```

The `make_tables.php` file is a one-time script: You should never have to run it again, unless you needed to drop all of your tables and recreate them. So, rather than explain all of the code in the page, let's just look at one of the SQL statements:

```
CREATE TABLE IF NOT EXISTS char_main (
  id int(11) NOT NULL auto_increment,
  alias varchar(40) NOT NULL default '',
  real_name varchar(80) NOT NULL default '',
  lair_id int(11) NOT NULL default 0,
  align enum('good','evil') NOT NULL default 'good',
  PRIMARY KEY (id)
)
```

The syntax for creating a table in SQL is the following:

```
CREATE [TEMPORARY] TABLE [IF NOT EXISTS] tbl_name
    [(create_definition,...)] [table_options] [select_statement]
```

Obviously, we are not using the TEMPORARY keyword. We want this table to be permanent and exist after our connection with the database. We are using the IF NOT EXISTS keyword, but only if this page is loaded twice. If you attempt to load the page again, MySQL will not attempt to re-create the tables, and will not generate an error.

Our table name in this case is char_main. The columns we create are id, alias, real_name, lair_id, and alias, which are the names we came up with earlier.

Let's look at each column:

❑   id int(11) NOT NULL auto_increment: The id column is set as an integer, with 11 maximum places. An integer datatype can contain the values -2147483648 to 2147483648. A sharp observer would note that the max value is only ten digits. The eleventh digit is for negative values.

      NOT NULL will force a value into the column. With some exceptions, numeric columns will default to 0, and string columns will default to an empty string (' '). Very rarely will we allow a column to carry a NULL value.

      The code auto_increment causes the column to increase the highest value in the table by 1, and store it in this column. A column set to auto_increment does not have a default value.

❑   alias varchar(40) NOT NULL default ' ': the alias column is set as a varchar datatype, a string of 0 to 255 characters. We are allotting 40 characters, which should be enough for any character name. A varchar differs from a char datatype by the way space is allotted for the column.

      A varchar datatype occupies only the space it needs, whereas char datatypes will always take up the space allotted to them by adding spaces at the end. The only time you really need to use the char datatype is for strings of less than three characters (such as the State column in the char_zipcode table).

❑   real_name varchar(80) NOT NULL default ' ': Similar to alias. We are allotting 80 characters, which should be enough for our needs.

❑   Note that we did not separate the real_name column into first_name and last_name columns. If you wanted to do that, you certainly could, but in this small application it really isn't necessary. On the other hand, in a human resources application for your company, having separate columns for first and last name is almost a requirement, so that you can do things such as greet employees by their first names in a company memo.

❑ `lair_id int(11) NOT NULL default 0`: Our foreign key to the `char_lair` table is also an integer of length 11, with a default value of 0.

❑ `align enum('good','evil') NOT NULL default 'good'`: the `align` column can be one of two values: "good" or "evil." Because of this, we use an `enum` datatype, and default it to "good." (Everyone has some good in them, right?)

You now have a database. You have tables. If you just had a way to enter some data into your tables in your database, you'd have an application you could give to your users, where they could store information about their favorite superheroes and villains.

You could enter the data with some query statements in PHPMyAdmin, but that probably wouldn't be too efficient, not to mention that your users wouldn't have any access to it. You need some sort of interface for them that they can use to create and edit data.

Let's design some Web pages for them.

Creating the Comic Character Application

It's back to the drawing board. Literally. Get away from your computer. We're going to put together some ideas for a Web application.

First of all, you need a page to display a list of comic book characters along with some information about them. It doesn't need to include every detail about them (such as the location of their secret lair), but it should have enough data so that users can distinguish who they are and read a little bit of information about them.

We will list the following information:

❑ Character name (alias)

❑ Real name

❑ Alignment (good or evil)

❑ Powers

❑ Enemies

We also need a character input form. This form will serve two purposes. It will allow us to create a new character, in which case the form will load with blank fields and a `create` button, or it will allow us to edit an existing character, in which case it will load with the fields filled in, and an `update` button. We'll also have a `reset` button that either clears the new form, or restores the edited form fields. A `delete` button should also be available when editing an existing character.

The fields on our form will be as follows:

❑ Character name (alias)

❑ Real name

❑ Powers (multiple select field)

❑ Lair address, city, state, and ZIP

❑ Alignment (radio button: good/evil, default good)

❑ Enemies (multiple select field)

We also need a form for adding/deleting powers. This form will be relatively simple and will contain the following elements:

❑ Checkbox list of every power currently available

❑ Delete Selected button

❑ A text field to enter a new power

❑ An Add Power button

We also need a PHP script that can handle all database inserts, deletes, and so on. We call this a *transaction page,* and it simply does a required job and redirects the user on to another page. This page handles *all* transactions for the character application (with redirect), including the following:

❑ Inserting a new character (character listing page)

❑ Editing an existing character (character listing page)

❑ Deleting a character (character listing page)

❑ Adding a new power (power editor page)

❑ Deleting a power (power editor page)

That's basically all there is to the application. Four pages (five if you count the `config.php` file you created earlier—it will be used again) shouldn't be too difficult. Let's write them first, and then we'll talk about how they work.

Try It Out   **The Comic Book Character Site**

Some of these files are a bit long. Don't let that scare you. Most of the code consists of SQL statements, and we explain them clearly for you in the "How It Works" section that follows. Remember that this code can also be downloaded from the Web site (www.wrox.com).

Let's start with a short one.

1.   Enter the following code in your favorite PHP editor, and save it as `poweredit.php`:

```php
<?php
require('config.php');

$conn = mysql_connect(SQL_HOST, SQL_USER, SQL_PASS)
    or die('Could not connect to MySQL database. ' . mysql_error());
mysql_select_db(SQL_DB, $conn);

$sql = "SELECT id, power FROM char_power ORDER BY power";
```

```php
$result = mysql_query($sql) or die(mysql_error());
if (mysql_num_rows($result) > 0) {
 while ($row = mysql_fetch_assoc($result)) {
  $pwrlist[$row['id']] = $row['power'];
 }
 $numpwr = count($pwrlist);
 $thresh = 5;
 $maxcols = 3;
 $cols = min($maxcols, (ceil(count($pwrlist)/$thresh)));
 $percol = ceil(count($pwrlist)/$cols);
 $powerchk = '';
 $i = 0;
 foreach ($pwrlist as $id => $pwr) {
  if (($i>0) && ($i%$percol == 0))
     $powerchk .= "</td>\n<td valign='top'>";
  $powerchk .= "<input type='checkbox' name='powers[]'
     value='$id'> $pwr<br />\n";
  $i++;
 }
 $delbutton = " <tr>
  <td colspan=\"$cols\" bgcolor=\"#CCCCFF\" align=\"center\">
   <input type=\"submit\" name=\"action\" value=\"Delete Powers\">
   <font size=\"2\" color=\"#990000\"><br /><br />
   deleting will remove all associated powers
   <br />from characters as well — select wisely</font>
  </td>
 </tr>";
} else {
 $powerchk = "<div style=\"text-align:center;width:300;
 font-family:Tahoma,Verdana,Arial\">No Powers entered...</div>";
}

?>
<html>
<head>
<title>Add/Delete Powers</title>
</head>
<body>
<img src="CBA_Tiny.gif" align="left" hspace="10">
<h1>Comic Book<br />Appreciation</h1><br />
<h3>Editing Character Powers</h3>
<form action="char_transact.php" method="post" name="theform">
<table border="0" cellpadding="5">
 <tr bgcolor="#FFCCCC">
  <td valign="top"><?php echo $powerchk;?></td>
 </tr>
 <?php echo $delbutton; ?>
 <tr>
  <td colspan="<?php echo $cols;?>" bgcolor="#CCCCFF" align="center">
   <input type="text" name="newpower" value="" size=20>
   <input type="submit" name="action" value="Add Power">
  </td>
 </tr>
</table>
```

```
</form>
<a href="charlist.php">Return to Home Page</a>
</body>
</html>
```

2. Enter the following code, and save it as `charlist.php`:

```
<?php
require('config.php');

$ord = $_GET['o'];
if (is_numeric($ord)){
 $ord = round(min(max($ord, 1), 3));
} else {
 $ord = 1;
}
$order = array(
    1 => 'alias ASC',
    2 => 'name ASC',
    3 => 'align ASC, alias ASC'
);

$conn = mysql_connect(SQL_HOST, SQL_USER, SQL_PASS)
 or die('Could not connect to MySQL database. ' . mysql_error());
mysql_select_db(SQL_DB,$conn);

$sql = "SELECT c.id, p.power FROM char_main c JOIN char_power p JOIN
    char_power_link pk ON c.id = pk.char_id AND p.id = pk.power_id";

$result = mysql_query($sql) or die(mysql_error());
if (mysql_num_rows($result) > 0) {
 while ($row = mysql_fetch_assoc($result)) {
  $p[$row['id']][] = $row['power'];
 }
 foreach ($p as $key => $value) {
  $powers[$key] = implode(", ", $value);
 }
}

$sql = "SELECT c.id, n.alias FROM char_main c JOIN char_good_bad_link
    gb JOIN char_main n ON (c.id = gb.good_id AND n.id = gb.bad_id)
    OR (n.id = gb.good_id AND c.id = gb.bad_id)";

$result = mysql_query($sql) or die(mysql_error());
if (mysql_num_rows($result) > 0) {
 while ($row = mysql_fetch_assoc($result)) {
  $e[$row['id']][] = $row['alias'];
 }
 foreach ($e as $key => $value) {
  $enemies[$key] = implode(", ", $value);
 }
}
$table = "<table><tr><td align=\"center\">No characters currently
     exist.</td></tr></table>"
```

```
?>

<html>
<head>
<title>Comic Book Appreciation</title>
</head>
<body>
<img src='CBA_Tiny.gif' align='left' hspace='10'>
<h1>Comic Book<br />Appreciation</h1><br />
<h3>Character Database</h3>

<?php
$sql = "SELECT id, alias, real_name AS name, align
    FROM char_main ORDER BY ". $order[$ord];

$result = mysql_query($sql) or die(mysql_error());
if (mysql_num_rows($result) > 0) {
  $table = "<table border='0' cellpadding='5'>";
  $table .= "<tr bgcolor='#FFCCCC'><th>";
  $table .= "<a href='" . $_SERVER['PHP_SELF'] . "?o=1'>Alias</a>";
  $table .= "</th><th><a href='" . $_SERVER['PHP_SELF'] . "?o=2'>";
  $table .= "Name</a></th><th><a href='" . $_SERVER['PHP_SELF'];
  $table .= "?o=3'>Alignment</a></th><th>Powers</th>";
  $table .= "<th>Enemies</th></tr>";

  // build each table row
  while ($row = mysql_fetch_assoc($result)) {
    $bg = ($bg=='F2F2FF'?'E2E2F2':'F2F2FF');
    $pow = ($powers[$row['id']]==''?'none':$powers[$row['id']]);
    $ene = ($enemies[$row['id']]==''?'none':$enemies[$row['id']]);
    $table .= "<tr bgcolor='#" . $bg . "'><td><a href='charedit.php?c="
      . $row['id'] . "'>" . $row['alias']. "</a></td><td>"
      . $row['name'] . "</td><td align='center'>" . $row['align']
      . "</td><td>" . $pow . "</td><td align='center'>" . $ene
      . "</td></tr>";
  }

  $table .= "</table>";
  $table = str_replace('evil', '<font color="red">evil</font>', $table);
  $table = str_replace('good', '<font color="darkgreen">good</font>',
    $table);

}
echo $table;
?>
<br /><a href="charedit.php">New Character</a> &bull;
<a href="poweredit.php">Edit Powers</a>
</body>
</html>
```

3. (Two down, two to go.) Enter the next block of code and save it as `charedit.php`:

```
<?php
require('config.php');

$char = $_GET['c'];
```

```php
if ($char == '' || !is_numeric($char)) $char='0';
$subtype = "Create";
$subhead = "Please enter character data and click '$subtype
   Character.'";
$tablebg = '#EEEEFF';

$conn = mysql_connect(SQL_HOST, SQL_USER, SQL_PASS)
 or die('Could not connect to MySQL database. ' . mysql_error());
mysql_select_db(SQL_DB,$conn);

$sql = "SELECT id, power FROM char_power";
$result = mysql_query($sql);
if (mysql_num_rows($result) > 0) {
 While ($row = mysql_fetch_assoc($result)) {
  $pwrlist[$row['id']] = $row['power'];
 }
}

$sql = "SELECT id, alias FROM char_main WHERE id != $char";
$result = mysql_query($sql) or die(mysql_error());
if (mysql_num_rows($result) > 0) {
 $row = mysql_fetch_assoc($result);
 $charlist[$row['id']] = $row['alias'];
}

if ($char != '0') {
 $sql = "SELECT c.alias, c.real_name AS name, c.align, l.lair_addr
    AS address, z.city, z.state, z.id AS zip FROM char_main c,
    char_lair l, char_zipcode z WHERE z.id = l.zip_id AND
    c.lair_id = l.id AND c.id = $char";
 $result = mysql_query($sql) or die(mysql_error());
 $ch = mysql_fetch_assoc($result);

 if (is_array($ch)) {
  $subtype = "Update";
  $tablebg = '#EEFFEE';
  $subhead = "Edit data for <i>" . $ch['alias'] . "</i> and click
     '$subtype Character.'";

  $sql = "SELECT p.id FROM char_main c JOIN char_power p
     JOIN char_power_link pk ON c.id = pk.char_id
     AND p.id = pk.power_id WHERE c.id = $char";
  $result = mysql_query($sql) or die(mysql_error());
  if (mysql_num_rows($result) > 0) {
   While ($row = mysql_fetch_assoc($result)) {
    $powers[$row['id']] = 'selected';
   }
  }

  // get list of character's enemies
  $sql = "SELECT n.id FROM char_main c JOIN char_good_bad_link gb
     JOIN char_main n ON (c.id = gb.good_id AND n.id = gb.bad_id)
     OR (n.id = gb.good_id AND c.id = gb.bad_id) WHERE
     c.id = $char";
  $result = mysql_query($sql) or die(mysql_error());
```

```
      if (mysql_num_rows($result) > 0) {
       While ($row = mysql_fetch_assoc($result)) {
        $enemies[$row['id']] = 'selected';
       }
      }
     }
    }
    ?>

    <html>
    <head>
    <title>Character Editor</title>
    </head>
    <body>
    <img src='CBA_Tiny.gif' align='left' hspace='10'>
    <h1>Comic Book<br />Appreciation</h1><br />
    <h3><?php echo $subhead;?></h3>

    <form action='char_transact.php' name='theform' method='post'>
    <table border='0' cellpadding='15' bgcolor='<?php echo $tablebg;?>'>
     <tr>
      <td>Character Name:</td>
      <td><input type='text' name='alias' size='41'
       value='<?php echo $ch['alias'];?>'
    >
      </td>
     </tr>
     <tr>
      <td>Real Name:</td>
      <td><input type='text' name='name' size='41'
       value='<?php echo $ch['name'];?>'
    >
      </td>
     </tr>
     <tr>
      <td>Powers:<br /><font size=2 color='#990000'>
       (Ctrl-click to<br />select multiple<br />powers)</font>
      </td>
      <td>
       <select multiple='multiple' name='powers[]' size='4'>
       <?php
        foreach ($pwrlist as $key => $value) {
         echo "<option value='$key' " . $powers[$key] .
            ">$value</option>\n";
        }
       ?>
       </select>
      </td>
     </tr>

     <tr>
      <td>Lair Location:<br /><font size=2 color='#990000'>
       (address,<br />city, state, zip)</font>
```

```
  </td>
 <td><input type='text' name='address' size='41'
  value='<?php echo $ch['address'];?>'
 ><br />
  <input type='text' name='city' value='<?php echo $ch['city'];?>'
 >
  <input type='text' name='state' size='2'
  value='<?php echo $ch['state'];?>' >
  <input type='text' name='zip' size='10'
  value='<?php echo $ch['zip'];?>' >
 </td>
</tr>

<tr>
 <td>Alignment:</td>

 <td><input type='radio' name='align' value='good'<?php
    echo($ch['align']=='good' ? ' checked="checked"' : '');?>>
  good<br />
  <input type='radio' name='align' value='evil'<?php
    echo($ch['align']=='evil' ? ' checked="checked"' : '');?>>
  evil
 </td>
</tr>
<?php if (is_array($charlist)) { ?>
<tr>
 <td>Enemies:<br /><font size=2 color='#990000'>
  (Ctrl-click to<br />select multiple<br />enemies)</font>
 </td>
 <td>
  <select multiple='multiple' name='enemies[]' size='4'>";
<?php
 foreach ($charlist as $key => $value) {
  echo "<option value='$key' ".$enemies[$key].">$value</option>\n";
 }
?>
  </select>
 </td>
</tr>
<?php }?>
 <tr>
  <td colspan=2>
   <input type='submit' name='action'
   value='<?php echo $subtype;?> Character'>
   <input type="reset">
<?php if ($subtype == "Update"){?>
       
   <input type='submit' name='action' value='Delete Character'>
<?php }?>
  </td>
 </tr>
</table>
```

```
<input type='hidden' name='cid' value='<?php echo $char;?>'>
</form>
<a href='charlist.php'>Return to Home Page</a>
</body>
</html>
```

4. Okay, only one more now. This code is the longest, but that's because it contains a lot of SQL statements. It's not as bad as it looks. But if you want to download this code from the Web site, go ahead, and be guilt-free. Consider it our gift to you. If you are typing it, you know the drill. After entering it, save this one as `char_transact.php`:

```php
<?php
require('config.php');
foreach($_POST as $key => $value) {
 $$key = $value;

}

$conn = mysql_connect(SQL_HOST, SQL_USER, SQL_PASS)
 or die('Could not connect to MySQL database. ' . mysql_error());
mysql_select_db(SQL_DB,$conn);

switch ($action) {
 case "Create Character":
  $sql = "INSERT IGNORE INTO char_zipcode (id, city, state)
   VALUES ('$zip', '$city', '$state')";
  $result = mysql_query($sql) or die(mysql_error());

  $sql = "INSERT INTO char_lair (id, zip_id, lair_addr)
   VALUES (NULL, '$zip', '$address')";
  $result = mysql_query($sql) or die(mysql_error());
  if ($result) $lairid = mysql_insert_id($conn);

  $sql = "INSERT INTO char_main (id, lair_id, alias, real_name, align)
   VALUES (NULL, '$lairid', '$alias', '$name', '$align')";
  $result = mysql_query($sql) or die(mysql_error());
  if ($result) $charid = mysql_insert_id($conn);

  if ($powers != "") {
   $val = "";
   foreach ($powers as $key => $id) {
    $val[] = "('$charid', '$id')";
   }
   $values = implode(',', $val);
   $sql = "INSERT IGNORE INTO char_power_link (char_id, power_id)
    VALUES $values";
   $result = mysql_query($sql) or die(mysql_error());
  }

  if ($enemies != '') {
   $val = "";
   foreach ($enemies as $key => $id) {
    $val[] = "('$charid', '$id')";
```

```
        }
        $values = implode(',', $val);
        if ($align = 'good') {
         $cols = '(good_id, bad_id)';
        } else {
         $cols = '(bad_id, good_id)';
        }
        $sql = "INSERT IGNORE INTO char_good_bad_link $cols
         VALUES $values";
        $result = mysql_query($sql) or die(mysql_error());
       }

       $redirect = 'charlist.php';
       break;

   case "Delete Character":
       $sql = "DELETE FROM char_main, char_lair USING char_main m,
        char_lair l WHERE m.lair_id = l.id AND m.id = $cid";
       $result = mysql_query($sql) or die(mysql_error());

       $sql = "DELETE FROM char_power_link WHERE char_id = $cid";
       $result = mysql_query($sql) or die(mysql_error());

       $sql = "DELETE FROM char_good_bad_link WHERE good_id = $cid
        OR bad_id = $cid";
       $result = mysql_query($sql) or die(mysql_error());

       $redirect = 'charlist.php';
       break;
   case "Update Character":
       $sql = "INSERT IGNORE INTO char_zipcode (id, city, state)
        VALUES ('$zip', '$city', '$state')";
       $result = mysql_query($sql) or die(mysql_error());

       $sql = "UPDATE char_lair l, char_main m SET l.zip_id='$zip',
        l.lair_addr='$address', alias='$alias', real_name='$name',
        align='$align' WHERE m.id = $cid AND m.lair_id = l.id";
       $result = mysql_query($sql) or die(mysql_error());

       $sql = "DELETE FROM char_power_link WHERE char_id = $cid";
       $result = mysql_query($sql) or die(mysql_error());

       if ($powers != "") {
        $val = "";
        foreach ($powers as $key => $id) {
         $val[] = "('$cid', '$id')";
        }
        $values = implode(',', $val);
        $sql = "INSERT IGNORE INTO char_power_link (char_id, power_id)
         VALUES $values";
        $result = mysql_query($sql) or die(mysql_error());
       }

       $sql = "DELETE FROM char_good_bad_link WHERE good_id = $cid OR
```

```
     bad_id = $cid";
   $result = mysql_query($sql) or die(mysql_error());

   if ($enemies != '') {
    $val = "";
    foreach ($enemies as $key => $id) {
     $val[] = "('$cid', '$id')";
    }
    $values = implode(',', $val);
    if ($align == 'good') {
     $cols = '(good_id, bad_id)';
    } else {
     $cols = '(bad_id, good_id)';
    }
    $sql = "INSERT IGNORE INTO char_good_bad_link $cols
     VALUES $values";
    $result = mysql_query($sql) or die(mysql_error());
   }

   $redirect = 'charlist.php';
   break;

  case "Delete Powers":
   if ($powers != "") {
    $powerlist = implode(',', $powers);

    $sql = "DELETE FROM char_power WHERE id IN ($powerlist)";
    $result = mysql_query($sql) or die(mysql_error());

    $sql = "DELETE FROM char_power_link
     WHERE power_id IN ($powerlist)";
    $result = mysql_query($sql) or die(mysql_error());
   }

   $redirect = 'poweredit.php';
   break;

  case "Add Power":
   if ($newpower != '') {
    $sql = "INSERT IGNORE INTO char_power (id, power)
     VALUES (NULL, '$newpower')";
    $result = mysql_query($sql) or die(mysql_error());
   }

   $redirect = 'poweredit.php';
   break;

  default:

   $redirect = 'charlist.php';
   break;
 }
header("Location: $redirect");
?>
```

Excellent work! We hope you typed everything correctly. (Remember, if your code is exactly as you see it in this chapter, and it doesn't work correctly, it's because we're testing your debugging and problem solving skills.)

Before we run through the code and figure out how it works, let's play with it a bit.

1. Open your browser, and point it to the location of `charlist.php`.

This is your Character Database home page. It should look something like Figure 9-1. If the logo is missing, you can download it from the Web site, edit the four pages to eliminate the image, or change it to anything you want. Because you don't currently have any characters to look at, let's move on.

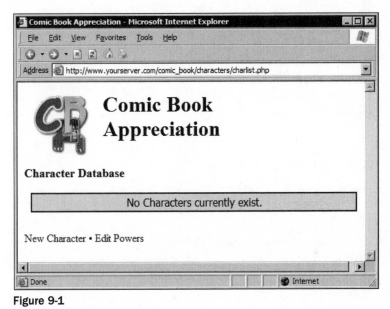

Figure 9-1

2. Click "Edit Powers."

When the page appears (see Figure 9-2), it initially will be empty.

3. Enter an ultra-cool superpower such as invisibility or x-ray vision in the text box, and click Add Power.

If you need help with power ideas, here are a few: super strength, invisibility, x-ray vision, speed, soccer mom, stretchable, flight, breathes underwater. Add a total of six powers. Moving on . . .

You should now see a new button and a list of powers with checkboxes next to them.

4. Check one or two powers and click Delete Powers. They should go away.

5. When you finish editing the powers, click the link at the bottom, "Return to Home Page," which takes you back to the Character List page (which of course still has no characters).

Figure 9-2

6. Click the link New Character.

A shiny new page appears (with a blue background), ready for your data input (see Figure 9-3). You will notice that the powers you entered are now choices in the Powers field. (Relational databases rule!)

7. Enter the appropriate data, and click Create Character.

You should be taken to the home page, where you'll now see the character you entered (as in Figure 9-4).

8. If you click New Character again, you should now see an extra field for Enemies. You can select any previously created character in the database as the current character's enemy.

9. From the home page, click one of your characters' names.

The Character Editor page loads again, but now the background is green, and the character's data will be automatically entered into the fields (see Figure 9-5). If you look at the URL for this page, you see ?c=x at the end, where x is the character's number.

10. Change some of the data, and click Update Character.

You are taken back to the home page, and you should immediately see the results of your changes. In fact, if you selected an enemy for this character, you should see the results change in the enemy's row as well.

Figure 9-3

Are you starting to see the benefits of relational databases? Are you ready to get under the hood and figure out what you just typed in those 499 (yes, 499!) lines of code? Let's go.

How It Works

Let's start off with `poweredit.php`. It's not too long, and it will allow us to get our feet wet with SQL, PHP, and HTML.

Figure 9-4

poweredit.php

You will see this on every page, but we will mention it this one time only. We include the `config.php` file that contains the constants used in the next couple of lines. By putting these constants in an included file, we can make any required changes in one place. We use the `require` command instead of `include` because of the way PHP works: An included file will not stop the processing of the rest of the page, whereas a required file, if not found, would immediately stop processing.

```
require('config.php');
```

Next, a connection to the server is made, and the appropriate database is selected. Notice the use of the constants we defined in `config.php`:

```
$conn = mysql_connect(SQL_HOST, SQL_USER, SQL_PASS)
    or die('Could not connect to MySQL database. ' . mysql_error());
mysql_select_db(SQL_DB,$conn);
```

What follows is a somewhat simple SQL select statement. It is grabbing the `id` and `power` columns from the `char_power` table, and sorting them by power. This way when we iterate through them later and put the data on the Web page, they will be in alphabetical order.

```
$sql = "SELECT id, power FROM char_power ORDER BY power";
```

This executes the SQL statement and throws an error if there are any problems:

```
$result = mysql_query($sql) or die(mysql_error());
```

Figure 9-5

Now we check to make sure at least one row was returned. If so, we iterate through each row, building up an array of powers, using the power id as the array key. Note the use of `mysql_fetch_assoc`. Other options are `mysql_fetch_row` and `mysql_fetch_array`. Because we only need an associative array (which uses field names as keys instead of a numerical index), `mysql_fetch_assoc` works nicely.

```
if (mysql_num_rows($result) > 0) {
  While ($row = mysql_fetch_assoc($result)) {
   $pwrlist[$row['id']] = $row['power'];
  }
```

When retrieving data from the database, we will usually need to retrieve appropriate ids so that we can later insert or update the correct record. In this case, the id serves as the key to the array, making it easy to retrieve the values. We could have certainly used a multi-value array, but that gets a little more confusing, and it's just not necessary here. Just be sure you understand that many times in this application (and many apps using relational databases) you will use the table id as an array key.

Now we're going to get a little tricky. Because our list of powers could get quite large, we want to try to distribute them across multiple columns. However, we'd like to distribute them fairly evenly. The following 13 lines of code do this for us (if math is not interesting to you at all, or you simply don't want to know how this part of the code works, skip this section).

First, we get a count of the number of powers in our array. Next, we set the threshold to 5 lines (after which a second column will be created), and a maximum number of columns (in this case, 3).

```
$numpwr = count($pwrlist);
$thresh = 5;
$maxcols = 3;
```

Next, we determine how many columns to create. Let's assume there are 7 powers to display. First, we divide the count by the threshold (7/5), which gives us 1.4. Next, we use ceil() to round up to the nearest integer (ceil (1.4) = 2). Then we take the smaller of the two values (3 and 2), and store it in the $cols variable. In this example, $cols would equal 2.

To figure out how many powers go into each column, we divide the count by the number of columns, and round up to the nearest integer. In this case, ceil(7/2) = 4. So, we'll have two columns, with four values in each column (the last column will contain the remainder of powers if there are less than four).

```
$powerchk is a string that will contain each power, with a checkbox attached to it.
For now, we initialize it to an empty string ''. $cols = min($maxcols,
(ceil(count($pwrlist)/$thresh)));
  $percol = ceil(count($pwrlist)/$cols);
  $powerchk = '';
```

Now we loop through each element of the $pwrlist array, which contains the id as the key ($id), and power as the value ($pwr). Our counter $i will start at 0 and increment each time through the loop. In each loop, we add the <input> tag to create the checkbox, using the id as the value, and the name of the power as the label. When our counter reaches a value that is divisible by $percol, we add a close table definition and start a new one.

```
$i = 0;
foreach ($pwrlist as $id => $pwr) {
  if (($i>0) && ($i%$percol == 0))
     $powerchk .= "</td>\n<td valign='top'>";
  $powerchk .= "<input type='checkbox' name='powers[]'
     value='$id'> $pwr<br />\n";
  $i++;
}
```

In our example, increments 0, 1, 2, and 3 end up in the first column. When $i reaches 4 (the value of $percol), we start a new column. If this is confusing, don't worry. You can play around with it by changing your $thresh and $maxcols values, and adding a bunch of random power values to see how the table is built. For now, let's check out the rest of the code.

This is the rest of our if loop. If there is even one power, a row is created that contains a delete button. If not, we create a row that simply states that no powers have yet been entered.

```
$delbutton = " <tr>
  <td colspan='$cols' bgcolor='#CCCCFF' align='center'>
    <input type='submit' name='action' value='Delete Powers'>
    <font size='2' color='#990000'><br /><br />
    deleting will remove all associated powers
    <br />from characters as well — select wisely</font>
  </td>
</tr>";
} else {
$powerchk = "<div style='text-align:center;width:300;
font-family:Tahoma,Verdana,Arial'>No Powers entered...</div>";
}
?>
```

We have left off some of the HTML. We assume you know HTML well enough that we don't need to explain it. As you can see in the <form> tag, when the user clicks the Add Power or Delete Powers button, we'll be sending values to char_transact.php:

```
<form action='char_transact.php' method='post' name='theform'>
```

At this point, $powerchk either contains the No Powers display, or the built up table columns. Either way, we insert $powerchk into the table. Note the open and close table definitions (<td valign="top"> and </td>). We didn't add them to $powerchk earlier, but we *did* add the internal close/open definitions to create the columns as necessary.

```
<table border='0' cellpadding='5'>
  <tr bgcolor='#FFCCCC'>
    <td valign='top'><?php echo $powerchk;?></td>
```

In the following, $delbutton either contains the row with the delete button (if powers were found), or it's blank. That is how we control when it shows up, and this is where it's inserted into the table.

```
<?php echo $delbutton; ?>
```

The following deals with the add button. Notice that it is called 'action' and that it has a value of Add Power. When submitting a form, PHP passes these values on to the next page. Because we are using the post method on our form, we will have a $_POST variable called 'action' that contains the value of the button. Because of this, and because all of our forms load char_transact.php, all of our buttons are named 'action', and have different values so that we can determine what to do with the data that is sent. We go into more detail about this when we look at char_transact.php.

```
<input type='submit' name='action' value='Add Power'>
```

charlist.php

The `charlist.php` page has an optional parameter that can be passed: `?o=x`, where x is 1, 2, or 3. This code retrieves that variable if it exists, and converts it to the appropriate value if necessary. If some smart-alec types o=4 in the browser, the code return 3. If no value or a bad value is passed, it will default to 1. The value is stored in `$ord`.

```
$ord = $_GET['o'];
if (is_numeric($ord)){
 $ord = round(min(max($ord, 1), 3));
} else {
 $ord = 1;
}
$order = array(
   1 => 'alias ASC',
   2 => 'name ASC',
   3 => 'align ASC, alias ASC'
);
```

This value determines which column our character display will be sorted on: 1 is by alias, 2 is by real name, and 3 is by alignment and then alias. We will use the value `$ord` as the key to our order array, which will be appended to the appropriate SQL statement later.

Make a connection, and choose a database. You know the drill by now.

```
$conn = mysql_connect(SQL_HOST, SQL_USER, SQL_PASS)
  or die('Could not connect to MySQL database. ' . mysql_error());
mysql_select_db(SQL_DB,$conn);
```

Ah . . . our first `JOIN`. This `select` statement might look confusing to the uninitiated, but it is not that complicated. First, let's look at the `JOIN` statements. We are joining three tables, using the `char_power_link` table to link the `char_power` table and the `char_main` table. This is a many-to-many (M:N) relationship. We define how they are joined with the `ON` statement. As you can see, we are linking up the character table to the link table using the character id, and we're linking the power table to the link table using the power id. With that link established, you can see that we are grabbing the character's id and the powers assigned to each character.

```
$sql = "SELECT c.id, p.power FROM char_main c JOIN char_power p JOIN
    char_power_link pk ON c.id = pk.char_id AND p.id = pk.power_id";
$result = mysql_query($sql) or die(mysql_error());
```

Notice our use of aliases for the tables. The character table is `c`, the power link table is `pk`, and the power table is `p`. This allows us to refer to the appropriate columns with a shorter syntax (for example `pk.char_id` instead of `char_power_link.char_id`). It is not necessary to use `table.column` syntax if the column name is unique across all tables. However, it is a good practice to keep so that you are always aware of which data you are accessing. It is required, of course, for column names that are duplicated across multiple tables (such as id). Some might recommend that you *always* use unique names for all of your fields, but we prefer the practice of naming all primary keys "id" and using proper `table.column` syntax in our SQL queries.

Next, we are creating a multidimensional array. That's fancy talk for an array with more than one index. This one is two-dimensional. Think of a two-dimensional array as being like a spreadsheet, and it isn't difficult to understand.

```
if (mysql_num_rows($result) > 0) {
  while ($row = mysql_fetch_assoc($result)) {
    $p[$row['id']][] = $row['power'];
  }
```

The trick here is that we have multiple powers for the same id. By adding [] to the $p array, a new array item is created for each row that has the same id. The end result is that you have a $p array of *x* characters, each element of which contains a $p[x] array of *y* powers. That is a multidimensional array.

Now we go back through our temporary array $p, and pull out each array that it holds. The $key variable contains the character id, and $value contains the array of that character's powers. We then implode the powers into a comma-separated list of powers, and store that in the $powers array, using the character id ($key) as the array index. We end up with an array that contains a list of powers for each character.

```
foreach ($p as $key => $value) {
  $powers[$key] = implode(", ", $value);
}
```

Oh boy, another JOIN. This one is similar to the previous M:N query, with a couple of exceptions. First of all, we are linking the character table twice. You can see that we are creating two instances of that table, one called c for "character" and one called n for "nemesis." This distinction is very important.

```
$sql = "SELECT c.id, n.alias FROM char_main c JOIN char_good_bad_link
    gb JOIN char_main n ON (c.id = gb.good_id AND n.id = gb.bad_id)
    OR (n.id = gb.good_id AND c.id = gb.bad_id)";
```

The other exception is the ON statement. We have characters that we are attempting to link to other characters as "enemies." Call them opponents, or nemesis, or whatever. Typically, you expect good versus evil and vice-versa. However, we are allowing *any* character to be the enemy of *any other* character. That makes linking more interesting because we are using a table with a bad_id and a good_id. If you have two evil characters that are enemies, which one gets stored in the good_id column?

The answer is that it doesn't matter. What we want to do is to make sure that we not only don't have any duplicates in the char_good_bad_link table, but also that we don't have what we call *reverse duplication*. In other words, if you have a row with good_id=3 and bad_id=7, then good_id=7 and bad_id=3 must be considered a duplicate. There is no way to prevent that in MySQL using primary keys, so we must take care of that contingency in our code. We do that in a couple of places.

In this instance, we are combining two queries in one. The first one grabs all instances of each character where the character's id is in the good_id field and his enemies' IDs are in the bad_id field. The second part of the ON statement reverses that, and pulls all instances of each character where the character's ID is in the bad_id field and his enemies' ids are in the good_id field. This does not prevent reverse duplication (that is handled elsewhere), but it does make sure we have grabbed every possible link to a character's enemy.

This code is virtually identical to the multidimensional powers array. This time, we are creating a multi-dimensional array of each character and that character's enemies. We then implode the enemies list and store it in the $enemies array, using the character's id as the array index.

```
$result = mysql_query($sql) or die(mysql_error());
if (mysql_num_rows($result) > 0) {
 while ($row = mysql_fetch_assoc($result)) {
  $e[$row['id']][] = $row['alias'];
 }
 foreach ($e as $key => $value) {
  $enemies[$key] = implode(", ", $value);
 }
}
```

We are going to build a table of characters in a moment. In case there are no characters to display (as when you first tested your charlist.php page), we want to display a "No characters" message. This code builds the $table variable (even though it doesn't contain an actual table) using a <div> tag. If any characters do exist, this variable will be overwritten with an actual table of data.

```
$table = "<table><tr><td align=\"center\">No characters currently
    exist.</td></tr></table>"

?>
```

Next is another simple SQL SELECT, pulling the appropriate data: character's id, alias, real name, alignment, and address info. Note the $order array. We set that value at the beginning of this page, using the ?_GET value "o" in the URL. This is where it's used to sort the characters.

```
$sql = "SELECT id, alias, real_name AS name, align
  FROM char_main ORDER BY ". $order[$ord];
$result = mysql_query($sql) or die(mysql_error());
```

We are building up the table of characters, as long as we returned at least one record from the database. Note the first three columns' links. They refer back to this same page, adding the ?o=x parameter. This will re-sort the data and display it sorted on the column the user clicked.

```
if (mysql_num_rows($result) > 0) {
 $table = "<table border='0' cellpadding='5'>";
 $table .= "<tr bgcolor='#FFCCCC'><th>";
 $table .= "<a href='" . $_SERVER['PHP_SELF'] . "?o=1'>Alias</a>";
 $table .= "</th><th><a href='" . $_SERVER['PHP_SELF'] . "?o=2'>";
 $table .= "Name</a></th><th><a href='" . $_SERVER['PHP_SELF'];
 $table .= "?o=3'>Alignment</a></th><th>Powers</th>";
 $table .= "<th>Enemies</th></tr>";
```

Next, we alternate the background colors of the table, to make it a little easier to read.

```
// build each table row
 while ($row = mysql_fetch_assoc($result)) {
  $bg = ($bg=='F2F2FF'?'E2E2F2':'F2F2FF');
```

Remember the power and enemy arrays we built earlier? We use the character's id to grab the list of values and put them into a variable to be inserted shortly into the appropriate table cell.

```
$pow = ($powers[$row['id']]==''?'none':$powers[$row['id']]);
  $ene = ($enemies[$row['id']]==''?'none':$enemies[$row['id']]);
```

The table is built, row by row, inserting the appropriate data in each cell; then it's closed:

```
$table .= "<tr bgcolor='#" . $bg . "'><td><a href='charedit.php?c="
    . $row['id'] . "'>" . $row['alias']. "</a></td><td>"
    . $row['name'] . "</td><td align='center'>" . $row['align']
    . "</td><td>" . $pow . "</td><td align='center'>" . $ene
    . "</td></tr>";
$table .= "</table>";
```

Just for kicks, and to make them more visible, we change the color of the "good" and "evil" values in the table. This isn't necessary, but it makes the values pop out more.

```
$table = str_replace('evil', '<font color="red">evil</font>', $table);
$table = str_replace('good', '<font color="darkgreen">good</font>',
    $table);
```

This variable contains either the <div> tag we created earlier or the table of character data. It's inserted in the page here.

```
echo $table;
```

charedit.php

This file does double-duty, so it's a little longer. But a lot of it is HTML, and much of what it does we have already done before, so this shouldn't be too difficult.

The default functionality of this page is New Character mode. If there is a value in $char other than 0, we will pull the data and change the default values.

```
$char = $_GET['c'];
if ($char == '' || !is_numeric($char)) $char='0';
$subtype = "Create";
$subhead = "Please enter character data and click '$subtype
    Character.'";
$tablebg = '#EEEEFF';
```

Get all powers, and put them into an array to be accessed later (when building the power select field on the form).

```
$sql = "SELECT id, power FROM char_power";
$result = mysql_query($sql);
if (mysql_num_rows($result) > 0) {
 While ($row = mysql_fetch_assoc($result)) {
  $pwrlist[$row['id']] = $row['power'];
 }
}
```

All characters except the chosen character will be pulled from the database to be used for the Enemies field. If the character id is not valid, then *all* characters will be pulled for the Enemies field.

```
$sql = "SELECT id, alias FROM char_main WHERE id != $char";
$result = mysql_query($sql) or die(mysql_error());
if (mysql_num_rows($result) > 0) {
 $row = mysql_fetch_assoc($result);
 $charlist[$row['id']] = $row['alias'];
}
```

If there is a character id, attempt to pull the data from the database. This SQL statement is also a JOIN, although the JOIN keyword is not used. You can identify such a JOIN because there are two or more tables, and the WHERE keyword is matching columns from each of the tables. The JOIN in this case is implied. Once all the tables are joined, all the appropriate fields are pulled as long as the character id in the character table matches $char. If there is no match, no records will be returned. If there is a match, one record is returned and the row is stored in $ch.

```
if ($char != '0') {
 $sql = "SELECT c.alias, c.real_name AS name, c.align, l.lair_addr
    AS address, z.city, z.state, z.id AS zip FROM char_main c,
    char_lair l, char_zipcode z WHERE z.id = l.zip_id AND
    c.lair_id = l.id AND c.id = $char";
 $result = mysql_query($sql) or die(mysql_error());
 $ch = mysql_fetch_assoc($result);
```

Once we determine there was a record retrieved, we alter the default variables to reflect the edited document. The background is green, and we are "Updating" rather than "Creating."

```
if (is_array($ch)) {
 $subtype = "Update";
 $tablebg = '#EEFFEE';
 $subhead = "Edit data for <i>" . $ch['alias'] . "</i> and click
    '$subtype Character.'";
```

The next SQL statement retrieves all powers associated with this character. All we really need is the id so that we can create a $powers array with each element containing the word "selected." This will be used in the Powers field on the form, so that each power assigned to the character will be automatically selected.

```
$sql = "SELECT p.id FROM char_main c JOIN char_power p
    JOIN char_power_link pk ON c.id = pk.char_id
    AND p.id = pk.power_id WHERE c.id = $char";
$result = mysql_query($sql) or die(mysql_error());
if (mysql_num_rows($result) > 0) {
 While ($row = mysql_fetch_assoc($result)) {
  $powers[$row['id']] = 'selected';
 }
}
```

Now we do exactly the same thing with the character's enemies. Note the similarity in this SQL statement to the one in charlist.php. The only difference is that we want only the enemies that match our character.

```
// get list of character's enemies
$sql = "SELECT n.id FROM char_main c JOIN char_good_bad_link gb
    JOIN char_main n ON (c.id = gb.good_id AND n.id = gb.bad_id)
    OR (n.id = gb.good_id AND c.id = gb.bad_id) WHERE
    c.id = $char";
$result = mysql_query($sql) or die(mysql_error());
if (mysql_num_rows($result) > 0) {
 While ($row = mysql_fetch_assoc($result)) {
  $enemies[$row['id']] = 'selected';
 }
}
```

We next build the table in HTML, and insert values into the appropriate places as defaults. This is how we fill in the fields with character data. Note the use of the PHP tag. We don't recommend using the shortcut `<?=$variable?>` because some servers don't have short PHP tags enabled. Using the full syntax guarantees that your code will work, regardless of what server it is on.

```
<td>Character Name:</td>
<td><input type='text' name='alias' size='41'
 value='<?php echo $ch['alias'];?>'
 onfocus='this.select();'>
</td>
```

Now we build the Powers select field. As we loop through each power in the `$pwrlist` array (which contains *all* powers), we concatenate the `$powers` array value for that power ("selected"). If that power's key (from `$pwrlist`) doesn't exist in the `$powers` array, `$powers[$key]` will simply be blank instead of "selected." In this way, we build a field of *all* powers where the character's chosen powers are selected in the list. Neato, huh?

```
<td>Powers:<br /><font size=2 color='#990000'>
 (Ctrl-click to<br />select multiple<br />powers)</font>
</td>
<td>
 <select multiple='multiple' name='powers[]' size='4'>
 <?php
  foreach ($pwrlist as $key => $value) {
   echo "    <option value='$key' " . $powers[$key] .
      ">$value</option>\n";
  }
 ?>
 </select>
</td>
```

Note the `[]` in the select *name* attribute. That is necessary for PHP to recognize the variable as an array when it gets POSTed to the next page. This is a requirement for any field that might post with multiple values.

The following portion creates a set of radio buttons for "good" and "evil." The character's alignment is selected with the `checked` attribute.

```
    <td><input type='radio' name='align' value='good'<?php
      echo($ch['align']=='good' ? ' checked="checked"' : '');?>>
    good<br />
    <input type='radio' name='align' value='evil'<?php
      echo($ch['align']=='evil' ? ' checked="checked"' : '');?>>
    evil
    </td>
```

Remember what we did with the Powers field? Ditto all of that for the Enemies field. The only difference here is that if there are no values in the $charlist variable (list of all characters except the chosen character), the Enemies field will not show up on the form.

```
    <?php if (is_array($charlist)) { ?>
     <tr>
      <td>Enemies:<br /><font size=2 color='#990000'>
      (Ctrl-click to<br />select multiple<br />enemies)</font>
      </td>
      <td>
      <select multiple='multiple' name='enemies[]' size='4'>";
    <?php
     foreach ($charlist as $key => $value) {
      echo "        <option value='$key' " . $enemies[$key] .
          ">$value</option>\n";
     }
```

If the character entry form is not in Update mode, then we will hide the Delete Character button (you can't delete a character you haven't created yet):

```
    <?php if ($subtype == "Update"){?>
          
      <input type='submit' name='action' value='Delete Character'>
    <?php }?>
```

Finally, the character id is not passed through any form fields, so we create a hidden field to hold that information. We need that id if we are going to do an update to an existing character. Of course, if we are creating a new character, then the id will be created for us when we insert all the appropriate data.

```
    <input type='hidden' name='cid' value='<?php echo $char;?>'>
```

char_transact.php

And so, finally, we come to the workhorse of the character database application: char_transact.php. It looks like there is a lot happening on this page, but it's not that complicated. There are simply many different tasks that are performed by this page, depending on how the data got here. Let's open her up and see what makes her tick.

On many PHP servers, the php.ini option register_globals is set to ON. That registers all $_REQUEST variables (POST, GET, and COOKIE) as global variables. In other words, if your form posted a field called username using the post method, then this page could access it as $username in addition to $_POST['username']. We're not going to go into the security problems you might have by setting register_globals = ON. However, we do recommend that you set it to OFF, if you have control over that. In fact, it is set to OFF by default in PHP versions after 4.2.0. (If you would like more information about this, visit www.php.net/register_globals.)

You should always assume that `register_globals` is turned `OFF` to make your application more portable, and for this reason, we assume that we have access to the posted variables through the `$_POST` array only. What we are doing here is looping through `$_POST` and setting each variable ourselves. If username was passed as `$_POST['username']`, then it will now be accessible as `$username`, regardless of the `register_globals` setting.

```
foreach($_POST as $key => $value) {
  $$key = $value;


}
```

Remember that each button is named `action` and that each one has a different value. In the code that follows, we determine which button was clicked, and run the appropriate code. For example, if the Delete Character button was clicked, we want to run the SQL commands only for removing character data.

```
switch ($action) {
```

The `switch` command is a fancy way of providing a multiple choice. It is easier to read than a complex `if...else` statement. The only "gotcha" you need to be aware of is to use `break;` at the end of each case to prevent the rest of the code in the other case blocks from executing.

The `INSERT` query that follows is relatively simple. In plain English: "Insert the values `$zip`, `$city`, and `$state` into the columns `id`, `city`, and `state` in the `char_zipcode` table." The `IGNORE` keyword is a very cool option that allows you do an insert without first using a `SELECT` query to see if the data is already in the table. In this case, you know there might already be a record for this Zip code. So, `IGNORE` tells the query "If you see this Zip code in the database already, don't do the `INSERT`."

```
case "Create Character":
 $sql = "INSERT IGNORE INTO char_zipcode (id, city, state)
  VALUES ('$zip', '$city', '$state')";
 $result = mysql_query($sql) or die(mysql_error());
```

Note that the `IGNORE` statement compares primary keys only. Therefore, even if another Zip code is in the database with the same state, the `INSERT` still takes place. Using `IGNORE` when inserting into a table where the primary key is automatically incremented has no effect at all; the `INSERT` will *always* happen in that case. This might seem obvious to you, but just keep this fact in mind; with some complex tables it won't be so intuitive.

In the INSERT that follows, you see the use of `NULL` as the first value. When you insert `NULL` into a column, MySQL does the following: If the column allows `NULL` values, it inserts the `NULL`; if it does not allow `NULL` (the column is set to `NOT NULL`), it will set the column to the default value. If a default value has not been determined, then the standard default for the datatype is inserted (empty string for varchar/char, 0 for integer, and so on). If, as is the case here, the column is set to auto_increment, then the next highest available integer for that column is inserted. In our case, id is the primary key, so this is what we want to happen.

```
$sql = "INSERT INTO char_lair (id, zip_id, lair_addr)
 VALUES (NULL, '$zip', '$address')";
$result = mysql_query($sql) or die(mysql_error());
```

We also could have left out the id field from the insert, and inserted values into the zip_id and lair_addr columns only. MySQL treats ignored columns as if you had attempted to insert NULL into them. We like to specify every column when doing an insert. If you needed to modify your SQL statement later, having all the columns in the INSERT query gives you a nice placeholder so all you have to do is modify the inserted value.

The following is a neat little function. Assuming the insert worked properly ($result returned TRUE), the mysql_insert_id() function will return the value of the last auto_increment from the last run query. This works only after running a query on a table with an auto_incremented column. In this case it returns the primary key value of the row we just inserted into the char_lair table. We will need that value to insert into the char_main table.

```
if ($result) $lairid = mysql_insert_id($conn);
```

The connection variable is optional, but we think it's a good habit to always include it. If you omit it, it will use the most recently opened connection. In a simple application like ours, that's not a problem; in a more complex application where you might have more than one connection, it could get confusing.

Again, note the use of NULL for the primary key id, and the use of mysql_insert_id() to return the primary key in the following:

```
$sql = "INSERT INTO char_main (id, lair_id, alias, real_name, align)
 VALUES (NULL, '$lairid', '$alias', '$name', '$align')";
$result = mysql_query($sql) or die(mysql_error());
if ($result) $charid = mysql_insert_id($conn);
```

We are always interested in minimizing the number of times we run a query on the database. Each hit takes precious time, which can be noticeable in a more complex application. At this point, we need to figure out how to insert all powers with only one SQL command:

```
if ($powers != "") {
 $val = "";
 foreach ($powers as $key => $id) {
  $val[] = "('$charid', '$id')";
 }
 $values = implode(',', $val);
 $sql = "INSERT IGNORE INTO char_power_link (char_id, power_id)
  VALUES $values";
 $result = mysql_query($sql) or die(mysql_error());
}
```

There are a couple of concerns here. First, if there is already a power for this user (there shouldn't be; it's a new character, but always be prepared), we need to not insert the row. We already know how to take care of this by using the IGNORE keyword.

Second, we must insert multiple rows of data with only one query. Easy enough; all we have to do is supply a comma-separated list of value groupings that matches up to the column grouping in the query. For example:

```
INSERT INTO table (col1, col2) VALUES (val1, val2), (val3, val4)
```

We accomplish this by looping through the $powers array and putting the values for character id and power id into a new array. We then concatenate that array with a comma separator, and *voilà!* There are your multiple rows of data to insert.

We then do the same thing with the $enemies array that we did with $powers. This time, however, we insert into the columns based on whether the character is good or evil. It doesn't really matter too much which column gets which id, but for the most part we want evil character ids in the bad_id column.

```
if ($enemies != '') {
 $val = "";
 foreach ($enemies as $key => $id) {
  $val[] = "('$charid', '$id')";
 }
 $values = implode(',', $val);
 if ($align = 'good') {
  $cols = '(good_id, bad_id)';
 } else {
  $cols = '(bad_id, good_id)';
 }
 $sql = "INSERT IGNORE INTO char_good_bad_link $cols
  VALUES $values";
 $result = mysql_query($sql) or die(mysql_error());
}
```

When it comes to the char_good_bad_link table, we have a little bit of referential integrity that we have to handle (beyond what MySQL does for us). Namely, we don't want to have a good_id/bad_id combination to match up to a bad_id/good_id combination. For the purposes of a relational database, that isn't bad, but for our purposes that is considered a duplication. We will handle this contingency when updating a character, but because this is a new character (with a brand new id), we don't have to worry about that just yet.

We're done inserting new character data, so we now set the page we are going to load next, and break out of the switch statement.

```
$redirect = 'charlist.php';
break;
```

When deleting a character, we simply remove all instances of it from all relevant tables. In order to remove the relevant data from the char_lair table, we have to JOIN it to the char_main table by matching up the lair id's first. Then we delete all matching rows where the character id matches.

```
case "Delete Character":
 $sql = "DELETE FROM char_main, char_lair USING char_main m,
  char_lair 1 WHERE m.lair_id = 1.id AND m.id = $cid";
 $result = mysql_query($sql) or die(mysql_error());

 $sql = "DELETE FROM char_power_link WHERE char_id = $cid";
 $result = mysql_query($sql) or die(mysql_error());
```

We don't really need to put the results of the mysql_query command in a variable. We like to do this as a matter of habit because if we ever need the return value later, it will be available for us to use. In the case of a DELETE, you don't get a result set, you get a return value of either TRUE or FALSE.

Remembering that our char_good_bad_link needs to maintain what we call "reverse" referential integrity (1, 3 matches 3, 1), we remove all rows that contain the character's id in either column:

```
$sql = "DELETE FROM char_good_bad_link WHERE good_id = $cid
OR bad_id = $cid";
$result = mysql_query($sql) or die(mysql_error());
```

Updating a character is where things get interesting. First of all, we can simply do an INSERT IGNORE on the Zip code table. If the address and Zip code change, we don't really need to delete the old data because it might be used for other characters—it's perfectly fine to leave the old data alone. So, we just do an INSERT IGNORE as we did for a new character, and leave it at that.

```
case "Update Character":
$sql = "INSERT IGNORE INTO char_zipcode (id, city, state)
VALUES ('$zip', '$city', '$state')";
$result = mysql_query($sql) or die(mysql_error());
```

Here is our first UPDATE query, and incidentally, the only one we use in the entire application. It is very similar to INSERT and SELECT queries, with the exception of the SET keyword. The SET keyword tells MySQL what columns to set, and what values to set them to. The old values in the row are overwritten. This is a JOIN query because there is more than one table. The WHERE keyword specifies both the linking column (lair_id) and the condition that only rows for this character will be updated.

```
$sql = "UPDATE char_lair l, char_main m SET l.zip_id='$zip',
l.lair_addr='$address', alias='$alias', real_name='$name',
align='$align' WHERE m.id = $cid AND m.lair_id = l.id";
$result = mysql_query($sql) or die(mysql_error());
```

Because the char_power_link table does not have an automatically incremented column as the primary key, we don't have to do an update to the table. An update is possible, but it is much easier to simply delete all the old links of character to power, and insert new link rows. In some cases, we may be deleting and inserting the same data (for instance, we might be adding flight as a power, but invisibility did not change; invisibility will still be deleted and reinserted). When updating data in an M:N relationship, you will usually simply delete the old data, and insert the updated/new data.

```
$sql = "DELETE FROM char_power_link WHERE char_id = $cid";
$result = mysql_query($sql) or die(mysql_error());

if ($powers != "") {
 $val = "";
 foreach ($powers as $key => $id) {
  $val[] = "('$cid', '$id')";
 }
 $values = implode(',', $val);
 $sql = "INSERT IGNORE INTO char_power_link (char_id, power_id)
  VALUES $values";
 $result = mysql_query($sql) or die(mysql_error());
}
```

This brings us to the Enemies data, where not only do we have to maintain referential integrity, but we have to worry about updating rows where our id can be present in either of the two linking columns. We must maintain our own "reverse" referential integrity.

```
$sql = "DELETE FROM char_good_bad_link WHERE good_id = $cid OR
 bad_id = $cid";
$result = mysql_query($sql) or die(mysql_error());

if ($enemies != '') {
 $val = "";
 foreach ($enemies as $key => $id) {
  $val[] = "('$cid', '$id')";
 }
 $values = implode(',', $val);
 if ($align == 'good') {
  $cols = '(good_id, bad_id)';
 } else {
  $cols = '(bad_id, good_id)';
 }
 $sql = "INSERT IGNORE INTO char_good_bad_link $cols
  VALUES $values";
 $result = mysql_query($sql) or die(mysql_error());
}
```

How did we deal with referential integrity? It turns out that it takes care of itself when we follow the same method we employed when updating the char_power_link table. By simply running the same DELETE query we ran when deleting a character, and then immediately running the same INSERT query we ran when creating a new character, we ensure that only one set of rows exists to match up each character to his/her enemy. It's simple, elegant, and it works!

By this time, queries should seem quite familiar to you. The DELETE query is one of the simplest of the SQL statements. In these DELETE queries, we need to delete each power that was selected on the Add/Delete Power page. We must do this not only in the char_power table but in the char_power_link table as well. (In our application, if a power is removed, we remove that power from the characters as well.) In order to perform a DELETE on multiple rows, we use the IN keyword, with which each id in the supplied comma-separated list of power IDs is matched against the id, and each matching row is deleted.

```
case "Delete Powers":
 if ($powers != "") {
  $powerlist = implode(',', $powers);

  $sql = "DELETE FROM char_power WHERE id IN ($powerlist)";
  $result = mysql_query($sql) or die(mysql_error());

  $sql = "DELETE FROM char_power_link
   WHERE power_id IN ($powerlist)";
  $result = mysql_query($sql) or die(mysql_error());
 }
```

When adding a power, we first check to make sure a value was passed (no need to run a query if there is nothing to add), and then attempt to insert the value into the power table. Once again, we use the IGNORE keyword in what follows to avoid duplication of power. We have mentioned that you really use IGNORE only on tables that have a primary key that is not autogenerated. There is an exception. IGNORE will not allow any duplicate data in any column that is designated as UNIQUE. In our char_power table, the power column is a UNIQUE column, so attempting to insert a duplicate value would result in an error. The IGNORE keyword prevents the insertion, so we don't get an error returned. If the power already exists, we simply return to the poweredit.php page and await further instructions.

```
case "Add Power":
 if ($newpower != '') {
  $sql = "INSERT IGNORE INTO char_power (id, power)
   VALUES (NULL, '$newpower')";
  $result = mysql_query($sql) or die(mysql_error());
 }
```

You should always have a default: option in your case statements. You don't need to do anything there, but it is good programming practice to include it. In this case, we are simply going to redirect the user back to the charlist.php page.

```
default:
 $redirect = 'charlist.php';
 break;
```

Finally, we reach the last command of char_transact.php. In order to use the header() function, no data can have been previously sent to the client. If it has, you will get an error. In our case, char_transact.php has no data sent to the client, so our header() function will work as advertised.

```
header("Location: $redirect");
```

Each case sets a destination page after running its queries. This command will now send the user to that destination.

One tremendous advantage to using a transaction page in this manner is that, because no data was sent to the client browser, once the browser gets to the destination page the history will have no memory of this page. Further, if the user refreshes his or her browser, it won't re-execute the transaction.. This makes for a very clean application.

For example, let's say a user starts on the Character List page. He or she clicks the Edit Powers link. From the Edit Powers page, the user enters a new power and clicks Add Power. The user might do this five times, adding five new powers. Each time, the PHP server submits the form to the transaction page and redirects the user back to the power page. However, if the user then clicks Back on his or her browser, the user is taken back to the Character List page, as if he or she just came from there. This is almost intuitive to the average user, and is the way applications should work.

Summary

Whew! We covered a lot of ground in this chapter. You learned about how to plan the design of your application, including database design. You learned how to normalize your data, so that it can easily be linked and manipulated. You created a brand new database for your Web site, and started building your Web site by creating tables, and creating the Web application needed to access and update those tables.

Congratulations! You just created your first, fully functioning Web application with a relational database backend. (That's going to look *so* good on your resume.)

This chapter is only the beginning, however. With the knowledge you gained here, you can create almost any application you desire. Here are some examples of what you could do:

❏ **Content Management (CMS):** Create a data entry systems that will allow users and administrators to alter the content of the Web site and your database without knowing any HTML.

❏ **Maintain a database of users visiting your site:** You can enable user authentication, e-mail your users to give them exciting news, sign them up for newsletters, and so on.

❏ **Create an online e-commerce site:** Create shopping carts where users can store the merchandise they will purchase. (This can be daunting—many choose to use a third-party shopping cart application.)

❏ **Create an online discussion forum where your users can go to discuss how wonderful your site looks!**

These are just a few ideas. In fact, we are going to show you how to do each of these things over the course of upcoming chapters. With a little imagination, you can come up with solutions to almost any problem you might face in building your site.

If any of the ideas presented in this chapter are difficult for you to grasp, that's okay. It is a lot of material, especially if you are a beginning programmer. The great thing about a book is that you can keep coming back! We will also be revisiting many of these concepts in later chapters. For example, in Chapter 15 where we teach you to build your own forum, we will go through database normalization again on a new set of databases. You will also have many more opportunities to create SQL queries, some familiar and some new.

For now, take some time to play with your new toy, the Character Database. You have the basic knowledge for creating even the most complex sites. You have the first incarnation installed on your server.

Now all you need to do is let all of your friends and family know about your cool new site. If only you knew how to send e-mails using PHP. Well, we'll handle that in Chapter 10.

10

E-mailing with PHP

So far, the chapters in this book have walked you through the creation of a comprehensive Web site. You have designed your site so that users can add and modify data, which is being stored in databases. You have built pages dynamically for your users, ensuring they have a rich and unique experience when they visit your Web site. You are even displaying helpful error messages in case something goes wrong. Now it's time to get a little more interactive with your users with e-mail. But we are not talking about standard e-mail, in which you write to your mother to tell her about the cool site you've been building. (You did tell her, didn't you? She would be so proud.) We're talking about sending out e-mails using PHP.

Why would you want a server-side scripting language to send e-mails? Perhaps you want to create a simple feedback form to be submitted to an administrator. Or maybe you want certain errors to be automatically e-mailed to the Webmaster. Or perhaps you would like to create an application that allows users to send their friends and family electronic postcards. (Nod your head in vigorous agreement here because that is exactly what we are going to do!)

Specifically, this chapter covers:

❑ Sending a basic e-mail

❑ Sending an e-mail formatted with HTML

❑ Multipart messages

❑ Sending images

❑ Getting confirmation

Setting Up PHP to Use E-mail

We aren't going to delve too deeply into the setup of a mail server for PHP, but here are the basics.

If you are in a *NIX (UNIX, Linux, and so on) environment, you will most likely have sendmail installed on your server. If you are using a hosting service, check with your service provider to make sure send-mail or some equivalent is being used.

If you are not using sendmail, or you have Apache installed on a Windows server, you have a couple of choices. You can use your existing SMTP (Simple Mail Transport Protocol) service, or you can install a mail server such as Mailtraq on your computer. If you have questions or concerns about setting up or using a mail server, there are many online resources available to help you. We suggest using a search engine.

Once you have your mail server squared away, you'll need to modify your `php.ini`. There are a couple of parameters you need to set. Of course, if you are using a hosting service, they should already have these parameters set up.

❑ **SMTP:** Set this to the IP address or DNS name of your SMTP server. For example, if you have a mail server installed on the same server as your PHP server, you should be able to set SMTP to `localhost`. This applies to Windows installations only.

❑ **smtp_port:** Set this to the port PHP uses to connect to the SMTP server. This applies to Windows installations only, and is valid for PHP version 4.3 and above.

❑ **sendmail_from:** The From address used by default by the PHP `mail()` command.

❑ **sendmail_path:** The path to the sendmail program (*NIX servers only). For most servers, this is usr/sbin/sendmail.

That's just about all there is to setting up PHP for e-mail. We will test to make sure it works correctly in the next section, "Sending an E-mail."

More information about setting up PHP for mail can be found at `http://us3.php.net/manual/en/ref.mail.php`.

Sending an E-mail

The actual method of sending an e-mail is quite simple. Of course, it can be made much more complex with the addition of headers, and sending HTML and images. However, we are going to start off with something simple.

Try It Out   **Sending a Simple E-mail**

This example is just about the simplest code you can write to send an e-mail. Of course, it's not very flex-ible, but it does demonstrate the `mail()` function quite well.

1.   Start your favorite text/PHP/HTML editor. Notepad works just fine.

2.   Enter the following code. Make sure you put your own e-mail address in as the first parameter:

```php
<?php
mail("your@e-mailaddress.com", "Hello World", "Hi, world. Prepare for our arrival.
We're starving!");
?>
```

3. Save the text file as firstmail.php and load it in your browser. You should see a blank page and should receive an e-mail shortly at the address entered as the first parameter.

Pretty cool, huh? That's all there is to it!

How It Works

The mail() function automatically sends an e-mail, using the following format:

```
Mail(to, subject, message, headers, other_parameters)
```

The parameters headers and other_parameters are optional. If you want to send a message to multiple recipients, their addresses must be separated with a comma in the to parameter:

```
Mail("first@e-mail.com, second@e-mail.com", "Hi", "Whazzup??")
```

We will cover the headers parameter soon. The other_parameters are beyond the scope of this book, but if you want more information about the mail() function, point your browser to www.php.net/manual/en/function.mail.php.

You may have noticed when receiving this e-mail that there was no From address (or, your service provider may have automatically put in a bogus address. Ours says "Nobody." In the next example, you'll see how to add a "From:" parameter to your e-mail, and you'll collect information from the user before sending the e-mail. Let's dig in!

Try It Out   Collecting Data and Sending an E-mail

You are going to create two Web pages, postcard.php and pc_sendmail.php. The file postcard.php will collect the data you are going to send. The file pc_sendmail.php will actually send the message, using the data you enter.

1. Start up your favorite text/PHP/HTML editor, and enter the following code:

```
<html>
E-mail
<head>
<title>Enter E-mail Data</title>
</head>
<body>
<form name="theform" method="post" action="sendmail.php">
<table>
 <tr>
  <td>To:</td>
  <td><input type="text" name="to" size="50"></td>
 </tr>
 <tr>
  <td>From:</td>
  <td><input type="text" name="from" size="50"></td>
 </tr>
 <tr>
  <td>Subject:</td>
  <td><input type="text" name="subject" size="50"></td>
```

```
   </tr>
   <tr>
    <td valign="top">Message:</td>
    <td>
     <textarea cols="60" rows="10" name="message"
     >Enter your message here</textarea>
    </td>
   </tr>
   <tr>
    <td></td>
    <td>
     <input type="submit" value="Send">
     <input type="reset" value="Reset the form">
    </td>
   </tr>
  </table>
  </form>
  </body>
  </html>
```

2. Save the page as `postcard.php`. Note that `postcard.php` doesn't actually have any PHP code in it. It simply collects the required data in an HTML form. You give it a .php extension in case you decide to add PHP code to it later (and you will).

3. Start a new text document and enter the following code:

```
<html>

<head>
<title>Mail Sent!</title>
</head>
<body>
<?php
$to = $_POST["to"];
$from = $_POST["from"];
$subject = $_POST["subject"];
$message = $_POST["message"];
$headers = "From: " . $from . "\r\n";
$mailsent = mail($to, $subject, $message, $headers);
if ($mailsent) {
  echo "Congrats! The following message has been sent: <br><br>";
  echo "<b>To:</b> $to<br>";
  echo "<b>From:</b> $from<br>";
  echo "<b>Subject:</b> $subject<br>";
  echo "<b>Message:</b><br>";
  echo $message;
} else {
  echo "There was an error...";
}
?>
</body>
</html>
```

4. Save this page as `pc_sendmail.php`. This second page will take the values entered into the first page, and send them in an e-mail.

5. Load up the first page, `postcard.php`, in your browser, and enter some data. Make sure you use valid e-mail addresses so that you can verify their receipt. It should look something like Figure 10-1.

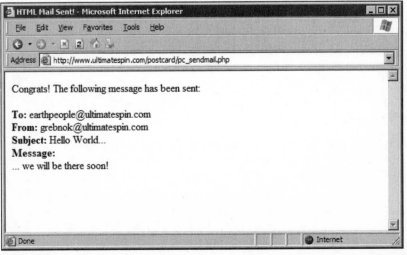

Figure 10-1

6. Click the Send button. A second page appears, similar to the one shown in Figure 10-2.

Figure 10-2

289

7. Open your e-mail client and check your e-mail (which should look like the one shown in Figure 10-3).

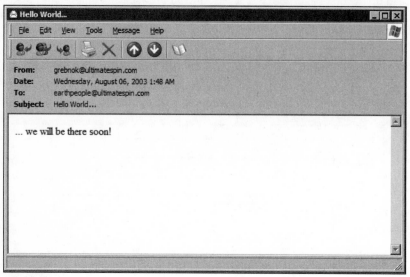

Figure 10-3

How It Works

We are going to assume that you know HTML well enough that we don't have to explain `postcard.php` in great detail. Just remember that if your `pc_sendmail.php` page is not in the same folder as `postcard.php`, you have to provide the correct path:

```
<form name="theform" method="post" action="yourdir/sendmail.php">
```

Once the user presses the Send button, `pc_sendmail.php` is loaded. The first step in your PHP code assigns all the fields from `postcard.php` to variables. This step is not necessary if `register_globals` is set to `On` in your `php.ini` file, but I strongly recommend you use this code anyway, in case `register_globals` is ever turned `Off`:

```
$to = $_POST["to"];
$from = $_POST["from"];
$subject = $_POST["subject"];
$message = $_POST["message"];
```

In order to specify from whom the e-mail is coming, use the optional fourth parameter for the `mail()` function, `headers`. We explain headers in more detail in the section "Sending HTML by Using Headers," later in this chapter.

```
$headers = "From: " . $from . "\r\n";
```

The `mail()` function returns a value of True if it is successful and False if it fails. You will use this function to make your application a little more user-friendly:

```
$mailsent = mail($to, $subject, $message, $headers);
if ($mailsent) {
  echo "Congrats! The following message has been sent: <br><br>";
  echo "<b>To:</b> $to<br>";
  echo "<b>From:</b> $from<br>";
  echo "<b>Subject:</b> $subject<br><br>";
  echo "<b>Message:</b><br>";
  echo $message;
} else {
  echo "There was an error...";
}
?>
```

Of course, you can modify this to handle errors more elegantly. Use the knowledge you acquired in Chapter 8 to do so.

You have now created your first PHP e-mail application. Congratulations! (Call your mother! She'll be so proud.) But you'll probably soon get tired of ugly, plain text e-mails. I'm sure you're champing at the bit to create colorful, formatted e-mails, right? How else are you going to enable users to send some pretty postcards? Okay, let's do something about that!

Dressing Up Your E-mails with HTML

Because you are creating a postcard application, sending plain-text e-mails just won't do. You want to dress them up a bit, and make them look professional, yet attractive. So, let's add a bit of HTML to your e-mail code to dress it up!

Try It Out   Sending HTML Code in an E-mail

First, let's try a little experiment. This step isn't vital, but it will help illustrate a later point about headers.

1. Go to Step 5 of the previous "Try It Out" section and send another e-mail. This time, put some HTML in the message. An example would be:

```
<h3>Hello World!</h3><br>Prepare for our arrival.<br><br><b>We are starving!!!</b>
```

2. When you have entered all relevant data in the form, click the Send button, and check your e-mail. It should look something like the e-mail shown in Figure 10-4.

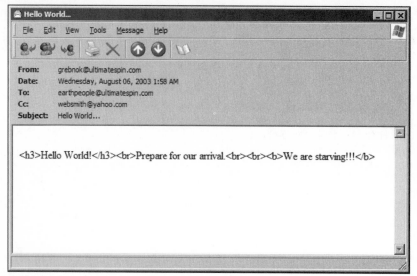

Figure 10-4

How It Works

Perhaps this heading should be "How It *Doesn't* Work." That's because your e-mail client does not know that it has received HTML. Why? Because you didn't tell it! In order for any HTML-capable client to display HTML, the client needs to be told that the incoming e-mail is going to have some HTML tags on it. Only then will it know how to properly display your message.

Try It Out **Sending HTML by Using Headers**

You need a way for your e-mail to tell the client it contains HTML. This is accomplished by using headers. You already saw how we used headers to include a "From:" parameter. Now you are going to use a similar header to tell the client that the e-mail message contains HTML.

1. Edit your copy of `pc_sendmail.php` in your favorite text editor. Back up `pc_sendmail.php` before making changes if you want to keep the old version.

2. Make the following modifications to this file. Modifications are shown in bold:

```
<html>

<head>
<title>HTML Mail Sent!</title>
</head>
<body>
<?php
$to = $_POST["to"];
$from = $_POST["from"];
$subject = $_POST["subject"];
$message = $_POST["message"];
$headers = "MIME-Version: 1.0\r\n";
```

```
$headers .= "Content-type: text/html; charset=iso-8859-1\r\n";
$headers .= "Content-Transfer-Encoding: 7bit\r\n";
$headers .= "From: " . $from . "\r\n";
$mailsent = mail($to, $subject, $message, $headers);
if ($mailsent) {
  echo "Congrats! The following message has been sent: <br><br>";
  echo "<b>To:</b> $to<br>";
  echo "<b>From:</b> $from<br>";
  echo "<b>Subject:</b> $subject<br>";
  echo "<b>Message:</b><br>";
  echo $message;
} else {
  echo "There was an error...";
}
?>
</body>
</html>
```

3. Save the file.

4. Load postcard.php into your browser and fill in the fields with appropriate information. Be sure to include some HTML in the message field, such as:

    `<h3>Hello World!</h3><br>Prepare for our arrival.<br><br><b>We are starving!!!</b>`

5. Click the Send button, and open your e-mail client to see the new message, which will look something like Figure 10-5.

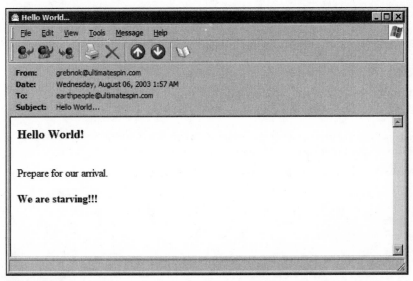

Figure 10-5

How It Works

We added a couple of new lines to the variable $headers. This allows you to do many additional things with your e-mail, including adding HTML. This line is required in order to use extended MIME capabilities (such as HTML).

```
$headers = "MIME-Version: 1.0\r\n";
```

Note the \r\n. This is a carriage return and new line, which must be entered between each header. UNIX sometimes allows just \n, but to be on the safe side, we will always use \r\n.

The following indicates that we will be using HTML in our message:

```
$headers .= "Content-type: text/html; charset=iso-8859-1\r\n";
$headers .= "Content-Transfer-Encoding: 7bit\r\n";
```

It is concatenated to the $headers variable.

That's all there is to adding HTML to your messages. All you have to do is tell the e-mail client to expect HTML, and it will work. You can really get fancy now—with tables, stylesheets, images, and so on.

However, there is still a concern—what about e-mail programs that don't accept or recognize HTML? What happens to them? You certainly want this application to be as user-friendly as possible, right? Not to worry—we'll take care of them with multipart (or mixed) messages.

Multipart Messages

You want to be able to send your postcards to anyone. However, some people don't have HTML capabilities in their e-mail client. Therefore, you will send your postcards using both plain text and HTML.

Try It Out   **Multipart Messages**

In order to send messages with both plain text and HTML, you will use Mixed Messages. (Don't worry. This is one time when it's okay to send your significant other a mixed message.) Here's how to do it:

1.   Edit your copy of postcard.php in your favorite text editor. Back up postcard.php before making changes if you want to keep the old version.

2.   Make the following modifications (shown here in bold) to postcard.php:

```
<html>
<head>
<title>Enter Data</title>
</head>
<body>
<form name="theform" method="post" action="sendmail.php">
<table>
  <tr>
   <td>To:</td>
   <td><input type="text" name="to" size="50"></td>
  </tr>
  <tr>
```

```
   <td>From:</td>
   <td>
      <input type="text" name="from" size="50">
   </td>
 </tr>
 <tr>
 <td>CC:</td>
 <td>
      <input type="text" name="cc" size="50">
 </td>
 </tr>
 <tr>
 <td>Bcc:</td>
 <td><input type="text" name="bcc" size="50"></td>
 </tr>
 <tr>
   <td>Subject:</td>
   <td><input type="text" name="subject" size="50"></td>
 </tr>
 <tr>
 <td valign="top">Message:</td>
 <td>
      <textarea cols="60" rows="10" name="message"
      >Enter your message here</textarea>
 </td>
 </tr>
 <tr>
   <td></td>
   <td>
      <input type="submit" value="Send">
      <input type="reset" value="Reset the form">
   </td>
 </tr>
 </table>
</form>
</body>
</html>
```

3. Edit your copy of pc_sendmail.php in your favorite text editor. Back up pc_sendmail.php before making changes if you want to keep the old version.

4. Make the following changes to pc_sendmail.php. Modifications are shown in bold:

```
<html>
<head>
<title>Multipart Mail Sent!</title>
</head>
<body>
<?php
$to = $_POST["to"];
$cc = $_POST["cc"];
$bcc = $_POST["bcc"];
$from = $_POST["from"];
```

295

```php
$subject = $_POST["subject"];
$messagebody = $_POST["message"];
$boundary = "==MP_Bound_xyccr948x==";
$headers = "MIME-Version: 1.0\r\n";
$headers .= "Content-type: multipart/alternative; boundary=\"$boundary\"\r\n";
$headers .= "CC: " . $cc . "\r\n";
$headers .= "BCC: " . $bcc . "\r\n";
$headers .= "From: " . $from . "\r\n";
$message = "This is a Multipart Message in MIME format\n";
$message .= "--$boundary\n";
$message .= "Content-type: text/html; charset=iso-8859-1\n";
$message .= "Content-Transfer-Encoding: 7bit\n\n";
$message .= $messagebody . "\n";
$message .= "--$boundary\n";
$message .= "Content-Type: text/plain; charset=\"iso-8859-1\"\n";
$message .= "Content-Transfer-Encoding: 7bit\n\n";
$message .= $messagebody . "\n";
$message .= "--$boundary--";
$mailsent = mail($to, $subject, $message, $headers);
if ($mailsent) {
  echo "Congrats! The following message has been sent: <br><br>";
  echo "<b>To:</b> $to<br>";
  echo "<b>From:</b> $from<br>";
  echo "<b>Subject:</b> $subject<br>";
  echo "<b>Message:</b><br>";
  echo $message;
} else {
  echo "There was an error...";
}
?>
</body>
</html>
```

How It Works

Multipart messages are not really that complicated. You must tell the e-mail client that data is coming in multiple parts—in this instance, plain text and HTML. This is done in the header:

```php
$headers .= "Content-type: multipart/alternative;
  boundary=\"$boundary\"\r\n";
```

This tells the e-mail client to look for additional "Content-type" information in the message, which includes boundary information. The boundary is what separates the multiple parts of the message. It begins with two dashes (--), and goes at the beginning of the message, between each part, and at the end. There is *no* significance to the content of this boundary. The key here is to make it as unique as possible so that it most likely is not a value that would be repeated anywhere within the message. You can use symbols, numbers, and letters in any combination. Many people choose to use a random number generator or an md5() hash. The method you use is entirely up to you.

The following line simply tells older e-mail programs why they may not see the information they expected in their browser. It's not necessary, but it's user-friendly:

```
$message = "This is a Multipart Message in MIME format\n";
```

The HTML portion of our e-mail follows. Note the double dashes (--) in front of the boundary. Also note the use of two new lines (\n\n) on the Content-Transfer-Encoding line. Do not neglect those—the code will not work correctly without them.

```
$message .= "--$boundary\n";
$message .= "Content-type: text/html; charset=iso-8859-1\n";
$message .= "Content-Transfer-Encoding: 7bit\n\n";
$message .= $messagebody . "\n";
```

Next is the text portion of our e-mail. Note the similarity to the HTML portion. You do not need to include the same $messagebody here. In fact, you would usually include an alternate message in text format.

```
$message .= "--$boundary\n";
$message .= "Content-Type: text/plain; charset=\"iso-8859-1\"\n";
$message .= "Content-Transfer-Encoding: 7bit\n\n";
$message .= $messagebody . "\n";
```

This is the final boundary. Note the double dashes (--) at the end. This signifies that it's the end of the e-mail.

```
$message .= "--$boundary--";
```

Our boundary in this case was set by the following line:

```
$boundary = "==MP_Bound_xyccr948x==";
```

Storing Images

In order to create a postcard application, you need to have digital postcards available for the user to choose from. For the purposes of our site, we'll have four postcards. If you are ambitious, you can add more, and we hope that you will!

Try It Out   Storing Images

Let's add some nice postcards to the application, shall we? You can create your own, or you can download the images from the Web site (www.wrox.com).

1.   First, store your postcard images in a folder on your Apache server. We have ours in the folder postcards/. Place them anywhere you like, but remember where they are!

2. Start up your favorite PHP editor, and type the following code. Make sure you enter your own server, username, password, and database name:

```php
<?php
$conn = mysql_connect("yourserver", "joeuser", "yourpass");
mysql_select_db("yourdatabase", $conn);
?>
```

3. Save this file as `conn_comic.php` in the `includes/` folder.

You can call it whatever you like, but we are going to be including it in a few files using the `require()` function, so you'll have to remember to use the filename you came up with. Or, you could go with the name we came up with, because we took the time to come up with such a clever name, and have used it in subsequent PHP pages.

4. Enter the following code, and save it as `db_insertpics.php`.

If you used the four pictures we provided for you and put them in the `postcards/` folder, you need not change this file. If you are using a different number of postcards, or have created your own, make sure you modify this code to reflect those changes. And, if you have named the `conn_comic.inc` file something you think is more clever than our name, make sure you reflect that change here.

```php
<?php
require("./includes/conn_comic.php");
$path = "http" . ($_SERVER["HTTPS"]=="on"?"s":"") .
  "://" . $_SERVER['SERVER_NAME'] .
  strrev(strstr(strrev($_SERVER['PHP_SELF']),"/"));
$imagepath = $path . "postcards/";
$imgURL = array('punyearth.gif', 'grebnok.gif', 'sympathy.gif',
  'congrats.gif');
$imgDESC = array('Wish you were here!', 'See you soon!',
  'Our Sympathies', 'Congratulations!');

for ($i=0; $i<4; $i++) {
  $sql = "INSERT INTO images ( images.img_url , images.img_desc )
          VALUES ( '$imagepath$imgURL[$i]', '$imgDESC[$i]')";
  $success = mysql_query($sql, $conn) or die(mysql_error());
}
echo "done."
?>
```

How It Works

Connect to the server using the correct username and password.

```php
$conn = mysql_connect("yourserver", "joeuser", "yourpass");
```

Create the database. Call it "postcard." If it is successful, print "Database created" to the screen and move on.

```php
$sql = "CREATE DATABASE postcard";
$success = mysql_query($sql, $conn) or die(mysql_error());
Echo "Database created. . .";
```

Now that you've created the database, select that database.

```
mysql_select_db("postcard", $conn);
```

Create the `images` table in the database, containing three columns. If it is successful, print "images table created" to the screen and move on.

```
$sql = "CREATE TABLE images (id int NOT NULL primary key
    auto_increment, img_url VARCHAR (255) NOT NULL,
    img_desc text )";
$success = mysql_query($sql, $conn) or die(mysql_error());
echo "'images' table created. . ."
```

Now create two arrays of values to place in the `images` table. We need to know the location of the post-cards entered previously in Step 1, and their descriptions. Each URL corresponds to a description in the other array.

```
$imgURL = array('/postcards/punyearth.gif', '/postcards/grebnok.gif',
    '/postcards/sympathy.gif', '/postcards/congrats.gif');
$imgDESC = array('Wish you were here!', 'See you soon!', 'Our
    Sympathies', 'Congratulations!');
```

Loop through the arrays, pulling the location and description text and inserting them into the images table. If there are no errors, print "Data entered" to the screen and you're done.

```
for ($i=0; $i<4; $i++) {
    $sql = "INSERT INTO images
    ( images.img_url , images.img_desc )
    VALUES ( '$imgURL[$i]', '$imgDESC[$i]')";
    $success = mysql_query($sql, $conn) or die(mysql_error());
}
Echo "Data entered. . .";
```

When running this PHP script, if anything goes wrong, make sure you delete the postcard database before running it again. Otherwise, you will get an error (database exists) and it will stop executing.

If you need further information on MySQL commands, check out Appendix F, or visit www.mysql.com/documentation/index.html.

We include the code to view and use the images in the next section, "Getting Confirmation."

Getting Confirmation

So far, you have a pretty cool postcard application. Any user can send a postcard to whomever he or she wants, and PHP takes care of mailing it. Unfortunately, there is still a small problem with the application.

As the application stands right now, it is quite easy for the user to use any e-mail address in the "From" field. This is a bad thing because nasty e-mails can be sent on someone else's behalf, and you don't want that, do you? In order to prevent such maliciousness, you must first send a confirmation e-mail to the

"From" address. Once you get the confirmation, you know the user entered a good e-mail address, and you can go ahead and send the e-mail.

This act of achieving confirmation is the first step toward creating a workflow application. We look at workflow applications in more detail in Chapter 12, but for now just understand that a workflow application is one that requires input from various parties before it reaches its final destination.

Try It Out   Getting Confirmation

In order to accommodate this workflow, your application must undergo a metamorphosis from what it was in the past. The `pc_sendmail.php` script must be split into two separate processes, such that, in between the two processes, you wait for confirmation. (You may want to save your old `postcard.php` and `pc_sendmail.php` files and start new files from scratch before making this change.)

Much of the code we have used so far in `pc_sendmail.php` will be recycled. If you are an experienced developer, we are sure you know very well how to cannibalize your old code! If you are not familiar with cannibalization, now is the time to learn. Sometimes you need to write a function that you have written before in another application. With a couple of modifications, it would work in your new app. So, you copy and paste it into your new application and make the necessary changes. Voila, your first cannibalization!

In order to confirm an e-mail address, the postcard information needs to be temporarily stored in a table, to be retrieved later on, once confirmation has been established:

1. Open your favorite PHP editor and create a new PHP file called `db_makeconfirm.php`:

    Make sure you use the correct server, username, and password.

```php
<?php
$conn = mysql_connect("yourserver", "joeuser", "yourpass");
mysql_select_db("postcard", $conn);
$sql = <<<EOD
CREATE TABLE confirm (
   id int NOT NULL PRIMARY KEY AUTO_INCREMENT,
   validator VARCHAR (32) NOT NULL,
   to_e-mail VARCHAR (100) NOT NULL,
   toname VARCHAR (50) NOT NULL,
   from_e-mail VARCHAR (100) NOT NULL,
   fromname VARCHAR (50) NOT NULL,
   bcc_e-mail VARCHAR (100),
   cc_e-mail VARCHAR (100),
   subject VARCHAR (255),
   postcard VARCHAR (255) NOT NULL,
   message text
)
EOD;
$query = mysql_query($sql, $conn) or die(mysql_error());
echo "Table <i>confirm</i> created."
?>
```

2. Run `db_makeconfirm.php`, and then check your MySQL server to make sure the confirm table was indeed created in the database.

3. Enter the new and improved `postcard.php` in your favorite PHP editor and save it:

```
<html>
<head>
<title>Enter E-mail Data</title>
</head>
<body>
<form name="theform" method="post" action="sendconf.php">
<center>
<table width="640" border="0" cellpadding="4" cellspacing="0">
 <tr>
  <td colspan="4"><H2>Postcard Sender</H2></td>
 </tr>
 <tr bgcolor="#CCCCCC">
  <td>To:</td>
  <td><input type="text" name="toname" size="30"></td>
  <td>e-mail:</td>
  <td><input type="text" name="to" size="40"></td>
 </tr>
 <tr>
  <td>From:</td>
  <td><input type="text" name="fromname" size="30"></td>
  <td>e-mail:</td>
  <td><input type="text" name="from" size="40"></td>
 </tr>
 <tr bgcolor="#CCCCCC">
  <td>CC:</td>
  <td><input type="text" name="cc" size="40"></td>
  <td>Bcc:</td>
  <td><input type="text" name="bcc" size="40"></td>
 </tr>
 <tr>
  <td colspan="2">Choose a Postcard:
   <select name="postcard[]" onchange="changepostcard(this.value)">
   <?php
    include("./includes/conn_comic.inc");
    $sql = "SELECT * FROM images ORDER BY img_desc";
    $images = mysql_query($sql, $conn) or die(mysql_error());
    $iloop = 0;
    while ($imagearray = mysql_fetch_array($images)) {
      $iloop++;
      //$iid = $imagearray['id'];
      $iurl = $imagearray['img_url'];
      $idesc = $imagearray['img_desc'];
      if ($iloop == 1) {
        echo "<option selected value=\"$iurl\">
         $idesc</option>\n";
        $image_url = $imagearray['img_url'];
      } else {
        echo "<option value=\"$iurl\">$idesc</option>\n";
      }
    }
   ?>
   </select><br>
  </td>
```

```
    <td>Subject:</td>
    <td><input type="text" name="subject" size="40"></td>
   </tr>
   <tr>
    <td colspan="2"><img src="<?php echo($image_url)?>" width=320
       height=240 border=0 id="postcard"></td>
    <td valign="top"> </td>
    <td align="right">
     <textarea cols="30" rows="12" name="message"
      >Enter your message here</textarea>
     <input type="submit" value="Send">
     <input type="reset" value="Reset the form">
    </td>
   </tr>
  </table>
 </center>
</form>
<script language="Javascript">
function changepostcard(imgurl) {
 window.document.theform.postcard.src = imgurl;
}
</script>
</body>
</html>
```

4. Next write `pc_sendconf.php`, the page that sends out the confirmation e-mail to the user. Remember that much of this code can be pulled (cannibalized) from `pc_sendmail.php`.

```
<html>
<head>
<title>HTML Mail Sent!</title>
</head>
<body>
<?php
$to = $_POST["to"];
$toname = $_POST["toname"];
$cc = $_POST["cc"];
$bcc = $_POST["bcc"];
$from = $_POST["from"];
$fromname = $_POST["fromname"];
$subject = $_POST["subject"];
if (!empty($_POST["postcard"])) {
   foreach($_POST["postcard"] as $value) {
     $postcard = $value;
   }
}
$messagebody = $_POST["message"];
$boundary = "==MP_Bound_xyccr948x==";
$headers = "MIME-Version: 1.0\r\n";
$headers .= "Content-type: multipart/alternative; boundary=\"$boundary\"\r\n";
$headers .= "From: no-reply@postcardorama.com\r\n";
$html_msg .= "<center>";
$html_msg .= "<table width=\"500\" border=0 cellpadding=\"4\">";
$html_msg .= "<tr><td>Greetings, $toname!";
```

```php
$html_msg .= "</td></tr><tr><td>";
$html_msg .= "$fromname has sent you a postcard today.<br>Enjoy!";
$html_msg .= "</td></tr><tr><td align=\"center\">";
$html_msg .= "<img src=\"$postcard\" border=\"0\">";
$html_msg .= "</td></tr><tr><td align=center>";
$html_msg .= $messagebody . "\n";
$html_msg .= "</td></tr></table></center>";
$temp=gettimeofday();
$msec=(int)$temp["usec"];
$msgid = md5(time() . $msec);
$conn = mysql_connect("yourserver", "joeuser", "yourpass");
mysql_select_db("postcard", $conn);
$sql = "INSERT INTO confirm (validator, to_e-mail, toname, from_e-mail, fromname,
bcc_e-mail, cc_e-mail, subject, postcard, message) VALUES (\"$msgid\", \"$to\",
\"$toname\", \"$from\", \"$fromname\", \"$bcc\", \"$cc\", \"$subject\",
\"$postcard\", \"$messagebody\")";
$query = mysql_query($sql, $conn) or die(mysql_error());
$confirmsubject = "Please Confirm your postcard";
$confirmmessage = "Hello " . $fromname . ",\n\n";
$confirmmessage .= "Please click on the link below to confirm that
  you would like to send this postcard:\n\n";
$confirmmessage .= $html_msg . "\n\n";
$confirmmessage .= "<a href=\"http://localhost/wrox/confirmmail.php
  ?id=$msgid\">Click here to confirm</a>";
$textconfirm = "Hello " . $fromname . ",\n\n";
$textconfirm .= "Please visit the following URL to confirm your
  postcard:\n\n";
$textconfirm .= "http://localhost/wrox/confirmmail.php
  ?id=\"$msgid\"";
$message = "This is a Multipart Message in MIME format\n";
$message .= "--$boundary\n";
$message .= "Content-type: text/html; charset=iso-8859-1\n";
$message .= "Content-Transfer-Encoding: 7bit\n\n";
$message .= $confirmmessage . "\n";
$message .= "--$boundary\n";
$message .= "Content-Type: text/plain; charset=\"iso-8859-1\"\n";
$message .= "Content-Transfer-Encoding: 7bit\n\n";
$message .= $textconfirm . "\n";
$message .= "--$boundary--";
$mailsent = mail($from, $confirmsubject, $message, $headers);
if ($mailsent) {
  echo "Here is the postcard you wish to send.<br>";
  echo "A confirmation e-mail has been sent to $from.<br>";
  echo "Open your e-mail and click on the link to confirm that you would
        like to send this postcard to $toname.<br><br>";
  echo "<b>Subject:</b> $subject<br>";
  echo "<b>Message:</b><br>";
  echo $html_msg;
} else {
  echo "There was an error sending the e-mail.";
}
?>
</body>
</html>
```

5.   Next is `pc_confirm.php`. This file is loaded in the browser with an ID in the URL to designate which saved postcard is awaiting confirmation, and it then sends the postcard to the intended recipient. Again, parts can be pulled from the old `pc_sendmail.php` file.

```php
<?php
$id = $_GET['id'];
require('./includes/conn_comic.inc');
$sql = "SELECT * FROM confirm WHERE validator = '$id'";
$query = mysql_query($sql, $conn) or die(mysql_error());
$pcarray = mysql_fetch_array($query);
if (!is_array($pcarray)) {
  echo "Oops! Nothing to confirm. Please contact
        your administrator";
  exit;
}
$to = $pcarray["to_e-mail"];
$toname = $pcarray["toname"];
$from = $pcarray["from_e-mail"];
$fromname = $pcarray["fromname"];
$bcc = $pcarray["bcc_e-mail"];
$cc = $pcarray["cc_e-mail"];
$subject = $pcarray["subject"];
$postcard = $pcarray["postcard"];
$messagebody = $pcarray["message"];

$boundary = "==MP_Bound_xyccr948x==";
$headers = "MIME-Version: 1.0\r\n";
$headers .= "Content-type: multipart/alternative; boundary=\"$boundary\"\r\n";
if (!$cc == "") {
  $headers .= "CC: " . $cc . "\r\n";
}
if (!$bcc == "") {
  $headers .= "BCC: " . $bcc . "\r\n";
}
$headers .= "From: " . $from . "\r\n";

$html_msg .= "<center>";
$html_msg .= "<table width=\"500\" border=0 cellpadding=\"4\">";
$html_msg .= "<tr><td>Greetings, $toname!";
$html_msg .= "</td></tr><tr><td>";
$html_msg .= "$fromname has sent you a postcard today.<br>Enjoy!";
$html_msg .= "</td></tr><tr><td align=\"center\">";
$html_msg .= "<img src=\"$postcard\" border=\"0\">";
$html_msg .= "</td></tr><tr><td align=center>";
$html_msg .= $messagebody . "\n";
$html_msg .= "</td></tr></table></center>";

$message = "This is a Multipart Message in MIME format\n";
$message .= "--$boundary\n";
$message .= "Content-type: text/html; charset=iso-8859-1\n";
$message .= "Content-Transfer-Encoding: 7bit\n\n";
$message .= $html_msg . "\n";
$message .= "--$boundary\n";
$message .= "Content-Type: text/plain; charset=\"iso-8859-1\"\n";
```

```
$message .= "Content-Transfer-Encoding: 7bit\n\n";
$message .= $messagebody . "\n";
$message .= "-$boundary-";
$mailsent = mail($to, $subject, $message, $headers);
?>
<html>
<head>
<title>Postcard Sent!</title>
</head>
<body>
<?php
if ($mailsent) {
  echo "Congrats! The following message has been sent: <br><br>";
  echo "<b>To:</b> $to<br>";
  echo "<b>From:</b> $from<br>";
  echo "<b>Subject:</b> $subject<br>";
  echo "<b>Message:</b><br>";
  echo $html_msg;
} else {
  echo "There was an error...";
}
?>
</body>
</html>
```

6. Let's create a form that allows a user to view the postcard. Call this one `viewpostcard.php`. (Funny how the name matches the functionality, isn't it?) The great thing about `viewpost card.php` is that most of it is very similar to `pc_confirm.php`. Yes, now you get to cannibalize some of your own code!

```
<?php
$id = $_GET['id'];
require('./includes/conn_comic.inc');
$sql = "SELECT * FROM confirm WHERE validator = '$id'";
$query = mysql_query($sql, $conn) or die(mysql_error());
$pcarray = mysql_fetch_array($query);
$path = "http" . ($_SERVER["HTTPS"]=="on"?"s":"") .
  "://" . $_SERVER['SERVER_NAME'] .
  strrev(strstr(strrev($_SERVER['PHP_SELF']),"/"));
if (!is_array($pcarray)) {
 echo "Oops! Can't find a postcard. Please contact your
   administrator.";
 exit;
}
$to = $pcarray["to_e-mail"];
$toname = $pcarray["toname"];
$from = $pcarray["from_e-mail"];
$fromname = $pcarray["fromname"];
$bcc = $pcarray["bcc_e-mail"];
$cc = $pcarray["cc_e-mail"];
$subject = $pcarray["subject"];
$postcard = $pcarray["postcard"];
$messagebody = $pcarray["message"];

$html_msg .= "<table width=\"500\" border=0 cellpadding=\"4\">";
```

```
$html_msg .= "<tr><td>Greetings, $toname!";
$html_msg .= "</td></tr><tr><td>";
$html_msg .= "$fromname has sent you a postcard today.<br>Enjoy!";
$html_msg .= "</td></tr><tr><td align=\"center\">";
$html_msg .= "<img src=\"$postcard\" border=\"0\">";
$html_msg .= "</td></tr><tr><td align=center>";
$html_msg .= $messagebody . "\n";
$html_msg .= "</td></tr></table>";

echo <<<EOD
  <html>
  <head>
  <title>Viewing postcard for $toname</title>
  </head>
  <body>
  $html_msg
  </body>
  </html>
EOD;
?>
```

7. Load `postcard.php` in your browser to verify that it works. The results should look similar to what's shown in Figure 10-6.

Figure 10-6

8. Enter the appropriate data; remember to put in your valid e-mail address in the From: email field.

9. In the Choose a Postcard field, select a postcard from the drop-down list, enter a message, and click the Send button. A screen similar to the one shown in Figure 10-7 loads.

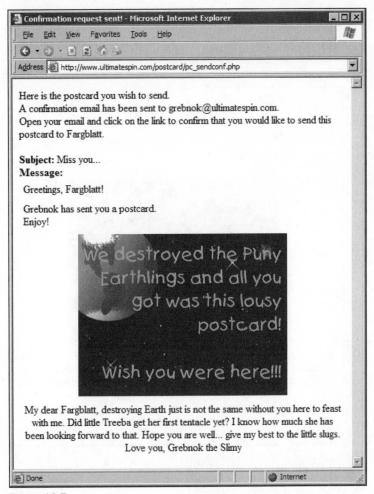

Figure 10-7

10. Check your e-mail. You should receive an e-mail that looks something like Figure 10-8.

Note the text attachment; this is the part of the e-mail that users would see if their e-mail client did not support HTML. They would see something similar to this:

```
Hello Grebnok,
Please visit the following URL to confirm your postcard:
http://www.ultimatespin.com/wrox/pc_confirm.php?id=8d3ba748a0aea409fd6b6005be67f262
```

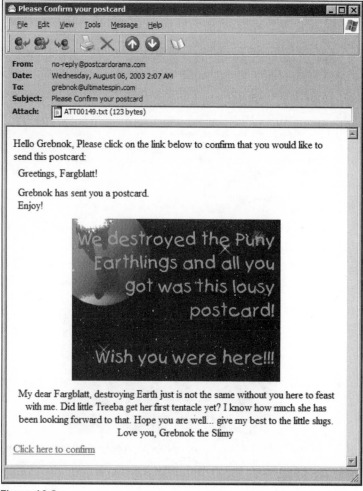

Figure 10-8

11. Click the link at the bottom of the e-mail to confirm that you want to send the postcard.

12. Open the e-mail account this postcard was sent to (see Figure 10-9).

   You did send it to an e-mail address you have access to, right? If you sent this to your little sister, we sure hope you didn't scare her!

How It Works

Your application is getting more complex. However, it is still fairly basic in its functionality. Here's what it does:

❑ The user loads `postcard.php` and fills out all the fields. He or she also selects a postcard to be sent. In the From field, the user enters his or her e-mail address.

❑ After clicking Send, the user receives an e-mail showing him or her what the postcard and message look like. A link is provided at the bottom of the e-mail asking the user to click to confirm the postcard.

❑ Once the user clicks the confirmation link, the postcard is sent to the intended recipient.

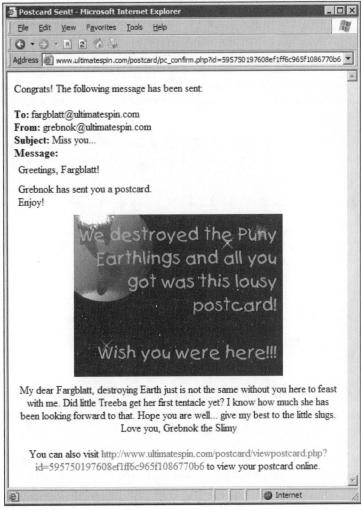

Figure 10-9

By now, you should be fairly familiar with using PHP to access MySQL. The file db_makeconfirm.php is pretty standard:

```
$sql = <<<EOD
CREATE TABLE confirm (
  id int NOT NULL PRIMARY KEY AUTO_INCREMENT,
  validator VARCHAR (32) NOT NULL,
```

```
    to_e-mail VARCHAR (100) NOT NULL,
    toname VARCHAR (50) NOT NULL,
    from_e-mail VARCHAR (100) NOT NULL,
    fromname VARCHAR (50) NOT NULL,
    bcc_e-mail VARCHAR (100),
    cc_e-mail VARCHAR (100),
    subject VARCHAR (255),
    postcard VARCHAR (255) NOT NULL,
    message text
)
EOD;
```

Note the use of the heredoc syntax. This makes the SQL statement a little easier to read. It also allows you to get a more accurate indication of where errors occur because errors usually tell you the line number on which they occurred.

Now let's take a look at the postcard.php file. This is your standard HTML form tag. Make sure sendconf.php is in the same directory as postcard.php. If not, then you will need to provide the proper path for sendconf.php:

```
<form name="theform" method="post" action="sendconf.php">
```

Next is a simple select statement. It will be followed by PHP code that builds the list of postcards the user will be able to select. Note the square brackets after postcard[]. These are required so that PHP is able to access the $postcard variable as a proper array:

```
<select name="postcard[]" onchange="changepostcard(this.value)">
```

You then connect to the MySQL server and open a connection to the postcard database:

```
$conn = mysql_connect("yourserver", "joeuser", "yourpass");
mysql_select_db("postcard", $conn);
```

This gets all image data and puts it into the $images array:

```
$sql = "SELECT * FROM images ORDER BY img_desc";
$images = mysql_query($sql, $conn) or die(mysql_error());
```

You are tracking $iloop; if $iloop == 1$iloop == 1, the first option tag will be selected by default on the form. This assures you that when the page first loads, you'll see a postcard.

```
$iloop = 0;
```

Next you loop through the $images array, constructing the rest of your HTML select tag (options). The $image_url variable is set to the default image's URL:

```
while ($imagearray = mysql_fetch_array($images)) {
 $iloop++;
 //$iid = $imagearray['id'];
 $iurl = $imagearray['img_url'];
 $idesc = $imagearray['img_desc'];
 if ($iloop == 1) {
```

```
      echo "<option selected value=\"$iurl\">$idesc</option>\n";
      $image_url = $imagearray['img_url'];
   } else {
      echo "<option value=\"$iurl\">$idesc</option>\n";
   }
}
?>
```

Then you place the default image on the page, just below the select box. You are going to use JavaScript to change this image whenever the user selects a different postcard from the select box. This enables you to minimize the number of times this page has to reload.

```
<img src="<?php echo($image_url)?>" width=320 height=240 border=0
 id="postcard">
```

What follows, of course, is the JavaScript function that changes the image. It should be pretty self-explanatory if you know JavaScript. If you don't know JavaScript, *this is the JavaScript function that changes the image*. Perhaps you should buy *JavaScript For Dummies, Third Edition*, by Emily A. Vander Veer (Wiley, 2000).

```
<script language="Javascript">
function changepostcard(imgurl) {
 window.document.theform.postcard.src = imgurl;
}
</script>
```

Now you move on to `sendconf.php`. Much of it is similar to `pc_sendmail.php`, so we'll just touch on some of the more important points:

```
if (!empty($_POST["postcard"])) {
 foreach($_POST["postcard"] as $value) {
  $postcard = $value;
 }
}
```

Remember, `$postcard` is an array. A simpler method of getting the value of the postcard would have been to use the 0 key of the `$postcard` array:

```
$postcard = $_POST["postcard"][0];
```

However, to ensure that you get the first value in the `$postcard` array regardless of the key, you use the `foreach()` loop. You must use the `if` statement because if there is no `$postcard` array, `foreach()` returns an "invalid argument" warning. Yes, we know that currently a postcard value is always posted to the `sendconf.php` page, but if you make a change to `postcard.php` (for instance, to make the postcard image optional), you don't want `sendconf.php` to break, right? Let's move on.

Your `sendconf.php` script performs an extra step you did not take care of in `pc_sendmail.php`. You must temporarily store the postcard data while you await confirmation.

```
$temp=gettimeofday();
$msec=(int)$temp["usec"];
$msgid = md5(time() . $msec);
```

Note the use of a new PHP function, md5(). This returns a 128-bit "fingerprint," or "hash," of the message passed to it. For example, the md5 hash of "Hello World" is b10a8db164e0754105b7a99be72e3fe5. It is designed as a one-way encryption of the data passed in to it, so you cannot reverse it to discover the original value.

By passing in a time value, you can be fairly certain that the md5 hash returned will be a unique value, which you use as a unique ID for the data. It is not 100 percent guaranteed to be unique, but because it is generated based on the current time in seconds and contains 32 alphanumeric characters, you can be reasonably sure it will be unique.

> *If you are interested in finding out more information about the md5 hash, visit RFC 1321: The MD5 Message-Digest Algorithm at* www.faqs.org/rfcs/rfc1321.

```
$conn = mysql_connect("yourserver", "joeuser", "yourpass");
mysql_select_db("postcard", $conn);
$sql = "INSERT INTO confirm (validator, to_e-mail, toname, from_e-mail,
    fromname, bcc_e-mail, cc_e-mail, subject, postcard, message) VALUES
    (\"$msgid\", \"$to\", \"$toname\", \"$from\", \"$fromname\",
    \"$bcc\", \"$cc\", \"$subject\", \"$postcard\",
    \"$messagebody\")";
$query = mysql_query($sql, $conn) or die(mysql_error());
```

Next, you store the postcard data temporarily until it is validated. When the user clicks the confirmation link in the e-mail to send it, the postcard is sent on to its intended recipient.

```
$confirmsubject = "Please Confirm your postcard";
$confirmmessage = "Hello " . $fromname . ",\n\n";
$confirmmessage .= "Please click on the link below to confirm that
    you would like to send this postcard:\n\n";
$confirmmessage .= $html_msg . "\n\n";
$confirmmessage .= "<a href=\"http://localhost/wrox/confirmmail.php
    ?id=$msgid\">Click here to confirm</a>";
$textconfirm = "Hello " . $fromname . ",\n\n";
$textconfirm .= "Please visit the following URL to confirm your
    postcard:\n\n";
$textconfirm .= "http://localhost/wrox/confirmmail.php
    ?id=\"$msgid\"";
$message = "This is a Multipart Message in MIME format\n";
$message .= "—$boundary\n";
$message .= "Content-type: text/html; charset=iso-8859-1\n";
$message .= "Content-Transfer-Encoding: 7bit\n\n";
$message .= $confirmmessage . "\n";
$message .= "—$boundary\n";
$message .= "Content-Type: text/plain; charset=\"iso-8859-1\"\n";
$message .= "Content-Transfer-Encoding: 7bit\n\n";
$message .= $textconfirm . "\n";
$message .= "—$boundary—";
```

The variable $confirmmessage is the HTML version of the confirmation e-mail. The variable $textconfirm is the plain text version. The variable $message is the entire message, coded to send both plain and HTML e-mails. Note where you insert the $confirmmessage and $textconfirm variables in the multipart message.

Finally, the following sends the e-mail. Don't be confused by the variable $from. That actually controls who this e-mail is being sent *to*. That's the whole idea behind sending out this confirmation e-mail.

```
$mailsent = mail($from, $confirmsubject, $message, $headers);
```

When the user receives the confirmation e-mail, there is a link at the bottom:

```
$confirmmessage .= "<a href=\"http://localhost/confirmmail.php
    ?id=$msgid\">Click here to confirm</a>";
```

When the user clicks the link, confirmmail.php is loaded in his or her browser, appended with ?id= plus the unique validation ID. This is used within confirmmail.php to access the proper postcard in the database, compose the e-mail, and send it on its way. A quick reminder: If you always set your variables like this, you never have to worry about the register_globals setting in your php.ini file.

```
$id = $_GET['id'];
```

The following gets all postcards that match your ID. Of course, there should always be just one match, because $id is unique.

```
$sql = "SELECT * FROM confirm WHERE validator = '$id'";
```

The array $pcarray contains all of the postcard data you need to send the postcard to its intended recipient:

```
$query = mysql_query($sql, $conn) or die(mysql_error());
$pcarray = mysql_fetch_array($query);
```

Here's a little insurance to make sure you don't try to send out a postcard if no postcard data exists. (Of course, you will think of a much more elegant error message, won't you?) This might be a good place for the PHP header() function to redirect the user to a "more information" error page.

```
if (!is_array($pcarray)) {
  echo "Oops! Nothing to confirm. Please contact your administrator";
  exit;
}
```

The following lines are not entirely necessary. They do make life easier, however, if you have to refer to the values multiple times. It's also good to have your variables in a centralized location; if something goes wrong, you have one place to look.

```
$to = $pcarray["to_e-mail"];
$toname = $pcarray["toname"];
$from = $pcarray["from_e-mail"];
$fromname = $pcarray["fromname"];
$bcc = $pcarray["bcc_e-mail"];
$cc = $pcarray["cc_e-mail"];
$subject = $pcarray["subject"];
$postcard = $pcarray["postcard"];
$messagebody = $pcarray["message"];
```

What follows is pretty standard stuff; you did this before in `pc_sendmail.php`. Here's a quick review: To create a multipart message, use the Content-type of multipart/alternative, and a boundary that contains unique alphanumeric text to designate the HTML and text portions of the e-mail.

```php
$boundary = "==MP_Bound_xyccr948x==";
$headers = "MIME-Version: 1.0\r\n";
$headers .= "Content-type: multipart/alternative; boundary=\"$boundary\"\r\n";
if (!$cc == "") {
 $headers .= "CC: " . $cc . "\r\n";
}
if (!$bcc == "") {
 $headers .= "BCC: " . $bcc . "\r\n";
}
$headers .= "From: " . $from . "\r\n";

$html_msg .= "<center>";
$html_msg .= "<table width=\"500\" border=0 cellpadding=\"4\">";
$html_msg .= "<tr><td>Greetings, $toname!";
$html_msg .= "</td></tr><tr><td>";
$html_msg .= "$fromname has sent you a postcard today.<br>Enjoy!";
$html_msg .= "</td></tr><tr><td align=\"center\">";
$html_msg .= "<img src=\"$postcard\" border=\"0\">";
$html_msg .= "</td></tr><tr><td align=center>";
$html_msg .= $messagebody . "\n";
$html_msg .= "</td></tr></table></center>";

$message = "This is a Multipart Message in MIME format\n";
$message .= "-$boundary\n";
$message .= "Content-type: text/html; charset=iso-8859-1\n";
$message .= "Content-Transfer-Encoding: 7bit\n\n";
$message .= $html_msg . "\n";
$message .= "-$boundary\n";
$message .= "Content-Type: text/plain; charset=\"iso-8859-1\"\n";
$message .= "Content-Transfer-Encoding: 7bit\n\n";
$message .= $messagebody . "\n";
$message .= "-$boundary-";
$mailsent = mail($to, $subject, $message, $headers);
?>
```

Until now, nothing has been sent to the browser. That is a good thing. For example, if you had received any errors, and wished to use the `header()` function to redirect the user to a different page, it works only if no text has already been sent to the browser. The lesson here is: Don't put your <html> (and other) tags in the code until you are ready to send text to the user's browser.

```php
<html>
<head>
<title>Postcard Sent!</title>
</head>
<body>
<?php
if ($mailsent) {
 echo "Congrats! The following message has been sent: <br><br>";
 echo "<b>To:</b> $to<br>";
```

```
    echo "<b>From:</b> $from<br>";
    echo "<b>Subject:</b> $subject<br>";
    echo "<b>Message:</b><br>";
    echo $html_msg;
    } else {
    echo "There was an error...";
    }
?>
</body>
</html>
```

Summary

In this chapter, you've looked at PHP's mail() function and learned how to use it by creating a postcard application. You may have seen similar applications at Hallmark's or Yahoo!'s Web sites. Your application is not as complex as theirs, but with a little bit more work, it shouldn't be too difficult to offer users some terrific features.

The mail() function gives PHP the capability to communicate with the outside world, whether it be with users of the Web site, Web site or server administrators, or even another server. There are many opportunities to use mail(): A simple form on the Web page that a user fills out to describe a technical problem can be immediately mailed to a tech support person, for example. Or, the PHP server can send the Web site administrator an e-mail any time a Web page displays a fatal error. Complicated workflow applications can be created, such as content management applications.

User Logins, Profiles, and Personalization

In this chapter, you learn to manipulate Web pages with user logins, profiles, and personalization using PHP's session and cookie functions. You create a useful login and personalization application that you can use in conjunction with the applications you have created thus far.

Session and cookie functions are two of the most fundamental, important, and useful functions you will encounter in the PHP programming language. Not convinced about the value of these yet? Think about it this way: You wouldn't want just anyone guessing where you have your important files and messing with information to change your Web site in any way he or she wanted, would you? Well, with htaccess, and better yet, PHP sessions, you can combat hackers or the general public from "stumbling" onto your sensitive files and directories.

Specifically, we will be showing you how to:

- ❑ Restrict access to files/directories via htaccess
- ❑ Use PHP to accomplish the same function as htaccess, but with more control and functionality
- ❑ Store user and admin information in a database to utilize database-driven logins
- ❑ Create a registration system with required and optional fields for users to sign up
- ❑ Take a quick look at cookies to keep login information between sessions
- ❑ Create a navigation system dependent on whether or not a user has logged in

The Easiest Way to Protect Your Files

Using htaccess is a simple and quick solution to restricting access to files or directory structures. Some Web sites contain sensitive information that you don't want the public to access. Or perhaps you have an administration section where administrators can change the content of the public site, such as in a news or upcoming events section; you don't want just anybody to change that content.

In this section, you protect a folder so that when a user visits a page in that directory, a dialog box pops up requiring that a username and password be entered.

Try It Out   **Creating htaccess and htpasswd Files**

First of all, let's take a look at your Apache configuration file, `httpd.conf`. The Linux example is located at something similar to /usr/local/apache/conf, and the Windows example will be something similar to: c:\FoxServ\Apache\conf.

Follow these steps:

1. Open the `httpd.conf` file and look for the following lines around line 270 or so. By default the lines are likely to look like this and will reside in the <Directory /> section that contains your Web root:

    ```
    #
    # AllowOverride controls what directives may be placed in .htaccess
    # files.
    # It can be "All", "None", or any combination of the keywords:
    # Options FileInfo AuthConfig Limit
    #
    AllowOverride None
    #
    ```

2. For htaccess capabilities, change the lines to look like this:

    ```
    #
    # AllowOverride controls what directives may be placed in .htaccess files.
    # It can be "All", "None", or any combination of the keywords:
    # Options FileInfo AuthConfig Limit
    #
    AllowOverride AuthConfig
    #
    ```

3. Create a text file named `.htaccess` in the directory that you wish to restrict access to. This file will require only the following lines to function correctly:

    ```
    AuthType Basic
    AuthUserFile /usr/local/apache/htdocs/protected #or your windows path
    AuthName "Restricted"
    <LIMIT GET POST>
    require valid-user
    </LIMIT>
    ```

4. Now, when creating the password file and adding your first user, you need to separate the installation based on your operating system selection. Create your password file in your main login directory by completing these steps:

    For Linux htaccess installation:

a. Go to your command prompt and type the following:

```
/usr/local/apache/bin -c /usr/local/apache/htdocs/protected john
```

Note: Use the location of your apache installation's htpasswd command, if not located in /usr/bin.

b. You will be prompted to enter john's password; enter it as doe. You will then be required to re-enter the password for confirmation. That's it; your Linux htaccess installation is complete.

For Windows htaccess installation:

a. To run htpasswd, go to Start⇨Run and type **cmd** to run commands from the command prompt. The command prompt should look like Figure 11-1.

Figure 11-1

b. Navigate to the c:\FoxServ\Apache\bin directory (or wherever your htpasswd.exe program resides), using the cd command and run htpasswd with the following syntax at the prompt (>):

```
c:\>cd "FoxServ\Apache\bin"
c:\FoxServ\Apache\bin>htpasswd users john
```

c. At the prompt to enter john's password, enter it as **doe**; you will then be required to re-enter the password for confirmation. That's it; your Windows htaccess installation is complete.

5. Navigate to a file in your protected directory, and you should see a screen similar to Figure 11-2.

Assuming you enter the appropriate username and password, you will be allowed to view the page you are requesting, along with any file or folder that resides there. However, if you fail to enter the appropriate username and password three consecutive times, or press Cancel, you will see a screen similar to that shown in Figure 11-3.

Figure 11-2

How It Works

When you request the page, Apache checks for `.htaccess` files in every folder from the Web site's document root all the way down to the file that you are requesting. Apache then opens the file and interprets it. It does this by reading which directory to protect, according to your file path, and then by reading to whom to allow access. We gave access to valid users only, as in the example of john, so no anonymous users will be allowed access. Anonymous users will see the screen shown previously in Figure 11-3.

Because no usernames or passwords are submitted with your initial request, Apache sends a message back to the browser, requesting you to enter a username and password to access this section of the site. Therefore, a dialog box is displayed, and you can submit the username and password by entering them there. Once these are accepted, you will be allowed to view the site. Also, your Web browser will remember to automatically submit this username and password when accessing the particular folder and throughout the directory tree for the rest of the browser session.

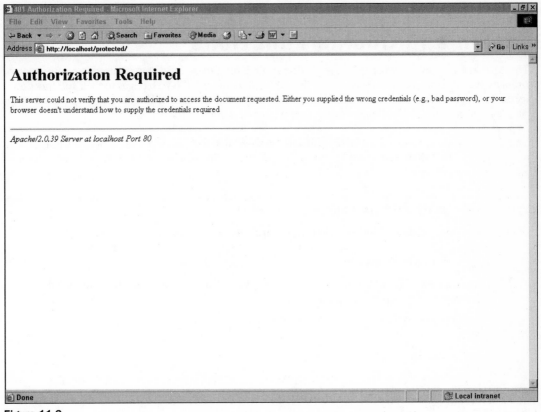

Figure 11-3

There are some problems and drawbacks to using htaccess:

❑ The dialog box that pops up is ugly.

❑ Your third-party hosting company may not allow the use of htaccess.

❑ It's easier to use brute force attacks with htaccess than when you use program-driven login authorization.

❑ It's not easy to customize "on the fly" for a dynamic, user-driven Web site.

Those are just some of the drawbacks to htaccess. Luckily for you, you can use PHP to solve the access problem to your Web-based files. You are likely to still have to use htaccess to protect files such as downloadable images, PDFs, Zip files, and other files that can't contain PHP code.

Friendlier Logins Using PHP's Session and Cookie Functions

This section is not just for restricted access to certain PHP files; these functions are used to require that users of your Web site be authorized before they are allowed to use the Web pages to their full functionality. Keep in mind that this is really useful only when protecting sections of Web pages, not for protecting all files and directories. (This will make more sense when we jump into the code.)

This form of authorization could be used in an administration area of a Web site where the administrator can change content that is viewable by the public. Note that this can be used in conjunction with htaccess for higher security, if needed.

Try It Out   Using PHP for Logins

Now let's use some code within PHP itself to authorize the user's username and password:

1. Open your favorite text editor.

2. Create a new PHP file, saving it as `template.php`. This file will be the template we'll use to illustrate how you protect a page.

3. Start off each Web page you wish to protect with this code:

```php
<?php
include 'auth.inc.php';
?>
<html>
<head>
     <title>Beginning PHP, Apache, MySQL Web Development</title>
</head>
<body>
<h1>This is the Template Page</h1>
</body>
</html>
```

The preceding template file is just an example of what you would do to protect a PHP page. In a real working situation, you can replace everything between the opening and closing <body> tags to protect any PHP page that you feel necessary.

This takes us to the authorization file, which is checking to see if the user has successfully started a session by logging in. If not, the user is redirected to the login page.

4. Use the following code to create a page and save it as `auth.inc.php`.

```php
<?php
session_start();
if ($_SESSION['logged'] != 1)
{
$redirect = $_SERVER['PHP_SELF'];
header("Refresh: 5; URL=login.php?redirect=$redirect");
echo "You are being redirected to the login page!<br>";
echo "(If your browser doesn't support this, <a
href=\"login.php?redirect=$redirect\">click here</a>)";
die();
}
?>
```

5. Now that you have the template page and the authorization page done, let's create the login page that you use to create the sessions that allow you to gain access to your protected pages. Enter the following code, which actually does the login authorization and the creation of the session for the user once he or she has successfully provided the correct username and password.

```php
<?php
session_start();
$_SESSION['logged'] = 0;

if (isset($_POST['submit']))
{
    if ($_POST['username'] == "wroxbooks" && $_POST['password'] == "aregreat")
    {
    $_SESSION['logged'] = 1;
    header ("Refresh: 5; URL=" . $_POST['redirect'] . "");
    echo "You are being redirected to your original page request!<br>";
    echo "(If your browser doesn't support this, <a href=\"" .
$_POST['redirect']. "\">click here</a>)";
    }
    else
    {
    ?>
    <html>
    <head>
    <title>Beginning PHP, Apache, MySQL Web Development</title>
    </head>
    <body>
    Invalid Username and/or Password<br><br>
    <form action="login.php" method="post">
    <input type="hidden" name="redirect" value="<?php echo $_POST['redirect'];
?>">
    Username: <input type="text" name="username"><br>
    Password: <input type="password" name="password"><br><br>
    <input type="submit" name="submit" value="Login">
    </form>
    <?php
    }
}
else
{
?>
<html>
<head>
<title>Beginning PHP, Apache, MySQL Web Development</title>
</head>
<body>
You must be logged in to view this page<br><br>
<form action="login.php" method="post">
<input type="hidden" name="redirect" value="<?php echo $_GET['redirect']; ?>">
Username: <input type="text" name="username"><br>
Password: <input type="password" name="password"><br><br>
<input type="submit" name="submit" value="Login">
</form>
<?php
```

```
    }
    ?>
    </body>
    </html>
```

This may seem to be a less-than-useful example, but it shows that you can protect pages so not just any Joe Shmoe can gain access to them. In fact, this example would work just fine if you need to have just one or two users and/or administrators share usernames and passwords.

Later in the chapter, we will show you how you can use PHP in conjunction with MySQL to create user-driven login systems. We also show you how to allow multiple administrators, multiple usernames and passwords, and privilege levels that can be managed with the MySQL database.

How It Works

Now that you have all the code typed in, you can navigate to the `template.php` page you created. Because you haven't logged in, the `auth.inc.php` file we included redirects you to the `login.php` page that requires you to log in to view the initial page you requested.

Try inputting the incorrect information so you can see how the login page works. You will see a screen similar to the one shown in Figure 11-4.

Figure 11-4

Input the correct information: `wroxbooks` for the username, and `aregreat` for the password. At this point, you are redirected to the page you originally requested because you supplied the information correctly. You will see a screen similar to Figure 11-5.

Figure 11-5

This is a very useful way to protect your PHP files to limit use to logged-in users and administrators. However, there are a couple of minor drawbacks that you will solve later when you integrate the database-driven system:

❑   This is manageable only for a few users with login information.

❑   It's somewhat labor intensive when the need to move to a user-driven database system arises.

Using Database-Driven Information

We will now show you what you can do with a database-driven Web site. Obviously, we will be using a MySQL database as our preferred database, but keep in mind that PHP can be used with many other databases as well.

We will first set up a couple of tables in our database. For this we will show you the table schema you will need. We call our database `registration` and our tables `admin` and `user_info`. You can then go ahead and create the tables as necessary using one of the methods you learned in previous chapters.

1. First of all, create an administration table schema called `admin`.

   You won't be using this table information until the last section of the chapter, but because you are creating table schemas you may as well do it now. This is where you can keep track of your administrators managing your system.

```
CREATE TABLE admin (
 username varchar(50) NOT NULL,
 password varchar(255) NOT NULL,
 first_name varchar(50) NOT NULL,
 last_name varchar(50) NOT NULL,
 email varchar(50) NOT NULL,
 admin_level int(2) NOT NULL,
 id int(10) NOT NULL auto_increment,
 PRIMARY KEY (id)
);
```

2. Create a table to store users and their information. Call this table `user_info` and create it with the following schema:

```
CREATE TABLE user_info (
 email varchar(50) NOT NULL,
 username varchar(50) NOT NULL,
 password varchar(255) NOT NULL,
 first_name varchar(50) NOT NULL,
 last_name varchar(50) NOT NULL,
 city varchar(50) default NULL,
 state varchar(50) default NULL,
 hobbies varchar(255) default NULL,
 id int(10) NOT NULL default '0'
);
```

3. Add a couple of administrators to your database, using your preferred method.

   We will add two as an example; you can add as many as you wish. For this example, we will use John Doe and Jane Doe. Keep in mind that we will be using these in all the examples we create here:

```
INSERT INTO admin ( username , password , first_name , last_name , email
, admin_level , id )
VALUES (
'johndoe', PASSWORD( 'jane' ) , 'John', 'Doe', 'john@johndoe.com', '1', ''
);
```

   and

```
INSERT INTO admin ( username , password , first_name , last_name , email
      , admin_level , `id` )
VALUES (
```

```
'janedoe', PASSWORD( 'john' ) , 'Jane', 'Doe', 'jane@janedoe.com', '2', ''
);
```

We now have a couple of administrators set up in our admin table, so we can begin to create the registration portion of our PHP code to allow users to register and login and update their information or delete their accounts if needed. We will, again, be using sessions to track our users, and we will also be using some cookie information to keep persistent logins between sessions should the user want that option.

Try It Out   **Session Tracking with PHP and MySQL**

In this section, you create a user login system. You will create it so that the user is required to input a username, password, first name, last name, and e-mail address. The other fields will be optional.

1. First, create an index page that looks for login information similar to the previous example, but don't include an authorization page so that you can show different content based on whether the user is logged in or not. This allows the user the chance to log in if he or she wishes to. Call this page index.php, and use the following code to create it:

```php
<?php
session_start();
if ($_SESSION['user_logged'] == "" || $_SESSION['user_password'] == "")
{
include "unlogged_user.php";
}
else
{
include "logged_user.php";
}
?>
```

That page checks for whether a user is logged in or not.

2. Create unlogged_user.php and logged_user.php so you can have different content show up depending on whether or not a user is logged in. This first page will be unlogged_user.php, and will simply contain some information about the benefits registering provides and how to go about registering:

```html
<html>
<head>
        <title>Beginning PHP, Apache, MySQL Web Development</title>
</head>
<body>
<h1>Welcome to the home page!</h1>
You are currently not logged into our system.<br>
Once logged in, you will have access to your personal area, along with other user
information.<br>
If you have already registered, <a href="user_login.php">click here</a> to login,
or if you would like to create an account, <a href="register.php">click here</a> to
register.
</body>
</html>
```

3. Next, create the page that tells a user he or she is logged in; then you can show links to the user's own personal area (which you create later) to allow him or her to update personal information, or delete their account entirely. Call this one `logged_user.php` and use the following code:

```
<html>
<head>
      <title>Beginning PHP, Apache, MySQL Web Development</title>
</head>
<body>
<h1>Welcome to the home page!</h1>
And thank you for logging into our system.<br>
You may now <a href="user_personal.php">click here</a>
to go into your own personal information area, and
update or remove your information should you wish to do so.
</body>
</html>
```

4. Create a page called `conn.inc.php` to include in your pages for your MySQL connection information:

```
<?php
$conn = mysql_connect("localhost", "wrox_user ", "wrox_pass") or
die(mysql_error());
$db = mysql_select_db("registration") or die(mysql_error());
?>
```

5. Create the registration page, making sure you include the optional fields and that the username chosen by the user registering isn't the same as an existing username. Call it `register.php` (it's a lot of code all at once, but we explain it all later when we get this system together).

    Should users not fill out some required field, or use an already registered username, we will notify them, and keep what had previously been entered in the appropriate fields so they don't have to re-enter everything.

```
<?php
session_start();
include "conn.inc.php";
?>
<html>
<head>
      <title>Beginning PHP, Apache, MySQL Web Development</title>
</head>
<body>
<?php
if ($_POST['submit'] == "Register")
{
      if ($_POST['username'] != "" && $_POST['password'] != "" &&
$_POST['first_name'] != "" && $_POST['last_name'] != "" &&
      $_POST['email'] != "")
      {
            $check_user = $_POST['username'];

            $query = "SELECT username FROM user_info WHERE username =
'$check_user';";
```

```php
            $result = mysql_query($query) or die(mysql_error());

            if (mysql_num_rows($result) != 0)
            {
?>
                <font color="#ff0000"><b>The Username, <?php echo $_POST['username']
; ?>, is already in use, please choose another!</b></font>
                <form action="register.php" method="post">
                Username: <input type="text" name="username"><br>
                Password: <input type="password" name="password" value="<?php echo
                    $_POST['password']; ?>"><br>
                Email: <input type="text" name="email" value="<?php echo
$_POST['email']; ?>"><br>
                First Name: <input type="text" name="first_name" value="<?php echo
$_POST['first_name']; ?>"><br>
                Last Name: <input type="text" name="last_name" value="<?php echo
$_POST['last_name']; ?>"><br>
                City: <input type="text" name="city" value="<?php echo
$_POST['city']; ?>"><br>
                State: <input type="text" name="state" value="<?php echo
$_POST['state']; ?>"><br>
                Hobbies/Interests: (choose at least one)<br>
                <select name="hobbies[]" size="10" multiple>
        <option value="Golfing"<?php if (in_array("Golfing",
$_POST['hobbies'])) echo " selected"; ?>>Golfing</option>
                <option value="Hunting"<?php if (in_array("Hunting",
$_POST['hobbies'])) echo " selected"; ?>>Hunting</option>
                <option value="Reading"<?php if (in_array("Reading",
$_POST['hobbies'])) echo " selected"; ?>>Reading</option>
                <option value="Dancing"<?php if (in_array("Dancing",
$_POST['hobbies'])) echo " selected"; ?>>Dancing</option>
                <option value="Internet"<?php if (in_array("Internet",
$_POST['hobbies'])) echo " selected"; ?>>Internet</option>
                <option value="Flying"<?php if (in_array("Flying",
$_POST['hobbies'])) echo " selected"; ?>>Flying</option>
                <option value="Traveling"<?php if (in_array("Traveling",
$_POST['hobbies'])) echo " selected"; ?>>Traveling</option>
                <option value="Exercising"<?php if (in_array("Exercising",
$_POST['hobbies'])) echo " selected"; ?>>Exercising</option>
                <option value="Computers"<?php if (in_array("Computers",
$_POST['hobbies'])) echo " selected"; ?>>Computers</option>
                <option value="Other Than Listed"<?php if (in_array("Other Than
Listed", $_POST['hobbies'])) echo " selected"; ?>>Other Than
Listed</option>
                </select><br><br>
                <input type="submit" name="submit" value="Register">   <input
type="reset" value="Clear">
                </form>
<?php
            }
            else
            {
            $query = "INSERT INTO user_info(username, password, email, first_name,
last_name, city, state, hobbies) VALUES ('" . $_POST['username'] .
```

```
"', (password('"
. $_POST['password'] . "')), '" . $_POST['email'] . "', '" .
$_POST['first_name'] .
"', '" . $_POST['last_name'] . "', '" . $_POST['city'] . "', '" .
 $_POST['state'] .
"', '" . implode(", ", $_POST['hobbies']) . "');";
            $result = mysql_query($query) or die(mysql_error());
            $_SESSION['user_logged'] = $_POST['username'];
            $_SESSION['user_password'] = $_POST['password'];
?>
            Thank you, <?php echo $_POST['first_name'] . ", " . $_POST['last_name'];
?> for registering!<br>
            <a href="index.php">Click here</a> to continue.
<?php
        }
    }
    else
    {
?>          <font color="#ff0000"><b>The Username, Password, Email, First Name, and
            Last Name fields are required!</b></font>
            <form action="register.php" method="post">
            Username: <input type="text" name="username" value="<?php echo
                $_POST['username']; ?>"><br>
Password: <input type="password" name="password" value="<?php echo
$_POST['password']; ?>"><br>
            Email: <input type="text" name="email" value="<?php echo $_POST['email'];
 ?>"><br>
            First Name: <input type="text" name="first_name" value="<?php echo
$_POST['first_name']; ?>"><br>
            Last Name: <input type="text" name="last_name" value="<?php echo
$_POST['last_name']; ?>"><br>
            City: <input type="text" name="city" value="<?php echo $_POST['city'];
?>"><br>
            State: <input type="text" name="state" value="<?php echo $_POST['state'];
?>"><br>
            Hobbies/Interests: (choose at least one)<br>
            <select name="hobbies[]" size="10" multiple>
            <option value="Golfing"<?php if (in_array("Golfing", $_POST['hobbies']))
echo " selected"; ?>>Golfing</option>
            <option value="Hunting"<?php if (in_array("Hunting", $_POST['hobbies']))
echo " selected"; ?>>Hunting</option>
            <option value="Reading"<?php if (in_array("Reading", $_POST['hobbies']))
echo " selected"; ?>>Reading</option>
            <option value="Dancing"<?php if (in_array("Dancing", $_POST['hobbies']))
echo " selected"; ?>>Dancing</option>
            <option value="Internet"<?php if (in_array("Internet",
$_POST['hobbies']))
echo " selected"; ?>>Internet</option>
            <option value="Flying"<?php if (in_array("Flying", $_POST['hobbies']))
echo
                " selected"; ?>>Flying</option>
            <option value="Traveling"<?php if (in_array("Traveling",
$_POST['hobbies'])) echo " selected"; ?>>Traveling</option>
            <option value="Exercising"<?php if (in_array("Exercising",
```

```
$_POST['hobbies'])) echo " selected"; ?>>Exercising</option>
        <option value="Computers"<?php if (in_array("Computers",
$_POST['hobbies'])) echo " selected"; ?>>Computers</option>
        <option value="Other Than Listed"<?php if (in_array("Other Than Listed",
$_POST['hobbies'])) echo " selected"; ?>>Other Than Listed</option>
        </select><br><br>
        <input type="submit" name="submit" value="Register">   <input
type="reset" value="Clear">
        </form>
<?php
     }
}
else
{
?>
Welcome to the registration page!<br>
The Username, Password, Email, First Name, and Last Name fields are required!
<form action="register.php" method="post">
Username: <input type="text" name="username"><br>
Password: <input type="password" name="password"><br>
Email: <input type="text" name="email"><br>
First Name: <input type="text" name="first_name"><br>
Last Name: <input type="text" name="last_name"><br>
City: <input type="text" name="city"><br>
State: <input type="text" name="state"><br>
Hobbies/Interests: (choose at least one)<br>
<select name="hobbies[]" size="10" multiple>
<option value="Golfing">Golfing</option>
<option value="Hunting">Hunting</option>
<option value="Reading">Reading</option>
<option value="Dancing">Dancing</option>
<option value="Internet">Internet</option>
<option value="Flying">Flying</option>
<option value="Traveling">Traveling</option>
<option value="Exercising">Exercising</option>
<option value="Computers">Computers</option>
<option value="Other Than Listed">Other Than Listed</option>
</select><br><br>
<input type="submit" name="submit" value="Register">   <input type="reset"
    value="Clear">
</form>
<?php
}
?>
</body>
</html>
```

Let's recap quickly what you've done:

❑   You have an index page that checks whether or not a user is logged in.

❑   Based on that check, it either tells the user to log in or register to allow them access to their personal information area.

❑ You have the registration area covered, along with the login process, and are keeping them tracked with their session information.

Now that you have accomplished all that, you can create the area where each user is allowed to change his or her information or delete the account. Call this page `user_personal.php`, but first you will create a slightly modified authorization page, which checks whether or not the user is logged in and, if he or she is not, redirects the user to your also slightly modified login page:

1. Enter the first set of code and call it `auth_user.inc.php`:

```
<?
session_start();
if ($_SESSION['user_logged'] == "" || $_SESSION['user_password'] == "")
{
    $redirect = $_SERVER['PHP_SELF'];
    header("Refresh: 5; URL=user_login.php?redirect=$redirect");
    echo "You are currently not logged in, we are redirecting you, be
        patient!<br>";
    echo "(If your browser doesn't support this, <a
        href=\"user_login.php?redirect=$redirect\">click here</a>)";
    die();
}
else {}
?>
```

2. Create the modified login page. Call this one `user_login.php`.

The modification is in the way that you check the username and password against usernames and passwords stored in the MySQL database. Previously, you just hard-coded a username and password in the code.

```
<?php
session_start();
include "conn.inc.php";
if (isset($_POST['submit']))
{
    $query = "SELECT username, password FROM user_info WHERE username = '" .
        $_POST['username'] . "' AND password = (password('" . $_POST['password']
        . "'));";
    $result = mysql_query($query) or die(mysql_error());

    if (mysql_num_rows($result) == 1)
    {
        $_SESSION['user_logged'] = $_POST['username'];
        $_SESSION['user_password'] = $_POST['password'];
        header ("Refresh: 5; URL=" . $_POST['redirect'] . "");
        echo "You are being redirected to your original page request!<br>";
        echo "(If your browser doesn't support this, <a href=\"" .
            $_POST['redirect']. "\">click here</a>)";
    }
    else
    {
?>
        <html>
```

```
        <head>
        <title>Beginning PHP, Apache, MySQL Web Development</title>
        </head>
        <body>
        Invalid Username and/or Password<br>
        Not registered? <a href="register.php">Click here</a> to register.<br>
        <form action="user_login.php" method="post">
        <input type="hidden" name="redirect" value="<?php echo
$_POST['redirect'];
                ?>">
        Username: <input type="text" name="username"><br>
        Password: <input type="password" name="password"><br><br>
        <input type="submit" name="submit" value="Login">
        </form>
<?
    }
}
else
{
if ($_SERVER['HTTP_REFERER'] == "" || $_SERVER['HTTP_REFERER'] ==
    "http://localhost/index.php")
{
$redirect = "/index.php";
}
else
{
$redirect = $_GET['redirect'];
}
?>
        <html>
        <head>
        <title>Beginning PHP, Apache, MySQL Web Development</title>
        </head>
        <body>
        Login below by supplying your username/password...<br>
        Or <a href="register.php">click here</a> to register.<br><br>
        <form action="user_login.php" method="post">
        <input type="hidden" name="redirect" value="<? echo $redirect; ?>">
        Username: <input type="text" name="username"><br>
        Password: <input type="password" name="password"><br><br>
        <input type="submit" name="submit" value="Login">
        </form>
        </body>
        </html>
<?php
}
?>
```

3. Create the `user_personal.php` page with the following code:

```php
<?php
session_start();
include "auth_user.inc.php";
include "conn.inc.php";
?>
```

```html
<html>
<head>
     <title>Beginning PHP, Apache, MySQL Web Development</title>
</head>
<body>
<h1>Welcome to your personal information area</h1>
Here you can update your personal information, or delete your account.<br>
Your information as we currently have it is shown below:<br>
<a href="index.php">Click here</a> to return to the home page<br><br>
<?php
$query = "SELECT * FROM user_info WHERE username = '" . $_SESSION['user_logged'].
"'
 AND password = (password('" . $_SESSION['user_password'] . "'));";
$result = mysql_query($query) or die(mysql_error());

$row = mysql_fetch_array($result);
?>
First Name: <?php echo $row['first_name']; ?><br>
Last Name: <?php echo $row['last_name']; ?><br>
City: <?php echo $row['city']; ?><br>
State: <?php echo $row['state']; ?><br>
Email: <?php echo $row['email']; ?><br>
Hobbies/Interests: <?php echo $row['hobbies']; ?><br><br>
<a href="update_account.php">Update Account</a> | 
<a href="delete_account.php">Delete Account</a>
</body>
</html>
```

You may have noticed that there are links in the preceding code to pages that you haven't created yet. Let's do that now. One page will allow a logged-in user to update his or her account. The other will allow the user to delete the account upon confirming that that is the intention.

1. Create the first page update_account.php with the following code:

```php
<?php
session_start();
include "auth_user.inc.php";
include "conn.inc.php";
?>
<html>
<head>
     <title>Beginning PHP, Apache, MySQL Web Development</title>
</head>
<body>
<h1>Update Account Information</h1>
Here you can update your account information for viewing in your profile.<br><br>
<?php
if ($_POST['submit'] == "Update")
{
     $query_update = "UPDATE user_info SET email = '" . $_POST['email'] . "', city
          = '" . $_POST['city'] . "', state = '" . $_POST['state'] . "', hobbies =
          '" . implode(", ", $_POST['hobbies']) . "' WHERE username = '" .
          $_SESSION['user_logged']. "' AND password = (password('" .
          $_SESSION['user_password'] . "';";
```

```php
    $result_update = mysql_query($query_update) or die(mysql_error());

    $query = "SELECT * FROM user_info WHERE username = '" .
        $_SESSION['user_logged']. "' AND password = (password('" .
        $_SESSION['user_password'] . "'));";
    $result = mysql_query($query) or die(mysql_error());

    $row = mysql_fetch_array($result);
    $hobbies = explode(", ", $row['hobbies'])
?>
    <b>Your account information has been updated.</b><br>
    <a href="user_personal.php">Click here</a> to return to your account.
    <form action="update_account.php" method="post">
    Email: <input type="text" name="email" value="<?php echo $row['email'];
?>"><br>
    City: <input type="text" name="city" value="<?php echo $row['city']; ?>"><br>
    State: <input type="text" name="state" value="<?php echo $row['state'];
?>"><br>
    Hobbies/Interests: (choose at least one)<br>
    <select name="hobbies[]" size="10" multiple>
    <option value="Golfing"<?php if (in_array("Golfing", $hobbies)) echo "
selected";
 ?>>Golfing</option>
    <option value="Hunting"<?php if (in_array("Hunting", $hobbies)) echo "
selected";
        ?>>Hunting</option>
    <option value="Reading"<?php if (in_array("Reading", $hobbies)) echo "
selected";
        ?>>Reading</option>
    <option value="Dancing"<?php if (in_array("Dancing", $hobbies)) echo "
selected";
        ?>>Dancing</option>
    <option value="Internet"<?php if (in_array("Internet", $hobbies)) echo "
        selected"; ?>>Internet</option>
    <option value="Flying"<?php if (in_array("Flying", $hobbies)) echo "
selected";
        ?>>Flying</option>
    <option value="Traveling"<?php if (in_array("Traveling", $hobbies)) echo "
        selected"; ?>>Traveling</option>
    <option value="Exercising"<?php if (in_array("Exercising", $hobbies)) echo "
        selected"; ?>>Exercising</option>
    <option value="Computers"<?php if (in_array("Computers", $hobbies)) echo "
        selected"; ?>>Computers</option>
    <option value="Other Than Listed"<?php if (in_array("Other Than Listed",
        $hobbies)) echo " selected"; ?>>Other Than Listed</option>
    </select><br><br>
    <input type="submit" name="submit" value="Update">   <input type="button"
        value="Cancel" onclick="history.go(-1);">
    </form>
<?php
}
else
{
    $query = "SELECT * FROM user_info WHERE username = '" .
```

```
    $_SESSION['user_logged']. "' AND password = (password('" .
    $_SESSION['user_password'] . "'));";
        $result = mysql_query($query) or die(mysql_error());

        $row = mysql_fetch_array($result);
        $hobbies = explode(", ", $row['hobbies'])
?>
        <form action="update_account.php" method="post">
        Email: <input type="text" name="email" value="<?php echo $row['email'];
?>"><br>
        City: <input type="text" name="city" value="<?php echo $row['city']; ?>"><br>
        State: <input type="text" name="state" value="<?php echo $row['state'];
?>"><br>
        Hobbies/Interests: (choose at least one)<br>
        <select name="hobbies[]" size="10" multiple>
        <option value="Golfing"<?php if (in_array("Golfing", $hobbies)) echo "
selected";
 ?>>Golfing</option>
        <option value="Hunting"<?php if (in_array("Hunting", $hobbies)) echo "
selected";
 ?>>Hunting</option>
        <option value="Reading"<?php if (in_array("Reading", $hobbies)) echo "
selected";
 ?>>Reading</option>
        <option value="Dancing"<?php if (in_array("Dancing", $hobbies)) echo "
selected";
 ?>>Dancing</option>
        <option value="Internet"<?php if (in_array("Internet", $hobbies)) echo "
 selected"; ?>>Internet</option>
        <option value="Flying"<?php if (in_array("Flying", $hobbies)) echo "
selected";
 ?>>Flying</option>
        <option value="Traveling"<?php if (in_array("Traveling", $hobbies)) echo "
 selected"; ?>>Traveling</option>
        <option value="Exercising"<?php if (in_array("Exercising", $hobbies)) echo "
 selected"; ?>>Exercising</option>
        <option value="Computers"<?php if (in_array("Computers", $hobbies)) echo "
 selected"; ?>>Computers</option>
        <option value="Other Than Listed"<?php if (in_array("Other Than Listed"
, $hobbies)) echo " selected"; ?>>Other Than Listed</option>
        </select><br><br>
        <input type="submit" name="submit" value="Update">   <input type="button"
 value="Cancel" onclick="history.go(-1);">
        </form>
<?php
}
?>
</body>
</html>
```

2. Create the next page (call it delete_account.php) to allow users to delete their accounts, using the following code:

```
<?php
session_start();
include "auth_user.inc.php";
```

```
    include "conn.inc.php";

    if ($_POST['submit'] == "Yes")
    {
        $query_delete = "DELETE FROM user_info WHERE username = '" .
            $_SESSION['user_logged']. "' AND password = (password('" .
            $_SESSION['user_password'] . "'));";
        $result_delete = mysql_query($query_delete) or die(mysql_error());

        $_SESSION['user_logged'] = "";
        $_SESSION['user_password'] = "";

        header("Refresh: 5; URL=index.php");
        echo "Your account has been deleted! You are being sent to the home
            page!<br>";
        echo "(If your browser doesn't support this, <a href=\"index.php\">click
            here</a>)";
        die();
    }
    else
    {
    ?>
    <html>
    <head>
    <title>Beginning PHP, Apache, MySQL Web Development</title>
    <body>
    Are you sure you want to delete your account?<br>
    There is no way to retrieve your account once you confirm!<br>
    <form action="delete_account.php" method="post">
    <input type="submit" name="submit" value="Yes">   <input type="button" value="
            No " onclick="history.go(-1);">
    </form>
    </body>
    </html>
    <?php
    }
    ?>
```

That's all the code for now. It was a lot to absorb all at once, but it will make more sense when we explain what we are doing in the next section.

How It Works

Well, let's imagine new users coming to this section of the site for the first time. They navigate to the index.php page and initially see a screen similar to the one shown in Figure 11-6.

The users obviously haven't logged in yet, so they are not allowed to do anything else here. They are given the choice to log in if they have registered before, or they can register to activate an account.

Should the users decide to log in, they will be presented with the same options as when you created the previous login pages. The page should look like the one in Figure 11-7.

Figure 11-6

Users will be required to supply the usernames and passwords they chose for themselves. The only difference between this login portion and the previous one you created is that the authorization is coming from a MySQL database, rather than hard coding of the authorization into the pages themselves. Should a user not enter the information correctly, he or she will be asked for the information again, and have the option to register from that page as well.

Should the user choose to register, he or she will see a page similar to the one in Figure 11-8.

Now the user can fill in information and register to be a user of this site. Once the user fills in the information and hits the register button, the code checks whether or not the required fields have been filled out. If one (or more) of the required fields is not filled out, the form appears again with the information entered still in the form, and an error message stating the problem. The page will look similar to the one shown in Figure 11-9.

Figure 11-7

Figure 11-8

Figure 11-9

A user can now fill in the missing information and continue. A check is performed after the required fields are satisfied to see if the username chosen is already taken. Should that be the case, the form again retains any information that has been filled out, and a different error message appears on the screen stating that the username is taken. The username field is erased so users know that they need to choose another username. The screen will look like that in Figure 11-10.

Now the user can choose another username and complete the registration process. Once the user chooses a username that is *not* already taken, the registration is complete. Once the registration is complete, the user is automatically logged in for this session using the username and password as the session values, and he or she will be redirected to the home page. After being redirected, the user's screen should look similar to Figure 11-11.

Now the logged-in users are able to navigate to their own personal information pages where they can update their information at any time and are also allowed to delete their account from this location.

The Username, jeremys, is already in use, please choose another!

Username:
Password: ``*******``
Email: jeremys@cloverfish.net
First Name: Jeremy
Last Name: Stolz
City: West Fargo
State: North Dakota
Hobbies/Interests: (choose at least one)

Golfing
Hunting
Reading
Dancing
Internet
Flying
Traveling
Exercising
Computers
Other Than Listed

Register   Clear

Figure 11-10

Welcome to the home page!

Thank you for logging into our system.
You may now click here to go into your own personal information area, and update or remove your information should you wish to do so.

Figure 11-11

The beauty of sessions and keeping track of users is that you don't have to worry about passing information about the users with form data, or passing it through the query string or address bar. All the data is stored temporarily on the server where the Web site resides. You also don't have to worry about people trying to put parameters into the address bar to fake the identity of another user. The session data is unavailable to users on the site, so only if they had access to the server itself would they be able to obtain the user-supplied data.

Now we will look at the pages where the user's information is displayed, and where a user can update or delete his or her account. The display page simply displays the previously entered user information. The update page is also straightforward: It shows a form will the user's previously entered data and gives the user the ability to update it if he or she wishes, or simply cancel the update and return to the previous screen. The delete page merely asks if the user is sure he or she wants to delete the account and gives the option of returning to the previous screen. The user's information display page should look something like the one shown in Figure 11-12.

When users choose to update their accounts, they will see a screen similar to Figure 11-13.

Figure 11-12

Figure 11-13

Should they update their information, they will be told that the information was indeed updated and then they will be allowed to update the information again if they wish (for example if on review they realize they input something incorrectly). That page will look like the one in Figure 11-14.

Finally, the delete page looks similar to the one shown in Figure 11-15. This appears once users choose the Delete Account link on the display page. From here, if users choose Yes, their account is deleted, their logged in session will be destroyed, and they will be redirected to the index page.

That's it for the user portion of the registration system. We show you an administration section later in the chapter, where you can allow certain levels of admins to have different privileges from others. But now, let's move on to a quick cookie example, which you can implement into the previous registration system.

Figure 11-14

Figure 11-15

Try It Out   Cookie Tracking with PHP

Here's a quick example of how to use a cookie in a page to see if the users have a corresponding cookie stored on their machines. Then, if you wish, you can implement this into your login system to allow persistent logins between single browser sessions. We will be supplying the cookie's value through the code, but if you were to implement it, you could use the session variable in the cookie value portion. We use five small pages for this example. We will give you all of them and then explain how they work.

1.   Create the first file, `setcookie.php`:

```
<html>
<head>
      <title>Beginning PHP, Apache, MySQL Web Development</title>
</head>
<body>
<h1>This is the Set Cookie Page</h1>
<a href="setcookie_un.php">Click here</a> to set your cookies.
</body>
</html>
```

2.   Create the second file, `setcookie_un.php`:

```
<?php
$username = "jeremys";
setcookie('username', $username, time() + 60 * 60 * 24 * 30); // sets cookie for 30
days
header("Location: setcookie_pw.php");
?>
```

3.   Create the third file, `setcookie_pw.php`:

```
<?php
$password = "apache";
setcookie('password', $password, time() + 60 * 60 * 24 * 30); // sets cookie for 30
days
header("Location: cookies_set.php");
?>
```

4.   Create the fourth file, `cookies_set.php`:

```
<html>
<head>
      <title>Beginning PHP, Apache, MySQL Web Development</title>
</head>
<body>
<h1>This is the Set Cookie Page</h1>
Your cookies have been set.<br>
<a href="testcookie.php">Click here</a> to test your cookies.
</body>
</html>
```

5. Finally, create the fifth file, `testcookie.php`:

```
<html>
<head>
    <title>Beginning PHP, Apache, MySQL Web Development</title>
</head>
<body>
<h1>This is the Test Cookie Page</h1>
<?php
if ($_COOKIE['username'] == "" || $_COOKIE['password'] == "")
{
?>
No cookies were set.<br>
<a href="setcookie.php">Click here</a> to set your cookies.
<?php
}
else
{
?>
Your cookies were set:<br>
Username cookie value: <b><?php echo $_COOKIE['username']; ?></b><br>
Password cookie value: <b><?php echo $_COOKIE['password']; ?></b><br>
<?php
}
?>
</body>
</html>
```

How It Works

We ran through the previous cookie example to show you how you can keep persistent logins between single browser sessions. As you may have noticed, some of the pages are just display or navigation pages. For that reason, we won't explain those. We will focus instead on `setcookie_un.php`, `setcookie_pw.php`, and `testcookie.php`.

The `setcookie_un.php` page does just what the name says: It sets the cookie for the username, which is just hard coded for this example. It then uses a header redirect to send you to the next page.

That next page is `setcookie_pw.php`, which does the same as `setcookie_un.php`, except that it is setting the cookie for the password. Then you're redirected to a simple display page that tells you your cookies have been set.

You can then navigate to `testcookie.php`. This page checks to see if the cookie values are valid. If they are not, it says, "No cookies were set," and you can try to set the cookies again. If you are successful in your login, the screen will look like the one in Figure 11-16.

Should you need to delete or end a cookie, simply run some code (such as the code that follows) to end the cookie from the user's browser.

```
setcookie('username', "", time() - 3600);
```

Figure 11-16

This sets the username cookie for one hour ago and sets the username value to an empty string, thereby making the username cookie unavailable to the Web site the user is logged into.

Now that you have some cookie knowledge, you can use it in the login system if you want. Although cookies are a good way to keep persistent logins between browser sessions, they can be altered and/or spoofed by a user because the cookie is stored on the client machine. That is generally why many systems house their main login information with sessions and use cookies as a subfeature only.

Now let's move on to the last portion of this chapter. We will show you how logged-in admins can change information and delete information based on their access privileges. You may notice similarities between this system and the user login system and you'd be right. Remember that the more you practice, the easier this will be when you are writing systems like this for your clients.

Try It Out   **Administration Section**

In this section, administrators are required to log in before they can view the users signed up in the user registration database. Once they are logged in, only certain privileged admins will be allowed to perform certain operations. For this example, admins with a privilege level of 1 are allowed to update user accounts and delete user accounts. Admins with a privilege level of 2 are allowed to update user information; they will not be allowed to delete a user's account. This would be useful if a user was, for some reason, unable to log into the site and the administrator needed to reset passwords, change usernames, and so on, but you don't want just any administrator to be allowed to do everything the main administrator does.

The code for all the pages follows. Key the pages in, and save them in a folder called admin in your Web directory. We will explain how they work after showing you the code.

1.   Create the first file, `conn.inc.php`:

```php
<?php
$conn = mysql_connect("localhost", "jcstolz", "r3minyL") or die(mysql_error());
$db = mysql_select_db("registration") or die(mysql_error());
?>
```

2.   Create the second file, `auth_admin.inc.php`:

```php
<?php
session_start();
if ($_SESSION['admin_logged'] == "" || $_SESSION['admin_password'] == "")
{
    $redirect = $_SERVER['PHP_SELF'];
    header("Refresh: 5; URL=admin_login.php?redirect=$redirect");
    echo "You are currently not logged in, we are redirecting you, be
        patient!<br>";
    echo "(If your browser doesn't support this, <a
        href=\"login.php?redirect=$redirect\">click here</a>)";
    die();
}
else {}
?>
```

3.   Create the third file, saving it as `index.php`:

```php
<?php
session_start();
if ($_SESSION['admin_logged'] == "" || $_SESSION['admin_password'] == "")
{
include "unlogged_admin.php";
}
else
{
include "logged_admin.php";
}
?>
```

4. Create the fourth file, `logged_admin.php`:

```
<html>
<head>
     <title>Beginning PHP, Apache, MySQL Web Development</title>
</head>
<body>
<h1>Welcome to the Admin Area!</h1>
You are currently logged in.<br>
<a href="admin_area.php">Click here</a> to access your administrator tools.
</body>
</html>
```

5. Create and save the fifth file as `unlogged_admin.php`:

```
<html>
<head>
     <title>Beginning PHP, Apache, MySQL Web Development</title>
</head>
<body>
<h1>Welcome to the Admin Area!</h1>
You are currently not logged in.<br>
Once logged in, you will have access to your administrator tools.<br>
<a href="admin_login.php">Click here</a> to login.
</body>
</html>
```

6. Create the sixth file, `admin_login.php`:

```
<?php
session_start();
include "conn.inc.php";
if (isset($_POST['submit']))
{
     $query = "SELECT username, password, admin_level FROM admin WHERE username =
'" . $_POST['username'] . "' AND password = (password('" . $_POST['password'] .
"'));";
     $result = mysql_query($query) or die(mysql_error());

     $row = mysql_fetch_array($result);
     $admin_level = $row['admin_level'];

     if (mysql_num_rows($result) == 1)
     {
          $_SESSION['admin_logged'] = $_POST['username'];
          $_SESSION['admin_password'] = $_POST['password'];
          $_SESSION['admin_level'] = $row['admin_level'];
          header ("Refresh: 5; URL=" . $_POST['redirect'] . "");
          echo "You are being redirected to your original page request!<br>";
          echo "(If your browser doesn't support this, <a href=\"" .
               $_POST['redirect']. "\">click here</a>)";
     }
```

```
        else
        {
?>
            <html>
            <head>
            <title>Beginning PHP, Apache, MySQL Web Development</title>
            </head>
            <body>
            Invalid Username and/or Password<br>
            <form action="admin_login.php" method="post">
            <input type="hidden" name="redirect" value="<?php echo
$_POST['redirect'];
                    ?>">
            Username: <input type="text" name="username"><br>
            Password: <input type="password" name="password"><br><br>
            <input type="submit" name="submit" value="Login">
            </form>
<?php
        }
}
else
{
    if ($_SERVER['HTTP_REFERER'] == "" || $_SERVER['HTTP_REFERER'] ==
        "http://localhost/admin/index.php" || $_SERVER['HTTP_REFERER'] ==
        "http://localhost/admin/")
    {
        $redirect = "/admin/index.php";
    }
    else
    {
        $redirect = $_GET['redirect'];
    }
?>
    <html>
    <head>
    <title>Beginning PHP, Apache, MySQL Web Development</title>
    </head>
    <body>
    Login below by supplying your username/password...<br>
    <form action="admin_login.php" method="post">
    <input type="hidden" name="redirect" value="<?php echo $redirect; ?>">
    Username: <input type="text" name="username"><br>
    Password: <input type="password" name="password"><br><br>
    <input type="submit" name="submit" value="Login">
    </form>
    </body>
    </html>
<?php
}
?>
```

7. Create the seventh file and save it as `admin_area.php`:

```
<?php
session_start();
include "auth_admin.inc.php";
```

```php
include "conn.inc.php";
?>
<html>
<head>
     <title>Beginning PHP, Apache, MySQL Web Development</title>
</head>
<body>
<h1>Admin Area</h1>
Below is a list of users and your available administrator privileges.<br><br>
<?php
if ($_SESSION['admin_level'] == "1")
{
$query = "SELECT first_name, last_name, id FROM user_info ORDER BY last_name;";
$result = mysql_query($query) or die(mysql_error());

while ($row = mysql_fetch_array($result))
{
echo $row['first_name']; ?> <?php echo $row['last_name'];
?>
  <a href="update_user.php?id=<?php echo $row['id']; ?>">Update User</a>
|
<a href="delete_user.php?id=<?php echo $row['id']; ?>">Delete User</a><br>
<?php
}
}
else
{
$query = "SELECT first_name, last_name, id FROM user_info ORDER BY last_name;";
$result = mysql_query($query) or die(mysql_error());

while ($row = mysql_fetch_array($result))
{
echo $row['first_name']; ?> <?php echo $row['last_name'];
?>
  <a href="update_user.php?id=<?php echo $row['id']; ?>">Update
User</a><br>
<?php
}
}
?>
</body>
</html>
```

8. Create the eighth file, `update_user.php`:

```php
<?php
session_start();
include "auth_admin.inc.php";
include "conn.inc.php";
?>
<html>
<head>
     <title>Beginning PHP, Apache, MySQL Web Development</title>
</head>
<body>
<h1>Update User Information</h1>
```

```php
<?php
if ($_POST['submit'] == "Update")
{
    $query_update = "UPDATE user_info SET username = '" . $_POST['username'] . "',
        password = (password('" . $_POST['password'] . "')), first_name = '" .
        $_POST['first_name'] . "', last_name = '" . $_POST['last_name'] . "',
        email = '" . $_POST['email'] . "', city = '" . $_POST['city'] . "',
        state = '" . $_POST['state'] . "', hobbies = '" . implode(", ",
        $_POST['hobbies']) .
            "' WHERE id = '" . $_POST['id'] . "';";
    $result_update = mysql_query($query_update) or die(mysql_error());

    $query = "SELECT * FROM user_info WHERE id = '" . $_POST['id'] . "';";
    $result = mysql_query($query) or die(mysql_error());

    $row = mysql_fetch_array($result);
    $hobbies = explode(", ", $row['hobbies'])
?>
    <b>User information has been updated.</b><br>
    <a href="admin_area.php">Click here</a> to return to the admin area.
    <form action="update_user.php" method="post">
    <input type="hidden" name="id" value="<?php echo $_POST['id']; ?>">
    Username: <input type="text" name="username" value="<?php echo
$row['username'];
        ?>"><br>
    Password: <input type="password" name="password" value=""> Not displayed<br>
    First Name: <input type="text" name="first_name" value="<?php echo
        $row['first_name']; ?>"><br>
    Last Name: <input type="text" name="last_name" value="<?php echo
        $row['last_name']; ?>"><br>
    Email: <input type="text" name="email" value="<?php echo $row['email'];
?>"><br>
    City: <input type="text" name="city" value="<?php echo $row['city']; ?>"><br>
    State: <input type="text" name="state" value="<?php echo $row['state'];
?>"><br>
    Hobbies/Interests: (choose at least one)<br>
    <select name="hobbies[]" size="10" multiple>
    <option value="Golfing"<?php if (in_array("Golfing", $hobbies)) echo "
selected";
        ?>>Golfing</option>
    <option value="Hunting"<?php if (in_array("Hunting", $hobbies)) echo "
selected";
        ?>>Hunting</option>
    <option value="Reading"<?php if (in_array("Reading", $hobbies)) echo "
selected";
        ?>>Reading</option>
    <option value="Dancing"<?php if (in_array("Dancing", $hobbies)) echo "
selected";
        ?>>Dancing</option>
    <option value="Internet"<?php if (in_array("Internet", $hobbies)) echo "
        selected"; ?>>Internet</option>
    <option value="Flying"<?php if (in_array("Flying", $hobbies)) echo "
selected";
        ?>>Flying</option>
```

```php
      <option value="Traveling"<?php if (in_array("Traveling", $hobbies)) echo "
            selected"; ?>>Traveling</option>
      <option value="Exercising"<?php if (in_array("Exercising", $hobbies)) echo "
            selected"; ?>>Exercising</option>
      <option value="Computers"<?php if (in_array("Computers", $hobbies)) echo "
            selected"; ?>>Computers</option>
      <option value="Other Than Listed"<?php if (in_array("Other Than Listed",
            $hobbies)) echo " selected"; ?>>Other Than Listed</option>
      </select><br><br>
      <input type="submit" name="submit" value="Update">
      </form>
<?php
}
else
{
      $query = "SELECT * FROM user_info WHERE id = '" . $_GET['id'] . "';";
      $result = mysql_query($query) or die(mysql_error());

      $row = mysql_fetch_array($result);
      $hobbies = explode(", ", $row['hobbies'])
?>
      <form action="update_user.php" method="post">
      <input type="hidden" name="id" value="<?php echo $_GET['id']; ?>">
      Username: <input type="text" name="username" value="<?php echo
$row['username'];
            ?>"><br>
      Password: <input type="password" name="password" value=""> Not displayed<br>
      First Name: <input type="text" name="first_name" value="<?php Echo
            $row['first_name']; ?>"><br>
      Last Name: <input type="text" name="last_name" value="<?php Echo
            $row['last_name']; ?>"><br>
      Email: <input type="text" name="email" value="<?php echo $row['email'];
?>"><br>
      City: <input type="text" name="city" value="<?php echo $row['city']; ?>"><br>
      State: <input type="text" name="state" value="<?php echo $row['state'];
?>"><br>
      Hobbies/Interests: (choose at least one)<br>
      <select name="hobbies[]" size="10" multiple>
      <option value="Golfing"<?php if (in_array("Golfing", $hobbies)) echo "
selected";
            ?>>Golfing</option>
      <option value="Hunting"<?php if (in_array("Hunting", $hobbies)) echo "
selected";
            ?>>Hunting</option>
      <option value="Reading"<?php if (in_array("Reading", $hobbies)) echo "
selected";
            ?>>Reading</option>
      <option value="Dancing"<?php if (in_array("Dancing", $hobbies)) echo "
selected";
            ?>>Dancing</option>
      <option value="Internet"<?php if (in_array("Internet", $hobbies)) echo "
            selected"; ?>>Internet</option>
      <option value="Flying"<?php if (in_array("Flying", $hobbies)) echo "
selected";
```

```
        ?>>Flying</option>
    <option value="Traveling"<?php if (in_array("Traveling", $hobbies)) echo "
        selected"; ?>>Traveling</option>
    <option value="Exercising"<?php if (in_array("Exercising", $hobbies)) echo "
        selected"; ?>>Exercising</option>
    <option value="Computers"<?php if (in_array("Computers", $hobbies)) echo "
        selected"; ?>>Computers</option>
    <option value="Other Than Listed"<?php if (in_array("Other Than Listed",
        $hobbies)) echo " selected"; ?>>Other Than Listed</option>
    </select><br><br>
    <input type="submit" name="submit" value="Update">   <input type="button"
        value="Cancel" onclick="history.go(-1);">
    </form>
<?php
}
?>
</body>
</html>
```

9. Finally, create the ninth file, `delete_user.php`:

```php
<?php
session_start();
include "auth_admin.inc.php";
include "conn.inc.php";
if ($_SESSION['admin_level'] == "1")
{
    if ($_POST['submit'] == "Yes")
    {
        $query_delete = "DELETE FROM user_info WHERE id = '" . $_POST['id'] .
            "';";
        $result_delete = mysql_query($query_delete) or die(mysql_error());

        $_SESSION['user_logged'] = "";
        $_SESSION['user_password'] = "";

        header("Refresh: 5; URL=admin_area.php");
        echo "Account has been deleted! You are being sent to the admin
            area!<br>";
        echo "(If your browser doesn't support this, <a
            href=\"admin_area.php\">click here</a>)";
        die();
    }
    else
    {
?>
        <html>
        <head>
        <title>Beginning PHP, Apache, MySQL Web Development</title>
        <body>
        <h1>Admin Area</h1>
        Are you sure you want to delete this user's account?<br>
        There is no way to retrieve your account once you confirm!<br>
```

```
              <form action="delete_user.php" method="post">
              <input type="hidden" name="id" value="<?php echo $_GET['id']; ?>">
              <input type="submit" name="submit" value="Yes">   <input
                  type="button" value=" No " onclick="history.go(-1);">
              </form>
              </body>
              </html>
        <?php
          }
      }
      else
      {
      ?>
      You don't have a high enough privilege to delete a user.<br>
      <a href="admin_area.php">Click here</a> to go back.
      <?php
      }
      ?>
      </body>
      </html>
```

How It Works

Now we'll explain how a typical run through with an admin (we'll call him Joe) works. Some of the pages you keyed in don't really need explaining so we won't discuss those.

When our administrator goes to the admin area, Joe is told whether or not he is logged in. If he is, he can go to his personal administration area where he is able to do whatever he is allowed to do.

The authorization is the same as the previous example so you can refer to previous figures for examples of how those pages look. We will show you what screens look like when administrators with different levels log in and go to the admin area.

> *You keyed in all the code needed to do every aspect of the admin section, but this functionality is very similar to the update and delete aspects of the user section so we won't cover those.*

When an admin with a privilege level of 2 logs in, the screen should look like the one in Figure 11-17.

Now notice in Figure 11-17 that the admin logged in here is able to update the user but is not allowed to delete the user because we did a check with the first `if` statement to see what the admin's level is. Should Joe log in with a level of 1, he would see something similar to Figure 11-18.

Depending on what link he chooses and whether he has a high enough admin level, the admin will be able to update or delete the user's account. To guard against an admin of lower level trying to navigate to the delete page and supply a user ID through the query string, we inserted a line of code that checks the admin level and notifies the admin that he or she doesn't have privileges to delete a user's account. We then provide a link back to the admin area.

Now that you have learned how to use database-driven information with an administration section, you should be on your way to creating login systems for your own personal site or for your clients.

Figure 11-17

Figure 11-18

Summary

By now, you've got a good understanding of the power of PHP and its session and cookie functions, along with MySQL and database-driven information. With these two powerful programs, along with Apache, you have some great tools to further your Web development skills. Just think about the possibilities you can explore with all you learned in this chapter. You can:

❑   Restrict access to files/directories via htaccess.

❑   Use PHP to accomplish the same as htaccess but with more control and functionality.

❑   Store user and admin information in a database to utilize database-driven logins.

❑   Create a registration system for users to sign up with the required and optional fields.

❑   Use cookies to retain login information between sessions.

❑   Create a navigation system dependent on whether or not a user has logged in.

Building a Content Management System

Whatever the reason, people these days seem to get bored easily. One of your jobs as the Web site administrator is not only to figure out how to get as many people to visit your site as possible but how to keep them there and keep them coming *back*.

There are many things you can focus on to get the masses to your site, such as word of mouth, advertising, and search engines. To keep your users at your site, the experts give plenty of hints, such as making your site easy to navigate, making sure your pages load quickly, and giving the user a personal experience. Getting your users to return, however, is how you keep your site going over time.

Getting Your Users to Return

Take a moment to think about all the sites you return to. You know . . . the ones you have saved in your bookmark list in your browser. With the exception of sites you had to visit such as those in the "research" folder, what do most of those sites have in common?

Most likely, each site periodically has new information. You might visit a news site each day or look up the weather in your area. Perhaps you are interested in your daily horoscope, or maybe you belong to an online message board and would like to read new posts. In each case, the content gets updated on a regular basis—sometimes daily, sometimes weekly, and sometimes even hourly. Can you imagine how much work the Web site developers must have to do to update the content every day?

Actually, if the site is designed well, the designer shouldn't have to enter *any* content.

Content

According to the Merriam-Webster dictionary, the term "content" refers to the "events, physical detail, and information in a work of art."

Wow . . . "a work of art." That might be stretching it a little bit, but your Web site is certainly a collection of events, details, and information. In other words, your site contains lots of content. You don't want to have to maintain all that content, do you? It would be very nice to offload some of that work to others.

In fact, all a Web site developer should ever have to do is maintain the site design itself (update some HTML, change a background color, fix a bug in the PHP code, for example). The content should be completely separate from the design of the site, and should be maintained by other people. Because the content is separate from the design, those content people don't have to know anything about Web site design! But once you have your content separated, you need to figure out how to manage it.

Management

Assuming you have a lot of content, entering it into your site will most likely take a lot of work. What you need to do is come up with a way to organize it, categorize it, and push the content to your Web site. You will need a number of people, each assigned a certain role, working together to create the content and mold it into the appropriate form for presentation on the Web site.

Of course, you want this process to be efficient, and you definitely need to have the appropriate tools to the do the job.

System

Chapter 9 showed you how to create your own databases and tables and how to create Web pages used to insert, delete, update, and retrieve the information in those tables. In Chapter 11, you learned how to authenticate and recognize your users by making them log in to your Web site. Armed with this knowledge, we could create a system of Web pages designed to allow users to create new content (authors), edit that content (editors), and publish it. By assigning users to certain roles, you can manage who has access to certain functions within the site.

Putting It All Together

So, it seems that we need a group of Web site pages and tables, and an organized set of rules, that will give us the means to gather information, format it, and present it to the world for its enjoyment. In other words, we need a *system* in place to allow us to *manage* our Web site *content* (separately from the site design).

We need a Content Management System (or CMS, as we'll refer to it from now on).

There are many degrees of content management. On some sites, this might simply refer to a message board, where users sign up to post messages to each other about their favorite color of lint. Another site might have reporters in the field writing news stories and sending them in to be published online. Yet another site might not only allow users to update content, but will allow administrators to change the layout of the site, including colors and images.

As you have no doubt figured out, the term *CMS* refers not only to the application used to enter content but to the people responsible for entering content, and to the rules they must follow. Without proper rules, and without the people to make it happen, no CMS application in the world is going to help you.

It's up to you to find the people. We'll help you establish the rules. Are you ready? Good, let's get started.

Getting Started

Typically, this is where we throw you into a "Try It Out" section and have you enter code. shortly. First, we want to let you know that this is a relatively large application, larger than ⌐y you have done so far in this book. If you don't want to type it all in, that's not a problem—just go to the Web site and download it. Just make sure you go through the "How It Works" section to learn and understand the important concepts. You can download the code from here:

```
www.wrox.com
```

The CMS application you are going to build will allow registered users to post articles. Those articles will be labeled "pending" until a user with the proper permissions publishes the article. Once it's published, it will show up as the newest article on the home page. Unregistered users will be able to read articles but will not be able to post new ones.

Registered users will also be able to post comments about an article. When a visitor views a full article, all comments will be displayed below it. Sound simple? We're going to do it with about 20 PHP pages. That may sound like a lot, but it's fairly typical of a standard Web application such as this. There are pages for display (index, admin, pending articles, article review, and so on), editing (compose, user account, control panel), and transaction files (for users and articles). There are also some files used as includes (such as header and footer). Don't worry—some are only a few lines long. The whole application contains around 1,000 lines of code, which is pretty short by many application standards.

Let's do some coding.

Try It Out   The Content Management System Application

As we mentioned, there are around 20 PHP pages. Enter each of these files in your favorite PHP editor, and save them with the given filename. We're going to give you the filename of each one, and introductions whenever necessary. Make sure all files are saved in the same directory on your Web server. Ours are saved in a directory called "CMS."

1. The first file is conn.php. This file will go at the top of each page in the application where you need to connect to the database.

    Be sure to enter in your own host, username, password, and database. (If you don't have a database created yet, you'll need to create one first. Chapter 9 helps you with that if you need it.)

```php
<?php

define('SQL_HOST','yourhost');
define('SQL_USER','joeuser');
define('SQL_PASS','yourpassword');
define('SQL_DB','yourdatabase');

$conn = mysql_connect(SQL_HOST,SQL_USER,SQL_PASS)
  or die('Could not connect to the database; ' . mysql_error());

mysql_select_db(SQL_DB,$conn)
  or die('Could not select database; ' . mysql_error());

?>
```

2. Now you need to create your database tables. You can do this on your MySQL server, or you can simply use the following `cmstables.php` file. It will create your tables, as well as insert your first user so that you can begin administering the site immediately.

```php
<?php
require_once 'conn.php';

$sql = <<<EOS
CREATE TABLE IF NOT EXISTS cms_access_levels (
 access_lvl tinyint(4) NOT NULL auto_increment,
 access_name varchar(50) NOT NULL default '',
 PRIMARY KEY (access_lvl)
)
EOS;
$result = mysql_query($sql) or die(mysql_error());

$sql = "INSERT IGNORE INTO cms_access_levels
 VALUES (1,'User')";
$result = mysql_query($sql) or die(mysql_error());
$sql = "INSERT IGNORE INTO cms_access_levels
 VALUES (2,'Moderator')";
$result = mysql_query($sql) or die(mysql_error());
$sql = "INSERT IGNORE INTO cms_access_levels
 VALUES (3,'Administrator')";
$result = mysql_query($sql) or die(mysql_error());

$sql = <<<EOS
CREATE TABLE IF NOT EXISTS cms_articles (
 article_id int(11) NOT NULL auto_increment,
 author_id int(11) NOT NULL default '0',
 is_published tinyint(1) NOT NULL default '0',
 date_submitted datetime NOT NULL default '0000-00-00 00:00:00',
 date_published datetime NOT NULL default '0000-00-00 00:00:00',
 title varchar(255) NOT NULL default '',
 body mediumtext NOT NULL,
 PRIMARY KEY (article_id),
 KEY IdxArticle (author_id,date_submitted),
 FULLTEXT KEY IdxText (title,body)
)
EOS;
$result = mysql_query($sql) or die(mysql_error());

$sql = <<<EOS
CREATE TABLE IF NOT EXISTS cms_comments (
 comment_id int(11) NOT NULL auto_increment,
 article_id int(11) NOT NULL default '0',
 comment_date datetime NOT NULL default '0000-00-00 00:00:00',
 comment_user int(11) NOT NULL default '0',
 comment text NOT NULL,
 PRIMARY KEY (comment_id),
 KEY IdxComment (article_id)
)
EOS;
```

```
$result = mysql_query($sql) or die(mysql_error());

$sql = <<<EOS
CREATE TABLE IF NOT EXISTS cms_users (
 user_id int(11) NOT NULL auto_increment,
 e-mail varchar(255) NOT NULL default '',
 passwd varchar(50) NOT NULL default '',
 name varchar(100) NOT NULL default '',
 access_lvl tinyint(4) NOT NULL default '1',
 PRIMARY KEY (user_id),
 UNIQUE KEY uniq_e-mail (e-mail)
)
EOS;
$result = mysql_query($sql) or die(mysql_error());

$admine-mail = "admin@yoursite.com";
$adminpass = "admin";
$adminname = "Admin";

$sql = "INSERT IGNORE INTO cms_users VALUES (NULL,
 '$admine-mail', '$adminpass', '$adminname', 3)";
$result = mysql_query($sql) or die(mysql_error());

echo "<html><head><title>CMS Tables Created</title></head><body>";
echo "CMS Tables created. Here is your initial login information:\n";
echo "<ul><li><strong>login</strong>: " . $admine-mail . "</li>\n";
echo "<li><strong>password</strong>: " . $adminpass . "</li></ul>\n";
echo "<a href='login.php'>Login</a> to the site now.";
echo "</body></html>"
?>
```

3. Some functions are used on many different pages. Those are included in the file outputfunctions .php, which is included at the top of each appropriate page:

```php
<?php

function trimBody($theText, $lmt=500, $s_chr="\n", $s_cnt=2) {
 $pos = 0;
 $trimmed = FALSE;
 for ($i = 1; $i <= $s_cnt; $i++) {
  if ($tmp = strpos($theText,$s_chr,$pos)) {
   $pos = $tmp;
   $trimmed = TRUE;
  } else {
   $pos = strlen($theText) - 1;
   $trimmed = FALSE;
   break;
  }
 }
 $theText = substr($theText,0,$pos);

 if (strlen($theText) > $lmt) {
  $theText = substr($theText,0,$lmt);
```

```
   $theText = substr($theText,0,strrpos($theText,' '));
   $trimmed = TRUE;
 }
 if ($trimmed) $theText .= '...';
 return $theText;
}

function outputStory($article, $only_snippet=FALSE) {
 global $conn;

 if ($article) {
  $sql = "SELECT ar.*,usr.name " .
      "FROM cms_articles ar " .
      "LEFT OUTER JOIN cms_users usr " .
      "ON ar.author_id = usr.user_id " .
      "WHERE ar.article_id = " . $article;
  $result = mysql_query($sql,$conn);

  if ($row = mysql_fetch_array($result)) {
   echo '<h3>' . htmlspecialchars($row['title']) . "</h3>\n";
   echo "<h5><div class='byline'>By: " .
      htmlspecialchars($row['name']) .
      "</div>";
   echo "<div class='pubdate'>";
   if ($row['is_published'] == 1) {
    echo date("F j, Y",strtotime($row['date_published']));
   } else {
    echo "not yet published";
   }
   echo "</div></h5>\n";
   if ($only_snippet) {
    echo "<p>\n";
    echo nl2br(htmlspecialchars(trimBody($row['body'])));
    echo "</p>\n";
    echo '<h4><a href="viewarticle.php?article=' .
       $row['article_id'] . "\">Full Story...</a></h4><br />\n";
   } else {
    echo "<p>\n";
    echo nl2br(htmlspecialchars($row['body']));
    echo "</p>\n";
   }
  }
 }
}

function showComments($article,$showLink=TRUE) {
 global $conn;
 if ($article) {
  $sql = "SELECT is_published " .
      "FROM cms_articles " .
      "WHERE article_id=" . $article;
  $result = mysql_query($sql,$conn)
   or die('Could not look up comments; ' . mysql_error());

  $row = mysql_fetch_array($result);
```

```php
    $is_published = $row['is_published'];

    $sql = "SELECT co.*,usr.name,usr.e-mail " .
        "FROM cms_comments co " .
        "LEFT OUTER JOIN cms_users usr " .
        "ON co.comment_user = usr.user_id " .
        "WHERE co.article_id=" . $article .
        " ORDER BY co.comment_date DESC";
    $result = mysql_query($sql,$conn)
     or die('Could not look up comments; ' . mysql_error());

    if ($showLink) {
     echo '<h4>' . mysql_num_rows($result) . 'Comments';
     if (isset($_SESSION['user_id']) and $is_published) {
      echo ' / <a href="comment.php?article=' . $_GET['article'] .
        '">Add one</a>';
     }
     echo "</h4>\n";
    }

    if (mysql_num_rows($result)) {
     echo "<div class=\"scroller\">\n";
     while ($row = mysql_fetch_array($result)) {
      echo "<span class='commentName'>" .
      htmlspecialchars($row['name']) .
      "</span><span class='commentDate'> (" .
      date("l F j, Y H:i",strtotime($row['comment_date'])) .
        ")</span>\n";
      echo "<p class='commentText'>\n" .
        nl2br(htmlspecialchars($row['comment'])) .
        "\n</p>\n";
     }
     echo "</div>\n";
    }
    echo "<br />\n";
   }
  }
?>
```

4. Two more files are included in various pages, header.php and footer.php. Enter those next. First, header.php:

```php
<?php session_start(); ?>
<html>
<head>
<title>BPAM CMS</title>
</head>
<body>
<div id="logobar">
 <div id="logoblob">
  <h1>Comic Book Appreciation</h1>
 </div>
<?php
 if (isset($_SESSION['name'])) {
  echo ' <div id="logowelcome">';
```

```
    echo '  Currently logged in as: '.$_SESSION['name'];
    echo ' </div>';
  }
?>

</div>
<div id="navright">
 <form method="get" action="search.php">
 <p class='head'>Search</p>
 <p>
   <input id="searchkeywords" type="text" name="keywords"
<?php
   if (isset($_GET['keywords'])) {
    echo ' value="' . htmlspecialchars($_GET['keywords']) . '" ';
   }
?>
   />
   <input id="searchbutton" class="submit" type="submit"
   value="Search" />
  </p>
 </form>
</div>
<div id="maincolumn">
 <div id='navigation'>
<?php
 echo '<a href="index.php">Articles</a>';
 if (!isset($_SESSION['user_id'])) {
  echo ' | <a href="login.php">Login</a>';
 } else {
  echo ' | <a href="compose.php">Compose</a>';

  if ($_SESSION['access_lvl'] > 1) {
   echo ' | <a href="pending.php">Review</a>';
  }

  if ($_SESSION['access_lvl'] > 2) {
   echo ' | <a href="admin.php">Admin</a>';
  }
  echo ' | <a href="cpanel.php">Control Panel</a>';
  echo ' | <a href="transact-user.php?action=Logout">Logout</a>';
 }
?>
 </div>
 <div id="articles">
```

5. And now enter footer.php. (This one's a toughie. You might want to take a break first.)

```
 </div>
 </div>
 </body>
</html>
```

6. Now another big one, `http.php`. This one is used for redirections:

```php
<?php
function redirect($url) {
 if (!headers_sent()) {
  header('Location: http://' . $_SERVER['HTTP_HOST'] .
   dirname($_SERVER['PHP_SELF']) . '/' . $url);
 } else {
  die('Could not redirect; Headers already sent (output).');
 }
}
?>
```

Whew. All this coding, and nothing yet to show on the screen! There are two more files to go that don't output anything. These are the workhorses of the application, so they are a bit longer than the rest.

7. First, create `transact-user.php`:

```php
<?php
require_once 'conn.php';
require_once 'http.php';

if (isset($_REQUEST['action'])) {
 switch ($_REQUEST['action']) {
  case 'Login':
   if (isset($_POST['e-mail'])
     and isset($_POST['passwd']))
   {
    $sql = "SELECT user_id,access_lvl,name " .
        "FROM cms_users " .
        "WHERE e-mail='" . $_POST['e-mail'] . "' " .
        "AND passwd='" . $_POST['passwd'] . "'";
    $result = mysql_query($sql,$conn)
     or die('Could not look up user information; ' . mysql_error());

    if ($row = mysql_fetch_array($result)) {
     session_start();
     $_SESSION['user_id'] = $row['user_id'];
     $_SESSION['access_lvl'] = $row['access_lvl'];
     $_SESSION['name'] = $row['name'];
    }
   }
   redirect('index.php');
   break;

  case 'Logout':
   session_start();
   session_unset();
   session_destroy();

   redirect('index.php');
```

```
    break;

case 'Create Account':
 if (isset($_POST['name'])
   and isset($_POST['e-mail'])
   and isset($_POST['passwd'])
   and isset($_POST['passwd2'])
   and $_POST['passwd'] == $_POST['passwd2'])
 {
  $sql = "INSERT INTO cms_users (e-mail,name,passwd) " .
      "VALUES ('" . $_POST['e-mail'] . "','" .
      $_POST['name'] . "','" . $_POST['passwd'] . "')";

  mysql_query($sql,$conn)
   or die('Could not create user account; ' . mysql_error());

  session_start();
  $_SESSION['user_id'] = mysql_insert_id($conn);
  $_SESSION['access_lvl'] = 1;
  $_SESSION['name'] = $_POST['name'];
 }
 redirect('index.php');
 break;

case 'Modify Account':
 if (isset($_POST['name'])
   and isset($_POST['e-mail'])
   and isset($_POST['accesslvl'])
   and isset($_POST['userid']))
 {
  $sql = "UPDATE cms_users " .
      "SET e-mail='" . $_POST['e-mail'] .
      "', name='" . $_POST['name'] .
      "', access_lvl=" . $_POST['accesslvl'] . " " .
      " WHERE user_id=" . $_POST['userid'];

  mysql_query($sql,$conn)
   or die('Could not update user account; ' . mysql_error());
 }
 redirect('admin.php');
 break;

case 'Send my reminder!':
 if (isset($_POST['e-mail'])) {
  $sql = "SELECT passwd FROM cms_users " .
      "WHERE e-mail='" . $_POST['e-mail'] . "'";

  $result = mysql_query($sql,$conn)
   or die('Could not look up password; ' . mysql_error());

  if (mysql_num_rows($result)) {
   $row = mysql_fetch_array($result);

   $subject = 'Comic site password reminder';
   $body = "Just a reminder, your password for the " .
```

```
                        "Comic Book Appreciation site is: " . $row['passwd'] .
                        "\n\nYou can use this to log in at http://" .
                        $_SERVER['HTTP_HOST'] .
                        dirname($_SERVER['PHP_SELF']) . '/';

            mail($_POST['e-mail'],$subject,$body)
              or die('Could not send reminder e-mail.');
          }
        }
      redirect('login.php');
      break;

    case 'Change my info':
      session_start();

      if (isset($_POST['name'])
        and isset($_POST['e-mail'])
        and isset($_SESSION['user_id']))
      {
       $sql = "UPDATE cms_users " .
            "SET e-mail='" . $_POST['e-mail'] .
            "', name='" . $_POST['name'] . "' " .
            "WHERE user_id=" . $_SESSION['user_id'];

        mysql_query($sql,$conn)
          or die('Could not update user account; ' . mysql_error());
      }
      redirect('cpanel.php');
      break;
   }
 }
?>
```

8. Now enter `transact-article.php`:

```
<?
session_start();
require_once 'conn.php';
require_once 'http.php';

if (isset($_REQUEST['action'])) {
 switch ($_REQUEST['action']) {
  case 'Submit New Article':
   if (isset($_POST['title'])
     and isset($_POST['body'])
     and isset($_SESSION['user_id']))
   {
    $sql = "INSERT INTO cms_articles " .
        "(title,body,author_id,date_submitted) " .
        "VALUES ('" . $_POST['title'] .
        "','" . $_POST['body'] .
        "'," . $_SESSION['user_id'] . ",'" .
        date("Y-m-d H:i:s",time()) . "')";

    mysql_query($sql,$conn)
```

```
     or die('Could not submit article; ' . mysql_error());
  }
  redirect('index.php');
  break;

case 'Edit':
  redirect('compose.php?a=edit&article=' . $_POST['article']);
  break;

case 'Save Changes':
  if (isset($_POST['title'])
    and isset($_POST['body'])
    and isset($_POST['article']))
  {
   $sql = "UPDATE cms_articles " .
       "SET title='" . $_POST['title'] .
       "', body='" . $_POST['body'] . "', date_submitted='" .
       date("Y-m-d H:i:s",time()) . "' " .
       "WHERE article_id=" . $_POST['article'];
   if (isset($_POST['authorid'])) {
    $sql .= " AND author_id=" . $_POST['authorid'];
   }

   mysql_query($sql,$conn)
    or die('Could not update article; ' . mysql_error());
  }

  if (isset($_POST['authorid'])) {
   redirect('cpanel.php');
  } else {
   redirect('pending.php');
  }
  break;

case 'Publish':
  if ($_POST['article']) {
   $sql = "UPDATE cms_articles " .
       "SET is_published=1,date_published='" .
       date("Y-m-d H:i:s",time()) . "' " .
       "WHERE article_id=" . $_POST['article'];
   mysql_query($sql,$conn)
    or die('Could not publish article; ' . mysql_error());
  }
  redirect('pending.php');
  break;

case 'Retract':
  if ($_POST['article']) {
   $sql = "UPDATE cms_articles " .
       "SET is_published=0,date_published='' " .
       "WHERE article_id=" . $_POST['article'];
   mysql_query($sql,$conn)
    or die('Could not retract article; ' . mysql_error());
  }
  redirect('pending.php');
```

```php
      break;

  case 'Delete':
    if ($_POST['article']) {
     $sql = "DELETE FROM cms_articles " .
         "WHERE is_published=0 " .
          "AND " . "article_id=" . $_POST['article'];
     mysql_query($sql,$conn)
       or die('Could not delete article; ' . mysql_error());
    }
    redirect('pending.php');
    break;

  case 'Submit Comment':
    if (isset($_POST['article'])
      and $_POST['article']
      and isset($_POST['comment'])
      and $_POST['comment'])
    {
     $sql = "INSERT INTO cms_comments " .
         "(article_id,comment_date,comment_user,comment) " .
         "VALUES (" . $_POST['article'] . ",'" .
         date("Y-m-d H:i:s",time()) .
         "'," . $_SESSION['user_id'] .
         ",'" . $_POST['comment'] . "');";
     mysql_query($sql,$conn)
       or die('Could add comment; ' . mysql_error());
    }
    redirect('viewarticle.php?article=' . $_POST['article']);
    break;

  case 'remove':
    if (isset($_GET['article'])
      and isset($_SESSION['user_id']))
    {
     $sql = "DELETE FROM cms_articles " .
         "WHERE article_id=" . $_GET['article'] .
         " AND author_id=" . $_SESSION['user_id'];
     mysql_query($sql,$conn)
       or die('Could not remove article; ' . mysql_error());
    }
    redirect('cpanel.php');
    break;
 }
} else {
 redirect('index.php');
}
?>
```

9. Okay, time to enter the "real" pages. Let's do these in order of largest files to smallest, so things will go a little quicker at the end. Let's start off with cpanel.php:

```php
<?php
require_once 'conn.php';
require_once 'header.php';
```

```php
$sql = "SELECT name,e-mail " .
    "FROM cms_users " .
    "WHERE user_id=" . $_SESSION['user_id'];
$result = mysql_query($sql,$conn)
 or die('Could not look up user data; ' . mysql_error());

$user = mysql_fetch_array($result);
?>
<form method="post" action="transact-user.php">

<p>Name:<br />
 <input type="text" id="name" name="name"
  value="<?php echo htmlspecialchars($user['name']); ?>" /></p>

<p>E-mail:<br />
 <input type="text" id="e-mail" name="e-mail"
  value="<?php echo htmlspecialchars($user['e-mail']); ?>" /></p>

<p><input type="submit" class="submit" name="action"
  value="Change my info" /></p>

</form>

<h2>Pending Articles</h2>
<div class="scroller">
 <table>
<?php

$sql = "SELECT article_id, title, date_submitted " .
    "FROM cms_articles " .
    "WHERE is_published=0 " .
    "AND author_id=" . $_SESSION['user_id'] . " " .
    "ORDER BY date_submitted";
$result = mysql_query($sql,$conn)
 or die('Could not get list of pending articles; ' . mysql_error());

if (mysql_num_rows($result) == 0) {
 echo "  <em>No pending articles available</em>";
} else {
 while ($row = mysql_fetch_array($result)) {
  echo "<tr>\n";
  echo '<td><a href="reviewarticle.php?article=' .
     $row['article_id'] . '">' . htmlspecialchars($row['title']) .
     "</a> (submitted " .
     date("F j, Y",strtotime($row['date_submitted'])) .
     ")</td>\n";
  echo "</tr>\n";
 }
}
?>
 </table>
</div>
<br />

<h2>Published Articles</h2>
```

```
<div class="scroller">
 <table>
<?php

$sql = "SELECT article_id, title,date_published " .
    "FROM cms_articles " .
    "WHERE is_published=1 " .
    "AND author_id=" . $_SESSION['user_id'] . " " .
    "ORDER BY date_submitted";
$result = mysql_query($sql,$conn)
 or die('Could not get list of pending articles; ' . mysql_error());

if (mysql_num_rows($result) == 0) {
 echo "  <em>No published articles available</em>";
} else {
 while ($row = mysql_fetch_array($result)) {
  echo "<tr>\n";
  echo '<td><a href="viewarticle.php?article=' .
    $row['article_id'] . '">' . htmlspecialchars($row['title']) .
    "</a> (published " .
     date("F j, Y",strtotime($row['date_published'])) .
     ")</td>\n";
  echo "</tr>\n";
 }
}
?>
 </table>
</div>
<br />
<?php require_once 'footer.php'; ?>
```

10. Create useraccount.php:

```
<?php
require_once 'conn.php';

$userid = '';
$name = '';
$e-mail = '';
$password = '';
$accesslvl = '';
if (isset($_GET['userid'])) {
 $sql = "SELECT * FROM cms_users WHERE user_id=" . $_GET['userid'];
 $result = mysql_query($sql,$conn)
  or die('Could not look up user data; ' . mysql_error());

 $row = mysql_fetch_array($result);
 $userid = $_GET['userid'];
 $name = $row['name'];
 $e-mail = $row['e-mail'];
 $accesslvl = $row['access_lvl'];
}

require_once 'header.php';
```

```php
echo "<form method=\"post\" action=\"transact-user.php\">\n";

if ($userid) {
 echo "<h1>Modify Account</h1>\n";
} else {
 echo "<h1>Create Account</h1>\n";
}
?>

<p>
 Full name:<br />
 <input type="text" class="txtinput" name="name" maxlength="100"
  value="<?php echo htmlspecialchars($name); ?>" />
</p>
<p>
 E-mail Address:<br />
 <input type="text" class="txtinput" name="e-mail" maxlength="255"
  value="<?php echo htmlspecialchars($e-mail); ?>" />
</p>
<?php

if (isset($_SESSION['access_lvl'])
  and $_SESSION['access_lvl'] == 3)
{
 echo "<fieldset>\n";
 echo " <legend>Access Level</legend>\n";

 $sql = "SELECT * FROM cms_access_levels ORDER BY access_lvl DESC";
 $result = mysql_query($sql,$conn)
  or die('Could not list access levels; ' . mysql_error());

 while ($row = mysql_fetch_array($result)) {
  echo ' <input type="radio" class="radio" id="acl_' .
    $row['access_lvl'] . '" name="accesslvl" value="' .
    $row['access_lvl'] . '" ';

  if ($row['access_lvl'] == $accesslvl) {
   echo 'checked="checked" ';
  }
  echo '/>' . $row['access_name'] . "<br />\n";
 }
?>
</fieldset>
<p>
 <input type="hidden" name="userid" value="<?php echo $userid; ?>" />
 <input type="submit" class="submit" name="action"
  value="Modify Account" />
</p>
<?php } else { ?>
<p>
 Password:<br />
 <input type="password" id="passwd" name="passwd" maxlength="50" />
</p>
<p>
```

```
 Password (again):<br />
 <input type="password" id="passwd2" name="passwd2" maxlength="50" />
</p>
<p>
 <input type="submit" class="submit" name="action"
  value="Create Account" />
</p>
<?php } ?>
</form>

<?php require_once 'footer.php'; ?>
```

11. Create `compose.php`:

```php
<?php

require_once 'conn.php';

$title = '';
$body = '';
$article = '';
$authorid = '';
if (isset($_GET['a'])
  and $_GET['a'] == 'edit'
  and isset($_GET['article'])
  and $_GET['article']) {
 $sql = "SELECT title,body,author_id FROM cms_articles WHERE article_id=" .
    $_GET['article'];
 $result = mysql_query($sql,$conn)
  or die('Could not retrieve article data; ' . mysql_error());

 $row = mysql_fetch_array($result);

 $title = $row['title'];
 $body = $row['body'];
 $article = $_GET['article'];
 $authorid = $row['author_id'];
}
require_once 'header.php';
?>

<form method="post" action="transact-article.php">

<h2>Compose Article</h2>

<p>
 Title:<br />
 <input type="text" class="title" name="title" maxlength="255"
  value="<?php echo htmlspecialchars($title); ?>" />
</p>
<p>
 Body:<br />
 <textarea class="body" name="body" rows="10" cols="60"><?php
```

```
        echo htmlspecialchars($body); ?></textarea>
</p>
<p>
<?php
echo '<input type="hidden" name="article" value="' .
    $article . "\" />\n";

if ($_SESSION['access_lvl'] < 2) {
 echo '<input type="hidden" name="authorid" value="' .
    $authorid . "\" />\n";
}

if ($article) {
 echo '<input type="submit" class="submit" name="action" ' .
    "value=\"Save Changes\" />\n";
} else {
 echo '<input type="submit" class="submit" name="action" ' .
    "value=\"Submit New Article\" />\n";
}
?>
</p>
</form>

<?php require_once 'footer.php'; ?>
```

12. Create `reviewarticle.php`:

```
<?php
require_once 'conn.php';
require_once 'outputfunctions.php';
require_once 'header.php';
?>

<form method="post" action="transact-article.php">

<h2>Article Review</h2>
<?php

outputStory($_GET['article']);

$sql = "SELECT ar.*, usr.name, usr.access_lvl " .
    "FROM cms_articles ar INNER JOIN cms_users usr " .
    "ON ar.author_id = usr.user_id " .
    "WHERE article_id=" . $_GET['article'];

$result = mysql_query($sql,$conn)
 or die('Could not retrieve article info; ' . mysql_error());

$row = mysql_fetch_array($result);

if ($row['date_published'] and $row['is_published']) {
 echo '<h4>Published: ' .
    date("l F j, Y H:i",strtotime($row['date_published'])) .
```

```
          "</h4>\n";
}
echo "<p><br />\n";
if ($row['is_published']) {
 $buttonType = "Retract";
} else {
 $buttonType = "Publish";
}

echo "<input type='submit' class='submit' " .
    "name='action' value='Edit' /> ";
if (($row['access_lvl'] > 1) or ($_SESSION['access_lvl'] > 1)) {
 echo "<input type='submit' class='submit' " .
     "name='action' value='$buttonType' /> ";
}
echo "<input type='submit' class='submit' " .
    "name='action' value='Delete' /> ";
?>

<input type="hidden" name="article"
 value="<?php echo $_GET['article'] ?> " />
</p>

</form>

<?php require_once 'footer.php'; ?>
```

13. Create `pending.php`:

```
<?php
require_once 'conn.php';
require_once 'header.php';

$a_artTypes = array(
 "Pending" => "submitted",
 "Published" => "published"
);

echo "<h2>Article Availability</h2>\n";
$i=-1;
foreach ($a_artTypes as $k => $v) {
 $i++;
 echo "<h3>" . $k . " Articles</h3>\n";
 echo "<p>\n";
 echo " <div class='scroller'>\n";

 $sql = "SELECT article_id, title, date_".$v.
     " FROM cms_articles " .
     "WHERE is_published=" . $i .
     " ORDER BY title";

 $result = mysql_query($sql,$conn)
   or die('Could not get list of pending articles; ' . mysql_error());
```

```php
    if (mysql_num_rows($result) == 0) {
     echo "  <em>No " . $k . " articles available</em>";
    } else {
     while ($row = mysql_fetch_array($result)) {
      echo '  <a href="reviewarticle.php?article=' .
        $row['article_id'] . '">' . htmlspecialchars($row['title']) .
        "</a> ($v " .
        date("F j, Y",strtotime($row['date_'.$v])) .
        ")<br />\n";
     }
    }
    echo "  </div>\n";
    echo "</p>\n";
   }

   require_once 'footer.php';
   ?>
```

14. Create `admin.php`:

```php
<?php

require_once 'conn.php';
require_once 'header.php';

$a_users = array(1 => "Users","Moderators","Admins");

function echoUserList($lvl) {
 global $a_users;
 $sql = "SELECT user_id, name, e-mail FROM cms_users " .
    "WHERE access_lvl = $lvl ORDER BY name";

 $result = mysql_query($sql) or die(mysql_error());

 if (mysql_num_rows($result) == 0) {
  echo "<em>No " . $a_users[$lvl] . " created.</em>";
 } else {
  while ($row = mysql_fetch_array($result)) {
   if ($row['user_id'] == $_SESSION['user_id']) {
    echo htmlspecialchars($row['name']) . "<br />\n";
   } else {
    echo '<a href="useraccount.php?userid=' . $row['user_id'] .
       '" title="' . htmlspecialchars($row['e-mail']) . '">' .
       htmlspecialchars($row['name']) . "</a><br />\n";
   }
  }
 }
}
?>
<h2>User Administration</h2>
<?php
 for($i=1;$i<=3;$i++) {
  echo "<h3>". $a_users[$i] . "</h3>\n" .
```

```
  "<div class='scroller'>\n";
  echoUserList($i);
  echo "\n</div>\n";
 }
?>
<br />
<?php require_once 'footer.php'; ?>
```

15. Create `comment.php`:

```php
<?php

require_once 'conn.php';
require_once 'outputfunctions.php';
require_once 'header.php';

outputStory($_GET['article']);

?>

<h1>Add a comment</h1>

<form method="post" action="transact-article.php">

<p>
 Comment:<br />
 <textarea id="comment" name="comment" rows="10" cols="60"></textarea>
</p>

<p>
 <input type="submit" class="submit" name="action"
  value="Submit Comment" />
 <input type="hidden" name="article"
  value="<?php echo $_GET['article']; ?>" />
</p>

</form>

<?php

showComments($_GET['article'],FALSE);

require_once 'footer.php';

?>
```

16. Create `search.php`:

```php
<?php
require_once 'conn.php';
require_once 'outputfunctions.php';
require_once 'header.php';

$result = NULL;
if (isset($_GET['keywords'])) {
```

```
    $sql = "SELECT article_id FROM cms_articles " .
        "WHERE MATCH (title,body) " .
        "AGAINST ('" . $_GET['keywords'] . "') " .
        "ORDER BY MATCH (title,body) " .
        "AGAINST ('" . $_GET['keywords'] . "') DESC";

    $result = mysql_query($sql,$conn)
        or die('Could not perform search; ' . mysql_error());
}

echo "<h1>Search Results</h1>\n";

if ($result and !mysql_num_rows($result)) {
    echo "<p>No articles found that match the search terms.</p>\n";
} else {
    while ($row = mysql_fetch_array($result)) {
        outputStory($row['article_id'],TRUE);
    }
}

require_once 'footer.php';
?>
```

17. Create `login.php`:

```
<?php require_once 'header.php'; ?>

<form method="post" action="transact-user.php">

<h1>Member Login</h1>

<p>
 E-mail Address:<br />
 <input type="text" name="e-mail" maxlength="255" value="" />
</p>
<p>
 Password:<br />
 <input type="password" name="passwd" maxlength="50" />
</p>
<p>
 <input type="submit" class="submit" name="action" value="Login" />
</p>

<p>
 Not a member yet? <a href="useraccount.php">Create a new account!</a>
</p>
<p>
 <a href="forgotpass.php">Forgot your password?</a>
</p>

</form>

<?php require_once 'footer.php'; ?>
```

18. Create `index.php`:

```php
<?php
require_once 'conn.php';
require_once 'outputfunctions.php';
require_once 'header.php';

$sql = "SELECT article_id FROM cms_articles WHERE is_published=1 " .
    "ORDER BY date_published DESC";

$result = mysql_query($sql,$conn);

if (mysql_num_rows($result) == 0) {
 echo "  <br />\n";
 echo "  There are currently no articles to view.\n";
} else {
 while ($row = mysql_fetch_array($result)) {
  outputStory($row['article_id'],TRUE);
 }
}

require_once 'footer.php';
?>
```

19. Create `forgotpass.php`:

```php
<?php require_once 'header.php'; ?>

<form method="post" action="transact-user.php">

<h1>E-mail Password Reminder</h1>

<p>
 Forgot your password? Just enter your e-mail address, and we'll e-mail
 your password to you!
</p>

<p>
 E-mail Address:<br />
 <input type="text" id="e-mail" name="e-mail" />
</p>

<p>
 <input type="submit" class="submit" name="action" value="Send my reminder!" />
</p>
</form>

<?php require_once 'footer.php'; ?>
```

20. Create `viewarticle.php`:

```php
<?php
require_once 'conn.php';
require_once 'outputfunctions.php';
require_once 'header.php';
```

```
outputStory($_GET['article']);

showComments($_GET['article'],TRUE);

require_once 'footer.php';
?>
```

That last one was a doozy, huh?

Now that you have typed all of that in (except for those of you who downloaded it from the Web site), we know there may be a few parts of the application where you thought "Huh? What in the world does *this* do?" Wouldn't it be cool if there was a section where we tell you how it works? All in good time. Let's put this application through its paces first!

1.   If you have not already done so, load CMStables.php in your browser. If it runs with no errors, you should see a screen similar to Figure 12-1. It will look a little different, of course, if you used your own username, e-mail, and password values.

Figure 12-1

2. Once you have run the file, we recommend that you immediately remove it from your server. You don't want anyone getting hold of your password. We also recommend that you change your password immediately.

3. Click the Login link on the page, or open `login.php` in your browser. Enter your e-mail address and password and click the Login button (see Figure 12-2).

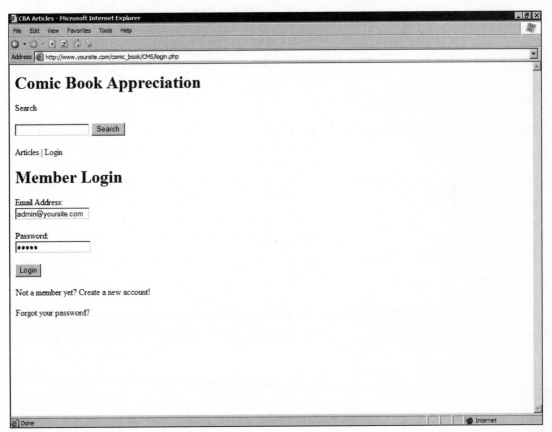

Figure 12-2

You should now see a simple screen similar to Figure 12-3. There is not much to see yet, because you haven't written any articles. You should, however, see many more menu options.

4. Click the Compose link to load `compose.php` (see Figure 12-4).

5. Enter a title and some text for the article. When you are done, click Submit New Article.

You will be taken back to the index page, but there will still be no article. The article you just wrote is pending review.

Figure 12-3

Figure 12-4

6. Click the Review link.

The Review page `pending.php` loads (see Figure 12-5) with a list of all pending and published articles. Right now, there is only one pending article—the one you just wrote.

7. Click the article.

You will be taken to `reviewarticle.php`. It should look similar to Figure 12-6. You have the option to edit, publish, or delete the article.

Figure 12-5

8. Click the Publish button. You will be taken back to `pending.php`, and the article will now be listed under Published Articles.

9. Click the Articles link, and you will be taken back to the index page. This time, the article should appear on the page (see Figure 12-7).

Figure 12-6

Figure 12-7

10. We're going to skip the next two menu items (we'll come back to them). For now, click the Logout link.

11. Next, click Login, and click "Create a new account!" You should see a screen similar to Figure 12-8.

Figure 12-8

12. Enter data into each field and click Create Account. For this example, we will enter the following:

- ❑ Full Name: George Smith
- ❑ E-mail Address: gsmith05523@hotmail.com
- ❑ Password: phprocks
- ❑ Password (again): phprocks

Once you create a new user, you will be automatically logged in as that user. You should notice that you can see the article you recently created, but you cannot see the Review or Admin menu items. Review is available to Moderators or Admins (levels 2 or 3) only, and Admin is available to Admins only (level 3). Your initial account was created at level 3, but the account you just created defaulted to level 1 (User).

13. Click Control Panel.

You should see a screen similar to the one shown in Figure 12-9. Here you can change your user information (user name and e-mail), and see what articles have been written for the site. (At this point, you have no articles pending or written.)

Figure 12-9

14. Go ahead and log out, and then log back in using your admin account. When you are logged in, click the Admin link. You should see a screen similar to Figure 12-10.

You should see George Smith (or whatever name you used) under Users. You will notice your Admin name under Admins, but it is not a link. You can alter your own account from your Control Panel.

Figure 12-10

15. Click the user listed under Users.

You should see a page similar to that in Figure 12-11. Notice that you can change the user's name and password just as you can in the Control Panel. However, notice also the addition of the Access Level option. You can set any user to be a User, Moderator, or Admin. User is the default for new users.

And that is your new CMS application. Not too complicated, is it? There are a couple of other things you can do (such as retracting a published article), but we'll leave those to you to find. For now, it's time to look under the hood to see how this thing works!

Figure 12-11

How It Works

Nineteen files make up this CMS application. An additional file is used once to create the tables, making 20 files in all. That may seem like a lot to you, but the use of transaction pages and include files increases the number substantially. If you did not have certain parts of the application broken out into separate files, you would certainly have fewer files, but each file would be *much* larger. Our primary purpose in separating out the application into so many files is to reduce code redundancy.

Connect to the Data Source

Your first step in creating this application is to connect to the database. Most of your pages will require this connection, so putting it in a separate included file is the best solution. This file is conn.php:

```
define('SQL_HOST','yourhost');
define('SQL_USER','joeuser');
define('SQL_PASS','yourpassword');
define('SQL_DB','yourdatabase');

$conn = mysql_connect(SQL_HOST,SQL_USER,SQL_PASS)
```

```
    or die('Could not connect to the database; ' . mysql_error());

 mysql_select_db(SQL_DB,$conn)
   or die('Could not select database; ' . mysql_error());
```

The code in conn.php simply defines the constants, connects to the server, and then selects the database to be used. If you are using more than one database, then you simply need to change the mysql_select_db command to access the appropriate database before running any SQL commands.

Create the Database Tables

Once conn.php is created, you can create your database tables. Do this with CMStables.php.

First, connect to the database.

```
    require_once 'conn.php';
```

Next, create the table needed for access levels. All of the fields, their datatypes, and other parameters are defined in this SQL statement. We use IF NOT EXISTS so that the CREATE command does nothing if the table already exists. If you wanted CMStables.php to always create a new, clean version of the app, then you could remove the IF NOT EXISTS and run the SQL command DROP TABLE tablename before re-creating the table.

```
$sql = <<<EOS
CREATE TABLE IF NOT EXISTS cms_access_levels (
 access_lvl tinyint(4) NOT NULL auto_increment,
 access_name varchar(50) NOT NULL default '',
 PRIMARY KEY (access_lvl)
)
EOS;
$result = mysql_query($sql) or die(mysql_error());
```

The next lines insert data into your newly created cms_access_levels table. These access levels are used throughout the CMS application to determine what different users have access to.

```
$sql = "INSERT IGNORE INTO cms_access_levels VALUES (1,'User')";
$result = mysql_query($sql) or die(mysql_error());
```

We won't include every SQL statement from CMStables.php. If you are knowledgeable enough to read this book, then we think you can figure out the rest of the SQL commands. However, we are showing you the following command to illustrate the use of keys.

```
$sql = <<<EOS
CREATE TABLE IF NOT EXISTS cms_articles (
 article_id int(11) NOT NULL auto_increment,
 author_id int(11) NOT NULL default '0',
 is_published tinyint(1) NOT NULL default '0',
 date_submitted datetime NOT NULL default '0000-00-00 00:00:00',
 date_published datetime NOT NULL default '0000-00-00 00:00:00',
 title varchar(255) NOT NULL default '',
 body mediumtext NOT NULL,
 PRIMARY KEY (article_id),
```

```
    KEY IdxArticle (author_id,date_submitted),
    FULLTEXT KEY IdxText (title,body)
)
EOS;
$result = mysql_query($sql) or die(mysql_error());
```

The PRIMARY KEY, you may remember from Chapter 9, is what ensures that each row is unique because it is the unique identifier for each row in the table.

The keyword KEY is similar to PRIMARY KEY, and in fact can be substituted for PRIMARY KEY in most cases. In this particular case, we are using KEY as a synonym for INDEX, which allows subsequent SQL statements to find data very quickly. Because we will be looking for articles by author and by date, those are the fields used to create the index.

> *For more information on how MySQL uses indexes, visit* www.mysql.com/doc/en/MySQL_indexes.html.

We also allow users of the CMS application to search for articles based on text entered in a search string. In order to perform such a search (which we allow for the title and body fields), we use the FULLTEXT KEY keyword when creating our table. This is identical to using FULLTEXT INDEX.

When creating the cms_users table, we use the previous keywords to create both PRIMARY KEY to uniquely identify table rows, and UNIQUE KEY to ensure that each user's e-mail address is unique.

```
    PRIMARY KEY (user_id),
    UNIQUE KEY uniq_e-mail (e-mail)
```

After creating the cms_users table, we insert one record so that the administrator is able to log in with Admin permissions. This allows you to immediately administer the site as needed. This data is echoed to the screen to provide you with some feedback that everything has worked as you expected.

```
$sql = "INSERT IGNORE INTO cms_users VALUES (NULL, '$admine-mail', '$adminpass',
'$adminname', 3)";
$result = mysql_query($sql) or die(mysql_error());

echo "<html><head><title>CMS Tables Created</title></head><body>";
echo "CMS Tables created. Here is your initial login information:\n";
echo "<ul><li><strong>login</strong>: " . $admine-mail . "</li>\n";
echo "<li><strong>password</strong>: " . $adminpass . "</li></ul>\n";
echo "<a href='login.php'>Login</a> to the site now.";
echo "<a href='login.php'>Login</a> to the site now.";
```

Create Reusable Functions

Many of the pages require functions that can be used over and over again. Because of this, we will include these reusable functions in the outputfunctions.php file.

```
function trimBody($theText, $lmt=500, $s_chr="\n", $s_cnt=2) {
```

The function trimBody() will take a text input and return a shortened (trimmed) version for display on a page. If an article is very long, you might want to show only the first couple of sentences, or only the first paragraph. If the article is trimmed, you should end the trimmed text with ellipses (. . .).

The first parameter, $theText, is the text you want trimmed. The second parameter ($lmt) is the absolute longest text string you want returned, expressed in number of characters. The default value, if none is supplied, is 500 characters. The third parameter ($s_chr) is the "stop character." We will trim the document to this character. The default value is a newline (\n). The last parameter is $s_cnt, or "stop count." Given the stop character (in this case \n), we will trim after we reach the number designated by $s_cnt. In this case we default to 2, so we will trim the text after the second newline character.

You must first initialize the variables. The variable $pos keeps track of the current position of the character you are examining. The variable $trimmed tells you whether or not the text has been trimmed.

```
$pos = 0;
$trimmed = FALSE;
```

You then loop through the text $s_cnt times. If you find the character within the text on the last loop through, then $trimmed will be true, and $theText will be trimmed to that character. If not, $trimmed will be false, and $theText will contain the full text string. (This might happen if you were trimming the string to the third newline and it were only two paragraphs long, for example.)

```
for ($i = 1; $i <= $s_cnt; $i++)
  if ($tmp = strpos($theText,$s_chr,$pos)) {
    $pos = $tmp;
    $trimmed = TRUE;
  } else {
    $pos = strlen($theText) - 1;
    $trimmed = FALSE;
    break;
  }
}
$theText = substr($theText,0,$pos);
```

If the returned string is now longer than our limit, you trim it to the exact length of the limit.

```
if (strlen($theText) > $lmt)
  $theText = substr($theText,0,$lmt);
```

After doing this, you might have cut off a word. In the interest of keeping your trimmed text clean, you trim back to the last space, and then set $trimmed = true.

```
  $theText = substr($theText,0,strrpos($theText,' '));
  $trimmed = TRUE;
}
```

If you have trimmed the text at all, you add the ellipses, and return the trimmed text back to where the function was called.

```
  if ($trimmed) $theText .= '...';
  return $theText;
}
```

The `trimBody` function is quite flexible. You can trim text to 50 characters (by setting `$s_chr = "xyz"` and `$s_cnt = 999`), or trim it to the first sentence (setting `$s_chr = "."` and `$s_cnt = 1`). You can also set the default values to anything you want.

Our next function, `outputStory()`, takes two arguments. The argument `$article` is the ID of the article you want to display, and `$only_snippet` is either `TRUE` or `FALSE` to indicate whether you should trim it using the `trimBody()` function you just created. You will not be returning a value to the calling script. Instead, you send the results directly to the screen. Because of this, `outputStory()` should be used in the location where you want the story echoed.

```
function outputStory($article, $only_snippet=FALSE) {
```

In order for the function to access the `$conn` variable, you have to declare it global. Otherwise, it will use its own `$conn` variable, which currently does not contain anything. Essentially, you are saying "Use the `$conn` variable that was declared outside of this function." Remember that `$conn` is created in `conn.php`, which is included at the top of `outputfunctions.php`.

```
global $conn;
```

If the article ID was passed as expected, then you run the rest of the function. The first step is to select the article from the database, including all the author data for that article:

```
if ($article) {
  $sql = "SELECT ar.*,usr.name " .
      "FROM cms_articles ar " .
      "LEFT OUTER JOIN cms_users usr " .
      "ON ar.author_id = usr.user_id " .
      "WHERE ar.article_id = " . $article;
  $result = mysql_query($sql,$conn);
```

The rest of the function is fairly straightforward. It combines the data retrieved from the database with HTML to format it for the screen. There are a few things we want to point out, however.

First, you'll notice that we use the `trimBody()` function we just wrote, but only if we passed `TRUE` in as the second parameter of the `outputStory()` function. Second, we use the `htmlspecialchars()` PHP function to convert any text in our article that might cause HTML problems (such as <, >, &, and so on) to their entity equivalents (`&lt;`, `&gt;`, and `&amp;`, respectively, and so on). Third, newline characters in HTML are essentially ignored. In order for HTML to properly display text with newlines, you need to insert `<br />` for every newline in the text. PHP provides a neat function to do this: `nl2br()`, which we use here:

```
if ($only_snippet) {
  ...
  echo nl2br(htmlspecialchars(trimBody($row['body'])));
  ...
} else {
  ...
  echo nl2br(htmlspecialchars($row['body']));
  ...
}
```

The end result is that the article gets displayed on the page just as intended when it was entered, and is trimmed if specified.

The last function in `outputFunctions()` is `showComments()`. You pass the article ID and a Boolean value that determines whether or not to show a link to allow users to add their own comments:

```
function showComments($article,$showLink=TRUE) {
```

Declare `$conn` to be global, so you can access it within the function `global $conn;`.

You will need to know later whether or not this article has been published. So, you grab the value of the field `is_published` from the article for use later:

```
$sql = "SELECT is_published " .
    "FROM cms_articles " .
    "WHERE article_id=" . $article;
$result = mysql_query($sql,$conn)
 or die('Could not look up comments; ' . mysql_error());

$row = mysql_fetch_array($result);
$is_published = $row['is_published'];
```

Next, you grab all of the comments associated with this article, including the user's name and e-mail address for each comment:

```
$sql = "SELECT co.*,usr.name,usr.e-mail " .
    "FROM cms_comments co " .
    "LEFT OUTER JOIN cms_users usr " .
    "ON co.comment_user = usr.user_id " .
    "WHERE co.article_id=" . $article .
    " ORDER BY co.comment_date DESC";
$result = mysql_query($sql,$conn)
 or die('Could not look up comments; ' . mysql_error());
```

As with the `outputStory()` function, you just want to output out HTML whenever the `outputComments` function is called. If you passed TRUE as the second parameter to this function, then you put a header on the page that says "Comments," along with a link for the user to add his or her own comment (if this is a registered user and the article is published). If there are 0 comments, this is all the user will see, and he or she will still be able to add a new comment.

```
if ($showLink) {
 echo '<h4>' . mysql_num_rows($result) . 'Comments';
 if (isset($_SESSION['user_id']) and $is_published) {
  echo ' / <a href="comment.php?article=' . $_GET['article'] .
     '">Add one</a>';
 }
 echo "</h4>\n";
}
```

If there are comments, loop through each comment and display the comments below the article, with the newest comments first.

```
      if (mysql_num_rows($result)) {
        echo "<div class=\"scroller\">\n";
        while ($row = mysql_fetch_array($result)) {
```

You'll notice the <span> and </span> tags, as well as <div> tags. These are not currently being used, but they will allow you to use CSS (cascading style sheets) to change how your pages are displayed. We may include a CSS file or two on the Web site to demonstrate this, but for now, describing CSS is beyond the scope of this book.

```
        echo "<span class='commentName'>" .
        htmlspecialchars($row['name']) .
        "</span><span class='commentDate'> (" .
        date("l F j, Y H:i",strtotime($row['comment_date'])) .
           ")</span>\n";
        echo "<p class='commentText'>\n" .
           nl2br(htmlspecialchars($row['comment'])) .
           "\n</p>\n";
      }
```

Again, notice the use of htmlspecialchars() and nl2br() in the previous code. Get used to using them; they are very important for converting text entered in a text box into readable text on an HTML page.

The date function is quite powerful. It allows you to take the standard date value entered in a datetime field in MySQL and format it in many ways. In this case, the datetime of 2003-09-19 17:39:24 will be displayed as Friday September 19, 2003 17:39. There are many options for displaying dates. For more information about this, visit www.php.net/date.

The outputFunctions.php file is included on each page that needs one of its functions. If you have any other functions that you might want to add to your application, simply add it to this file, and make sure this file is included in the page.

Two additional files are included on every page that displays information on the Web: header.php and footer.php. Let's look at header.php now. (We won't look at footer.php, which should be self-evident.)

```
    <?php session_start(); ?>
```

This is the very first line of our page, and a very important one. Login information is stored using Sessions. Sessions allow you to store values to be used elsewhere on the site. This makes Sessions ideal for storing login data. By using session_start() at the beginning of your page, you are telling the application to allow you access to $_SESSION variables. Now you can set and retrieve session variables.

For a more detailed discussion of sessions, visit www.php.net/session.

Here's our first example of session variables. Once session_start() has been initialized, the variable $_SESSION['name'] should be available to you, as long as the user has logged in. So, if isset($_SESSION['name']) returns FALSE, you know the user is not logged in.

```
    if (isset($_SESSION['name'])) {
      echo ' <div id="logowelcome">';
      echo '  Currently logged in as: '.$_SESSION['name'];
      echo ' </div>';
    }
```

The following is the search form, displayed on every page. We did not discuss this functionality earlier; we hope you discovered this little gem in your explorations of the application. Now you get to see how it works. Note that there really isn't anything special going on here; it is a standard form that posts the keywords field to `search.php`. If there are keywords in the URL, they will be prefilled in the keywords field. We look at the search results page a little later.

```html
<form method="get" action="search.php">
 <p class='head'>Search</p>
 <p>
  <input id="searchkeywords" type="text" name="keywords"
<?php
  if (isset($_GET['keywords'])) {
   echo ' value="' . htmlspecialchars($_GET['keywords']) . '" ';
  }
?>
  />
  <input id="searchbutton" class="submit" type="submit"
  value="Search" />
 </p>
</form>
```

In most cases, there are three values you save as session variables: the user's name, login ID, and access level. You use those values to determine what menu items to display. Here are the options:

❑ **Article:** All users

❑ **Login:** All users *not* logged in

❑ **Compose:** All logged in users

❑ **Review:** All logged in users with access level 2 or more

❑ **Admin:** All logged in users with access level 3 or more

❑ **Control Panel:** All logged in users

❑ **Logout:** All logged in users

```php
echo '<a href="index.php">Articles</a>';
if (!isset($_SESSION['user_id'])) {
 echo ' | <a href="login.php">Login</a>';
} else {
 echo ' | <a href="compose.php">Compose</a>';

 if ($_SESSION['access_lvl'] > 1) {
  echo ' | <a href="pending.php">Review</a>';
 }

 if ($_SESSION['access_lvl'] > 2) {
  echo ' | <a href="admin.php">Admin</a>';
 }
 echo ' | <a href="cpanel.php">Control Panel</a>';
 echo ' | <a href="transact-user.php?action=Logout">Logout</a>';
}
```

So, that's `header.php`. It displays the title, login status, and appropriate menu items based on the user level.

Next, let's take a look at `http.php`, the last of our included files:

```
function redirect($url) {
 if (!headers_sent()) {
  header('Location: http://' . $_SERVER['HTTP_HOST'] .
   dirname($_SERVER['PHP_SELF']) . '/' . $url);
 } else {
  die('Could not redirect; Headers already sent (output).');
 }
}
```

You may have noticed that this is another function, and wondered why we didn't include it in the `outputFunctions.php` file. We certainly could have, but we made the choice to separate them for two reasons. First, `outputFunctions.php` is for functions that output data to be displayed on the screen, either directly or indirectly (as with `trimBody()`). The `http.php` file is used for browser functions; in this case, we have only one of those—redirection. Second, the redirection function and the output functions are used at different times. By grouping functions with similar functionality, we minimize the size of included files.

Transaction Pages

So now we come to the tasty, gooey center of our application: the transaction pages. Any time data is posted from a form, it's handled by either the `transact-user.php` or `transact-article.php` page. We use two different files simply to make the code more manageable.

Let's take a look at the `transact-user.php` file first.

The application needs to access the database, and to redirect users to various pages after completing transactions. We take care of the former with `conn.php`, and the latter with `http.php`. Because transaction pages don't display anything on the screen, we don't need the `header.php`, `footer.php`, or `outputFunctions.php` files included.

```
require_once 'conn.php';
require_once 'http.php';
```

The `$_REQUEST['action']` variable contains either the name of the button you clicked on the previous page, or a GET request in the URL (such as `?action=delete`). If `$_REQUEST['action']` is empty, then you don't do any transactions, and simply redirect the user to the `index.php` page:

```
if (isset($_REQUEST['action'])) {.
```

You use `switch()` in what follows because of its flexibility. If you expand the functionality of this application, you could end up adding many more "actions." In this `transact-user.php` page, it is a simple matter of adding a new case: condition. You could certainly use if . . . else statements instead of switch, but in the long run they can be cumbersome to work with.

```
switch ($_REQUEST['action']) {
```

The e-mail and password are what you use to log in. If both are not passed, the user will not be logged in.

```
case 'Login':
 if (isset($_POST['e-mail'])
   and isset($_POST['passwd']))
 {
```

This gets the user's information. If a row is returned, it verifies that the login e-mail address and password supplied are correct.

```
$sql = "SELECT user_id,access_lvl,name " .
   "FROM cms_users " .
   "WHERE e-mail='" . $_POST['e-mail'] . "' " .
   "AND passwd='" . $_POST['passwd'] . "'";
$result = mysql_query($sql,$conn)
 or die('Could not lookup user information; ' . mysql_error());

if ($row = mysql_fetch_array($result)) {
```

Again, in order to retrieve or set session variables, you must first use the command `session_start()`. Once you do, you set three variables to be used throughout the application: user ID, access level, and user name:

```
session_start();
$_SESSION['user_id'] = $row['user_id'];
$_SESSION['access_lvl'] = $row['access_lvl'];
$_SESSION['name'] = $row['name'];
 }
}
```

Next, you redirect the user back to the home page (`index.php`). The break function is required at the end of each case statement. Otherwise, the code in the next case runs as well, and you don't want that because it logs the user out!

```
redirect('index.php');
break;
```

Logout is quite simple, really. If no session variables exist with the user ID, access level, and user name, then the application knows you are not logged in. Therefore, you first use `session_start()` to tell PHP you are accessing session variables. Then, you unset the session, which clears all the session variables, and finally you destroy the session, which destroys all of the data registered to a session. Both `session_unset()` and `session_destroy()` are used to completely remove all login data.

```
case 'Logout':
 session_start();
 session_unset();
 session_destroy();

 redirect('index.php');
 break;
```

In order to create an account, all of the fields must be filled in, and the two password fields must match.

```
case 'Create Account':
  if (isset($_POST['name'])
    and isset($_POST['e-mail'])
    and isset($_POST['accesslvl'])

    and $_POST['passwd'] == $_POST['passwd2']))
  {
```

We insert the user's information into the database...   `$sql = "INSERT INTO cms_users (e-mail,name,passwd) " .`

```
        "VALUES ('" . $_POST['e-mail'] . "','" .
        $_POST['name'] . "','" . $_POST['passwd'] . "')";

    mysql_query($sql,$conn)
      or die('Could not create user account; ' . mysql_error());
```

Then set the appropriate session variables. This has the effect of logging in the user after he or she registers.

```
    session_start();
    $_SESSION['user_id'] = mysql_insert_id($conn);
    $_SESSION['access_lvl'] = 1;
    $_SESSION['name'] = $_POST['name'];
  }
  redirect('index.php');
  break;
```

When an account is modified, all of the fields must have data. As long as they do, the user's account is updated in the database, and the user is redirected to the admin.php page:

```
case 'Modify Account':
  if (isset($_POST['name'])
    and isset($_POST['e-mail'])
    and isset($_POST['accesslvl'])
    and isset($_POST['userid']))
  {
  $sql = "UPDATE cms_users " .
      "SET e-mail='" . $_POST['e-mail'] .
      "', name='" . $_POST['name'] .
      "', access_lvl=" . $_POST['accesslvl'] . " " .
      " WHERE user_id=" . $_POST['userid'];

    mysql_query($sql,$conn)
      or die('Could not update user account; ' . mysql_error());
  }
  redirect('admin.php');
  break;
```

It's time to revisit the mail() function we introduced in Chapter 10. This will be a simple e-mail, but there is no reason you can't take your wealth of knowledge from Chapter 10 and send an HTML-enabled e-mail to your users. It's not necessary, of course, but it's your application. Do what you will!

```
case 'Send my reminder!':
  if (isset($_POST['e-mail'])) {
    $sql = "SELECT passwd FROM cms_users " .
        "WHERE e-mail='" . $_POST['e-mail'] . "'";

    $result = mysql_query($sql,$conn)
      or die('Could not look up password; ' . mysql_error());
```

If you find a record, you get it, create a subject and body for your e-mail message (including the long lost password), and send it on its merry way.

```
    if (mysql_num_rows($result)) {
      $row = mysql_fetch_array($result);
      $subject = 'Comic site password reminder';
      $body = "Just a reminder, your password for the " .
          "Comicbook appreciation site is: " . $row['passwd'] .
          "\n\nYou can use this to log in at http://" .
          $_SERVER['HTTP_HOST'] .
          dirname($_SERVER['PHP_SELF']) . '/';

    mail($_POST['e-mail'],$subject,$body)
      or die('Could not send reminder e-mail.');
    }
```

We assume, of course, that the user will immediately open his or her e-mail to read the password. We conveniently deposit users in the login page so they can enter their e-mail address and password.

```
  }
  redirect('login.php');
  break;
```

The following code may look *very* familiar. It is virtually identical to the previous Modify Account case, except this time, the user is changing his or her own data. Because of this, the access level does not get updated.

```
case 'Change my info':
  session_start();

  if (isset($_POST['name'])
    and isset($_POST['e-mail'])
    and isset($_SESSION['user_id']))
  {
    $sql = "UPDATE cms_users " .
        "SET e-mail='" . $_POST['e-mail'] .
        "', name='" . $_POST['name'] . "' " .
        "WHERE user_id=" . $_SESSION['user_id'];

    mysql_query($sql,$conn)
      or die('Could not update user account; ' . mysql_error());
  }
  redirect('cpanel.php');
  break;
```

The following is the end of your switch statement. It's easy to forget to close it, something that is the cause of much debugging grief. We are here to remind you to close your switch!

```
}
```

Remember the if statement at the beginning? If the $_REQUEST['action'] variable is not set, you simply redirect the user to index.php. What are they doing loading the transact-user.php file, anyway?

```
} else {
 redirect('index.php');
}
```

That wasn't so bad, was it? It's a lot of code, but much of it is fairly similar. Check some variables, run some SQL code, redirect the user. That's pretty much how most transactions work.

transact-article.php

Want to look at some more? Great! Let's take a look at transact-article.php. This time, we'll simply point out some of the more interesting things we might not have covered yet, or things that bear repeating.

Yes, this bears repeating. You know what the following does, right? It registers the session variables that invariably will need to be set in order to run some of these transactions. This gives you access to the data for the currently logged-in user:

```
session_start();
```

The transact-article.php page requires connection to the database, and redirects users to various pages using the redirect() function. The following two include files provide this functionality, respectively.

```
require_once 'conn.php';
require_once 'http.php';
```

You need to make sure that a button was pressed, or an action is specified in the URL (such as ?action=twiddleThumbs).

```
if (isset($_REQUEST['action'])) {
```

There are a lot of actions that can happen in this file. The switch() statement is a more elegant way of choosing your transactions than if . . . else.

```
switch ($_REQUEST['action']) {
```

You first ensure that the title and body were both entered and that the user is logged in (tested by the presence of the user_id session variable).

```
case 'Submit New Article':
 if (isset($_POST['title'])
    and isset($_POST['body'])
    and isset($_SESSION['user_id']))
  {
```

You insert the article into the database, including the user ID and the date. The datetime is formatted in a standard MySQL datetime format that can be stored in a datetime column. When you retrieve that datetime to be displayed on the Web, you can format it any way that you want. The standard datetime format for September 21, 2003, 12:42 a.m. is 2003-09-21 00:42:00.

```
        $sql = "INSERT INTO cms_articles " .
            "(title,body,author_id,date_submitted) " .
            "VALUES ('" . $_POST['title'] . "','" . $_POST['body'] .
            "'," . $_SESSION['user_id'] . ",'" .
            date("Y-m-d H:i:s",time()) . "')";

    mysql_query($sql,$conn)
      or die('Could not submit article; ' . mysql_error());
    }
    redirect('index.php');
    break;
```

The Edit case is simple. The compose.php page is set up to retrieve an article and preload it into the title and body fields if the appropriate data is entered in the URL. You simply need to add a=edit and article=xx to the URL and redirect the user to that URL.

```
    case 'Edit':
        redirect('compose.php?a=edit&article=' . $_POST['article']);
        break;
```

Make sure the title and body fields have been filled in, and that the hidden field "article" contains a value. If you were composing a new document, the hidden field would not contain anything, and you'd know something was wrong. (You can't use the Save Changes feature for a new document.)

```
    case 'Save Changes':
        if (isset($_POST['title'])
          and isset($_POST['body'])
          and isset($_POST['article']))
        {
```

Next you send the article to the database. If the hidden field authorid has a value, then a user is editing her or his own document, and you must add the condition to match the author_id to the SQL statement.

```
    $sql = "UPDATE cms_articles SET title='" . $_POST['title'] .
            "',body='" . $_POST['body'] . "',date_submitted='" .
            date("Y-m-d H:i:s",time()) . "' WHERE article_id=" .
            $_POST['article'];

        if (isset($_POST['authorid'])) {
          $sql .= " AND author_id=" . $_POST['authorid'];
        }
        mysql_query($sql,$conn)
          or die('Could not update article; ' . mysql_error());
        }
```

You then redirect the user to either the control panel, if the user is editing his or her own document, or the review page, if the user is a moderator or admin editing someone else's document.

```
if (isset($_POST['authorid'])) {
 redirect('cpanel.php');
} else {
 redirect('pending.php');
}
break;
```

Next you make sure the article ID was passed. If it was, modify the article in the database to set the is_published column to 1, and set the date_published datetime column to the current date and time (formatted in MySQL datetime format).

```
case 'Publish':
    if ($_POST['article']) {
    $sql = "UPDATE cms_articles " .
        "SET is_published=1,date_published='" .
        date("Y-m-d H:i:s",time()) . "' WHERE article_id=" .
        $_POST['article'];

    mysql_query($sql,$conn)
      or die('Could not publish article; ' . mysql_error());
    }
    redirect('pending.php');
    break;
```

This next case is actually quite similar to the Publish case, only this time, after checking the article ID, you set is_published to 0 and erase the date_published field. Retracting an article in this case simply returns it to its pre-published state, but you might think of better ways to retract an article. Perhaps you could have separate columns for is_retracted and retract_date. There is no right or wrong way to do it, and, of course, it depends on the needs of your own site.

```
case 'Retract':
    if ($_POST['article']) {
    $sql = "UPDATE cms_articles SET is_published=0,date_published=''
      WHERE article_id=" . $_POST['article'];

    mysql_query($sql,$conn)
      or die('Could not retract article; ' . mysql_error());
    }
    redirect('pending.php');
    break;
```

Check to see that an article ID was passed, and simply delete the record. Don't prompt the user with "Are you sure?" here because that was already handled with a JavaScript prompt before we got to this point.

```
case 'Delete':
    if ($_POST['article']) {
    $sql = "DELETE FROM cms_articles WHERE is_published=0 AND " .
```

```
            "article_id=" . $_POST['article'];

  mysql_query($sql,$conn)
    or die('Could not delete article; ' . mysql_error());
  }
  redirect('pending.php');
  break;
```

If the article ID was passed, and the comment field is filled in, process this transaction.

```
case 'Submit Comment':
  if (isset($_POST['article'])
    and isset($_POST['comment']))
  {
```

Insert the article ID, the comment date (in MySQL datetime format), the user ID, and the actual comment into the database. When this has been accomplished, redirect the user to the article so he or she can see the newly saved comment.

```
$sql = "INSERT INTO cms_comments " .
       "(article_id,comment_date,comment_user,comment) " .
       "VALUES (" . $_POST['article'] . ",'" .
       date("Y-m-d H:i:s",time()) .
       "'," . $_SESSION['user_id'] .
       ",'" . $_POST['comment'] . "');";

  mysql_query($sql,$conn)
    or die('Could add comment; ' . mysql_error());
  }
  redirect('viewarticle.php?article=' . $_POST['article']);
  break;
```

This is a case where the action is passed in the URL (?action=remove&article=123). Verify that the article ID was passed and that the user is logged in.

```
case 'remove':
  if (isset($_GET['article'])
    and isset($_SESSION['user_id']))
  {
```

We currently allow only users to delete their own articles. You might modify this transaction to allow moderators and admins to delete any article, but for now only users can delete the articles they have written.

```
$sql = "DELETE FROM cms_articles WHERE article_id=" .
       $_GET['article'] . " AND author_id=" .
       $_SESSION['user_id'];

  mysql_query($sql,$conn)
    or die('Could not remove article; ' . mysql_error());
  }
  redirect('cpanel.php');
  break;
```

Once again, don't forget to close your switch statement:

```
}
```

And again, if a user has somehow loaded this page without any posted variables, he or she is immediately redirected to the home page.

```
} else {
 redirect('index.php');
}
```

cpanel.php

Now let's take a look at our first actual Web page, cpanel.php. The Control Panel page cpanel.php is used to allow users to change their user names and e-mail addresses. They can also see all of the articles they have written, categorized by Pending and Published articles.

As always, you need to connect to the database. And, as always, conn.php takes care of that. This time, we are displaying a Web page. We load up header.php, which is our standard header for all Web display pages.

```
require_once 'conn.php';
require_once 'header.php';
```

We first go out to the database and get the user's name and e-mail address.

```
$sql = "SELECT name,e-mail " .
    "FROM cms_users " .
    "WHERE user_id=" . $_SESSION['user_id'];
$result = mysql_query($sql,$conn)
 or die('Could not look up user data; ' . mysql_error());
$user = mysql_fetch_array($result);
```

You will be entering and exiting PHP mode throughout this file and in the other Web pages. This gives you great flexibility and makes the page a lot easier to read. The next line exits PHP code:

```
?>
```

The following form uses the post method. Notice the action. You already created that file. You know that when a submit button is clicked on this page, transact-user.php loads, the appropriate code runs, and the user is redirected to the control panel.

```
<form method="post" action="transact-user.php">
```

Note the use of htmlspecialchars(). This prevents strange characters such as < or > from messing up the page. These characters will be displayed using their entity equivalents (such as < and >).

```
<p>Name:<br />
 <input type="text" id="name" name="name"
  value="<?php echo htmlspecialchars($user['name']); ?>" /></p>
```

The rest of the form is standard HTML. Now you need to display Pending and Published articles. Time to drop back into PHP:

```
<p>E-mail:
<br />
 <input type="text" id="e-mail" name="e-mail"
  value="<?php echo htmlspecialchars($user['e-mail']); ?>" /></p>

<p><input type="submit" class="submit" name="action"
  value="Change my info" /></p>

</form>

<h2>Pending Articles</h2>
<div class="scroller">
 <table>
```

This code gets all pending articles written by this user. They are ordered by date_submitted, with the oldest being first. Please note that if there are no pending articles, this will *not* return a MySQL error. You will still get a result set, but there won't be any rows. We handle that contingency next.

```
<?php
$sql = "SELECT article_id, title, date_submitted " .
    "FROM cms_articles " .
    "WHERE is_published=0 " .
    "AND author_id=" . $_SESSION['user_id'] . " " .
    "ORDER BY date_submitted";
$result = mysql_query($sql,$conn)
 or die('Could not get list of pending articles; ' . mysql_error());
```

If there are no pending articles, we simply state so and move on. Otherwise...if

```
(mysql_num_rows($result) == 0) {
 echo "  <em>No pending articles available</em>";
} else {
```

You loop through each pending article and display the title (with a link to the article), along with the date/time it was submitted.

```
while ($row = mysql_fetch_array($result)) {
  echo "<tr>\n";
  echo '<td><a href="reviewarticle.php?article=' .
    $row['article_id'] . '">' . htmlspecialchars($row['title']) .
    "</a> (submitted " .
    date("F j, Y",strtotime($row['date_submitted'])) .
    ")</td>\n";
  echo "</tr>\n";
 }
}
```

Yada, yada, yada. Don't you love knowing HTML?

```
Ah... more PHP!?>
 </table>
</div>
<br />

<h2>Published Articles</h2>
<div class="scroller">
 <table>
```

Okay, this next code is almost identical to the code used to display pending articles. This time, display them using the date_published column.

```php
<?php
$sql = "SELECT article_id, title,date_published " .
    "FROM cms_articles " .
    "WHERE is_published=1 " .
    "AND author_id=" . $_SESSION['user_id'] . " " .
    "ORDER BY date_submitted";
$result = mysql_query($sql,$conn)
 or die('Could not get list of pending articles; ' . mysql_error());

if (mysql_num_rows($result) == 0) {
 echo "  <em>No published articles available</em>";
} else {
 while ($row = mysql_fetch_array($result)) {
  echo "<tr>\n";
  echo '<td><a href="viewarticle.php?article=' .
     $row['article_id'] . '">' . htmlspecialchars($row['title']) .
     "</a> (published " .
      date("F j, Y",strtotime($row['date_published'])) .
      ")</td>\n";
  echo "</tr>\n";
 }
}
```

footer.php

Then load the footer. It is only a few lines of HTML for now, but some day you will want to put a menu, or perhaps a copyright line. The great thing is, even if your site uses 300 pages, you will have to add that information in only one place: footer.php.

```
?>
 </table>
</div>
<br />
<?php require_once 'footer.php'; ?>
```

Now let's take a look at the next Web display page, useraccount.php. First thing you'll notice is our old friend conn.php. But where is header.php? No worries—it will show up soon. As long as you don't echo anything to the page yet, you're okay.

```php
<?php
require_once 'conn.php';
```

You need to retrieve all of the data for this user. Set all the variables to empty to ensure the values you retrieve are "fresh." As long as the user is logged in, those variables will fill up with the appropriate data. If there is no user logged in, this page will create a new user. Neato, huh?

```php
$userid = '';
$name = '';
$e-mail = '';
$password = '';
$accesslvl = '';
if (isset($_GET['userid'])) {
 $sql = "SELECT * FROM cms_users WHERE user_id=" . $_GET['userid'];
 $result = mysql_query($sql,$conn)
  or die('Could not look up user data; ' . mysql_error());

 $row = mysql_fetch_array($result);
 $userid = $_GET['userid'];
 $name = $row['name'];
 $e-mail = $row['e-mail'];
 $accesslvl = $row['access_lvl'];
}
```

Here's the header! We told you not to worry.

```php
require_once 'header.php';
```

What follows is no different from that last page we looked at, but we're using PHP to echo it to the page.

```php
echo "<form method=\"post\" action=\"transact-user.php\">\n";
```

You could have just as easily written this as:

```php
?>
<form method="post" action="transact-user.php">
<?php
```

If the user is logged in, then this page contains the user's current data. Therefore, you need to modify his account. Otherwise, it's a new user, and you need to *create* an account. The title reflects this.

```php
if ($userid) {
 echo "<h1>Modify Account</h1>\n";
} else {
 echo "<h1>Create Account</h1>\n";
}
?>
```

Here's some more boring HTML. Once again, note the use of `htmlspecialchars()` to prevent weird symbols from messing up the page.

```
<p>
 Full name:<br />
 <input type="text" class="txtinput" name="name" maxlength="100"
  value="<?php echo htmlspecialchars($name); ?>" />
<p>
</p>
 E-mail Address:<br />
 <input type="text" class="txtinput" name="e-mail" maxlength="255"
  value="<?php echo htmlspecialchars($e-mail); ?>" />
</p>
```

If the user has Admin access, do the following:

```
<?php
if (isset($_SESSION['access_lvl'])
  and $_SESSION['access_lvl'] == 3)
{
```

While we do assume that most readers have a fundamental knowledge of HTML, many of you may not be familiar with `<fieldset>` and `<legend>`. We simply suggest you enter them and see how they are displayed on the page; using `<fieldset>` and `<legend>` is a great way to group many of your form fields.

> We recommend you visit www.w3.org/TR/REC-html40/interact/forms.html#h-17.10 for more information.

```
echo "<fieldset>\n";
echo " <legend>Access Level</legend>\n";
```

First, go get all of the access levels from the database:

```
$sql = "SELECT * FROM cms_access_levels ORDER BY access_lvl DESC";
$result = mysql_query($sql,$conn)
 or die('Could not list access levels; ' . mysql_error());
```

Then cycle through each one, displaying them as radio buttons on the page.

```
while ($row = mysql_fetch_array($result)) {
 echo ' <input type="radio" class="radio" id="acl_' .
   $row['access_lvl'] . '" name="accesslvl" value="' .
   $row['access_lvl'] . '" ';

 if ($row['access_lvl'] == $accesslvl) {
  echo 'checked="checked" ';
 }
 echo '/>' . $row['access_name'] . "<br />\n";
}
```

The next page requires the user ID. Because this is not entered in a form field, create a hidden field to carry the data over to the transaction page.

```
?>
</fieldset>
<p>
 <input type="hidden" name="userid" value="<?php echo $userid; ?>" />
 <input type="submit" class="submit" name="action"
  value="Modify Account" />
</p>
```

A short but sweet PHP tag ends the first part of the `if` statement and adds an `else` clause. This is a very flexible way of using `if...else` commands with standard HTML. Because you can enter and exit PHP at any time, your pages are very flexible and easy to read.

The rest of this code is loaded if you are *not* an admin type.

```
<?php } else { ?>
```

If you are not an admin, you must be here to create a new account. Therefore, it asks you for your password:

```
<p>
 Password:<br />
 <input type="password" id="passwd" name="passwd" maxlength="50" />
</p>
<p>
 Password (again):<br />
 <input type="password" id="passwd2" name="passwd2" maxlength="50" />
</p>
<p>
 <input type="submit" class="submit" name="action"
  value="Create Account" />
</p>
```

Then comes the end of the `if` statement and the end of the form:

```
<?php } ?>
</form>
```

And there is your footer page again, closing things off neatly:

```
<?php require_once 'footer.php'; ?>
```

compose.php

We're almost there. Next, we tackle `compose.php`, the page where you create new articles. Instantiate the variables you are going to be using:

```
<?php
require_once 'conn.php';

$title = '';
$body = '';
$article = '';
$authorid = '';
```

If you are editing an article, instead of composing a brand new one, you must go out to the database and retrieve the article.

```
if (isset($_GET['a'])
  and $_GET['a'] == 'edit'
  and isset($_GET['article'])) {
$sql = "SELECT title,body,author_id " .
    "FROM cms_articles WHERE article_id=" . $_GET['article'];

$result = mysql_query($sql,$conn)
  or die('Could not retrieve article data; ' . mysql_error());

$row = mysql_fetch_array($result);

$title = $row['title'];
$body = $row['body'];
$article = $_GET['article'];
$authorid = $row['author_id'];
}
```

Load the prerequisite header.php:

```
require_once 'header.php';
```

What follows is more standard HTML stuff. You know what htmlspecialchars() does, don't you? Of course you do. If not, go back a page or two and review.

```
?>

<form method="post" action="transact-article.php">

<h2>Compose Article</h2>

<p>
 Title:<br />
 <input type="text" class="title" name="title" maxlength="255"
  value="<?php echo htmlspecialchars($title); ?>" />
</p>
<p>
 Body:<br />
 <textarea class="body" name="body" rows="10" cols="60"><?php
  echo htmlspecialchars($body); ?></textarea>
</p>
<p>
```

The article ID must be carried over to the transaction page if you are modifying an existing article. The following hidden input field will do this for you.

```
<?php
echo '<input type="hidden" name="article" value="' .
   $article . "\" />\n";
```

You also need to pass the author ID if the original author is editing his or her own document.

```php
if ($_SESSION['access_lvl'] < 2) {
  echo '<input type="hidden" name="authorid" value="' .
    $authorid . "\" />\n";
}
```

If the article is being modified, display the Save Changes submit button. If it's a new article, display the Submit New Article button.

```php
if ($article) {
  echo '<input type="submit" class="submit" name="action" ' .
    "value=\"Save Changes\" />\n";
} else {
  echo '<input type="submit" class="submit" name="action" ' .
    "value=\"Submit New Article\" />\n";
}
```

And so it ends, footer and all. Clean and simple.

```php
?>
</p>
</form>
<?php require_once 'footer.php'; ?>
```

On to `reviewarticle.php`. This time, you need to use one of the functions in `outputfunctions.php`, so you include it at the top of your page.

```php
<?php
require_once 'conn.php';
require_once 'outputfunctions.php';
require_once 'header.php';
?>
```

First, you display the title of the page, and then use the `outputStory()` function to display the article on the page.

```php
<form method="post" action="transact-article.php">

<h2>Article Review</h2>
<?php

outputStory($_GET['article']);
```

It is important to note that we passed only one variable to the function `outputStory()`, even though `outputStory()` takes two arguments. The second argument is `$only_snippet`, which defaults to FALSE. Because we did not use the second parameter, PHP automatically uses its default value. If there were no default value assigned, then attempting to call `outputStory()` with only one argument would result in a PHP warning telling us that we are missing an argument. This allows for more flexible functions.

In this Web page, we want to display additional data about the document, such as when it was published, and who wrote it. We used the previous SQL statement to retrieve this additional information. Yes, outputStory() retrieves this data, too, but if you modified outputStory() so that articles did not display their author or publish date, you would still want it displayed on this review page.

```
$sql = "SELECT ar.*, usr.name, usr.access_lvl " .
    "FROM cms_articles ar INNER JOIN cms_users usr " .
    "ON ar.author_id = usr.user_id " .
    "WHERE article_id=" . $_GET['article'];

$result = mysql_query($sql,$conn)
 or die('Could not retrieve article info; ' . mysql_error());

$row = mysql_fetch_array($result);
if ($row['date_published'] and $row['is_published']) {
 echo '<h4>Published: ' .
    date("l F j, Y H:i",strtotime($row['date_published'])) .
    "</h4>\n";
}
```

If the document is published, you have an option to retract the article. If it is still pending, then you can publish it.

```
echo "<p><br />\n";
if ($row['is_published']) {
 $buttonType = "Retract";
} else {
 $buttonType = "Publish";
}
```

Now add the edit button. This allows the user to edit the article:

```
echo "<input type='submit' class='submit' " .
    "name='action' value='Edit' /> ";
```

Add the Retract or Publish button, used to retract a published article, or publish a pending article. Only moderators and admins are allowed to retract and publish articles.

```
if (($row['access_lvl'] > 1) or ($_SESSION['access_lvl'] > 1)) {
 echo "<input type='submit' class='submit' " .
    "name='action' value='$buttonType' /> ";
}
```

Next insert the Delete button, used to remove articles. The Delete code in transact-article.php currently allows only pending articles to be deleted. (Here's an exercise for you: Make this button show up only if the document is pending. And we bet you thought your homework would come up only at the end of the chapter, didn't you?)

```
echo "<input type='submit' class='submit' " .
    "name='action' value='Delete' /> ";
?>
```

And they all lived happily ever after. The End.

```
Next comes pending.php:<input type="hidden" name="article"
 value="<?php echo $_GET['article'] ?> " />
</p>

</form>

<?php require_once 'footer.php'; ?>
```

Feeling a little *déjà vu?* Good.

```
<?php
require_once 'conn.php';
require_once 'header.php';
```

Oooh . . . an associative array. This is one of PHP's advantages. Other server-side scripting languages such as ASP/VBScript do not use associative arrays, and we think they are very useful little things. What are you going to use this one for? Read on, dear reader, and we'll show you.

```
$a_artTypes = array(
 "Pending" => "submitted",
 "Published" => "published"
);
```

The following is where you use your associative array. You are displaying pending, or submitted, articles, and then displaying published ones. In the interests of conserving code (because we're lazy, remember?), you loop through the array and substitute the appropriate values where necessary. The variable $k holds the array key, and $v holds the array value. We also set $i to -1 because it will be incremented immediately inside the loop:

```
echo "<h2>Article Availability</h2>\n";
$i=-1;
foreach ($a_artTypes as $k => $v) {
...right here. $i++;
```

Here's your first use of the array key. The first pass through, this will read "Pending Articles." Next time through, it will read "Published Articles." Clever?

```
echo "<h3>" . $k . " Articles</h3>\n";
```

Notice that we are using $v in what follows to create the field date_submitted in the first loop, and date_published in the second. We are also using $i to first compare is_published to 0, and then to 1 in the next loop.

```
echo "<p>\n";
 echo " <div class='scroller'>\n";

$sql = "SELECT article_id, title, date_".$v.
    " FROM cms_articles " .
    "WHERE is_published=" . $i .
```

```
          " ORDER BY title";

   $result = mysql_query($sql,$conn)
    or die('Could not get list of pending articles; ' . mysql_error());
```

Again, the array key is used, if no articles are returned. Now you can see why we used an associative array.

```
   if (mysql_num_rows($result) == 0) {
    echo "  <em>No " . $k . " articles available</em>";
```

If rows are returned, you then loop through each article and display the title (linked to reviewarticle.php) and the date it was either submitted (pass one) or published (pass two).

```
   } else {
    while ($row = mysql_fetch_array($result)) {
     echo '  <a href="reviewarticle.php?article=' .
       $row['article_id'] . '">' . htmlspecialchars($row['title']) .
       "</a> ($v " .
       date("F j, Y",strtotime($row['date_'.$v])) .
       ")<br />\n";
    }
```

And so ends another exciting day in the CMS saga. Stay tuned while we look at our next file, admin.php.

```
   }
   echo "  </div>\n";
   echo "</p>\n";
   }

   require_once 'footer.php';
   ?>
```

Guess what? You guessed it. Our good friends conn.php and header.php are back. Okay, let's move on . . .

```
   <?php
   require_once 'conn.php';
   require_once 'header.php';
```

Is this an associative array? Actually, it is a normal array, but it is not zero-based. The way PHP works when creating arrays is ingenious. What this line tells PHP is "Create a normal array, but start the number index at 1." We could have assigned indices to the other values as well, but this is not necessary. PHP knows that "Moderators" has an index of 2, and "Admins" has an index of 3. Now how cool is that?

```
   $a_users = array(1 => "Users","Moderators","Admins");
```

Hey, a function. Shouldn't this go in an include file, such as outputfunctions.php? Perhaps, and you could certainly do that if you wanted to. However, this function is very specific to this file, so it really doesn't need to go in an include file. It's up to you, really.

```
   function echoUserList($lvl) {
```

In order to use the array we created earlier within this function, we must declare it global. Now the function can access the data in the array.

```
global $a_users;
```

This function will be called more than once. Each time, a different value will be contained in the $lvl variable. The following SQL pulls the appropriate data according to the $lvl value:

```
$sql = "SELECT user_id, name, e-mail FROM cms_users " .
    "WHERE access_lvl = $lvl ORDER BY name";

$result = mysql_query($sql) or die(mysql_error());
```

If no users are found in the database for this access level, we display a message explaining that those users were not found. This is done by using the array we created earlier:

```
if (mysql_num_rows($result) == 0) {
  echo "<em>No " . $a_users[$lvl] . " created.</em>";
```

A user cannot modify his or her own record. Instead, his or her name is shown in plain text, with no link.

```
} else {
  while ($row = mysql_fetch_array($result)) {
    if ($row['user_id'] == $_SESSION['user_id']) {
      echo htmlspecialchars($row['name']) . "<br />\n";
```

Otherwise, the user's name is displayed on the screen, as a link that loads useraccount.php.

```
} else {
  echo '<a href="useraccount.php?userid=' . $row['user_id'] .
    '" title="' . htmlspecialchars($row['e-mail']) . '">' .
    htmlspecialchars($row['name']) . "</a><br />\n";
}
```

Here's the end of the function. Note that nothing has been output to the screen yet.

```
    }
  }
}
```

First you display the page title:

```
?>
<h2>User Administration</h2>
```

Then you loop through the code three times, running the function each time with a different level value:

```
<?php
 for($i=1;$i<=3;$i++) {
   echo "<h3>". $a_users[$i] . "</h3>\n" .
   "<div class='scroller'>\n";
   echoUserList($i);
   echo "\n</div>\n";
 }
?>
```

And then you're done.

```
<br />
<?php require_once 'footer.php'; ?>
```

comment.php

The next page is `comment.php`. Include the necessary files:

```php
<?php
require_once 'conn.php';
require_once 'outputfunctions.php';
require_once 'header.php';
```

Then display the appropriate article at the top of the page:

```php
outputStory($_GET['article']);
```

Then add the page title:

```php
?>
<h1>Add a comment</h1>
```

A simple text area is used to enter a new comment:

```html
<form method="post" action="transact-article.php">

<p>
 Comment:<br />
 <textarea id="comment" name="comment" rows="10" cols="60"></textarea>
</p>
```

The next bit deals with the submit button and a hidden field for the article ID. This is needed to send the article ID to the next page:

```html
<p>
 <input type="submit" class="submit" name="action"
  value="Submit Comment" />
 <input type="hidden" name="article"
  value="<?php echo $_GET['article']; ?>" />
</p>
```

Display all the current comments for this article on this page:

```php
</form>

<?php

showComments($_GET['article'],FALSE);
```

And that's it! They're getting easier, aren't they? Stay with us—only a few more short ones.

search.php

Next, begin `search.php`.

```
require_once 'footer.php';
?>
```

Include the necessary files:

```
<?php
require_once 'conn.php';
require_once 'outputfunctions.php';
require_once 'header.php';
```

As long as you passed keywords, you do a search. In the following SQL statement, you'll notice the `MATCH` and `AGAINST` keywords. This is the syntax used to do a text search in those fields. They must be full-text indexed fields in order to perform this search. Visit `www.mysql.com/doc/en/Fulltext_Search.html` for more information on full-text indexed fields.

```
$result = NULL;
if (isset($_GET['keywords'])) {
 $sql = "SELECT article_id FROM cms_articles " .
     "WHERE MATCH (title,body) " .
     "AGAINST ('" . $_GET['keywords'] . "') " .
     "ORDER BY MATCH (title,body) " .
     "AGAINST ('" . $_GET['keywords'] . "') DESC";

 $result = mysql_query($sql,$conn)
   or die('Could not perform search; ' . mysql_error());
}
```

If you didn't find a match, say so:

```
echo "<h1>Search Results</h1>\n";

if ($result and !mysql_num_rows($result)) {
 echo "<p>No articles found that match the search terms.</p>\n";
```

Otherwise, loop through the results and display them as snippets on the screen:

```
} else {
 while ($row = mysql_fetch_array($result)) {
  outputStory($row['article_id'],TRUE);
 }
}
```

Let's move on to `index.php`:

```
require_once 'footer.php';
?>
```

Include the standard files:

```php
<?php
require_once 'conn.php';
require_once 'outputfunctions.php';
require_once 'header.php';
```

Retrieve all published articles, with the most recent articles listed first:

```php
$sql = "SELECT article_id FROM cms_articles WHERE is_published=1 " .
    "ORDER BY date_published DESC";

$result = mysql_query($sql,$conn);
```

If no articles are published, let the user know. This is optional, of course. If this were part of a larger page, such as a portal application, then you might simply want to put something else in place of the article list.

```php
if (mysql_num_rows($result) == 0) {
  echo "  <br />\n";
  echo "  There are currently no articles to view.\n";
```

Go through each article ID retrieved, and display the articles (trimmed) on the page:

```php
} else {
  while ($row = mysql_fetch_array($result)) {
    outputStory($row['article_id'],TRUE);
  }
}
```

Then you can tidy up afterwards:

```php
require_once 'footer.php';
?>
```

forgotpass.php and viewarticle.php

The next page, forgotpass.php, is another simple form with a header and footer, and HTML. It's used simply to send an e-mail to the user to remind him or her of a password.

The last page, viewarticle.php, is very short, yet it illustrates the nature of included files and functions wonderfully.

As you can see, there is no content displayed directly with viewarticle. It simply includes the necessary files and uses two functions to display the article and all of the comments.

```php
<?php
require_once 'conn.php';
require_once 'outputfunctions.php';
require_once 'header.php';

outputStory($_GET['article']);
```

```
    showComments($_GET['article'],TRUE);

    require_once 'footer.php';
    ?>
```

You may notice that we don't worry about the situation in which an article is not passed. As it stands, if you load `viewarticle.php` without the `"article"` parameter in the URL, you will simply get a page that consists of the site title, search, and a menu (all included in `header.php`). The rest will be blank. If that's the desired result, then that's fine. You may decide to redirect the user back to the home page if `$_GET['article']` is empty. If you do, don't forget to include `http.php` and use `redirect()` *before* `header.php`.

You may have noticed that we left out two pages, `login.php` and `forgotpass.php`. They are important pages, of course, but are mostly simple HTML. The includes at the top and bottom for `header.php` and `footer.php` are the only PHP. We're sure you can figure out how those two pages work.

Summary

Well, if you didn't have writer's cramp before, you probably do now. We hope this application has given you some insight into the separation of content and design. Because of the way the application was designed, you can easily modify the look and feel of the application by either directly altering your header and footer files, or using a CSS file to set up different styles. This won't matter to your users, who will still be able to enter articles without ever having to worry about what the article will look like on the Web when it's published.

We also hope that you understand the importance of updating your site often enough to draw users back again and again. By adding an application like this to your site, and allowing users to add content for you, you create a dynamically changing site with fresh information. Just think about all the ways you could implement such a design:

❑ Creating a message board. (We examine this in more detail in Chapter 15.)

❑ Adding a daily comic. Perhaps you have an artist who can draw you a comic every day. You could create an application that allows him or her to upload comic strips, and allows users to comment on them. You can see an example of this online at www.userfriendly.org.

❑ Compiling photo journals. A while back, there was a project in which photographers went all over the world, and in a 24-hour period, they took their pictures and uploaded the digital images, and people in the central office typed up descriptions and allowed people to view them online. It was a very ambitious project and a perfect example of a CMS application.

The bottom line is that if you have content that you want to be able to update on a regular basis, you definitely want to implement a CMS application. And now, you have the basic tools to build one on your own!

Perhaps you should send your users an e-mail to tell them of your improved functionality. We'll do that in Chapter 13.

13

Mailing Lists

Ah, yes. The mailing list. Two simple, innocent words that never meant anyone any harm. That is, until a few years ago, when someone decided to put the two together, and junk mail was born. Oh sure, mailing lists are used for more than junk mail. After all, how else are you going to receive your Quilting Monthly magazine unless your name and address are on a list? What does this have to do with PHP? In the world of e-mail and your incredible new Web site, it is a perfect way for you to communicate with all of your users! You might need to let every user know that your site has moved to a new address. Maybe you want to send out a monthly newsletter. Whatever the reason, you will occasionally need to send e-mails to many people, and you will need a relatively easy way to do so.

Specifically, we are going to discuss the following:

❑ Administering a mailing list

❑ Creating a mailing list

❑ Spam

❑ Opt-in and opt-out

So, are you ready to learn how to spam your Web site users? We hope not, because that is not what we are going to do. Yes, we are going to use mailing lists. And yes, we are going to send out "mass" e-mails. However, we are going to be responsible, and send e-mails only to those people who have agreed to be recipients. Right? Let's get started.

First Things First

Before you actually create the mailing list, you must have something that you intend to send to your recipients. The train of thought usually goes like this: You decide that you have some information you want to share with your users. This can be a newsletter, information about the next comic convention, or Web site updates they may want to know about. You format the information you wish to share, using plain text or HTML. You try to figure out how you are going to e-mail this information to *every* member of your Web site. If you can figure out how to send it, you hope that your users will be able to read and appreciate what you sent with their many types of e-mail clients.

What Do You Want to Send Today?

The first question is what you will send. You may already have some ideas. Maybe not. Suffice it to say there are many different reasons to send out bulk messages. Here are a few:

- ❑ **Web site notifications:** These are important tidbits of information about your Web site. You will want to let your users know you've improved the level of security for online transactions on your site, for example.

- ❑ **Newsletters:** If you had a family Web site, for example, and wanted to let your whole family know about the new addition to your family, you could send them a newsletter.

- ❑ **Important announcements:** "Our site will be down for 5 days. Sorry for the inconvenience. We'll let you know when it is back up." (Oooh . . . an opportunity for *two* mailings!)

- ❑ **Advertising:** Perhaps you've partnered with an online comic book store to offer deals on rare comics to your members, for example.

We are going to send out two different e-mails: Web site change notifications and a newsletter. The former will be sent to all members of the Web site. The latter will be sent to those who subscribe to the newsletter only.

We are going to use HTML in our mass e-mail, of course. Because Chapter 10 taught you how to send HTML in an e-mail, this should pose no problem at all. You can also e-mail links to an online version of the HTML you are sending, so that those with text e-mail clients can see your hard work, as well.

Coding the Application

The first thing you're going to do is to create the administration page, where you can add and remove mailing lists. There are a few scripts to tackle, but because they all rely on each other to work, you need to enter them all now. Hey . . . you're the one who wanted to write some code. Let's get cracking!

Try It Out   Mailing List Administration

First, you're going to create the file that will hold the server, username, password, and database values:

1. Open your favorite text editor, and enter the following code, making sure you use the proper values for your server:

```php
<?php

define('SQL_HOST','yourhost');
define('SQL_USER','joeuser');
define('SQL_PASS','yourpass');
define('SQL_DB','yourdatabase');
define('ADMIN_E-MAIL', 'your@e-mailaddress.com');

?>
```

2. Save the file as `config.php`.

3. Now you're going to create the tables. You can create them with your MySQL tool (such as PHPMyAdmin), or you can simply enter the following code, save it as `sql.php` on your server, and load it in your browser:

```php
<?php
require('config.php');

$conn = mysql_connect(SQL_HOST, SQL_USER, SQL_PASS)
 or die('Could not connect to MySQL database. ' . mysql_error());

$sql = "CREATE DATABASE IF NOT EXISTS" . SQL_DB . ";";

$res = mysql_query($sql) or die(mysql_error());

mysql_select_db(SQL_DB,$conn);

$sql1 = <<<EOS
 CREATE TABLE IF NOT EXISTS ml_lists (
  ml_id int(11) NOT NULL auto_increment,
  listname varchar(255) NOT NULL default '',
  PRIMARY KEY (ml_id)
 ) TYPE=MyISAM;
EOS;

$sql2 = <<<EOS
 CREATE TABLE IF NOT EXISTS ml_subscriptions (
  ml_id int(11) NOT NULL default '0',
  user_id int(11) NOT NULL default '0',
  pending tinyint(1) NOT NULL default '1',
  PRIMARY KEY (ml_id,user_id)
 ) TYPE=MyISAM;
EOS;

$sql3 = <<<EOS
 CREATE TABLE IF NOT EXISTS ml_users (
  user_id int(11) NOT NULL auto_increment,
  firstname varchar(255) default '',
  lastname varchar(255) default '',
  e-mail varchar(255) NOT NULL default '',
  PRIMARY KEY (user_id)
 ) TYPE=MyISAM;
EOS;

$res = mysql_query($sql1) or die(mysql_error());
$res = mysql_query($sql2) or die(mysql_error());
$res = mysql_query($sql3) or die(mysql_error());
echo "Done.";
?>
```

4. Next, you will create the admin page, where the administrator (that's you!) can create, delete, and rename mailing lists. Create the following code, and save it as `admin.php`:

```php
<?php
require('config.php');
```

```
?>

<html>
<head>
<title>Mailing List Administration</title>
</head>
<body>

<form method="post" action="admin_transact.php">

<p>
 Add Mailing List:<br />
 <input type="text" name="listname" maxlength="255" />
 <input type="submit" name="action" value="Add New Mailing List" />
</p>

<p>
 Delete Mailing List:<br />
 <select name="ml_id">
<?php

$conn = mysql_connect(SQL_HOST, SQL_USER, SQL_PASS)
 or die('Could not connect to MySQL database. ' . mysql_error());

mysql_select_db(SQL_DB,$conn);

$sql = "SELECT * FROM ml_lists ORDER BY listname;";
$result = mysql_query($sql)
 or die('Invalid query: ' . mysql_error());

while ($row = mysql_fetch_array($result))
{
 echo " <option value=\"" . $row['ml_id'] . "\">" . $row['listname']
  . "</option>\n";
}

?>
 </select>
 <input type="submit" name="action" value="Delete Mailing List" />
</p>

</form>

<p>
 <a href="quickmsg.php">Send a quick message to users</a>
</p>

</body>
</html>
```

5. The administrator needs the ability to send e-mails to the members of various mailing lists. Otherwise, what was the point of creating the mailing lists in the first place? Okay, you know the routine: Enter the following code, and save it as `quickmsg.php`:

```php
<?php
require('config.php');
?>

<html>
<head>
<title>Quick Message</title>
</head>
<body>

<form method="post" action="admin_transact.php">

<p>
 Choose Mailing List:<br />
 <select name="ml_id">
  <option value="all">All</option>
<?php

$conn = mysql_connect(SQL_HOST, SQL_USER, SQL_PASS)
 or die('Could not connect to MySQL database. ' . mysql_error());

mysql_select_db(SQL_DB,$conn);

$sql = "SELECT * FROM ml_lists ORDER BY listname;";
$result = mysql_query($sql)
 or die('Invalid query: ' . mysql_error());

while ($row = mysql_fetch_array($result))
{
 echo "  <option value=\"" . $row['ml_id'] . "\">" . $row['listname']
    . "</option>\n";
}

?>
 </select>
</p>

<p>Compose Message:</p>

<p>
 Subject:<br />
 <input type="text" name="subject" />
</p>

<p>
 Message:<br />
 <textarea name="msg" rows="10" cols="60"></textarea>
</p>

<p>
 <input type="submit" name="action" value="Send Message" />
</p>

</form>

<p>
```

```
        <a href="admin.php">Back to mailing list administration</a>
    </p>

    </body>
    </html>
```

6. Okay, one more script. When the administrator clicks a button, you need to have a page that handles the transactions. Enter the following, and save it as admin_transact.php:

```php
<?php
require('config.php');

$conn = mysql_connect(SQL_HOST, SQL_USER, SQL_PASS)
 or die('Could not connect to MySQL database. ' . mysql_error());

mysql_select_db(SQL_DB,$conn);

if (isset($_POST['action']))
{
 switch ($_POST['action'])
 {
  case 'Add New Mailing List':
    $sql = "INSERT INTO ml_lists (listname) VALUES ('" .
        $_POST['listname'] . "');";
   mysql_query($sql)
    or die('Could not add mailing list. ' . mysql_error());
   break;

  case 'Delete Mailing List':
    $sql = "DELETE FROM ml_lists WHERE ml_id=" . $_POST['ml_id'];
   mysql_query($sql)
    or die('Could not delete mailing list. ' . mysql_error());
$sql = "DELETE FROM ml_subscriptions WHERE ml_id=" .
        $_POST['ml_id'];
   mysql_query($sql)
    or die('Could not delete mailing list subscriptions. ' .
    mysql_error());
   break;

  case 'Send Message':
   if ((isset($_POST['msg'])) and (isset($_POST['ml_id'])))
   {
    if (is_numeric($_POST['ml_id'])) {
     $sql = "SELECT listname FROM ml_lists WHERE ml_id='" .
        $_POST['ml_id'] . "'";
     $result = mysql_query($sql,$conn)
      or die(mysql_error());
     $row = mysql_fetch_array($result);
     $listname = $row['listname'];
    } else {
     $listname = "Master";
    }

    $sql = "SELECT DISTINCT usr.e-mail, usr.firstname, usr.user_id ".
        "FROM ml_users usr " .
```

```
            "INNER JOIN ml_subscriptions mls " .
            "ON usr.user_id = mls.user_id " .
            "WHERE mls.pending=0";
    if ($_POST['ml_id'] != 'all')
    {
     $sql .= " AND mls.ml_id=" . $_POST['ml_id'];
    }

    $result = mysql_query($sql) or die('Could not get list of
        e-mail addresses. ' . mysql_error());

    $headers = "From: " . ADMIN_E-MAIL . "\r\n";
    while ($row = mysql_fetch_array($result))
    {
    if (is_numeric($_POST['ml_id'])) {
     $ft = " You are receiving this message as a member of the ";
     $ft .= $listname . "\n mailing list. If you have received";
     $ft .= "this e-mail in error, or would like to\n remove your";
     $ft .= "name from this mailing list, please visit the";
     $ft .= "following URL:\n";
     $ft .= " http://" . $_SERVER['HTTP_HOST'] .
        dirname($_SERVER['PHP_SELF']) . "/remove.php?u=" .
        $row['user_id'] . "&ml=" . $_POST['ml_id'];
    } else {
     $ft = " You are receiving this e-mail because you subscribed";
     $ft .= " to one or more\n mailing lists. Visit the following";
     $ft .= " URL to change your subscriptions:\n";
     $ft .= " http://" . $_SERVER['HTTP_HOST'] .
        dirname($_SERVER['PHP_SELF']) . "/user.php?u=" .
        $row['user_id'];
    }
     $msg = stripslashes($_POST['msg']) . "\n\n";
     $msg .= "————\n";
     $msg .= $ft;

     mail($row['e-mail'],
        stripslashes($_POST['subject']),
        $msg,$headers) or die('Could not send e-mail.');
    }
   }
   break;
 }
}

header('Location: admin.php');

?>
```

That's it for now. You still have the user functions to worry about, but you'll tackle those in a bit. For now, let's load a few of these pages in your browser to see them in action; then we'll figure out how they work.

The first page of the mailing list application we want to take a look at is the Mailing List Administrator page. Load admin.php in your browser. As you can see in Figure 13-1, you can create a new mailing list, delete an existing mailing list, or send a quick message to users. Feel free to create a couple of new mailing lists. Go crazy, have fun, get wacky. Good. Let's move on.

Figure 13-1

Click the link at the bottom of the Mailing List Administrator page, "Send a quick message to users." A new page appears where you can compose a new message and send it to either a single mailing list, or all users (see Figure 13-2). If you just created these pages, you don't have any users yet. You can compose a message, but it won't go to anyone. You'll need to create the user pages first, which you'll do shortly.

How It Works

You first file, config.php, contains just five lines:

```
define('SQL_HOST','yourhost');
define('SQL_USER','joeuser');
define('SQL_PASS','yourpass');
define('SQL_DB','yourdatabase');
define('ADMIN_E-MAIL', 'your@e-mailaddress.com');
```

These constants are created separately so that in the event that you make a change such as moving the application to another server, or changing the password, it can be done in only one location. If this data were in each file, any change would require modification of several files.

Figure 13-2

Include `config.php` in each file that requires access to MySQL like so:

```
require('config.php');
```

You use `require()` instead of `include()` because if the file is not loaded, you want to halt loading of the page. Another option would be to use `include()`, and then immediately test for the existence of one of the constants. If it does not exist, you could then redirect the user to another page, which makes for a more user-friendly experience.

As you can see here, the constants from `config.php` are used to make your connection:

```
$conn = mysql_connect(SQL_HOST, SQL_USER, SQL_PASS)
 or die('Could not connect to MySQL database. ' . mysql_error());

$sql = "CREATE DATABASE IF NOT EXISTS" . SQL_DB . ";";

$res = mysql_query($sql) or die(mysql_error());

mysql_select_db(SQL_DB,$conn);
```

Take notice of the CREATE DATABASE statement. There are a couple of things you should be aware of about creating databases. If you already have a database (one that you created in another chapter, or if your site is already using a database), it's better to keep your mailing list tables in that database. You don't need extra databases because if your Web site spans multiple databases, you will need to create multiple connections to those databases, and that is extra overhead that is just not necessary.

In addition, if there are any relationships between your tables from this application and tables from other apps, they need to be in the same database. For example, if you have a user table that stores your registered users for all applications, all of the applications that rely on that user table should reside in the same database.

If you do need to create a new database, the CREATE DATABASE command may still not work if your site is hosted by an Internet service provider (ISP). Some ISPs don't allow programmed creation of databases. If this is the case, you may need to go through your ISP to create the database (through PHPMyAdmin, for example) and run sql.php. Just be sure to put the proper database name in the code. See Chapter 9 for more information about creating databases.

This SQL is used to create the tables in your database:

```
$sql1 = <<<EOS
 CREATE TABLE IF NOT EXISTS ml_lists (
  ml_id int(11) NOT NULL auto_increment,
  listname varchar(255) NOT NULL default '',
  PRIMARY KEY (ml_id)
 ) TYPE=MyISAM;
EOS;

$sql2 = <<<EOS
 CREATE TABLE IF NOT EXISTS ml_subscriptions (
  ml_id int(11) NOT NULL default '0',
  user_id int(11) NOT NULL default '0',
  pending tinyint(1) NOT NULL default '1',
  PRIMARY KEY (ml_id,user_id)
 ) TYPE=MyISAM;
EOS;

$sql3 = <<<EOS
 CREATE TABLE IF NOT EXISTS ml_users (
  user_id int(11) NOT NULL auto_increment,
  firstname varchar(255) default '',
  lastname varchar(255) default '',
  e-mail varchar(255) NOT NULL default '',
  PRIMARY KEY (user_id)
 ) TYPE=MyISAM;
EOS;
```

Note there are three tables: ml_lists, ml_users, and ml_subscriptions. The ml_lists table contains two columns: the unique ID (ml_id) and the name of the mailing list (listname). The ml_users table contains four columns: the unique id (user_id), first and last name (firstname, lastname), and e-mail address (e-mail).

The ml_subscriptions table is where most of the "work" is done when it comes to mailing lists. It contains three columns: ml_id, user_id, and pending. The combination of ml_id and user_id must be unique. (You don't want to have the same user subscribed to the same mailing list more than once, right?). The pending column is used to determine whether or not a user has confirmed his or her subscription. We discuss the use of the pending column later in this chapter.

The following lines simply run the SQL queries to create the tables. As long as all three tables are created (or already exist), you will see "Done" echoed to the screen. Otherwise, you will see an error message.

```
$res = mysql_query($sql1) or die(mysql_error());
$res = mysql_query($sql2) or die(mysql_error());
$res = mysql_query($sql3) or die(mysql_error());
echo "Done.";
```

Next, let's take a look at admin.php:

```
require('config.php');
```

Now you should see why we put the connection values in a separate file. By doing this, all you need is a single line to include the constants, and you can use them in this page.

Let's pause here for a moment and talk about form submittal. A common practice is to post a form back to itself, and you certainly could have done that here. When your page contains data that needs to be inserted into a database, however, you need to think twice about a self-posting form. If the user were to refresh or reload the page, all of your database functions would run again, and that could be disastrous. You would end up with duplicate data, or delete records you didn't mean to delete.

Obviously, you don't want anything like that to happen, so in order to minimize the probability, you post to a separate form called admin_transact.php. This page handles all of the necessary database transactions, and then redirects back to the page from which you came. If the user reloads the page at that point, no harm will come to your database.

```
<form method="post" action="admin_transact.php">
```

You might notice that all of your buttons have the same name, "action," each with a different value. When posting the form, you will be accessing the $_POST['action'] variable to see which button was pressed, and perform the appropriate actions. This allows you to use one script for multiple transactions, rather than having to create a page with multiple forms, each posting to a different transaction page.

```
<input type="submit" name="action" value="Add New Mailing List" />
```

Now you get all of the mailing lists available and wrap them in option tags so that they will appear on your page in a drop-down select box.

```
<select name="ml_id">
<?php

$conn = mysql_connect(SQL_HOST, SQL_USER, SQL_PASS)
```

```
      or die('Could not connect to MySQL database. ' . mysql_error());

   mysql_select_db(SQL_DB, $conn);

   $sql = "SELECT * FROM ml_lists ORDER BY listname;";
   $result = mysql_query($sql)
     or die('Invalid query: ' . mysql_error());

   while ($row = mysql_fetch_array($result))
   {
     echo "  <option value=\"" . $row['ml_id'] . "\">" .
        $row['listname'] . "</option>\n";
   }

   ?>
   </select>
```

This is the link to the e-mail portion of the admin's functions, which is pretty self-explanatory:

```
   <a href="quickmsg.php">Send a quick message to users</a>
```

You should be able to figure out quickmsg.php fairly easily. Most of it is HTML, and the PHP code is practically identical to the code used to build the select in admin.php. Feel free to cannibalize your own code as often as you need.

Finally, we come to the real workhorse of the Mailing List Administrator application, admin_transact .php. This page is the one to which you post your forms, and it will process that information, update the database tables, and send out e-mails as required. Let's take a look under the hood:

```
   require('config.php');
```

Remember seeing the preceding line in admin.php? Having your connection data in one file and including it in each page makes your code much more efficient. Of course, you already knew that. Let's move on to create the connection to the database, and select it so that you can work with it:

```
   $conn = mysql_connect(SQL_HOST, SQL_USER, SQL_PASS)
     or die('Could not connect to MySQL database. ' . mysql_error());

   mysql_select_db(SQL_DB, $conn);
```

Did the user click an "action" button?

```
   if (isset($_POST['action']))
   {
```

Depending on which button was clicked, you're going to perform one of three actions: create a new mailing list, delete an old mailing list, or send a message to the users subscribing to a mailing list:

```
   switch ($_POST['action'])
     {
```

Not only must you delete the mailing list, like this:

```
case 'Add New Mailing List':
    $sql = "INSERT INTO ml_lists (listname) VALUES ('" .
        $_POST['listname'] . "');";
    mysql_query($sql)
     or die('Could not add mailing list. ' . mysql_error());
    break;

  case 'Delete Mailing List':
    mysql_query("DELETE FROM ml_lists WHERE ml_id=" . $_POST['ml_id'])
     or die('Could not delete mailing list. ' . mysql_error());
```

if anyone was subscribed to that mailing list, you must delete those subscriptions, too:

```
$sql = "DELETE FROM ml_subscriptions WHERE ml_id=" .
        $_POST['ml_id'];
    mysql_query($sql)
     or die('Could not delete mailing list subscriptions. ' .
     mysql_error());
    break;
```

When you send a message, you want to let the user know which mailing list you are referring to. If the mailing list ID (ml_id) is "all" instead of a number, you will want to reflect that as well:

```
case 'Send Message':
    if ((isset($_POST['msg'])) and (isset($_POST['ml_id'])))
    {
     if (is_numeric($_POST['ml_id'])) {
      $sql = "SELECT listname FROM ml_lists WHERE ml_id='" .
        $_POST['ml_id'] . "'";
      $result = mysql_query($sql, $conn)
       or die(mysql_error());
      $row = mysql_fetch_array($result);
      $listname = $row['listname'];
     } else {
      $listname = "Master";
     }
```

What follows is a more complicated SQL statement than you've written thus far, but not too difficult. What's happening here is that you are grabbing the e-mails, first names, and user id's from the ml_users table where the mailing list id (ml_id) matches their user id in the ml_subscriptions table. This is done by using the INNER JOIN command in SQL. You also *must not* send any e-mails or newsletters to those that are awaiting subscription confirmation, so select only those where pending = 0, or false. If pending = 1 (true), then that row is ignored.

```
$sql = "SELECT DISTINCT usr.e-mail, usr.firstname, usr.user_id" .
        "FROM ml_users usr " .
        "INNER JOIN ml_subscriptions mls " .
        "ON usr.user_id = mls.user_id " .
        "WHERE mls.pending=0";
```

If the administrator did not choose "all" in the select list, you must limit your selection to the specific users that are subscribed to the mailing list the administrator selected. You do this by tacking on the AND condition:

```
if ($_POST['ml_id'] != 'all')
{
  $sql .= " AND mls.ml_id=" . $_POST['ml_id'];
}
```

Now execute the previous SQL statement, and return the results:

```
$result = mysql_query($sql) or die('Could not get list of
    e-mail addresses. ' . mysql_error());
```

You may remember the next step from Chapter 10. This is how you add the From: header to an e-mail. It is fairly self-explanatory:

```
$headers = "From: " . ADMIN_E-MAIL . "\r\n";
```

The following pretty piece of work is nothing more than a way to build up a custom message, depending on whether the administrator is sending the e-mail to *all* mailing lists, or to a specific one:

```
while ($row = mysql_fetch_array($result))
  {
  if (is_numeric($_POST['ml_id'])) {
    $ft = " You are receiving this message as a member of the ";
    $ft .= $listname . "\n mailing list. If you have received";
    $ft .= "this e-mail in error, or would like to\n remove your";
    $ft .= "name from this mailing list, please visit the";
    $ft .= "following URL:\n";
    $ft .= " http://" . $_SERVER['HTTP_HOST'] .
        dirname($_SERVER['PHP_SELF']) . "/remove.php?u=" .
        $row['user_id'] . "&ml=" . $_POST['ml_id'];
  } else {
    $ft = " You are receiving this e-mail because you subscribed";
    $ft .= " to one or more\n mailing lists. Visit the following";
    $ft .= " URL to change your subscriptions:\n";
    $ft .= " http://" . $_SERVER['HTTP_HOST'] .
        dirname($_SERVER['PHP_SELF']) . "/user.php?u=" .
        $row['user_id'];
  }
```

Wrap the message entered on the `quickmsg.php` form inside some extra disclaimer text before you send it off to the `mail()` function:

```
$msg = stripslashes($_POST['msg']) . "\n\n";
$msg .= "--------------\n";
$msg .= $ft;

mail($row['e-mail'],
    stripslashes($_POST['subject']),
    $msg,$headers) or die('Could not send e-mail.');
}
```

And away it goes, before you loop back to the top of your `while` loop and do it again with the next user. Notice that you are looping through *each* e-mail address you have, and sending an e-mail to each one using the `mail()` command. It is important to note that the page will not finish loading until it has sent every e-mail. This works fine if you have a few e-mail addresses (a hundred or less). It has the added benefit of allowing you (with slight modifications to the code) to personalize each e-mail with the person's first name ("Dear Billy-Bob,").

If you need to send to more people and don't want to deal with the long wait time, we recommend putting all of your e-mail addresses in the BCC: field of the mail, using headers (as discussed in Chapter 10). You can't personalize the e-mail, but the page will load much faster.

Of course, some day your site will be extremely popular, and you might have thousands of e-mails to send. At that point, it might be time to start looking at a professional mailing list management application. That, however, is beyond the scope of this book.

After the page is done with its transactions, redirect the user to the `admin.php` page. Most of the time, this happens so quickly that you don't notice the redirection at all.

```
header('Location: admin.php');
```

Sign Me Up!

Now it's time to look at the other half of the application, the Mailing List Signup form. This is the page you send your users to that enables them to sign up for any of the mailing lists that you have created. This application consists of `user.php`, `user_transact.php`, `thanks.php`, and `remove.php`. As always, you'll also be using the `config.php` file that you already created.

On the surface, when you view the page from the Web, it looks like a simple application. However, there's a lot going on inside. So let's open it up and see what's under the hood!

Try It Out   Mailing List Signup

The first page you are going to create is the actual signup form:

1. Enter the following code in your favorite PHP editor and save it as `user.php`:

```php
<?php
require('config.php');
?>

<html>
<head>
<title>Mailing List Signup</title>
</head>
<body>

<form method="post" action="user_transact.php">

<p>
  Sign up for Mailing List:<br />
```

```
</p>

<?php

$conn = mysql_connect(SQL_HOST, SQL_USER, SQL_PASS)
 or die('Could not connect to MySQL database. ' . mysql_error());

mysql_select_db(SQL_DB,$conn);

if (isset($_GET['u']))
{
 $uid = $_GET['u'];
 $sql = "SELECT * FROM ml_users WHERE user_id = '$uid';";
 $result = mysql_query($sql)
  or die('Invalid query: ' . mysql_error());
 if (mysql_num_rows($result)) {
  $row = mysql_fetch_array($result);
  $e-mail = $row['e-mail'];
 } else {
  $e-mail = "";
 }
}
?>

<p>
 E-mail Address:<br />
 <input type="text" name="e-mail" size="40" value="<?php echo
    $e-mail;?>"/>
</p>

<p>
 If you aren't currently a member, please provide
 your name:<br /><br />
 First Name:<br />
 <input type="text" name="firstname" /><br />
 Last Name:<br />
 <input type="text" name="lastname" /><br />
</p>

<p>
 Select the mailing lists you want to receive:<br />
 <select name="ml_id">

<?php
$result = mysql_query("SELECT * FROM ml_lists ORDER BY listname;")
 or die('Invalid query: ' . mysql_error());

while ($row = mysql_fetch_array($result))
{
 echo "  <option value=\"" . $row['ml_id'] . "\">" .
    $row['listname'] . "</option>\n";
}

?>
```

```
    </select>
  </p>

  <p>
   <input type="submit" name="action"
      value="Subscribe" />
  </p>

  </form>

  </body>
  </html>
```

2. Enter the transaction page by entering the following code in your PHP editor and saving it as user_transact.php:

```php
<?php
require('config.php');

$conn = mysql_connect(SQL_HOST, SQL_USER, SQL_PASS)
 or die('Could not connect to MySQL database. ' . mysql_error());

mysql_select_db(SQL_DB,$conn);

if (isset($_REQUEST['action']))
{
 $headers = "From: " . ADMIN_E-MAIL . "\r\n";
 switch ($_REQUEST['action'])
 {
  case 'Remove':
   $sql = "SELECT user_id FROM ml_users " .
       "WHERE e-mail='" . $_POST['e-mail'] . "';";
   $result = mysql_query($sql,$conn);

   if (mysql_num_rows($result))
   {
    $row = mysql_fetch_array($result);
    $user_id = $row['user_id'];
    $url = "http://" . $_SERVER['HTTP_HOST'] .
       dirname($_SERVER['PHP_SELF']) .
       "/remove.php?u=" . $user_id .
       "&ml=" . $_POST['ml_id'];
    header("Location: $url");
    exit();
   }
   $redirect = 'user.php';
   break;
  case 'Subscribe':
   $sql = "SELECT user_id FROM ml_users " .
       "WHERE e-mail='" . $_POST['e-mail'] . "';";
   $result = mysql_query($sql,$conn);

   if (!mysql_num_rows($result))
   {
```

```php
    $sql = "INSERT INTO ml_users " .
        "(firstname,lastname,e-mail) " .
        "VALUES ('" . $_POST['firstname'] . "'," .
        "'" . $_POST['lastname'] . "'," .
        "'" . $_POST['e-mail'] . "');";
  $result = mysql_query($sql, $conn);
  $user_id = mysql_insert_id($conn);
}
else
{
  $row = mysql_fetch_array($result);
  $user_id = $row['user_id'];
}

$sql = "INSERT INTO ml_subscriptions (user_id,ml_id) " .
    "VALUES ('" . $user_id . "','" . $_POST['ml_id'] . "')";
mysql_query($sql,$conn);

$sql = "SELECT listname FROM ml_lists " .
    "WHERE ml_id=" . $_POST['ml_id'];
$result = mysql_query($sql,$conn);
$row = mysql_fetch_array($result);
$listname = $row['listname'];

$url = "http://" . $_SERVER['HTTP_HOST'] .
    dirname($_SERVER['PHP_SELF']) .
    "/user_transact.php?u=" . $user_id .
    "&ml=" . $_POST['ml_id'] . "&action=confirm";

$subject = 'Mailing list confirmation';
$body = "Hello " . $_POST['firstname'] . "\n" .
    "Our records indicate that you have subscribed to the " .
    $listname . " mailing list.\n\n" .
    "If you did not subscribe, please accept our apologies. " .
    "You will not be subscribed if you do not visit the " .
    "confirmation URL.\n\n" .
    "If you subscribed, please confirm this by visiting the " .
    "following URL:\n" . $url;

mail($_POST['e-mail'],$subject,$body,$headers);

$redirect = "thanks.php?u=" . $user_id . "&ml=" .
    $_POST['ml_id'] . "&t=s";
break;


case 'confirm':

  if (isset($_GET['u']) & isset($_GET['ml']))
  {
  $sql = "UPDATE ml_subscriptions SET pending=0 " .
      "WHERE user_id=" . $_GET['u'] .
      " AND ml_id=" . $_GET['ml'];
  mysql_query($sql, $conn);

  $sql = "SELECT listname FROM ml_lists " .
```

```php
            "WHERE ml_id=" . $_GET['ml'];
      $result = mysql_query($sql,$conn);

      $row = mysql_fetch_array($result);
      $listname = $row['listname'];

      $sql = "SELECT * FROM ml_users " .
            "WHERE user_id='" . $_GET['u'] . "';";
      $result = mysql_query($sql,$conn);
      $row = mysql_fetch_array($result);
      $firstname = $row['firstname'];
      $e-mail = $row['e-mail'];

      $url = "http://" . $_SERVER['HTTP_HOST'] .
            dirname($_SERVER['PHP_SELF']) .
            "/remove.php?u=" . $_GET['u'] .
            "&ml=" . $_GET['ml'];

      // Send out confirmed e-mail
      $subject = 'Mailing List Subscription Confirmed';
      $body = "Hello " . $firstname . ",\n" .
            "Thank you for subscribing to the " .
            $listname . " mailing list. Welcome!\n\n" .
            "If you did not subscribe, please accept our apologies.\n".
            "You can remove this subscription immediately by ".
            "visiting the following URL:\n" . $url;

      mail($e-mail,$subject,$body,$headers);

      $redirect = "thanks.php?u=" . $_GET['u'] . "&ml=" .
            $_GET['ml'] . "&t=s";
    } else {
      $redirect = 'user.php';
    }
    break;

  default:
    $redirect = 'user.php';
 }
}

header('Location: ' . $redirect);

?>
```

3. You may have noticed when entering the last bit of code that you are redirecting your users to a page called thanks.php. It would probably be a good idea to create that page now by entering the following code and saving it as thanks.php:

```php
<?php
require('config.php');
?>

<html>
<head>
```

```php
<title>Thank You</title>
</head>
<body>

<?php
$conn = mysql_connect(SQL_HOST, SQL_USER, SQL_PASS)
  or die('Could not connect to MySQL database. ' . mysql_error());

mysql_select_db(SQL_DB,$conn);

if (isset($_GET['u']))
{
 $uid = $_GET['u'];
 $sql = "SELECT * FROM ml_users WHERE user_id = '$uid';";
 $result = mysql_query($sql)
  or die('Invalid query: ' . mysql_error());
 if (mysql_num_rows($result)) {
  $row = mysql_fetch_array($result);
  $msg = "<h2>Thank You, " . $row['firstname'] . "</h2><br /><br />";
  $e-mail = $row['e-mail'];
 } else {
  die("No match for user id " . $uid);
 }
}

if (isset($_GET['ml']))
{
 $ml_id = $_GET['ml'];
 $sql = "SELECT * FROM ml_lists WHERE ml_id = '" . $ml_id . "';";
 $result = mysql_query($sql)
  or die('Invalid query: ' . mysql_error());
 if (mysql_num_rows($result)) {
  $row = mysql_fetch_array($result);
  $msg .= "Thank you for subscribing to the <i>" .
     $row['listname'] . "</i> mailing list.<br />";
 } else {
  die ("Could not find Mailing List $ml_id");
 }
} else {
 die ("Mailing List id missing.");
}

if (!isset($_GET['t'])) die("Missing Type");
switch ($_GET['t'])
{
 case 'c':
  $msg .= "A confirmation request has been sent " .
     "to <b>$e-mail</b>.<br /><br />";
  break;
 case 's':
  $msg .= "A subscription notification has been " .
     "sent to you at <b>$e-mail</b>.<br /><br />";
}
$msg .= "<a href='user.php?u=$uid'>" .
    "Return to Mailing List Signup page</a>";
```

```
echo $msg;
?>

</body>
</html>
```

4. One more file to go, and it's a short one. The e-mail that you send has a link on it allowing your users to remove themselves from the mailing list, if they desire. Enter that file now, and save it as `remove.php`:

```php
<?php
require('config.php');

$conn = mysql_connect(SQL_HOST, SQL_USER, SQL_PASS)
 or die('Could not connect to MySQL database. ' . mysql_error());

mysql_select_db(SQL_DB,$conn);

if ((isset($_GET['u'])) and (isset($_GET['ml'])))
{
 $sql = "DELETE FROM ml_subscriptions " .
     "WHERE user_id=" . $_GET['u'] .
     " AND ml_id=" . $_GET['ml'];
 $result = mysql_query($sql,$conn);
} else {
 die("Incorrect parameters passed for deletion");
}

if ($result) {
 $msg = "<h2>Removal Successful</h2>";
} else {
 $msg = "<h2>Removal Failed</h2>";
}

$ml_id = $_GET['ml'];
$sql = "SELECT * FROM ml_lists WHERE ml_id = '" . $ml_id . "';";
$result = mysql_query($sql)
 or die('Invalid query: ' . mysql_error());
if (mysql_num_rows($result)) {
 $row = mysql_fetch_array($result);
 $msg .= "You have been removed from the <i>" .
     $row['listname'] . "</i> mailing list.<br />";
} else {
 $msg .= "Sorry, could not find Mailing List id#{$ml_id}");
}

$msg .= "<a href='user.php?u=" . $_GET['u'] .
     "'>Return to Mailing List Signup page</a>";
echo $msg;
?>
```

Excellent job! Now it's time to test your code and figure out how it works. Follow these steps:

1. Open your browser and open `user.php`. You should see a form that looks very much like the one in Figure 13-3.

Figure 13-3

2. Enter your e-mail address and your first and last name, choose a mailing list to subscribe to, and click Subscribe.

You should see a Thank You screen (shown in Figure 13-4) and receive a confirmation e-mail at the e-mail address you entered.

3. Open the confirmation e-mail. There will be a link at the bottom (or a nonlinked URL if you are using a text e-mail client).

4. Click the link, and it takes you back to the Thank You page, this time thanking you for confirming your subscription.

You will get another e-mail informing you about your subscription, with a link that allows you to remove yourself from the mailing list. Don't click that link just yet. First you're going to send an e-mail to the mailing list you just subscribed to:

1. Open `admin.php`, and then click the link at the bottom, "Send a quick message to users."

2. In the Quick Message page, choose the mailing list that you just subscribed to in the previous steps, and enter a subject. Then type a quick message.

Figure 13-4

3. Click Send Message.

4. Open your e-mail client again, and read the message you should have received. At the bottom of this e-mail is a link you can click to remove yourself from the mailing list.

5. Now, click the link.

   You should see the Removal page (see Figure 13-5), with a message of success. If you send another message to that mailing list, the message should not be sent to your e-mail address.

Figure 13-5

How It Works

By now, you know how `config.php` works. You know why we use it. We won't insult your intelligence by explaining again how it's important to use this file to hold your MySQL connection info and password. We are also going to skip over parts of the code that we've touched on before. We certainly don't want to bore you!

Let's take a look at `user.php` instead, shall we?

user.php

Typically, `user.php` loads empty, without any extra data. Occasionally, you may return to this page from elsewhere, and will have the user id of the person loading the page. In this case, you tack on ?u=x to the end of the URL (where x is the user id, such as 3). This bit of code detects the presence of that value:

```
if (isset($_GET['u']))
{
```

and then puts it into a variable:

```
$uid = $_GET['u'];
```

and finally looks up the user's e-mail address:

```
$sql = "SELECT * FROM ml_users WHERE user_id = '$uid';";
 $result = mysql_query($sql)
   or die('Invalid query: ' . mysql_error());
```

If you find a row, grab the e-mail address and stick it into a variable:

```
if (mysql_num_rows($result)) {
  $row = mysql_fetch_array($result);
  $e-mail = $row['e-mail'];
} else {
  $e-mail = "";
}
```

Then use that e-mail address as the default value for the e-mail field on the form. (How clever is that?)

```
E-mail Address:<br />
 <input type="text" name="e-mail" size="40" value="<?php echo
    $e-mail;?>"/>
```

The following code is very similar to the code used on the `admin.php` page. It loops through the existing mailing lists in the database and formats them on the page as options for the select field.

```
<select name="ml_id">

<?php
$result = mysql_query("SELECT * FROM ml_lists ORDER BY listname;")
 or die('Invalid query: ' . mysql_error());

while ($row = mysql_fetch_array($result))
```

```
 {
  echo "  <option value=\"" . $row['ml_id'] . "\">" .
     $row['listname'] . "</option>\n";
 }

 ?>
 </select>
```

The rest of user.php is boring HTML. Let's take a look at the meat and potatoes of the user side of things next.

user_transact.php

This is where the action happens, for the most part. Let's take a look, shall we?

First, make the connection to the server, and select the database:

```
$conn = mysql_connect(SQL_HOST, SQL_USER, SQL_PASS)
 or die('Could not connect to MySQL database. ' . mysql_error());

mysql_select_db(SQL_DB, $conn);
```

You will be building the e-mail message later. The parameter $headers will be the fourth parameter of the mail() function, and will insert a From address in the e-mail.

```
$headers = "From: " . ADMIN_E-MAIL . "\r\n";
```

For more information about headers, see Chapter 10. When loading user_transact.php, you either clicked a button named 'action' (POST), or action is in the URL as ?action=xyz (GET). Because it can come across as a POST or a GET, you use $_REQUEST to grab the value. The variable $_REQUEST is your "catch-all" predefined variable, which contains an associative array of all $_GET, $_POST, and $_COOKIE variables.

```
if (isset($_REQUEST['action']))
{
```

Current accepted values for 'action' are 'Remove,' 'Subscribe,' and 'confirm.' switch ($_REQUEST['action'])

```
   {
```

If 'action' = 'Remove', you look up the user id in the ml_users database. If you find a user_id, you pass that id on to remove.php, along with the mailing list id. Your job is done, so you redirect the user to remove.php.

```
case 'Remove':
   $sql = "SELECT user_id FROM ml_users " .
       "WHERE e-mail='" . $_POST['e-mail'] . "';";
   $result = mysql_query($sql, $conn);

   if (mysql_num_rows($result))
```

```
    {
     $row = mysql_fetch_array($result);
     $user_id = $row['user_id'];
     $url = "http://" . $_SERVER['HTTP_HOST'] .
         dirname($_SERVER['PHP_SELF']) .
         "/remove.php?u=" . $user_id .
         "&ml=" . $_POST['ml_id'];
     header("Location: $url");
     exit();
    }
    $redirect = 'user.php';
    break;
```

Note the `exit()` function immediately following `header()`. This is important, so the rest of the page is not loaded. The end of each case statement contains a break so that the rest of the case statements are not executed.

If the user clicks the Subscribe button, a number of things have to happen. First, you must look up the e-mail address that was provided to see if the user already exists:

```
case 'Subscribe':
    $sql = "SELECT user_id FROM ml_users " .
        "WHERE e-mail='" . $_POST['e-mail'] . "';";
    $result = mysql_query($sql,$conn);
```

If the user does not exist (no rows were returned from your query), you will insert a new record in the ml_users table. MySQL automatically assigns a user id.

```
if (!mysql_num_rows($result))
    {
     $sql = "INSERT INTO ml_users " .
         "(firstname,lastname,e-mail) " .
         "VALUES ('" . $_POST['firstname'] . "'," .
         "'" . $_POST['lastname'] . "'," .
         "'" . $_POST['e-mail'] . "');";
     $result = mysql_query($sql, $conn);
```

To retrieve that user id, use the PHP function `mysql_insert_id`. The variable `$conn` is optional, but it's usually a good idea to include it. If you omit it, it will automatically use the last open connection. The `mysql_insert_id` function will return a valid value only if the last SQL statement run resulted in a column being automatically incremented. In this case that did happen—the column is user_id, which is the value you need for the next part of our code.

```
$user_id = mysql_insert_id($conn);
    }
```

If the e-mail address was found in the database, you simply grab the user id from the record that was returned. Either way, you now have a `$user_id`. You also have a mailing list id, retrieved from `$_POST['ml_id']`. That's all you need to create a subscription record.

```
else
  {
   $row = mysql_fetch_array($result);
   $user_id = $row['user_id'];
  }
```

You may recall that the ml_subscriptions table contains three columns: user_id, ml_id, and pending. The first two values you have. The last one, pending, should be set to 1 until the user confirms the subscription. You initially set up the table to set pending to 1 as a default, so that column is automatically taken care of. So you now have all the data you need to create a subscription, and just like that, you insert the appropriate data into the subscriptions table.

```
$sql = "INSERT INTO ml_subscriptions (user_id,ml_id) " .
       "VALUES ('" . $user_id . "','" . $_POST['ml_id'] . "')";
mysql_query($sql,$conn);
```

Now all that is left to do is to notify the user. You do this in two ways: with a Thank You Web page that confirms that the subscription was processed, and with an e-mail to request confirmation because you don't want people to be able to sign other people up for mail. It's not a foolproof security measure, but it will stop most abuse.

You'll send the e-mail, and then redirect the user to the Thank You page. The first thing you do is get the name of the mailing list, using the mailing list id. That's because you want to tell the user in the e-mail which mailing list he or she subscribed to, and it wouldn't be too helpful to say it was mailing list #42!

```
$sql = "SELECT listname FROM ml_lists " .
       "WHERE ml_id=" . $_POST['ml_id'];
$result = mysql_query($sql,$conn);
$row = mysql_fetch_array($result);
$listname = $row['listname'];
```

Next, you build up the URL that will be at the bottom of the e-mail message. This URL directs the user back to this same page (user_transact.php), this time with an 'action' of 'confirm' (the third "action" choice, which we'll look at shortly).

```
$url = "http://" . $_SERVER['HTTP_HOST'] .
       dirname($_SERVER['PHP_SELF']) .
       "/user_transact.php?u=" . $user_id .
       "&ml=" . $_POST['ml_id'] . "&action=confirm";
```

Then you build the subject and body of the message, concatenating the URL to the bottom, and send it off with the mail() command:

```
$subject = 'Mailing list confirmation';
$body = "Hello " . $_POST['firstname'] . "\n" .
   "Our records indicate that you have subscribed to the " .
   $listname . " mailing list.\n\n" .
   "If you did not subscribe, please accept our apologies. " .
   "You will not be subscribed if you do not visit the " .
   "confirmation URL.\n\n" .
```

```
                "If you subscribed, please confirm this by visiting the " .
                "following URL:\n" . $url;

        mail($_POST['e-mail'],$subject,$body,$headers);
```

Once the mail has been sent, all that is left to do is send the user to the Thank You page. We will look at the Thank You page shortly.

```
        $redirect = "thanks.php?u=" . $user_id . "&ml=" .
            $_POST['ml_id'] . "&t=s";
        break;
```

When the user receives the confirmation e-mail, he or she clicks the link at the bottom, which loads user_transact.php again, this time with action=confirm. When confirming, you simply need to do one thing—change the pending flag for the appropriate subscription to 0. Once that is done, redirect the user to the Thank You page for confirmation, and send another e-mail informing the user of his or her new subscription. You will also provide an easy means of removal in the e-mail.

The first thing to do is make sure the user id and mailing list id were passed to the function. If not, you simply redirect the user to user.php.

```
        case 'confirm':

        if (isset($_GET['u']) & isset($_GET['ml']))
        {

        ...

        } else {
         $redirect = 'user.php';
        }
```

Next, find the subscription that matches the user id and mailing list id and update the pending column to 0. Remember that the user_id and ml_id columns combined make up a primary key, so there can be just one record for each set of possible values.

```
    $sql = "UPDATE ml_subscriptions SET pending=0 " .
            "WHERE user_id=" . $_GET['u'] .
            " AND ml_id=" . $_GET['ml'];
        mysql_query($sql, $conn);
```

Look familiar? It should—we are grabbing the mailing list name based on the mailing list id, just as we did for the Subscribe case. Looks like this is a prime candidate for a function:

```
    $sql = "SELECT listname FROM ml_lists " .
            "WHERE ml_id=" . $_GET['ml'];
        $result = mysql_query($sql,$conn);

        $row = mysql_fetch_array($result);
        $listname = $row['listname'];
```

Now you need to retrieve the user's e-mail address based on his or her user id, so you can send him or her an e-mail. This should also look familiar:

```
$sql = "SELECT * FROM ml_users " .
    "WHERE user_id='" . $_GET['u'] . "';";
$result = mysql_query($sql,$conn);
$row = mysql_fetch_array($result);
$firstname = $row['firstname'];
$e-mail = $row['e-mail'];
```

The body of this message is a little different. You are building the subject and body parameters for the `mail()` function and sending the mail to your user. Now you just need to send it on her way.

```
$url = "http://" . $_SERVER['HTTP_HOST'] .
        dirname($_SERVER['PHP_SELF']) .
        "/remove.php?u=" . $_GET['u'] .
        "&ml=" . $_GET['ml'];

$subject = 'Mailing List Subscription Confirmed';
$body = "Hello " . $firstname . ",\n" .
    "Thank you for subscribing to the " .
    $listname . " mailing list. Welcome!\n\n" .
    "If you did not subscribe, please accept our apologies.\n".
    "You can remove this subscription immediately by ".
    "visiting the following URL:\n" . $url;

mail($e-mail,$subject,$body,$headers);
```

Off your user goes, to the Thank You page:

```
$redirect = "thanks.php?u=" . $_GET['u'] . "&ml=" .
    $_GET['ml'] . "&t=s";
```

Finally, if `'action'` somehow is set to something other than `Remove`, `Subscribe`, or `confirm`, you will need to redirect the user somewhere else—in this case, `user.php`. The final line handles the redirection:

```
default:

    $redirect = 'user.php';
  }
}

header('Location: ' . $redirect);
```

The `user_transact.php` page is not terribly complicated. However, when you have a single page performing multiple tasks, you need to be careful that all situations are handled correctly.

thanks.php

Next let's look at the code in `thanks.php`. Most of it is familiar code that you have used elsewhere. You should have no problem breezing through this one:

Connect to the database:

```
$conn = mysql_connect(SQL_HOST, SQL_USER, SQL_PASS)
 or die('Could not connect to MySQL database. ' . mysql_error());

mysql_select_db(SQL_DB,$conn);
```

Get user info based on the user id. If you find it, display the title "Thank You," followed by the user's first name. Also grab the user's e-mail address. You'll use it later.

```
if (isset($_GET['u']))
{
 $uid = $_GET['u'];
 $sql = "SELECT * FROM ml_users WHERE user_id = '$uid';";
 $result = mysql_query($sql)
  or die('Invalid query: ' . mysql_error());
 if (mysql_num_rows($result)) {
  $row = mysql_fetch_array($result);
  $msg = "<h2>Thank You, " . $row['firstname'] . "</h2><br /><br />";
  $e-mail = $row['e-mail'];
 } else {
  die("No match for user id " . $uid);
 }
}
```

Next, you get the listname, based on the mailing list id. If you find it, you build the message to include "Thanks for subscribing." Once you get past this point, you know you have the user id and mailing list id.

```
if (isset($_GET['ml']))
{
 $ml_id = $_GET['ml'];
 $sql = "SELECT * FROM ml_lists WHERE ml_id = '" . $ml_id . "';";
 $result = mysql_query($sql)
  or die('Invalid query: ' . mysql_error());
 if (mysql_num_rows($result)) {
  $row = mysql_fetch_array($result);
  $msg .= "Thank you for subscribing to the <i>" .
     $row['listname'] . "</i> mailing list.<br />";
 } else {
  die ("Could not find Mailing List $ml_id");
 }
} else {
 die ("Mailing List id missing.");
}
```

Now all you have to do is determine the type of message you're displaying.

```
if (!isset($_GET['t'])) die("Missing Type");
```

It is crucial that the type be set. If not, stop processing this page. You don't know what to thank the user for.

Then comes the custom part of the message. Currently, there are two types of Thank You messages: "A confirmation request has been sent to . . .", and "A subscription notification has been sent . . ."

```
switch ($_GET['t'])
{
 case 'c':
  $msg .= "A confirmation request has been sent " .
      "to <b>$e-mail</b>.<br /><br />";
  break;
 case 's':
  $msg .= "A subscription notification has been " .
      "sent to you at <b>$e-mail</b>.<br /><br />";
}
```

Finally, you finish the page by putting a link back to user.php, and displaying the page.

```
$msg .= "<a href='user.php?u=$uid'>" .
     "Return to Mailing List Signup page</a>";
echo $msg;
```

remove.php

There are two ways for a user to remove him or herself from a mailing list. The first way is for the user to go to user.php, enter the e-mail address, choose the mailing list, and click the Remove button. The second way is via a link that you conveniently include at the end of e-mails that are sent to the mailing list recipients.

The remove.php page requires two parameters, user ID and mailing list ID. You are removing a database record from the ml_subscriptions table, and you will recall that those two values are what make each record unique. You can easily get that data from the e-mail link; it's embedded as part of the URL.

However, the user.php form forces you to take one extra step. You get the mailing list id from the mailing list choice, but you have only an e-mail address for the user. Therefore, you will need to do a lookup with that e-mail address. As you'll no doubt recall, the Remove button on user.php loads the user_transact.php page, and when the 'action' is Remove, you do a lookup for user_id based on the e-mail address, and build the URL for remove.php. You then redirect the user to remove.php with the correct parameters. Time for remove.php to do its job!

You can't just assume that remove.php received the appropriate variables. You test to ensure they are set and run the DELETE query.

```
if ((isset($_GET['u'])) and (isset($_GET['ml'])))
{
 $sql = "DELETE FROM ml_subscriptions " .
     "WHERE user_id=" . $_GET['u'] .
     " AND ml_id=" . $_GET['ml'];
 $result = mysql_query($sql,$conn);
} else {
 die("Incorrect parameters passed for deletion");
}
```

That was easy, but there are a couple of things you still need to do, like build the page! Don't quit on us now. Of course, first, you must make sure the deletion worked. Announce the results in big letters!

```
if ($result) {
  $msg = "<h2>Removal Successful</h2>";
} else {
  $msg = "<h2>Removal Failed</h2>";
}
```

Using the mailing list id, you do a lookup for the name of the mailing list and build the page's message:

```
$ml_id = $_GET['ml'];
$sql = "SELECT * FROM ml_lists WHERE ml_id = '" . $ml_id . "';";
$result = mysql_query($sql)
  or die('Invalid query: ' . mysql_error());
if (mysql_num_rows($result)) {
  $row = mysql_fetch_array($result);
  $msg .= "You have been removed from the <i>" .
      $row['listname'] . "</i> mailing list.<br />";
} else {
  $msg .= "Sorry, could not find Mailing List id#{$ml_id}");
}
```

Finally, you add a link back to `user.php` at the bottom of the page and echo it to the screen.

```
$msg .= "<a href='user.php?u=" . $_GET['u'] .
    "'>Return to Mailing List Signup page</a>";
echo $msg;
```

Mailing List Ethics

There are a couple of ethical issues you should know about when dealing with the world of mailing lists, namely spam and opt-in/opt-out. This section represents our personal soap box for airing our opinions about them.

A Word About Spam (and SPAM)

With the advent of the computer, mailing lists have been brought to a whole new level. Now you can be (and no doubt are) told on a daily basis that Candy really wants you to visit her Web site, and that a little blue pill will solve all of your personal problems. Yes, occasionally an e-mail sits in your Inbox informing you of new job postings, new posts on PHPBuilder.com, or tour dates for Jimmy Buffett. But we think you know what mailing lists are primarily used for: spam!

For those of you just crawling out of a suspended animation chamber, *spam* is a term used to describe a "shotgun" approach to advertising. You simply send your e-mail advertisement to as many people as you possibly can, in the hopes that a certain small percentage of them will actually respond. The term "spam" was given to this practice in honor of the famous Monty Python sketch in which restaurant patrons choose their meal from a menu in which every dish contains SPAM. (Back in the 1930s, the wonderful people at Hormel blessed us with a delicious luncheon meat called Spiced Ham. A contest and a $100 prize later, it was renamed "SPAM." The rest is history. Really—visit their Web site, www.spam.com, to learn more.)

In the Monty Python sketch, a group of Vikings drowns out the sketch with choruses of "Spam, spam, spam, spam . . ." Although it is a very funny sketch, e-mail spam does not seem to elicit the same response.

What is our point? SPAM is a luncheon meat. You spell it in all capital letters, and you enjoy it on your sandwiches. Spam is another name for UCE, or unsolicited commercial e-mail. It is spelled in all lowercase, and we shun it.

The bottom line: Don't use mailing lists to send spam. Your mother would be *very* disappointed.

Opt-In vs. Opt-Out

You may have heard these terms before. What do they mean? To most of your users, probably not much. They simply answer the questions on your registration, read the fine print (as all users do, of course), and click the Submit button.

However, you aren't a user any more. At least, not on your own site. You are the administrator. You need to understand the difference between opt-in and opt-out because it may mean the difference between annoyance and acceptance for your users.

Opt-in and opt-out are fancy ways of saying "What is the default choice for our users?" Opt-in means the user is not currently scheduled to receive that newsletter, but he or she may *opt* to subscribe. Obviously, opt-out is the opposite—your user will automatically receive notifications unless he or she *opts* to remove him- or herself from that mailing list.

Why the difference? As the administrator, you may sometimes have to walk a fine line between satisfying your advertisers (the ones giving you money to keep your site alive) and your users (the ones visiting your site, keeping your advertisers happy by driving up the number of hits). If an advertiser pays you enough, you might agree to automatically send advertisements from that company unless the user explicitly chooses not to receive them (opt-out).

However, you might have a newsletter you send once per week that contains, for example, details of comic conventions throughout the country (or even the world). Not all visitors to your site will be interested in that, but if any are, they can subscribe to the newsletter so they will always be notified (opt-in).

As we mentioned, you walk a fine line when choosing between the two. Because this is a new Web site for you, the decision might not be that difficult. But as your site grows, interest increases, and companies want to advertise with you, you'll need to make these important decisions. For now, we suggest you make all mailing lists opt-in, with the exception of important site announcements.

Summary

You have just created a nice, relatively simple maillist subscription application. You have the ability to create new mailing lists, delete old ones, and send e-mails to multiple recipients. Users can subscribe and unsubscribe to any mailing lists, and you added a step for confirmation to help stamp out abuse.

We hope you come away from this chapter with an understanding of the difference between good, informative mass e-mails and spam.

Mailing lists are good. Spam is bad. Any questions? Good. Next let's take a look at how to sell your SPAM collection on your Web site.

Online Selling: A Quick Way to E-Commerce

Some of us cringe when we hear the word "e-commerce" and the phrase "selling over the Internet." Perhaps we've had a bad experience ourselves, or the thought of opening an online store is just too overwhelming. Even though this is the part of the book that all geeks out there probably dread reading, we're here to show you that e-commerce is really not so bad, and that pretty much anyone can do it.

However, just because anyone can do it doesn't mean it's always done the right way. Done the wrong way, your site can look downright cheesy, but done the right way, your site can look professional and inviting, and become an excellent resource for your visitors and potential customers. There are definite, if unwritten, guidelines for selling things over the Web and we want to make sure you do things the right way.

Selling things from your Web site can not only make you some extra cash; it can enhance your relationship with your Web site visitors (if e-commerce is not your site's primary function). In the case of our comic book fan site, offering pertinent items can make your site more interactive and interesting and bring visitors back again to see what new items you have for sale. True comic book fans will appreciate the niche of items you are providing, especially if some of the items are unique or hard to come by.

In this chapter, we discuss:

- ❑ Creating a simple shopping cart script
- ❑ Other ideas to improve your script
- ❑ E-commerce basics

Adding E-Commerce to the Comic Book Fan Site

It's time to show you how you can easily incorporate an e-commerce section on our Comic Book Appreciation fan site. You will need a few things to get started:

- ❑ Something to sell

- ❑ Some mechanism for your customers to pick what they want to buy

- ❑ Some way for your customers to pay for what they want to buy

- ❑ Some process to get the merchandise to your customers

Let's break it down (break dancing gear optional) and talk about each of these things individually. The first two we can help you with; the second two are really outside the scope of this book, beyond a general discussion.

Something to Sell

Before you can sell something, you have to have something to sell. Duh. Next topic. No, seriously, retailers spend millions researching what will sell and what won't, what the hottest trends are, and what the latest technology has to offer. All that being said, your ideas for products will probably come from one or more of the following categories:

- ❑ **Your own knowledge:** You will most likely know what your customers want based on your inherent knowledge of the focus of your Web site. For example, if you have a site for collectors of old tractors, you probably know what products would appeal to your typical customer because *you* are the typical customer.

- ❑ **Something you yourself couldn't easily find:** You also may have been looking for a specific product or group of products, only to find that they do not exist on one particular site until you create it and pull them all together. (For example, www.giftsforengineers.com was created to be a compilation of products that appeal to engineers.)

- ❑ **Your own inventions:** Another item you might sell from your site is a new invention or design you have created from your little old brain. Many budding artists and inventors sell their stuff on the Web, where they can reach a multitude of potential buyers.

- ❑ **Promotion of your site:** Many other Web sites offer promotional items for sale that tout the URL of their site. This acts as a "win-win" for both parties; the customers can proclaim their support for a cool site and the site makes a few bucks and gets its name out there for all to see.

So whether you're reinventing the wheel, selling specific types of wheels, taking a bunch of wheels and putting them together, or selling wheels with your name on them, you must create a product base, and it may not be as easy as it looks.

For our CBA site, we will be selling items from a few different categories. To spice things up a bit, we decided it would be great to have some fun with this:

❑ T-shirts, bumper stickers, and coffee mugs with the CBA logo, from the promotional category

❑ Superhero suits customizable with color schemes and monogrammed torso letters

❑ Two different types of grappling hooks for all our superheroes' needs

We will be expanding on these products later and adding them to our product catalog (that is, the `products` table in our database).

A Shopping Cart

Now that we know what we are going to sell, we have to have some way for our customers to choose the specific products they want to buy; this involves a shopping cart. You can hook yourself up with ready-made shopping cart software, or you can use a cart straight from a programming script, such as PHP (or CGI, or whatever). Because we're on this topic, we may as well get a little crazy and talk a little bit about the pros and cons of each.

Shopping Cart Software

There are numerous shopping cart software programs that can easily hook your customers up and make it easy for them to pick what they want. While these programs can be expensive, they can also take care of things such as security, complex product option selection, maintaining customer information, and keeping track of previously placed orders.

An example of shopping cart software is Cart32. Available at www.cart32.com, this is a widely used shopping cart program that provides numerous configuration options for a Webmaster. Features include Web-based administration of your cart and pending/sent orders, the ability to use your own database or theirs to store product and customer information, automatic credit card processing and e-mail confirmations, complex product options and discount structures, online tracking through the major shipping carriers for your customers to track their orders, inventory management, and customization of the look of your cart. The costs are $29.95 to set up and $29.95 per month if you have Cart32 host the cart portion of your site for you. Many Web hosting companies have chosen Cart32 for the cart they offer to their customers.

These types of software programs are popular because they enable you to get your store up and running with relative ease and because they take care of the security issues for you.

Your Own Cart Software Code

Remember that whenever you depend on someone else to supply a portion of your site, you are at the mercy of their servers and their software. If they are hosting your shopping cart for you, when their site is down, so is yours. If their servers catch a virus, it affects you and your customers, too. Plus, there may be a function you need that they don't offer, or the cost may be prohibitive for your newly created site. Whatever the reason, some of you may want to code your own script, and for those of you brave enough to tread these waters, let's go!

We'll start with a very simple shopping cart system that will consist of several files:

- ❑ **create.php:** Creates the main database and the necessary tables.
- ❑ **createtemp.php:** Creates a temporary table to store shopping cart information before the customer actually checks out.
- ❑ **products.php:** Populates the database with product information.
- ❑ **cbashop.php:** Acts as the home page for our little store and lists our available products.
- ❑ **getprod.php:** Retrieves detailed information about a single product.
- ❑ **add.php:** Adds a product to our shopping cart.
- ❑ **cart.php:** Displays the contents of our shopping cart.
- ❑ **change.php:** Allows us to change the quantity of an item in our shopping cart.
- ❑ **delete.php:** Deletes an item from the shopping cart.
- ❑ **checkout.php:** The first step in the checkout process; this is where the customer enters billing and shipping information.
- ❑ **checkout2.php:** The second step in the checkout process; this is where customers verify the accuracy of their orders and make any last-minute changes.
- ❑ **checkout3.php:** The final step of the checkout process, where the customer actually sends the order to us, and receives an order number and confirmation. The information is put into the database and deleted from the temporary table, a customer number is assigned (if it's a new customer), and an order number is assigned, as well. E-mail confirmations are sent to the customer and to us.

Try It Out   Defining the Database and Tables

1. Open your text editor and type the following code:

```php
<?php
//connect to the database - either include a connection variable file or
//type the following lines:
$connect = mysql_connect("localhost", "root", "mysqlpass") or
     die ("Hey loser, check your server connection.");

//Create the ecommerce database
if (mysql_create_db("ecommerce")) {
     echo "Woo hoo! Database created!";
}
else echo "Sorry, try creating the database again.";
mysql_select_db ("ecommerce");

//Define the product table
$query = "CREATE TABLE products (
     prodnum CHAR(5) NOT NULL,
     name VARCHAR(20) NOT NULL,
     proddesc TEXT NOT NULL,
     price DEC (6,2) NOT NULL,
     dateadded DATE NOT NULL,
```

```
        PRIMARY KEY(prodnum))";

$product = mysql_query($query)
     or die(mysql_error());

//Define the customer table
$query2 = "CREATE TABLE customers (
     custnum INT(6) NOT NULL AUTO_INCREMENT,
     firstname VARCHAR (15) NOT NULL,
     lastname VARCHAR (50) NOT NULL,
     add1 VARCHAR (50) NOT NULL,
     add2 VARCHAR (50),
     city VARCHAR (50) NOT NULL,
     state CHAR (2) NOT NULL,
     zip CHAR (5) NOT NULL,
     phone CHAR (12) NOT NULL,
     fax CHAR (12),
     email VARCHAR (50) NOT NULL,
     PRIMARY KEY (custnum))";

$customers = mysql_query($query2)
     or die(mysql_error());

//Define the general order table
$query3 = "CREATE TABLE ordermain (
     ordernum INT(6) NOT NULL AUTO_INCREMENT,
     orderdate DATE NOT NULL,
     custnum INT(6) NOT NULL,
     subtotal DEC (7,2) NOT NULL,
     shipping DEC (6,2),
     tax DEC(6,2),
     total DEC(7,2) NOT NULL,
     shipfirst VARCHAR(15) NOT NULL,
     shiplast VARCHAR(50) NOT NULL,
     shipcompany VARCHAR (50),
     shipadd1 VARCHAR (50) NOT NULL,
     shipadd2 VARCHAR(50),
     shipcity VARCHAR(50) NOT NULL,
     shipstate CHAR(2) NOT NULL,
     shipzip CHAR(5) NOT NULL,
     shipphone CHAR(12) NOT NULL,
     shipemail VARCHAR(50),
     PRIMARY KEY(ordernum) ";

$ordermain = mysql_query($query3)
     or die(mysql_error());

//Define the order details table
$query4 = "CREATE TABLE orderdet (
     ordernum INT (6) NOT NULL,
     qty INT(3) NOT NULL,
     prodnum CHAR(5) NOT NULL,
     KEY(ordernum))";

$orderdet = mysql_query($query4)
```

```
        or die(mysql_error());

  ?>
```

2. Save this as `create.php`.

3. Run the file from your browser.

How It Works

You can see that several things are accomplished in this script. We now have a new database called "ecommerce" with four tables in it. The first table is named `products` and contains the list of products available.

Fieldname	Type	Description of What It Stores
prodnum	CHAR(5)	The individual product number assigned to each product.
name	VARCHAR(20)	A brief title for the product, such as "CBA Logo T-shirt."
proddesc	TEXT	A longer description we can use on the individual page for that product. May contain HTML code.
price	DEC(6,2)	Price of the product up to 999.99.
dateadded	DATE	Date the product was added to the site.

The next table is named `customers` and contains the list of customers and their information.

Fieldname	Type	Description of What It Stores
custnum	INT(6)	The individual customer number assigned to each customer. This will auto increment.
firstname	VARCHAR(15)	Customer's first name.
lastname	VARCHAR(50)	Customer's last name.
add1	VARCHAR(50)	Customer's address: line 1.
add2	VARCHAR(50)	Customer's address: line 2 (can be null).
city	VARCHAR(50)	Customer's city.
state	CHAR(2)	Customer's state.
zip	CHAR(5)	Customer's zip code.
phone	CHAR(12)	Customer's phone number (in xxx-xxx-xxxx format).
fax	CHAR(12)	Customer's fax number (same format as phone number, can be null).
email	VARCHAR(50)	Customer's e-mail address.

The next table you create is called `ordermain` and contains the main order information.

Fieldname	Type	Description of What It Stores
ordernum	INT(6)	The individual number assigned to each order. This will auto-increment and is the primary key.
orderdate	DATE	Date the order was placed.
custnum	INT(6)	Number of the customer who placed the order.
subtotal	DEC(7,2)	Subtotal of the order before tax and shipping, up to 9999.99.
shipping	DEC(6,2)	Shipping costs for the order, up to 999.99.
tax	DEC(6,2)	Tax on the order, up to 999.99.
total	DEC(7,2)	Total of the order, up to 9999.99.
shipfirst	VARCHAR(15)	First name of the shipping contact for this order.
shiplast	VARCHAR(50)	Last name of the shipping contact.
shipadd1	VARCHAR(50)	Shipping contact's address: line 1.
shipadd2	VARCHAR(50)	Shipping contact's address: line 2 (can be null).
shipcity	VARCHAR(50)	Shipping contact's city.
shipstate	CHAR(2)	Shipping contact's state.
shipzip	CHAR(5)	Shipping contact's zip code.
shipphone	CHAR(12)	Shipping contact's phone number (in xxx-xxx-xxxx format).
shipemail	VARCHAR(50)	Shipping contact's e-mail address.

The fourth and final table is named `orderdet` and contains a detailed list of the products in each order.

Fieldname	Type	Description of What It Stores
ordernum	INT(6)	The order number (note this is designated a "key" and not "primary key."
qty	INT (3)	How many of the item the customer wants.
productnum	CHAR(5)	The product associated with this order.

We now have a mechanism set up so that we can store all our products, all our customers, and all the information associated with the orders they place.

Try It Out   Adding Your Products

Now let's begin by filling the `products` database:

1. Open your text editor and type the following program:

```php
<?php
//connect to the database - either include a connection variable file or
//type the following lines:
$connect = mysql_connect("localhost", "root", "mysqlpass") or
    die ("Hey loser, check your server connection.");
mysql_select_db ("ecommerce");

$query = "INSERT INTO products VALUES (
    '00001', 'CBA Logo T-shirt',
    'This T-shirt will show off your CBA connection.
    Our t-shirts are high quality and 100% preshrunk cotton.',
    17.95, '2003-08-01'),
    ('00002','CBA Bumper Sticker',
    'Let the world know you are a proud supporter of the
    CBA Web site with this colorful bumper sticker.',
    5.95, '2003-08-01'),
    ('00003', 'CBA Coffee Mug',
    'With the CBA logo looking back at you over your
    morning cup of coffee, you\'re sure to have a great
    start to your day. Our mugs are microwave and dishwasher
    safe.',
    8.95, '2003-08-01'),
    ('00004', 'Superhero Body Suit',
    'We have a complete selection of colors and sizes for you
    to choose from. This body suit is sleek, stylish, and
    won\'t hinder your crime-fighting or evil scheming abilities.
    We also offer your choice in monogrammed letter applique.',
    99.95, '2003-08-01'),
    ('00005', 'Small Grappling Hook',
    'This specialized hook will get you out of the tightest
    places. Specially designed for portability and stealth,
    please be aware that this hook does come with a weight limit.',
    139.95, '2003-08-01'),
    ('00006', 'Large Grappling Hook',
    'For all your heavy-duty building-to-building swinging needs,
    this large version of our grappling hook will safely transport
    you throughout the city. Please be advised however that at
    50 pounds, this is hardly the hook to use if you\'re a lightweight.',
    199.95, '2003-08-01')";

$result = mysql_query($query)
    or die(mysql_error());
echo "Products added successfully!";

?>
```

2. Save it as `products.php`.

3. Open the file in your browser.

How It Works

We started our script with a connection to the MySQL server; then we made sure our database was the "active" one.

We then inserted each of our products into the `products` table, while keeping the values in the same order as we used when creating the table:

- ❏ `prodnum`
- ❏ `name`
- ❏ `proddesc`
- ❏ `price`
- ❏ `dateadded`

You'll notice that although we assigned sequential numbers to our products, we are not using the auto-increment feature, because in the real world, you may wish to assign product numbers based on category, distributor/manufacturer, or other numbering scheme; these product IDs may include letters and numbers.

Because we had no errors and our query didn't die, we should have seen the "Products added successfully" statement, and our products should now be in the database.

If you don't have faith and believe that they're really in there, you can reaffirm your query with this small test program (save this as `producttest.php` and run it from your browser):

```php
<?php
//connect to the database - either include a connection variable file or
//type the following lines:
$connect = mysql_connect("localhost", "root", "mysqlpass") or
    die ("Hey loser, check your server connection.");
mysql_select_db ("ecommerce");
$query = "SELECT * FROM products";
$results = mysql_query($query)
    or die(mysql_error());

?>
<HTML>
<HEAD>
<TITLE>Product List</TITLE>
</HEAD>
<BODY>
<table>
    <tr>
    <td width='10%'>Product Number</td>
    <td width='20%'>Name</td>
    <td width='50%'>Description</td>
    <td width='10%'>Price</td>
    <td width='10%'>Date Added</td>
    </tr>
    <tr>
```

```php
<?php
while ($row = mysql_fetch_array($results)) {
    extract ($row);
    echo "<td width='10%'>";
    echo $prodnum;
    echo "</td><td width='20%'>";
    echo $name;
    echo "</td><td width='50%'>";
    echo $proddesc;
    echo "</td><td width='10%'>";
    echo $price;
    echo "</td><td width='10%'>";
    echo $dateadded;
    echo "</td></tr>";
    }
?>

    </table>
</BODY>
</HTML>
```

This program asks MySQL to give you all the products from the `products` table and populate an HTML table with the results. Each row is created while the rows are still being fetched. When it's complete, you should see the screen depicted in Figure 14-1.

Product Number	Name	Description	Price	Date Added
00001	CBA Logo T-shirt	This T-shirt will show off your CBA connection. Our t-shirts are high quality and 100% preshrunk cotton.	17.95	2003-08-01
00002	CBA Bumper Sticker	Let the world know you are a proud supporter of the CBA website with this colorful bumper sticker.	5.95	2003-08-01
00003	CBA Cofee Mug	With the CBA logo looking back at you over your morning cup of coffee, you're sure to have a great start to your day. Our mugs are microwave and dishwasher safe.	8.95	2003-08-01
00004	Superhero Body Suit	We have a complete selection of colors and sizes for you to choose from. This body suit is sleek, stylish, and won't hinder your crime-fighting or evil scheming abilities. We also offer your choice in monogrammed letter applique.	99.95	2003-08-01
00005	Small Grappling Hook	This specialized hook will get you out of the tightest places. Specially designed for portability and stealth, please be aware that this hook does come with a weight limit.	139.95	2003-08-01
00006	Large Grappling Hook	For all your heavy-duty building-to-building swinging needs, this large version of our grappling hook will safely transport you throughout the city. Please be advised however that at 50 pounds, this is hardly the hook to use if you're a lightweight.	199.95	2003-08-01

Figure 14-1

Now that we have everything ready to go, let's write the code that shows us more information about a specific product.

Creating the Store Home Page

Open your text editor and save the following as cbashop.php. This will act as our e-commerce home page and will list all the available products we have for sale. Unfortunately, we can't give you the images through this book, but you can download them from our source Web site, www.wrox.com.

```php
<?php
//connect to the database - either include a connection variable file or
//type the following lines:
$connect = mysql_connect("localhost", "root", "mysqlpass") or
    die ("Hey loser, check your server connection.");
mysql_select_db ("ecommerce");
$query = "SELECT * FROM products";
$results = mysql_query($query)
    or die(mysql_error());

?>
<HTML>
<HEAD>
<TITLE>Comic Book Appreciation Site Product List</TITLE>
</HEAD>
<BODY>
<div align='center'>
Thanks for visiting our site! Please see our list of awesome
products below, and click on the link for more information:
<br><br>
<table width='300'>
    <tr>
<?php

// Show only Name, Price and Image
while ($row = mysql_fetch_array($results)) {
    extract ($row);
    echo "<td>";
    echo "<a href = 'getprod.php?prodid=" . $prodnum ."'>";
    echo "THUMBNAIL<br>IMAGE</td></a>";
    echo "<td>";
    echo "<a href = 'getprod.php?prodid=" . $prodnum ."'>";
    echo $name;
    echo "</td></a>";
    echo "<td>";
    echo "<a href = 'getprod.php?prodid=" . $prodnum ."'>";
    echo $price;
    echo "</td></a></tr>";
    }

?>

    </table>
    </div>
</BODY>
</HTML>
```

Your screen should now look like that shown in Figure 14-2.

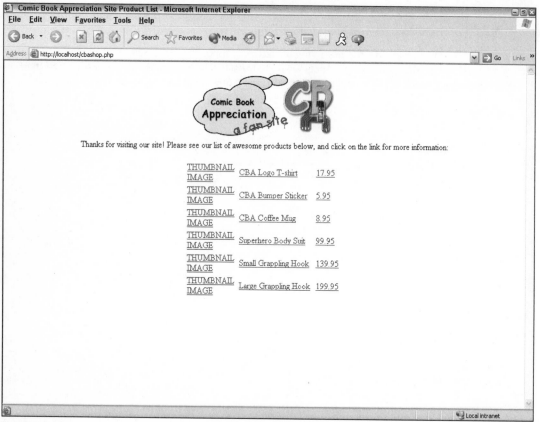

Figure 14-2

How It Works

First, we connected to the database just like we do every time. You might consider putting this info in an include file for simplicity's sake. Then we listed our intro information, "welcome to our site," blah blah blah—you know the routine. We've tried to keep it simple here, but in the real world this would look a lot fancier.

Then we got to the meat of the page, the actual products. We had our table populate a new row so long as there were results still being retrieved from the database with our `while` statements. When the query was finished getting results, we ended the table.

We also included a link to each of our products from either the picture of the item, the name of the item, or the price of the item. You can see an example in these lines:

```
echo "<a href = 'getprod.php?prodid=" . $prodnum ."'>";
    echo "THUMBNAIL<br>IMAGE</td></a>";
```

The URL then becomes `http://localhost/getprod.php?prodid=0001`, or something similar, depending on what product the user clicks. The program inserts the product ID number and sends it to the server so that the appropriate data can be retrieved.

Try It Out   Viewing the Products

You are now going to create the page that displays the details of each product. You know the drill. . . . When you're done entering this in your text editor, save this file as `getprod.php`.

```php
<?php
session_start();
//connect to the database - either include a connection variable file or
//type the following lines:
$connect = mysql_connect("localhost", "root", "mysqlpass") or
    die ("Hey loser, check your server connection.");
mysql_select_db ("ecommerce");
$prodid=$_REQUEST['prodid'];
$query = "SELECT * FROM products WHERE prodnum='$prodid'";
$results = mysql_query($query)
    or die(mysql_error());
$row = mysql_fetch_array($results);
extract ($row);
?>
<HTML>
<HEAD>
<TITLE><?php echo $name ?></TITLE>
</HEAD>
<BODY>
<div align='center'>
<table width='500' cellpadding = '5'>
    <tr>
<?php
    echo "<td>IMAGE</td>";
    echo "<td>";
    echo "<strong>";
    echo $name;
    echo "</strong><br>";
    echo $proddesc;
    echo "<br>";
    echo "Product Number: ";
    echo $prodnum;
    echo "<br>Price: ";
    echo $price;
    echo "</td>";
?>
    </tr>

    <tr>
    <td>
      </td>
      <td><form method="POST" action="add.php">
    Quantity:
        <input type="text" name="qty" size="2">
```

```
              <input type="hidden" name="prodnum" value="<?php echo $prodnum ?>">
          <input type="submit" name="Submit" value="Add to cart">
          </form>

          <form method = "POST" action="cart.php">
       <input type="submit" name="Submit" value="View cart">
          </form>
          </td>
          </tr>

</table>
<a href="cbashop.php">Go back to the main page</a>
</div>
</BODY>
</HTML>
```

We chose to click the Superhero Body Suit, so our screen looks like that shown in Figure 14-3 (again, the images would be shown in place of the "IMAGE" marker there).

Figure 14-3

How It Works

First, we start a session for the customer. Then we again connect to the database. From there we have the following:

```
$prodid=$_REQUEST['prodid'];
$query = "SELECT * FROM products WHERE prodnum='$prodid'";
$results = mysql_query($query)
     or die(mysql_error());
$row = mysql_fetch_array($results);
extract ($row);
```

In this block of code, we first take prodid, which came from the URL, and rename it so we can easily use it in our MySQL queries. In the next line, we query the products table for the appropriate product ID. We then run the query and extract the results so we can use them.

In the next several lines, we build a table and display the information straight from the database. Then we have the following:

```
<td><form method = "POST" action="add.php">
Quantity:
        <input type="text" name="qty" size="2">
        <input type="hidden" name="prodnum" value="<?php echo $prodnum ?>">
    <input type="submit" name="Submit" value="Add to cart">
    </form>
```

Here we have created a form that calls to action the add.php file (which we'll create in a moment) and passes the only real variables we care about: the product number (prodnum) and the quantity (qty).

The following gives the customer the option of viewing the current contents of the shopping cart. You can also supply this in the form of a link, but we chose to offer it as a button in this case.

```
        <form method = "POST" action="cart.php">
    <input type="submit" name="Submit" value="View cart">
    </form>
    </td>
```

We also gave our customers the option to return to the main page.

Try It Out   Creating a Table for the Shopping Cart

Create a temporary table to store the items in the customer's cart before he or she checks out.

This file will be called createtemp.php:

```
<?php
//connect to the database - either include a connection variable file or
//type the following lines:
$connect = mysql_connect("localhost", "root", "mysqlpass") or
```

```
        die ("Hey loser, check your server connection.");

mysql_select_db ("ecommerce");

//Define the temp table
$query = "CREATE TABLE carttemp(
     hidden INT(10) NOT NULL AUTO_INCREMENT,
     sess CHAR(50) NOT NULL,
     prodnum CHAR(5) NOT NULL,
     quan INT(3) NOT NULL,
     PRIMARY KEY (hidden),
     KEY(sess))";

$temp = mysql_query($query)
     or die(mysql_error());
?>
```

How It Works

Hey, guess what? You're right: We had to connect to the database again.

Then we created a temporary table that will "hold" the items while the customer continues browsing and before they actually check out. We didn't want to populate the other tables with this information yet because our customers may decide not to go through with the order and we would have assigned them order numbers for orders that are never sent. This can really mess up your accounting and tracking systems.

To keep each entry separate, we create a `hidden` field that will simply act as a primary key and allow us to later delete only one row from our shopping cart. The `sess` field is used to temporarily store our session ID (which is assigned by the browser) to allow us to link the information from this particular shopping session, and keep it all together.

Try It Out   Adding Products to the Cart

Now create the `add.php` file that will allow us to add products to our cart:

```php
<?php
session_id();
session_start();
$connect = mysql_connect("localhost", "root", "mysqlpass") or
     die ("Hey loser, check your server connection.");
mysql_select_db ("ecommerce");
$qty =$_POST['qty'];
$prodnum = $_POST['prodnum'];
$sess =session_id();

$query = "INSERT INTO carttemp (sess, quan, prodnum)
        VALUES ('$sess','$qty','$prodnum')";
$results = mysql_query($query)
     or die(mysql_error());

include("cart.php");
?>
```

How It Works

We must call the `session_id()` function before the `session_start()` function so `session_id()` value doesn't get overwritten and the current session ID is maintained. The `session_id()` function simply returns the current session ID (assigned by the browser) and lets us use its value later on in the script (which, conveniently enough, we did, through our $sess variable).

We again rename our POST variables for simplicity's sake in our queries and then run our `insert` query to put the information we have collected in the temporary table.

The next to last line is where we include our shopping cart, so the customer can see that, yes, the product was successfully added into the cart, and he or she can view all the products in there.

Try It Out   Viewing the Shopping Cart

Now let's create the actual shopping cart, `cart.php`:

```php
<?php
session_id();
session_start();
//connect to the database
$connect = mysql_connect("localhost", "root", "mysqlpass") or
     die ("Hey loser, check your server connection.");
mysql_select_db ("ecommerce");
?>
<HTML>
<HEAD>
<TITLE>Here is Your Shopping Cart!</TITLE>
</HEAD>
<BODY>
<div align="center">
You currently have

<?php
$sessid = session_id();

//display number of products in cart
    $query = "SELECT * from carttemp WHERE sess = '$sessid'";
    $results = mysql_query($query)
        or die (mysql_query());
    $rows = mysql_num_rows($results);
    echo $rows;
?>

product(s) in your cart.<br>

  <table border="1" align="center" cellpadding="5">
      <tr>
          <td>Quantity</td>
          <td>Item Image</td>
          <td>Item Name</td>
          <td>Price Each</td>
          <td>Extended Price</td>
```

```
            <td></td>
            <td></td>
    <tr>
    <?php
        while ($row = mysql_fetch_array($results)) {
            extract ($row);
            $prod = "SELECT * FROM products WHERE prodnum =
            '$prodnum'";
            $prod2 = mysql_query($prod);
            $prod3 = mysql_fetch_array($prod2);
            extract ($prod3);
            echo "<td><form method = 'POST' action='change.php'>
                <input type='hidden' name='prodnum'
                    value='$prodnum'>
                <input type='hidden' name='sessid'
                    value='$sessid'>
                <input type='hidden' name='hidden'
                    value='$hidden'>
                <input type='text' name='qty' size='2'
                    value='$quan'>";
            echo "</td>";
            echo "<td>";
            echo "<a href = 'getprod.php?prodid=" .
                $prodnum ."'>";
            echo "THUMBNAIL<br>IMAGE</td></a>";
            echo "<td>";
            echo "<a href = 'getprod.php?prodid=" .
                $prodnum ."'>";
            echo $name;
            echo "</td></a>";
            echo "<td align='right'>";
            echo $price;
            echo "</td>";
            echo "<td align='right'>";
    //get extended price
            $extprice = number_format($price * $quan, 2);
            echo $extprice;
            echo "</td>";
            echo "<td>";
            echo "<input type='submit' name='Submit'
                    value='Change Qty'>
                </form></td>";
            echo "<td>";
            echo "<form method = 'POST' action='delete.php'>
                <input type='hidden' name='prodnum'
                    value='$prodnum'>
                <input type='hidden' name='qty' value='$quan'>
                <input type='hidden' name='hidden'
                    value='$hidden'>
                <input type='hidden' name='sessid'
                    value='$sessid'>";
            echo "<input type='submit' name='Submit'
                    value='Delete Item'>
                </form></td>";
            echo "</tr>";
```

```
                //add extended price to total
                $total = $extprice + $total;


            }
?>
<tr>
<td colspan='4' align='right'>Your total before shipping is:</td>
<td align='right'> <?php echo number_format($total, 2) ?></td>
<td></td>
<td></td>
</tr>
</table>
<form method="POST" action="checkout.php">
<input type='submit' name='Submit' value='Proceed to Checkout'>
</form>
<a href="cbashop.php">Go back to the main page</a>
</div>
</BODY>
</HTML>
```

We decided that we would need only one Superhero Body Suit, so we added one to our cart. Our screen now looks like that in Figure 14-4.

Figure 14-4

How It Works

Now, looking at our code, you can see the following:

```
<div align="center">
You currently have

<?php
$sessid = session_id();

//display number of products in cart
    $query = "SELECT * from carttemp WHERE sess = '$sessid'";
    $results = mysql_query($query)
        or die (mysql_query());
    $rows = mysql_num_rows($results);
    echo $rows;
?>

product(s) in your cart.<br>
```

We want to display the total number of items in our cart, so we start in HTML and we flip over to PHP where we query our temporary table to see what is in there for the current session. We get the total number of rows and that tells us how many entries are in our cart. Of course, this doesn't check for duplicates—it's only a start. We then flip back over to HTML to finish our sentence, and the result is:

```
You currently have 1 product(s) in your cart.
```

We then populate our table much in the same way we did in `cbashop.php`, except this time we're pulling the information from our temporary table. Because we also wanted to provide a link to the product detail page for each product (in case our customers forgot what they ordered), we had to also grab info from our `products` table.

We then come to these lines:

```
//get extended price
        $extprice = number_format($price * $quan, 2);
        echo $extprice;
```

This is where we show our customers the extended price for each item based on how many they are ordering.

Likewise, we keep a tally of their order with these lines:

```
//add extended price to total
        $total = $extprice + $total;
```

We also allow them to change the quantities or delete an item altogether, with two more files, `change.php` and `delete.php`, respectively. We use these files as "actions" in our HTML forms, and pass the variables as needed, as in these lines:

```
echo "<input type='submit' name='Submit'
                    value='Change Qty'>
                </form></td>";
```

```
          echo "<td>";
          echo "<form method = 'POST' action='delete.php'>
               <input type='hidden' name='prodnum'
                      value='$prodnum'>
               <input type='hidden' name='qty' value='$quan'>
               <input type='hidden' name='hidden'
                      value='$hidden'>
               <input type='hidden' name='sessid'
                      value='$sessid'>";
          echo "<input type='submit' name='Submit'
                      value='Delete Item'>
               </form></td>";
```

We then give customers the option of proceeding to the checkout or going back to the main page for more shopping with these lines:

```
<form method="POST" action="checkout.php">
<input type='submit' name='Submit' value='Proceed to Checkout'>
</form>
<a href="cbashop.php">Go back to the main page</a>
```

Try It Out   Changing Items in the Cart

Let's go ahead and type change.php:

```php
<?php
session_id();
session_start();
$connect = mysql_connect("localhost", "root", "mysqlpass") or
     die ("Hey loser, check your server connection.");
mysql_select_db ("ecommerce");
$qty =$_POST['qty'];
$hidden = $_POST['hidden'];
$sess = $_POST['sessid'];

$query = "UPDATE carttemp
     SET quan = '$qty'
     WHERE hidden = '$hidden'";
$results = mysql_query($query)
     or die(mysql_error());

echo "Quantity Updated.<br>      ";
include("cart.php");
?>
```

And delete.php:

```php
<?php
session_id();
session_start();
$connect = mysql_connect("localhost", "root", "mysqlpass") or
     die ("Hey loser, check your server connection.");
mysql_select_db ("ecommerce");
$qty =$_POST['qty'];
```

```
$hidden = $_POST['hidden'];
$sess = $_POST['sessid'];

$query = "DELETE FROM carttemp WHERE hidden = '$hidden'";
$results = mysql_query($query)
    or die(mysql_error());

echo "<div align='center'>
    Item Deleted.<br>
    <br></div>     ";
include("cart.php");
?>
```

How It Works

Our change.php file updates the quantity of whatever line item is clicked with these lines:

```
$query = "UPDATE carttemp
    SET quan = '$qty'
 WHERE hidden = '$hidden'";
```

Likewise, with the delete.php file, the items are deleted with this line:

```
$query = "DELETE FROM carttemp WHERE hidden = '$hidden'";
```

In each of the files, we then display the cart once again so that our customers can see what their cart currently contains.

Try It Out   ## Checking Out: Step One

Now let's create the checkout.php file, the first of three checkout files. This is one hefty file, so get your typing fingers ready:

```
<?php
session_id();
session_start();
?>
<HTML>
<HEAD>
<TITLE>Step 1 of 3 - Billing and Shipping Information</TITLE>
</HEAD>
<BODY>
<strong>Order Checkout</strong><br>
<strong>Step 1 - Please Enter Billing and Shipping Information</strong><br>
Step 2 - Please Verify Accuracy of Order Information and Send Order<br>
Step 3 - Order Confirmation and Receipt<br>

<form method="post" action="checkout2.php">

  <table width="300" border="1" align="left">
    <tr>
      <td colspan="2" bgcolor="#0000FF">
        <div align="center"><font size="3" color="#FFFFFF">Billing Information
          </font></div>
```

```
      </td>
    </tr>
    <tr>
      <td width="50%">
        <div align="right">First Name</div>
      </td>
      <td width="50%">
        <input type="text" name="firstname" maxlength="15">
      </td>
    </tr>
    <tr>
      <td width="50%">
        <div align="right">Last Name</div>
      </td>
      <td width="50%">
        <input type="text" name="lastname" maxlength="50">
      </td>
    </tr>
    <tr>
      <td width="50%">
        <div align="right">Billing Address</div>
      </td>
      <td width="50%">
        <input type="text" name="add1" maxlength="50">
      </td>
    </tr>
    <tr>
      <td width="50%">
        <div align="right">Billing Address 2</div>
      </td>
      <td width="50%">
        <input type="text" name="add2" maxlength="50">
      </td>
    </tr>
    <tr>
      <td width="50%">
        <div align="right">City</div>
      </td>
      <td width="50%">
        <input type="text" name="city" maxlength="50">
      </td>
    </tr>
    <tr>
      <td width="50%">
        <div align="right">State</div>
      </td>
      <td width="50%">
        <input type="text" name="state" size="2" maxlength="2">
      </td>
    </tr>
    <tr>
      <td width="50%">
        <div align="right">Zip</div>
      </td>
      <td width="50%">
```

```
        <input type="text" name="zip" maxlength="5" size="5">
      </td>
  </tr>
  <tr>
    <td width="50%">
      <div align="right">Phone Number</div>
    </td>
    <td width="50%">
      <input type="text" name="phone" size="12" maxlength="12">
    </td>
  </tr>
  <tr>
    <td width="50%">
      <div align="right">Fax Number</div>
    </td>
    <td width="50%">
      <input type="text" name="fax" maxlength="12" size="12">
    </td>
  </tr>
  <tr>
    <td width="50%">
      <div align="right">E-Mail Address</div>
    </td>
    <td width="50%">
      <input type="text" name="email" maxlength="50">
    </td>
  </tr>
</table>
<table width="300" border="1">
  <tr bgcolor="#990000">
    <td colspan="2">
      <div align="center"><font size="3" color="#FFFFFF">Shipping Information
        </font></div>
    </td>
  </tr>
  <tr>
    <td width="50%">
      <div align="right">Shipping Info same as Billing</div>
    </td>
    <td width="50%">
      <input type="checkbox" name="same">
    </td>
  </tr>
  <tr>
    <td width="50%">
      <div align="right">First Name</div>
    </td>
    <td width="50%">
      <input type="text" name="shipfirst" maxlength="15">
    </td>
  </tr>
  <tr>
    <td width="50%">
      <div align="right">Last Name</div>
```

```
      </td>
      <td width="50%">
        <input type="text" name="shiplast" maxlength="50">
      </td>
    </tr>
    <tr>
      <td width="50%">
        <div align="right">Billing Address</div>
      </td>
      <td width="50%">
        <input type="text" name="shipadd1" maxlength="50">
      </td>
    </tr>
    <tr>
      <td width="50%">
        <div align="right">Billing Address 2</div>
      </td>
      <td width="50%">
        <input type="text" name="shipadd2" maxlength="50">
      </td>
    </tr>
    <tr>
      <td width="50%">
        <div align="right">City</div>
      </td>
      <td width="50%">
        <input type="text" name="shipcity" maxlength="50">
      </td>
    </tr>
    <tr>
      <td width="50%">
        <div align="right">State</div>
      </td>
      <td width="50%">
        <input type="text" name="shipstate" size="2" maxlength="2">
      </td>
    </tr>
    <tr>
      <td width="50%">
        <div align="right">Zip</div>
      </td>
      <td width="50%">
        <input type="text" name="shipzip" maxlength="5" size="5">
      </td>
    </tr>
    <tr>
      <td width="50%">
        <div align="right">Phone Number</div>
      </td>
      <td width="50%">
        <input type="text" name="shipphone" size="12" maxlength="12">
      </td>
    </tr>
    <tr>
```

```
        <td width="50%">
          <div align="right">E-Mail Address</div>
    </td>
        <td width="50%">
          <input type="text" name="shipemail" maxlength="50">
        </td>
      </tr>
    </table>
    <p>
      <input type="submit" name="Submit" value="Proceed to Next Step —&gt;">
    </p>
    </form>

  </BODY>
  </HTML>
```

Figure 14-5 shows what our screen looks like when we make the choice to check out after putting one Superhero Body Suit in our cart.

Figure 14-5

How It Works

The following is the step that asks for our customer's billing and shipping information. We start with a little intro, and we let the customer know what step he or she is currently on. Then we set up the form that will collect all the information and submit it to the next page of the checkout process:

```
<form method="post" action="checkout2.php">
```

The rest is pretty much no-brainer type stuff, just getting the variables and passing them along to checkout2.php.

Try It Out   **Checking Out: Step Two**

Let's complete checkout2.php so customers can verify that all the information is accurate, and to give customers a chance to make any last minute changes.

```php
<?php
session_id();
session_start();
//connect to the database
$connect = mysql_connect("localhost", "root", "mysqlpass") or
    die ("Hey loser, check your server connection.");
mysql_select_db ("ecommerce");
if ($_POST['same'] == 'on') {
    $_POST['shipfirst'] = $_POST['firstname'];
    $_POST['shiplast'] = $_POST['lastname'];
    $_POST['shipadd1'] = $_POST['add1'];
    $_POST['shipadd2'] = $_POST['add2'];
    $_POST['shipcity'] = $_POST['city'];
    $_POST['shipstate'] = $_POST['state'];
    $_POST['shipzip'] = $_POST['zip'];
    $_POST['shipphone'] = $_POST['phone'];
    $_POST['shipemail'] = $_POST['email'];
    }
?>
<HTML>
<HEAD>
<TITLE>Step 2 of 3 - Verify Order Accuracy</TITLE>
</HEAD>
<BODY>
Step 1 - Please Enter Billing and Shipping Information<br>
<strong>Step 2 - Please Verify Accuracy and Make Any Necessary
    Changes</strong><br>
Step 3 - Order Confirmation and Receipt<br>

<form method="post" action="checkout3.php">
  <table width="300" border="1" align="left">
    <tr>
      <td colspan="2" bgcolor="#0000FF">
        <div align="center"><font size="3" color="#FFFFFF">Billing
          Information
          </font></div>
```

```
      </td>
    </tr>
    <tr>
      <td width="50%">
        <div align="right">First Name</div>
      </td>
      <td width="50%">
        <input type="text" name="firstname" maxlength="15"
          value="<?php echo $_POST['firstname']?> ">
      </td>
    </tr>
    <tr>
      <td width="50%">
        <div align="right">Last Name</div>
      </td>
      <td width="50%">
        <input type="text" name="lastname" maxlength="50"
          value="<?php echo $_POST['lastname']?>">
      </td>
    </tr>
    <tr>
      <td width="50%">
        <div align="right">Billing Address</div>
      </td>
      <td width="50%">
        <input type="text" name="add1" maxlength="50"
          value="<?php echo $_POST['add1']?>">
      </td>
    </tr>
    <tr>
      <td width="50%">
        <div align="right">Billing Address 2</div>
      </td>
      <td width="50%">
        <input type="text" name="add2" maxlength="50"
          value="<?php echo $_POST['add2']?>">
      </td>
    </tr>
    <tr>
      <td width="50%">
        <div align="right">City</div>
      </td>
      <td width="50%">
        <input type="text" name="city" maxlength="50"
          value="<?php echo $_POST['city']?> ">
      </td>
    </tr>
    <tr>
      <td width="50%">
        <div align="right">State</div>
      </td>
      <td width="50%">
        <input type="text" name="state" size="2" maxlength="2"
```

```
                       value="<?php echo $_POST['state']?>">
      </td>
   </tr>
   <tr>
      <td width="50%">
        <div align="right">Zip</div>
      </td>
      <td width="50%">
        <input type="text" name="zip" maxlength="5" size="5"
              value="<?php echo $_POST['zip']?>">
      </td>
   </tr>
   <tr>
      <td width="50%">
        <div align="right">Phone Number</div>
      </td>
      <td width="50%">
        <input type="text" name="phone" size="12" maxlength="12"
          value="<?php echo $_POST['phone']?>">
      </td>
   </tr>
   <tr>
      <td width="50%">
        <div align="right">Fax Number</div>
      </td>
      <td width="50%">
        <input type="text" name="fax" maxlength="12" size="12"
          value="<?php echo $_POST['fax']?>">
      </td>
   </tr>
   <tr>
      <td width="50%">
        <div align="right">E-Mail Address</div>
      </td>
      <td width="50%">
        <input type="text" name="email" maxlength="50"
          value="<?php echo $_POST['email']?>">
      </td>
   </tr>
</table>
<table width="300" border="1">
  <tr bgcolor="#990000">
    <td colspan="2">
      <div align="center"><font size="3" color="#FFFFFF">Shipping
              Information
        </font></div>
    </td>
  </tr>
  <tr>
    <td width="50%">
      <div align="right">Shipping Info same as Billing</div>
    </td>
    <td width="50%">
```

```
          <input type="checkbox" name="same"></td>
    </tr>
    <tr>
      <td width="50%">
        <div align="right">First Name</div>
      </td>
      <td width="50%">
        <input type="text" name="shipfirst" maxlength="15"
          value="<?php echo $_POST['shipfirst']?>">
      </td>
    </tr>
    <tr>
      <td width="50%">
        <div align="right">Last Name</div>
      </td>
      <td width="50%">
        <input type="text" name="shiplast" maxlength="50"
          value="<?php echo $_POST['shiplast']?>">
      </td>
    </tr>
    <tr>
      <td width="50%">
        <div align="right">Billing Address</div>
      </td>
      <td width="50%">
        <input type="text" name="shipadd1" maxlength="50"
          value="<?php echo $_POST['shipadd1']?>">
      </td>
    </tr>
    <tr>
      <td width="50%">
        <div align="right">Billing Address 2</div>
      </td>
      <td width="50%">
        <input type="text" name="shipadd2" maxlength="50"
          value="<?php echo $_POST['shipadd2']?>">
      </td>
    </tr>
    <tr>
      <td width="50%">
        <div align="right">City</div>
      </td>
      <td width="50%">
        <input type="text" name="shipcity" maxlength="50"
          value="<?php echo $_POST['shipcity']?>">
      </td>
    </tr>
    <tr>
      <td width="50%">
        <div align="right">State</div>
      </td>
      <td width="50%">
        <input type="text" name="shipstate" size="2" maxlength="2"
```

```
                              value="<?php echo $_POST['shipstate']?>">
          </td>
       </tr>
       <tr>
          <td width="50%">
            <div align="right">Zip</div>
          </td>
          <td width="50%">
            <input type="text" name="shipzip" maxlength="5" size="5"
              value="<?php echo $_POST['shipzip']?>">
          </td>
       </tr>
       <tr>
          <td width="50%">
            <div align="right">Phone Number</div>
          </td>
          <td width="50%">
            <input type="text" name="shipphone" size="12" maxlength="12"
              value="<?php echo $_POST['shipphone']?>">
          </td>
       </tr>
       <tr>
          <td width="50%">
            <div align="right">E-Mail Address</div>
          </td>
          <td width="50%">
            <input type="text" name="shipemail" maxlength="50"
              value="<?php echo $_POST['shipemail']?>">
          </td>
       </tr>
     </table>

<table border="1" align="left" cellpadding="5">
       <tr>
            <td>Quantity</td>
            <td>Item Image</td>
            <td>Item Name</td>
            <td>Price Each</td>
            <td>Extended Price</td>
            <td></td>
            <td></td>
       </tr>
        <tr>
        <?php
         $sessid = session_id();
         $query = "SELECT * FROM carttemp WHERE sess = '$sessid'";
        $results = mysql_query($query)
            or die (mysql_query());
            while ($row = mysql_fetch_array($results)) {
                extract ($row);
                $prod = "SELECT * FROM products WHERE
                    prodnum = '$prodnum'";
                $prod2 = mysql_query($prod);
```

```
                $prod3 = mysql_fetch_array($prod2);
                extract ($prod3);
                echo "<td>";
                echo $quan;
                echo "</td>";
                echo "<td>";
                echo "<a href = 'getprod.php?prodid=" .
                      $prodnum ."'>";
                echo "THUMBNAIL<br>IMAGE</td></a>";
                echo "<td>";
                echo "<a href = 'getprod.php?prodid=" .
                      $prodnum ."'>";
                echo $name;
                echo "</td></a>";
                echo "<td align='right'>";
                echo $price;
                echo "</td>";
                echo "<td align='right'>";
        //get extended price
                $extprice = number_format($price * $quan, 2);
                echo $extprice;
                echo "</td>";
                echo "<td>";
                echo "<a href='cart.php'>Make Changes to Cart</a>";
                echo "</td>";
                echo "</tr>";
        //add extended price to total
                $total = $extprice + $total;

                }
?>
<tr>
<td colspan='4' align='right'>Your total before shipping is:</td>
<td align='right'> <?php echo number_format($total, 2) ?></td>
<td></td>
<td></td>
</tr>
</table>
<input type="hidden" name="total" value="<?php echo $total?>">
  <p>
    <input type="submit" name="Submit" value="Send Order -&gt;">
  </p>
  </form>


  </BODY>
  </HTML>
```

If you entered the information in checkout.php, your screen should look like that in Figure 14-6.

Figure 14-6

How It Works

In the code, you see the standard connection lines and our session lines. Then we check to see if the billing info is the same as the shipping info, and, if so, we populate the shipping table with the billing information, as follows:

```
if ($_POST['same'] == 'on') {
    $_POST['shipfirst'] = $_POST['firstname'];
    $_POST['shiplast'] = $_POST['lastname'];
    $_POST['shipadd1'] = $_POST['add1'];
    $_POST['shipadd2'] = $_POST['add2'];
    $_POST['shipcity'] = $_POST['city'];
    $_POST['shipstate'] = $_POST['state'];
    $_POST['shipzip'] = $_POST['zip'];
    $_POST['shipphone'] = $_POST['phone'];
    $_POST['shipemail'] = $_POST['email'];
    }
```

The rest of the script is pretty similar to previous pages. We show the billing and shipping information as we did in checkout1.php and we show our cart contents as we did in cart.php. We decided in this case to keep our shopping cart changes in the cart.php file itself, so we provided a link to cart.php.

Just another point worth mentioning: We passed the $total variable in a hidden field instead of retabulating it in the next page; we needed to access it early on in the code. This just makes life a lot easier.

We also set our form action to be checkout3.php, where it all happens.

Try It Out   Checking Out: Step Three

For our final file, we want to complete checkout3.php. Numerous things will be going on in this file, and we'll talk about them in a minute.

```php
<?php
session_id();
session_start();
//connect to the database - either include a connection variable file or
//type the following lines:
$connect = mysql_connect("localhost", "root", "mysqlpass") or
      die ("Hey loser, check your server connection.");
mysql_select_db ("ecommerce");
//Let's make the variables easy to access in our queries
$firstname = $_POST['firstname'];
$lastname = $_POST['lastname'];
$firstname = $_POST['firstname'];
$add1 = $_POST['add1'];
$add2 = $_POST['add2'];
$city = $_POST['city'];
$state = $_POST['state'];
$zip = $_POST['zip'];
$phone = $_POST['phone'];
$fax = $_POST['fax'];
$email = $_POST['email'];
$shipfirst = $_POST['shipfirst'];
$shiplast = $_POST['shiplast'];
$shipadd1 = $_POST['shipadd1'];
$shipadd2 = $_POST['shipadd2'];
$shipcity = $_POST['shipcity'];
$shipstate = $_POST['shipstate'];
$shipzip = $_POST['shipzip'];
$shipstate = $_POST['shipstate'];
$shipphone = $_POST['shipphone'];
$shipemail = $_POST['shipemail'];
$total = $_POST['total'];
$sessid = session_id();
$today = date("Y-m-d");
//1) Assign Customer Number to new Customer, or find existing customer number
      $query = "SELECT * FROM customers WHERE
            (firstname = '$firstname' AND
            lastname = '$lastname' AND
            add1 = '$add1' AND
            add2 = '$add2' AND
```

```
                city = '$city')";
        $results = mysql_query($query)
                or (mysql_error());
        $rows = mysql_num_rows($results);

        if ($rows < 1) {
                //assign new custnum
                $query2 = "INSERT INTO customers (
                firstname, lastname, add1, add2, city, state, zip, phone, fax, email)
                 VALUES (
                '$firstname',
                '$lastname',
                '$add1',
                '$add2',
                '$city',
                '$state',
                '$zip',
                '$phone',
                '$fax',
                '$email')";
                $insert = mysql_query($query2)
                        or (mysql_error());
                $custid = mysql_insert_id();
        }
        //If custid exists, we want to make it equal to custnum
        if($custid) $custnum = $custid;
//2) Insert Info into ordermain
        //determine shipping costs based on order total (25% of total)
        $shipping = $total * 0.25;

        $query3 = "INSERT INTO ordermain (orderdate, custnum, subtotal,
                shipping, shipfirst, shiplast, shipadd1, shipadd2,
                shipcity, shipstate, shipzip, shipphone, shipemail)
                VALUES (
                '$today',
                '$custnum',
                '$total',
                '$shipping'
                '$shipfirst',
                '$shiplast',
                '$shipadd1',
                '$shipadd2',
                '$shipcity',
                '$shipstate',
                '$shipzip',
                '$shipphone',
                '$shipemail')";
        $insert2 = mysql_query($query3)
                or (mysql_error());
        $orderid = mysql_insert_id();

//3) Insert Info into orderdet
        //find the correct cart information being temporarily stored
        $query = "SELECT * from carttemp WHERE sess='$sessid'";
```

```
        $results = mysql_query($query)
            or (mysql_error());

        //put the data into the database one row at a time
        while ($row = mysql_fetch_array($results)) {
                extract ($row);
                $query4 = "INSERT INTO orderdet (ordernum, qty, prodnum)
                    VALUES (
                    '$orderid',
                    '$quan',
                    '$prodnum')";
                $insert4 = mysql_query($query4)
                    or (mysql_error());
        }

//4)delete from temporary table
    $query="DELETE FROM carttemp WHERE sess='$sessid'";
    $delete = mysql_query($query);


//5)email confirmations to us and to the customer
/* recipients */
$to = "<" . $email .">";

/* subject */
$subject = "Order Confirmation";

/* message */
    /* top of message */
    $message = "
      <html>
      <head>
      <title>Order Confirmation</title>
      </head>
      <body>
    Here is a recap of your order:<br><br>
    Order date:";
$message .= $today;
$message .= "
    <br>
     Order Number: ";
$message .= $orderid;
$message .= "
    <table width='50%' border='0'>
     <tr>
       <td>
        <p><font size='2'>Bill to:<br>";
$message .= $firstname;
$message .= " ";
$message .= $lastname;
$message .= "<br>";
$message .= $add1;
$message .= "<br>";
if ($add2) $message .= $add2 . "<br>";
```

```
$message .= $city . ", " . $state . " " . $zip;
$message .= "</p></td>
   <td>
     <p><font size='2'>Ship to:<br>";
$message .= $shipfirst . " " . $shiplast;
$message .= "<br>";
$message .= $shipadd1 . "<br>";
if ($shipadd2) $message .= $shipadd2 . "<br>";
$message .= $shipcity . ", " . $shipstate . " " . $shipzip;
$message .= "</font></p>
    </td>
   </tr>
  </table>
  <hr noshade width='250px' align='left'>
 <table cellpadding='5'>
   <tr>";

//grab the contents of the order and insert them
//into the message field

    $query = "SELECT * from orderdet WHERE ordernum = '$orderid'";
    $results = mysql_query($query)
        or die (mysql_query());
        while ($row = mysql_fetch_array($results)) {
            extract ($row);
            $prod = "SELECT * FROM products
                    WHERE prodnum = '$prodnum'";
            $prod2 = mysql_query($prod);
            $prod3 = mysql_fetch_array($prod2);
            extract ($prod3);
            $message .= "<td><font size='2'>";
            $message .= $quan;
            $message .= "</font></td>";
            $message .="<td><font size='2'>";
            $message .= $name;
            $message .= "</font></td>";
            $message .= "<td align='right'><font size='2'>";
            $message .= $price;
            $message .= "</font></td>";
            $message .= "<td align='right'><font size='2'>";
        //get extended price
            $extprice = number_format($price * $quan, 2);
            $message .= $extprice;
            $message .= "</font></td>";
            $message .= "</tr>";
            }

$message .= "<tr>
    <td colspan='3' align='right'><font size='2'>
      Your total before shipping is:</font>
    </td>
    <td align='right'><font size='2'>";
$message .= number_format($total, 2);
$message .= "</font>
```

```
          </td>
        </tr>
        <tr>
          <td colspan='3' align='right'><font size='2'>
            Shipping Costs:</font>
          </td>
          <td align='right'><font size='2'>";
   $message .= number_format($shipping, 2);
   $message .= "</font>
          </td>
        </tr>
      <tr>
          <td colspan='3' align='right'><font size='2'>
           Your final total is:</font>
          </td>
          <td align='right'><font size='2'> ";
   $message .= number_format(($total + $shipping), 2);
   $message .= "</font>
          </td>
        </tr>
      </table>
</body>
</html>";

/* headers */
$headers = "MIME-Version: 1.0\r\n";
$headers .= "Content-type: text/html; charset=iso-8859-1\r\n";
$headers .= "From: <storeemail@email.com>\r\n";
$headers .= "Cc: <storeemail@email.com>\r\n";
$headers .= "X-Mailer: PHP / ".phpversion()."\r\n";

/* mail it */
mail ($to, $subject, $message, $headers);


//6)show them their order & give them an order number
?>
<HTML>
<HEAD>
<TITLE>Thank you for your order!</TITLE>
</HEAD>
<BODY>
Step 1 - Please Enter Billing and Shipping Information<br>
Step 2 - Please Verify Accuracy and Make Any Necessary Changes<br>
<strong>Step 3 - Order Confirmation and Receipt</strong><br><br>

Thank you for your order!<br><br>
Your order number is <?php echo $orderid ?>. Please print this page or retain
this number for your records.<br>
<br>
Here is a recap of your order:<br><br>
Order date: <?php echo $today ?><br>


<table width="50%" border="0">
```

```
  <tr>
    <td>
      <p><font size="2">Bill to:<br>
        <?php echo $firstname . " " . $lastname ?><br>
        <?php echo $add1 ?><br>
        <?php if ($add2) echo $add2 . "<br>"?>
        <?php echo $city . ", " . $state . "  " . $zip ?> </font></p>
    </td>
    <td>
      <p><font size="2">Ship to:<br>
        <?php echo $shipfirst . " " . $shiplast ?><br>
        <?php echo $shipadd1 ?><br>
        <?php if ($shipadd2) echo $shipadd2 . "<br>"?>
        <?php echo $shipcity . ", " . $shipstate . "  " . $shipzip ?> </font></p>
    </td>
  </tr>
</table>
<hr noshade width='250px' align='left'>
<table cellpadding="5">
    <tr>
    <?php
    $query = "SELECT * from orderdet WHERE ordernum = '$orderid'";
    $results = mysql_query($query)
         or die (mysql_query());
         while ($row = mysql_fetch_array($results)) {
             extract ($row);
             $prod = "SELECT * FROM products WHERE prodnum = '$prodnum'";
             $prod2 = mysql_query($prod);
             $prod3 = mysql_fetch_array($prod2);
             extract ($prod3);
             echo "<td><font size='2'>";
             echo $quan;
             echo "</font></td>";
             echo "<td><font size='2'>";
             echo $name;
             echo "</font></td>";
             echo "<td align='right'><font size='2'>";
             echo $price;
             echo "</font></td>";
             echo "<td align='right'><font size='2'>";
        //get extended price
             $extprice = number_format($price * $quan, 2);
             echo $extprice;
             echo "</font></td>";
             echo "</tr>";
             }
?>
<tr>
<td colspan='3' align='right'><font size='2'>
Your total before shipping is:</font>
</td>
<td align='right'><font size='2'>
    <?php echo number_format($total, 2) ?></font>
</td>
</tr>
```

```
<tr>
<td colspan='3' align='right'><font size='2'>
Shipping Costs:</font>
</td>
<td align='right'><font size='2'>
    <?php echo number_format($shipping, 2) ?></font>
</td>
</tr>
<tr>
<td colspan='3' align='right'><font size='2'>
Your final total is:</font>
</td>
<td align='right'><font size='2'>
    <?php echo number_format(($total + $shipping), 2) ?></font>
</td>
</tr>
</table>
</BODY>
</HTML>
```

See Figure 14-7 for a copy of the confirmation of our order.

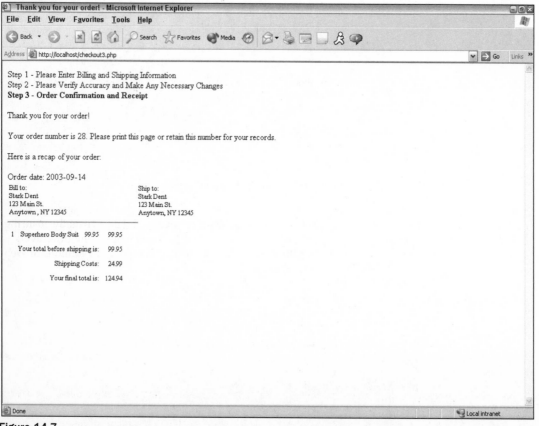

Figure 14-7

How It Works

Of course, there are comments throughout the code, but here is a rundown of what this script accomplishes.

❑ Before we can enter anything else, we have to determine whether or not our customer is new or returning. If he or she is a returning customer, we want to keep the existing customer number, and if new, he or she will be assigned the next customer number in line. Of course, this is not a fail-safe plan: We check for the same first name, last name, two lines of address, and city. A returning customer would just have to abbreviate something differently to be considered "new." We talk more about this later in this chapter.

We use the PHP function `mysql_insert_id()` to get the auto-increment value that was just added into the database. This helps us make sure we are keeping all the information from the same order together.

❑ Once we have the customer information entered in the database, we can then enter the order-specific information. This includes the date and order number, as well as the shipping information associated with this order. We also tabulated the shipping costs as a percentage of total cost of the order (25 percent), but obviously you can set your shipping costs to be whatever you like.

❑ We can then enter the order detail information with all the specific items that have been placed in the shopping cart.

❑ We then delete the temporary information, as we don't need it anymore.

❑ We also send a confirmation e-mail to our customer, and one to ourselves to let us know an order was placed.

❑ We display the order confirmation on the page to let the customer know immediately that the order was received and to give him or her an order number.

This is the end of our simple shopping cart script.

E-Commerce, Any Way You Slice It

As we briefly mentioned before, you can integrate e-commerce into your site the right way and you can do it the wrong way. To prevent yourself from looking like a complete idiot and virtually ensuring e-commerce failure, we highly recommend doing things the right way. Good word-of-mouth travels slowly, but we all know how quickly bad word-of-mouth spreads. Also, with so many millions of Web sites out there competing for attention, we want to elevate yours above the rest.

This may sound harsh, but here are some things to remember about some of the more challenging characteristics of your potential customers:

❑ **Your customers are impatient.** They don't want to have to wait for your pages to load or for answers to their questions. They are busy people, just like you, and if they don't find what they need right away, they're outta there and on to something else.

❑ **Your customers are distrustful.** Who wants their personal information strewn about all over the Web? You certainly don't, and they don't either. They don't want their credit card number to be used by every geek in your office, and they don't want to give you tons of money and never see the product they purchased. They don't want to order from you one week and have you go bankrupt the next.

❑ **Your customers want a lot for a little.** In this age of Web site competition, where people can compare prices with a few mouse clicks, they are striving to get the best deal they can. They want to make sure they are getting the best deal, but they also appreciate the value-added services of a high-quality Web site.

❑ **Your customers are generally lazy.** They don't want to have to put any effort into trying to find the right product on your site or figuring out what you're trying to say or what your policies are. They don't want to work at trying to get the checkout process to work, and they don't want to have to filter through pages and pages of text to glean information.

❑ **Your customers aren't very forgiving.** You basically have one chance to make a good first impression on your customers. Nothing can eliminate a sale (and future sales for that matter) faster than a bad experience. Whether it is something minor such as spelling mistakes and broken images on your site or something major such as selling faulty merchandise, your customers are likely to remember something bad a lot longer than something good. They will also be more likely to share a bad experience more quickly than they will a good one.

❑ **Your customers may not be as technically savvy as you are.** Yes, there are actually people out there who still use dial-up with 56K. There are people out there who still use 14" monitors and there are people out there who have never made an online purchase in their lives. Remember these people and don't leave them behind totally when designing your site. If you do, you are alienating a huge percentage of the population.

Don't worry: Satisfying e-commerce customers is not hard, but a little effort can really go a long way. We've included some general guidelines to follow. After reading them, you may think, "Well, duh, no kidding," but you'd be surprised at how many big, well-known companies don't follow them.

Information Is Everything

Your customers have to get as much information as possible about your product because they can't actually see, feel, touch, and smell what you have to offer. Your site is your window to your customers, and they have to depend on what you're telling them to make their purchasing decision. Whatever blanks you leave in your product description, policies, company history, or checkout process will have to be filled in by the customer's imagination. While that may be good in certain circumstances, you do not want your customers to make incorrect assumptions that leave them dissatisfied after the fact, or for their uncertainty to prevent the sale altogether.

Besides textual information, graphics are a very important part of the sale. There is a fine balance between adding too many graphics to your site, which causes your potential patrons to wait longer than they need to, and providing enough high-quality pictures so they can actually see what they're getting.

Importance of Trust

Let's talk for a minute about trust over the Web. We all know that most of the proclaimed 14-year-old females in those online chat rooms are really 40-year-old fat guys sitting in their living rooms. Things are not always as they seem in the online world, and because of that, as an e-commerce retailer, you are at a disadvantage over those with a physical storefront and salespeople. And then there's the old saying "caveat emptor" ("buyer beware") that goes along with any purchase/sales transaction. "Trust" must be established and it certainly is an uphill battle. If you're an established business already, and you have spent years building product or brand name recognition, don't think that switching to e-commerce will be so easy. Yes, if your business has an established reputation you may have an easier time than some unknown entity, like "Joe's House of Beauty," but people still want to know what they're getting and be assured that they're not going to get ripped off.

Privacy Policy

Users want to know that their personal information will not be sold and they won't end up on 47 spam e-mail lists. They also want to make sure they won't be on an annoying telemarketing phone list or receive junk snail mail. The only way they can be assured this won't happen is if you provide a clear, concise privacy policy in an easy-to-find place on your site.

Return Policy

Returns are a sometimes overlooked part of a company's e-commerce venture. There have to be processes in place for accepting returns, shipping out replacement merchandise, or issuing credits in exchange. Your users will need to know where you stand on returns, what your requirements are for accepting them and how they will be handled once they reach your warehouse (or basement).

If you are a relatively (or completely) unknown entity, you may want to consider providing a 100 percent money back guarantee or something similar to try and build trust with your potential customers. You may get burned once or twice on this and it may require more work from you, but overall it can be a very beneficial asset to you, especially if your customers are riding the fence on a potential purchase.

Whatever you decide, you should think long and hard about how you want to handle returned merchandise, and then make sure your customers understand your decisions in order to avoid misunderstandings later on.

Warm Bodies

Who doesn't love a nice, warm body? In this age of technology, sometimes it's nice just to talk to an actual living, breathing person who can help you answer a question or find what you are looking for. If you can manage this in your e-commerce business, it is another great feature that will undoubtedly pay for itself in those "on the fence" purchasing decisions. You can provide personal customer service in a few ways:

- ❑ Give your customers a phone number (preferably toll-free) where they can have access to your customer service staff, or just you, if you're a one-man show.

- ❑ Offer online customer service chat for your customers, where you can address customer questions or concerns without having to pay someone to wait for the phone to ring.

- ❑ Provide a customer service e-mail address for questions and problems. Although this isn't the optimal solution, as many people don't want to wait for answers to their questions, at least this gives customers an outlet to vent their frustrations and then move on to something else. It also gives you a chance to prepare a proper reply and respond accordingly.

Professional Look

When designing your site, you want to make sure it doesn't look "homemade" and that it appears as professional as possible. Professional equals credible in the minds of your customers, and it helps to build that elusive trusting relationship.

Here are some ways to improve the look of your site:

- ❑ Spend some time viewing other e-commerce sites. What do you personally like about them? What don't you like? By emulating the big guys, you can look big, too.

- ❑ Invest in a few Web site design books or do some online research. Numerous articles and books have been written on the topic, and you may as well not re-invent the wheel.

- ❑ If you use a template of some sort, please, please, please do us a favor and make sure you remove all generic instances. We've seen sites with a title bar that reads "Insert Description Here." This is not a good look, trust us.

- ❑ *Spell check* your document. Spell checkers are available in nearly all text editors, so spelling mistakes are pretty much unacceptable and can really undermine your professional look.

Secure Credit Card Processing

Nothing will make your customers feel better than knowing their credit card information is safe and won't get stolen along the way. Make sure you are using a secure encryption method to transfer sensitive information, such as SSL, and make sure your customers understand how safe their information is. It's a good idea to not get too technical; just explain the security process in layman's terms.

If it's possible, it's a good idea to have a third party (such as Verisign) verify that your site is secure and prominently display its seal somewhere on your site.

Easy Navigation

You want to make sure your customers are able to move around your site and find what they need. Remember the rule from earlier in this section: They do not want to work too hard, or they will lose interest and go somewhere else.

Common Links

Make sure you have clear links to every area of your site, and put the common links near the top where they can be seen easily. Common links include a customer's shopping cart, customer service, or user login.

Search Function

You should give your customers a way to easily find what they're looking for. An accurate and quick search engine is essential to accomplish this. There are many ways to add this feature to your site, either through coding it by hand in PHP or hooking up with third-party software. Another way to improve your search engine is to make sure you include misspellings and not-so-common terms to give your customers the best results possible.

Typical Design

It's been long enough now that most people are accustomed to seeing navigation links either at the top or to the left side of a page. By keeping with this general scheme, you can ensure that your customers will know where to look to find what they need.

Competitive Pricing

If you are selling items that are available from other sources, it's important to remember that your store can easily be compared with numerous other stores selling the same thing. If your prices are way out of line, your customers will get a good chuckle and then promptly click back to their Google search. Do your research, and make sure you are in line with similar products being sold on the Web. Not all customers base their decision solely on price, but they definitely don't want to be taken for a ride, unless you have a Lamborghini Diablo, and that's a different story.

Appropriate Merchandise

There are only a handful of stores on the Web that can get away with carrying a wide range of unrelated products, and, no offense, but chances are, you aren't one of them. Be sure you are carrying items that are related to your overall site and to each other, or you will confuse your customers and detract from your look and focus.

Timely Delivery

In this world of "overnight this" and "immediately download that," it is no longer acceptable to ask for six to eight weeks to deliver your merchandise to your customers. The only exception is if you are creating something custom made or if your customers are preordering something that hasn't been officially released yet. The typical lead time for standard products to ship to a customer is roughly two to three business days. If you can do better than that, your customers will be happy, and if not, you need to make sure your customer realizes it will take longer and give an explanation.

It is also important to provide numerous shipping options to your customers and let them decide how quickly they need your products and how much they are willing to spend to get them faster.

Communication

Because you are isolated from your customers, communication is essential to building strong relationships. Your customers want to know that you received their order, when the order is ready to ship, and when it ships. They appreciate getting a tracking number so they can see where their package is every step of the way. Some companies even track each outgoing package and let their customers know when they think the package has been delivered, in case there are any misunderstandings. All of this can be communicated via e-mail. Your customers will definitely appreciate being kept in the loop, and knowing that their order has not been lost somewhere along the order fulfillment and delivery chain.

Customer Feedback

The online world presents an interesting dilemma for e-commerce retailers in that you must operate your store in a bubble. You can't tell what your customers are thinking or how they react to your site. You know you're relatively successful at something only if you have sales and relatively unsuccessful if you don't. Figuring out which of our rules you're breaking can be a tricky endeavor. That's when your customer feedback can make or break you.

You always want to give your customers an outlet to express their concerns or problems, and it can give you a warm fuzzy feeling to get some positive feedback once in a while. To encourage your customers to provide you with feedback you should do two things:

❑ Give them an incentive to complete a survey, or provide some sort of feedback. Free shipping, a discount on their next order, or a free gift of some sort are some good possibilities.

❑ Make it easy for your customers to complete a survey, but make sure it provides you with valuable feedback. Don't just ask for their comments; ask them to rate certain areas of your site. Also, don't give them 100 questions, but a maximum of 15–20. After that, people lose interest and their special gift isn't worth it.

By sticking to the preceding guidelines and advice, you will increase the quality and quantity of your customer feedback and increase your ability to tap into one of your most valuable resources.

Summary

Now that you have the know-how to add e-commerce to your site, you should feel comfortable making your site as competitive and professional as any other site out there. You should be able to set up a simple shopping cart, and, with time, you will be able to continue to add features to really enhance your cart and your site in general. E-commerce concepts aren't difficult to comprehend, and by following the simple guidelines we've outlined, you will be well on your way. Although e-commerce retailers don't typically enjoy overnight success, adding e-commerce to your site can really augment what you're currently doing and may grow to something big over time.

Exercises

We know we're not perfect, so before you start naming all the things we didn't accomplish in our shopping cart scripts, we'll save you the trouble and list them for you. As a matter of fact, we did these things on purpose because we wanted to give you some homework.

Anyway, here are the things you can work on, and hints are in Appendix A in case you need to cheat:

❑ **Allow for options.** You may have noticed that we didn't let our customers pick the size of their T-shirt or size and color of the Superhero Body Suit. Alter the codes to allow for these options.

❑ **Allow for payment.** Because of copyright issues, we weren't able to actually hook you up with Paypal or one of the other payment processors available. Decide how you want to accept payment, and then alter the code accordingly.

❑ **Allow for tax.** Many states require that you charge sales tax on the orders shipped to the state where you have a physical presence, and some states require sales tax on all online orders. Set your code to check for customers in your own state and add the appropriate sales tax to those orders only.

❑ **Check for mistakes.** We have not included any mechanism to check for required fields, or for mismatched types (such as a bogus e-mail address). Add these checks in your code.

❑ **Allow for registering, login, and order tracking.** Some customers like to check the status of their orders.

Creating a Bulletin Board System

People don't like to be alone because we are social animals. Throughout our brief history as civilized human beings, we have consistently maintained some sort of connection to other people, whether it be the family unit, clans, chess clubs, or AA meetings.

With the advent of the computer, many geeks found themselves shut in a room for long periods, becoming the modern equivalent of the social outcast. (How many of us have joked about not knowing what the sun looks like?)

Enter Dennis C. Hayes, Ward Christensen, and Randy Seuss, three very smart men who together made it possible for you to communicate with other computer geeks without ever having to look at their faces.

History of the Computer Bulletin Board

D. C. Hayes is the inventor of the modem; indeed, one brand of modems was named for him. He is the father of PC-to-PC communication and is at the top of the list of people responsible for the 807 America Online disks you received in the mail last year.

Ward Christensen is the creator of Xmodem, a program that allowed users to send and receive files. It was the precursor to many file transfer programs, including FTP, which we still use today.

In February 1978, Christensen teamed up with Randy Seuss to create the first program that allowed users to communicate with one another over a modem. They called it a bulletin board system because it emulated the bulletin board they used at their local computer club. (Yes, they were serious geeks!) They named the board Chicago Bulletin Board System (CBBS).

Bulletin boards began cropping up all over the country and were soon very popular places to communicate with other people. Suddenly, geeks were no longer pariahs, but could actually interact with others. Sure, non-BBS users still saw them as outcasts, but what did they know? They were just common civilians, unwise to the ways of computers.

The only problem was that you had to dial in to the specific BBS you wanted to connect to. There was no network of computers that enabled you to jump from BBS to BBS. Over time, communication speed has increased to the point where modems are no longer the preferred connection device. With the arrival of the Internet, people had a place to connect one time, and could "surf" from site to site. BBS's began to go the way of the dinosaur.

Fortunately, BBS's didn't become extinct. They still exist today, but they have evolved. These days, a BBS is simply a Web site that does what the BBS of old did—it allows users to log in and communicate with others about a common interest. If you want to talk to other people about your collection of Barbie doll shoes, chances are there is a BBS out there for it.

Many BBS's refer to themselves as *forums*. By definition, a forum is a gathering place where people can meet and discuss different topics. That is a very apt definition for a BBS. However, we are going to clarify it a little further, for use in the computer world. By our definition (and the way we'll use it in this chapter), a forum is a place to talk to other people about a common interest. A bulletin board is the location in which the forum exists, which may house multiple forums. Therefore, you might visit a book BBS to find different forums for science fiction, nonfiction, authors, and more.

Your Bulletin Board

This brings us to the reason for this chapter. You are going to create a Bulletin Board System. Once you create the BBS, it will be up to you to create any type of forums within it that you need.

No doubt, you have visited many bulletin boards by now and are aware of the different features they have to offer. Some of them have many bells and whistles, and are very slick programs. PHPBB and Vbulletin are two of those very nice applications. Yours will not have quite the feature set these offer (unless you are ambitious and decide to expand the app you write).

You have probably seen some very simple boards out there, too. Some are nothing more than a couple of input boxes for Subject and Body, with no authentication. Those are fine for some Web sites, but not for us. This is the last application of the book, and we're going to put a few features in this thing. We are also going to use cascading style sheets (CSS) to alter the look of the page because, let's face it, the apps up to now have been fairly plain. Because of the extended feature set of this app, CSS will help you position things on the page a little better.

Don't worry if you don't know CSS; it's not a requirement. We will provide you with a CSS file, downloadable from the Web site. If you know how, you can write your own style sheet, or modify the one we provide. Otherwise, simply use the one we give you and you'll be fine. The application will work fine without the CSS, but as you will see, it will be much prettier and better laid out with it.

Here is a list of some of the more prominent features of the bulletin board you will build:

❑ **User authentication:** You want to keep track of who is posting what. You can certainly allow anonymous access (hmm . . . might make a good exercise . . .), but this app will require users to log in before they can post. Users will *not* have to log in to read posts, however.

❑ **Search:** This is the key to any good board, in our opinion. This will allow users to see if their question has already been answered, as well as enable people to find posts that discuss the topic they want to talk about.

❑ **Admin screen:** There will be a few features of the site that can be modified in the admin screen. These will be fairly limited, but we hope that the implementation will inspire you to figure out what other parts of the bulletin board you can include in the Admin section.

❑ **Regular expressions:** We include BBcodes in the application. If you have never seen them, these are special codes that give the user a limited ability to format their posts. For example, by placing [b] and [/b] around words they will become bold (for example, [b]some words[/b] will become **some words**). We will be using regular expressions for this feature.

❑ **Pagination:** You don't want to have 328 posts on a single page. For one, it's a bit long for users to read. Second, PHP takes a while to render such a page, especially if there are images in the posts. For this reason, we offer page links at the bottom to load different pages. To enable this, you will be creating a pagination function.

These are most of the major features of the board. There will be a few more bells and whistles added, but we won't spoil the surprise yet. We want to give you plenty of "ooh," "aah," and "You're a genius!" moments later.

Try It Out   The Bulletin Board Code

This is a large application—the biggest in the book. It consists of about 1,800 lines of code. Are you scared yet? Well, don't be. The hardest part is the typing, and if you want to avoid that, you can always download the code from the Web site:

```
www.wrox.com
```

If you do download the code and want to skip what follows and jump ahead to read the explanation of the code, go now to the next Try It Out section.

The first thing you will need to do is create a database. If you have already created a database for the other apps in this book, we recommend you use the same database. There is no need to create a new one. This app uses the prefix forum_ for its tables, so there should be no conflict.

If you do not have a database created, then Chapter 9 will help you create one. Do that, and then come back. We'll wait . . . .

There are around 20 PHP files to enter. We are simply going to list them one after another, giving you the filename of each, and a short explanation of what the file is for. Save each file in the same folder.

Do your typing finger warm-ups, and let's get started!

1. Open your favorite PHP editor. Remember to save early, and save often!

2. Create `conn.php`: This is the file that connects the application to the database.

   This file will be included at the top of almost every other page, and contains all of your connection information. Substitute the appropriate data for your host, username, password, and database.

```php
<?php
define('SQL_HOST','localhost');
define('SQL_USER','buzzly_comic');
define('SQL_PASS','spiderman');
define('SQL_DB','buzzly_comicsite');

$conn = mysql_connect(SQL_HOST,SQL_USER,SQL_PASS)
  or die('Could not connect to the database; ' . mysql_error());

mysql_select_db(SQL_DB,$conn)
  or die('Could not select database; ' . mysql_error());
?>
```

3. Enter `setup.php`.

   Once you have your database created, and `conn.php` saved, this file creates all of the necessary tables in your database.

```php
<?php
require_once "conn.php";
$adminemail = "admin@yoursite.com";
$adminpass = "admin";
$adminname = "Admin";

/******* Access Levels Table ****************************************/
$sql = <<<EOS
CREATE TABLE forum_access_levels (
  access_lvl tinyint(4) NOT NULL auto_increment,
  access_name varchar(50) NOT NULL default '',
  PRIMARY KEY (access_lvl)
)
EOS;
$result = mysql_query($sql);
switch(mysql_errno()) {
  case 1050:
    break;
  case 0:
    $sql = "INSERT IGNORE INTO forum_access_levels
      VALUES (1,'User')";
    $result = mysql_query($sql) or die(mysql_error());
    $sql = "INSERT IGNORE INTO forum_access_levels
      VALUES (2,'Moderator')";
    $result = mysql_query($sql) or die(mysql_error());
    $sql = "INSERT IGNORE INTO forum_access_levels
      VALUES (3,'Administrator')";
    $result = mysql_query($sql) or die(mysql_error());
    break;
```

```
      default:
        die(mysql_error());
        break;
    }
    $a_tables[] = "forum_access_levels";

    /******* Admin Table *************************************************/
    $sql = <<<EOS
    CREATE TABLE  forum_admin (
      id int(11) NOT NULL auto_increment,
      title varchar(100) NOT NULL default '',
      value varchar(255) NOT NULL default '',
      constant varchar(100) NOT NULL default '',
      PRIMARY KEY  (id)
    )
    EOS;
    $result = mysql_query($sql);
    switch(mysql_errno()) {
      case 1050:
        break;
      case 0:
        $sql = "INSERT INTO forum_admin VALUES (NULL,
          'Board Title', 'Comic Book Appreciation Forums', 'title')";
        $result = mysql_query($sql) or die(mysql_error());
        $sql = "INSERT INTO forum_admin VALUES (NULL, ".
              "'Board Description', 'The place to discuss your favorite ".
              "comic books, movies, and more!', 'description')";
        $result = mysql_query($sql) or die(mysql_error());
        $sql = "INSERT INTO forum_admin VALUES (NULL, ".
              "'Admin Email', '$adminemail', 'admin_email')";
        $result = mysql_query($sql) or die(mysql_error());
        $sql = "INSERT INTO forum_admin VALUES (NULL, 'Copyright', ".
              "'(c) 2003 CBA Inc.  All rights reserved.', ".
              "'copyright')";
        $result = mysql_query($sql) or die(mysql_error());
        $sql = "INSERT INTO forum_admin VALUES (NULL, ".
              "'Board Titlebar', 'CBA Forums', 'titlebar')";
        $result = mysql_query($sql) or die(mysql_error());
        $sql = "INSERT INTO forum_admin VALUES (NULL, ".
              "'Pagination Limit', '10', 'pageLimit')";
        $result = mysql_query($sql) or die(mysql_error());
        $sql = "INSERT INTO forum_admin VALUES (NULL, ".
              "'Pagination Range', '7', 'pageRange')";
        $result = mysql_query($sql) or die(mysql_error());
        break;
      default:
        die(mysql_error());
        break;
    }
    $a_tables[] = "forum_admin";

    /******* BBcode Table *************************************************/
    $sql = <<<EOS
```

```
CREATE TABLE IF NOT EXISTS forum_bbcode (
  id int(11) NOT NULL auto_increment,
  template varchar(255) NOT NULL default '',
  replacement varchar(255) NOT NULL default '',
  PRIMARY KEY (id)
)
EOS;
$result = mysql_query($sql) or die(mysql_error());
$a_tables[] = "forum_bbcode";

/******* Forum Table ************************************************/
$sql = <<<EOS
CREATE TABLE forum_forum (
  id int(11) NOT NULL auto_increment,
  forum_name varchar(100) NOT NULL default '',
  forum_desc varchar(255) NOT NULL default '',
  forum_moderator int(11) NOT NULL default '0',
  PRIMARY KEY (id)
)
EOS;
$result = mysql_query($sql);
switch(mysql_errno()) {
  case 1050:
    break;
  case 0:
    $sql = "INSERT INTO forum_forum VALUES (NULL, 'New Forum', ".
           "'This is the initial forum created when installing the ".
           "database.  Change the name and the description after ".
           "installation.', 1)";
    $result = mysql_query($sql) or die(mysql_error());
    break;
  default:
    die(mysql_error());
    break;
}
$a_tables[] = "forum_forum";

/******* Post Count Table ************************************************/
$sql = <<<EOS
CREATE TABLE forum_postcount (
  user_id int(11) NOT NULL default '0',
  count int(9) NOT NULL default '0',
  PRIMARY KEY (user_id)
)
EOS;
$result = mysql_query($sql);
switch(mysql_errno()) {
  case 1050:
    break;
  case 0:
    $sql = "INSERT INTO forum_postcount VALUES (1,1)";
    $result = mysql_query($sql) or die(mysql_error());
    break;
```

```
      default:
        die(mysql_error());
        break;
    }
    $a_tables[] = "forum_postcount";

    /****** Posts Table **************************************************/
    $sql = <<<EOS
    CREATE TABLE  forum_posts (
      id int(11) NOT NULL auto_increment,
      topic_id int(11) NOT NULL default '0',
      forum_id int(11) NOT NULL default '0',
      author_id int(11) NOT NULL default '0',
      update_id int(11) NOT NULL default '0',
      date_posted datetime NOT NULL default '0000-00-00 00:00:00',
      date_updated datetime NOT NULL default '0000-00-00 00:00:00',
      subject varchar(255) NOT NULL default '',
      body mediumtext NOT NULL,
      PRIMARY KEY  (id),
      KEY IdxArticle (forum_id,topic_id,author_id,date_posted),
      FULLTEXT KEY IdxText (subject,body)
    )
    EOS;
    $result = mysql_query($sql);
    switch(mysql_errno()) {
      case 1050:
        break;
      case 0:
        $sql = "INSERT INTO forum_posts VALUES (NULL, 0, 1, 1, 0, '".
        date("Y-m-d H:i:s", time())."', 0, 'Welcome', 'Welcome to your ".
        "new Bulletin Board System. Do not forget to change your admin ".
        "password after installation. Have fun!')";
        $result = mysql_query($sql) or die(mysql_error());
        break;
      default:
        die(mysql_error());
        break;
    }
    $a_tables[] = "forum_posts";

    /****** Users Table **************************************************/
    $sql = <<<EOS
    CREATE TABLE  forum_users (
      id int(11) NOT NULL auto_increment,
      email varchar(255) NOT NULL default '',
      passwd varchar(50) NOT NULL default '',
      name varchar(100) NOT NULL default '',
      access_lvl tinyint(4) NOT NULL default '1',
      signature varchar(255) NOT NULL default '',
      date_joined datetime NOT NULL default '0000-00-00 00:00:00',
      last_login datetime NOT NULL default '0000-00-00 00:00:00',
      PRIMARY KEY  (id),
      UNIQUE KEY uniq_email (email)
```

```
)
EOS;
$result = mysql_query($sql);
switch(mysql_errno()) {
  case 1050:
    break;
  case 0:
    $datetime = date("Y-m-d H:i:s",time());
    $sql = "INSERT IGNORE INTO forum_users VALUES (NULL, ".
           "'$adminemail', '$adminpass', '$adminname', 3, '', ".
           "'$datetime', 0)";
    $result = mysql_query($sql) or die(mysql_error());
    break;
  default:
    die(mysql_error());
    break;
}
$a_tables[] = "forum_users";

/******* Display Results **********************************************/
require("config.php");
echo "<html><head><title>Forum Tables Created " .
    $datetime . "</title>";
echo "<link rel='stylesheet' type='text/css' ";
echo "href='forum_styles.css'>";
echo "</head><body>";
echo "<div class='bodysmall'>";
echo "<h1>".$admin['title']['value']."</h1>";
echo "<H3>Forum Tables created:</h3>\n<ul>";
foreach ($a_tables as $table) {
  $table = str_replace("forum_","",$table);
  $table = str_replace("_", " ",$table);
  $table = ucWords($table);
  echo "<li>$table</li>\n";
}
echo "</ul>\n<h3>Here is your initial login information:</h3>\n";
echo "<ul><li><strong>login</strong>: " . $adminemail . "</li>\n";
echo "<li><strong>password</strong>: " . $adminpass . "</li></ul>\n";
echo "<h3><a href='login.php?e=".$adminemail."'>Log In</a> ";
echo "to the site now.</h3></div>";
echo "<div class='copyright'>".$admin['copyright']['value']."</div>";
echo "</body></html>";
?>
```

4. Create functions.php. Okay, this is a big one. This file contains most of the major functions that the board uses.

```
<?php
function trimBody($theText, $lmt=100, $s_chr="@@@", $s_cnt=1) {
  $pos = 0;
  $trimmed = FALSE;
  for ($i = 1; $i <= $s_cnt; $i++) {
    if ($tmp = strpos($theText,$s_chr,$pos)) {
```

```
      $pos = $tmp;
      $trimmed = TRUE;
    } else {
      $pos = strlen($theText);
      $trimmed = FALSE;
      break;
    }
  }
  $theText = substr($theText,0,$pos);

  if (strlen($theText) > $lmt) {
    $theText = substr($theText,0,$lmt);
    $theText = substr($theText,0,strrpos($theText,' '));
    $trimmed = TRUE;
  }
  if ($trimmed) $theText .= '...';
  return $theText;
}

function msgBox($m, $t, $d="index.php", $s="Info") {
  $theMsg = "<div id='requestConfirm" . $s . "'>";
  $theMsg .= "<h2>" . $t . "</h2>\n";
  $theMsg .= "<p>" . $m . "</p>";
  $theMsg .= "<p><a href='" . $d . "' ";
  $theMsg .= "class='buttonlink'>";
  $theMsg .= "Yes</a>";
  $theMsg .= "<a href='index.php' class='buttonlink'>";
  $theMsg .= "No</a></p>";
  $theMsg .= "</div>";
  return $theMsg;
}

function getForum($id) {
  $sql = "SELECT forum_name as name, forum_desc as description, " .
            "forum_moderator as mod " .
         "FROM forum_forum " .
         "WHERE id = " . $id;
  $result = mysql_query($sql)
    or die(mysql_error() . "<br>" . $sql);
  $row = mysql_fetch_array($result);
  return $row;
}

function getForumID($topicid) {
  $sql = "SELECT forum_id FROM forum_posts WHERE id=$topicid";
  $result = mysql_query($sql)
    or die(mysql_error() . "<br>" . $sql);
  $row = mysql_fetch_array($result);
  return $row['forum_id'];
}

function breadcrumb($id, $getfrom="F") {
  $sep = "<span class='bcsep'>";
```

```
  $sep .= " &middot; ";
  $sep .= "</span>";
  if ($getfrom == "P") {
    $sql = "SELECT forum_id, subject FROM forum_posts ".
           "WHERE id = " . $id;
    $result = mysql_query($sql)
       or die(mysql_error() . "<br>" . $sql);
    $row = mysql_fetch_array($result);
    $id = $row['forum_id'];
    $topic = $row['subject'];
  }
  $row = getForum($id);
  $bc = "<a href='index.php'>Home</a>$sep";
  switch ($getfrom) {
    case "P":
      $bc .= "<a href='viewforum.php?f=$id'>".$row['name'].
             "</a>$sep".$topic;
      break;
    case "F":
      $bc .= $row['name'];
      break;
    default:
  }
  return "<h4 class='breadcrumb'>" . $bc . "</h4>";
}

function showTopic($topicid, $showfull=TRUE) {
  global $conn;
  global $userid;
  global $limit;

  echo breadcrumb($topicid, "P");
  if (isset($_GET['page'])) {
    $page = $_GET['page'];
  } else {
    $page = 1;
  }
  if ($limit == "") $limit = 25;
  $start = ($page - 1) * $limit;
  if (isset($_SESSION['user_id'])) {
    echo topicReplyBar($topicid, getForumID($topicid), "right");
  }
  $sql = "SELECT SQL_CALC_FOUND_ROWS ".
         "p.id, p.subject, p.body, p.date_posted, " .
         "p.date_updated, u.name as author, u.id as author_id, " .
         "u.signature as sig, c.count as postcount, " .
         "p.forum_id as forum_id, f.forum_moderator as mod, " .
         "p.update_id, u2.name as updated_by " .
      "FROM forum_forum f " .
      "JOIN forum_posts p " .
      "ON f.id = p.forum_id " .
      "JOIN forum_users u " .
      "ON u.id = p.author_id " .
      "LEFT JOIN forum_users u2 " .
```

```
            "ON u2.id = p.update_id " .
            "LEFT JOIN forum_postcount c " .
            "ON u.id = c.user_id " .
            "WHERE (p.topic_id = $topicid OR p.id = $topicid) " .
            "ORDER BY p.topic_id, p.date_posted " .
            "LIMIT $start,$limit";
$result = mysql_query($sql,$conn)
    or die(mysql_error() . "<br>" . $sql);
$pagelinks = paginate($limit);
if (mysql_num_rows($result) == 0) {
    $msg = "There are currently no posts.  Would you " .
           "like to be the first person to create a thread?";
    $title = "No Posts...";
    $dest = "compose.php?forumid=" . $forumid;
    $sev = "Info";
    $message = msgBox($msg,$title,$dest,$sev);
    echo $message;
} else {
    echo "<table class='forumtable' cellspacing='0' ";
    echo "cellpadding='2'><tr>";
    echo "<th class='author'>Author</th>";
    echo "<th class='post'>Post</th>";
    echo "</tr>";
    while ($row = mysql_fetch_array($result)) {
        $lastupdate = "";
        $editlink = "";
        $dellink = "";
        $replylink = " ";
        $pcount = "";
        $pdate = "";
        $sig = "";
        if ($showfull) {
            $body = $row['body'];
            if (isset($_SESSION['user_id'])) {
                $replylink = "<a href='compose.php?forumid=".
                    $row['forum_id']."&topicid=$topicid&reid=".$row['id'].
                    "' class='buttonlink'>REPLY</a> ";
            } else {
                $replylink = "";
            }
            if ($row['update_id'] > 0) {
            $lastupdate = "<p class='smallNote'>Last updated: " .
                $row['date_updated'] . " by " .
                $row['updated_by'] . "</p>";
            }
            if (($userid == $row['author_id']) or
                ($userid == $row['mod']) or
                ($_SESSION['access_lvl'] > 2)) {
                $editlink = "<a href='compose.php?a=edit&post=".$row['id'].
                    "' class='buttonlink'>EDIT</a> ";
                $dellink = "<a href='transact-affirm.php?action=deletepost&".
                    "id=" . $row['id'] .
                    "' class='buttonlink'>DELETE</a> ";
            }
```

```php
            $pcount = "<br /><span class='textsmall'>Posts: " .
                ($row['postcount']==""?"0":$row['postcount']) . "</span>";
            $pdate = $row['date_posted'];
            $sig = ($row['sig'] != ""?"<p class='sig'>".
                    bbcode(nl2br($row['sig'])):"")."</p>";
        } else {
            $body = trimBody($body);
        }
        $rowclass = ($rowclass == "row1"?"row2":"row1");
        echo "<tr class='$rowclass'>";
        echo "<td class='author'>" . $row['author'];
        echo $pcount;
        echo "</td><td class='post'><p>";
        if (isset($_SESSION['user_id'])
            and ($_SESSION['last_login'] < $row['date_posted'])) {
          echo NEWPOST . " ";
        }
        if (isset($_GET['page'])) $pagelink = "&page=" . $_GET['page'];
        echo "<a name='post" . $row['id'] .
            "' href='viewtopic.php?t=" . $topicid . $pagelink . "#post" .
            $row['id'] . "'>".POSTLINK."</a>";
        if (isset($row['subject'])) {
          echo " <strong>" . $row['subject'] . "</strong>";
        }
        echo "</p><p>" . bbcode(nl2br(htmlspecialchars($body))) . "</p>";
        echo $sig;
        echo $lastupdate;
        echo "</td></tr>";
        echo "<tr class='$rowclass'><td class='authorfooter'>";
        echo $pdate . "</td><td class='threadfooter'>";
        echo $replylink;
        echo $editlink;
        echo $dellink;
        echo "</td></tr>\n";
      }
      echo "</table>";
      echo $pagelinks;
      echo "<p>".NEWPOST." = New Post     ";
      echo POSTLINK." = Post link (use to bookmark)</p>";
  }
}

function isParent($page) {
  $currentpage = $_SERVER['PHP_SELF'];
  if (strpos($currentpage, $page) === false) {
    return FALSE;
  } else {
    return TRUE;
  }
}

function topicReplyBar($topicid,$forumid,$pos="right") {
  $html = "<p class='buttonBar" . $pos . "'>";
  if ($topicid > 0) {
```

```
            $html .= "<a href='compose.php?forumid=$forumid".
              "&topicid=$topicid&reid=$topicid' class='buttonlink'>Reply ".
              "to Thread</a>";
    }
    if ($forumid > 0) {
        $html .= "<a href='compose.php?forumid=$forumid' ".
          "class='buttonlink'>New Thread</a>";
    }
    $html .= "</p>";
    return $html;
}

function userOptionList($level) {
    $sql = "SELECT id, name, access_lvl " .
           "FROM forum_users " .
           "WHERE access_lvl=" . $level . " " .
           "ORDER BY name";
    $result = mysql_query($sql) or die(mysql_error());

    while ($row = mysql_fetch_array($result)) {
        echo "<option value='". $row['id'] . "'>" .
           htmlspecialchars($row['name']) . "</options>";
    }
}

function paginate($limit=10) {
    global $admin;

    $sql = "SELECT FOUND_ROWS();";
    $result = mysql_query($sql) or die(mysql_error());
    $row = mysql_fetch_array($result);
    $numrows = $row[0];
    $pagelinks = "<div class=pagelinks>";
    if ($numrows > $limit) {
        if(isset($_GET['page'])){
            $page = $_GET['page'];
        } else {
            $page = 1;
        }
        $currpage = $_SERVER['PHP_SELF'] . "?" . $_SERVER['QUERY_STRING'];
        $currpage = str_replace("&page=".$page,"",$currpage);

        if($page == 1){
            $pagelinks .= "<span class='pageprevdead'>&lt; PREV</span>";
        }else{
            $pageprev = $page - 1;
            $pagelinks .= "<a class='pageprevlink' href='" . $currpage .
              "&page=" . $pageprev . "'>&lt; PREV</a>";
        }

        $numofpages = ceil($numrows / $limit);
        $range = $admin['pageRange']['value'];
        if ($range == "" or $range == 0) $range = 7;
        $lrange = max(1,$page-(($range-1)/2));
```

```php
    $rrange = min($numofpages,$page+(($range-1)/2));
    if (($rrange - $lrange) < ($range - 1)) {
      if ($lrange == 1) {
        $rrange = min($lrange + ($range-1), $numofpages);
      } else {
        $lrange = max($rrange - ($range-1), 0);
      }
    }

    if ($lrange > 1) {
      $pagelinks .= "..";
    } else {
      $pagelinks .= "  ";
    }
    for($i = 1; $i <= $numofpages; $i++){
      if($i == $page){
        $pagelinks .= "<span class='pagenumdead'>$i</span>";
      }else{
        if ($lrange <= $i and $i <= $rrange) {
          $pagelinks .= "<a class='pagenumlink' href='" . $currpage .
          "&page=" . $i . "'>" . $i . "</a>";
        }
      }
    }
    if ($rrange < $numofpages) {
      $pagelinks .= "..";
    } else {
      $pagelinks .= "  ";
    }

    if(($numrows - ($limit * $page)) > 0){
      $pagenext = $page + 1;
      $pagelinks .= "<a class='pagenextlink' href='" . $currpage .
        "&page=" . $pagenext . "'>NEXT &gt;</a>";
    } else {
      $pagelinks .= "<span class='pagenextdead'>NEXT &gt;</span>";
    }
  } else {
    $pagelinks .= "<span class='pageprevdead'>
      &lt; PREV</span>  ";
    $pagelinks .= "<span class='pagenextdead'>
      NEXT &gt;</span>  ";
  }
  $pagelinks .= "</div>";
  return $pagelinks;
}

function bbcode($data) {
  $sql = "SELECT * FROM forum_bbcode";
  $result = mysql_query($sql);
  if (mysql_num_rows($result) > 0) {
    while($row = mysql_fetch_array($result)) {
      $bbcode['tpl'][] =
        "§" . html_entity_decode($row['template'],ENT_QUOTES). "§i";
```

```
        $bbcode['rep'][] =
            html_entity_decode($row['replacement'],ENT_QUOTES);
    }
    $data1 = preg_replace($bbcode['tpl'],$bbcode['rep'],$data);
    $count = 1;
    while (($data1 != $data) and ($count < 4)) {
        $count++;
        $data = $data1;
        $data1 = preg_replace($bbcode['tpl'],$bbcode['rep'],$data);
    }
  }

  return $data;
}
?>
```

5. Enter `http.php`.

This is for various functions used for navigating around the site. It contains the `redirect()` function.

```
<?php
function redirect($url) {
  if (!headers_sent()) {
    header('Location: http://' . $_SERVER['HTTP_HOST'] .
      dirname($_SERVER['PHP_SELF']) . '/' . $url);
  } else {
    die('Could not redirect; Headers already sent (output).');
  }
}
?>
```

6. Create `config.php`.

This sets up any constants or variables you may need in the app. It loads admin settings and BBcodes into arrays to be used by the board.

```
<?php
require_once 'conn.php';
require_once 'functions.php';

$sql = 'SELECT * FROM forum_admin';
$result = mysql_query($sql) or die(mysql_error());

while ($row = mysql_fetch_array($result)) {
   $admin[$row['constant']]['title'] = $row['title'];
   $admin[$row['constant']]['value'] = $row['value'];
}

$sql = 'SELECT * FROM forum_bbcode';
$result = mysql_query($sql) or die(mysql_error());

while ($row = mysql_fetch_array($result)) {
   $bbcode[$row['id']]['template'] = $row['template'];
   $bbcode[$row['id']]['replacement'] = $row['replacement'];
```

```
   }

// define constants here:
  define("NEWPOST",
          "<span class='newpost'>&raquo;</span>");
  define("POSTLINK",
          "<span class='postlink'>&diams;</span>");
?>
```

7. Create `header.php`. This goes at the top of each page that gets displayed.

```php
<?php
session_start();
require_once 'config.php';
$title = $admin[titlebar][value];
if ($pageTitle != "") {
  $title .= " :: " . $pageTitle;
}
$userid = $_SESSION['user_id'];
$access_lvl = $_SESSION['access_lvl'];
$username = $_SESSION['name'];
?>
<html>
<head>
<title><?php echo $title; ?></title>
<link rel="stylesheet" type="text/css" href="forum_styles.css">
</head>
<body>
<div class="body">
<div id="header">
  <form method="get" action="search.php" id="searchbar">
    <input id="searchkeywords" type="text" name="keywords"
    <?php
      if (isset($_GET['keywords'])) {
        echo ' value="' . htmlspecialchars($_GET['keywords']) . '" ';
      }
      echo 'onfocus="this.select();" '
    ?>
      />
      <input id="searchbutton" class="submit" type="submit"
      value="Search" />
  </form>
  <h1 id="sitetitle"><?php echo $admin['title']['value'];?></h1>
  <div id="login">
  <?php
    if (isset($_SESSION['name'])) {
      echo 'Welcome, '.$_SESSION['name'];
    }
  ?>
  </div>
  <p id="subtitle"><?php echo $admin['description']['value']; ?></p>
</div>
<div id="subheader">
  <div id='navigation'>
```

```php
<?php
echo '    <a href="index.php">Home</a>';
if (!isset($_SESSION['user_id'])) {
  echo ' | <a href="login.php">Log In</a>';
  echo ' | <a href="useraccount.php">Register</a>';
} else {
  echo ' | <a href="transact-user.php?action=Logout">';
  echo "Log out " . $_SESSION['name'] . "</a>";
  if ($_SESSION['access_lvl'] > 2) {
    echo ' | <a href="admin.php">Admin</a>';
  }
  echo ' | <a href="useraccount.php">Profile</a>';
}
?>
</div>
</div>
```

8. Enter `footer.php`, which places a footer at the bottom of each page that gets displayed:

```php
</div>
<div class="copyright">
  <?php echo $admin[copyright][value]; ?>
</div>
</body>
</html>
```

9. Create `index.php`, the home page. This is the page users first see when they view the board.

```php
<?php
require_once 'conn.php';
require_once 'functions.php';
require_once 'header.php';

$sql = <<<EOS
  SELECT f.id as id, f.forum_name as forum, f.forum_desc as description,
         count(forum_id) as threads, u.name as mod
         FROM forum_forum f
         LEFT JOIN forum_posts p
         ON f.id = p.forum_id
         AND p.topic_id=0
         LEFT JOIN forum_users u
         ON f.forum_moderator = u.id
         GROUP BY f.id
EOS;
$result = mysql_query($sql)
  or die(mysql_error());
if (mysql_num_rows($result) == 0) {
  echo "    <br />\n";
  echo "    There are currently no forums to view.\n";
} else {
  echo "<table class='forumtable' cellspacing='0' ";
  echo "cellspacing='0'><tr>";
  echo "<th class='forum'>Forum</th>";
  echo "<th class='threadcount'>Threads</th>";
  echo "<th class='moderator'>Moderator</th>";
```

```
    echo "</tr>";
    while ($row = mysql_fetch_array($result)) {
        $rowclass = ($rowclass == "row1"?"row2":"row1");
        echo "<tr class='$rowclass'>";
        echo "<td class='firstcolumn'><a href='viewforum.php?f=" . $row['id'] . "'>";
        echo $row['forum'] . "</a><br />";
        echo "<span class='forumdesc'>" . $row['description'];
        echo "</span></td>";
        echo "<td class='center'>" . $row['threads'] . "</td>";
        echo "<td class='center'>" . $row['mod'] . "</td>";
        echo "</tr>\n";
    }
    echo "</table>";
}

require_once 'footer.php';
?>
```

10.   Enter `login.php`, the login page. (Guess what it's used for?)

```
<?php require_once 'header.php';?>
<form name="theForm" method="post" action="transact-user.php">
<h3>Member Login</h3>
<p>
    Email Address:<br />
    <input type="text" name="email" maxlength="255" value="<?php
    echo $_GET['e'];?>" />
</p>
<p>
    Password:<br />
    <input type="password" name="passwd" maxlength="50" />
</p>
<p>
    <input type="submit" class="submit" name="action" value="Login" />
</p>

<p>
    Not a member yet? <a href="useraccount.php">Create a new account!</a>
</p>
<p>
    <a href="forgotpass.php">Forgot your password?</a>
</p>
</form>
<?php require_once 'footer.php'; ?>
```

11.   Create `forgotpass.php`. This page is displayed if the user forgets his or her password.

```
<?php require_once 'header.php'; ?>
<form method="post" action="transact-user.php">
<h3>Email Password Reminder</h3>
<p>
    Forgot your password? Just enter your email address, and we'll email
    your password to you!
</p>
<p>
```

```
     Email Address:<br />
     <input type="text" id="email" name="email" />
   </p>
   <p>
     <input type="submit" class="submit" name="action" value="Send my reminder!" />
   </p>
   </form>
   <?php require_once 'footer.php'; ?>
```

12. Enter admin.php. This is the page used to edit different board attributes, user information, forums, and more.

```php
<?php
require_once 'header.php';
?>

<script type="text/Javascript">
  <!--
  function delBBCode(id) {
    window.location = "transact-admin.php?action=deleteBBCode&b=" + id;
  }
  function delForum(id) {
    window.location = "transact-affirm.php?action=deleteForum&f=" + id;
  }
}
//-->
</script>

<?php
$sql = "SELECT access_lvl, access_name FROM forum_access_levels " .
       "ORDER by access_lvl DESC";
$result = mysql_query($sql) or die(mysql_error());
while ($row = mysql_fetch_array($result)) {
  $a_users[$row['access_lvl']] = $row['access_name'];
}

$menuoption = "boardadmin"; // default
if (isset($_GET['option'])) $menuoption = $_GET['option'];

$menuItems = array(
  "boardadmin" => "Board Admin",
  "edituser" => "Users",
  "forums" => "Forums",
  "bbcode" => "BBcode"
  );
echo "<p class='menu'>|";
foreach ($menuItems as $key => $value) {
  if ($menuoption != $key) {
    echo "<a href='" . $_SESSION['PHP_SELF'] . "?option=$key'>";
  }
  echo " $value ";
  if ($menuoption != $key) echo "</a>";
  echo "|";
}
```

```php
echo "</p>";

switch ($menuoption) {
  case 'boardadmin':
  ?>
    <h3>Board Administration</h3>
    <form id='adminForm' method='post' action='transact-admin.php'>
    <table cellspacing='0' class='forumtable'>
    <tr>
      <th>Title</th><th>Value</th><th>Parameter</th>
    </tr>
  <?php
    foreach ($admin as $k => $v) {
      echo "<tr><td>". $v['title'] . "</td><td>" .
        "<input type='text' name='". $k . "' " .
        "value='" . $v['value'] . "' size='60'>" .
        "</td><td>$k</td></tr>\n";
    }
  ?>
    </table>
    <p class='buttonBar'>
      <input class='submit' type='submit' name="action"
        id="Update" value='Update'>
    </p>
    </form>
  <?php
    break;
  case 'edituser':
  ?>
    <h3>User Administration</h3>
    <div id="users">
    <form name="myform" action="transact-admin.php" method="post">
    Please select a user to admin:<br>
    <select id='userlist' name='userlist[]'>
  <?php
      foreach ($a_users as $key => $value) {
        echo "<optgroup label='". $value . "'>\n";
        userOptionList($key);
        echo "\n</optgroup>\n";
      }
  ?>
    </select>
    <input class="submit"  type="submit" name="action"
          value="Modify User">
    </form>
    </div>
  <?php
    break;
  case 'forums':
    ?>
    <h2>Forum Administration</h2>
    <table class='forumtable' cellspacing='0'>
    <tr><th class="forum">Forum</th><th> </th><th> </th></tr>
    <?php
```

```php
    $sql = "SELECT * FROM forum_forum";
    $result = mysql_query($sql) or die(mysql_error());
    while ($row = mysql_fetch_array($result)) {
      echo "<tr><td><span class='forumname'>" . $row['forum_name'] .
          "</span><br><span class='forumdesc'>" . $row['forum_desc'] .
          "</span></td><td>" . "<a href='editforum.php?forum=" .
          $row['id'] . "'>Edit</a></td><td>" .
          "<a href='#' onclick='delForum(". $row['id'] .
          ");'>" . "Delete</a></td></tr>";
    }
    ?>
    </table>
    <p class='buttonBar'>
      <a href='editforum.php' class='buttonlink'>New Forum</a>
    </p>
  <?php
  break;
case 'bbcode':
  ?>
    <h3>BBcode Administration</h3>
    <form id='bbcodeForm' method='post' action='transact-admin.php'>
    <table cellspacing='0' class='forumtable'>
    <tr>
      <th class='template'>Template</th>
      <th class='replacement'>Replacement</th>
      <th class='action'>Action</th>
    </tr>
  <?php
    if (isset($bbcode)) {
      foreach ($bbcode as $k => $v) {
        echo "<tr class='row1'><td>" .
          "<input class='mono' type='text' name='bbcode_t". $k . "' " .
          "value='" . $v['template'] . "' size='32'>" .
          "</td><td>" .
          "<input class='mono' type='text' name='bbcode_r". $k . "' " .
          "value='" . $v['replacement'] . "' size='32'>" .
          "</td><td><input type='button' class='submit' " .
          "name='action' id='DelBBCode' value='Delete' " .
          "onclick='delBBCode(".$k.");'>" .
          "</td></tr>\n";
      }
    }
  ?>
    <tr class='row2'><td colspan='3'> </td></tr>
    <tr class='row2'><td>
    <input class='mono' type='text' name='bbcode-tnew' size='32'>
    </td><td>
    <input class='mono' type='text' name='bbcode-rnew' size='32'>
    </td><td>
    <input type='submit' class='submit' name='action'
      id='AddBBCode' value='Add New'>
    </td></tr>
    </table>
    <p class='buttonBar'>
```

```
        <input class='submit' type='submit' name="action"
          id="Update" value='Update BBCodes'>
      </p>
      </form>
    <?php
      break;
      default:
  }
  ?>
  </script>
  <?php require_once 'footer.php'; ?>
```

13. Create useraccount.php. Users access this page to edit their own profiles.

```php
<?php
require_once 'header.php';

$userid = $username = $useremail = $password = $accesslvl = '';
$mode = "Create";
if (isset($_SESSION['user_id'])) {
  $userid = $_SESSION['user_id'];
  $mode = "Edit";
  if (isset($_GET['user'])) {
    if (($_SESSION['user_id'] == $_GET['user'])
        || ($_SESSION['access_lvl'] > 2)) {
      $userid = $_GET['user'];
      $mode = "Modify";
    }
  }
  $sql = "SELECT * FROM forum_users WHERE id=$userid";
  $result = mysql_query($sql)
    or die('Could not look up user data; ' . mysql_error());

  $row = mysql_fetch_array($result);
  $username = $row['name'];
  $useremail = $row['email'];
  $accesslvl = $row['access_lvl'];
  $signature = $row['signature'];
}

echo "<h3>$mode Account</h3>\n";
echo "<form method=\"post\" action=\"transact-user.php\">\n";
?>

<p>
  Full name:<br />
  <input type="text" class="txtinput" name="name" maxlength="100"
    value="<?php echo htmlspecialchars($username); ?>" />
</p>
<?php
  if ($mode == "Edit") {
?>
<p>
  Email Address:<br />
  <input type="text" class="txtinput" name="email" maxlength="255"
```

```php
    value="<?php echo htmlspecialchars($useremail); ?>" />
</p>
<?php
  }
if ($mode == "Modify") {
  echo "<div><fieldset>\n";
  echo "  <legend>Access Level</legend>\n";

  $sql = "SELECT * FROM forum_access_levels ORDER BY access_lvl DESC";
  $result = mysql_query($sql,$conn)
    or die('Could not list access levels; ' . mysql_error());

  while ($row = mysql_fetch_array($result)) {
    echo '  <input type="radio" class="radio" id="acl_' .
        $row['access_lvl'] . '" name="accesslvl" value="' .
        $row['access_lvl'] . '" ';

    if ($row['access_lvl'] == $accesslvl) {
      echo 'checked="checked" ';
    }
    echo '/>' . $row['access_name'] . "<br />\n";
  }
  echo "</fieldset></div>";
}
if ($mode != "Modify") echo "<div id='passwords'>";
if ($mode == "Edit") {
  if ($_GET['error'] == "nopassedit") {
    echo "<span class='error'>Could not modify passwords.";
    echo " Please try again.</span><br />";
  }
?>
<p>
  Old Password:<br />
  <input type="password" id="oldpasswd"
    name="oldpasswd" maxlength="50" />
</p>
<?php
}
if ($mode != "Modify") {
?>
<p>
  New Password:<br />
  <input type="password" id="passwd" name="passwd" maxlength="50" />
</p>
<p>
  Password Verification:<br />
  <input type="password" id="passwd2" name="passwd2" maxlength="50" />
</p>
<?php }
if ($mode != "Modify") echo "</div>";
if ($mode != "Create") {
?>
<p>
  Signature:<br />
  <textarea name="signature" id="signature" cols=60 rows=5><?php
```

```
        echo $signature;?></textarea>
  </p>
  <?php } ?>
  <p>
    <input type="submit" class="submit" name="action"
      value="<?php echo $mode;?> Account" />
  </p>
  <?php if ($mode == "Edit") {?>
  <input type="hidden" name="accesslvl"
    value="<?php echo $accesslvl; ?>" />
  <?php } ?>
  <input type="hidden" name="userid" value="<?php echo $userid; ?>" />
  </form>
  <?php require_once 'footer.php'; ?>
```

14. Enter `editforum.php`, which is used to edit forum details:

```
<?php
if (isset($_GET['forum'])) {
  $action="Edit";
} else {
  $action="Add";
}
$pageTitle = "$action Forum";
require_once 'header.php';

$forum = 0;
$fname = '';
$fdesc = '';
$fmod = '';
$userid = 0;

if (isset($_GET['forum'])) {
  $forum = $_GET['forum'];
  $sql = "SELECT forum_name, forum_desc, u.name, u.id " .
         "FROM forum_forum f " .
         "LEFT JOIN forum_users u " .
         "ON f.forum_moderator = u.id " .
         "WHERE f.id = $forum";
  $result = mysql_query($sql) or die(mysql_error());
  if ($row = mysql_fetch_array($result)) {
    $fname = $row['forum_name'];
    $fdesc = $row['forum_desc'];
    $fmod = $row['name'];
    $userid = $row['id'];
  }
}
echo "<h2>$action forum</h2>";
?>
<form name="forumedit" action="transact-admin.php" method="post">
<table class="forumtable" cellspacing='0'>
<tr><th colspan='2'>General Forum Settings</th></tr>
<tr>
  <td>Forum Name</td>
  <td>
```

```
        <input type='text' name='forumname'
          value="<?php echo $fname;?>">
      </td>
    </tr>
    <tr>
      <td>Forum Description</td>
      <td>
        <input type='text' name='forumdesc' size='75'
          value="<?php echo $fdesc;?>">
      </td>
    </tr>
    <tr>
      <td>Forum Moderator</td>
      <td>
        <select id="moderator" name="forummod[]">
        <option value='0'>unmoderated</option>
        <?php
        $sql = "SELECT * FROM forum_users ".
               "WHERE access_lvl > 1";
        $result = mysql_query($sql) or die(mysql_error());
        while ($row = mysql_fetch_array($result)) {
          echo "<option value='" . $row['id'] . "'";
          if ($userid == $row['id']) echo " selected='selected'";
          echo ">" . $row['name'] . "</option>";
        }
        ?>
        </select>
      </td>
    </tr>
    <tr>
      <td colspan='2'>
        <input class="submit" type="submit" name="action"
          value="<?php echo $action;?> Forum">
      </td>
    </tr>
  </table>
  <input type="hidden" name="forum_id" value="<?php echo $forum;?>">
</form>
<?php require_once 'footer.php';?>
```

15. Create `viewtopic.php`, which displays all of the posts in a thread:

```
<?php
require_once 'conn.php';
require_once 'functions.php';
require_once 'http.php';
if (!isset($_GET['t'])) redirect('index.php');
require_once 'header.php';

$topicid = $_GET['t'];
$limit = $admin['pageLimit']['value'];

showTopic($topicid,TRUE);

require_once 'footer.php';
?>
```

16. Create `viewforum.php`, which displays all of the threads (topics) for a forum:

```php
<?php
require_once 'conn.php';
require_once 'functions.php';
require_once 'http.php';
if (!isset($_GET['f'])) redirect('index.php');
require_once 'header.php';

$forumid = $_GET['f'];
$forum = getForum($forumid);

  echo breadcrumb($forumid, "F");
  if (isset($_GET['page'])) {
    $page = $_GET['page'];
  } else {
    $page = 1;
  }
  $limit = $admin['pageLimit']['value'];
  if ($limit == "") $limit = 25;
  $start = ($page - 1) * $admin['pageLimit']['value'];

  $sql = "CREATE TEMPORARY TABLE tmp ( ".
         "topic_id INT(11) NOT NULL DEFAULT 0, ".
         "postdate datetime NOT NULL default '0000-00-00 00:00:00');";
  mysql_query($sql) or die(mysql_error()."<br>".$sql);

  $sql = "LOCK TABLES forum_users READ,forum_posts READ;";
  mysql_query($sql) or die(mysql_error()."<br>".$sql);

  $sql = "INSERT INTO tmp SELECT topic_id,MAX(date_posted) ".
         "FROM forum_posts ".
         "WHERE forum_id = $forumid ".
         "AND topic_id > 0 ".
         "GROUP BY topic_id;";
  mysql_query($sql) or die(mysql_error()."<br>".$sql);

  $sql = "UNLOCK TABLES";
  mysql_query($sql) or die(mysql_error()."<br>".$sql);

  //die('stop');
  $sql = "SELECT SQL_CALC_FOUND_ROWS ".
           "t.id as topic_id, t.subject as t_subject, ".
           "u.name as t_author, count(p.id) as numreplies, ".
           "t.date_posted as t_posted, tmp.postdate as re_posted ".
         "FROM forum_users u ".
         "JOIN forum_posts t ".
         "ON t.author_id = u.id ".
         "LEFT JOIN tmp ".
         "ON t.id = tmp.topic_id ".
         "LEFT JOIN forum_posts p ".
         "ON p.topic_id = t.id ".
         "WHERE t.forum_id = $forumid ".
         "AND t.topic_id = 0 ".
         "GROUP BY t.id ".
```

```php
            "ORDER BY re_posted DESC " .
            "LIMIT $start, $limit";
    $result = mysql_query($sql)
      or die(mysql_error()."<br>".$sql);
      $numrows = mysql_num_rows($result);
    if ($numrows == 0) {
      $msg = "There are currently no posts.  Would you " .
             "like to be the first person to create a thread?";
      $title = "Welcome to " . $forum['name'];
      $dest = "compose.php?forumid=" . $forumid;
      $sev = "Info";
      $message = msgBox($msg,$title,$dest,$sev);
      echo $message;
    } else {
      if (isset($_SESSION['user_id'])) {
        echo topicReplyBar(0, $_GET['f'], "right");
      }
      echo "<table class='forumtable' cellspacing='0' ";
      echo "cellpadding='2'><tr>";
      echo "<th class='thread'>Thread</th>";
      echo "<th class='author'>Author</th>";
      echo "<th class='replies'>Replies</th>";
      echo "<th class='lastpost'>Last Post</th>";
      echo "</tr>";
      while ($row = mysql_fetch_array($result)) {
        $rowclass = ($rowclass == "row1"?"row2":"row1");
        if ($row['re_posted']=="") {
          $lastpost = $row['t_posted'];
        } else {
          $lastpost = $row['re_posted'];
        }
        if ((isset($_SESSION['user_id'])) and
            ($_SESSION['last_login'] < $lastpost)) {
          $newpost = true;
        } else {
          $newpost = false;
        }
        echo "<tr class='$rowclass'>";
        echo "<td class='thread'>".($newpost?NEWPOST." ":"");
        echo "<a href='viewtopic.php?t=";
        echo $row['topic_id'] . "'>" . $row['t_subject'] . "</a></td>";
        echo "<td class='author'>" . $row['t_author'] . "</td>";
        echo "<td class='replies'>" . $row['numreplies'] . "</td>";
        echo "<td class='lastpost'>" . $lastpost . "</td>";
        echo "</tr>\n";
      }
      echo "</table>";
      echo paginate($limit);
      echo "<p>".NEWPOST." = New Post(s)</p>";
    }
    $sql = "DROP TABLE tmp;";
    mysql_query($sql) or die(mysql_error()."<br>".$sql);

require_once 'footer.php';
?>
```

17. Enter `compose.php`, the form used to enter the subject and body of a post:

```php
<?php
require_once 'conn.php';
require_once 'functions.php';
require_once 'header.php';

$subject = '';
$topicid = $_GET['topicid'];
$forumid = $_GET['forumid'];
$reid = $_GET['reid'];
$body = '';
$post = '';
$authorid = $_SESSION['user_id'];
$edit_mode=FALSE;

if (isset($_GET['a'])
    and $_GET['a'] == 'edit'
    and isset($_GET['post'])
    and $_GET['post']){
  $edit_mode=TRUE;
}

require_once 'header.php';

if (!isset($_SESSION['user_id'])) {
  echo "<div class='notice'>" .
      "You must be logged in to post.  Please <a href='" .
      "login.php'>Log in</a> before posting a message." .
      "</div>";
} elseif ($edit_mode and $_SESSION['user_id'] != $authorid) {
  echo "<div class='noauth'>" .
      "You are not authorized to edit this post.  Please contact " .
      "your administrator.</div>";
} else {
  if ($edit_mode) {
    $sql = "SELECT * FROM forum_posts p, forum_forum f " .
          "WHERE p.id = " . $_GET['post'].
          " AND p.forum_id = f.id";
    $result = mysql_query($sql,$conn)
      or die('Could not retrieve post data; ' . mysql_error());

    $row = mysql_fetch_array($result);

    $subject = $row['subject'];
    $topicid = $row['topic_id'];
    $forumid = $row['forum_id'];
    $body = $row['body'];
    $post = $_GET['post'];
    $authorid = $row['author_id'];
  } else {

    if ($topicid == "") {
      $topicid = 0;
      $topicname = "New Topic";
```

```php
    } else {
      if ($reid != "") {
        $sql = "SELECT subject FROM forum_posts WHERE id = " . $reid;
        $result = mysql_query($sql,$conn)
          or die('Could not retrieve topic; ' . mysql_error());
        if (mysql_num_rows($result) > 0) {
          $row = mysql_fetch_array($result);
          $re = preg_replace("/(re: )/i","",$row['subject']);
        }
      }
      $sql = "SELECT subject FROM forum_posts WHERE id = ";
      $sql .= $topicid . " AND topic_id = 0 AND forum_id = $forumid;";
      $result = mysql_query($sql,$conn)
        or die('Could not retrieve topic; ' . mysql_error());
      if (mysql_num_rows($result) > 0) {
        $row = mysql_fetch_array($result);
        $topicname = "Reply to <em>" . $row['subject'] . "</em>\n";
        $subject = ($re == "")?"":"Re: " . $re);
      } else {
        $topicname = "Reply";
        $topicid = 0;
      }
    }
  }
}
if ($forumid == "" or $forumid == 0) $forumid=1;
$sql = "SELECT forum_name FROM forum_forum WHERE id = '";
$sql .= $forumid . "'";
$result = mysql_query($sql,$conn)
  or die('Could not retrieve forum name; ' . mysql_error());
$row = mysql_fetch_array($result);
$forumname = $row['forum_name'];

?>

  <form id="forumpost" method="post" action="transact-post.php">

  <h3><?php echo $edit_mode
                ?"Edit Post"
                :"$forumname: $topicname";?>
  </h3>
  <p>
    Subject:<br />
    <input type="text" class="subject" name="subject" maxlength="255"
      value="<?php echo $subject; ?>" />
  </p>
  <p>
    Body:<br />
    <textarea class="body" name="body" rows="10" cols="60"><?php
      echo $body; ?></textarea>
  </p>
  <p>
  <?php

  if ($edit_mode) {
    echo '<input type="submit" class="submit" name="action" ' .
```

```
                  "value=\"Save Changes\" />\n";
    } else {
      echo '<input type="submit" class="submit" name="action" ' .
           "value=\"Submit New Post\" />\n";
    }
    ?>
    </p>
    <?php
    echo "<input type='hidden' name='post' value='$post'>\n";
    echo "<input type='hidden' name='topic_id' value='$topicid'>\n";
    echo "<input type='hidden' name='forum_id' value='$forumid'>\n";
    echo "<input type='hidden' name='author_id' value='$authorid'>\n";
    echo "</form>\n";
  }
  require_once 'footer.php';
  ?>
```

18. Create `search.php`, which displays the user's search results:

```php
<?php
require_once 'conn.php';
require_once 'functions.php';
require_once 'header.php';

$result = NULL;
if (isset($_GET['keywords'])) {
  $sql = "SELECT *, MATCH (subject,body) " .
         "AGAINST ('" . $_GET['keywords'] . "') AS score " .
         "FROM forum_posts " .
         "WHERE MATCH (subject,body) " .
         "AGAINST ('" . $_GET['keywords'] . "') " .
         "ORDER BY score DESC";

  $result = mysql_query($sql,$conn)
    or die('Could not perform search; ' . mysql_error());
}

echo "<table class='forumtable' width='100%' " .
     "cellspacing='0'>\n";
echo "<tr><th class='searchHeader'>Search Results</th></tr>\n";

if ($result and !mysql_num_rows($result)) {
  echo "<tr class='row1'><td>No articles found that match the ";
  echo "search term(s) '<strong>" . $_GET['keywords'] . "</strong>'";
  if ($access_lvl > 2) echo "<p>SQL: $sql</p>";
  echo "</td></tr>\n";
} else {
  while ($row = mysql_fetch_array($result)) {
    $rowclass = ($rowclass == "row1"?"row2":"row1");
    echo "<tr class='$rowclass'>\n<td>\n";
    $topicid=($row['topic_id']==0?$row['id']:$row['topic_id']);
    echo "<p class='searchSubject'>\n<a href='viewtopic.php?t=" .
         $topicid . "#post" . $row['id'] . "'>" .
         $row['subject'] . "</a>\n";
    echo "</p>\n";
```

```
        echo "<p class='searchBody'>\n";
        echo htmlspecialchars(trimBody($row['body']));
        if ($access_lvl > 2) {
          echo "<br /><br />relevance: " . $row['score'];
        }
        echo "\n</p>\n";
        echo "</td>\n</tr>\n\n";
    }
}
echo "</table>";

require_once 'footer.php';
?>
```

19. Create `transact-admin.php`, one of four transaction pages.

Admin forms post to this page, which manipulates the data and then redirects the user to another page. Transaction pages do not send any data to the client unless there is an error.

```php
<?php
session_start();
require_once 'conn.php';
require_once 'http.php';

if (isset($_REQUEST['action'])) {
  switch ($_REQUEST['action']) {
    case 'Add Forum':
      if (isset($_POST['forumname'])
          and $_POST['forumname'] != ""
          and isset($_POST['forumdesc'])
          and $_POST['forumdesc'] != "")
      {
        $sql = "INSERT IGNORE INTO forum_forum " .
               "VALUES (NULL, '" .
               htmlspecialchars($_POST['forumname'], ENT_QUOTES) .
               "', '" .
               htmlspecialchars($_POST['forumdesc'], ENT_QUOTES) .
               "', " . $_POST['forummod'][0] . ")";
        mysql_query($sql) or die(mysql_error());
      }
      redirect('admin.php?option=forums');
      break;
    case 'Edit Forum':
      if (isset($_POST['forumname'])
          and $_POST['forumname'] != ""
          and isset($_POST['forumdesc'])
          and $_POST['forumdesc'] != "")
      {
        $sql = "UPDATE forum_forum " .
               "SET forum_name = '" . $_POST['forumname'] .
               "', forum_desc = '" . $_POST['forumdesc'] .
               "', forum_moderator = " . $_POST['forummod'][0] .
               " WHERE id = " . $_POST['forum_id'];
        mysql_query($sql) or die(mysql_error());
      }
```

```
      redirect('admin.php?option=forums');
      break;
    case 'Modify User':
      redirect("useraccount.php?user=" . $_POST['userlist'][0]);
      break;
    case 'Update':
      foreach($_POST as $key => $value) {
        if ($key != 'action') {
          $sql = "UPDATE forum_admin SET value='$value' ".
                 "WHERE constant = '$key'";
          mysql_query($sql) or die(mysql_error());
        }
      }
      redirect('admin.php');
      break;
    case "deleteForum":
      $sql = "DELETE FROM forum_forum WHERE id=" . $_GET['f'];
      mysql_query($sql) or die(mysql_error());
      $sql = "DELETE FROM forum_posts WHERE forum_id=" . $_GET['f'];
      mysql_query($sql) or die(mysql_error());
      redirect('admin.php?option=forums');
      break;
    case "Add New":
      $sql = "INSERT INTO forum_bbcode " .
             "VALUES (NULL,'".
             htmlentities($_POST['bbcode-tnew'],ENT_QUOTES)."','".
             htmlentities($_POST['bbcode-rnew'],ENT_QUOTES)."');";
      mysql_query($sql) or die(mysql_error()."<br>".$sql);
      redirect('admin.php?option=bbcode');
      break;
    case "deleteBBCode":
      if (isset($_GET['b'])) {
        $bbcodeid = $_GET['b'];
        $sql = "DELETE FROM forum_bbcode WHERE id=" . $bbcodeid;
        mysql_query($sql) or die(mysql_error());
      }
      redirect('admin.php?option=bbcode');
      break;
    case 'Update BBCodes':
      foreach($_POST as $key => $value) {
        if (substr($key,0,7) == 'bbcode_') {
          $bbid = str_replace("bbcode_", "", $key);
          if (substr($bbid,0,1) == 't') {
            $col = "template";
          } else {
            $col = "replacement";
          }
          $id = substr($bbid,1);
          $sql = "UPDATE forum_bbcode SET $col='$value' ".
                 "WHERE id=$id";
          mysql_query($sql) or die(mysql_error());
        }
      }
      redirect('admin.php?option=bbcode');
      break;
```

```
        default:
          redirect('index.php');
      }
    } else {
      redirect('index.php');
    }
    ?>
```

20. Enter `transact-post.php`, the second of four transaction pages. This one deals with forum posts.

```php
<?php
session_start();
require_once 'conn.php';
require_once 'http.php';

if (isset($_REQUEST['action'])) {
  switch (strtoupper($_REQUEST['action'])) {
    case 'SUBMIT NEW POST':
      if (isset($_POST['subject'])
          and isset($_POST['body'])
          and isset($_SESSION['user_id']))
      {
        $sql = "INSERT INTO forum_posts VALUES (" .
               "NULL," . $_POST['topic_id'] .
               "," . $_POST['forum_id'] .
               "," . $_SESSION['user_id'] .
               ",0" .
               ",'" . date("Y-m-d H:i:s",time()) .
               "',0" .
               ",'" . $_POST['subject'] .
               "','" . $_POST['body'] . "')";

        mysql_query($sql,$conn)
          or die('Could not post: ' . mysql_error() . "<br>$sql");
        $postid = mysql_insert_id();

        $sql = "INSERT IGNORE INTO forum_postcount VALUES (" .
               $_SESSION['user_id'] . ",0);";
        mysql_query($sql,$conn)
          or die(mysql_error());

        $sql = "UPDATE forum_postcount SET count = count + 1 " .
               "WHERE user_id = " . $_SESSION['user_id'];
        mysql_query($sql,$conn)
          or die(mysql_error());

      }
      $topicid=($_POST['topic_id']==0?$postid:$_POST['topic_id']);
      redirect('viewtopic.php?t=' . $topicid . '#post' . $postid);
      break;

    case 'NEW TOPIC':
      redirect('compose.php?f=' . $_POST['forum_id']);

    case 'EDIT':
```

```php
        redirect('compose.php?a=edit&post=' . $_POST['topic_id']);
        break;

    case 'SAVE CHANGES':
        if (isset($_POST['subject'])
            and isset($_POST['body']))
        {
          $sql = "UPDATE forum_posts " .
                 "SET subject='" . $_POST['subject'] .
                 "', update_id=" . $_SESSION['user_id'] .
                 ", body='" . $_POST['body'] . "', date_updated='" .
                 date("Y-m-d H:i:s",time()) . "' " .
                 "WHERE id=" . $_POST['post'];
          if (isset($_POST['author_id'])) {
            $sql .= " AND author_id=" . $_POST['author_id'];
          }

          mysql_query($sql,$conn)
            or die('Could not update post; ' . mysql_error());
        }
        $redirID = ($_POST['topic_id'] == 0?$_POST['post']:
          $_POST['topic_id']);
            redirect('viewtopic.php?t=' . $redirID);
        break;

    case 'DELETE':
        if ($_REQUEST['post']) {
          $sql = "DELETE FROM forum_posts " .
                 "WHERE " . "id=" . $_REQUEST['post'];
          mysql_query($sql,$conn)
            or die('Could not delete post; ' . mysql_error());
        }
        redirect($_REQUEST['r']);
        break;
    }
} else {
  redirect('index.php');
}
?>
```

21. Create `transact-user.php`, the third of four transaction pages. This one handles functions related to the users (such as logging in).

```php
<?php
require_once 'conn.php';
require_once 'http.php';

if (isset($_REQUEST['action'])) {
  switch ($_REQUEST['action']) {
    case 'Login':
      if (isset($_POST['email'])
          and isset($_POST['passwd']))
        {
```

```
            $sql = "SELECT id,access_lvl,name,last_login " .
                    "FROM forum_users " .
"WHERE email='" . $_POST['email'] . "' " .
                    "AND passwd='" . $_POST['passwd'] . "'";
            $result = mysql_query($sql,$conn)
              or die('Could not look up user information; ' . mysql_error());

            if ($row = mysql_fetch_array($result)) {
              session_start();
              $_SESSION['user_id'] = $row['id'];
              $_SESSION['access_lvl'] = $row['access_lvl'];
              $_SESSION['name'] = $row['name'];
              $_SESSION['last_login'] = $row['last_login'];
              $sql = "UPDATE forum_users SET last_login = '".
                      date("Y-m-d H:i:s",time()) . "' ".
                      "WHERE id = ". $row['id'];
              mysql_query($sql,$conn)
                or die(mysql_error()."<br>".$sql);
            }
          }
          redirect('index.php');
          break;

      case 'Logout':
        session_start();
        session_unset();
        session_destroy();

        redirect('index.php');
        break;

      case 'Create Account':
        if (isset($_POST['name'])
            and isset($_POST['email'])
            and isset($_POST['passwd'])
            and isset($_POST['passwd2'])
            and $_POST['passwd'] == $_POST['passwd2'])
        {
          $sql = "INSERT INTO forum_users ".
                  "(email,name,passwd,date_joined,last_login) " .
                  "VALUES ('" . $_POST['email'] . "','" .
                  $_POST['name'] . "','" . $_POST['passwd'] . "','".
                  date("Y-m-d H:i:s",time()). "','".
                  date("Y-m-d H:i:s",time()). "')";

          mysql_query($sql,$conn)
            or die('Could not create user account; ' . mysql_error());

          session_start();
          $_SESSION['user_id'] = mysql_insert_id($conn);
          $_SESSION['access_lvl'] = 1;
          $_SESSION['name'] = $_POST['name'];
          $_SESSION['login_time'] = date("Y-m-d H:i:s",time());
```

```php
      }
      redirect('index.php');
      break;

  case 'Modify Account':
    if (isset($_POST['name'])
        and isset($_POST['email'])
        and isset($_POST['accesslvl'])
        and isset($_POST['userid']))
    {
      $sql = "UPDATE forum_users " .
             "SET email='" . $_POST['email'] .
             "', name='" . $_POST['name'] .
             "', access_lvl=" . $_POST['accesslvl'] .
             ", signature='" . $_POST['signature'] . "' " .
             " WHERE id=" . $_POST['userid'];

      mysql_query($sql,$conn)
        or die('Could not update user account... ' . mysql_error() .
             '<br>SQL: ' . $sql);
    }
    redirect('admin.php');
    break;

  case 'Edit Account':
    if (isset($_POST['name'])
        and isset($_POST['email'])
        and isset($_POST['accesslvl'])
        and isset($_POST['userid']))
    {
      $chg_pw=FALSE;
      if (isset($_POST['oldpasswd'])
          and $_POST['oldpasswd'] != '') {
        $sql = "SELECT passwd FROM forum_users " .
               "WHERE id=" . $_POST['userid'];
        $result = mysql_query($sql) or die(mysql_error());
        if ($row = mysql_fetch_array($result)) {
          if (($row['passwd'] == $_POST['oldpasswd'])
              and (isset($_POST['passwd']))
              and (isset($_POST['passwd2']))
              and ($_POST['passwd'] == $_POST['passwd2']))
          {
            $chg_pw = TRUE;
          } else {
            redirect('useraccount.php?error=nopassedit');
            break;
          }
        }
      }
      $sql = "UPDATE forum_users " .
             "SET email='" . $_POST['email'] .
```

```
                      "', name='" . $_POST['name'] .
                      "', access_lvl=" . $_POST['accesslvl'] .
                      "', signature='" . $_POST['signature'];
            if ($chg_pw) {
              $sql .= "', passwd='" . $_POST['passwd'];
            }
            $sql .= "' WHERE id=" . $_POST['userid'];
mysql_query($sql,$conn)
            or die('Could not update user account... ' . mysql_error() .
                  '<br>SQL: ' . $sql);
          }
          redirect('useraccount.php?blah=' . $_POST['userid']);
          break;

      case 'Send my reminder!':
          if (isset($_POST['email'])) {
            $sql = "SELECT passwd FROM forum_users " .
                  "WHERE email='" . $_POST['email'] . "'";

            $result = mysql_query($sql,$conn)
              or die('Could not look up password; ' . mysql_error());

            if (mysql_num_rows($result)) {
              $row = mysql_fetch_array($result);

              $subject = 'Comic site password reminder';
              $body = "Just a reminder, your password for the " .
                    "Comic Book Appreciation site is: " . $row['passwd'] .
                    "\n\nYou can use this to log in at http://" .
                    $_SERVER['HTTP_HOST'] .
                    dirname($_SERVER['PHP_SELF']) . '/login.php?e='.
                    $_POST['email'];
              $headers = "From: admin@yoursite.com\r\n";

              mail($_POST['email'],$subject,$body,$headers)
                or die('Could not send reminder email.');
            }
          }
          redirect('login.php');
          break;
    }
  }
?>
```

22. Create `transact-affirm.php`.

This is the only "transaction page" that does send data to the client. If a function requires confirmation, the user is sent here and redirected forward.

```php
<?php
require_once 'conn.php';
require_once 'functions.php';
require_once 'http.php';
require_once 'header.php';
?>
<script type='text/javascript'>
<!--
function deletePost(id,redir) {
  if (id > 0) {
    window.location = "transact-post.php?action=delete&post=" +
      id + "&r=" + redir;
  } else {
history.back();
  }
}
function deleteForum(id) {
  if (id > 0) {
    window.location = "transact-admin.php?action=deleteForum&f=" + id;
  } else {
    history.back();
  }
}
//-->
</script>
<?php
switch (strtoupper($_REQUEST['action'])) {
  case "DELETEPOST":
    $sql = "SELECT * FROM forum_posts WHERE id=" . $_REQUEST['id'];
    $result = mysql_query($sql);
    $row = mysql_fetch_array($result);
    if ($row['topic_id'] > 0) {
      $msg = "Are you sure you wish to delete the post<br>".
        "<em>".$row['subject']."</em>?";
      $redir = htmlspecialchars("viewtopic.php?t=" . $row['topic_id']);
    } else {
      $msg = "If you delete this post, all replies will be deleted ".
        "as well.  Are you sure you wish to delete the entire ".
        "thread<br><em>".$row['subject']."</em>?";
      $redir = htmlspecialchars("viewforum.php?f=" . $row['forum_id']);
    }
    echo "<div id='requestConfirmWarn'>";
    echo "<h2>DELETE POST?</h2>\n";
    echo "<p>" . $msg . "</p>";
    echo "<p><input class='confirm' type='button' value='Delete' ";
    echo "onclick='deletePost(" . $row['id'] .
      ",\"" . $redir . "\");'>";
    echo "<input class='confirm' type='button' value='Cancel' ";
    echo "onclick='history.back()'></p>";
    echo "</div>";
    break;
```

```
   case "DELETEFORUM":
      $sql = "SELECT * FROM forum_forum WHERE id=" . $_REQUEST['f'];
      $result = mysql_query($sql);
      $row = mysql_fetch_array($result);
      $msg = "If you delete this forum, all topics and replies will be".
         " deleted as well.  Are you sure you wish to delete the entire ".
         "forum<br><em>".$row['forum_name']."</em>?";
      echo "<div id='requestConfirmWarn'>";
      echo "<h2>DELETE FORUM?</h2>\n";
      echo "<p>" . $msg . "</p>";
      echo "<p><input class='confirm' type='button' value='Delete' ";
      echo "onclick='deleteForum(" . $_REQUEST['f'] . ");'>";
      echo "<input class='confirm' type='button' value='Cancel' ";
      echo "onclick='history.back()'></p>";
      echo "</div>";

   default:
   }
require_once 'footer.php';
?>
```

Excellent. We are sure you typed all 1,800 lines of code without a single mistake. Let's move on to the application and see how it works, shall we?

Try It Out   The Bulletin Board Application

Let's work our way through a fresh installation of the Comic Book Appreciation Bulletin Board System. (That is a mouthful, so from now on, we'll refer to it as the "CBA board.")

Note that many screens are involved in this application. You have probably seen a bulletin board application before, so we are not going to show you each and every screen as we describe the application, just some of the more important screens.

If you have not already done so, your first step should be to create the CBA board tables.

1.   Load `setup.php` in your browser.

You should see a screen similar to Figure 15-1, informing you that the databases have been created and reminding you of your initial login e-mail and password.

If you downloaded the application from the Web site, your screen should look very similar to Figure 15-1. However, if you entered the code from the book, it will look quite different. The reason for this is that you are missing a file, `forum_styles.css`, that modifies the way the page looks. You can download this file from the Web site if you would like to use it, although it is not required. All screenshots in this chapter utilize the `forum_styles.css` style sheet. Although CSS is beyond the scope of this book, we will discuss `forum_styles.css` briefly in the "How It Works" section that follows this "Try It Out" section.

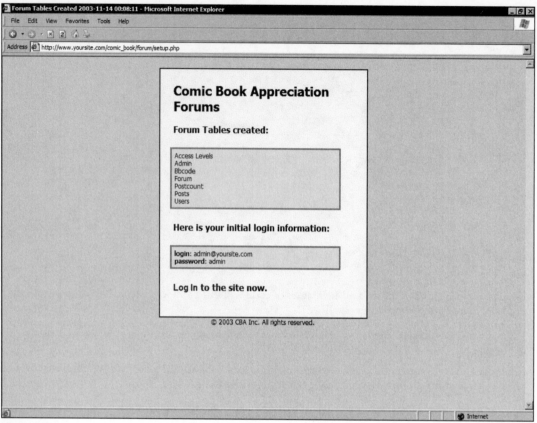

Figure 15-1

2. Click the Log In link at the bottom of the setup page. You are taken to the login page, and the e-mail address is filled in for you.

Observe the link at the bottom of the login screen, "Forget your password?" If a user cannot remember her password, she can click this link and submit her e-mail address. If she is verified to be a valid user, her password will be sent to the e-mail address given. You can try this out yourself if you like, assuming you are using a legitimate e-mail address (and not the admin@yoursite.com default).

3. Enter your password and click the Login button. You should now see the home page of the CBA board application (see Figure 15-2).

You are now logged in as the administrator of the CBA board application. As the administrator, you have complete control of your application. There are three other roles that apply to the board: Moderator, User, and Anonymous. Technically "Anonymous" isn't really a role, but if you are not logged in, the system does not know who you are and treats you as "anonymous."

Figure 15-2

We are going to create a couple of new user identities to demonstrate the difference between the various roles.

1. Log out, and click Register. You should see a screen similar to the one shown in Figure 15-3.

2. Enter a username. This name will be used for display purposes.

3. Enter your e-mail address. This doesn't have to be a real address unless you want to be able to have your password e-mailed to you.

4. Enter your password twice for verification.

5. Click the Create Account button.

   Your account will be created, and you will be automatically logged in with your new account.

Figure 15-3

6. Repeat Steps 2 through 5 to create one more account.

7. Log out, and then Log back in with your original admin account.

    If you don't remember the e-mail and password, just run `setup.php` again in your browser. Don't worry—your tables won't be re-created.

8. Now that you are logged in as the site administrator, you should see a menu item called "Admin." Click it.

    This brings you to the administration page (see Figure 15-4). The values in the fields you now see are used in the application. For instance, the first field, Board Title, is "Comic Book Appreciation Forums."

9. Edit the Board Title field to read "Comic Book Appreciation Bulletin Board" and click Update.

    The title at the top of the page should change accordingly.

Figure 15-4

10. Complete the other fields in the administration page:

❑ Board Description

❑ Admin Email

❑ Copyright

❑ Board Titlebar

Most of those should be fairly self-explanatory. The last two fields control how many posts you see on one page and how many pages you have access to at one time.

11. Change Pagination Limit to 3 and click the Update button.

12. Click the Administration menu "Users."

This displays the User Administration screen; from here you can select a user from the drop-down menu, and edit user details.

13. Choose one of the user profiles you created in Step 5 and click "Modify User."

From this page (see Figure 15-5), you can modify a user's name, access level, and signature.

Figure 15-5

14. Change the user's access level to Moderator and click "Modify Account."

15. Now, click the Administration menu "Forums." You should see a list of the forums available for your board. If this is your initial installation, you will have only one forum—called New Forum. You can edit this forum, delete it, and/or create a new forum. Feel free to create as many forums as you want. Note that when creating or editing a forum, you can choose a moderator. The user's account you edited in Step 13 is now available as a choice in the Moderator field.

16. Click the Administration menu item "BBcodes."

You will see a form where you can enter a "template" and "replacement." This allows you to designate words or phrases that will be replaced by different words or phrases. For instance, you can enter the phrase "very hard" in the template field, and "cats and dogs" in the replacement field. Once you click the Add New button, these will be added to the database. Note that the real power of this page is in the use of regular expressions. If you are not familiar with regular expressions, we explain how they work in the "How It Works" section.

17. Enter the following template and replacement values exactly as they are shown. Remember to click Add New after entering each one:

Target	Replacement
`\[url\]([^[]+?)\[/url\]`	`<a href="$1" target="_blank">$1</a>`
`\[img\]([^[]+?)\[/img\]`	`<img src="$1">`
`\[i\]([^[]+?)\[/i\]`	`<i>$1</i>`
`\[b\]([^[]+?)\[/b\]`	`<b>$1</b>`
`\[u\]([^[]+?)\[/u\]`	`<u>$1</u>`
`\[url=([^]]+?)\]`	`<a href="$1" target="_blank">`
`\[/url\]`	`</a>`
`very hard`	`cats and dogs`

That's it for the administration functions. There are not too many, but we are sure you will think of many things to add down the road.

18. Click the Profile menu item on the main menu.

This screen should look familiar. It is the same page we used to modify user accounts. However, because you are now looking at the page as a user and not as an admin, you have access that allows you to modify different data.

19. Add a short signature. Your name should be enough for now.

Okay, you have goofed off enough. Let's create a few posts:

1. Click the Home menu item on the main menu.

You should now see a screen similar to Figure 15-6. If you did not make any changes to the forums, there will be just one forum called "New Forum." If you did make changes, you should see your forums listed here.

2. Click the first forum on the page.

3. If you are prompted to create a new thread, click "yes." Otherwise, click New Thread.

4. Enter any subject you like, and any text in the body. Somewhere in the body field, include the phrase "It was raining very hard today."

5. When you are done, click the button Submit New Post.

You should now see your post on the screen (see Figure 15-7). Note that although you typed in "very hard" in your post, it now reads "cats and dogs." That is the BBcode tool at work. We'll look at that in more detail in the "How It Works" section that follows this "Try It Out" section.

Figure 15-6

6. Click Reply to Thread and repeat Steps 4 and 5 to create at least three more posts.

After creating the last post, note that the Next/Prev buttons become available at the bottom of the thread. Because we changed our Pagination Limit to 3 in the steps, we can see only three posts on this page. You can see that you can click the number 2, or click "Next" and it will take you to the next (up to 3) posts.

Let's look at one more function, Search. After that, we'll delve a little deeper into the application to see how it ticks.

Up at the top of the screen, you should see a text box with a button labeled "Search." Enter the word "raining" and click the Search button.

If you followed Step 4 in the previous series of steps, you should see at least one document returned in the search results. If you are still logged in as the administrator, you should also see the SQL statement that was used to find that document, and a score value. We explain that later in "How It Works."

Figure 15-7

That's just about it for the Bulletin Board application. It's not overly complex, but it does have a few useful features. When you are done with this chapter (and the book), you should be armed with enough knowledge to add your own ideas to this and the other applications.

But now, let's take a look under the covers.

How It Works

As we stated before, we are not going to show you how the app works page by page, line by line. Not only is it a very large application that would take too many pages to explain, but most of the code of the Bulletin Board application has been explained in previous chapters. So far, we have shown you how to write a SQL statement, how to work with arrays, and how to create reusable functions.

We will concentrate on some of the new concepts introduced in this application, such as pagination and regular expressions. Let's start with the setup.php file.

setup.php

We're doing things a little differently here from the way we did them in other chapters. Previously, when creating a database, we used CREATE TABLE IF NOT EXISTS. That is a good way to create a new table yet avoid errors if the table already exists. But what if data needs to be inserted into the table? How do you know whether or not the table was just created or already existed? By using the CREATE TABLE command, you can't know.

Instead, we are going to trap the error caused by creating an existing table. If the error occurs, then we know the table already exists, and we will skip over the data insertions and continue with the next table. If any other error occurs, we will halt execution with the die() command, as usual.

First, we create our SQL statement and then run it with the mysql_query command. Note the creation of a full text index for the subject and body fields. This makes searches much faster (which we will cover shortly). Also note the absence of the "IF NOT EXISTS" keywords.

```
$sql = <<<EOS
CREATE TABLE forum_posts (
  id int(11) NOT NULL auto_increment,
  topic_id int(11) NOT NULL default '0',
  forum_id int(11) NOT NULL default '0',
  author_id int(11) NOT NULL default '0',
  update_id int(11) NOT NULL default '0',
  date_posted datetime NOT NULL default '0000-00-00 00:00:00',
  date_updated datetime NOT NULL default '0000-00-00 00:00:00',
  subject varchar(255) NOT NULL default '',
  body mediumtext NOT NULL,
  PRIMARY KEY (id),
  KEY IdxArticle (forum_id,topic_id,author_id,date_posted),
  FULLTEXT KEY IdxText (subject,body)
)
EOS;
$result = mysql_query($sql);
```

Next, we test for the error condition caused by the table existing in the database. The error code is 1050 and is returned by the function mysql_errno(). If we receive that particular error code, everything is okay, but no insert will take place. If there is no error, the table creation worked, and we insert our new data. Any other error code halts the program.

```
switch(mysql_errno()) {
  case 1050:
    break;
  case 0:
    $sql = "INSERT INTO forum_posts VALUES (NULL, 0, 1, 1, 0, '".
    date("Y-m-d H:i:s", time())."', 0, 'Welcome', 'Welcome to your ".
    "new Bulletin Board System. Do not forget to change your admin ".
    "password after installation. Have fun!')";
    $result = mysql_query($sql) or die(mysql_error());
    break;
  default:
    die(mysql_error());
    break;
}
```

You may assume we have a vast knowledge of MySQL just because we know that the error code for creating a table that already exists is 1050. The fact is, we did *not* know the code: We simply ran a CREATE query on a table we knew already existed, and echoed the resulting `mysql_errno()` to the screen. We then knew the code and could trap for it.

Why do we give away such a secret? Some day you may find yourself trying to trap a particular error condition in your code, and you won't know the code you are looking for. Rather than scouring the Internet hoping to find the code, you can usually induce the error yourself and echo the resulting code number to the screen. Once you have the code number, you can trap for it, just as we did in the preceding code.

One last comment about `setup.php` before we move on: You may notice that in some cases we *did* use IF NOT EXISTS. If you do not need to know whether you are duplicating a table, then IF NOT EXISTS will work nicely. We included it only in cases where we did not need to insert any data.

Next, let's take a look at our login procedure. There isn't much new to see here, but it gives us a chance to discuss authentication with you for a moment.

A Last Look at User Authentication

The CBA board uses user authentication, but it is by no means totally secure. For a board application, it is probably secure enough. However, if this were human resources data containing sensitive information, you might want to make it a bit more secure.

> *This book does not attempt to help you create a virtual Fort Knox. If you have such a need, we strongly suggest you look for a good book on security, and perhaps look at a few online resources. A good start is* `www.w3.org/Security/Faq/`.

Let's take a look at our security model, and see where there might be some places to improve it a bit. If you look at most of the PHP pages that make up the application, you see where we check for a user's access level before displaying certain items. For example, take a look at `header.php`.

Because `header.php` is included at the top of almost every Web page, we do most of our user authentication there. By checking for the existence of the `user_id` session variable, we know the user is logged in. By checking if `access_lvl` is greater than 2, we know whether the user has administrator access. This allows us to customize the main menu depending on whether the user is logged in, and what access level he or she possesses. It also allows us to address the user by name.

```
echo '    <a href="index.php">Home</a>';
if (!isset($_SESSION['user_id'])) {
   echo ' | <a href="login.php">Log In</a>';
   echo ' | <a href="useraccount.php">Register</a>';
} else {
   echo ' | <a href="transact-user.php?action=Logout">';
   echo "Log out " . $_SESSION['name'] . "</a>";
   if ($_SESSION['access_lvl'] > 2) {
      echo ' | <a href="admin.php">Admin</a>';
   }
   echo ' | <a href="useraccount.php">Profile</a>';
}
```

So, if users are not logged in, we give them links to log in or register as a new user. If they are logged in, they can log out or view their profile. And, if they are administrators, they will have access to the admin functions.

That brings us to the `admin.php` page. We were able to get here by clicking the Admin link, which is available only if you are logged in as the administrator. So far, so good. What if the user attempts to access the `admin.php` page directly?

Try it yourself. Load `index.php` in your browser, and then make sure you are logged out. Once you are logged out, load `admin.php` by typing it directly in the address bar of your browser. It should load with no problem. Now, edit one of the fields on the main admin page. Again, nothing is stopping you. Indeed, when you click the Update button, the data will be saved.

But wait . . . you are not logged in! How is this possible? Simple. You have not checked the user's credentials once he or she got into the page.

Just as you are responsible for checking IDs in your bar in case underage patrons slip in, you are responsible for the users' access to your entire site. If you don't want certain people to access a page, you not only have to bar access to any link loading the page, but kick them off the page if they are successful in loading it.

Fortunately, this is easy to do. At the top of your page, simply check their credentials (Those are up to you. Do they need a certain access level? Do they just need to be logged in?), and then redirect them to another page if they don't pass (`shameonyou.php`, or simply back to `index.php`).

You can do other things to make your site more secure. Most are way beyond the scope of the book. A look at the link we gave you earlier should help you if you are interested in learning more about security. Just don't ever think you are "secure enough" if you haven't considered the risk of unauthorized access.

While we are still visiting `admin.php`, let's take a closer look at it.

admin.php

The file `admin.php` is set up in four different areas: board administration, user admin, forum admin, and BBcode admin. A lot is going on in this page. We'll tackle each area, one at a time. First let's look at board administration.

Board Administration

Looking at the code, you will see that we simply build our table of fields by looping through an array called `$admin`.

```
foreach ($admin as $k => $v) {
  echo "<tr><td>". $v['title'] . "</td><td>" .
    "<input type='text' name='". $k . "' " .
    "value='" . $v['value'] . "' size='60'>" .
    "</td><td>$k</td></tr>\n";
}
```

The array $admin is associative. The key is a unique identifier for the data, which is associated with a value and a title. For example, the title bar's title is "Board Titlebar" and the value is "CBA Forums." It is represented in the $admin array as follows:

```
$admin['titlebar']['title'] = "Board Titlebar"
$admin['titlebar']['value'] = "CBA Forums"
```

By looping through the $admin array, we can extract each piece of data and use it to build our form. But the question is, where is $admin populated? It is certainly not created anywhere in admin.php.

If you look at the top of admin.php, you'll notice that header.php is included. The array is not built in header.php either, but looking at the top of header.php you will notice another included file, config.php. A quick look into config.php uncovers the fact that $admin is loaded there. Note also that $bbcode is also being built. We'll see that used shortly.

```
$sql = 'SELECT * FROM forum_admin';
$result = mysql_query($sql) or die(mysql_error());

while ($row = mysql_fetch_array($result)) {
   $admin[$row['constant']]['title'] = $row['title'];
   $admin[$row['constant']]['value'] = $row['value'];
}

$sql = 'SELECT * FROM forum_bbcode';
$result = mysql_query($sql) or die(mysql_error());

while ($row = mysql_fetch_array($result)) {
   $bbcode[$row['id']]['template'] = $row['template'];
   $bbcode[$row['id']]['replacement'] = $row['replacement'];
}
```

Notice that $admin (and $bbcode) are built by looping through the entire admin (and BBcode) table. This is important because it illustrates how the board administration page contains every piece of data contained in the admin table. These values are available, and are used, throughout the application. For example, header.php uses some of the $admin data:

```
$title = $admin['titlebar']['value'];
 ...
<title><?php echo $title; ?></title>
 ...
  <h1 id="sitetitle"><?php echo $admin['title']['value'];?></h1>
 ...
  <p id="subtitle"><?php echo $admin['description']['value']; ?></p>
```

You may also notice the lack of any way to add or delete admin values. There is a good reason for this. The $admin values are available at the code level. Because of this, you don't want to be able to delete a value that the code is relying on. You also don't need to create new values because the code wouldn't use the new values in any case.

However, you may find the need to create a new row of data in the admin table to be used in your board application. For example, we are using a style sheet to alter the appearance of the application. Perhaps you want the ability to dynamically change the style sheet used by changing a value in the admin page, rather than editing the `header.php` file.

The good news is that once you add a new row of data to the admin table, it is automatically detected by the board administration page and displayed. The bottom line? If you feel you need a new, administrator-controlled value in your application, simply add the appropriate row of data to your admin table (using phpMyAdmin, if you like), and access it in your code using the `$admin['key']['value']` and `$admin['key']['title']` syntax.

User Administration

Users require a similar treatment, although this treatment is just a bit different from the `$admin` array.

The first thing we need to do is gather up all of the access levels, along with their names. That is done with the following code, which results in a numerical array of Access Levels:

```
$sql = "SELECT access_lvl, access_name FROM forum_access_levels " .
       "ORDER by access_lvl DESC";
$result = mysql_query($sql) or die(mysql_error());
while ($row = mysql_fetch_array($result)) {
  $a_users[$row['access_lvl']] = $row['access_name'];
}
```

Next, we create an HTML select field, dynamically building up the options. By looping through the access level array we just created, we can also use the `optgroup` tag to categorize the select list by access level. (Aren't we so clever?)

```
    <select id='userlist' name='userlist[]'>
<?php
    foreach ($a_users as $key => $value) {
      echo "<optgroup label='". $value . "'>\n";
      userOptionList($key);
      echo "\n</optgroup>\n";
    }
?>
    </select>
```

Note that you create the list of users by calling the `userOptionList()` function. This function resides in `functions.php` and is called once for each access level. A list of `<option>` tags is output, each containing the appropriate user information.

```
function userOptionList($level) {
  $sql = "SELECT id, name, access_lvl " .
         "FROM forum_users " .
         "WHERE access_lvl=" . $level . " " .
         "ORDER BY name";
  $result = mysql_query($sql) or die(mysql_error());

  while ($row = mysql_fetch_array($result)) {
```

```
        echo "<option value='". $row['id'] . "'>" .
            htmlspecialchars($row['name']) . "</options>";
    }
}
```

That's really all there is to it. When the appropriate user is chosen, his or her ID is passed on to the `transact-admin.php` transaction page, where the admin user is redirected to the `useraccount.php` page for that user.

Let's take a gander at the forum administration page next.

Forum Administration

This part is pretty straightforward. We look up all of the forums in the forum table and then list them with their descriptions, plus a link for editing and a link for deleting. Choosing delete takes the administrator to `transact-affirm.php`, which prompts the user for confirmation before deleting the forum. This is a safety precaution because deleting a forum results in the deletion of all posts within that forum as well. We leave it to you to explore `transact-affirm.php` on your own. It is a fairly self-explanatory page, and by now you should have no problem figuring out how it works.

BBcode Administration

Now we come to the real neat stuff. This is really part of a larger topic of discussion involving regular expressions. Therefore, we believe it deserves its own heading.

Regular expressions

If you are not familiar with regular expressions, one look at a typical regular expression might prompt you to wonder just who would consider it "regular." However, just like any language, once you learn what the syntax means, regular expressions are not that difficult. With the right combination of commands, however, regular expressions can be very powerful.

A regular expression (often abbreviated "regex" or "regexp") is a pattern of symbols and letters used to match text. Once a match is found, it can either be displayed, erased, or replaced with something else. If you have ever used `*.php` to list all PHP files in a directory, then you have used a regex pattern.

So, how do regular expressions apply to an application such as this one? Good question. Imagine that this site catered to children (as it might, in fact, because many children are comic book fans). You might want to prevent the usage of obscene words on your site, so that it is a friendly place that parents appreciate and allow their children to visit. By using regular expressions, you can scan a post before it gets displayed on the screen and replace any vulgarities with cleaner prose.

The topic of regular expressions could easily fill a book by itself. Indeed, there are many places to learn more about regular expressions than you will learn in this chapter. You can start with the PHP manual by visiting www.php.net/pcre.

The two types of regex functions

In PHP, there are two basic types of regular expression functions: POSIX and PCRE.

POSIX stands for Portable Operating System Interface (don't ask about the X; we think geeks just like to use X wherever they can). POSIX is a set of standard operating system interfaces based on the UNIX operating system. The term POSIX, therefore, does not actually refer to the regular expressions themselves, but describes the source of the regular expression syntax. It is more proper to refer to them as POSIX-style regular expressions. POSIX-style regular expressions are implemented in PHP by using the `ereg()` functions, such as `ereg()`, `eregi()`, and `ereg_replace()`.

PCRE stands for Perl Compatible Regular Expressions. They are usually faster than POSIX-style regular expressions, and for that reason along with the fact that PCRE regular expressions are usually more powerful, most developers choose to use PCRE functions such as `preg_match()` and `preg_replace()`.

Chapter 7 briefly introduced you to a POSIX-style regular expression. Here we show you PCRE. It is ultimately up to you which you choose to use. However, for a thorough understanding of both styles, make sure you read the PHP manual.

How to write a PCRE regex

So, what does a regex look like? We will demonstrate different regex patterns using the `preg_replace()` function. The `preg_replace()` function takes three arguments: the search pattern (the needle), the replacement pattern, and the text to be searched (the haystack). The regex pattern is contained in `$needle`:

```
$result = preg_replace($needle, $replacement, $haystack);
```

When creating your regex pattern, you must use delimiters to define the boundaries of your regex. The delimiters can be any character except alphanumeric. Most use the forward slash character (/). This is not a requirement; use any character you are comfortable with. Just remember that if you use the same character within your pattern, it must be escaped by a preceding backslash (\ ).

There are many ways to designate search patterns in your regexp. The simplest is the literal: What you are looking for is literally entered in your pattern, usually within parentheses:

```
preg_replace('/(goose)/', 'pinch', 'Do not goose me, please');
```

If you are looking for one of a group of patterns, separate them with the pipe (|):

```
/(goose|duck|egret)/
```

To look for specific characters, put them in square brackets. All of the following are legal regex expressions:

`/[abc]/`	Matches the letter a, b, or c
`/[a-z]/`	Matches any lowercase letter
`/[a-zA-Z0-9]/`	Matches any alphanumeric character
`/[^aeiou]/`	Matches any consonant (^ means "not")

In order to specify the number of times a character should or can be repeated, there are a few options:

. (period)	Matches any single character except newlines
?	Matches any 0 or 1 character
*	Matches any 0 or more characters
+	Matches any 1 or more characters
{x}	Matches any x characters (such as {5})
{x,y}	Matches any x through y characters (such as {2,4})

> *There is much more to regular expressions than this list covers. For a complete list, visit* www.php.net/manual/en/pcre.pattern.syntax.php.

In addition to pattern matching, there are modifiers that change the "rules" of your pattern. These go on the right side of the right-hand delimiter. For the complete list of modifiers, visit www.php.net/manual/en/pcre.pattern.modifiers.php; for now, here is a partial list:

i	Caseless: Pattern matches any uppercase and lowercase.
s	Dot (.) matches all characters, *including newlines*.
e	Very powerful! After pattern matching, evaluates the result as PHP.

In Step 19 of the previous "Try It Out" section, you entered a few strange patterns in the BBcode Administration page. We will clear up the mystery of those values for you, and show you how they work. Before we do that, however, let's look at how BBcodes are implemented. Once you see where the replacements take place, we will look at the actual patterns.

If you take a look at the showTopic() function defined in functions.php, you'll see a line that looks like this:

```
echo "</p><p>" . bbcode(nl2br(htmlspecialchars($body))) . "</p>";
```

The variable $body contains the text we want to display on the screen. However, before we do that, we have a couple of "cleanup" tasks to perform. First, we want to convert (and not render) any HTML that might exist in the form to the HTML equivalents, so that the HTML is displayed in the body as it was entered. This will prevent malicious users from inputting HTML that can break your page. The function htmlspecialchars() will take care of that for us.

Once all of the HTML has been converted to the HTML entity equivalents, enter <br /> tags for every newline entered in the body of the post. PHP has a handy tool for that, of course: nl2br().

Finally, perform all of the replacements we have set up on the BBcode administration page. That is accomplished using our own function, bbcode(), which runs through each of the target/replacement pairs in the BBcode database, replacing any relevant text in the body. It does this recursively (a max of four iterations) until no more matches are found.

```
function bbcode($data) {
  $sql = "SELECT * FROM forum_bbcode";
  $result = mysql_query($sql);
  if (mysql_num_rows($result) > 0) {
    while($row = mysql_fetch_array($result)) {
      $bbcode['tpl'][] =
        "§" . html_entity_decode($row['template'],ENT_QUOTES). "§i";
      $bbcode['rep'][] =
        html_entity_decode($row['replacement'],ENT_QUOTES);
    }
    $data1 = preg_replace($bbcode['tpl'],$bbcode['rep'],$data);
    $count = 1;
    while (($data1 != $data) and ($count < 4)) {
      $count++;
      $data = $data1;
      $data1 = preg_replace($bbcode['tpl'],$bbcode['rep'],$data);
    }
  }

  return $data;
}
```

Because regex uses many odd characters in the pattern, before storing the data in our table we use `htmlentities()` to convert the data into something MySQL can safely store. For that reason, when retrieving the data, we must perform `html_entity_decode()`. Note the use of the § character as a delimiter. Because it is not a character used in regex patterns, it's a perfect delimiter. To use the character, make sure your numlock is enabled, hold down your Alt key, and type **0167**. Alternatively, you could use a different non-alphanumeric character as your delimiter.

Also note the use of the *i* modifier after the right-hand modifier. This specifies that we do not care about upper or lower case matching. If you want to use case matching, feel free to remove this modifier.

As you can see from the code, `$row['template']` contains the regex pattern. The array variable `$row['replacement']` contains the replacement pattern. Now, let's look at some of the pattern/replacement pairs you entered earlier:

Pattern	Replacement	Explanation
very hard	cats and dogs	This is a very simple replacement, using a literal pattern match. It replaces the words "very hard" with the words "cats and dogs" in any post or signature. You saw evidence of this in one of your posts.
\[/url\]	</a>	Replaces any instance of [/url] in the body with </a>. Note that the opening and closing square brackets must be delimited to show that you want to match them literally.
\[b\]([^[]+?)\[/b\]	$1	Now we're getting into some interesting stuff. This pattern matches [b]some text here[/b] and replaces it with some text here.

The last pattern deserves a bit of explanation, as it introduces a couple of new concepts. The parentheses are there so we can use what we call *back references*. Note the $1 in the replacement pattern. This tells the function "Take whatever you found in the first set of parentheses and put it here." If we had a more complex pattern with a second set of parentheses, we would refer to the data matched within those parentheses using $2.

Within those parentheses, we are matching any character at all *except* a left square bracket. The + tells the expression to match from 1 to any number of those characters. If you wanted the expression to match 0 or more, use * instead of +.

The ? can be very confusing, especially for those not familiar with regular expressions. Because it is immediately preceded by a quantifier (+), it does not mean 0 characters or 1 character as it usually does. In this case, it is telling the regex not to be greedy.

Imagine the following text:

```
Hello, [b]George[/b], how are [b]you[/b] doing today?
```

If we ran the regex pattern §\[b\]([^[]+)\[/b\]§i against that text (note the lack of ?), the regex would be "greedy" and match the maximum sized pattern it could find by default. The result is that the preceding text would be altered like so:

```
Hello, <b>George[/b], how are [b]you</b> doing today?
```

This isn't good in this particular case because we are trying to style "George" and "you" in boldface. We use the ? in our pattern after the + to tell the regex pattern to be *ungreedy*, so that it finds the smallest matches. By adding in the ?, the result would be

```
Hello, <b>George</b>, how are <b>you</b> doing today?
```

which of course is the intended result.

We know regular expressions can be a bit confusing. Take the time to learn them, though. If you understand them well, they can be your biggest ally. You will be surprised at the sort of patterns you can match with regex.

For more information on regular expressions, visit the following pages in the PHP manual:

❑   http://www.php.net/manual/en/ref.pcre.php

❑   http://www.php.net/manual/en/pcre.pattern.modifiers.php

❑   http://www.php.net/manual/en/pcre.pattern.syntax.php

Searching

A bulletin board would not be worth much unless you had the ability to search for old posts. Visit any bulletin board you might be familiar with, and most likely you will find a search function there.

There are many types of searches. The simplest requires that you enter text into an input field, and when you hit the Search button, it looks for any of the text you entered. That is the search we created for this application.

Searches can get very complicated, too. You might want to search posts by the date they were entered, or by author. You might want to find a range of dates. You might even want to be able to designate how the result page is sorted. These capabilities are not currently available in the CBA Forums, but if you feel ambitious enough, feel free to beef up your search.

The actual search mechanism is fairly simple. You have a single text field with a Search button that submits your form. The search.php page captures the search term, and builds a relatively simple SQL statement that is designed to return matching rows. We then simply iterate through those rows and display the data on the screen. It's not that much different than displaying a forum or thread on the page. The only real difference is the SQL statement.

```
if (isset($_GET['keywords'])) {
  $sql = "SELECT *, MATCH (subject,body) " .
         "AGAINST ('" . $_GET['keywords'] . "') AS score " .
         "FROM forum_posts " .
         "WHERE MATCH (subject,body) " .
         "AGAINST ('" . $_GET['keywords'] . "') " .
         "ORDER BY score DESC";

  $result = mysql_query($sql,$conn)
    or die('Could not perform search; ' . mysql_error());
}
```

The bulk of the work of a search happens in the database. It stands to reason, then, that the more efficient and well-built our database is, the faster our data will be retrieved. In order to maximize the efficiency, we create an index for the fields to be searched. In this case, we index the subject and body columns of our forum_posts table. You can see how this works in the CREATE TABLE command in setup.php:

```
CREATE TABLE  forum_posts (
  id int(11) NOT NULL auto_increment,
  topic_id int(11) NOT NULL default '0',
  forum_id int(11) NOT NULL default '0',
  author_id int(11) NOT NULL default '0',
  update_id int(11) NOT NULL default '0',
  date_posted datetime NOT NULL default '0000-00-00 00:00:00',
  date_updated datetime NOT NULL default '0000-00-00 00:00:00',
  subject varchar(255) NOT NULL default '',
  body mediumtext NOT NULL,
  PRIMARY KEY  (id),
  KEY IdxArticle (forum_id,topic_id,author_id,date_posted),
  FULLTEXT KEY IdxText (subject,body)
)
```

Note that after creating each of the columns, we set the Primary Key, a Key, and a Fulltext Key. We discussed Primary Keys in Chapter 9. These help us create and track unique records. The KEY is another term for INDEX. As you can see, we have created in index for forum_id, topic_id, author_id, and date_posted. An index makes searching for rows *much* faster.

For more information on keys (indexes), visit www.mysql.com/doc/en/MySQL_indexes.html.

As you can see from the last line of the SQL query, we create a Fulltext index with the subject and body columns. This allows us to quickly find the records we are searching for.

Let's take a look at the SQL statement that does the actual search. Let's assume you are looking for the word "Board."

```
SELECT *, MATCH (subject,body) AGAINST ('Board') AS score
FROM forum_posts
WHERE MATCH (subject,body) AGAINST ('Board')
ORDER BY score DESC
```

In order to understand how this returns records, you must understand the MATCH command. MATCH returns a score value that rates how relevant the match was for each and every row in the table. According to the MySQL manual, it is based on the "number of words in the row, the number of unique words in that row, the total number of words in the collection, and the number of documents (rows) that contain a particular word."

Note that the same MATCH command is used twice. Fortunately, the MySQL optimizer caches the results of the MATCH command the first time it is run, and will not run it twice. Because the MATCH command returns a zero (0) for rows that do not match at all, putting MATCH in the WHERE clause prevents those rows from returning. If you do not put in the WHERE clause, all rows in the table will be returned, and they will not be sorted.

Using MATCH in the WHERE clause causes the rows to be returned sorted by relevance. This is not intuitive to all users, however, so we like to put in ORDER BY score DESC just for good measure, although it is not required.

For more information on Fulltext Indexes, visit www.mysql.com/doc/en/Fulltext_Search.html.

Pagination

If you are not familiar with pagination, then we suggest you do a quick search on Google.com. Search for the term Spider-Man. Don't get caught up looking at the sites your search returns! When your search results are displayed, scroll to the bottom of the page. You should see some links that will take you to more pages of search results, with the option of clicking next, previous, or a specific numbered page.

That, friend, is pagination, and we are going to teach you how to do it for your own pages. (No need to thank us. Just send money.)

If you visit the PHPBuilder.com forums, you may see this question asked over and over again: "How do I add PREV/NEXT buttons to the bottom of my pages?" We have yet to see a good, comprehensive answer. Indeed, you may even run screaming after we explain it to you. But, we hope to finally clear the air, and give you a tool that will allow you to paginate almost any set of data returned from MySQL. So let's get started.

When paginating your data, there are a few things you should have. The first, of course, is a large set of data that you can't display on one page. You also need to know how many rows of data you will display per page, and how many total records you have in your result set. For our purposes, we also need to know how many pages you will have access to at one time. For example, if you had 40 pages of data to display, you might want to show links only for pages 1 through 10, or 12 through 21, and so forth. We call this the *range*.

Let's take a look at how we paginate a page of posts. Most of the code can be located in functions.php.

In viewtopic.php, you can see that we create a variable called $limit and that it is grabbed from the $admin array that gets set in config.php:

```
$limit = $admin['pageLimit']['value'];
```

Now we take a look at showTopic() in functions.php. We will list the rows relevant to pagination only:

```
global $limit;
...
if (isset($_GET['page'])) {
  $page = $_GET['page'];
} else {
  $page = 1;
}
if ($limit == "") $limit = 25;
$start = ($page - 1) * $limit;
```

Declaring $limit global makes the variable (set in viewtopic.php) available to the function. If we don't pass $page to the Web page, we assume we are on page 1. Otherwise, we set $page to the value passed to us in the URL. By knowing the page, and the limit (number of posts per page), we can calculate our $start value (which will be used by the LIMIT statement in the SQL used to retrieve rows). For example, if we are on page 3, and our limit is 25 posts per page, then the third page will display rows 51 through 75.

Here is the whole SQL statement for returning posts. It is long, but not overly complex. It is simply four tables joined by the JOIN statement. Please note the first line and the last line of the SQL statement:

```
SELECT SQL_CALC_FOUND_ROWS " .
        "p.id, p.subject, p.body, p.date_posted, " .
        "p.date_updated, u.name as author, u.id as author_id, " .
        "u.signature as sig, c.count as postcount, " .
        "p.forum_id as forum_id, f.forum_moderator as mod, " .
        "p.update_id, u2.name as updated_by " .
    "FROM forum_forum f " .
    "JOIN forum_posts p " .
    "ON f.id = p.forum_id " .
    "JOIN forum_users u " .
    "ON u.id = p.author_id " .
    "LEFT JOIN forum_users u2 " .
    "ON u2.id = p.update_id " .
    "LEFT JOIN forum_postcount c " .
    "ON u.id = c.user_id " .
    "WHERE (p.topic_id = $topicid OR p.id = $topicid) " .
    "ORDER BY p.topic_id, p.date_posted ".
```

```
        "LIMIT $start,$limit";
    $result = mysql_query($sql,$conn)
      or die(mysql_error() . "<br>" . $sql);
    $pagelinks = paginate($limit);
```

This query will return a maximum of the number of rows in $limit. The problem is, we need to know how many rows *would have returned* if LIMIT had not been used. Fortunately, MySQL provides a means for us to find out.

In the first line, we are using the SQL command SQL_CALC_FOUND_ROWS. This doesn't do anything to the query directly. It slows it down slightly, but it does allow us to subsequently run the SQL command:

```
    $sql = "SELECT FOUND_ROWS();";
```

This command, when run, returns the number of rows that SQL_CALC_FOUND_ROWS found. Although SQL_CALC_FOUND_ROWS makes the query take a little longer, it is still more efficient than running the query a second time with the COUNT(*) parameter.

Okay. We have our numbers; time to create the page links.

```
    function paginate($limit=10) {
      global $admin;

      $sql = "SELECT FOUND_ROWS();";
      $result = mysql_query($sql) or die(mysql_error());
      $row = mysql_fetch_array($result);
      $numrows = $row[0];
      $pagelinks = "<div class=pagelinks>";
      if ($numrows > $limit) {
        if(isset($_GET['page'])){
          $page = $_GET['page'];
        } else {
          $page = 1;
        }
    ...
      } else {
        $pagelinks .= "<span class='pageprevdead'>
          &lt; PREV</span>  ";
        $pagelinks .= "<span class='pagenextdead'>
          NEXT &gt;</span>  ";
      }
```

Our paginate function takes one parameter, $limit. If $limit is not passed in to the function, then we set $limit to a default value of 10.

Because our focus is now in a function, in order for the code to access the admin variables (such as range and limit), $admin must be declared global.

As you can see, by using SELECT FOUND_ROWS(), $numrows contains the number of rows your query returns. As long as the number of rows is larger than our limit, we'll generate the pagination links. Otherwise, we'll just display inactive links.

Next, we grab the page variable, if it is set. If not, we set $page to 1.

Our next step is to determine whether the <PREV link should be activated or not. Obviously, if we are on page 1, there is no previous page. Otherwise, the previous page is the current page number minus 1:

```
if($page == 1){
    $pagelinks .= "<span class='pageprevdead'>&lt; PREV</span>";
}else{
    $pageprev = $page - 1;
    $pagelinks .= "<a class='pageprevlink' href='" . $currpage .
      "&page=" . $pageprev . "'>&lt; PREV</a>";
}
```

The next bit of code does a bit of math. We are determining a few things in this code block. First, the number of pages is determined by dividing the total number of rows returned by our previous SELECT FOUND_ROWS() query ($numrows) by the number of posts per page ($limit) and rounding up.

Next, the range is grabbed from the global variable $admin['pagerange']['value] and stored in $range. If it's not available, then $range defaults to 7. This value determines how many pages are accessible via a link at the bottom of the page. For example, if the range is 5, there are 13 pages, and you are currently viewing page 6, you will have access to pages 4, 5, 6, 7, and 8:

```
< PREV .. [4] [5] 6 [7] [8] .. NEXT >
```

The ".." tells you that there are more pages in that direction (before or after).

```
$numofpages = ceil($numrows / $limit);
$range = $admin['pageRange']['value'];
if ($range == "" or $range == 0) $range = 7;
```

The next few lines determine what range of pages to show you. In the previous example, if the $range is 5, but you are viewing page 2 out of 13 pages, the code should be smart enough to allow you access to pages 1 through 5:

```
< PREV  [1] 2 [3] [4] [5] .. NEXT >
```

As you can see, you are viewing page 2, you can directly get to pages 1 through 5, and there are more pages past 5. The piece of logic that determines which pages are available is the following:

```
$lrange = max(1,$page-(($range-1)/2));
$rrange = min($numofpages,$page+(($range-1)/2));
if (($rrange - $lrange) < ($range - 1)) {
  if ($lrange == 1) {
    $rrange = min($lrange + ($range-1), $numofpages);
  } else {
    $lrange = max($rrange - ($range-1), 0);
  }
}
```

Then, the next part of the code renders the space between PREV and NEXT. If the lower range is higher than 1, put ".." in to show that there are more pages by clicking <PREV. Then, use the $lrange and

$rrange values to build the page number links. If the link corresponds to the current page, don't make it a link. Next, if the high end of the range of pages is lower than the total number of pages available, put in the ".." to show that there are more pages by clicking NEXT>.

```
if ($lrange > 1) {
  $pagelinks .= "..";
} else {
  $pagelinks .= "  ";
}
for($i = 1; $i <= $numofpages; $i++){
  if($i == $page){
    $pagelinks .= "<span class='pagenumdead'>$i</span>";
  }else{
    if ($lrange <= $i and $i <= $rrange) {
      $pagelinks .= "<a class='pagenumlink' href='" . $currpage .
      "&page=" . $i . "'>" . $i . "</a>";
    }
  }
}
if ($rrange < $numofpages) {
  $pagelinks .= "..";
} else {
  $pagelinks .= "  ";
}
```

The last part is to render NEXT> as clickable or not, depending on whether or not you are looking at the last post of the thread. Doing this is relatively simple:

```
if(($numrows - ($limit * $page)) > 0){
  $pagenext = $page + 1;
  $pagelinks .= "<a class='pagenextlink' href='" . $currpage .
    "&page=" . $pagenext . "'>NEXT &gt;</a>";
} else {
  $pagelinks .= "<span class='pagenextdead'>NEXT &gt;</span>";
}
```

You may notice that this code generates simple text links for the pages. This is true. However, each element is surrounded by <span> tags, which allows us to use style sheets to easily modify the look of these links.

Voilà! You have a terrific, customizable, dynamically built pagination function.

Breadcrumbs

Once upon a time, there were two skinny little yahoos named Hansel and Gretel. They didn't want to get lost in the forest, blah blah blah, so Hansel got the bright idea of dropping crumbs of bread so that they could find their way back. Birds ate the bread, the kids got lost, and they ate a house. Hansel got fat eating German chocolates and candies while sitting in a cage, and Gretel was forced to do chores. Then one day they stuffed a little old lady in an oven and ran home. The End.

Except for the fact that the birds ate their trail, Hansel had the right idea. By placing a trail of crumbs behind themselves, they should have been able to navigate out of any dark forest.

Some time ago, Yahoo! came along, giving us the ability to find Web sites based on categories. Because there are so many sites out there that are very specialized, some of them might be in a sub-sub-sub-sub-category.

For example, let's say you wanted to view some sites in the Yahoo! directory about PHP. You click the Computers and Internet category. Hmmm. Next, click Software, then Internet, World Wide Web, Servers, (ah, getting close we think), Server Side Scripting, and (yes, finally!) PHP. Or, you could have simply done a search for "PHP" and clicked the categories link near the top of the page.

Now that you have been to this page, wouldn't it be nice to remember how you got here? If you look near the top of the screen, you should see something that looks like this:

```
Directory > Computers and Internet > Software > Internet >
     World Wide Web > Servers >Server Side Scripting > PHP
```

It is a map of subdirectories telling you exactly how to get to the category you are looking at. Someone (probably a fan of gingerbread houses, but don't quote me on that) saw this "map" and decided to call it a breadcrumb list. The name has stuck.

The truth is, breadcrumbs are very helpful, and they make a lot of sense for a bulletin board forum. They can give you a map from the post you are reading, to the thread it was in, to the forum the thread was in, to the category the forum was in, to the home page. Perhaps it would look like this:

```
Home > Comic Book Movies > Spider-Man > This movie rocked! > I agree
```

By allowing you to click on any part of the breadcrumb, you can easily navigate to another part of the site.

We have implemented breadcrumbs for this application, and we will show you how it was done. There are many different ways you could implement a breadcrumb system (such as by folder structure). This is just one, and it is relatively simple.

The function itself takes two arguments, $id and $getfrom. The argument $getfrom will either be "F" for forum, or "P" for post. The default is "F."

```
function breadcrumb($id, $getfrom="F") {
```

There is usually a standard separator for crumbs. Some people use >, but we like to use a bullet, or dot. If you prefer to use >, then use the HTML entity > in place of ·:

```
$sep = "<span class='bcsep'>";
$sep .= " &middot; ";
$sep .= "</span>";
```

If we are in a post, then we want our breadcrumb to include a link to the forum, along with a non-linked indication of what thread we are in. We pass in the topic_id to retrieve the right topic and get the forum_id from that topic and put it into the $id field. We also extract the name of the topic.

```
if ($getfrom == "P") {
    $sql = "SELECT forum_id, subject FROM forum_posts ".
           "WHERE id = " . $id;
    $result = mysql_query($sql)
        or die(mysql_error() . "<br>" . $sql);
    $row = mysql_fetch_array($result);
    $id = $row['forum_id'];
    $topic = $row['subject'];
}
```

Next, we run `getForum` on the `$id` that is now a forum_id. It returns a row that contains the name and description of the forum. We don't currently use description, but you could if you wanted to use it as the `alt` or `title` attribute for the breadcrumb. At this point, we begin building the breadcrumb in the variable `$bc`; Home is always first, and then the separator. Next is either a link to the forum (if looking at a post), or simply the forum listed without a link. Next comes the thread title for the post we are looking at.

```
$row = getForum($id);
$bc = "<a href='index.php'>Home</a>$sep";
switch ($getfrom) {
    case "P":
        $bc .= "<a href='viewforum.php?f=$id'>".$row['name'].
               "</a>$sep".$topic;
        break;
    case "F":
        $bc .= $row['name'];
        break;
    default:
}
return "<h4 class='breadcrumb'>" . $bc . "</h4>";
}
```

As we said, this breadcrumb is not that difficult. We are sure that armed with all of the PHP knowledge you now have, you could come up with a very impressive breadcrumb function.

Going Out in Style

As promised, here is the section on cascading style sheets (CSS). Unfortunately, because CSS is beyond the scope of this book, we are not going to give you a handy tutorial on how to implement them. However, you have come a long way to get here, and your education would not be complete without at least learning a little bit about CSS.

If you are not familiar with CSS, we recommend getting a book, or reading an online tutorial. There are some excellent sites dedicated to teaching people how to make their Web pages CSS-compliant. We recommend you take a look at the following pages:

❑ **www.w3schools.com/css/default.asp:** A great site at which to start learning the basics of CSS.

❑ **http://hotwired.lycos.com/webmonkey/authoring/stylesheets/tutorials/tutorial1.html:** A long URL, yes, but an excellent tutorial. It's very funny, too. We strongly recommend you check this one out. In fact, put www.webmonkey.com in your favorites list. There are many articles there you will want to read.

❑ **www.zeldman.com:** Jeffrey Zeldman's very informative site. If you get into CSS and XHTML compliance, you will hear his name *many* times. Get his book—you can link to it from his Web site.

❑ **www.alistapart.com:** Many very informative articles on everything from CSS to XML to typography. The authors of these articles are considered by some to be the gods of CSS and XHTML compliance.

So there you have it. You do not need to know a single bit of CSS to do every example in this book, including this chapter. But if you are ambitious enough to have read this far and have written most of the applications in the book, We are sure a little thing like CSS will be no problem for you. Happy coding!

Afterthoughts

Congratulations! You have just completed the creation of a fully functioning bulletin board system. It is more powerful than some of the simpler ones you'll find, but it is certainly not the most complex. There are many things you could still do to this application that could really make it sing, if you were so inclined.

What else could you add to this application? Perhaps you have a few ideas already, based on what you have seen on other forums. If you need some ideas, here is a short list to get you started:

❑ **Avatars:** Allow your users to upload (or choose from your site) a small image that can be placed under his or her username.

❑ **Smilies!** Most forums will replace smilies with a graphical representation of some sort. Create some smilies yourself (or find good ones on the Internet that are not copyrighted), store them in an images folder on your Web site, and use regular expressions to replace smilies with the appropriate images.

❑ **User profiles:** Allow users to add more information to their profiles, such as hobbies, location, age, sex, and so on. Also allow them to add their AIM, Yahoo! IM, and MSN IDs. Make their usernames into a link that allows other users to contact them via e-mail or Instant Messenger. Make sure you include a checkbox to allow users to hide their e-mail address, if they want to.

❑ **Quoting:** What is a forum without the ability to quote relevant text? Allow users to quote all or part of a post. We leave it up to you to figure out how to implement it.

❑ **Polls:** A very popular option, polls allow users to post a short questionnaire for their peers to answer. Install a poll option when posting a new topic, and display a graph of the results at the top of the thread.

That should keep you busy for a while. Good luck!

Summary

Now you have created a community where your visitors can hang their hats and stay a while. Combined with all of the other applications you have built, you should no doubt have a very cool, integrated Web site up and running in no time! Congratulations on making it this far. This chapter was long, with a lot of code. Most of it was not overly difficult; indeed, most of the code was stuff you did in other chapters. But we hope that by the time you have read this whole chapter, you will feel comfortable creating a Web site from the ground up, using PHP and MySQL installed on an Apache server.

Exercises

If you would like to test out how much you have learned from this chapter, take the time to do these little exercises. Not only will they help you learn; they will allow you to add some extra features to your bulletin board application.

❑   Add code to admin.php to prevent unauthorized users from loading the page. Redirect them back to index.php.

❑   Create a regular expression that recognizes an e-mail address in a post and turns it into a link.

❑   Add a bit of code to the pagination function to allow the user to go to the first page or last page. For example, if there are 14 pages, and the user is on page 8, and the range is 7, it should look something like this:

```
<PREV [1] .. [5] [6] [7] 8 [9] [10] [11] .. [14] NEXT >
```

Part IV: Advanced Users

Using Log Files to Improve Your Site

The cool thing about being a Web developer is that sometimes you get to act like Big Brother and keep close tabs on what your visitors are doing. Although it may seem voyeuristic to some, analyzing what goes on at your site can give you valuable information that will enable you to make your site better.

Some examples of the types of information you can glean from logs include:

❑ What IP addresses your visitors are using so you can get a geographical location for your most common visitors; this helps with language and international issues

❑ What browsers your visitors are using so you can make sure your site is readable by your most common visitors

❑ What times and days your visitors are visiting so you can schedule maintenance during slow times or special events during busier times

❑ What pages are the most popular on your site so you can gauge the success or failure of certain pages and remove the dead weight

❑ Whether or not your traffic is increasing so you can determine if your site is becoming more well-known or stagnating itself into oblivion

❑ What pages and processes are causing problems so you can fix them—duh

❑ If you're using user authentication on your site, what users are logging in when and what their activity is so you can see who your MVPs are and perhaps offer them special Web site features (or maybe a beer at the local bar)

This chapter is all about logs, and in it we cover the following:

❑ What logs look like and what information they contain

❑ Where you can find them on your system

❑ What resources you can use to help analyze your statistics

❑ How you can use the information to improve your site

What Is a Log?

A *log* is a text file saved on your server; this file appends itself every time something happens, such as when a file is requested by someone or when an error occurs. Here are three types of logs:

❑ Access Logs track every hit.

❑ Error Logs track every error or warning.

❑ Custom Logs track whatever information you tell them to.

Where Are These Logs?

Log files are in different locations, depending on what program created them and what their function is. Most are available in a folder outside the scope of your Web site so that users don't have access to them.

Apache

Apache keeps access logs and error logs. If Apache has been installed on your server, the default location is \<apache install directory>\logs.

The typical access log entry looks like this:

```
127.0.0.1 - george [29/Aug/2003:13:55:36 -0500] "GET /index.php?xyz=123 HTTP/1.0"
200 2326 "http://www.yourserver.com/cms/index.php" "Mozilla/4.08 [en] (Win98; I
;Nav)"
```

All of this information is on one line of the log, and is built by Apache according to the LogFormat directive in the mod_log_config module. The typical config looks like this:

```
LogFormat "%h %l %u %t \"%r\" %>s %b" common
```

The config string that built the above line used the combined format, and looks like this:

```
LogFormat "%h %l %u %t \"%r\" %>s %b \"%{Referer}i\" \"%{User-agent}i\""
        combined
```

Although the LogFormat directive is beyond the scope of this book, we will list each parameter here so that you can understand what each piece of the log is and how it's broken down:

❑ **%h (127.0.0.1):** The address of the client currently accessing your server. This can be an IP address or a hostname (if HostNameLookups is turned on on your server).

❑ **%l (-):** The RFC 1413 identity of the client. This is usually a hyphen (-) to indicate that Apache was not able to obtain the information.

❑ **%u (george):** The username of the client. This is set if the page is using HTTP User Authentication. Otherwise, you see a hyphen (-).

❑ **%t ([29/Aug/2003:13:55:36 -0500]):** The date/time the client accessed your server.

    ❑ The format for this is as follows: [day/month/year:hour:minute:second zone]

    ❑ day = 2 digits

    ❑ month = 3 letters

    ❑ year = 4 digits

    ❑ hour = 2 digits

    ❑ minute = 2 digits

    ❑ second = 2 digits

    ❑ zone = (`+' | `-') 4 digits

❑ **\"%r\" ("GET /index.php?xyz=123 HTTP/1.0"):** The request line from the client. This is wrapped in quotes, which have to be escaped. This is actually multiple information, which could be built using other parameters:

    ❑ %m (request method), in this case, GET

    ❑ %U (URL), in this case, /index.php

    ❑ %q (query string), in this case, ?xyz=123

    ❑ %H (protocol), in this case, HTTP/1.0

    ❑ \"%m %U%p %H\" is the functional equivalent of \"%r\"

❑ **%>s (200):** The status code sent back to the client. In this case, because it starts with a "2," we know it was a successful request.

❑ **%b (2326):** The size of the object returned to the client in bytes (not including headers). If no content is returned, the value is hyphen (-), or "0" if %B is used.

❑ **\"%{Referer}i\" ("http://www.yourserver.com/cms/index.php"):** The address of the page the client came from. This is useful for compiling information about where your users heard about your Web site.

❑ **\"%{User-agent}i\" ("Mozilla/4.08 [en] (Win98; I ;Nav)"):** User-Agent HTTP request header information. This is the information the client's browser sends about itself. This is very useful for determining how many people are using certain browsers, such as Internet Explorer.

If the preceding information looks like Greek to you, don't worry. There are ways of getting the information without understanding any programming, and methods of reading the information to build statistics, charts, graphs, and other things that are much easier to read. We share those methods with you shortly.

Here is what the typical error log entry looks like:

```
[Wed Aug 27 14:32:52 2003] [warning] [client 69.129.21.24] File does
    not exist: /home/grebnol/public_html/index.php
```

The information in the error log is pretty self-explanatory. It is free-form and descriptive, but typically most error logs capture the date/time, the error severity, the client IP address, the error message, and the object the client was requesting.

Because the error message is also contained in the Apache access log, it makes more sense to pull the data out of the access log. For example, the preceding error will show up in the access log with access code 404.

PHP

PHP also keeps a log of errors for you, but as we discussed in Chapter 1, the default setting for this feature is set to "off" in your php.ini file. You have to turn it on to enable error logging, which we highly recommend. Also, don't forget to tell your php.ini file where you want the error log to be saved.

The typical error log entry looks like this:

```
[01-Sep-2003 18:42:03] PHP Parse error:  parse error, unexpected '}' in
C:\Program Files\Apache Group\Apache2\test\deleteme.php on line 14
```

As in the other logs we have looked at, the logs themselves are relatively straightforward, and their purpose is to keep track of all of the errors that occurred when your PHP pages were being accessed.

In the preceding example, you can see that there was a parse error in the file deleteme.php on line 14, which merits our attention. Anyone attempting to see the contents of this file will see only the parse error until we get it fixed.

A regular check of the PHP error log should be on your "to-do" list, just to make sure there aren't any errors in your code.

MySQL

As if that's not enough, MySQL also logs queries and errors that pertain to database transactions. By default, the error log is stored as hostname.err in the data directory (in Windows and UNIX both). You can specify where the error log is saved by issuing the following command from the command prompt when starting the MySQL server:

```
mysqld —log-error[=filename].
```

Here is a typical entry in the error log:

```
030812  0:28:02  InnoDB: Started
MySql: ready for connections.
Version: '4.0.14-max-debug'  socket: ''  port: 3306
```

This lets us know that the MySQL server started successfully, what version is currently running, and what socket and port it is configured for. It also gives us the date and time that the server began running (in the first line). It should also be noted that this log cannot be accessed while the server is running; you will need to stop the server to open this file.

MySQL also allows us to view every query that is sent to the server. To specify where the general query log is located, you would type the following command when starting the MySQL server;

```
mysqld —log[=file]
```

Again, by default, this file will be stored in the "data" directory with the name *hostname*.log file, unless you specify otherwise. An entry in the general query log looks like this:

```
 /usr/local/mysql/libexec/mysqld, Version: 4.0.16-log, started with:
Tcp port: 3306  Unix socket: /tmp/mysql.sock
Time              Id Command      Argument
031109 21:33:34    1 Connect      buzzly_comic@localhost on
                   1 Init DB      buzzly_comicsite
                   1 Query        SELECT * FROM forum_admin
                   1 Query        SELECT * FROM forum_bbcode
                   1 Quit
031109 21:33:50    2 Connect      buzzly_comic@localhost on
                   2 Init DB      buzzly_comicsite
                   2 Query        SELECT id,access_lvl,name,last_login FROM
forum_users
WHERE email='admin@yoursite.com' AND passwd='admin'
                   2 Query        UPDATE forum_users SET last_login = '2003-11-09
21:33:50'
WHERE id = 1
                   2 Quit
                   3 Connect      buzzly_comic@localhost on
                   3 Init DB      buzzly_comicsite
                   3 Query        SELECT * FROM forum_admin
                   3 Query        SELECT * FROM forum_bbcode
```

If you are interested in seeing only the queries that changed data, you should view the binary log file instead of the general query file. With previous versions of PHP you would have used the update log, but it is highly recommended that you begin using the binary log instead.

The update log will be phased out with the release of PHP 5.0.

This file is also saved by default in your "data" directory, with the filename of hostname-bin unless you specify otherwise. You would activate this log by typing the following at the command prompt:

```
mysqld —log-bin[=file_name]
```

An entry in the binary log looks like this:

```
# at 4
#031109 21:29:46 server id 1  log pos 4          Start: binlog v 3, server v 4.0.16-
log
created 031109 21:29:46 at startup
# at 79
#031109 21:33:50 server id 1  log_pos 79 Query           thread_id=2 exec_time=0
error_code=0
use buzzly_comicsite;
SET TIMESTAMP=1068431630;
UPDATE forum_users SET last_login = '2003-11-09 21:33:50' WHERE id = 1;
# at 196
#031109 21:34:52 server id 1  log_pos 196         Query         thread_id=8
exec_time=0
error_code=0
SET TIMESTAMP=1068431692;
UPDATE forum_users SET email='admin@yoursite.com', name='Admin', access_lvl=3,
signature='Testing, testing, 123.'  WHERE id=1;
```

Unlike the other logs in this chapter that could be accessed with Wordpad or Notepad, you must access the binary log using the `mysqlbinlog` utility. At the command prompt, you would type **mysqlbinlog** to see the parameters for this software. Your screen will look something like the one shown in Figure 16-1.

Figure 16-1

As you can see, there are many parameters you can set to glean the specific information you are looking for.

Now That I Know What and Where They Are, What Do I Do with Them?

There are numerous software programs out there that live to help you take this gobbledy-gook and make sense out of it. Note that most of these programs are used for analyzing Web server activity, and not MySQL or PHP logs.

Webalizer

Webalizer can be found at www.webalizer.com and is a proud part of the wonderful open source community we talked about in Chapter 1. It provides reports in an easy-to-read HTML format with pretty charts and such that can be read by just about anyone, including the higher-ups. Its main purpose is to spit out reports on server activity, most specifically Apache. It is meant for use on UNIX systems, and thus far, isn't compatible with Windows. If you set your Apache config files to do DNS server lookups, then your reports with Webalizer will show those instead of simple IP addresses. This program is also known for its incredible speed, as it can process 10,000 records in a matter of one second.

You can see a sample screenshot in Figure 16-2, also available at the Webalizer Web site.

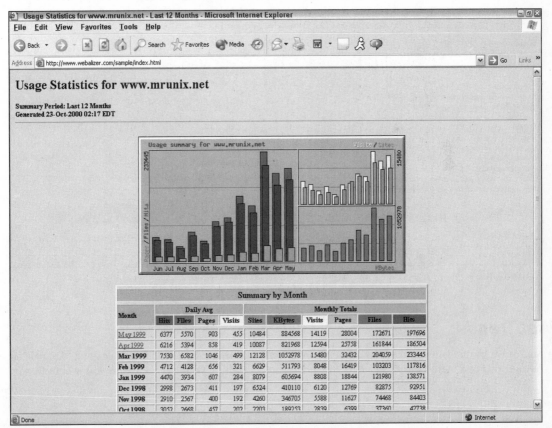

Figure 16-2

Analog

Another open source contender for helping you make sense of your log files is Analog, which you can find at www.analog.cx. While it's a little rough around the edges, it's still a powerful tool that can be customized to show what you want to see. By using the add-on, Report Magic (available at www.reportmagic.org), you can generate all kinds of fancy 3-D charts and graphs and really impress your superiors (or your dog if you're a one-man or one-woman show).

You can see sample screenshots in Figures 16-3, 16-4, and 16-5, also available at the Analog Web site.

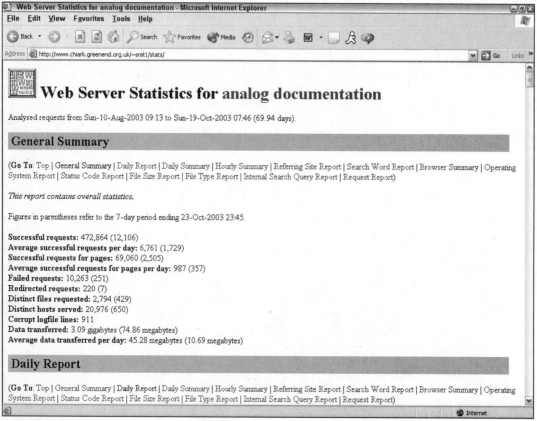

Figure 16-3

WebTrends

If you've got some money to throw around, WebTrends (www.netiq.com) is another good log analyzer program. For a mere $499 it can pretty much tell you everything you ever wanted to know about your

Web site. It works on numerous platforms, including Apache, and you are really given a lot of control over what your output looks like. We recommend this type of software if you have a high-powered server and are supporting a high-powered client who wants fancy stuff like his own logo on his own reports. The customization is really a great feature.

This software also offers a SmartSource data option that allows you to track specific things about your Web site with the use of client-side server tags in your HTML. This bypasses the whole "log" step and sends the info straight to the WebTrends software. It can even perform a DNS lookup at report generation if you forget to enable this option in your config files, or if you want to reduce server activity.

Again, this powerful software is not for the feint of heart and should be reserved for the heavy-duty users.

You can see a sample screenshot—provided by the WebTrends Web site—in Figure 16-6.

Figure 16-4

Figure 16-5

Figure 16-6

AWStats

Another of our open source buddies, AWStats can be found at `http://awstats.sourceforge.net/`. Don't be fooled by its price tag—this free software provides numerous features also offered by the big guys. Unlike some of the other open source stats programs, AWStats can track the number of unique visitors; entry and exit pages; search engines and keywords used to find the site; and browser details of each visitor, such as version and screen size.

AWStats also allows the Web administrator to set up customized reports for tracking something of specific interest for his or her specific needs, which is a welcome addition to this software package.

You can see a sample screenshot in Figure 16-7, also available at the AWStats Web site.

Figure 16-7

HTTP Analyze

One more stats program for you to investigate can be found at `www.http-analyze.org/`. Another open source favorite, this program works on any log file that is in the NCSA Common Logfile Format or W3C

Extended File Format, and thus works great with Apache. It should be noted that HTTP Analyze is supported by both UNIX and Windows systems. It also provides several different options for viewing data, all in HTML and easy-to-read formats.

You can see a sample screenshot in Figure 16-8, also available at the HTTP Analyze Web site.

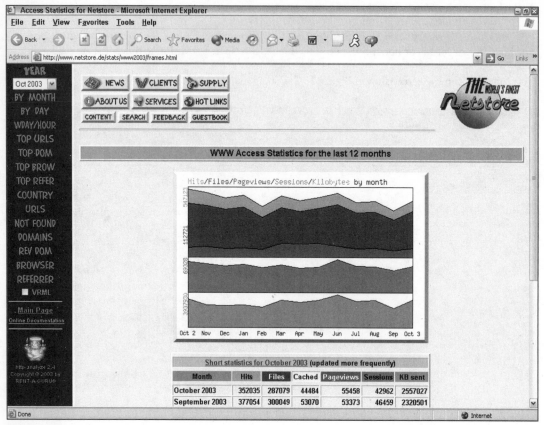

Figure 16-8

What Do the Reports Mean?

So now you have all these beautiful reports, and you go to your boss and proudly display your charts and graphs and expect a big pat on the back. But what happens when he or she says to you, "So?"

Let's talk a minute about what the reports mean to you, so you have a nice, neat, witty response.

Earlier in the chapter, we touched on how using the stats can help you improve your site. Your logs are, in many cases, your only source of feedback from your visitors. You can't know what you're doing right or wrong without any feedback, so as your only tangible evidence, these stats are really quite valuable. There are several different areas you probably want to pay attention to, depending on the specific needs of your site.

User Preferences and Information

You can't please all of the people all of the time, but you can certainly try. You care about what your users like so you obviously want to tailor your site to the most common visitor, and try to minimize the number of visitors who won't have the optimal viewing experience. You want to know what percentage of visitors are using which browsers so you can be sure and test your site against the most popular browsers of your audience. You also care about how many unique and not-so-unique visitors are coming to your site so you can tell if your site is gaining a new following, while maintaining its current one. You also want to know what screen size they are using, so you can again tailor the look of your site to be the best it can be for the most visitors.

Number of Hits and Page Views

Remember, a "hit" is any request made to the server, whereas a "page view" is a request for a page (such as an HTML page). Hits can consist of images, sound files, or anything that requires activity from the server. This number doesn't really give you an accurate count of how many people are viewing a page, so you typically go by page views.

You want to see which pages get the most page views, and are the most popular so that if you need to make something known about your site, you can make sure it appears on those pages. For example, say you have a new product to promote—if no one ever visits the "new products" page, it won't do you much good to only post it there. If the homepage of your site is the most popular, you want to also post that information on that page, so you make sure that everybody who visits your site knows about your new product.

You also want to be able to look at the pages that are doing well and compare them with the pages that aren't doing so well. Is the content of both pages clear and concise? What is it about the popular pages that makes them so great? Can you make your losers closer to the winners in page design, content, or positioning?

Trends over Time

It's rewarding to see your site become more popular as time goes on, but it creates a big pit in your stomach if things are going downhill. Tracking popularity over time can help you discern if interest in your site is waning, or if it is perhaps more popular around certain seasons of the year. If your site sells golf equipment and you notice a dip in page views during the winter months, obviously you don't have much to worry about, as your business is a seasonal business and this dip is understandable. Perhaps you notice that during the winter months your average visitor is coming from Florida (makes sense, eh?). Perhaps you can work with marketing to develop an advertising strategy tailored to the loyal Floridians during those months. (Yes, we said "Work with marketing." It happens, get over it!)

Referring Sites

If you can discern where people are finding your site, you will have a very valuable resource at your disposal. Are the search engines actually working in your favor? What keywords are people using to reach your site? Do you fare better with certain search engines than others? Are you getting referred from other, non-directory sites?

Perhaps you have a site that sells bowling equipment, and you notice through your stats that the Professional Bowlers Association has your site listed on its own site as a resource for its visitors, and has referred the majority of your visitors. Perhaps then you decide you want to offer a special discount to PBA members as a "thank you." Increasing your Web site traffic can be as simple as getting yourself listed on as many other sites as possible. Not only will it help people see you, it will help increase your listing in search engines such as Google that take into account criteria such as how many other places your Web site is listed.

Summary

You should now feel comfortable looking at and manipulating log files to benefit your site and your skills as a professional Web designer. You can choose to massage the data based on a program you have written yourself, or you may choose to utilize numerous other resources out there to provide you with fancy reports that let you know what is going on with your site. By paying attention to trends and popular pages in your site, you can get a better feel for who your visitor really is. This, in turn, enables you to continually improve your site.

At the very least, you will be able to speak intelligently to your boss when he or she asks "So what's going on with our Web site?"

Troubleshooting

Nothing is more frustrating than thinking you have all your "t's" crossed and your "i's" dotted, only to have your program blow up on you with a string of errors. Worse yet is having your program produce completely perplexing and unwanted results.

Well, you may find comfort in knowing that many developers experience the same types of obstacles. With this chapter, we hope to shed light on some potential problems you may encounter and suggest a few troubleshooting strategies.

Installation Troubleshooting

You're trying to access either PHP, MySQL, or Apache and you are running into problems. Perhaps for some reason they are not playing well with others and you are getting errors, or things aren't working the way they should be based on the installation instructions.

Many times, commonly seen errors or obstacles will be discussed on the source Web sites for each of the components. The source Web sites also provide detailed instructions for the particular system you are using, and we encourage you to read through them carefully to double-check yourself. Make sure you follow the instructions to the "t."

If while configuring PHP you receive an error that tells you that the server can't find a specific library, you can do one of two things:

❑   Check to make sure you've actually installed the library on your machine.

❑   Verify that the correct path has been specified in your configure command.

Parse Errors

You've seen it many times:

```
Parse error: parse error, expecting `','' or `';'' in
/foo/public_html/forum/index.php on line 25
```

Oh, the dreaded parse error! These are quite common, even with experienced programmers. Even with the best color-coded PHP text editors that check your syntax for you, one or two parse errors undoubtedly slip through. These can be very frustrating, but they are usually the simplest to fix, as they usually occur because of mistakes in your syntax, as opposed to your logic.

Cleanup on Line 26 . . . Oops, I Mean 94

When PHP displays a parse error, it includes a line number, which provides your first clue for solving the mystery. However, don't be fooled! Sometimes the line number can be misleading; in fact, at times the mistake will have occurred several lines up from the one identified by the server as the culprit.

Take a missing semicolon, for example. Without the semicolon to signify to the server that the line has come to an end, the server will continue to string subsequent lines together. It may not realize there is a problem until several lines later, and it will issue a parse error on the wrong line.

Elementary, My Dear Watson!

Sometimes the simplest answer is the right answer. Make sure you check to see that each of the following has been done:

- ❑ Each line ends with a semicolon.
- ❑ All quotes and parentheses are closed.
- ❑ All of your functions and control statements (if, which, and so on) end with a curly brace (}).
- ❑ All single and double quotes are nested properly.

If you get into the habit of checking your syntax regularly as you write your code, you will greatly decrease the risk of introducing parse errors. You may want to use an editor that is familiar with PHP and can color-code your programs. This makes it much easier to recognize when you have misspelled a function or forgotten to close your quotes. We use two programs:

- ❑ **UltraEdit (www.ultraedit.com):** This one is very customizable and easy to use. There is a small fee to register, but it's well worth it.
- ❑ **PHPEdit (www.phpedit.com):** This program is extremely powerful and free. It includes a context-sensitive manual for PHP, MySQL, and HTML. The program also has dynamic color coding, depending on whether you are currently typing in HTML or PHP. We have been using this one for a while now, and we are very impressed with it.

Empty Variables

You just built a large page that collects 50 fields of information from your users. There are no parse errors. You fill in the form online and click the submit button. The next page loads, just as it should. The only problem is that none of the variables seem to have been passed on to the new form!

This actually happens quite often. The first possible cause is that you are expecting your values to be posted, but you forgot to use `method="post"` on your form. By default, forms use the `get` method.

How do you solve this? Check the address of your second page. Are the variables in the query string? If so, mystery solved.

The Ultimate Bait-and-Switch

Another very common problem, addressed ad nauseam in this book, is a setting in your `php.ini` file called `register_globals`. If you have recently upgraded your server, or migrated your code to a different server, this just may be the reason you no longer have access to your variables.

As of PHP version 4.2.0, the PHP directive `register_globals` changed from a default value of "on" to a default value of "off." This was a controversial decision, and the cause of a lot of heartache with developers who wrote their programs on the assumption that it would always default to "on." When `register_globals` is set to "off," you must access your posted variables through the `$_POST` array.

For example, prior to 4.2.0, if you had `register_globals` set to the default of "on," you could post a form field called `first_name`, and the variable on the subsequent page could immediately be accessed as `$first_name`. It was determined that this could be a big security risk, so it was changed in PHP 4.2.0. Now, if you kept `register_globals` set to the default of "off," you'd have to access your posted form field `first_name` through the `$_POST` array, as `$_POST['first_name']`.

You can do a couple of things to fix this problem. The most obvious, of course, is to set the `register_globals` setting to "on" in your `php.ini` file. However, because of the recognized security risk, this is no longer the recommended course of action. For a more detailed discussion of this, visit the following URL:

```
www.php.net/register_globals
```

A better solution is to always access your variables via the `$_POST` array. If you want, you can always set your variables:

```
$first_name = $_POST['first_name'];
```

If you have a large number of `$_POST` variables, use this loop to convert them all to the more familiar format:

```
foreach($_POST as $key => $value) {
    $$key = $value;
}
```

If `$_POST['first_name']` is set to George, the preceding code will set `$key` to `first_name` and `$value` to George. Then, it sets `$first_name = George`. It will loop through every posted field, setting each variable. This is a good temporary fix to make your pages work, but we strongly recommend that, from this point forward, you always assume that `register_globals` is off, and you will never run into this particular problem again.

Consistent and Valid Variable Names

First you should make sure that your variable names are appropriate and valid according to the naming rules, as outlined in Chapter 2. Make sure you aren't beginning any variable name with a number, or trying to use a predefined variable for your variable name such as `$php_errormsg`. A complete list of these can be found at the PHP manual, `http://us2.php.net/manual/en/reserved.variables.php`.

Also, check the case you are using when referencing variables, as variable names are case-sensitive. The same holds true for database and table names. Make sure you are referencing them consistently, and if you make a change to a variable name after the fact, be sure to change all the instances of the variable name.

It is easier to maintain consistent variable names if you pick a naming convention and stick with it throughout your scripts. For example, if you always name your variables with a prefix of `$var_`, you can easily spot them in the code. This convention ties into the discussion in Chapter 2 regarding good coding practices.

Open a New Browser

Sometimes if you are working with sessions, and you are in the testing phase of your scripts, there may be an extraneous session setting hanging out there that could be preventing you from obtaining the desired results, and altering your variable values.

You can clear all session variables (provided you haven't changed your config files as we discuss in Chapter 2) by simply closing the browser and opening a new one, instead of just hitting Refresh or Reload.

"Headers Already Sent" Error

You may encounter an error message that looks like this:

```
Warning: Cannot modify header information - headers already sent by (output started
at C:\Program Files\Apache Group\Apache2\test\headererror.php:1) in C:\Program
Files\Apache Group\Apache2\test\headererror.php on line 2
```

This is a common error when working with sessions and cookies. It can occur if you try to set them after you have sent HTML code to the server. The server has to deal with these before any HTML output is sent to the server, which means that these lines must be the first in the code before any HTML code or `echo` statement. If you have even a trailing leading space before your first `<?php` line of code, you will see this error.

If you need to set cookie or session variables within the body of your code, you need to rethink your logic to accommodate this limitation. As we discuss in Chapter 2, those variables need to be addressed at the beginning of your code for them to be parsed correctly by the PHP server.

There are ways to get around this error, using the output buffer to suppress these errors. The output buffer is used to store all HTML output in a buffer until you are ready to send it to the browser. The command ob_start is used to begin the output buffering process, and ob_end_flush will send all of the stored HTML output to the browser, empty the buffer, and end the output storing process. This will let you cheat the system and store session and cookie variables in the body of the code, as well as allow you to use the header("location:") function in the body of the code. While this is not recommended for beginners, as it is more important for you to learn to code well, and according to the "rules," this can be a useful set of functions for a more experienced programmer. If you would like to learn more about the output buffer functions, you can find a complete list of them in Appendix C, or visit www.php.net.

General Debugging Tips

We have listed a few tips for general debugging purposes that can help you out of many sticky spots.

Using echo

Occasionally, you might want to read the server's mind and see what it thinks is going on. One way to do this is to echo out variable names periodically in your code. This will let you verify that the server is parsing everything correctly.

You can use echo in a step-by-step process as you follow the path of your variable, to see how the server is treating the variable throughout the code. This process would help, for example, if you wanted to perform a complex mathematical equation on a variable, and all you could tell from your output was that you were getting the wrong answer. You want to find out at what point the breakdown occurs, so you insert echo statements throughout each step of the equation to verify the accuracy of your calculation as it runs through the equation. You will then see the value of the variable as it changes.

The echo command can also be useful in if statements, foreach statements, functions, and so on to ensure that these loops are being called or processed correctly.

Let's see how echo can help us in a very simple example. Assume you have the following script:

```php
<?php
$curr_var = 0;

while ($curr_var < 20) {
    $abc = 2 * $curr_var;
    $curr_var ++;
}
echo $abc;
?>
```

By running this code in your browser, you get the number 38. What if you were expecting to get the number 40, or you wanted to check to see if your $abc variable was right? You could echo out the variable as it was processed to see how the program was working, as such:

```php
<?php
$curr_var = 0;

while ($curr_var < 20) {
    $abc = 2 * $curr_var;
    $curr_var ++;

    // debug lines
    echo $curr_var;
    echo "<br>";
}
echo $abc;
?>
```

You now see the numbers 1–20, plus your original answer of 38. It is easier for you to see that although the $curr_var goes to 20, it processes the answer only 19 times and so you get the answer of 38. Therefore, you should change the while statement as such:

```php
while ($curr_var <= 20) {
```

Now your while statement will process when $curr_var = 20, and you get a result of 40 at the end. (Okay, so you probably figured that out without the echo statement—work with us, here.) Use the comments as a reminder to yourself to delete the debugging lines when you have solved the problem, to avoid unwanted output to your browser when your page goes live.

Remember that arrays, although variables, behave a little differently. If you echo an array, all you will see on the screen is Array(). To view the contents of an array, instead of using echo, use print_r($array). Even with a multidimensional array, every value in the array will be echoed to the screen.

Divide and Conquer

Another good way to tackle a huge problem is to break it down into baby steps and test each one to make sure you are getting the correct result every step of the way. One small mistake in the beginning of a complex block of statements can have a snowball effect and completely alter your results at the end. By checking each step one by one, you can iron out those small bugs and can eventually get the intended results.

Test, Test, Test!

Many coders test their program out on their own system and as long as it works for them with their settings, they assume they are home free. To be completely thorough, you should test your code using every different environment available to you: different browsers, different preferences, different computer systems, and so on. If you have the opportunity and know-how, you should even try to hack through your own system to look for holes that might be exploited by someone a little less kind than you.

Where to Go for Help

Fortunately, the PHP community is growing. There are numerous sources online to help guide you through the murky waters should the going get tough. We have mentioned these numerous times in this book, but here they are again, one more time.

wrox.com

This book is specifically designed to provide help online in a companion Web site, so if you encounter trouble, we strongly encourage you to check out the book's sister site at www.wrox.com.

PHPBuilder.com

There are many PHP help Web sites out there, but our personal favorite tends to be PHPBuilder.com. You can find numerous articles, archives, snippets of useful code, and, most important, a well-developed and very helpful online community of fellow coders from all over the world with all levels of competency to assist you as quickly as they can. We have yet to find such a tight-knit and friendly community elsewhere, and we encourage you to post your questions in their forums.

If you are lucky, you might find one of the authors of this book lurking around at PHPBuilder.com. We are all regular contributors, and some of us are moderators. (Hint: check the Echo Lounge.)

Source Web Sites

You will see this time and time again, but like the other advice, we can't stress it enough. If you have a question about virtually anything, chances are the answer can be found at a source Web site. Each of these Web sites provides a very comprehensive manual that encompasses basically all known knowledge about the software at hand.

To refresh your memory, here they are:

- ❑ **PHP:** www.php.net (Useful hint: If you are looking for help with a function, such as echo, you can simply type **www.php.net/echo** in your browser and it takes you directly to the echo page. How nifty is that?)

  PHP also provides the manual in a Microsoft Windows Help format (CHM), which is very useful for Windows users. You can download the manual from the php.net Web site and install it on your local machine.

- ❑ **Apache:** www.apache.org
- ❑ **MySQL:** www.mysql.com

Search and Rescue

If you're experiencing problems with a script, chances are you aren't the first to experience the same obstacles. Use your favorite search engine (such as Google.com) to scour the Internet for articles, discussion forum posts, tutorials, or anything that discusses the problems you're having. This can be a very quick and easy way to keep from reinventing the wheel.

IRC Channels

You may require immediate assistance with your dilemma or question, and the IRC resource may be your solution. There are many PHP IRC channels out there: `irc://quakenet.org/php` and `irc://quakenet.org/phphelp` are good ones.

Summary

We hope we have helped you trudge through the slush and muck of debugging and working out the errors in your programs. Although you may not have found your "holy grail," we hope you will at least know where to search for it.

Answers to Exercises

This appendix supplies answers to the exercises we gave you at the end of many of the chapters. Keep in mind, as is always the case in programming, there is more than one way to skin a cat, and these are just our recommendations. If you were able to accomplish the given task in another way, then pat yourself on the back and take yourself to a movie because you're on your way!

Chapter 2

1. Go back to your `date.php` file and instead of displaying only the number of days in the current month, add a few lines that say:

The month is _____.

There are ____ days in this month.

There are _____ months left in the current year.

A: Your `date.php` file should look like something like this:

```
<html>
<head>
<title>How many days in this month?</title>
</head>
<body>
<?php

$monthname = date("F");
echo "The month is: " ;
echo $monthname;
echo "<br>";

echo "There are ";
$month=date("n");
if ($month==1) echo "31";
if ($month==2) echo "28 (unless it's a leap year)";
```

```
if ($month==3) echo "31";
if ($month==4) echo "30";
if ($month==5) echo "31";
if ($month==6) echo "30";
if ($month==7) echo "31";
if ($month==8) echo "31";
if ($month==9) echo "30";
if ($month==10) echo "31";
if ($month==11) echo "30";
if ($month==12) echo "31";
echo " days in this month.";

echo "<br>";

$monthsleft = 12-$month;

echo "There are ";
echo $monthsleft;
echo " months left in the year.";

?>
</body>
</html>
```

2. On your movie Web site, write a file that displays the following line at the bottom center of every page of your site, with a link to your e-mail address. Set your font size to 1.

This site developed by: <u>ENTER YOUR NAME HERE</u>.

A: The files of your movie site should all include these lines near the bottom of the script:

```
<?php
include "footer.php";
?>
```

Then you need to create the file footer.php, which consists of these lines:

```
<div align="center">
<font size="1">This site developed by <a href="mailto:johndoe@nothing.com">John
Doe</a></font>
</div>
```

3. Write a program that displays a different message based on the time of day. For example, if it is in the morning, have the site display "Good Morning!"

A: Your header.php page should include lines that resemble something like this:

```
<br>
<font size="2">
<?php
if ((date("G") >=5) AND (date("G") <= 11 )) echo "Good Morning!";
if ((date("G") >=12) AND (date("G") <=18)) echo "Good Afternoon!";
if ((date("G") >= 19) AND (date("G") <= 4)) echo "Good Evening!";
?>
</font>
```

4. Write a program that formats a block of text (to be input by the user) based on preferences chosen by the user. Give your user options for color of text, font choice, and size. Display the output on a new page.

A: This would be most easily accomplished by CSS but that is really beyond the scope of this book. Generally, you would include a form for your users, possibly on the login page, such as this:

```
<p>Enter your font choice:
<select name="font">
<option value="Verdana">Verdana</option>
<option value="Arial">Arial</option>
<option value="Times New Roman">Times New Roman</option>
</select>
</p>
<p>Enter your font size:
<select name="size">
<option value="1">1</option>
<option value="2">2</option>
<option value="3">3</option>
<option value="4">4</option>
</select>
</p>
<select name="menu">
<option value="black">Black</option>
<option value="red">Red</option>
<option value="green">Green</option>
<option value="purple">Purple</option>
</select>
</p>
```

If you didn't want to use CSS, you could store the variables with your session variables. You would add something like this to your `movie1.php` script, or whatever script is processing your font information:

```
$_SESSION['font']=$_POST['font'];
$_SESSION['size']=$_POST['size'];
$_SESSION['color']=$_POST['color'];
```

Then, every time you had text, you would echo in your session variable's value, like this:

```
echo "<font face='";
echo $_SESSION['font'];
echo "' size='";
echo $_SESSION['size'];
echo "' color='";
echo $_SESSION['color'];
echo "'>";
```

As you can see, this would be quite tedious to type everywhere you had text, so perhaps you would be better off putting this information in an include file, or using CSS.

5. In the program you created in Step 4, allow your users the option of saving the information for the next time they visit, and if they choose "yes," save the information in a cookie.

A: You would add a line like this to the end of your font preference form, wherever you've stored it:

```
Do you want to save these preferences for the next time you log in?
<input type="checkbox" name="pref" value="y">
```

Then at the very beginning of your `movie1.php` script (or again, wherever your script is that is processing the form variables) you would add a statement that looks something like this:

```
if ($_POST['pref']=='y') {
    setcookie('font', '$_POST['font'], time()+60);
    setcookie('size', '$_POST['size'], time()+60);
    setcookie('color', '$_POST['color'], time ()+60);
}
```

Then instead of accessing those variables through the session, you would access them through the cookie like this:

```
echo $_COOKIE['font'];
```

6. Using functions, write a program that keeps track of how many times a visitor has loaded the page.

A: Alter the following lines in your `moviesite.php` file:

```
//list the movies
    echo "<table>";


    $numlist = 1;
    while ($numlist <= $_POST["num"]) {
        echo "<tr>";
        echo "<td>";
        echo pos($favmovies);
        echo "</td">;
        next($favmovies);
        $numlist = $numlist + 1;
        echo "</tr>";
        }

    echo "</table>";
```

Chapter 3

1. Create a PHP program that prints the lead actor and director for each movie in the database.

A: Your program should look something like this:

```
<?php
//connect to MySQL
$connect = mysql_connect("localhost", "root", "mysqlpass") or
```

```
            die ("Hey loser, check your server connection.");

//make sure we're using the right database
mysql_select_db ("wiley");

//create function to get lead actor
function get_leadactor($lead_actor) {
global $actorname;
    $query2="SELECT people_fullname
        FROM people
        where people.people_id = $lead_actor";
        $results=mysql_query($query2)
            or die(mysql_error());
        $rows=mysql_fetch_array($results);
        extract ($rows);
        $actorname=$people_fullname;
}

//create a function to get director
function get_director($director) {
global $directorname;
    $query2="SELECT people_fullname
        FROM people
        where people.people_id = '$director'";
        $results=mysql_query($query2)
            or die(mysql_error());
        $rows=mysql_fetch_array($results);
        extract($rows);
        $directorname = $people_fullname;
}

//add a header row
echo "<table border='1'>\n";
echo "<tr>\n";
echo "<td><strong>Movie Name</strong></td>";
echo "<td><strong>Lead Actor</strong></td>";
echo "<td><strong>Director</strong></td>";
echo "</tr>";

//get the movies
$query="SELECT * FROM movie";
$results=mysql_query($query)
    or die(mysql_error());

while ($rows=mysql_fetch_assoc($results)) {
extract ($rows);

//call our functions to get specific info
get_leadactor($movie_leadactor);
get_director($movie_director);

//build the table
echo "<tr>\n";
    echo "<td>\n";
```

```
        echo $movie_name;
        echo "</td>\n";
        echo "<td>";
        echo $actorname;
        echo "</td>\n";
        echo "<td>\n";
        echo $directorname;
        echo "</td>\n";
echo "</tr>\n";
}
echo "</table>\n";
?>
```

2. Pick only comedies from the movie table, and show the movie name and year it was produced. Sort the list alphabetically.

A: Your code should look something like this:

```
<?php
//connect to MySQL
$connect = mysql_connect("localhost", "root", "mysqlpass") or
        die ("Hey loser, check your server connection.");

//make sure we're using the right database
mysql_select_db ("wiley");

$query="SELECT movie_name, movie_year
        FROM movie
        WHERE movie_type = 5
        ORDER BY movie_name";
$results=mysql_query($query)
        or die(mysql_error());
echo "<table>\n";
while ($rows=mysql_fetch_assoc($results)) {
echo "<tr>\n";
        foreach($rows as $value) {
        echo "<td>\n";
        echo $value;
        echo "</td>\n";
        }
echo "</tr><br>\n";
}
echo "</table>\n";
?>
```

3. Show each movie in the database on its own page, and give the user links in a "page 1, page 2 . . . " type navigation system.

A: Although you could do this many ways, a simple way is to manipulate the LIMIT clause in your SELECT statement as we have done through the URL here:

```
<?php
//connect to MySQL
$connect = mysql_connect("localhost", "root", "mysqlpass") or
```

```
        die ("Hey loser, check your server connection.");

    //make sure we're using the right database
    mysql_select_db ("wiley");

    //get our starting point for the query through the URL variable "offset"
    $offset=$_REQUEST['offset'];
    $query="SELECT movie_name, movie_year
        FROM movie
        ORDER BY movie_name
        LIMIT $offset,1";
    $results=mysql_query($query)
        or die(mysql_error());
    echo "<table>\n";
    while ($rows=mysql_fetch_assoc($results)) {
    echo "<tr>\n";
        foreach($rows as $value) {
        echo "<td>\n";
        echo $value;
        echo "</td>\n";
        }
    echo "</tr><br>\n";
    }
    echo "</table>\n";
    echo "<a href='page.php?offset=0'>Page 1</a><br>";
    echo "<a href='page.php?offset=1'>Page 2</a><br>";
    echo "<a href='page.php?offset=2'>Page 3</a><br>";
    ?>
```

Chapter 8

In Chapter 8 you were shown three short snippets of code and asked to spot the errors and figure out how to fix them. Then you were asked to create a little error-catching script to catch the errors.

1.

```
<?
$query = "select * from table_name where name = '" . $_POST['name'] . "';"
$result = mysql_query($result) or die(mysql_error());
?>
```

2.

```
<?
if ($_POST['first_name'] = "Jethro")
{
echo "Your name is " . $_POST['first_name'];
}
?>
```

3.

```
<?
$full_name = $_POST['mrmiss'] ". " $_POST['first_name'] " " $_POST['last_name'];
?>
```

A1. Parse error from lack of semicolon at the end of the statement; the semicolon there is for the SQL statement.

A2. You always need to check equality with double equals (= =), not single equals (=). Single equals is for setting a variable equal to a value.

A3. This is missing concatenation operators between the variables and the strings.

Chapter 14

❑ **Allow for options.** You may have noticed that we didn't let our customers pick the size of their T-shirt or size and color of the Superhero Body Suit. Alter the codes to allow for these options.

A: First, you need to alter your database tables to add size and color fields to enable the users to give you input. You should add these fields to your product and shopping cart-related tables. Your shopping cart should show these two options as extra columns.

❑ **Allow for payment.** Because of copyright issues, we weren't able to actually hook you up with Paypal or one of the other payment processors available. Decide how you want to accept payment, and then alter the code accordingly.

A: Again you need to alter your tables to add payment information. If your customer is paying with a credit card, you need to make sure the form is being submitted to you via SSL. You need a field for type of credit card, such as Visa, MasterCard, or Discover; you also need a field for expiration date. These fields must to be added in the main order information, as this information will be unique to each order.

If you are hooking up directly for instant payment processing through Verisign or another online merchant, you need to check with them for specific instructions on coding your shopping cart to match with their needs.

❑ **Allow for tax.** Many states require that you charge sales tax on the orders shipped to the state where you have a physical presence, and some states require sales tax on all online orders. Set your code to check for customers in your own state and add the appropriate sales tax to those orders only.

A: Because we allowed for a sales tax field already in the main order table, this requires a simple `if` statement in the final step of the order, where everything is processed. If the customer is having his or her order shipped within your state, then take whatever your tax rate is, multiply that by the customer's subtotal, and insert that number in the tax field when you're inserting all the other information.

❑ **Check for mistakes.** We have not included any mechanism to check for required fields, or for mismatched types (such as a bogus e-mail address). Add these checks in your code.

A: To check for weird characters and improperly formatted text, you should include statements that fix these potential problems. You can find such statements in Chapter 7 under validating user data.

❑ **Allow for registering, login, and order tracking.** Some customers like to check the status of their orders.

A: We discussed login and user authentication in Chapter 11. You apply these same principles here, and it is simply a matter of issuing a SELECT statement based on customer number and then displaying the results in a simple table. The only other change you should make is to add a field to the ordermain table that stores order status, such as "Shipped," "Cancelled," "Received," and so forth so customers can tell where in the order fulfillment process their order lies.

Chapter 15

❑ Add code to admin.php to prevent unauthorized users from loading the page. Redirect them back to index.php.

A: This block of code should go at the top of admin.php:

```php
<?php
include "http.php";
session_start();
if ($_SESSION['access_lvl'] < 3) redirect('index.php');
?>
```

❑ Create a regular expression that recognizes an e-mail address in a post and turns it into a link.

A: This is not the only answer but it gets the job done:

```
/[\w\-]+(\.[\w\-]+)*@[\w\-]+(\.[\w\-]+)+/
```

❑ Add a bit of code to the pagination function to allow the user to go to the first page or last page. For example, if there are 14 pages, and the user is on page 8, and the range is 7, it should look something like this:

```
<PREV [1] .. [5] [6] [7] 8 [9] [10] [11] .. [14] NEXT >
```

A: Replace the appropriate lines of code with the following code snippets:

```
if ($lrange > 1) {
    $pagelinks .= "<a class='pagenumlink' href='" . $currpage .
"&page=1'>[1]</a>..";
    } else {
    $pagelinks .= "  ";
    }

    if ($rrange < $numofpages) {
    $pagelinks .= "..<a class='pagenumlink' href='" . $currpage . "&page=".
$numofpages ."'>" . $numofpages . "</a>";
    } else {
    $pagelinks .= "  ";
    }
```

PHP Quick Reference

In this appendix, we have listed some quick reference notes for your use. Consider the information in this appendix to be your "cheat sheet." These topics are covered in depth in Chapter 2.

PHP Syntax

The basic PHP syntax is as follows:

```php
<?php
// enter lines of code, make sure they end with a semicolon;
?>
```

Displaying to Browser

To display text in a browser, use the following syntax:

```php
<?php
echo "Enter text here";      //echo text
echo $variable;              //echo values
echo "<br>";                 //echo HTML text
?>
```

Setting a Value to a Variable

To set a value to a variable, use the following syntax:

```php
<?php
$varname = value;        //for numeric
$varname = "value";      //for text
?>
```

Passing Variables

There are three ways to pass variables among pages in your Web site: through a URL, through sessions, and through a form.

Through a URL

To pass a variable through a URL, use the following HTML code:

```
<a href="http://www.localhost.com/index.php?varname=value">
```

Through Sessions

To pass a variable through a session, use the following PHP code:

```
<?php      //this must be the first line of the script, before HTML code
session_start()      //starts the session
$_SESSION['varname']=value      //sets values for the entire session
$_SESSION['varname2']=value
?>

<?php //this must be the first few lines of every page accessing
      session variables
session_start()
?>
```

Through a Form

A form must reference the PHP script that will parse the variables:

```
<?php
$_POST['varname']      //this is how you will access the
      values from the form
?>
```

if Statements

In order to use if statements, type the following syntax:

```
<?php if (this is true) execute this command ?>
```

or

```
<?php
if (this is true) {
execute command 1;
execute command 2;
```

```
execute command 3;
}
?>
```

else Statements

In order to use else statements, type the following syntax:

```
<?php
if (this is true) execute this command;
else execute this command
?>
```

or

```
else {
execute command 1;
execute command 2;
execute command 3;
}
?>
```

Nested if Statements

You can use nested if statements by using the following syntax:

```
<?php
if (this is true) {      //remember to use == for equals
    if (this is true) execute this command;
    if (this is true) execute this command;
    else execute this command;
}
?>
```

Including a File

To include a file, use the following syntax:

```
<?php include "header.php" ?>
```

Using Functions

Functions can be created and called using the following syntax:

```
<?php
function funcname()      //defines the function
```

```
{
    line of php code;
    line of php code;
    line of php code;
}
funcname()     //calls the function to execute
?>
```

Arrays

You can set the values for an array in one of two ways:

```
<?php
$name = array("firstname"=>"Albert", "lastname"=>"Einstein", "age"="124");

echo $name["firstname"];

?>
```

or

```
<?php
$name["firstname"] = "Albert";
$name["lastname"] = "Einstein";
$name["age"] = 124;
?>
```

If no keys are required, you can set the values for an array like this:

```
<?php
$flavor[] = "blue raspberry";
$flavor[] = "root beer";
$flavor[] = "pineapple";
?>
```

for

You can execute a block of code a specified number of times with the following `for` statement:

```
<?php
for ($n = 0; $n <= 10; $n=$n+1){
    //these lines will execute while the value 'n' is
             less than or greater than 10
    echo $n;
    echo "<br>";
}
```

foreach

You can apply the same block of code to each value in a specified array with the `foreach` statement:

```
foreach ($arrayvalue, as $currentvalue) {
    //these lines will execute as long as there is a value in $arrayvalue
    echo $currentvalue;
    echo "<br>\n";
}
```

C

PHP Functions

In this appendix, we have listed some of the functions that will be applicable to those of you using the Apache/PHP/MySQL components. PHP has numerous other functions available to you, and a complete listing can be found in the manual at the source Web site, www.php.net.

Note that some of the functions listed here have optional parameters that can be used to further specify the function (noted in brackets in our listing). In the interest of simplicity, some of those optional parameters have not been explained here, so you are encouraged to visit the source Web site for more information.

Apache/PHP Functions

PHP uses these functions with the Apache server.

PHP Function	Description
apache_child_terminate()	Stops the Apache server from running after the PHP script has been executed.
apache_lookup_uri(filename)	Returns information about the URI in filename as a class.
apache_note(note_name [, note_value])	Returns or sets values in the Apache notes tables as strings.
apache_request_headers()	Returns all HTTP headers as arrays.
apache_response_headers()	Returns all Apache response headers as arrays.
apache_setenv(variable, value[, bool])	Sets an Apache subprocess environment variable.

Table continued on following page

PHP Function	Description
`ascii2ebcdic(string)`	Converts ASCII code to EBCDIC, opposite of ebcdic2ascii.
`ebcdic2ascii(string)`	Converts EBCDIC to ASCII code, opposite of ascii2ebcdic.
`getallheaders()`	Returns all HTTP request headers as arrays.
`virtual(filename)`	Performs an Apache subrequest, returns an integer.

Array Functions

You can perform these functions on arrays of information.

Function	Description
`array([...])`	Depending on the parameters, this creates an array of values.
`array_change_key_case(array[, case])`	Converts the keys in the named array to either all uppercase or all lowercase.
`array_chunk(array, size[, keep_keys])`	Splits the array into chunks based on the named parameters.
`array_combine(keys, values)`	Combines two arrays with equal number of keys and values.
`array_count_values(array)`	Counts the number of times each value appears, and returns results in array format.
`array_diff_assoc(arrays)`	Finds the values from the first array that do not appear in subsequent arrays, but unlike `array_diff`, this takes key values into account.
`array_diff(arrays)`	Opposite of `array_intersect`, finds the values from the first array that do not appear in subsequent arrays, and returns results in array format.
`array_fill(array, number, value)`	Fills an array with named value, a named number of times.
`array_filter(array[, criteria])`	Returns only array values that fit the named criteria.
`array_flip(array)`	Flips the array values and keys and returns results in array format.
`array_intersect_assoc(arrays)`	Finds the values from the first array that do not appear in subsequent arrays, but unlike `array_intersect`, this takes key values into account.

Function	Description
array_intersect(arrays)	Opposite of array_diff, finds the values from the first array that appear in subsequent arrays, and returns results in array format.
array_key_exists(array, search)	Verifies whether or not a key exists for an array.
array_keys(array[, search_value])	Will find either all the keys in the named array, or those keys containing the search_value specified, and returns results in an array format.
array_map(criteria, array)	Applies a criterion to every element of the array.
array_merge(arrays)	Merges named arrays together and returns results in an array format. If two arrays have the same string keys, the later array will overwrite an earlier key, and if two arrays have the same numeric keys, the array will be appended instead of overwritten.
array_merge_recursive(arrays)	Similar to the array_merge function, but the values of the arrays are appended.
array_multisort(array[, mixed])	Sorts either a complex multidimensional array or several arrays at one time.
array_pad(array, pad_size, pad_value)	Copies the existing array and pads the named size and value, returns value in array format.
array_pop(array)	Similar to array_shift, except this deletes the last value of an array and returns what was deleted.
array_push(array, variables)	Similar to array_unshift, except this adds the named values to the end of the array and returns the updated number of values in the array.
array_rand(array [, number])	Chooses a random value from the named array and if "number" is specified, chooses "number" of random values from the named array. The random value that was chosen is returned (or if more than one value is chosen, results are returned in array format).
array_reduce(array, function)	Reduces the array to a single function based on the named parameters.
array_reverse(array)	Reverses the order of the values in the array, and results are returned in array format.
array_search(exp, array)	Searches the array for the named expression and returns the key if it exists.
array_shift(array)	Similar to array_pop, except this deletes the first value of an array and returns what was deleted. Opposite of array_unshift.

Table continued on following page

Function	Description
`array_slice(array, offset[, length])`	Based on the named offset, this will create a sub-array from the original array. New array that is returned will also be `length` (if named).
`array_splice(array, offset[, length, new_values])`	Based on the named offset, this will remove a section of the named array (and replace it with new values if they are named).
`array_sum(array)`	Calculates the sum of the values in the named array.
`array_unique(array)`	Deletes any duplicate values in array, and returns new array.
`array_unshift(array, variables)`	Similar to `array_push`, except this adds the named values to the beginning of an array and returns the number of updated values in the array. Opposite of `array_shift`.
`array_values(array)`	Returns an array with the values in the named array.
`array_walk(array, function [,parameter])`	Applies the named function (based on named parameters) to every value in the array.
`arsort(array)`	Sorts the array in descending order (while maintaining the key/value relationship).
`asort(array)`	Sorts the array in ascending order (while maintaining the key/value relationship).
`compact(variables)`	Merges the variables named into one array, returns results in array format.
`count(array)`	Equal to `sizeof`, this counts the number of values in the named array and returns the results in an integer format.
`current(array)`	Displays the values in the named array.
`each(array)`	Creates an array with the key and value of the current element of the named array, and returns results in array format.
`end(array)`	Sets the last value as the current value.
`extract(array[, type, prefix])`	Takes the named array and imports values into the symbol table. The `type` option directs server what to do if there is a conflict, and `prefix` adds a prefix to variable names.
`in_array(value, array)`	Lets you know whether or not a specified value exists in the array.

Function	Description
key(array)	Returns the key for the current value in the array.
krsort(array)	Sorts the keys in the array in reverse order and maintains the key/value relationship.
ksort(array)	Sorts the keys in the array and maintains the key/value relationship.
list(variables)	Lists the named variables.
natsort(array)	Uses "natural ordering" to sort alphanumeric strings (case-sensitive).
natcasesort(array)	Uses "natural ordering" to sort alphanumeric strings (case-insensitive).
next(array)	The opposite of prev, returns the value of the "next" element from the current element and returns false if the current element is the last element in the array.
pos(array)	Returns the value of the current element.
prev(array)	The opposite of next, returns the value of the element "before" the current element, and returns false if the current element is the first element in the array.
range(low, high)	Creates a new array of integers between the named parameters, and returns results in an array format.
reset(array)	Sets the current element as the first element in the array, and returns its value.
rsort(array)	The opposite of sort, this sorts the array in descending order.
shuffle(array)	Shuffles the array in random order.
sizeof(array)	Equal to count, returns the number of values in the array.
sort(array)	The opposite of rsort, this sorts the array in ascending order.
uasort(array, function)	Using the named function, this sorts the array accordingly and maintains the key/value relationship.
uksort(array, function)	Using the named function, this sorts the array by key.
usort(array, function)	Using the named function, this sorts the array by value.

Date/Time/Calendar Functions

The following are helpful functions built into PHP that you can use to work with dates, times, and calendar settings. Please note that if you have installed PHP on a Linux system, you will need to compile PHP with `--enable-calendar`.

Function	Description
`cal_days_in_month(calendar, month, year)`	Returns the number of days in the named month.
`cal_from_jd(julian_day, calendar)`	Converts a Julian Day Count into a date of a specified calendar.
`cal_info([calendar])`	Returns information about the named calendar.
`cal_to_jd(calendar, month, day, year)`	Converts a specified calendar date into a Julian Day Count.
`checkdate(month, day, year)`	Validates the named date and returns `true` or `false`.
`date(format [, timestamp])`	Returns the date (and time if named) of the local server based on named format. See next table for common formatting guidelines.
`easter_date([year])`	Gives the UNIX timestamp for midnight on Easter of the current year, or named year if present.
`easter_days([year])`	Calculates the number of days between March 21 and Easter of the current year, or named year if present.
`frenchtojd(french)`	Converts from French Republican calendar to Julian Day Count.
`getdate(timestamp)`	Creates an array with the named date/timestamps.
`gettimeofday`	Creates an array with the current time.
`gmdate(format[,timestamp])`	Formats a GMT date and time based on named parameters. See next table for common formatting guidelines.
`gmmktime([hour, minute, second, month, day, year, is_dst])`	Gives the UNIX timestamp for GMT time/day based on named parameters, or current time/day if not named.
`gmstrftime(format, timestamp)`	Formats a GMT/CUT date/time based on geography. See next table for common formatting guidelines.
`gregoriantojd(gregorian)`	Converts from Gregorian calendar to Julian Day Count.

Function	Description
`jddayofweek(julianday, mode)`	Gives day of week of Julian Day Count, based on format named in mode.
`jdmonthname(julianday, mode)`	Gives month of Julian Day Count, based on format named in mode.
`jdtofrench(julianday)`	Converts from Julian Day Count to French Republican calendar.
`jdtogregorian(julianday)`	Converts from Julian Day Count to Gregorian calendar.
`jdtojewish(julianday)`	Converts from Julian Day Count to Jewish calendar.
`jdtounix(julianday)`	Converts from Julian Day Count to UNIX timestamp.
`jewishtojd(jewish)`	Converts from Jewish calendar to Julian Day Count.
`juliantojd(julian)`	Converts from Julian calendar to Julian Day Count.
`localtime([timestamp, is_associative])`	Finds and returns local time in array format.
`microtime()`	Calculates and returns seconds and microseconds since 00:00:00 January 1, 1970.
`mktime([hour, minute, second, month, day, year])`	Gives the UNIX timestamp for time/day based on named parameters, or current time/day if not named.
`strftime(format [,timestamp])`	Based on format and current location, this will format the local time and date. See next table for common formatting guidelines.
`strtotime(time[, now])`	Converts a time/date format in common English into a UNIX timestamp.
`time()`	Gives current UNIX timestamp.
`unixtojd(timestamp)`	Converts from UNIX timestamp to Julian Day Count.

Dates can be formatted with the following formatting codes (in conjunction with `date()`):

Format Character	Description	What Is Returned
a	Lowercase ante meridiem and post meridiem.	am, pm
A	Uppercase ante meridiem and post meridiem.	AM, PM
B	Swatch Internet time.	000 through 999

Table continued on following page

Format Character	Description	What Is Returned
d	Day of the month in 2 digits with leading zeros.	01 to 31
D	Day of the week in text, abbreviated to three letters.	Mon through Sun
F	Month name in text format, unabbreviated.	January through December
g	Hour in 12-hour format, without leading zeros.	1 through 12
G	Hour in 24-hour format, without leading zeros.	0 through 23
h	Hour in 12-hour format, with leading zeros.	01 through 12
H	Hour in 24-hour format, with leading zeros.	00 through 23
i	Minutes with leading zeros.	00 to 59
I (capital "i")	Indicates if date is in daylight savings time.	1 if DST, 0 otherwise
j	Day of the month without leading zeros.	1 to 31
l (lowercase 'L')	Day of the week in text, unabbreviated.	Sunday through Saturday
L	Indicates if it's a leap year.	1 if it is a leap year, 0 otherwise
m	Month in numeric format, with leading zeros.	01 through 12
M	Month in text format, abbreviated to three letters.	Jan through Dec
n	Month in numeric format without leading zeros.	1 through 12
O	Difference to Greenwich time (GMT) in hours.	-0500
r	RFC 822 formatted date.	Mon, 25 Aug 2003 18:01:01 +0200
s	Seconds, with leading zeros.	00 through 59
S	English ordinal suffix for the day of the month, 2 characters.	st, nd, rd, or th
t	Number of days in the month.	28 through 31
T	Time zone setting of the server.	EST, MDT, and so on
U	Seconds since the Unix Epoch (January 1 1970 00:00:00 GMT).	
w	Day of the week in numeric format.	0 (for Sunday) through 6 (for Saturday)
W	ISO-8601 week number of year, weeks . starting on Monday	1–52

Format Character	Description	What Is Returned
Y	Year in numeric format in 4 digits.	2000, 2001, and so on
y	Year in numeric format in 2 digits.	00, 01, 02, and so on
z	Day of the year in numeric format.	0 through 366
Z	Time zone offset in seconds. The offset for time zones west of UTC is always negative, and for those east of UTC is always positive.	-43200 through 43200

Class/Object/Function Handling Functions

The functions in the table that follows are used when referencing and working with classes, objects, and custom functions in your PHP code.

Function	Description
call_user_func(function_name [, parameters])	Calls the named user-defined function.
call_user_func_array(function_name [, parameters])	Calls the named user-defined function based on the array of parameters.
call_user_method(method, object [, parameters])	Calls the user method from the named object.
call_user_method_array(method, object[, parameters])	Calls the user method with the array of named parameters.
class_exists(class_name)	Verifies whether or not the class has been defined.
create_function (arguments, code)	Creates a function based on the parameters and returns a unique name for the function.
func_get_arg(argument_num)	Returns an item from the argument list.
func_get_args()	Gets complete argument list.
func_num_args()	Returns the number of arguments in the argument list.
function_exists(function_name)	Verifies whether or not a function has been defined.
get_class(object_name)	Returns the name of the specified object's class.
get_class_methods(class_name)	Returns the methods for specified class, in an array format.

Table continued on following page

Function	Description
get_class_vars(class_name)	Returns the properties for the specified class, in an array format.
get_declared_classes()	Returns all the classes that have been defined, in an array format.
get_defined_functions()	Returns all the functions that have been defined, in an array format.
get_object_vars(object_name)	Returns the properties for the specified object, in an array format.
get_parent_class(object_name)	Returns the name of the specified object's parent class.
is_subclass_of(object_name, superclass)	Verifies whether or not object is a part of a subclass of the named superclass.
method_exists(object_name, method_name)	Verifies whether or not method has been defined.
register_shutdown_function (function)	Sets up named function to be executed when script has been processed.
register_tick_function(function)	Registers a function for execution upon every tick.
unregister_tick_function(function) register_tick_function.	Unregisters a function previously registered using

Directory and File Functions

These functions can modify your directory settings and allow you to work with files through your PHP script.

Function	Description
basename(path)	Returns the filename listed in named path.
chdir(directory)	Makes the named directory the current one.
chgrp(filename, group)	Assigns the named file to the named group.
chroot(directory)	Makes the named directory the root directory.
chmod(filename, mode)	Changes the mode of the named file.
chown(filename, owner)	Changes the owner of the named file.
clearstatcache()	Clears the file stat cache.
closedir(directory)	Closes the named directory.

Function	Description
copy(source, destination)	Copies the named source file to the named destination.
dir(directory)	Returns an object with the value of the named directory.
dirname(path)	Returns the directory listed in the named path.
disk_free_space(directory)	Equal to disk_free_space, returns the amount of free space in the named directory.
disk_total_space(directory)	Returns the amount of space in the named directory.
diskfreespace(directory)	Equal to disk_free_space, returns the amount of free space in the named directory.
getcwd()	Returns the name of the current directory.
fclosefile(file_pointer)	Closes the named file.
feof(file_pointer)	Verifies whether or not the end of file has been reached for the named file.
fflush(file_pointer)	Flushes the output to a file.
fgetc(file_pointer)	Returns the next character listed in the named file
fgetcsv(file_pointer, length[, delimiter])	Returns the next line in the named file.
fgets(file_pointer, length)	Returns a line of up to length -1 in the named file.
fegtss(file_pointer, length[, allowable_tags])	Returns a line of up to length -1in the named file, while removing all tags except those specified.
file(filename[, usepath])	Returns an entire file in an array format, with each line representing a new value in the array.
file_get_contents(filename)	Reads the entire file contents into a string.
file_exists(filename)	Verifies whether or not the named file exists.
fileatime(filename)	Returns the last time the named file was accessed.
filectime(filename)	Returns the last time the named file was changed (in UNIX timestamp format).
filegroup(filename)	Returns the owner of the named file's group.
fileinode(filename)	Returns the named file's inode number.
filemtime(filename)	Returns the last time the named file was modified.
fileowner(filename)	Returns the owner of the named file.

Table continued on following page

Function	Description
fileperms(filename)	Returns the permissions associated with the named file.
filesize(filename)	Returns the size of the named file.
filetype(filename)	Returns the type of the named file.
flock(file_pointer, operation[, wouldblock])	Locks or unlocks the named file.
fnmatch(pattern, exp)	Searches for a filename that matches the named parameters.
fopen(filename, mode[, usepath])	Opens the named file.
fpassthru(file_pointer)	Returns all remaining data in the named file.
fputs(file_pointer, string[, length])	Equal to fwrite, writes the named string to the named file.
fread(file_pointer, length)	Reads the named file up to the named length.
fscanf(handle, format[, var1, var2...])	Parses input based on the named format from the named file.
fseek(file_pointer, offset[, start])	Moves the file pointer in the named file by named offset spaces from start.
fstat(file_pointer)	Returns information about named file.
ftell(file_pointer)	Returns the position of the file pointer in the named file.
ftruncate(file_pointer, size)	Truncates the named file to the named size.
fwrite(file_pointer, strength[, length])	Equal to fputs, writes the named string to the named file.
glob(string)	Finds pathnames that match the named string.
is_dir(filename)	Verifies whether or not the named file is a directory.
is_executable(filename)	Verifies whether or not the named file is an executable.
is_file(filename)	Verifies whether or not the named file is a file.
is_link(filename)	Verifies whether or not the named file is a link.
is_readable(filename)	Verifies whether or not the named file is readable.
is_writeable(filename)	Verifies whether or not the named file is writeable.
is_uploaded_file(filename)	Verifies whether or not the named file has been uploaded using HTTP POST.
link(target, link)	Creates a new link.

Function	Description
`linkinfo(path)`	Returns all information about the named link.
`lstat(filename)`	Returns information about named file.
`mkdir(pathname, mode)`	Creates a directory based on specified pathname and mode.
`move_uploaded_file(filename, destination)`	Moves the named file to a different directory.
`opendir(path)`	Opens the named directory.
`parse_ini_file(filename)`	Parses the named configuration file.
`pathinfo(path)`	Returns information about the named path.
`pclose(file_pointer)`	Closes the named filepointer to a pipe.
`popen(command, mode)`	Opens a pipe with the named command.
`readdir(directory)`	Reads the named directory and returns the next entry.
`readfile(filename[, usepath])`	Reads the named file.
`readlink(path)`	Reads the named link and returns the target.
`realpath(path)`	Returns the absolute path.
`rename(name, newname)`	Renames the named file.
`rewind(file_pointer)`	Moves the pointer to the beginning of the file stream.
`rewinddir(directory)`	Moves the pointer to the beginning of the directory and resets the directory stream.
`rmdir(directory)`	Removes the named directory.
`scandir(directory[, sort_order])`	Lists the files and directories in the named path.
`set_file_buffer(file_pointer, buffer)`	Sets the file buffer for named file.
`stat(filename)`	Returns information about the named file.
`symlink(target, link)`	Creates a symbolic link.
`tempnam(directory, prefix)`	Creates a temporary file in the named directory.
`tmpfile()`	Creates a temporary file.
`touch(filename[, time])`	Sets the time the named file is modified.
`umask(mask)`	Modifies the current `umask`.
`unlink(filename)`	Deletes the named file.

Error Handling and Logging Functions

These functions can help you view and use errors to debug programs or alert you to potential problems in your scripts.

Function	Description
debug_backtrace()	Generates a backtrace and returns the information in an array format.
debug_print_backtrace()	Displays a generated backtrace.
error_log(message, message_type[, dest, extra_headers])	Adds an error message.
error_reporting([level])	Determines which PHP errors will be displayed.
restore_error_handler()	Restores error handler functions.
set_error_handler(error_handler)	Sets an error handler function.
trigger_error(error_message[, error_type])	Same as user_error, displays a user level error message.
user_error(error_message[, error_type])	Same as trigger_error, displays a user level error message.

HTTP Functions

These functions work with the HTTP protocol.

Function	Description
header(string)	Outputs the named HTTP header.
header_sent()	Verifies whether or not HTTP headers have been sent.
setcookie(name, [value, expiration, path, domain, secure])	Sends a cookie to the user based on the named parameters.

Image Functions

The following PHP functions enable you to manipulate and create images directly from your PHP code. Please note that you may need to have the GD library, which enables you to create dynamic images, installed to enable some of these functions. You can download GD from www.boutell.com/gd/.

Function	Description
exif_imagetype(filename)	Returns the type of named image file.
exif_read_data(filename)	Reads the EXIF headers in a JPEG or TIFF image, useful for reading digital images.
exif_thumbnail(filename[, width, height, type])	Reads the embedded thumbnail image of a JPEG or TIFF image.
gd_info()	Returns information about the currently installed GD library.
getimagesize(filename, [image_info])	Returns the size of the named file.
image_type_to_mime_type(type)	Gets the MIME-type for the named image type.
image2wbmp(image[, filename])	Outputs the image directly to a browser.
imagealphablending(image, blendmode)	Sets the blending mode for the named image.
imageantialias(image, on_off)	Toggles antialiasing on and off for the named image.
imagearc(name, cx, cy, width, height, start, end, col)	Draws a partial ellipse based on named parameters.
imagechar(name, font, x, y, c, col)	Draws a character horizontally based on named parameters.
imagecharup(name, font, x, y, c, col)	Draws a character vertically based on named parameters.
imagecolorallocate(name, red, green, blue)	Allocates a color for the named image and returns an identifier.
imagecolorallocatealpha(name, red, green, blue, transparent)	Similar to imagecolorallocate except allows the color to display at a certain level of transparency.
imagecolorat(name, x, y)	Indicates the color index of the pixel at the named coordinates.
imagecolorclosest(name, red, green, blue)	Returns the closest color in the palette of the named image.
imagecolorclosestalpha(name, red, green, blue, alpha)	Similar to imagecolorclosest, except takes into account the alpha (transparency) level.
imagecolorclosesthwb(name, red, green, blue)	Similar to imagecolorclosest, except also looks at hue, whiteness, and blackness.
imagecolordeallocate(name, red, green, blue)	Opposite of imagecolorallocate, deallocates the color for the named image.
imagecolorexact(name, red, green, blue)	Returns the exact color in the palette of the named image.

Table continued on following page

Function	Description
`imagecolorexactalpha(name, red, green, blue, alpha)`	Similar to `imagecolorexact`, except takes into account the alpha level.
`imagecolorresolve(name, red, green, blue)`	Returns either the index of the exact color or the closest color available in the palette of the named image.
`imagecolorresolvealpha(name, red, green, blue, alpha)`	Similar to `imagecolorresolve`, except takes into account the alpha level.
`imagecolorset(name, index, red, green, blue)`	Sets the color for the palette of the named file.
`imagecolorsforindex(name, index)`	Returns value for red, blue, and green for the specified index.
`imagecolorstotal(name)`	Returns the number of available colors in the palette of the named image.
`imagecolortransparent(name[, color])`	Sets named color as transparent in the named image.
`imagecopy(dest_name, source_name, dest_x, dest_y, source_x, source_y, source_width, source_height)`	Copies an image based on named parameters.
`imagecopymerge(dest_name, source_name, dest_x, dest_y, source_x, source_y, source_width, source_height, pct)`	Similar to `imagecopy`, but copies an image based on named parameters including percent (when set to 100, acts identically to `imagecopy`).
`imagecopymergegray(dest_name, source_name, dest_x, dest_y, source_x, source_y, source_width, source_height, pct)`	Similar to `imagecopymerge`, except copies image in grayscale.
`imagecopyresampled(dest_name, source_name, dest_x, dest_y, source_x, source_y, dest_width, dest_height, source_width, source_height)`	Copies and resizes a resampled image based on the named parameters.
`imagecopyresized(dest_name, source_name, dest_x, dest_y, source_x, source_y, dest_width, dest_height, source_width, source_height)`	Copies and resizes an image based on named parameters.
`imagecreate(width, height)`	Creates a new image based on named width and height.
`imagecreatefromgd2(name)`	Creates a new image from a GD file or URL.
`imagecreatefromgd2part(name, x, y, width, height)`	Creates a new image from a part of a GD file or URL.

Function	Description
imagecreatefromgd(name)	Creates a new image from a GD file or URL.
imagecreatefromgif(name)	Creates a new image from the named GIF file.
imagecreatefromjpeg(name)	Creates a new image from the named JPEG or JPG file.
imagecreatefrompng(name)	Creates a new image from the named PNG file.
imagecreatefromstring(name)	Creates a new image from an image stream in the named string.
imagecreatefromwbmp(name)	Creates a new image from named file or URL.
imagecreatefromxbm(name)	Creates a new image from named file or URL.
imagecreatefromxpm(name)	Creates a new image from named file or URL.
imagecreatetruecolor(x_size, y_size)	Returns an image identifier based on a black image according to the named parameters.
imagedashedline(name, x1, y1, x2, y2, color)	Draws a dashed line based on named parameters. Similar to imageline.
imagedestroy(name)	Deletes the named image.
imageellipse(name, cx, cy, width, height, color)	Draws an ellipse based on the named parameters.
imagefill(name, x, y, color)	Fills the entire image with one color based on the named parameters.
imagefilledarc(name, cx, cy, width, height, start, end, color, style)	Draws a filled partial ellipse based on the named parameters.
imagefilledellipse(name, cx, cy, width, height, color)	Draws a filled ellipse based on the named parameters.
imagefilledpolygon(name, points, num_of_points, color)	Draws a filled polygon based on the named parameters.
imagefilledrectangle(name, x1, y1, x2, y2, color)	Draws a filled rectangle based on the named parameters.
imagefilltoborder(name, x, y, border_color, color)	Fills the entire image with a color and outlines it with a border color, based on named parameters.
imagefontheight(font)	Returns the height of the named font in pixels.
imagefontwidth(font)	Returns the width of the named font in pixels.
imagegammacorrect(name, inputgamma, outputgamma)	Corrects the gamma levels in a GD image.

Table continued on following page

Function	Description
`imagegd2(name[, filename, chunk_size, type])`	Outputs the named GD file to the browser based on the named parameters.
`imagegd(name[, filename])`	Sends the named GD file to the browser.
`imagegif(name[, filename])`	Sends the named GIF image (filename) to another file or to a browser as the named image.
`imageinterlace(name[, interlace])`	Toggles whether or not interlacing is on or off for the named image.
`imagejpeg (name[, filename, quality])`	Sends the named JPEG image (filename) to another file or to a browser as the named image.
`imageline(name, x1, y1, x2, y2, color)`	Draws a solid line based on the named parameters. Similar to `imagedashedline`.
`imageloadfont(filename)`	Loads the named font.
`imagepallettecopy(destination, source)`	Copies the named color palette.
`imagepng(name[, filename])`	Sends the named PNG image (filename) to another file or to a browser as the named image.
`imagepolygon(name, points, num_of_points, color)`	Draws an empty polygon based on the named parameters.
`imagepsbbox(text, font, size, space, width, angle)`	Returns the coordinates for a text box using a PostScript font, based on named parameters.
`imagepsencodefont(encoding_file)`	Loads the named encoding vector for a PostScript font.
`imagepsextendfont(font_index, extend)`	Extends a PostScript font.
`imagepsfreefont(font_index)`	Frees the named PostScript font from memory.
`imagepsloadfont(filename)`	Loads the named PostScript font file.
`imagepsslantfont(font_index, slant)`	Slants the named PostScript font.
`imagepstext(name, text, font, size, foreground_color, background_color, x, y[, space, tightness, angle, antialias])`	Writes a text string using the named PostScript font and based on the named parameters.
`imagerectangle(name, x1, y1, x2, y2, color)`	Draws an empty rectangle based on the named parameters.
`imagerotate(name, angle, color)`	Rotates an image based on the named parameters.
`imagesavealpha(name, flag)`	Sets the flag to save with the image's alpha information.
`imagesetbrush(name, brush)`	Sets the brush for line drawing.

Function	Description
imagesetpixel(name, x, y, color)	Draws a pixel based on the named parameters.
imagesetstyle(name, style)	Sets the style for line drawing.
imagesetthickness(name, thickness)	Sets the thickness for line drawing.
imagesettile(name, tile)	Sets the tile image for fill functions.
imagestring(name, font, x, y, string, color)	Draws a horizontal string based on the named parameters.
imagestringup(name, font, x, y, string, color)	Draws a vertical string based on the named parameters.
imagesx(name)	Determines the width of the named image.
imagesy(name)	Determines the height of the named image.
imagetruecolortopallette(name, dither, colors)	Converts a true color image to a color palette based on the named parameters.
imagettfbbox(size, angle, font_filename, text)	Draws a text box using the named TrueType font and based on the named parameters.
imagettftext(name, size, angle, x, y, color, font_filename, text)	Writes a text string using the named TrueType font.
imagetypes()	Displays the image types supported by the PHP version currently being used.
iptcembed(data, filename)	Embeds International Press Telecommunications Council (IPTC) data into a JPEG file.
iptcparse(iptcblock)	Parses an IPTC block into tags.
jpeg2wbmp(jpegfilename, wbmpfilename, height, width, threshold)	Converts a JPEG file into a WBMP file.
png2wbmp(pngfilename, wbmpfilename, height, width, threshold)	Converts a PNG file into a WBMP file.
read_exif_data(filename)	Displays any EXIF headers from a JPEG file.

Mail Functions

Use these functions to send mail directly from your PHP script.

Function	Description
ezmlm_hash(addr)	Displays the hash value used by EZMLM scripts.
mail(to, subject, message[, headers])	Sends mail based on the named parameters.

Mathematical Functions

These functions allow you to perform mathematical calculations on your data while still in the PHP code.

Function	Description
abs(number)	Calculates the absolute value of a number.
acos(argument)	Calculates the arc cosine in radians.
asin(argument)	Calculates the arc sine in radians.
atan(argument)	Calculates the arc tangent in radians.
atan2(x, y)	Calculates the arc tangent of x and y.
base_convert(number, startbase, endbase)	Converts a number based on the named parameters.
bindec(binary_string)	Converts a binary string to a decimal, opposite of decbin.
ceil(number)	Rounds fractions to next highest integer.
cos(argument)	Calculates the cosine in radians.
decbin(number)	Converts a decimal to a binary string, opposite of bindec.
dechex(number)	Converts a decimal to hexadecimal, opposite of hexdec.
decoct(number)	Converts a decimal to octal, opposite of octdec.
deg2rad(number)	Converts degrees to radian, opposite of rad2deg.
exp(argument)	Calculates e to the named power.
floor(number)	Rounds fractions down to the next lowest integer.
getrandmax()	Calculates the maximum random value from the rand function.
hexdec(hex_string)	Converts hexadecimal to decimal, opposite of dechex.
lcg_value()	Calculates a pseudo random number between 0 and 1.
log(argument)	Calculates the natural log.
log10(argument)	Calculates the base 10 log.
max(num1, num2, ...)	Calculates the maximum of listed values.
min(num1, num2, ...)	Calculates the minimum of listed values.
mt_getrandmax()	Calculates the maximum random value from the mt_rand function.
mt_rand([min, max])	Generates a Mersenne Twister random value.
mt_srand(seed)	Seeds the Mersenne Twister random number generator.

Function	Description
number_format(number[, dec_places, dec_point, thousands])	Formats the number based on the named parameters.
octdec(octal_string)	Converts octal to decimal, opposite of decoct.
pi()	Returns pi.
pow(number, exp)	Calculates named number to the power of named exponent.
rad2deg(number)	Converts radians to decimal, opposite of deg2rad.
rand([min, max])	Generates a random integer based on named parameters if applicable.
round(number, [precision])	Rounds the named number to the nearest integer.
sin(argument)	Calculates the sine in radians.
sqrt(argument)	Calculates the square root.
srand(seed)	Seeds the random number generator.
tan(argument)	Calculates the tangent in radians.

Miscellaneous Functions

The table that follows lists useful functions that don't exactly fit anywhere else.

Function	Description
connection_aborted()	Verifies whether or not the client connection has been aborted.
connection_status()	Verifies the client connection status.
connection_timeout()	Verifies whether or not the script has timed out.
constant(name)	Returns the value of the named constant.
define(name, value[, case_insensitive])	Defines a constant based on the named parameters.
defined(name)	Verifies whether or not a named constant exists.
die(message)	Displays the message and ends execution of the script.
eval(string)	Evaluates the named string as PHP code.
exit()	Ends execution of the script.

Table continued on following page

Function	Description
get_browser([user_agent])	Returns information about the user's browser.
highlight_file(filename)	Displays a highlighted version of the named file.
highlight_string(str)	Displays a highlighted version of the named string.
ignore_user_abort([setting])	Allows a script to continue executing if the user aborts a connection.
iptcparse(iptcblock)	Parses the named IPTC block into an array.
leak(bytes)	Leaks the named amount of memory.
pack(format[, arg1, arg2...])	Packs the named arguments into a binary string.
show_source(filename)	Displays a highlighted version of source code of named file.
sleep(seconds)	Pauses execution of the script for named number of seconds
uniqid(prefix[, lcg])	Assigns a unique ID based on the current time and named prefix.
unpack(format, data)	Opposite of pack, this unpacks binary data into an array.
usleep(microseconds)	Pauses execution of the script for named number of microseconds.

MySQL Functions

The following table lists the PHP functions that can be used with your MySQL server for added functionality in your PHP script.

Function	Description
mysql_affected_rows([link_id])	Returns the number of rows of records affected by the previous command.
mysql_change_user(user, pass[, database, link_id])	Changes the user for the active database connection.
mysql_close([link_id])	Closes the active connection.
mysql_connect([hostname[:port] [:/path/to/socket], username, password])	Opens the connection to the server based on the named parameters. Similar to mysql_pconnect.
mysql_create_db(database [,link_id])	Creates a database.
mysql_data_seek(result_id, row_number)	Moves to the named row of the results.
mysql_db_name(result, row [,field])	Gets data for result.
mysql_db_query(database, query[, link_id])	Executes the named query on the named database and returns results.

Function	Description
mysql_drop_db(database[, link_id])	Erases the named database.
mysql_errno([link_id])	Displays the error number for the previous query.
mysql_error([link_id])	Displays the error message for the previous query.
mysql_escape_string(string)	Escapes the named string for use in a query.
mysql_fetch_array(result [, type])	Obtains the row of data based on the result from a previous query, returns result in an array format.
mysql_fetch_field(result[, field_offset])	Returns the field based on the result from a previous query.
mysql_fetch_lengths(result)	Returns the length of each field in the result from a previous query.
mysql_fetch_object(result[, type])	Obtains data based on the result from a previous query, returns result in an object format.
mysql_fetch_row(result)	Obtains the row of data based on the result from a previous query, returns result in an enumerated array.
mysql_field_flags(result, field)	Displays the field flag of the named field.
mysql_field_len(result, field)	Displays the field length of the named field.
mysql_field_name(result, field)	Displays the name of the named field.
mysql_field_seek(result, field_offset)	Moves to the named field of the results.
mysql_field_table(result, field)	Displays the table of the named field.
mysql_field_type(result, field)	Displays the type of the named field.
mysql_free_result(result)	Frees any memory still used by the result from a previous query.
mysql_get_client_info()	Returns the MySQL client information.
mysql_get_host_info([link_id])	Returns information about the server host.
mysql_get_proto_info([link_id])	Returns the protocol information.
mysql_get_server_info([link_id])	Returns information about the server.
mysql_info([link_id])	Gets information about the previous query.
mysql_insert_id([link_id])	Returns the ID value of the most recently inserted auto_increment field.
mysql_list_dbs([link_id])	Lists the databases on the MySQL server.

Table continued on following page

Function	Description
`mysql_list_fields(database, table[, link_id])`	Lists the fields in the named database and table.
`mysql_list_processes([link_id])`	Lists the processes.
`mysql_list_tables(database)`	Lists the tables in the named database.
`mysql_num_fields(result)`	Shows the number of fields in the result from a previous query.
`mysql_num_rows(result)`	Shows the number of rows in the result from a previous query.
`mysql_pconnect([hostname[:port] [:/path/to/socket], username, password])`	Opens a persistent connection to the server based on the named parameters. Similar to `mysql_connect`.
`mysql_ping([link_id])`	Pings the server connection to verify the connection is working properly.
`mysql_query(query[, link_id])`	Executes the named query.
`mysql_real_escape_string(string[, link_id])`	Escapes a string to be used in the query, and takes into account the charset of the connection.
`mysql_result(result, row[, field])`	Obtains the data located in the named field/row of the results.
`mysql_select_db(database[, link_id])`	Selects the named database and makes it current.
`mysql_stat([link_id])`	Gets current system status.
`mysql_thread_id([link_id])`	Returns current connection thread ID.
`mysql_tablename(result, index)`	Returns the table from which the result was obtained.
`mysql_unbuffered_query(query[, link_id])`	Queries the MySQL server without fetching and buffering the results.

Network Functions

The functions in the table that follows can be used to communicate with your network directly from PHP.

Function	Description
`checkdnsrr(host[, type])`	Equal to `dns_check_record`, searches for DNS records based on the named parameters.
`closelog()`	Closes connection to the system log, opposite of `openlog`.

Function	Description
debugger_off()	Turns off the PHP debugger.
debugger_on(server)	Turns on the PHP debugger and connects it to the named server.
define_syslog_variables()	Initializes syslog constants.
dns_check_record(host[, type])	Equal to checkdnsrr, searches for DNS records based on named parameters.
dns_get_mxr(host, mxhosts[, weight])	Equal to getmxrr, returns MX records based on the named host.
fsockopen([hostname, port, errno, errstr, timeout])	Opens a socket connection based on the named parameters.
gethostbyaddr(ip)	Returns the hostname based on the named IP address.
gethostbyname(host)	Returns the IP addressed based on the named host.
gethostbyname1(host)	Returns multiple IP addresses based on the named host.
getmxrr(host, mxhosts[, weight])	Equal to dns_get_mxr, returns MX records based on the named host.
getprotobyname(name)	Returns protocol number based on named protocol.
getprotobynumber(number)	Returns protocol name based on named protocol number.
getservbyname(service, protocol)	Returns a port number based on named parameters.
getservbyport(port, protocol)	Returns the service based on named parameters.
ip2long(ip)	Converts a string with an IP address into a proper address.
long2ip(proper_address)	Converts a proper address into an IP address with dotted format.
openlog(ident, option, facility)	Opens a connection to the system log, opposite of closelog
pfsockopen([hostname, port, errno, errstr, timeout])	Opens a persistent socket connection based on the named parameters.
socket_set_blocking(socket, mode)	Determines the blocking mode for the named socket.
socket_set_timeout(socket, seconds, microseconds)	Determines the socket timeout period.
syslog(priority, message)	Writes the named message to the system log.

Output Buffer Functions

The functions in the table that follows enable you to control the output buffer from PHP.

Function	Description
flush()	Flushes the output buffer.
ob_start()	Enables output buffering.
ob_get_contents()	Gets the contents of the output buffer.
ob_get_length()	Gets the length of the output buffer.
ob_end_flush()	Sends the output buffer contents and disables output buffering.
ob_end_clean()	Deletes the output buffer contents and disables output buffering.
ob_implicit_flush()	Toggles implicit flushing on and off.

PHP Configuration Information

With these functions, you can easily determine what your PHP is communicating to the server based on its setup, and alter configuration options from your PHP script.

Function	Description
assert(assertion)	Verifies whether or not an assertion is false.
assert_options(what,[value])	Returns the assert flags.
dl(library)	Loads the named extension library.
extension_loaded(name)	Verifies whether or not an extension library has been loaded.
get_cfg_var(var)	Returns the named configuration variable value.
get_current_user()	Returns the owner of the PHP script.
get_defined_constants()	Returns an array with all the defined constants and their values.
get_extension_funcs (module_name)	Returns the functions in the named module.
get_include_path()	Returns the current include_path configuration option.
get_included_files()	Returns an array containing the filenames of those included in the script with the include_once() function.

Function	Description
get_loaded_extensions()	Returns the compiled and loaded modules.
get_magic_quotes_gpc()	Returns the setting of magic_quotes_gpc.
get_magic_quotes_runtime()	Returns the setting of magic_quotes_runtime.
get_required_files()	Returns an array containing the filenames of those included in the script with the require_once() function.
getenv(var)	Returns the named environment variable value.
getlastmod()	Returns when the page was last modified.
getmygid()	Returns the group ID for the current script.
getmyinode()	Returns the inode of the script.
getmypid()	Returns the process ID for PHP.
getmyuid()	Returns the user ID for the owner of the PHP script.
getopt()	Returns array of options/argument pairs from the command line argument list.
getrusage([who])	Returns resource usage.
ini_alter(varname, newvalue)	Updates the php.ini file based on the named parameters.
ini_get_all([extension])	Returns configuration options.
ini_get(varname)	Returns the named value from the php.ini file.
ini_restore(varname)	Restores the previous value in the php.ini file.
ini_set(varname, newvalue)	Sets the named value in the php.ini file.
memory_get_usage()	Returns the amount of memory allocated to PHP.
php_ini_scanned_files()	Returns a list of parsed ini files from an additional directory.
php_logo_guid()	Returns the PHP logo GUID.
php_sapi_name()	Returns the interface between the Web server and PHP.
php_uname()	Returns information about the operating system running PHP.
phpcredits(flag)	Displays the credits for PHP.
phpinfo() configuration of PHP.	Displays information about the current environment and
phpversion()	Displays the currently running PHP version.
putenv(setting)	Sets the value of an environment variable.

Table continued on following page

Function	Description
restore_include_path()	Restores the include_path configuration option.
set_include_path(path)	Sets the include_path configuration option.
set_magic_quotes_runtime (newsetting)	Turns this feature on or off.
set_time_limit(seconds)	Sets the maximum amount of time a PHP script can run.
version_compare(string1, string2)	Compares two PHP version numbers.
zend_logo_guid()	Returns the Zend logo GUID.
zend_version()	Returns the current Zend engine.

Program Execution Functions

The functions in the table that follows allow PHP code to execute commands directly from the script.

Function	Description
escapeshellarg(arg)	Escapes a string to be used as a shell argument.
escapreshelllcmd(cmd)	Escapes shell metacharacters in the named command.
exec(command[, array, return_var])	Executes the named command and returns last line of results.
passthru(command[, return_var])	Executes the named command and returns the raw output.
system(command[, return_var])	Executes the named command and returns all output.

Spelling Functions

You can have PHP perform spell checks for you, as long as you supply a reference it can use.

Function	Description
aspell_check(link, word)	Using the named link as a reference, it will check the spelling of the named word.
aspell_check-raw(link, word)	Using the named link as a reference, it will check the spelling of the named word without changing the case or trimming the word.

Function	Description
aspell_new(master, individual)	Loads a named master dictionary and returns a link identifier.
aspell_suggest(link, word)	Using the named link as a reference, it will offer suggestions for spelling the named word, and return results in an array format.
pspell_add_to_personal(link, word)	Adds the named word to a personal dictionary.
pspell_add_to_session(link, word)	Adds the named word to a session's wordlist.
pspell_check(link, word)	Using the named link as a reference, it will check the spelling of the named word.
pspell_clear_session	Deletes a current session's wordlist.
pspell_config_create(language [, spelling, jargon, encoding])	Configures options to open a dictionary.
pspell_config_ignore(link, n)	Configures spell check so that words under *n* characters long will be ignored
pspell_config_mode(link, mode)	Changes the number of suggestions offered.
pspell_config_personal(link, file)	Sets the file that will contain a personal wordlist.
pspell_config_repl(link, file)	Sets the file that contains replacements pairs.
pspell_config_runtogether (link, flag)	Determines if run-together words are valid.
pspell_config_save_repl (link, flag)	Determines if replacement pairs should be saved with the personal wordlist.
pspell_new(language[, spelling, jargon, encoding, mode])	Loads a new dictionary with a personal wordlist.
pspell_save_wordlist(link)	Saves the personal wordlist to named link.
pspell_store_replacement(link, misspelled, correct)	Stores a replacement pair for a word.
pspell_suggest(link, word)	Suggests a list of alternatives for the named word.

Session Functions

The functions in the table that follows are useful when utilizing sessions in your PHP scripts.

Function	Description
`session_cache_limiter ([cache_limiter])`	Returns the cache limiter, or sets a new one.
`session_decode(string)`	Decodes the named session data.
`session_destroy()`	Destroys session data.
`session_encode()`	Encodes session data as a string.
`session_get_cookie_params()`	Gets information about session cookie configuration.
`session_id([id])`	Returns session ID, or sets a new one.
`session_is_registered(varname)`	Verifies whether or not named variable has been registered in current session.
`session_module_name ([module_name])`	Returns session module or sets new one.
`session_name([name])`	Returns session name or sets new one.
`session_register(name[, var1, var2...])`	Registers variables with the current session.
`session_save_path([path])`	Returns path where session data is saved, or sets a new one.
`session_set_cookie_params (expiration[, path, domain])`	Configures the session cookie based on the named parameters.
`session_set_save_handler(open, close, read, write, destroy, gc)`	Sets user-level session storage based on named parameters.
`session_start()`	Starts a new session.
`session_unregister(name)`	Unregisters session variables.
`session_unset()`	Releases all session variables.

String Functions

There are times when you need PHP to manipulate strings for you, and luckily there are many functions that help you do just that.

Function	Description
`addcslashes(string, charlist)`	Adds slashes before named characters in named string.
`addslashes(string)`	Adds slashes to quoted characters in the named strings for database queries.
`bin2hex(string)`	Converts binary data into ASCII hexadecimal format.

Function	Description
chop(string)	Deletes trailing spaces from the named string.
chr(ascii)	Returns the character based on the named ASCII code.
chunk_split(string[, length, div])	Divides named string by inserting the character named by div every length characters.
convert_cyr_string(string, from, to)	Converts named string from one Cyrillic character set to another.
count_chars(string[, mode])	Counts the number of characters in the named string.
crc32(string)	Calculates the crc32 of 32-bit lengths of string.
crypt(string[, char])	Using named 2-character parameter, this will DES-encrypt the named string.
echo(string)	Displays named string.
ereg(exp, string[, array])	Searches the named string for the named expression and stores the results in the named array.
ereg_replace(exp1, exp2, string)	Searches and replaces exp1 with exp2 in the named string.
eregi(exp, string[, array])	Searches the named string for the named expression (case-insensitive) and stores the results in the named array.
eregi_replace(exp1, exp2, string)	Searches and replaces exp1 with exp2 (case-insensitive) in the named string.
explode(separator, string[, limit])	Divides the named string using the named separator and returns results in array format, opposite of implode.
get_html_translation_table(table[, quote_styles])	Returns the named translation table.
get_meta_tags(filename[, path])	Returns meta tag information from named file.
hebrev(text[, max_chars_per_line])	Converts Hebrew text to visual text.
hebrevc(text[, max_chars_per_line])	Converts Hebrew text to visual text with newlines.
htmlentities(string[, quote_style])	Converts characters from named string into HTML entities.
htmlspecialchars(string[, quote_style])	Converts special characters from named string into HTML entities.
implode(delimiter, array_name)	Opposite of explode, this combines bits of the named array together using the named delimiter tag, equal to join.

Table continued on following page

Function	Description
join(delimiter, array_name)	Equal to implode, this combines bits of the named array together using the named delimiter tag.
levenshtein(str1, str2)	Calculates the Levenshtein distance between the two named strings.
ltrim(string)	Deletes spaces from the beginning of the named string.
md5_file(filename)	Calculates the MD5 hash of the named file.
md5(string)	Calculates the MD5 hash of the named string.
metaphone(string)	Calculates the metaphone key of the named string.
money_format(format, number)	Formats the number as a currency.
nl2br(string)	Inserts HTML code for before all line breaks in named string.
number_format(number, decimals)	Formats the number based on the named parameters.
ord(string)	Returns the ASCII code of the first character in the named string.
parse_str(string[, array])	Parses the string and stores results in named array.
print(string)	Displays the string and returns a value of 1 or 0 based on success of results.
printf(format[, arg1, arg2, ...])	Displays a formatted string based on the named parameters.
quoted_printable_decode(string)	Converts a quoted-printable string to an 8-bit string.
quotemeta(string)	Escapes meta characters in the named string.
rawurldecode(string)	Decodes the named URL-encoded string, opposite of rawurlencode.
rawurlencode(string)	URL-encodes the named string, opposite of rawurldecode.
rtrim(string)	Deletes trailing spaces from the end of the named string.
setlocale(category, locale)	For functions in the named category, this sets the locale information.
sha1_file(filename[, output])	Calculates the sha1 hash for a file.
sha1(string[, output])	Calculates the sha1 hash for a string.
similar_text(string1, string2[, percent])	Determines the similarity between two named strings.

Function	Description
soundex(string)	Determines soundex key of the named string.
split(exp, string[, limit])	Splits the named string using the named expression.
spliti(exp, string[, limit)	Splits the named string using the named expression (case-insensitive).
sprintf(format[, arg1, arg2...])	Displays the formatted string based on the named parameters.
sql_regcase(string)	Searches named string (case-insensitive) and returns a regular expression
sscanf(string, format[, var1, var2...])	Parses input from the named string based on named parameters.
str_ireplace(oldexp, newexp, string)	Similar to str_replace except it is case-insensitive.
str_pad(string, length[, pad_string, pad_type])	Pads the named string to the named length with another string.
str_repeat(string, number)	Repeats a named string a named number of times.
str_replace(oldexp, newexp, string)	Replaces one expression with another in named string.
str_rot13(string)	Performs the ROT13 encoding on the named string.
str_shuffle(string)	Randomly shuffles the string.
str_word_count(string[, format])	Counts the number of words in the string.
strcasecmp(string1, string2)	Compares two named strings, case-insensitive.
strchr(string, exp)	Locates named expression in named string.
strcmp(string1, string2)	Similar to strcasecamp, except comparison is case-sensitive.
strcoll(string1, string2)	Compares the two strings based on locale.
strcspn(string1, string2)	Returns the number of characters at the beginning of string1 that do not match string2, opposite of strspn.
strip_tags(string)	Removes HTML and PHP tags from the named string.
stripcslashes(string)	Removes C slashes from the named string.
stripslashes(string)	Removes escape slashes from the named string.
stristr(string, exp)	Finds all occurrences of a named expression in a named string (case-insensitive).

Table continued on following page

Function	Description
strlen(string)	Returns the length of the named string.
strnatcasecmp(string1, string2)	Using "natural order," compares two named strings (case-insensitive).
strncmp(string1, string2, n)	Compares first *n* characters of two named strings.
strpos(string, exp)	Returns numerical position of first occurrence of named expression in named string.
strrchr(string, exp)	Locates the last occurrence of named expression in named string.
strrev(string)	Reverses the named string.
strrpos(string, exp)	Returns numerical position of last occurrence of named expression in named string
strspn(string1, string2)	Returns the number of characters at the beginning of string1 that match string2, opposite of strcspn.
strstr(string, exp)	Finds all occurrences of a named expression in a named string (case-sensitive).
strtok(string1, string2)	Tokenizes named string based on named parameter, string2.
strtolower(string)	Converts named string to lowercase characters.
strtoupper(string)	Converts named string to uppercase characters.
strtr(string, exp1, exp2)	Translates characters based on the named parameters.
substr(string, start[, num_char])	Returns the named number of characters from the named start position in the named string.
substr_count(string, exp)	Returns the number of occurrences of named expression in the named string.
substr_replace(string, replacement, start[, num_char])	Replaces text within named string based on named parameters.
trim(string)	Deletes extra space at the beginning and end of the named string.
ucfirst(string)	Converts the first character to uppercase.
ucwords(string)	Converts the first character of each word to uppercase.
vprintf(format, arguments)	Displays a formatted string.
vsprintf(format, arguments)	Returns a formatted string as an array.
wordwrap(string[, width, break, cut])	Using the named break character, this will wrap the string based on the named parameters.

URL Functions

The functions in the table that follows allow you to handle URLs within your PHP code.

Function	Description
base64_decode(string)	Decodes an encoded string, opposite of base64_encode.
base64_encode(string)	Encodes a string, opposite of base64_decode.
parse_url(url)	Parses the URL into components.
urldecode(string)	Decodes an encoded string, opposite of urlencode.
urlencode(string)	Encodes a string, opposite of urldecode.

Variable Functions

Variables are a common tool used in PHP, and there are numerous functions to increase your ability to manipulate them.

Function	Description
doubleval(var)	Doubles the value of the variable.
empty(var)	Verifies whether or not the variable exists and has a non-zero value.
floatval(var)	Returns the float value of a variable.
get_defined_vars()	Returns all the defined variables in a script.
get_resource_type(handle)	Returns the resource type.
gettype(var)	Shows the field type of the variable.
import_request_variable (types[, prefix])	Imports GET/POST/Cookie variables into the global scope.
intval(var[, base])	Using the named base, this returns the integer value of the variable.
is_array(var)	Verifies whether or not the variable is an array.
is_bool(var)	Verifies whether or not the variable is Boolean.
is_callable(var)	Verifies whether or not the variable can be called as a function.
is_double(var)	Verifies whether or not the variable is a double.

Table continued on following page

Function	Description
is_float(var)	Verifies whether or not the variable is a float.
is_int(var)	Equal to is_integer and is_long, verifies whether or not the variable is an integer.
is_integer(var)	Equal to is_int and is_long, verifies whether or not the variable is an integer.
is_long(var)	Equal to is_int and is_integer, verifies whether or not the variable is an integer.
is_null(var)	Verifies whether or not the variable is null.
is_numeric(var)	Verifies whether or not the variable is a number or numeric string.
is_object(var)	Verifies whether or not the variable is an object.
is_real(var)	Verifies whether or not the variable is a real number.
is_resource(var)	Verifies whether or not the variable is a resource.
is_string(var)	Verifies whether or not the variable is a string.
isset(var)	Verifies whether or not the variable has been assigned a value.
print_r(exp[, return])	Displays readable information about a variable.
serialize(value)	Generates a storable version of variable.
settype(var, type)	Sets the named variable to the named type.
strval(var)	Returns the string value of the named variable.
unserialize(string)	Generates a PHP value from a stored version.
unset(var)	Deletes the named variable.
var_dump(exp)	Displays information about the named expression.
var_export(exp)	Outputs a string representation of the variable.

D

MySQL Data Types

See the table that follows for the potential data or field types in MySQL.

MySQL Field Type	Description
bigint(length)	Numeric field that stores integers from -9223372036854775808 to 9223372036854775807. (Adding the unsigned parameter allows storage of 0 to 18446744073709551615.) The parameter length limits the number of characters to be displayed.
bit	Equal to tinyint field.
blob	Equal to a text field, except it is case-sensitive when sorting and comparing. Stores up to 65535 characters.
bool	Equal to tinyint field.
boolean	Equal to tinyint field.
char(length)	Any characters can be in this field, but the field will have a fixed length.
date	Stores a date as yyyy-mm-dd.
datetime	Stores date and time as yyyy-mm-dd hh:mm:ss.
dec(length,dec)	Equal to decimal field.
decimal(length,dec)	Numeric field that can store decimals. Length limits the number of characters that will be displayed, and the dec parameter limits the number of decimal places that can be stored. A price field that would store prices up to 999.99, for example, would be defined as decimal(6,2).

Table continued on following page

MySQL Field Type	Description
double(length,dec)	A medium-sized floating point number that stores values from -1.7976931348623157E+308 to -2.2250738585072014E-308, 0, and 2.2250738585072014E-308 to 1.7976931348623157E+308. Length parameter determines how many characters will be displayed; dec parameter determines how many decimal places are displayed. (Adding the unsigned parameter allows only positive numbers to be stored.)
enum("option1", "option2", ...)	Allows only certain values to be stored in this field, such as true and false, or a list of states. 65535 different options can be allowed.
fixed(length,dec)	Equal to decimal field.
float(length,dec)	A small floating point number that stores values from -3.402823466E+38 to -1.175494351E-38, 0, and 1.175494351E-38 to 3.402823466E+38. Length parameter determines how many characters will be displayed; dec parameter determines how many decimal places are displayed. (Adding the unsigned parameter allows only positive numbers to be stored.)
float(precision)	Equal to float(length,dec) except the length and dec parameters are undefined. To be used with a true floating point number. (Adding the unsigned parameter allows only positive numbers to be stored.)
int(length)	Numeric field that stores integers from -2147483648 to +2147483647, but can be limited with the length parameter. Length limits the number of characters that can be shown, not the value. Mathematical functions can be performed on data in this field. Signifying the unsigned parameter permits positive integers (and zero) up to 4294967295.
longblob	Equal to longtext except it is case-sensitive when sorting and comparing.
longtext	Allows storage of up to 4294967295 characters.
mediumblob	Equal to mediumtext field except it is case-sensitive when sorting and comparing.
mediumint(length)	Numeric field that stores integers from -8388608 to 8388607. (Adding the unsigned parameter allows storage of 0 to 16777215.) Length limits the number of characters to be displayed.

MySQL Field Type	Description
mediumtext	Allows storage of up to 1677215 characters.
numeric(length,dec)	Equal to decimal field.
real(length,dec)	Equal to double field.
set("option1", "option2", ...)	Similar to enum field, but with set there can be none or more than one of the available options. Set allows up to 64 options.
smallint(length)	Numeric field that stores integers from -32768 to 32767. (Adding the unsigned parameter allows storage of 0 to 65535.) Length limits the number of characters to be displayed.
text	Any character can be in this field, and the maximum size of the data is 64K (65536 characters).
time	Stores time as hh:mm:ss.
timestamp	Stores date and time as yyyy-mm-dd hh:mm:ss. Useful for automatically capturing current date and time.
tinyblob	Equal to tinytext field, except it is case-sensitive when sorting and comparing.
tinyint(length)	Numeric field that stores integers from -128 to 127. (Adding the unsigned parameter allows storage of 0 to 255.) Length limits the number of characters to be shown.
tinytext	Allows storage of up to 255 characters.
varchar(length)	Any character can be in this field, and the data can vary from 1 to 255 characters. Maximum length of field is denoted in parentheses.
year(length)	Stores a year in 4-character format (by default). It is possible to specify a 2-year format by signifying so with the length parameter.

MySQL Quick Reference

In this appendix, we have listed some quick reference notes for your use. These topics are covered in more depth in Chapter 3 and on the MySQL Web site at www.mysql.com.

Database Manipulation Commands

Use the following commands to create and make changes to your database and tables.

Command	What it does
CREATE databasename	Creates the database
CREATE tablename (field1, field2, field3, and so on PRIMARY KEY(field))	Creates a new table
ALTER TABLE tablename WHERE condition	Modifies a table in the database
RENAME TABLE oldtablename TO newtablename	Renames a table in the database
INSERT INTO tablename (field1, field2, . . .) VALUES ("value1", "value2" . . .)	Inserts information into the table
UPDATE tablename SET field1=value1, field2=value2 . . . WHERE condition	Changes information already stored in the table
DROP tablename	Deletes the table
DROP database	Deletes the database
LOAD DATA INFILE "filename" INTO TABLE tablename	Loads a large quantity of data into the database

Connecting to the Database

Before you can connect to the database, you need four things:

- ❏ Database name
- ❏ Host Server name
- ❏ Username
- ❏ Password

Connect to the database using the following command (in PHP):

```
$connection =  mysql_connect("servername", "username", "password");
```

You then need to select the appropriate database by using the following command (in PHP):

```
<?php
$database = mysql_select_db("databasename", $connection)
       or die("couldn't find the database");
?>
```

Accessing the Database

MySQL commands are inserted within your PHP code to access the database in this way:

```
<?php
$query = mysql_query("UPDATE field1 FROM tablename WHERE condition1")
     or die("Couldn't find the table");
$result = mysql_fetch_array($query);
?>      //your information has now been updated
```

Retrieving Data from the Database

You can access the data stored in our tables with the following statement (you can use * to retrieve all fields):

```
SELECT field1, field2 FROM tablename
```

Condition Clauses

Use the following conditions in conjunction with this statement:

```
SELECT * FROM tablename WHERE
```

Conditions (use % for wildcard):

```
field = value
field > value
field < value
field >= value
field <= value
field != value
field BETWEEN value1 AND value2
field LIKE value
field NOT LIKE value
field IN (value1, value2, value3, etc)
field NOT IN (value1, value2, value3, etc)
```

Selecting from Multiple Tables

You can retrieve information from two or more tables at once by using the following statements:

```
SELECT table1.field, table2.field FROM table1, table2 WHERE
    table1.field = table2.field;
```

or

```
SELECT table1field, table2field FROM table1 LEFT JOIN table 2;
```

Sorting the Results

You can sort the results of the SELECT query by using the following clause at the end of the statement:

```
SELECT * FROM tablename WHERE field1=value1 ORDER BY field2 ASC|DESC
```

Limiting the Results

If you would like to limit the results returned from our query, you can modify your SELECT statement like this:

```
SELECT * FROM tablename WHERE field1=value1
ORDER BY field2 ASC
LIMIT offset, number_of_rows_to_be_returned
```

Comparison of Text Editors

There are many software programs out there that you can use to enter all your code. Some have better options than others, so we've put together a chart to help you compare apples with apples. This chart lists the editors alphabetically and compares common text editor features, such as syntax highlighting.

Many of these editors provide similar features, so your decision really depends on your budget, your needs, and how comfortable you are with each user interface.

You can read more about features not listed here, as many of these editors provide other unique benefits. We encourage you to visit the following Web sites to download these programs and get more information:

- ❑ AnyEdit: www.anyedit.org
- ❑ Dreamweaver MX 2004: www.macromedia.com
- ❑ EditPlus: www.editplus.com
- ❑ HTML-Kit: www.chami.com/html-kit/
- ❑ jEdit: www.jedit.org
- ❑ Notepad: www.microsoft.com
- ❑ PhpED: www.nusphere.com
- ❑ PHPEdit: www.phpedit.net
- ❑ SourceEdit: www.sourceedit.com
- ❑ TextPad: www.textpad.com
- ❑ UltraEdit-32: www.ultraedit.com
- ❑ WordPad: www.microsoft.com

Editor	Highlighted Syntax	Spell Checker	Built-in FTP Access	Block Mode Editing	Line Numbers	Word Wrap	PHP Code Auto-Completion	WYSIWYG Web Design Editor	Search and Replace	Price
AnyEdit	✓					✓	✓		✓	Free
Dreamweaver MX 2004	✓	✓	✓	✓	✓	✓	✓	✓	✓	$399
EditPlus	✓	✓	✓		✓	✓			✓	$30
HTML-Kit	✓	✓	✓		✓	✓	✓	✓	✓	Free
jEdit	✓			✓		✓			✓	Free
Notepad						✓			✓	Free
PhpED	✓	✓	✓	✓	✓	✓	✓		✓	$299
PHPEdit	✓			✓	✓	✓	✓		✓	Free
SourceEdit	✓		✓	✓	✓	✓	✓		✓	$79
TextPad		✓		✓	✓	✓			✓	$27
UltraEdit-32	✓	✓	✓	✓	✓	✓	✓		✓	$35
WordPad						✓			✓	Free

G

Choosing a Third-Party Host

Many people like to run their own servers out of their homes or offices, and that is a feasible solution for hosting, if you have the time. But hosting your own Web site can lead to more problems than it's worth. You need to think about backup power, keeping the security holes patched, regular maintenance, regular upgrades, and many other issues. And keep in mind that not only do you need to have a Web server running; you need to have something to take care of your domain name servers (DNS servers).

With third-party hosting solutions, you have trained IT professionals who make sure your Web server stays up and running 24 hours a day. It's their job to make sure your site is secure and always available for viewing.

Hosting Options

Should you decide to have a third party host your site, there are many options to choose from when making your hosting choice. Here are a few criteria to look at when outsourcing hosting:

- ❑ **Supported languages:** PHP, JAVA, CGI, and so on.
- ❑ **Supported databases:** MySQL, Postgresql, MSSQL, and so on.
- ❑ **Server control:** Super User Access
- ❑ **Server access:** Such as FTP, telnet, SSH, and so on.
- ❑ **Configuration ability:** Web Server settings/configurations, cron jobs, htaccess, and so on.
- ❑ **Administration GUIs:** E-mail, database, user setup, and so on.
- ❑ **Bandwidth usage:** Web site, e-mail, streaming media, database connections, and so on.
- ❑ **Price:** Based on features, contract time, and other criteria.

Keep in mind that you aren't likely to have every combination and possibility with every host, so it's important that you know enough about hosts to make a well-thought-out decision before jumping into a long contract. To that end, let's get into a little more detail about each of those topics.

Supported Languages

First of all, we will talk about the supported languages. Obviously, because you bought this book, we're assuming you are looking into using PHP, but there are other languages you may need to use. There may be a time when another language, such as JavaScript, is better suited for a job than PHP. For example, if you want live streaming audio or video on your site, you are likely to use a Java applet of some sort because PHP needs a request from the server to process information. PHP can do it with different calls to the server, but because it is more of a client request from the browser, a client-side language works much better for this task.

There may also be times when you need to use another programming language to accomplish something a client already has set up at a different host or server. If so, it is nice to at least have the option of using, say, a Perl script, rather than spending the time and money to redevelop the application in PHP.

Supported Databases

Again, because this book is geared toward MySQL, you will probably need a host that supports MySQL. However, there are many other databases you can use with PHP.

Here are just some of the databases that PHP can work with:

❑   MySQL

❑   PostgreSQL

❑   MS SQL Server

❑   MS Access

❑   Sybase

Depending on your situation, you may want to choose a host that has more than one of these databases set up by default. Some larger companies, for example, are using MSSQL as their database, usually because they are using ASP (Active Server Pages from Microsoft) for their programming. Should you need to convert any site to PHP, you will be glad to know that PHP can connect and work nicely with MSSQL as well. Also, keep in mind that you don't have to continue using the other databases; you can always port the data over to MySQL using PHP to ease the troubles of manual conversion.

Server Control and Access

Many hosts out there won't give a Web developer full access and/or control over their hosted domain. We tend to shy away from those hosts because you are more likely to run into problems with them when you want to do some custom configuration to the server.

Look into the type of access your host provides. Obviously, your host will give you FTP access so you can upload your files to the Web server. Some hosts, however, will give you FTP access but nothing else. The problem is that you are likely to run into a situation in which you want to configure your server. For this you will need either telnet or SSH access to use the command line.

In fact, the ability to configure is often necessary when performing tasks that usually aren't allowed by hosts by default. For example, consider htaccess. With htaccess, you can deny and allow access to certain files and directories based on the users you allow in the `htpasswd` file. (See Chapter 11 for more information on htaccess.)

Along with htaccess, most hosts allow you to use cron jobs, but are not likely to set them up for you. Therefore, you need to telnet into the server and edit the crontab file to allow you the ability to run scheduled tasks. There are countless configuration settings that you might want to change if your host allows you to configure them. Keep that in mind when choosing your hosting solution.

Administration GUIs

Certain hosts offer Administration GUIs (Graphical User Interfaces) or User Control Panels as a feature of their packages. A lot of people don't really care for GUIs, but when you don't have a choice, either because you don't have sufficient access to the server or you don't fully understand how to get things done through telnet, a point-and-click solution is a wonderful tool.

The interface can be as simple as one that allows you to view information about the server, or it can be as complex as one that allows you to install applications and programming languages with the click of a button. Also, keep in mind that if you have a client that wants to be able to administer its e-mail users, many of the control panels have utilities that allow the client to do so themselves. With such a feature, rather than having to call you or the hosting company to set up an e-mail account, the client can simply log on to the control panel and set up and delete users as the need arises.

Bandwidth and Site Usage

Bandwidth and site usage factor into the overall price of hosting. Hosting companies usually give out only so much bandwidth usage per site per month. Should you go over that amount, there is usually a hefty charge.

Consider the following issues when looking into bandwidth:

❑ Web site traffic

❑ E-mail usage

❑ Database connections

❑ Streaming media

If you have heavy activity in any or all of these areas, before you know it, you will get billed for bandwidth overusage. You need to consider how many people will visit your site on average. In addition, hosts count e-mail usage in the end-of-the-month calculation used to tally your bill. Some hosts will even go so far as to monitor your FTP access and count that toward the total bandwidth used.

Database connections don't really relate to bandwidth usage, but hosts often limit the amount of database connections you can make as another way to control the number of people allowed to visit the site at one time.

Finally, streaming media is very heavy on bandwidth; should you plan to use it as a form of conveying information to the end users of your site, your hosting bill could rise dramatically.

Pricing

You need to consider all the preceding areas when figuring out how much your host is worth to you. Rather than total price, look at the price per feature. You won't often get all the features you want for your site, but as long as you get most of them and you choose the host that has the lowest price per feature, you will probably make a wise hosting choice.

When using price to make your choice, ask yourself how much a particular feature is worth to you. Remember that some hosting companies require that you sign up for a full year and they won't offer a refund of any sort should you receive poor service and/or decide the service isn't worth the money you are paying. It's best to find a host that will allow you to choose either monthly, quarterly, or yearly hosting options. That way you don't have to wait a full year to leave if you're dissatisfied. Just keep in mind that when you choose a shorter option, such as monthly or quarterly, the host will often charge a little more than if you pay up front, or they may charge service setup fees that might be waived if you pay up front.

Making the Choice

When making your hosting decision, it's very important to consider the criteria outlined in this chapter. You really don't want to get stuck in a situation in which you are unhappy with the service you are receiving or, worse yet, your paying client is disappointed with services you recommended.

The following is a list of ten hosting options that we feel are the best bang for your buck. You may want to consider them when making your decision:

- ❑   www.olm.net
- ❑   www.lunarpages.com
- ❑   www.globat.com
- ❑   www.vervehosting.com
- ❑   www.ipowerweb.com
- ❑   www.websytz.com
- ❑   www.infiniology.com
- ❑   www.powweb.com
- ❑   www.inmotionhosting.com
- ❑   www.hostcolor.com

An Introduction to PEAR

PHP is a terrific scripting language. It is relatively easy to learn, especially if you already know other programming languages such as JavaScript, C++, or Perl. In no time at all, you can get some excellent pages up and running on your server, accessing databases, authenticating users, and providing dynamic, up-to-date content for your visitors.

So, you just spent six months creating your company's Web site. It's nearly perfect—users are being served up-to-the-minute content, and you have set up a complex Content Management System that enables almost anyone in the company to create new content. It's efficient, it's pretty, and you feel pretty darned good about it.

As you sit here thumbing through the appendixes, wondering if there are any more useful nuggets of information, in walks your boss, the IT Manager. She tells you once again what a fine job you did, congrats on the promotion—you know, the usual. As she gets up to leave, she stops in the doorway and casually mentions something that is going to completely overload your work schedule:

"Oh, by the way, HR is switching to an Oracle-based database accounting package. It's pretty slick. And we decided that since we'll be using Oracle anyway, all of our databases will be switched to Oracle. That won't be a problem, will it?"

Of course, the problem here stems from the way PHP accesses databases. The wonderful thing about PHP is that it supports a very wide variety of databases. The bad thing is that it has database-specific commands for each one.

Every developer has had this happen, so you are not alone. It might not be too difficult to change your code, but it will probably be time consuming, especially if you have hundreds of pages to update.

For example, to run a database query, do the following with various databases:

- ❑ **MySQL:** `mysql_query("SELECT * FROM table")`
- ❑ **Microsoft SQL:** `mssql_query("SELECT * FROM table")`
- ❑ **FrontBase:** `fbsql_query("SELECT * FROM table")`

❏ **Sybase:** `sybase_query("SELECT * FROM table")`

❏ **PostgreSQL:** `pgsql_query("SELECT * FROM table")`

Those may seem fairly simple to change, but this is just scratching the surface. Oracle doesn't even have a `_query()` function. You have to use `ora_parse()` on the SQL statement, and then run `ora_exec()`. You must also consider that there may be some specific functions you are using in MySQL that have no equivalent in Oracle. Perhaps you are even using very specific SQL statements in MySQL that are not supported in Oracle or are executed in a different way.

Now you can see how you might have your work cut out for you. Go ahead and give your IT Manager a resounding thump on the head for not foreseeing this change six months ago. (It's okay; just tell her I told you to do it.)

Wouldn't it be cool if there were a way to write your code more abstractly, so that when you run a function such as `get_query_results()`, it would be smart enough to know what type of database you are connecting to and perform all of the necessary steps to retrieve the data? Enter PEAR.

What Is PEAR?

PEAR is the PHP Extension and Add-on Repository. It is an extensive online collection of free PHP modules and classes for many different functions. Modules exist for XML parsing, database processing, user authentication, and more. In most cases, these modules make life easier for the developer by hiding the details of more complex functions and by providing a friendly programming interface and function set for accessing low-level functions. This is called abstraction, and the interface module is referred to as the abstraction layer.

This appendix does not provide you with installation instructions or step-by-step instructions on how to use any specific modules. Rather, our intention is to tell you about some of the more popular PEAR modules and explain what some of their benefits and pitfalls may be. We will include simple examples for clarification of some points, but they are not intended to be used as is.

If you would like more information about PEAR and the modules available, visit `http://pear.php.net`.

Requirements

PEAR is designed to be used with PHP version 4. Specifically, it will work with PHP versions 4.0.4 or newer. It is bundled with PHP, and the newest versions of PHP install PEAR by default. There is a very good chance that PEAR is already installed on your server, and you can begin using it right away.

For detailed installation instructions, visit `http://pear.php.net`.

The Packages

Many, many modules are available for PEAR. They are referred to as "packages," and they can be found at `http://pear.php.net/packages.php`. Packages are written by PHP developers using specific coding standards. Each package is developed by a team or individual, and must contain specific information such as documentation and a list of dependencies (both to and from other packages).

The packages are defined as "nodes" on a "tree." For example, the XML_Parser node is grouped with other XML packages. This grouping is for organizational purposes only—dependencies have nothing to do with the locations of nodes on a tree. The Mail package, for example, depends on the Net_SMTP package, even though they are not connected nodes.

PEAR package developers are required to follow a strict set of coding standards called, logically enough, the PEAR Coding Standards. One of the great things about PEAR (and open source development in general) is that anyone can develop a package and have it inserted into the package tree. ("PEAR tree"— isn't that clever? I'm just waiting for the first person to create a Partridge package.)

The big package we are going to discuss in this appendix is the database package PEAR DB. While there are many excellent packages, this one is probably the most widely used. Many love it, and many hate it. It definitely has its benefits, but it has a few downsides, too. We'll touch on those shortly.

We'll also take a look at a few other package nodes, including Authentication, Mail, Payment, XML, and HTML.

PEAR DB

Before you delve into PEAR, you must be aware that most PEAR packages use objects and classes. If you are not familiar with PHP's implementation of object-oriented programming, you may want to read the Classes and Objects section of the PHP manual (www.php.net/oop).

In order to use PEAR DB (also written as PEAR::DB), you must include the file db.php in your page. This is your "window" to the PEAR DB classes, and it is the only file you need to include. It will implement a class called DB_common, which is contained in the DB/common.php file.

In common.php, you find the code that is common across different databases and some basic utility functions. If necessary, some of the classes will be overwritten, depending on the specific database driver file you load.

This brings us to the third file: driver. This file is loaded dynamically, depending on which database you specify as the one you will use. If you are using MySQL, for example, DB/mysql.php is loaded. It implements a class called DB_mysql that extends DB_common, and contains classes and functions specific to the needs of MySQL databases.

What does all this mean? Basically, it's mostly transparent to you as far as database access goes. You include db.php in your page and specify the database you are accessing (along with user, password, host, and database, as usual), and PEAR DB does the rest.

Let's say you have a database with the following two tables. You may remember these tables from Chapter 9. Let's use these tables in an example to see how PEAR DB compares to standard database functions. All of our examples will use these two tables.

id	league_id	alias	real_name
1	2	Average Man	Bill Smith
2	2	The Flea	Tom Jacobs
3	1	Albino Dude	George White
4	3	Amazing Woman	Mary Jones

id	league
1	Amazing People
2	Dynamic Dudes
3	Stupendous Seven
4	Justice Network

Our first example uses MySQL-specific commands to retrieve all of the records and display them on the screen. For simplicity's sake, we will include the database constants in the same code. Just remember that the best coding practice is to put them into a separate `config.php` file and include them.

```php
<?php
$host = 'yourhost';
$uname = 'yourname';
$passwd = 'yourpass';
$db_name = 'yourdatabase';

$conn = mysql_connect($host, $uname, $passwd)
    or die('Could not connect to MySQL database. ' . mysql_error());

mysql_select_db($db_name,$conn);

$sql = "SELECT * FROM superhero s, league l WHERE l.id = s.league_id";
$result = mysql_query($sql) or die(mysql_error());

while ($row = mysql_fetch_array($result)) {
  echo $row['alias'] . " (" . $row['real_name'] . ") is a member of ";
  echo "the " . $row['league'] . " League.<br>";
}
?>
```

Here is what the code looks like if you use PEAR DB:

```php
<?php
$host = 'yourhost';
$uname = 'yourname';
$passwd = 'yourpass';
$db_name = 'yourdatabase';
$db_type = 'mysql';
```

```
require_once('DB.php');
$dsn = "$db_type://$uname:$passwd@$host/$db_name";
$conn = DB::connect($dsn);
if (DB::isError($conn))
  die ("Unable to connect: " . $conn->getMessage() . "\n");

$sql = "SELECT * FROM superhero s, league l WHERE l.id = s.league_id";
$result = $conn->query($sql);
if (DB::isError($result))
  die ("Query ($sql) failed: " . $result->getMessage() . "\n");

while ($row = $result->fetchRow(DB_FETCHMODE_ASSOC)) {
  echo $row['alias'] . " (" . $row['real_name'] . ") is a member of ";
  echo "the " . $row['league'] . " League.<br>";
}
?>
```

If you load either page in your browser, you will see the following on the screen:

```
Average Man (Bill Smith) is a member of the Dynamic Dudes League.
The Flea (Tom Jacobs) is a member of the Dynamic Dudes League.
Albino Dude (George White) is a member of the Amazing People League.
Amazing Woman (Mary Jones) is a member of the Stupendous Seven League.
```

The PEAR DB method takes more lines, and the syntax is a little different (which can be especially difficult if you are not familiar with objects). So why should you bother to use PEAR DB?

Remember that PEAR DB acts as an abstraction layer to help you interface with your database. If you look closely at the PEAR DB code, you'll notice that none of the functions seem to refer to the type of database you are accessing. In fact, they are quite generic. In contrast, the first code snippet uses mysql_ functions throughout the code. That's not a problem, as long as you always use MySQL.

Remember your IT Manager's passing comment? Your company has just decided to switch from MySQL to Oracle. Which one of these small code segments would you prefer to modify? Okay, perhaps even the MySQL code would take only a couple of minutes, but try to imagine this on a grand scale. Also remember that Oracle commands are different—you must pass the SQL statement to the server and commit it. MySQL doesn't work that way.

Now you should see the benefits of using PEAR DB's abstraction layer. In fact, by keeping the $db_type variable (or an SQL_DB_TYPE) constant in an included file, all you should have to do to make your *entire* Web site work with the new database is change the $db_type variable from mysql to oci8—theoretically, of course. This assumes that every SQL statement you used is compatible with both MySQL and Oracle (which is doubtful) and that every PEAR DB function you used for MySQL is compatible with Oracle (also doubtful). But at least you will have a lot less work to do.

There are definite benefits to using PEAR DB. For example PEAR DB:

❑ Enables you to easily change your code to work with any database backend supported by PEAR.

❑ Provides built-in error checking and error handling.

❏ Creates defaults for common methods (such as `fetchRow()`).

❏ Offers extended functionality—PEAR DB offers database functions that PHP does not natively provide. For example, a method (`DB::isManip`) tells you whether or not a SQL statement manipulates data or simply retrieves it. PHP has no equivalent function.

There are caveats to using PEAR DB as well. Some of these are:

❏ You must use SQL compatible with other databases or change your SQL statements when you change DB servers. You would have to do that without PEAR DB, of course, but you should know that PEAR DB does not solve this problem.

❏ PEAR DB is not as efficient as native PHP code, because you are running things in an abstraction layer, and there may be some very complicated things going on "under the hood."

❏ Not all database-specific functions are available through PEAR DB. For example, MySQL's function `mysql_fetch_object` has no PEAR DB equivalent. Workarounds exist for some functions (such as casting the results of a `fetchRow` to an object); of course, that defeats the purpose of having an abstraction layer.

So, should you install PEAR and use PEAR DB? Perhaps you should. You need to weigh the benefits against potential problems and determine if it's right for you. In the meantime, if you are working on a big PHP project, make sure you are absolutely sure what database you will be accessing. You can avoid a lot of headaches in the future (your IT Manager will thank you for that).

Other PEAR Packages

Pear::DB may be the most popular package available, but it is not the only package available. Let's take a look at a few of the other packages available in PEAR, including HTML, Authentication, Payment, and Mail.

For more information on PEAR DB and other PEAR packages, visit `http://pear.php.net`.

HTML

The HTML node contains quite a few packages, designed to make some HTML functions easier. A good example of this is HTML_BBCodeParser. This neat piece of code takes UBB style tags (`[b]`, `[img]`, and so on) and converts them to HTML (`<b>`, `<img>`, and so on). If you have ever been to a forum online (such as `www.phpbuilder.com/board`), you have seen these tags in action. This package allows you to create your own custom BBCode, and it claims to generate valid XHTML 1.0 code.

Other HTML packages include:

❏ HTML_Menu, which enables the easy creation and maintenance of an HTML menu navigation system

❏ HTML_QuickForm, which provides methods for creating, validating, and processing HTML forms.

❏ Pager for HTML pagination (1–10, 11–20, and so on).

Authentication

The Authentication packages attempt to make it a little easier to add user authentication to your site. Auth offers the capability to use several different methods of storing and retrieving login data, such as databases supported by PEAR, SMTP mail servers, and SAMBA, to name just a few. Auth_PrefManager offers a method of storing and retrieving user preference data, to be used any way you see fit.

Payment

How cool would it be to be able to link your site up to several different online payment and credit card processing companies? Now you can. These packages provide a means to connect to these systems:

- ❏ CyberCash online payment API.

- ❏ CyberMut, which allows you to use the CyberMut Payment system of the Credit Mutuel (French bank).

- ❏ Payment_Clieop creates a `clieop3` file for sending to a Dutch bank. We can't tell you how many times we have needed this!

- ❏ Payment_DTA creates German data transaction files.

- ❏ SPPLUS allows you to use the SPPLUS payment system with the Caisse d'Epargne (French bank).

- ❏ TCLink connects with credit card processing through the Trust Commerce gateway.

Very international, wouldn't you say?

Mail

The PEAR::Mail package provides functions for sending mail with PHP. It supports the `PHP mail()` function, SMTP, and sendmail. It also provides e-mail address validation conforming to RFC 822 standards.

Other Mail packages include mailparse, which provides functions for parsing a mail message; Mail_Mime, which handles the creation and manipulation of mime e-mails; and Mail_Queue, which puts large groups of e-mails in a queue to be sent later (great for very large mailing lists).

AMP Installation

This appendix will guide you through installation of Apache, MySQL, and PHP for both Windows and Linux operating systems.

Installing with Windows

By following our step-by-step guide, you will successfully have all three components installed on your Windows system. This guide includes instructions for Windows NT, Windows 2000, Windows XP, and Windows .NET 2003.

Install Apache

Apache will act as the server for your PHP/MySQL Web site. Installation is easy, as you will see.

This installation is for Windows NT, Windows 2000, Windows XP, and Windows .NET 2003. For other versions of Windows, complete installation instructions can be found at www.apache.org. Note that you must have TCP/IP running on your machine in order for your installation to be operational.

The following are the basic steps for installation:

1. Go to www.apache.org, and click the HTTP Server link.

   While the Apache Software Foundation provides many different software packages, this is the only one we are concerned with at this time.

2. Click "Download from a Mirror" to choose an FTP site for downloading.

3. Click the Win 32 Binary-MSI Installer link to download.

   If you experience problems downloading this file, you can try a different mirror site; click the drop-down box near the top of the screen to locate one.

4. Click the MSI file to initiate the installation wizard for the Apache software.

After accepting the installation agreement, you will see a screen that is equivalent to a readme.txt file—it gives basic information about the Apache software and where to go to find more information. We highly recommend that you read this file.

5. Click Next. You will see the Server Information screen.

6. Enter the following information:

- ❑ Domain name: For example, domainname.com
- ❑ Server name: For example, server.domainname.com
- ❑ Net administrator's e-mail address
- ❑ Who Are We Installing Apache For?

7. Select "All Users" if you want a server that will be available to anyone wishing to see your site or "Only the Current User" for a server that will be used for testing purposes before files are uploaded to a live server on another computer.

8. Click Next to select a setup type.

Typical installation is recommended for beginners and will suffice for most needs. Advanced users may feel more comfortable choosing Custom setup.

9. Click Next.

The Destination Folder screen appears.

10. If you do not want your Apache files saved in the default path, click Change and select an alternate path; then click Next.

The Ready to Install the Program screen appears.

11. Click Install to finish installation.

For configuration options and customization, please refer to Chapter 1 of this book.

Install PHP

This installation is for the PHP module on Windows 98, ME, and Windows 2000/XP/NT. For all other Windows versions, please refer to the source Web site, www.php.net.

The following are the steps for installing PHP:

1. Go to the PHP Web site at www.php.net.

2. Scroll down to the "downloads" section and click the appropriate link for the version you wish to install.

3. Scroll down to the Windows Binary section. If you are running your PHP on an Apache server, as we do in this book, click the PHP Package link to be able to run PHP on Apache Server.

4. Click any FTP site to begin the download.

5. Unzip your file using any standard unzip program and save it to the directory of your choice.

We recommend unzipping it to c:\ and then renaming it to c:\php\. It's best not to save your file in a directory with a space in it, as it can cause Web server problems.

6. Before you can run PHP, you will need to rename php.ini-dist to php.ini.

   By default, the PHP installation provides two copies of your common configuration file: php.ini-dist and php.ini-recommended. The php.ini-dist file is meant to be used for development purposes, while php.ini-recommended should be used when your site goes live, as it has additional security measures in place that the php.ini-dist does not have. Depending on your reason for using PHP, you would choose the php.ini file that best suits your needs. For the purposes of this book, we are going to be using the php.ini-dist file simply because it is easier to work with and will present you with fewer obstacles. Once you are more familiar with PHP in general, we encourage you to switch to the php.ini-recommended file as your default. Therefore, you need to rename the configuration file as indicated in this step in order for your PHP installation to be complete. Make sure to save your new php.ini file to your c:\windows directory so Apache can find it.

7. Copy php4ts.dll into the c:\program files\Apache Group\Apache2\bin directory so that Apache can find it.

   This file can be found in the c:\php directory, not the c:\php\dlls directory.

You now need to configure your PHP to run with Apache and MySQL. Please refer to Chapter 1 for more information on this step.

Install MySQL

MySQL is the database that holds all the data to be accessed by your Web site. This MySQL installation guide is for Windows 95, 98, 2000, NT, XP, and .NET 2003. For all other versions of Windows, please refer to the source Web site at www.mysql.com.

Proceed with the following steps to install MySQL:

1. Go to the source Web site, www.mysql.com, and click "downloads" on the navigation bar near the top of the page.

2. Scroll down to the latest stable version of MySQL, and click that link.

3. Scroll down to the Windows section of the downloadable files, and click Select a Mirror.

4. Find a mirror and click to download (you may choose either HTTP or FTP to download).

5. Unzip the file to a temporary directory of your choice.

6. Click setup.exe to run the installation program. You will see the first of the Installation Wizard screens.

7. Click Next to display the informational screen.

   We highly recommend that you read this screen before you continue.

8. Click Next, which brings you to the Choose Destination Location screen.

9. If the default directory is acceptable, simply click Next; otherwise, click Browse and select a different destination.

10. Click Next.

11. The next screen allows you to customize your installation; typical installation is sufficient for most users.

12. Click the setup type you prefer, and click Next to begin the installation.

After installing the appropriate files, the final screen will simply indicate the installation is complete. Click Finish to end the wizard.

You now need to configure your MySQL installation to fit your needs. See Chapter 1 for more information.

Installing with Linux

This section covers the installation of the three components of the AMP module using a Linux system.

In this instance, we will cover an installation from the source for all three AMP components. Other methods are available, such as RPM, deb, and ebuild. We've chosen to cover source installations instead because this method offers the most flexibility and works on nearly all UNIX-like systems.

Install MySQL

The following are the steps to install MySQL for a Linux system:

1. Go to the MySQL Web site (www.mysql.com) and download the latest stable version of the MySQL database server.

The link for this file is most likely located at the bottom under the heading Source Downloads.

2. Grab the tarball, named something along the lines of mysql-4.0.x.tar.gz.

3. Open a console window and change the directory (cd) to the folder where you downloaded the tarball.

4. If there isn't a user on the system dedicated to running the mysql daemon (typically mysql), you'll need to create one. To do this, in the console, enter the following commands:

```
> groupadd mysql
> useradd -g mysql mysql
```

5. Extract the tarball, and change to the directory it creates:

```
> tar -xzf mysql-VERSION.tar.gz
> cd mysql-VERSION
VERSION is the (sub)version of the mysql source tarball you downloaded, '0.15a'
```

6. Next, configure the source this way:

```
> ./configure -prefix=/usr/local/mysql
```

Using the --prefix switch tells the installer where to put the mysql libraries and binaries after they're built.

7. Compile the source:

```
> make
```

8. Install the libraries and binaries.

```
> make install
```

Note that you will need to be logged in as superuser (root) to perform this step and the following steps in the MySQL installation.

9. If this is the first time MySQL has been installed on your machine (in other words, not an upgrade), run this script to install the initial database/tables:

```
> scripts/mysql_install_db
```

10. Fix permissions on installed files, and copy over the default configuration file.

```
> chown -R root /usr/local/mysql
> chown -R mysql /usr/local/mysql/var
> chgrp -R mysql /usr/local/mysql
> cp support-files/my-medium.cnf /etc/my.cnf
```

Any changes you wish to make to customize MySQL should be made in this file.

11. Start the MySQL daemon:

```
> /usr/local/mysql/bin/mysqld_safe —user=mysql &
```

You'll probably want to add the previous command to whatever facilities are available to automatically start the daemon at boot. This varies by OS, so you'll need to find out what works on your system. Here is one easy way to add this that works with most systems (but may not be the "best" way):

```
> echo '/usr/local/mysql/bin/mysqld_safe —user=mysql &' >> /etc/rc.local
```

Install Apache

Follow these steps to install Apache:

1. Go to the Apache Web site (http://httpd.apache.org) and download the latest stable version of the Apache 2 Web server.

2. Grab the tarball, named something along the lines of httpd-2.0.x.tar.gz.

3. Open a console window, and change the directory (cd) to the folder where you downloaded the tarball.

4. Next, extract the tarball, and change to the directory it creates:

```
> tar -xzf httpd-2.0.47.tar.gz
> cd httpd-2.0.47
```

5. Configure the source:

```
> ./configure \
  —prefix=/usr/local/apache2 \
  —enable-so \
  —enable-mods-shared=max \
  —enable-modules=most
```

Using the `--prefix` switch tells the installer where to put the Apache server after it's built. For a complete list of configuration options, run `./configure -help`.

6. Compile the source:

```
> make
```

7. Install the server:

```
> make install
```

Note that you will need to be logged in as superuser (root) to perform this step and the following steps in the Apache installation.

8. Start the Apache daemon:

```
> /usr/local/apache2/bin/apachectl start
```

9. Add the command to start Apache to whatever boot scripts you like, so the server starts every time you reboot. For example:

```
> echo '/usr/local/apache2/bin/apachectl start
```

Install PHP

Follow these steps to install PHP:

1. Go to the PHP Web site (`www.php.net`) and download the latest stable version of PHP.

2. Grab the tarball, named something along the lines of `php-4.3.x.tar.gz`.

3. Open a console window, and change the directory (cd) to the folder where you downloaded the tarball.

4. Next, extract the tarball, and change to the directory it creates:

```
> tar -xzf php-4.3.3.tar.gz
> cd httpd-4.3.3
```

5. Configure the source:

```
> ./configure \
  —with-apxs2=/usr/local/apache2/bin/apxs \
  —with-mysql=/usr/local/mysql
```

Make sure you point to the correct locations for the Apache 2 apxs binary, and the base of the MySQL installation directory. There are numerous configuration options for PHP, and we would almost need a chapter just to describe them all. For a complete list of configuration options, run `./configure -help`.

6. Compile the source:

```
> make
```

7. Install PHP.

```
> make install
```

You will need to be logged in as superuser (root) to perform this step.

At this point, you should configure your php.ini file as you like and verify that the necessary directives have been placed in Apache's httpd.conf file. Refer to Chapter 1 for details on this.

Index

M

mail() **function**

  Content Management System and, 400–401

  e-mailing and, 286–287, 290–291, 315

  ErrorDocument and, 223

  mailing list and, 436–437, 450, 451

mail functions (PHP), 629

mail server, setting up for PHP, 285–286

mailing list. *See also* **e-mailing**

  administration page

    code for, 424–430

    explanation of, 430–437

  content for, 423–424

  ethics and, 454–455

  overview of, 423

  Quick Message page, 444

  Removal page, 445

  Signup form

    code for, 437–445

    explanation of, 446–454

  subscribing to, 5

  Thank You screen, 444, 445

maintainability, 158

make_table.php file, 249–250

management of content. *See* **Content Management System (CMS)**

manipulating string as array, 150

many-to-many relationship, 240, 245

map of subdirectories, 566

MATCH command (MySQL), 561

MATCH keyword, 419

mathematical functions (PHP), 45, 630–631

max_execution_time **setting (PHP), 19**

max_input_time **setting (PHP), 19**

md5() **function, 312**

mediumblob **field type (MySQL), 90**

mediumint(length) **field type (MySQL), 89**

mediumtext **field type (MySQL), 90**

memory_limit **setting (PHP), 19**

merchandise for e-commerce site, 501

message

  custom, building, 436

  multipart, e-mailing, 294–297

methods

  ErrorDocument (Apache) notification, 216–223

  GET (FORM element, HTML), 139

  POST (FORM element, HTML), 139, 140

  verification, 200

mktime() **function, 213**

modifying file

  coding practices and, 36

  copying before, 129

Monty Python sketch, 454–455

movie review Web site. *See also* **table**

  database, creating, 96–101

  inserting movie into database, 170–176

  overview of, 2, 9

  printing lead actor and director for each movie in database, 598–600

  showing each movie on own page, 600–601

  sorting by movie type and year produced, 600

  user input and, 192–202

  welcome message, adding, 66–68

moviedata.php file, 97–98

movie_details.php file

  creating, 123–124

  modifying, 129–130

  movie details, displaying, 126–128

  new information, displaying, 124–126

$movie_footer **variable, 116**

movie1.php file

  cookies and, 56–57

  creating, 49

  forms and, 59–60, 62

  functions and, 68–69

  sessions and, 52–53

  while command and, 80–81, 83

movie.php file

  checking dates and numbers, 203–206

  creating, 170–172

  editing, 182–185

  explanation of, 188–190

  user input and, 193–197

moviesite.php file

  array, adding to, 75–79

  creating, 42

  functions and, 69–72

  register_globals and, 48–49

  saving information on for next visit, 598

  URL variables and, 47

  variables and, 43

  while command and, 81–83

multidimensional array, 271

my.cnf **file (MySQL) configuration options, 24–27**

MyISAM table (MySQL), 93